D. H. Chamberlain.

(CHARLESTON, S. C., 1875.)

GOVERNOR CHAMBERLAIN'S ADMINISTRATION

IN

SOUTH CAROLINA

A CHAPTER OF RECONSTRUCTION IN THE SOUTHERN STATES

BY

WALTER ALLEN

"My highest ambition as Governor has been to make the ascendancy of the Republican party in South Carolina compatible with the attainment and maintenance of as high and pure a tone in the administration of public affairs as can be exhibited in the proudest Democratic State of the South. And it was also my fondest hope, by peaceful agencies, here in South Carolina, alone of all the Southern States, to have worked out, through the Republican party, the solution of the most difficult and one of the most interesting political and social problems which this century has presented."—D. H. CHAMBERLAIN, December 19, 1875.

Quem si non tenuit, magnis tamen excidit ausis

NEGRO UNIVERSITIES PRESS
NEW YORK

Originally published in 1888
by G. P. Putnam's Sons

Reprinted 1969 by
Negro Universities Press
A Division of Greenwood Publishing Corp.
New York

SBN 8371-1537-X

TO

ALICE INGERSOLL CHAMBERLAIN

WHOSE EARLY WEDDED LIFE WAS BOTH SHADOWED AND EXALTED BY THE EVENTS
HEREIN SET FORTH ; WHOSE FAITHFUL INTEREST PRESERVED IMPORTANT
PARTS OF THIS RECORD ; WHOSE WIFELY COUNSEL AND SYMPATHY
MADE HER A LARGE SHARER IN ALL THAT WAS ACHIEVED AND
ALL THAT WAS ENDURED BY HER HUSBAND WHILE
GOVERNOR OF SOUTH CAROLINA

AND TO

GRACE MASON WESTON ALLEN

THE AFFECTIONATE SHARER OF MY HUMBLER CARES AND TASKS

I dedicate this book

AS A TESTIMONY OF OBLIGATION AND ADMIRATION

W. A.

PREFACE.

THIS volume is what its title expresses; it is the record of
the Administration of Governor Chamberlain in South
Carolina, and nothing more. It was undertaken because it was
believed that the period covered by it, though brief, had a character and significance making it worthy of study and remembrance.
What is called "Reconstruction" was certainly a peculiar phase
of our American civil life. It presented new questions, new difficulties, social, political, legal, and constitutional. The result of
the overthrow and surrender of the armies of the South was to
present at once the novel and perplexing question, how to deal
with the civil Governments of the Southern States. The theories
put forward at that time seem now, many of them, grotesque,—
Mr. Sumner's theory of State suicide not the least so.

The question of the legal relation of those States to the Union
during and at the close of the war, has not yet passed beyond the
line of discussion and controversy. The Supreme Court of the
United States has announced the doctrine of "an indestructible
Union, composed of indestructible States."[1] Yet, the Reconstruction Acts of 1867 which proceeded on the theory of the destruction of the State Governments of the rebellious States, have
been carried into effect and recognized as valid by all branches of
the Federal Government.

It is not necessary to reconcile conflicting theories. What is
plain is that Reconstruction as it proceeded under the Acts of
Congress, involved the most serious consequences to all the people of the South. It involved directly a question never before
put to the test,—the effect of granting the suffrage at one stroke
to nearly 1,100,000 negroes, who were, in all senses of the word,

---

[1] *Texas* v. *White*, 7 Wall. 700.

slaves, a little more than two years before,—so distributed as to constitute an absolute majority of the whole voting population in four out of the eleven rebellious States.

That this tremendous step, this irrevocable plunge, was taken without full apprehension of its necessary consequences, is now clear. The Acts were passed with a certain gay courage by the Republican party, and then, in effect, the South was told to make what it could out of the situation. This is not saying the way chosen was not right and wise,—that it was not, in fact, the only right and wise solution of the unprecedented practical problem consistent with the genius of our institutions. Great evils incident to this plan of settlement have been experienced, but it is unreasonable to presume that another plan would have developed only blessings. So far as the promoters of the plan were actuated by a motive of securing the permanent ascendancy of the Republican party, in the South and in the nation, by means of the solid negro vote, the scheme has failed. But that is unimportant. The important considerations are whether, under another plan, at the end of twenty years, the emancipated race would have made greater progress and would have better prospects; whether the master race would be more favorable to the freedom and participation in citizenship of their former slaves; whether, on the whole, the Southern States would be nearer a realization of ideal republican Governments, wherein all citizens are contentedly subject to impartial laws, and contentedly enjoy an equality of rights. He is a rash man who ventures to answer these questions with a positive yes.

But whatever were the designs or motives of the authors of the Reconstruction measures, the work of carrying them out was of necessity committed to those who lived at the South. It is a mild statement to say that those on whom this responsibility fell were not generally well suited or qualified for such work. Sweeping denunciations are seldom just. Those who took part in Reconstruction at the South were not all, or nearly all, " Northern adventurers, Southern renegades, and depraved negroes." [1] Among all the classes so described were worthy and able men; but the crude forces with which they dealt were temporarily too

[1] See Protest against the new Constitution of S. C., pp. 6, 7.

strong for their control or resistance. Corruption ran riot ; dishonesty flourished in shameless effrontery ; incompetency became the rule in public offices.

In the progress of these conditions, efforts, well directed and patriotic, were made to stem the tide of misrule. Of all such efforts, that in South Carolina, of which Governor Chamberlain was the leader, was unquestionably the most sagacious and hopeful at the time, and it remains, and will remain always, the most interesting, on account of the peculiarly intense and dramatic incidents which characterized its course and end.

The object of this volume is to gather together and preserve the substance and material of a history rather than to draw the lessons or to state the ultimate results,—a work which it would be unwise for any one to attempt now. The records are presented as they stand, documents are given without modification or reserve, and the facts are left to speak for themselves, with only such incidental explanations and comments as seem to be necessary to a just understanding of the circumstances and conditions of each occasion. Numerous extracts from the newspapers of the day are given because they present the best mirror of the times and show how acts and events were regarded while they were occurring, thus preserving in a degree the atmosphere of public opinion breathed by the actors. If the result shall be, as it is believed it will be, to correct some grave misapprehensions, to recall many forgotten facts, to bring into view circumstances that have not been generally known or understood, and thus to clear up and illumine the actual quality and service of some of the actors, such a result will certainly justify and reward the labor. [1]

From the nature of the work that fell to his lot, the chief actor in this brief passage of history, not to say its hero, has been sub-

[1] The author's general aim can hardly be more accurately expressed than by the following extracts from the prefaces of two notable recent works.

" My aim has been . . . to furnish materials for an estimate, without undertaking an estimate or interposing any comments beyond what seemed necessary for the better understanding of the facts presented."—Pref. to Cabot's " Memoir of R. W. Emerson."

" We have done little more than coördinate material to serve posterity in forming that judgment which we have no desire to forestall."—Pref. to " Life of Wm. Lloyd Garrison," by his sons.

jected, in some quarters, to much dispraise, blame, and even obloquy. It cannot be doubted that he is a man of such quality as willingly to rest his claims to honorable remembrance on the truth of history,—the whole truth. It will not be disputed that for the period covered by this record he presents an interesting figure; nor will it be denied that he exhibited some high civic virtues and capacities, and did for South Carolina more than was hoped for at the time, and more than seemed within the power of one man. That he brought to his task great force of character, a strong purpose, admirable courage, high culture, and a powerful eloquence, is generally conceded. What he was, what he did, as well as the character of the events with which he was connected, will, however, best appear from a perusal of the record revealed in the following pages, in which no act or utterance that seemed to have importance regarding his aim and work has been wilfully suppressed. By such completeness could best be fulfilled, in respect of the subject in hand, what Tacitus conceived to be the main office of history: To prevent virtuous acts from being forgotten, and that evil words and deeds shall fear an infamous reputation with posterity.

The whole is submitted with the confidence—such confidence as Carlyle must have had in publishing the Letters of Cromwell —that the only condition indispensable to a just appreciation of one who bravely and honorably performed a hard duty is that what he did, why he did it, and how he did it, shall be fully and fairly set forth.

W. A.

28 YORK SQUARE, NEW HAVEN,
February 22, 1888.

TABLE OF CONTENTS.

CHAPTER I.

CHAPTER VII.

CHAPTER VIII.

CHAPTER IX.

CHAPTER X.

CHAPTER XI.

CHAPTER XXVII.

APPENDIX.

GOVERNOR CHAMBERLAIN'S ADMINISTRATION IN SOUTH CAROLINA.

CHAPTER I.

(INTRODUCTORY.)

The Settlement of South Carolina and the Character of its Settlers—Influence of Slavery; The Episode of Nullification—After the War of Rebellion; Reconstruction Policies—The Election of 1874.

I.

NO one of the colonies which became the original thirteen States had a more distinctive colonial character, or has had a more unique history in the Union, than South Carolina. This has resulted, in part, from the qualities and experiences of her early settlers, her locality, soil, climate, and physical environments, but, more than all, from the presence, from an early date in her history, of the institution and practices of slavery. Controversy over the moral character and political status of slavery has ceased. The argument on that point was closed with the defeat and extinction of the institution itself; but the fact remains, and will remain, that slavery was the one factor in the society of South Carolina—her social, ecclesiastical, moral, economic, and political forces—which most determined the character of her people and the course of her history, and accounts for all, or nearly all, her peculiarities.

Her early settlers were drawn from many sources: first, the English at Port Royal, afterwards transferred to the west bank of the Ashley River, and later to Oyster Point, where in 1680 the foundations of the present city of Charleston were laid; then other emigrants, from Europe, " a medley of different nations and principles," [1]—the Roundheads and Cavaliers of the Revolution of 1688, the Dutch from Nova-Belgia in 1674, and a colony of emigrants from the Barbadoes in 1671, bringing with them the first slaves ever held in South Carolina. Of this period of early settlement the historian of South Carolina says :

> " The inducements to emigration were so many and so various that every year brought new adventurers to the province. The friends of the proprietors were allured to it by the prospect of obtaining landed estates on easy terms ; while others took refuge in it from the frowns of fortune and the rigor of creditors. Young men reduced to misery by folly and excess embarked for the new settlement, where they had leisure to reform and where necessity taught them the unknown virtues of prudence and temperance. Restless spirits fond of revolution were gratified by emigration and found in a new country abundant scope for enterprise and adventures." [2]

The revocation of the Edict of Nantes in 1685 was the occasion of the influx of a large number of French Protestants, who brought, along with some of the stern virtues and religious strictness of the English Protestants, skill and industry in the arts, and a good degree of social culture and refinement—qualities and attainments which made them most useful settlers in the new State, leaders in all public affairs, and the progenitors of a brave, high-minded, and aristocratic portion of the population, thus realizing in an unexpected way the great project of the Admiral Coligny in 1562, of founding an asylum in America for the peaceful growth of French Protestantism.

In these years came also a colony of Massachusetts Congregationalists from Dorchester near Boston (1696), and over fifteen hundred of those subjects of poetry and pathos, the French Acadians of Nova Scotia. Scotland and the North of Ireland contributed freely to the best elements of the new colony, and furnished by emigrants and their immediate descendants a large majority of its preachers, physicians, lawyers, and schoolmasters, a special influence plainly traceable in all the after history.

On the whole, perhaps no colony in this country can be said to have been better settled. To such men and women dangers were tonic, privations were purifying. By a normal development the general standard of personal character and public conduct became high, self-respecting, and strong.

---

[1] Ramsay's " History of South Carolina," vol. i., p. 2.
[2] Ramsay, vol. i., pp. 3, 4.

Such qualities arising from such causes have characterized each of the leading periods of the history of the State, the period of the Proprietary Government from 1670 to 1719, the time of Lords Proprietors, Palatines, and Landgraves, culminating in the contest between the settlers and the proprietors, and followed by the period of Royal government from 1719 to 1774, as well as that of early settlement and struggles.

Three periods of war marked this earlier history, and gave the military character to the people which has never since been lost, —the period of the Spanish wars, that of the Indian wars, and that of the wars against the pirates.

The treaty of Paris between England and France in 1763 found South Carolina entering on a brilliant period of internal peace, development, and prosperity. The fourth period of her history, which may be called the Revolutionary period, extending from 1774 to 1783, is full of interest and illustrative of the special character of her people. South Carolina had no grievances peculiarly her own to incite her to the War of Independence. Her historian [1] says: " The first and second Georges were nursing fathers to the province; they performed to it the full duty of kings." Mr. Bancroft signally exalts her service :

" Be it remembered that the blessing of Union is due to the warmheartedness of South Carolina. 'She was all alive and felt at every pore.' And when we count up those who, above others, contributed to the great result, we are to name the inspired 'madman' James Otis, and the great statesman, the magnanimous, unwavering, faultless lover of his country, Christopher Gadsden." [2]

By the first formal census of South Carolina in 1790,—120 years after the first settlement at Port Royal,—the population of the State was 249,073, of whom the whites were 140,178 and the colored, 108,895 ; and by the census of 1800, the whole population was 345,591, whites 196,255, colored 149,336.

II.

Slavery is a powerful ingredient in any community ; it was in ancient times; it always must be, from the nature of the relations it involves. Almost absolute dominion over the person, even the life, of another,—absolute dominion, so far as legal right goes, over

[1] Ramsay.
[2] Hist. of U. S. [Ed. 1854], vol. v., pp. 294-5.

his will and actions,—cannot fail, in any age or among any people, to deeply affect the character of individuals and society. The effects are not wholly injurious, if judged by ordinary human standards. Slavery promotes in the master class the spirit of command, pride of blood, of race, of character. Personal courage and daring, patriotism, generosity, hospitality—the great patrician qualities—seem to a large extent to accompany and grow out of slavery. Certainly these and cognate qualities have marked the people of South Carolina in all periods. The brutalizing influences of slavery need less notice because, ordinarily, they are the only ones observed by those who look on from the outside ; but probably these influences were never more sadly exhibited than among the people of South Carolina.

Two great facts, or events, distinguish the history of South Carolina and illustrate the tendency of her people subsequent to the Revolution and the formation of the Union—the Nullification episode of 1835, and the Rebellion of 1861,—and each of these events throws light upon the portion of her annals of which this volume is to treat. Of each slavery was the inspiring cause. From 1783 to 1835, slavery had strengthened its hold in South Carolina and the South. From being deplored as a misfortune, or excused as a fact or a necessity, it had come to be defended in church and state as a relation sanctioned by the bible, advantageous on all grounds to the master race, and largely a blessing even to the slave race. It is not necessary to suppose that Calhoun and his followers were consciously aiming at all times to strengthen slavery ; we may even assume they were working in the belief that true political wisdom, their civil and political freedom, required the construction which they sought to put on the Constitution. None the less is it true and apparent that slavery was the only fact or influence alienating them from the old union of spirit that carried them shoulder to shoulder with the North, through the Revolution. If economic reasons moved them, it was in the habits and conditions which slavery created, that such reasons arose and were fostered. Slavery construed the Constitution and measured the Union for them, as it determined all things, whether they were conscious or unconscious of its controlling agency. It is vehemently denied by Southern writers and apologists that slavery was such a motive. Nullification and secession, it is averred, were simply political tenets or principles. But if this be true, those principles and tenets were first taught or suggested by the influence and interests of slavery. What gave heat and force to the great debate of Webster and Hayne in the Senate, was the different social conditions which the orators represented. But for this, that debate would have been academical and abstract. And the force which set the squadrons in the field in 1861, was the fear and rage inspired by the election of a President, and the triumph of a party, pledged to restrict slavery within the limits then bounding its possible progress.

The part of South Carolina in fomenting, precipitating, and waging the war intended to divide the Union is matter of common knowledge. The State suffered in large measure the losses and woes which war always imposes; and in the failure of the attempt which her leading spirits had so actively incited, attended as it was by the annihilation of all property in slaves and the system of slavery, thus violently revolutionizing the organic structure of their social and industrial as well as their political state, they and their sympathizers had an extraordinary share of the humiliation of defeat.

In 1850 the population of the State had risen to 668,507, the whites numbering 274,563 ; free colored, 8,960 ; slaves, 384,984.

III.

After the close of the war, two distinct and opposing plans were applied for the reconstruction, or restoration to the Union, of the State. The first, known as the Presidential plan, was quickly superseded by the second, known as the Congressional plan; but it had worked vast mischief by fostering delusive hopes, the reaction of which was manifest in long enduring bitterness. Under the latter plan, embodied in the Act of Congress of March 2, 1867, a convention was assembled in Charleston, January 14, 1868, "to frame a Constitution and Civil Government." The previous registration of voters made in ·October, 1867, showed a total of 125,328, of whom 46,346 were whites, and 78,982 blacks.

The feelings of the whites were probably correctly expressed at this time by the Address of the Conservative (Democratic) party issued at Columbia, November 6, 1867. It contains these words:

" We have shown that free labor, under the sudden emancipation policy of the government, is a disaster from which, under the most favorable circumstances, it will require years to recover. Add to this the policy which the Reconstruction Acts propose to enforce, and you place the South, politically and socially, under the heel of the negro ; these influences combined would drag to hopeless ruin the most prosperous community in the world. What do these Reconstruction Acts propose ? Not negro equality, merely, but negro supremacy. In the name, then, of humanity to both races, in the name of citizenship under the Constitution, in the name of our Anglo-Saxon blood and race, in the name of the civilization of the nineteenth century, in the name of magnanimity and the instincts of manhood, in the name of God and Nature, we protest against these Acts as destructive to the peace of society and the prosperity of the country, and the greatness and grandeur of our common future. The people of the South are powerless to avert the impending ruin. We have been overborne ; and the responsibility to posterity and to the world has passed into other hands."

On the question of holding a constitutional convention the vote cast in November, 1867, was 71,087 ; 130 whites and 68,876 blacks voting for it, and 2,801 whites against it. Of the delegates chosen to the convention thirty-four were whites and sixty-three blacks.

The new Constitution was adopted at an election held on the 14th, 15th, and 16th of April, 1868, all State officers to initiate its operation being elected at the same time. At this election the registration was 133,597 ; the vote for the Constitution 70,758 ; against it, 27,288 ; total vote, 98,046; not voting, 35,551.

Against the approval by Congress of this Constitution the Democratic State Central Committee forwarded a protest which concluded thus :

" We have thus suggested to your honorable body some of the prominent objections to your adoption of this Constitution. We waive all argument on the subject of its validity. It is a Constitution *de facto,* and that is the ground on which we approach your honorable body in the spirit of earnest remonstrance. The Constitution was the work of Northern adventurers, Southern renegades, and ignorant negroes. Not one per cent. of the white population of the State approves it, and not two per cent. of the negroes who voted for its adoption understood what this act of voting implied. That Constitution enfranchises every male negro over the age of twenty-one, and disfranchises many of the purest and best white men of the State. The negro being in a large numerical majority as compared with the whites, the effect is that the new Constitution establishes in this State negro supremacy with all its train of countless evils. A superior race—a portion, Senators and Representatives, of the same proud race to which it is your pride to belong—is put under the rule of an inferior race ; the abject slaves of yesterday, the flushed freedmen of to-day. And think you there can be any just, lasting reconstruction on this basis? The Committee respectfully reply, in behalf of their white fellow-citizens, that this cannot be. We do not mean to threaten resistance by arms, but the people of our State will never quietly submit to negro rule. We may have to pass under the yoke you have authorized, but by moral agencies, by political organization, by every peaceful means left us, we will keep up this contest until we have regained the political control handed down to us by an honored ancestry. This is a duty we owe to the land that is ours, to the graves that it contains, and to the race of which you and we are alike members—the proud Caucasian race, whose sovereignty on earth God has ordained, and they themselves have illustrated on the most brilliant pages of the world's history."

The new State officers took office July 9, 1868. In the first Legislature, which assembled on the same day, the Senate consisted of thirty-three members, of whom nine were negroes, and but seven were Democrats. The House of Representatives consisted of one hundred and twenty-four members, of whom forty-eight were white men, fourteen only of these being Democrats. The whole Legislature thus consisted of seventy-two white and eighty-five colored members.

At this date the entire funded debt of South Carolina amounted to $5,407,306.27. At the close of the four years (two terms) of Governor R. K. Scott's administration, December, 1872, the funded debt of the State amounted to $18,515,033.91, including past-due and unpaid interest for three years. During the period of this administration, no public works of any appreciable importance had been begun or completed. The entire increase of about thirteen million dollars may be said to represent only increased, extravagan., d profligate current expenditures.

In December, 1873, during the administration of Governor F. J. Moses, Jr., an Act was passed by the Legislature entitled " An Act to reduce the volume of the public debt and to provide for the payment of the same." [1] This Act recognized as valid, of principal and accrued interest of the public bonded debt, $11,480,-033.91, and declared invalid and not a debt of the State, $5,965,-000 of bonds known as " conversion " bonds. It provided for refunding the valid debt, so called, in new bonds of the State at fifty per centum of the par value of the bonds and coupons.

The financial and other history of the State from this time

[1] Statutes of S. C., vol. xv., p. 520.

until the inauguration of Governor Chamberlain in December, 1874, is revealed incidentally, but with all essential completeness, in the subsequent chapters.

IV.

The political campaign of 1874 in South Carolina was a distinct and determined effort on the part of a majority of the Republican party of the State to secure reforms in administration, and especially a reduction of public expenditures. Daniel H. Chamberlain,[1] who had held the office of Attorney General of the State during Governor Scott's administration, from 1868 to 1872, but had held no office for two years, was nominated for Governor by the Republican party. So loud was the demand for reform, that a respectable portion of the Republican party refused to support Mr. Chamberlain, on the alleged ground of want of confidence in his zeal and firmness as a reformer. This opposition took form in the nomination of John T. Green, of Sumter, a native South Carolinian, then a judge of the Circuit Court of the State. Judge Green was supported by the Democratic party, which made no separate nomination for Governor.

The platform originally adopted by the Republican party was accepted by the bolters as the exposition of their principles and aims, and the Democrats made no distinctive declaration of policy. Its provisions were as follows :

1. It re-affirms adhesion to the principles of the National Republican Convention at Philadelphia in 1872, as embodying the true ideas of American progress.

2. It maintains the authority of the general government to interfere for the protection of domestic tranquillity in the several States, and acknowledges with gratitude the interposition in this State.

3. It deprecates lawlessness in any form ; deplores violence, intimidation, or obstruction of personal or political rights by any party ; demands a universal respect and consideration for the elective franchise in the hands of the weakest, and declares that it shall hold men the enemies of equal rights who interfere with or deny a free and lawful exercise of the ballot to any citizen, of whatever party creed.

4. It pledges the party to continue scrupulously to enact and enforce the financial reforms promised two years ago, and in large measure fulfilled ; in proof of which it points to the following laws, viz.: The law to levy a specific tax ; the law to reduce the volume of the public debt ; the law to regulate public printing ; the law to regulate the disbursement of public funds ; and the law to reduce assessments.

[1] A sketch of Governor Chamberlain's previous life is given in the Appendix.

5. It pledges the party to reduce the public expenditures within the public revenue, and to secure the enactment of a law requiring officers who disburse moneys to give to the public monthly statements of all receipts and expenditures derivable from a moderate assessment and tax rate.

6. It earnestly entreats Congress to pass the Civil Rights Bill, which is absolutely essential to the enforcement of the constitutional guaranty of equal rights for all American citizens.

7. It pledges the party to maintain the settlement of the public debt as made last winter, and to reject all claims against which there is a suspicion.

8. It holds that all franchises granted by the State should be subservient to the public good ; that the charges for travel and freight should be equitable and uniform, and no unjust discrimination should be made between through and local travel and freight.

9. It advocates such modification of the present system of taxation as will prove of the largest advantage to the interests of the people, and promises most earnest endeavors for the enactment of such laws, and the encouragement of such means, as will most speedily develop the resources and build up the manufacturing and industrial prosperity of South Carolina, and the construction of such new railroads as will give the largest and cheapest facilities to all citizens.

10. It pledges protection, in the truest sense, to the property of the State, and to such wise, just, and humane laws as will perfect the education and elevation of the working classes.

11. That with a full faith in the justice of these principles, acknowledging the errors of the past, but feeling confident of the ability and determination to correct them, we appeal to all true Republicans to unite in bearing our candidates to victory, and we pledge our party to carry out, in the practical administration of the government, every principle inscribed on our standard in the interest of the whole people of the State.

The character of the struggle that ensued needs not to be set forth here, because references to it by participants on either side are so numerous in subsequent chapters that the reader will have no difficulty in understanding its nature. The result of the remarkably earnest and thorough canvass (Mr. Chamberlain himself speaking in nearly every one of the thirty-two counties of the State) was the election of the regular Republican ticket. Mr. Chamberlain received 80,403 votes, and Judge Green 68,814, the vote being the largest since 1868.

At the same time a new Legislature was elected, consisting of eighty-two Republicans and forty-two Democrats in the House of Representatives, and of twenty-two Republicans and eleven Democrats in the Senate, sixty-one of the Representatives and sixteen of the Senators being colored.

CHAPTER II.

M R. CHAMBERLAIN was inaugurated Governor December 1, 1874, and delivered the following Inaugural Address, which not only indicates clearly his own purposes for the future, but presents much information necessary for a just understanding of the character of past administrations and the situation which confronted the new one. It is a statement of facts and conditions fundamental to an intelligent estimate of what was afterwards accomplished.

Fellow-Citizens of the Senate and House of Representatives :

I have appeared before you to-day to assume the office of Governor, and to state my views of the action and policy on the part of our State Government which will best promote the public welfare.

Our recent political canvass presents one or two aspects which are significant of the will of the people. The two parties which sought supremacy were equally emphatic in their demand for the correction of existing abuses in the administration of our Government, and both presented to the public the same platform of principles and policy for the future conduct of public affairs. The remarkable spectacle was thus presented, among a people hitherto considered most widely divided in their political sympathies and aims, of an absolute identity of sentiment upon all the questions which were presented to the public by either party. It is true that a large minority of our citizens did not take part in either of the political conventions which presented the respective candidates for State officers, yet in the election, wherein the total number of votes cast was more than twelve thousand greater than in any previous election since 1868, only two parties appeared, both of which professed to seek similar ends by similar means. The result is that we who have been elected to office are united in the general objects which we seek and the general methods by which these objects are to be reached.

Without intending to overstate the extent to which our recent party combinations have bound us in respect to our future action, I congratulate all our people upon the substantial harmony of purpose which now prevails. I take strength and hope from that fact. If we are honest in our professions, I cannot find myself in antagonism to any member of the executive or legislative departments of our Government, except on matters of detail in our common pursuit of the same ends. I feel bound to say that, until experience shall correct me, I shall rely for support in the course which I intend to pursue, upon those members of the General Assembly who were opposed to me in the recent political contest as confidently as upon those who favored my election.

The paramount duty before us may be stated to be the practice and enforcement of economy and honesty in the administration of the Government. Fortunately our evils are chiefly evils of administration. Our State Constitution commands the undivided approval of our people. The body of our statute law is believed to be, in general, just and wise. The present demand is for a faithful application and enforcement of the existing Constitution and laws ; in a word, good administration.

Wise statesmanship aims at practical results, and concentrates its strength upon those measures which are of prime importance. I must be pardoned if I omit to catalogue all the matters of public interest to which consideration must be given by the General Assembly, and confine my attention to those topics which appear to be most pressing.

Our earliest and most earnest attention should be directed to the subject of the collection, appropriation, and disbursement of the public funds. These matters are fundamental. Our recent experience teaches us that a government cannot be strong in popular esteem which adopts unjust modes of taxation, imposes unnecessary taxes, expends the proceeds of taxation upon improper objects or in undue amounts, or permits loose and reckless methods in the disbursement of public funds.

THE TAX SYSTEM.

Our present tax system grows out of the provisions of the Constitution which are contained in Article I, Section 36, and Article IX, Section 1. The leading features of the system are an *ad valorem* valuation and a uniform and equal rate of assessment and taxation of all property, real, personal, and possessory, with certain specified exceptions. Under existing laws the taxpayer is required to make a statement, under oath, annually, to the County Auditor, of all his property subject to taxation, and to value the same "at its true value in money," or "usual selling price." It is the duty of the County Auditor to state opposite each taxpayer's name, in the return made by him, any amount which he believes ought to be added to the valuation to be made by the taxpayer, and to give notice of such recommendations to the taxpayer.

The returns are then submitted to a County Board of Equalization, composed of the County Auditor, County Treasurer, and "three intelligent taxpaying citizens," to be appointed by the Circuit Judge. This Board are required to equalize the valuation made by the tax-payer by raising the valuation of such property as, in their judgment, has been returned below its true value, and by reducing the valuation of such as, in their judgment, has been returned above its true value ; but they are forbidden to reduce the aggregate value of the real and per-sonal property of the county below the aggregate value as returned by the County Auditor. Under the construction placed upon the law by the present Comptroller General, in which I concur, the aggregate valuation of personal property in any county is absolutely fixed by the taxpay-ers themselves. The County Board of Equalization merely equalize the valuation of any specific personal property as compared with the average valuation of the other property of the county. A special Board of Equalization for the city of Charleston is provided for, with similar powers and duties.

The returns thus equalized stand, as to the valuations of personal property, as the basis of taxation ; but the valuations of real property in the several counties are submitted to a State Board of Equalization, composed of one member from each congressional district of the State, the Governor, Secretary of State, and Comptroller General, whose duty it is to add to, or deduct from, the aggregate valuation of the real property of each county, or of each town, city, or village in any county, such an amount as in their judgment will make the valuations represent the true value in money of the property. The returns thus equalized stand, as to valuations of real property, as the basis for taxation.

A special Board of Equalization is provided for, composed of the State Treasurer, Secretary of State, Comptroller General, and Attorney General, to equalize the value of the property of railroad companies, in a manner similar to that prescribed for the other Boards of Equal-ization.

A right of appeal is also given from the County Board of Equaliza-tion to the Comptroller General, who is authorized to make abatements in taxes in cases of erroneous or illegal assessments.

The leading purpose of a tax system which rests upon an *ad valorem* basis should be, in the language of our Constitution, to " secure a just valuation for taxation of all property," and to provide safe, convenient, and inexpensive methods for the collection of taxes. The *ad valorem* system being fixed by the Constitution, our attention must be directed to the practical means of carrying out this system.

Grave dissatisfaction with our tax laws has existed during the past six years. The most general and urgent complaint has been that the valuations placed upon the property of the State have been, to a large degree, capricious and excessive. It has also been believed that exces-sive valuations have been made in order to conceal the real extent of the burden of taxation. Without attempting to discuss the motives which prompted those who enforce the law, I express the opinion that the valuations made previous to the present year have been, to a great extent, unjust and oppressive. Whatever the causes, the result has been that property has born a valuation almost wholly arbitrary when different localities or separate pieces of similar property are compared, and excessive in amount when tested by any reasonable standard of value.

I see no reason to regard this injustice as a legitimate result of our present tax system. On the contrary, my most careful examination convinces me that the system will work out a just result if it can be placed in the hands of honest and competent officers. Undoubtedly the machinery for making valuations is somewhat complicated, if not intricate ; but the system will be seen, I think, upon a fair examination, to be adapted, in all its features to guarding the rights of the tax-payer in respect to assessments, whenever it is administered by those who regard the interest of the taxpayers.

During the past year a new assessment of real property, the fourth since 1868, has been made. It is not yet possible for me to judge of its correctness, but I am assured by those who have been familiar with the work during its progress that it approaches very nearly to the true value of the property. I am further informed that the aggregate valuation of all the property of the State under this assessment will fall from thirty to forty millions of dollars below the aggregate of the previous assessment. I have confidence that much has been done in this assessment to relieve the injustice of former assessments, but I call your attention to the subject as one of fundamental importance to the whole people. The people demand, and they have a right to demand, that property shall be valued for taxation at its true money value, as nearly as the imperfection of the human judgment will permit. If the present assessment does not reach this standard, then it is our duty to adopt such measures as will remove the remaining defects. I shall co-operate with the General Assembly in any measures calculated to attain the end contemplated by our Constitution and laws,—a just valuation for taxation of all property according to its true money value.

In this connection I may remark that so far as the working of our tax system depends upon faithful officers appointed by the Governor, I intend to see to it that no county shall have just cause of complaint. The appointment of County Auditors and County Treasurers now rests with the Governor, subject to the confirmation of the Senate. I commend to your careful consideration the question of making these officers elective by the people of the several counties. There are some arguments which might be urged in favor of either mode of selection. The only test which should be applied in determining the question is, which mode will with most certainty secure good officers and a faithful enforcement of the laws ?

My examination of the Act of the General Assembly of March 17, 1874, commonly called the " Taxation and Assessment Act," leads me to recommend that a full revision of that Act be made by some appropriate means by the General Assembly at this session, in conjunction with the Comptroller General, in order to remove inconsistencies and supply defects now apparent in the law.

I further recommend that the work of equalizing railroad property be given to the State Board of Equalization, provided for by Section 64 of the "Taxation and Assessment Act." I see no reason for placing this power in the hands of a board composed wholly of State officers as at present ; on the contrary, I see many reasons for giving to the property of our railroad companies all the protection afforded to other property.

REDUCTION OF EXPENSES.

Having secured a just valuation for taxation of the property of the State, our next duty will be to determine the rate per cent. of taxation necessary to support the Government. Upon this point the inflexible rule should be applied, of limiting the amount of taxes to the actual requirements of good government. It should especially be remembered that the people of this State are not now able to contribute one dollar of taxes beyond what the most rigid economy will warrant. Probably there will be very little dispute upon this general proposition. The work and difficulty will consist in applying it. I deem it my duty, therefore, to proceed to point out the specific measures which will, in my judgment, tend to bring us nearer to a correct rule of public expenditure.

The General Assembly at the last regular session of 1873-74 adopted the plan of making a specific levy of taxes for each object of public expenditure. I most earnestly urge that this plan be observed in the future. Its advantages are manifold and obvious. If the legislative branch is to have control of the public funds, no measure is so important to that end as the making of specific levies.

CONTINGENT FUNDS.

Assuming that the plan of specific levies will be continued, I proceed to indicate certain radical changes in the expenditure of public funds, which are demanded by a due regard for honesty and economy. Under this head I do not hesitate to characterize the whole system of contingent funds which has recently sprung up, as wrong in principle and mischievous and demoralizing in effect. During the past six years there has been appropriated and paid for contingent funds the astounding sum of $376,832.74. I venture the opinion that the State would have received equal benefit from one fifth of that sum, if expended with economy upon proper objects. In practice, a contingent fund is a sum of money which a public officer is allowed to draw and expend without the usual accountability. Some governments deem it necessary to entrust certain officers with a fund commonly called the "secret-service" fund, which may be expended for objects which might be defeated by publicity. I confess I am wholly unable to imagine any such objects in South Carolina. I think the people of this State should be able to trace every dollar of the public funds to the precise object on which it is expended. This cannot be done under our present system of contingent funds. I recommend, therefore, that the practice of appropriating contingent funds to be drawn and expended by different officers of the State without the usual accountability for such expenditures, be wholly discontinued. I recommend in place of that system, that distinct appropriations be made for all public objects which can be anticipated or enumerated, and then, that a small sum, not to exceed ten or twelve thousand dollars, if so much be necessary, be appropriated for contingent expenses, to be paid in specified amounts to the several officers who may require it, upon the warrant of the Comptroller General, drawn upon vouchers to be filed with the Comptroller General by the officers obtaining the warrant.

The records of the expenditure of this fund will thus be placed with the Comptroller General, where they will remain accessible to the people, and liable at any time to examination and publication. The reduction of public expenses by this system will not be inconsiderable, while the gain to official morality by the removal of opportunity for questionable uses of public funds will be great.

EXPENSES OF THE GENERAL ASSEMBLY.

Another subject demanding our most prompt and energetic action is the reduction of the expenses of the General Assembly. I cannot believe that any difference of opinion will exist upon this subject. The public, within and without the State, have united in pronouncing the expenditures heretofore made for legislative expenses, an intolerable abuse.

Since 1868 six regular and two special sessions of the General Assembly have been held. The total cost of those sessions has been $2,147,430.97. The average cost of each regular session has been $320,405.16. The lowest cost of any regular session was that of the regular session of 1868–69, amounting to $160,005.79; and the highest cost was that of the regular session of 1871–72, amounting to about $617,234.10. Besides these amounts now specified there are outstanding of bills payable issued on account of legislative expenses during the same period, $192,275.15. These figures render comment superfluous. The problem is to reduce these expenses to an economical limit.

The first and most obvious measure of reform is the shortening of the length of the sessions. I find the average length of the regular sessions since 1868 has been 105 days. It is clear that no public requirements will warrant sessions of such length in the future. I am aware that this may be regarded as a matter so peculiarly within the discretion of the General Assembly as to make any recommendations of mine impertinent. But my convictions of public duty upon this point are too clear to allow me, for any cause, to withhold the free expression of my views. I cannot see at present any reason of a public nature which can require a session of more than thirty days. If this General Assembly could set the example of a return to the former rule in this State of a final adjournment before the Christmas holidays, I am confident that they would receive the heartiest approval of all our people. I know of no services which could be rendered by remaining in session a longer period, which would be held as valuable by our constituents as the example of a return to rigid economy in this respect.

One cause of long sessions which I feel bound to specify, has been the passage of an inordinate number of special Acts of Incorporation. Whoever will examine the Acts of the General Assembly during the last six years will be convinced of the waste of time arising from this cause. The remedy is obvious. Let a General Incorporation Act be passed, or let the present Acts be duly revised and perfected, and then let all ordinary applications for corporate powers be made under the provisions of such Acts.

The second measure of retrenchment in legislative expenses which I urge, is a reduction of the number of subordinate officers and attachés of the General Assembly. Upon this point I am happy to speak in commendation of an Act passed by the last General Assembly. By that Act the total number of subordinate officers and attaches in both branches of the General Assembly is limited to fifty-seven. I trust your attention will be given to this subject, and that if, upon examination, the number therein provided for is found to be the lowest number consistent with the proper transaction of business, the law will remain undisturbed.

The third and most important means of reducing legislative expenses will be found in cutting off the gross abuses which have heretofore existed under the name of contingent or incidental legislative expenses. I am unable to obtain a statement of the precise amount expended during the last six years under this head. I find, however, that the average expenditure at each regular session since 1868, for attachés and contingent or incidental expenses, has been about $258,-424.65. Of this amount I estimate that not less than $190,000 have been expended for contingent legislative expenses at each regular session. If these figures do not teach their own lesson, then argument would be idle. Let it be borne in mind also that the amounts now stated represent only the actual payments made. There remains still a vast amount of unpaid claims in the form of legislative pay certificates, estimated at not less than $500,000.

In seeking a remedy for these startling grievances I am convinced that nothing is so essential as the establishment of a proper system of accountability in the payment of legislative expenses. Our present system is wholly anomalous, so far as I can learn from examining the systems prevailing in other States, and is wholly at variance with the general theory of our own State in the payment of other public expenses.

The Comptroller General is the proper auditing officer of the State. His office is intended to be the permanent depository of the written evidences of the expenditure of public funds. The separation of the duty of auditing from that of paying demands against the State is essential. The requirement of proper evidences of the character and validity of every demand made against the State, and the preservation of those evidences for public inspection, is also essential.

In order to meet these requirements, I recommend that all payments to be made on account of legislative expenses be made by the State Treasurer, upon warrants drawn by the Comptroller General, for which the vouchers shall be filed with the Comptroller General.

In the payment of members, subordinate officers, attachés, etc., the only voucher requisite would be a duly certified list of all persons who held these positions. The Comptroller General, having satisfied himself of the correctness of the lists furnished by the officers of the General Assembly and of the authority of law for their payment, would then draw his warrants upon the Treasurer for the proper sums of money.

In the payment of contingent expenses each branch of the General Assembly would, by committee or otherwise, make such audit as might be deemed necessary of such accounts, and order their payment. The vouchers thus accepted by the General Assembly would be sent to the office of the Comptroller General, and there remain forever exposed to the scrutiny of the public, and payment would be made by the Treasurer only on the warrant of the Comptroller General.

Let no one imagine that I feel any distrust of this General Assembly, or of its presiding officers, but I know that nothing is so vital in such matters as a correct system. Wise laws are expressions of correct rules of civil conduct. The best guaranty against individual dishonesty in financial transactions is a system which has no open doors to deception or fraud. Rigid accountability and constant exposure to publicity, I venture to pronounce the foremost requisites of a good system for the disbursement of public funds.

I respectfully and most earnestly urge immediate attention to this subject. Nothing can exceed it in importance. Consideration for the public good demands such action as will finally close the doors to a recurrence of the reckless expenditures which have attended our recent legislative sessions.

PUBLIC PRINTING.

I recommend that your earliest attention be directed to the matter of the public printing. The system which has prevailed for the past three years is utterly incapable of defense or excuse. The looseness of the system in theory is only equalled by its extravagance in practice. Under this system the Clerk of the Senate and the Clerk of the House of Representatives were empowered to contract for the public printing, and the drafts or orders for the payment of printing expenses were made payable upon the certificates of those officers alone, "out of any moneys in the Treasury not otherwise appropriated." No limit was fixed to the amount for which the contracts should be made. Under the system of making a general levy of taxes, no specific funds in the Treasury at any specified time were considered as specifically appropriated. The result was that under this system it was in the power of the clerks of the two houses to draw, on account of public printing, to an unlimited extent upon the public funds, without reference to the sufficiency of those funds to meet the demands of other appropriations.

More recently, however, the General Assembly has made definite appropriations for payment of printing accounts.

A few statistics will show how such a system has resulted in practice. The cost of the permanent and current printing from 1868 to the present time was $843,073.59. The cost of advertising the statutes, that is, of printing them in the newspapers, for the same period was $261,496.32 ; making a total cost of $1,104,569.91. During the past three years the cost to the State of permanent and current printing was $743,933.20, and the cost of printing the laws in newspapers for the same period was $174,696.66 ; making a total cost to the State of $918,629.86. Deducting from this last amount such items of printing as may be called extraordinary, including the republication of certain volumes of the statutes at large, the printing of the Ku-Klux trials, immigration reports, tax duplicates, and Supreme-Court decisions, amounting to $375,000, there remains as the cost of printing for three years the sum of $543,629.86, or an average annual cost of $181,209.95.

I offer no comment on these statistics. The only appropriate inquiry is, how shall such results be prevented hereafter ? I answer, by exterminating the present system, root and branch, and substituting a safe and economical system. Such a system can easily be pointed out. Let advertisement be made by order of the General Assembly for proposals for doing the necessary public printing of all kinds for the State for a fixed period, specifying the various kinds and amounts of printing required, with the option of ordering more work of any specified kind at fixed rates, and requiring a suitable bond to accompany each proposal, for the faithful execution of the work according to the proposals. Let these proposals be presented to the General Assembly and the most advantageous one be accepted. In this way the State may remove the present abuses and secure an honest and economical result.

In this connection I call your attention to an Act passed by the last General Assembly, entitled "An Act to regulate the public printing," to be found at page 707, of the Acts of 1873-74. This Act doubtless would have accomplished a good result but for the insertion of the last four lines of the first section It is evident that no proposal can ever be made under this Act, since the amount of work required to be done can never be estimated. If the lines referred to were expunged from this Act, it would serve as an illustration of the system which I have recommended.

I consider the cost of advertising or reprinting the Acts of the General Assembly in the newspapers of the State a wholly unnecessary expense, and I recommend the total discontinuance of the practice. If any laws are enacted which it is important should be published at once for the information of the people, it will be the interest of the newspapers to publish them as a matter of public information. If this is not done, a number of extra copies can be ordered by the General Assembly from the public printer at a trifling cost and be sent to the clerks of courts or other officers for distribution.

DEFICIENCIES.

Another reform which I urge upon the General Assembly is the keeping of the expenditures of the State within its receipts. Very little regard seems to have been hitherto paid to this obvious requirement of good administration. The existing deficiencies, running back to 1868, are simply enormous. The deficiencies for the fiscal year ending October 31, 1874, were $472,619.54. The deficiencies for the fiscal year ending October 31, 1873, were $540,328, of which about $440,000 have been paid during the last fiscal year, leaving about $100,000 still unpaid. The levy of taxes made the present year for payment of deficiencies for the last fiscal year will not be sufficient to pay more than one half the amount of such deficiencies. The evils of such a practice are serious. The amount of money needed should be first ascertained, and then a levy should be made adequate to raise that amount.

CERTIFICATES OF INDEBTEDNESS.

During the past year a class of State obligations called " certificates of indebtedness " was issued to the amount of $231,996, and the State Treasurer was directed to make other issues of the same obligations to the amount of about $340,000.

Fortunately the right of the General Assembly to authorize such issues has been contested in our Supreme Court, and thence carried, by writ of error, to the Supreme Court of the United States, where the cases are now pending. Without discussing the constitutional question involved, I feel called upon to express the hope that the General Assembly will not, under any circumstances, resort again to such an expedient. At a time when the national government is embarrassed with the great problem of restoring the national currency to a sound basis, let not this State further complicate the evils of an inconvertible paper medium by the introduction of another paper medium, which will necessarily circulate as money at rates greatly below its par value, but which has none of the qualities which belong to money, in its proper sense. To say that the people have gladly accepted the certificates of indebtedness does not prove that it is either honorable or honest in the State to issue them.

Another wide departure from correct administration has obtained for several years past—the issuing of orders, certificates, and warrants for the payment of money from the State treasury when no funds are on hand for their payment. I am not prepared to say that this practice can be immediately forbidden by law without too serious embarrassment to public interests, but I recommend the matter to the attention of the General Assembly. The evils of such a practice are great. It has already been forbidden in the administration of county affairs, and an effort should be made to return to a correct practice in this respect. The effect of such a practice upon the credit of the State is not essentially different from the case of an individual who should issue checks upon a bank when the b..nk held no funds applicable to their payment.

REDUCTION OF THE NUMBER OF OFFICERS.

An opinion prevails widely with the public that the number of public officers and the amount of salaries now allowed by law are greatly in excess of the public requirements. I am not now prepared to express an opinion upon a subject which requires so much care and investigation in order to reach a correct result. If any reductions of expenses can be made by abolishing offices or reducing salaries, I shall give my most hearty support to any plan which will accomplish that end, and I recommend that immediate attention be directed to the matter.

In this connection I call attention to the necessity of requiring County Treasurers, and perhaps County Auditors, to give bonds directly to the county. At present the bonds of these officers run to the State alone. It is questioned by some whether a suit can be maintained by the county upon such a bond ; but however that may be, in cases of default where the bond is inadequate to cover the whole loss, there is at present no law for determining in what way the unsecured remainder of loss shall be apportioned between county and State. It is plain that the county should be amply protected by adequate bonds for the custody and disbursement of county funds.

THE PUBLIC DEBT.

No subject will deserve greater attention or wiser action than the public debt of the State. At the last session of the General Assembly an Act was passed entitled " An Act to reduce the volume of the public debt and to provide for the payment of the same." By that Act the State Treasurer was authorized to issue in exchange for certain specified bonds and stocks of the State then outstanding, together with the coupons and interest orders which should become due on or before the 1st of January, 1874, new bonds or stocks equal in amount to fifty per centum of the face value of the bonds and stocks and coupons of interest orders presented for exchange. The bonds and stocks and coupons and interest orders thus specified as exchangeable, amounted to $11,-480,033.91. The remainder of the apparent funded debt of the State, consisting of what are known as " conversion bonds," and amounting to $5,965,000, was declared to have been " put on the market without any authority of law," and to be " absolutely null and void."

The new bonds and stocks authorized by this Act were required to " bear upon their face the declaration that the payment of the interest and the redemption of the principal is secured by the levy of an annual tax of two mills on the dollar upon the entire taxable property of the State, which declaration shall be considered a contract entered into between the State and every holder of said bonds and stocks."

It was further provided that these new bonds and stocks should bear six per cent. interest, payable semi-annually at the State Treasury and in New York, the first coupon to fall due July 1, 1874, and all coupons or interest orders upon said bonds or stocks were made receivable "in payment of all taxes due the State during the year in which they mature, except for tax levied for the public schools."

The faith, credit, and funds of the State were solemnly pledged for "the punctual payment of the interest and final redemption of the principal of said bonds and stocks, and for providing a surplus fund for that purpose."

Provision was also made for a fund, to be kept separate and apart from all other funds, and to be applied, first, to the annually accruing interest upon the new bonds and stocks ; second, to the extinguishment of the principal of the public debt by the annual purchase of bonds and stocks at the lowest market-price. The Act further contained provisions for a public registry of all the new bonds and stocks, and provided heavy penalties for any dereliction of duty on the part of any officer in the execution of the law.

The leading features of this scheme are the reduction of that part of the public debt which was considered valid to one half its par value, and the rejection of that part which was considered invalid. The Act was passed after long deliberation, and was at the time of its passage, and has since been, the object of public attention and discussion throughout the State. In the recent political canvass of this State, both parties especially pledged themselves to maintain this "settlement of the public debt." So far as I have learned the sentiment of the people of this State, they are wholly united in support of this measure. It must therefore be regarded, so far as legislative and popular influence and action can go, as a final settlement.

The ground upon which this measure rests as to its reduction of the volume of the debt, is the inability of the State to pay the debt in full. As to the part of the debt which is wholly rejected, it is held that it was issued without authority of law, and hence that it is not a legal obligation of the State.

During the five months since this Act was put in operation by the State officers, over two millions of dollars of the old bonds and stocks have been exchanged. When the entire outstanding valid debt shall have been exchanged, the principal of our public debt will amount to $5,740,016.95. The annual interest upon this amount will be $344,-402.02. The tax annually levied to pay the interest on this debt will at all times be held in readiness to pay all interest which accrues on the new bonds on and after July 1, 1874, whenever the exchange shall be effected.

Article XIV of the State Constitution, ratified January 29, 1873, forbids any increase of the public debt of the State by the loan of the credit of the State by guaranty, endorsement, or otherwise, until the question of such increase shall have been submitted to the qualified voters of the State at a general State election, and unless two thirds of the voters voting on this question shall be in favor of such increase. It is believed that this provision will be an effectual guard against any further increase of the public debt.

The Supreme Court of this State has decided that a provision, such as is contained in the present Act, for the levy of an annual tax is a contract between the State and its creditor, and is capable of enforcement by process of law directed against the proper officers of the State, and, furthermore, that such a provision operates of itself, not only as a levy of the tax, but as an appropriation of the proceeds of the levy to the purposes designated in the Act. Under this decision the provision for an annual tax remains a permanent levy and appropriation, and no further legislation is necessary from year to year to accomplish the purposes of the Act in this respect.

These provisions of law, together with the provision which makes all coupons or interest orders upon the new bonds receivable for taxes during the year in which they mature, give to the new bonds all the legal safeguards which it is possible to place around them.

I cannot believe that any party, nor even any man, will hereafter dare to interpose an objection to the prompt discharge of these new obligations of the State. Confidence in these matters is a plant of slow growth. Once trampled on and crushed, it revives with exceeding slowness, and flourishes only under long and tender care. If the experience of any State should have impressed this lesson, surely it is the experience of South Carolina. It now becomes our paramount duty to labor to restore our ruined State credit by the only means apparently left us—a prompt, unhesitating, and conscientious discharge of every obligation incurred under the law which authorizes the consolidation of the public debt. In this we may hope, little by little, to win back some part of that public credit, the loss of which is among the saddest calamities which have befallen our State.

BILLS OF THE BANK OF THE STATE.

I consider it my duty to call attention to the relations of the State to the bills of the Bank of the State. By the charter of the bank these bills were made receivable for taxes and other dues to the State. The insolvency of the bank has rendered the liability of the State the chief element of value in these bills. The State, by her proper officers, having refused to receive the bills in payment of taxes, proceedings were had in our courts to compel the reception of the bills issued prior to December 20, 1860, which were terminated in 1868 by funding such bills in bonds of the State. There then remained outstanding the bills issued by the bank after December 20, 1860. The State refusing to receive these bills, legal proceedings were again begun and continued in the courts of the State, and finally in the Supreme Court of the United States. In these cases it was decided, in October, 1873, that the bills in question were valid obligations which the State was bound to receive for taxes under the contract embraced in the charter of the bank. Owing to the embarrassed condition of the State at the time when these decisions were finally rendered, the State has continued to refuse all bills not specifically involved in the suits referred to. A large number of taxpayers have, however, tendered the bills in payment of taxes, and upon the refusal of the tax officers to receive them, have again resorted to the courts for the enforcement of their claims.   A large number of suits are now pending.   The collection of taxes in other funds from those who have tendered these bills, has been enjoined both by the State courts and the District Court of the United States.   It is certain that a much larger amount of the bills will be tendered in payment of the present levy of taxes, and if the collection of taxes is again enjoined by the courts, it is plain that great embarrassment will result to the State.   I cannot resist the conviction that it is impossible for the State finally to avoid the redemption of these bills.   When that time shall come the bills will fall, like an avalanche, on the Treasury, and being without value after redemption they will practically stop the ordinary supplies of the State.

I am therefore forced to recommend that the attention of the General Assembly be directed to the development of some plan by which these obligations may be met without disaster to the State.   Towards this end, I am, at present, able to make but one suggestion.   If the State should offer to receive these bills for all taxes now past due, and for a certain fraction of all future taxes, I am confident an arrangement might be effected by which the redemption of the bills may be distributed over a term of years, instead of being permitted to embarrass the State by their compulsory reception in one body.   A similar plan was adopted in the State of Tennessee, under like circumstances, in 1868.   I most earnestly advise that the matter be taken in hand by the General Assembly without delay.

JUSTICES OF THE PEACE AND CONSTABLES.

I call the attention of the General Assembly to the provisions of Sections 1, 21, 22, 23, and 24 of Article IV of the State Constitution. These sections provide for the election by the people of the several counties, of Justices of the Peace and Constables.   These provisions of the Constitution remain wholly dormant and nugatory.   In the place of the system thus established by the Constitution, we have a class of officers called Trial Justices, who exercise a jurisdiction similar to that given by the Constitution of the State to Justices of the Peace, and who are further authorized to appoint Constables.

The election by the people of Justices of the Peace and Constables is, without question, a constitutional right of the people, and unless the present system can be made more useful and satisfactory, the enforcement of the constitutional provisions referred to will, I am sure, be demanded by the people.   The General Assembly is responsible at all times for the failure to enforce the constitutional system.

Of the practical results of the Trial-Justice system as heretofore administered, I hear but one opinion, namely, that it is costly, inefficient, and oppressive.   The whole number of Trial Justices allowed by law is three hundred and forty-seven.   Even this number has, I am informed, been exceeded by some process in actual practice.   I am convinced that the number should be reduced immediately by at least one third. The incumbents of these offices are to a great extent deficient in the qualities which make a useful magistrate.

I leave the question of the enforcement of the constitutional system with the General Assembly without venturing an opinion of my own, but I shall deem it my duty, while the present system remains, to use the power of appointment now conferred on the Governor in such a way as to give to the people Trial Justices who will know the law and will use their powers to preserve the rights and protect the interests of all. This duty will be onerous and difficult, but I shall endeavor to discharge it without fear or favor.

BOARD OF STATE CANVASSERS.

The law in respect to the Board of State Canvassers requires amendment in some particulars in order to secure its useful and efficient working. Previous to the present year the general State election was held on the third Wednesday in October. The law required the Board of County Canvassers to meet on the Tuesday next following the election, and to make and transmit their returns to the Board of State Canvassers within ten days from the time of their first meeting. The Secretary of State was then required to convene the Board of State Canvassers on or before the tenth day of November next after the general election. By an amendment to the Constitution the general elections now take place on the first Tuesday following the first Monday of November, and the times for the meeting of the County and State Boards of Canvassers should now be changed so as to be in harmony with the change in the time of the general elections. As the law now stands the two Boards were required to meet on the same day in the present year.

Again, the Board of State Canvassers was originally intended to be composed of seven members, namely, the Secretary of State, Comptroller General, Attorney General, State Auditor, State Treasurer, Adjutant and Inspector General, and the Chairman of the Committee on Privileges and Elections of the House of Representatives. The office of State Auditor has since been abolished, and inasmuch as, by the Constitution, the terms of office of the Senators and Representatives chosen at a general election begin on the Monday following such election, there is no person holding the position of Chairman of the Committee on Privileges and Elections of the House of Representatives at the time of the meeting of the Board of State Canvassers. The Board is thus reduced to five members. I simply wish to call attention to this result, in order that the General Assembly may consider whether any change shall be made in the present condition of the Board.

I also call attention to the omission of any specific provisions of law for the action of the Board of State Canvassers in cases of special elections. The power heretofore exercised in such cases rests wholly on implication.

I also call attention to the present uncertainty of the law in respect to the nature of the powers conferred on the Board of State Canvassers, and the want of any provisions for enabling the Board to hear and determine cases of contested elections. It is held by many persons that the powers of the Board are wholly ministerial. If this be so, the requirement that the Board "shall decide all cases under protest or contest that may arise when the power to do so does not, by the Constitution, reside in some other body," seems to be of little force or value.

In addition to this grave question of power, the law provides no mode in which the Board may obtain testimony, so as to enable it to decide cases of contested elections upon proper evidence and with fairness to both parties.

The several matters now pointed out should receive the attention of the General Assembly.

REGISTRATION OF ELECTORS.

The Constitution of the State, in Section 3, Article VIII, declares that "it shall be the duty of the General Assembly to provide, from time to time, for the registration of all electors." No registration of electors has been made or provided for since the adoption of the Constitution. I recommend that this requirement of the Constitution be no longer disregarded. The obvious justice of a registration of electors, aside from the positive mandate of the Constitution, renders any argument in its favor needless.

COMMISSIONERS OF ELECTION.

Recent events have called public attention to the power claimed and exercised by the Governor, not only of appointing, but of summarily removing, the Commissioners of Election. The law requires the Governor to appoint the Commissioners of Election at least sixty days prior to the election. It is difficult to believe that it was intended to render this provision nugatory by allowing the Governor to remove them at will at any time before the election. I submit this subject to the General Assembly without further comment, except to say that the wisest mode of appointment of the Commissioners of Election, as well as the proper limitations of the power of appointment, are matters which demand the careful attention of the General Assembly.

INSURANCE DEPOSITS.

I call attention to the propriety of a revision or repeal of the present provisions of law requiring deposits by insurance companies of stocks or bonds of the State or United States for the protection of policy-holders within the State. Owing to the condition of the funded debt of the State, the deposits heretofore made by some companies have become nearly worthless. If protection to the policy-holders is to be secured by means of such deposits, the object in many instances is not now reached. The unequal effect of the present law upon companies already doing and those proposing to do business in the State, is likewise apparent. My own judgment inclines to the belief that good policy dictates the repeal of the present law. Free competition would then prevail, and our citizens would look for their security only to the history and character of the companies. In this way I think better results would be reached than under the present law.

SPECIAL TAX IN FAIRFIELD COUNTY.

The General Assembly by an Act approved March 13, 1872, provided for a tax of one half of a mill on the dollar on the property of those counties in which the writ of *habeas corpus* was suspended by the proclamation of the President of the United States in 1871, the proceeds to constitute a pension fund for the support of indigent widows and orphans of those persons who had been killed in those counties because of their political opinions. This tax has been levied for the past two years in Fairfield County; but there are no persons in that county who are entitled to the benefit of the fund. I recommend, therefore, that the law be amended so as to relieve that county from this tax.

THE PARDONING POWER.

I think it is proper that I should state on this occasion that, in the exercise of the power conferred on the Governor by the Constitution " to grant reprieves and pardons after conviction," I shall endeavor to keep in view the end for which our criminal laws are framed—the repression of crime and the protection of society. The occasions will be rare and attended by peculiar circumstances, on which I shall feel justified in setting aside the judgments of our courts and the verdicts of our juries.

EDUCATION AND SCHOOLS.

The great subject of education will demand your most serious attention. I wish I could impress upon the General Assembly and upon all our people the fundamental and incalculable importance of this subject in its relations to every other interest of the State. The peculiar evils and dangers to which the people of this State are exposed will find their certain and permanent cure only in the thorough diffusion of education. We have met here to-day to begin the great work of reform in our public affairs ; we find errors and abuses, and we seek to apply a remedy by the enactment of new laws or the change of old laws ; but let us know and remember that the complete accomplishment of our hopes for good government will never come until the common school shall reach and mold the minds of all those who exercise the political powers of the State. In vain shall we build, if we neglect this foundation. Stronger than our strongest statute, more beneficent than our wisest statesmanship, more enduring than any form of government or method of administration, is the silent influence of the school. There lies our hope. Show me the open door of the schoolhouse crowded with our children and youth, and I can look beyond the discouragements of this hour and discern that future South Carolina wherein intelligence and virtue shall everywhere uphold and guard her prosperity and honor.

I advise, therefore, in advance, against any reduction of public expenditure by reducing the appropriations for educational purposes. The aggregate amount expended for these purposes is not too great, but there is much occasion for efforts to make our school system more efficient. A perusal of the reports of the State Superintendent of Education will show that much has already been done. A few statistics will indicate the progress already made. The number of free common schools in the State in 1870, was 769. The number in 1873 was 2,017. The number of pupils in attendance in 1870 was 30,448. The number in 1873 was 83,753. The number of teachers employed in 1869 was 734. The number employed in 1873 was 2,310. I believe there has been a steady progress since 1870, not only in the number of our schools, but in their efficiency and standard of instruction.

There are, however, great hindrances in reaching satisfactory results. First of all, there is wanting such a general interest on the part of all our people as is essential to an efficient common-school system. Nothing can supply this want except the will of the people themselves. Perhaps the chief hindrance has been the want of capacity and devotion to their work on the part of the County School Commissioners. The powers of these Commissioners in the management of schools, the appointment of teachers, and the expenditure of school funds in their respective counties, are almost absolute. The relations of the State Superintendent to the County School Commissioners are almost wholly advisory.

I recommend that careful examination be made into this feature of the school system to ascertain whether any change can be made which will remedy the want of efficiency on the part of County School Commissioners.

In general, I recommend that careful attention be given to the school system in all its features. It is not enough to continue to make appropriations for school purposes. The whole number of persons in this State between the ages of six and sixteen, is 230,102, and of this number only 83,753 now attend schools—scarcely more than one third of the whole number. This fact suggests the need of greater efforts to extend our school system so that it may embrace a far greater number of our school population.

I have but one specific recommendation to make upon this subject. Our educational system at present consists of our common schools at one extreme, and our State University at the other. There is no proper intermediate link to connect these extremes. To reach the University the pupil must leave the common school and seek his preparation for the University elsewhere. I think the system should be so modified as to supply this defect, and this, I think, can be done without necessarily increasing the cost of the system. The plan I would propose is to select one or two of the most efficient of our present common schools in each county and elevate them to the grade of ordinary high schools, and open them upon proper conditions to the more advanced pupils in the common schools. To accomplish this end, I would suggest that a part, perhaps one fourth or one fifth, of the present appropriation for public schools in each county be assigned to the purpose now stated. I would further suggest that, for the present, the control of this class of schools be committed to a board of High-School Commissioners, to be selected in such a manner as to secure the best men in the State to aid in this effort to improve and perfect our school system. I am convinced that a plan substantially such as I have suggested would elevate the standard of our common schools and supply pupils with proper attainments for our University.

CONCLUSION.

Senators and Representatives: I have now made known to you my views upon those matters which seem to me to be of most urgent importance to our welfare as a State at the present time. Owing to the want of the information to be obtained from the reports of the various officers in charge of the several departments of the Government and the public institutions, I am obliged to omit the consideration of some topics which will necessarily command a part of your attention. At an early day it will be my duty to present to you some additional recommendations touching several important interests of the State.

The views now presented are the best contribution which it is in my power to make towards the removal of present evils and the restoration of good government. I offer them with deference to the General Assembly. To the accomplishment of the general results which I have indicated, so far as lies in my power, I am unalterably pledged. In the methods best adapted to accomplish those results I have no personal plans or wishes which I shall deem important in comparison with the results to be accomplished.

The work which lies before us is serious beyond that which falls to the lot of most generations of men. It is nothing less than the reëstablishment of society in this State upon the foundation of absolute equality of civil and political rights. The evils attending our first steps in this work have drawn upon us the frowns of the whole world. Those who opposed the policy upon which our State was restored to her practical relations with the Union have already visited us with the verdict of absolute condemnation. Those who framed and enforced that policy are filled with an anxiety for the result, in which fear often predominates over hope. The result, under Divine Providence, rests with us.

For myself I here avow the same confidence in the final result which I have hitherto felt. The evils which surround us are such as might well have been predicted by a sagacious mind before they appeared. They are deplorable, but they will be transitory. The great permanent influences which rule in civilized society are constantly at work, and will slowly lift us into a better life. Our foundations are strong and sure. Already we have seen the day when no party or

man in our State was bold enough to seek the favor of the people
except upon the most explicit pledges to remove our present abuses.
If we who are here to-day shall fail in our duty, others more honest
and capable will be called to our places.   Through us or through
others freedom and justice will bear sway in South Carolina.

I enter upon my duties as Governor with a just sense, as I hope, of
my own want of such wisdom and experience as the position demands.
I shall need the friendly aid not only of my political associates but of
all men who love our State.

We must move forward and upward to better things.   In performing my part of this work the highest favor I ask, next to the Divine
favor, which I now invoke, is that no man will urge me to do an
act inconsistent with the principles and pledges upon which the
people have intrusted us with our present powers.

From the Governor's exposure of the State finances, it appears
that during the six years from 1868 to 1874—the period of the
Scott and Moses administrations,—the expenditures of public
funds for the single item of executive contingent expenses
amounted to $376,832.74.   Another fact which appears is that,
during the same period, the expenditures for the Legislature—that
is, merely the *per-diem* salary and mileage of members, pay of
employés, cost of stationery, etc.—were $2,147,430.97, the average
cost of each session being $320,405.16.   Also, that besides these
extraordinary amounts which had been paid on account of legislative expenses, so called, there were then outstanding in the
community and unpaid, certificates, or bills payable for legislative
expenses, to the amount of $192,275.15.

The cost of the permanent and current legislative printing for
the same period was $843,073.59.   With $174,696.66, the cost
of printing the statutes in newspapers, added, the total cost of
public printing for this period was $918,629.86.   It appears,
also, that the existing unpaid deficiencies of the two preceding
years (1873–74) were over $575,000, together with a class of out-
standing indebtedness called "certificates of indebtedness," issued
in payment of current expenses, amounting to $231,996, with a
further authorized issue of $340,000.

In addition, therefore, to the increase of the public bonded
debt during six years by thirteen million dollars, there was a
further increase in the form of floating indebtedness, of nearly
or quite one million dollars.   The correction of this habit of

reckless extravagance was one of the reforms now to be vigorously undertaken, and he, upon whom the duty of leadership in the work had been imposed knew that wounds, such as had been inflicted upon the prosperity and credit of this State, could not be healed without being fearlessly probed and explored.[1]

Although Governor Chamberlain was elected under circumstances which might have warranted some discussion of the relations of the races, if not of the spirit of parties, in South Carolina, his Address contained no word which could be construed as an evidence of bitterness or partisanship. The Chief Magistrate recognized no difference, or reasons of difference, between any citizens, who sought with one purpose the things that would make for the establishment on firm foundations of the honor and prosperity of the commonwealth. When, in his first message to Congress, President Arthur made no reference to what had been known as "the Southern question," and by this significant silence implied that thenceforth all sections of the country should be regarded as loyal, having a common sentiment of nationality and a common interest in the general welfare, it was justly regarded as an evidence of wise statesmanship. In this wisdom he was anticipated by Governor Chamberlain under circumstances more provocative of indulgence in criticism and vindication.

---

[1] *Vulnera nisi tacta tractataque sanari non possunt.*—LIVY.

CHAPTER III.

TO say that Governor Chamberlain's first official utterance surprised the people of the State and the country, hardly does justice to the sentiment generally expressed. Although it was as far as possible from a sentimental address, but, on the contrary, was a plain, businesslike statement of the affairs of the State and, in its views and recommendations, was in strict accordance with the platform of his party and his own speeches before election, it attracted the attention of the country in a remarkable manner, and in South Carolina caused a profound sensation. For the first time, since the reorganization of the State Government, a Governor appeared able to know and unafraid to reveal to the uttermost both the facts and the causes of the evils under which the community labored, and to have an earnest intention of eradicating them. Without dissimulation and without extravagance he had portrayed the unfortunate condition of the State, the result in large part of causes for which his own party was responsible, the continuance of which he earnestly, even confidently, declared his purpose of preventing. In its spirit and temper, as well as in its substance, the Address was a different document from any thing that had before emanated from the Republican party in South Carolina, or in any Southern State, an indication of that rare phenomenon in any State—a party leader more concerned with the offences of his own supporters against honor and sound policy than with the misdoing of his opponents. It afforded the spectacle of a politician acting as if he believed parties should somewhat regard that most difficult and most ignored of all rules of conduct, " First

31

cast out the beam out of thine own eye." No wonder there was amazement everywhere.

The "white man's party" in the State hailed the Address with satisfaction, because it promised at least an effort to check the extravagance and demoralization which had become oppressive. They had found no fault with the Governor's professions and pledges heretofore, except that, with their experience of his party's conduct, ante-election professions of reform could not be trusted. They knew that he was by conviction, as well as by association and practice, an ardent supporter of the doctrine of equal rights; that he believed the freedmen capable of sharing on equal terms the duties and responsibilities of citizenship. They knew, also, that he was a Republican, that the Republican party in South Carolina, whatever might be the fact in the Northern States, contained a vast body of ignorance whose official representatives, with few exceptions, had been not only incompetent but venal, and they did not believe that any officer dependent upon that party would dare to rebuke or obstruct the corrupted inclinations of its local leaders. Therefore when this Governor, upon assuming the duties of his office, showed that he did not consider his election the complete triumph of reform, but, on the contrary, held that the real work was yet to be begun, and when he advanced a definite programme of aims and methods in which no element of insincerity or weakness appeared, they began to have hope that something would be effected. To them the Inaugural Address was an unexpected assurance of good intentions, and their representative journals commended it with heartiness, even while they still distrusted its author's firmness and fortitude.

It had a similar happy effect upon that portion of the people in the Northern States in whom the monstrous misgovernment of South Carolina had produced a wish for the overthrow of the party in power. Of course the Northern Democrats desired the defeat of the Republicans in South Carolina as a matter of partisan advantage, and during this administration they were, as a rule, far less just in their judgment of his actions than the Democrats of his own and other Southern States. But a large section of the Republican party in the North, represented by journals of high character and wide influence, had believed the demoralization of the party in that State so deep, complete, and scandalous, that it was incapable of reformation unless deprived of power and opportunity. Having little knowledge of the Republican candidate, except what was gathered from South Carolina papers, which, during the election canvass, did not acknowledge that he was any better than, or different from, the worst of his supporters, they had wished for his defeat, and they regretted his election as a new lease of power to the combination of cunning knaves with ignorant freedmen by which the South had been plundered, and their party everywhere subjected to taint and shame. To them the new Governor's Inaugural Address was a welcome surprise, kindling a hope that at last a man had appeared who would do something to redeem the name " carpet-bagger " from the reproach which had attached to it, not without good reason.

On the other hand, it must be acknowledged that a large proportion of the party that had supported Governor Chamberlain at the polls, including most of those who had been accomplices in the iniquity of the former administrations, were not less amazed, although their emotion was of another cast. That candidates and officials should profess devotion to economy, and justice, and reform, was nothing new. It had come to be understood among them that this was the proper thing to do, an expected hypocrisy, and in the art of it they were well versed. But there was in this Address a severely practical application of what they considered only the cant of politics, a deep-toned sincerity, an absence of congratulation and flattery, a suggestion of duty and labor and sacrifice, altogether so different from any thing before known of their party leaders, that they were at a loss what to think of it or of its author. They felt that he was committing himself too freely and too far; that he did not remember that he and they had secured their election, and that the time for exalting virtue and reiterating promises had gone by. Whether he was in earnest or only more audacious than themselves in insincerity, they were at first doubtful; but if he was not in earnest he was indiscreet, and if he was in earnest, he would have to be fought and put down, or their schemes of self-aggrandizement would be balked. They were dazed, but they were determined not to yield without a struggle. The nation has since witnessed a similar condition on a larger stage. The astonishment of the hitherto controlling forces of the Republican party of South Carolina, when Governor Chamberlain discovered to them that he meant to attempt to conduct his administration in fidelity to his and their public pledges, was not unlike the astonishment with which a large portion of the Democratic party received the post-election deliverances of Grover Cleveland regarding reform in the civil service, and his early efforts to make them good.

The succeeding pages are, in large part, the record of a struggle of which this Address was the signal, a struggle which in fierceness, obstinacy, and dramatic intensity is scarcely rivalled by any other that has occurred in this country of ours, between the honorable and the selfish elements comprised in one party, between wise statesmanship and unwise politics.

The following extracts from journals which had not been favorable to the election of Governor Chamberlain, show how strongly his first official utterance affected the opinions of intelligent observers who had despaired of securing good government for South Carolina through the Republican party there.

[From the Charleston (S. C.) *News and Courier*, December 11, 1874.]

The tone of every newspaper in the country, from Maine to California must be most encouraging to Governor Chamberlain. Every one of them takes him warmly by the hand, warns him of the task he has undertaken, urges him to stand unflinchingly by his purpose against all and every kind of opposition. There have been many governors elected in greater States than South Carolina during the past year, but no public expression has attracted so much comment and attention as the inaugural address of the Governor. This is a most remarkable uprising of the national sentiment in support of the Governor. It means just this : that the whole American press, representing the invincible genius of the republic, proposes to stand behind him like a giant, with his arm bared to strike down any opposition that attempts to weaken his hand, or wrench its grasp from the helm of this State, so long as it is true to the cause of the people. Mr. Chamberlain has placed his foot upon the rock of a living principle, with the eye of a great nation full upon him, and the light of a great future breaking all around him. He holds in his hand the heart of an heroic State, and upon his steady nerve depends the hope of a splendid national organization. The road he must travel will be hedged about with difficulty and danger and responsibility, but if he be faithful to his trust, the divinity of a high purpose will brush these things like a chaff from his path, and crown him with the gratitude of the nation.   We have an abiding faith—the faith of experience and hope—that in carrying out the letter and spirit of his inaugural, the Governor will not flinch nor be moved the breadth of a hair.   He will find a strength, not his own, that, if need be, will sustain him in vindicating the rights and interests of the poor people of this State.

[From another issue of the same journal.]

So long as he walks on the line that he has marked out for himself he will have the active support of the Conservative members of the General Assembly, and likewise the moral support, the aid and the comfort of the sixty thousand Conservatives whom those members represent.   What the people want—and all that they want— is the honest and economical administration which Governor Chamberlain has undertaken to give them ; and they will not, by any display of distrust, or by any recalcitrancy of conduct, add to the difficulties which he must encounter, who is resolved to restore to South Carolina that high public character and public credit which in other days were the pride and boast of her people.

[From the Florence (S. C.) *Pioneer*.]

The inaugural address was an able one, and if Mr. Chamberlain will carry out the policy for reform which he therein promises, and is backed by the Legislature, the good people of our State will be most agreeably disappointed, and will support him in his administration.

[From the Aiken (S. C.) *Courier-Journal*.]

We like the ring of Governor Chamberlain's inaugural message, and hope he will be able to carry out his programme to the letter, but knowing as we do many of his assistants and surroundings, and judging the others from these, we are of the opinion that they would clog the wheels of the governmental chariot, if drawn by the Archangel Gabriel himself.

[From the Anderson (S. C.) *Conservator*.]

It will be well for Mr. Chamberlain to understand at once, the success of his administration depends upon his identifying himself with the people and not with a few leaders, and that unless he exercises the functions of his high office, which he has received from the people, for their benefit, in correcting the abuses and corruptions which exist in all the departments of the government, his culture, learning, ability, and ambition will not save him from the fate of Scott and Moses.

[From the Greenville (S. C.) *News*.]

In many respects the Governor's message is full of good advice, and we hope the present Legislature will see to it, that much that he recommends will be carried into practical execution by appropriate and necessary enactment.   Economy and retrenchment should be the guarding [*sic*] policy in every thing.   We are pleased to realize that Mr. Chamberlain has taken such high position, and as the *News* has said before, we intend to support him in all his efforts to give us a good government.

[From *Harper's Weekly*, December 11, 1874.]

Governor Chamberlain's inaugural address is clearly the work of an able and sagacious man ; and should it prove to be the scheme of his official action, every honest and intelligent citizen of South Carolina will be satisfied.   . . .

It seems incredible that these should be the words of the successor of Moses, elected by the same party. They are full of good cheer, and we do not wonder that the inaugural address is considered to be able and statesmanlike, and that the " tax-payers " see the hope of good government and prosperity in the Governor's address. They must remember, however, that his task is most difficult, and that its successful accomplishment depends very much upon their hearty co-operation, not only by votes in the Legislature, but by sympathy and support in their newspapers. The just complaint of good citizens in this part of the country is that men of the class known as tax-payers have held contemptuously aloof from the work of government in the Southern States, and while constantly appealing for sympathy on the ground that they were the substantial and intelligent citizens, have made the worst instead of the best of the situation. They concede the ability of Governor Chamberlain. They have no right to distrust his sincerity until he gives them reason, which those who know him best have no fear that he will do. There is now a chance for South Carolina ; and Governor Chamberlain, in fulfilling his promise, will prove whether the tax-payers really wish the advantage of the State, or merely the possession of power.

[From The New York *Nation*, December 10, 1874.]

Mr. Chamberlain, the new Governor of South Carolina, delivered his inaugural address to the Legislature of that State last week, and it appears to have given great satisfaction to sound men of all parties. If he lives up to its promises and professions, and can get the Legislature to do so, he will prove the means of rescuing the State, and will be fairly entitled to a statue. The address is both able and interesting, but his descriptions of the abuses which have to be remedied are sometimes very amusing for the illustration they afford of the manners and morals of the class which has had charge of the State government since 1868. . . . What Mr. Chamberlain says about the public debt is probably what will most interest the outside world, and it is substantially this : that the Act of the last Assembly by which the State committed bankruptcy, and offered to compound with its creditors by giving new bonds for fifty per cent. of the par value of certain bonds, stocks, and coupons which the State was unable to pay, amounting in all to $11,480,033, and repudiating totally the " conversion bonds " put on the market by Kimpton, was a good settlement, and ought to be carried out. The new bonds are to be secured by the appropriation, for the payment of the principal and interest, of a tax of two mills on the dollar on the actual taxable property of the State, which is to be considered a contract between the State and its creditors. As no future increase of the State debt can be made under the existing Constitution without the approval of two thirds of the voters voting at a general State election, we dare say everybody but the holders of the conversion bonds will be satisfied with this arrangement ; but no civilized community ought to make such a proposal on such a state of facts without having previously committed to the penitentiary for a term of years, as part and parcel of the transaction, one or more of its financiers ; and, in this case, we have no hesitation in designating Scott, Parker, and Kimpton as persons from among whom the selection for this sacrifice ought to be made. In the meantime, we wish Mr. Chamberlain success and tenacity.

[From the Philadelphia *Ledger*.]

News of an honest and economical administration of the State Government of South Carolina is good news indeed. Governor Chamberlain, who has just been elected, was inaugurated on Tuesday, and his address, when one remembers that it comes from the candidate of the combination who have so long plundered that State, is of a most promising character. The South Carolina politicians, if the new Governor properly represents them, are to turn over a new leaf. The tax-payers of South Carolina, judging by the telegrams thence, seem to be much encouraged by the prospect of reform, and it is to be hoped the Governor will carry out the policy laid down. South Carolina sadly needs it.

CHAPTER IV.

The Governor and the Legislature—The First Conflict—He Defeats the Election of an Unfit Judge by the Legislature—Reluctant Approval of an Appropriation Bill—Message to the Legislature on the Subject—An Interesting Letter of Professor C. P. Pelham.

THOSE of the Republican party in the Legislature, a majority in party caucuses, who disapproved of the positive reform policy recommended by the Governor, made little public talk of the matter; but they were none the less resolved not to aid the "new departure" in any way that would be an acknowledgment on their part of previous wrong-doing. Unfortunately, ever since the freedmen had become citizens and politicians they had not wanted for leaders who suffered without rebuke, when they did not sanction and encourage, the disposition to make full use of power for personal advantage. Never having been trained in the exercise of responsibility, to them freedom and authority meant opportunity rather than duty, and they were incredulous regarding the motive of a magistrate who recommended an economy that would supply no perquisites, and set up standards of public service which would thwart the ambitions of some of the most active men in his party. In their view such aims were absurd, and they were confident of their ability to defeat any attempt to give them effect in the actual conduct of the State's affairs.

The first trial came soon. The occasion was the election by the Legislature of a judge to fill a vacancy in the Charleston circuit. The candidates for the office were W. J. Whipper, a shrewd, unscrupulous, negro politician, a lawyer, forsooth, but having neither the professional attainments nor the virtues of character suitable for a judicial office, who was regularly nominated by the Republican majority of the Legislature; Elihu C.

Baker, a lawyer from Massachusetts, who had been in the State but a short time, whose fitness in other particulars was not conspicuous, but who was supported by the few Republicans dissatisfied with Whipper; and Jacob P. Reed, a native of the State, a lawyer of good standing, and a reputable citizen. In accordance with a singular custom then prevailing, the candidates were invited and expected to attend a public meeting, or caucus, of members of the Legislature, to make addresses in their own behalf, and friends of the several candidates were expected to speak in behalf of their favorites. Seeing no other way of breaking the solid line of the misguided members of the Legislature arrayed in support of Whipper, Governor Chamberlain, against the strenuous advice of nearly all his friends, resolved to attend the meeting and state plainly his opinion of the candidates, especially of Whipper. It was an unprecedented proceeding; but it was the only way open to prevent a scandal upon the fame of the courts of South Carolina.

The account of the proceedings on this occasion which the correspondent of the Charleston *News and Courier* sent to that journal shows that the caucus, in the beginning, was an hilarious assembly. A band of music contributed to the enjoyment, and, apparently, the majority were so well assured of success that they thought they could afford to make merry as if the occasion had no serious significance. Mr. Whipper's address was a combination of story-telling, free-and-easy self-laudation, and denunciation of the Governor; Mr. Reed spoke briefly and modestly; Mr. Baker made a long oration. The Governor then addressed the assembly. His remarks and the subsequent proceedings, as reported by the same correspondent, were as follows:

He said he desired, if possible, to divest himself of the influence of Governor, and to appear as a private citizen to discuss the questions under consideration. He felt now, as he had never felt before, the responsibilities of his position and of his party. The eyes of the entire State and nation were upon them, and he had laid aside every consideration to come here to speak in behalf of the common welfare of the State. He disclaimed any desire to use any influence that did not belong to him as a simple member of the Republican party. The only fear that he entertained was whether he had the courage to do his duty. That duty was an unpleasant one, but it must be discharged.

In the selection of a Judge of the First Circuit a man must be selected

whose character is above suspicion. [Applause.] If the whole field
were open, and the circumstances were such that he could select, from
the educated men of the State, a candidate of ability and character and
learning, he was free to say that his choice would not fall upon any of
the three candidates named to-night. But he now proposed only to
discuss the merits of the three candidates named, and to inquire which
one of them came the nearest to the qualifications of a judge. There
were three qualifications to be considered. First, the candidate must
be a Republican ; second, he must be a man of ability, qualified to fill
the position ; and third, his character and integrity must be above suspicion. Here some one in the hall groaned very audibly, and there
was a general laugh. Without heeding the interruption, the Governor
went on to say that it was injustice to the Republican party to suppose
that they could do any thing merely because of their numerical majority.
They had seen a majority of forty thousand dwindle down to ten thousand in the last campaign under the pressure of just such mistakes.
They had no right, under any circumstances or under any political
pressure, to impose upon any community in this State a man to administer the laws whose character and reputation do not entitle him to the
full confidence of every man, woman, and child in the community.

He then compared the qualifications of the three candidates. He
was opposed to the election of General Whipper or of Mr. Baker to that
position, and it was his opinion that, of the three candidates named, the
one who best met the requirements of the position was Col. Reed. At
this stage there was a demonstration on the part of the Whipperites.
Green, of Beaufort, arose and asked the Governor if he was in favor of
selecting "eleventh-hour Republicans " to elect to office, which made a
very marked sensation and elicited unmistakable applause from the
crowd. This encouraged Jones, of Georgetown, who also propounded
a question. He wanted to know if Mr. Reed was not one of those
whom Mr. Chamberlain fought so hard against in the Ku-Klux
trials.

The Governor replied that, to his personal knowledge, Mr. Reed
was not only not connected in any way, but had no sympathy, with the
Ku-Klux, and that he had a great deal more respect for a Republican
who only turned over once than for one who had made a dozen somer-
saults. He was prepared both to trust and to indorse Mr. Reed. It
was always an event when such men as Orr, Green, Townsend, Maher,
Melton, announced themselves members of the Republican party. It
gave strength to the party. The accession of such men was the
strength and hope of the party in the future. He did not question
Whipper's republicanism, but in point of ability and legal learning he
was not equal to the position. The Republican party had no right, by
reason of its numerical strength, to pick up any and every man and put
him to discharge the duties of judge in a great commercial metropolis.
As to the integrity of Whipper, there were some matters connected with
his association with the Sinking Fund Commission that required explanation.

This assertion produced a marked sensation. Whipper arose, and in a violent harangue denounced the attack on him as low, base, and cowardly, at which his supporters applauded lustily.

Order being restored, the Governor went on to say that this was the most important judicial position in the State, next to the Chief Justiceship, and it should be filled with the best talent and character that the party could command. He regarded Mr. Reed as the best. He stood here because the Republican party in South Carolina was gone unless they stood up to their promises. This was the first opportunity they had to translate their professions of reform into action.

At the close of the Governor's speech Whipper took the stand and made a violent onslaught upon the Administration. He said the time for dictation from the Governor had passed. [Tremendous applause.] The attack on him was base and cowardly. It passed the bounds of decency. If he had defrauded the State, why did not the Governor of the State, who was on the Board, and who was then Attorney General, bring him to punishment? [Applause and yells from the crowd.] He would only say in conclusion that he defied all of them to prove that he (Whipper) owed the State a single dollar.

He was in turn followed by Green and W. H. Jones, both of whom attacked the Governor. By this time (ten o'clock) the crowd began to show decided symptoms of a riot, and most of the outsiders left the hall. The caucus then adjourned, and the members took their departure.

The issue of this extraordinary and daring proceeding was announced in the following despatch to the *News and Courier* :

COLUMBIA, S. C., December 11th.—This has been an exciting day, but it ends in the complete triumph of the Chamberlain Administration over the Whipper and Whittemore factions of the Republican party.

Early in the morning the prospect was that the Hon. J. P. Reed, the administration candidate, would be entirely out of the race, and there was some thought of bringing out a new man in the event that Whipper was not elected on the first ballot. Whipper's friends made a square issue on the question of color and of opposition to Chamberlain, and at 1 o'clock they counted on 89 votes, which are more than a majority on joint ballot. As soon, however, as the Conservatives saw that the Administration was attacked, and in danger of defeat, they rallied to the support of Colonel Reed, and their votes decided the election against Whipper.

The two houses met in joint assembly as agreed, and J. P. Reed, W. J. Whipper (colored), and Elihu C. Baker were nominated in short speeches. The first ballot was then had, and when the last name on the roll was called the vote stood Reed 73, Whipper 56, Baker 18, scattering 9 ; necessary to a choice, 79. Joe Crews (Rep.) changed his vote from Baker to Reed, and his example was followed by many others. The result of the ballot was then announced as follows : Reed 103, Whipper 40, Baker 10, scattering 3. The Charleston delegation cast every one of their twenty votes for Reed.

The Charleston *News and Courier* in its editorial comment on this result said :

For the victory that was won the people must thank Governor Chamberlain, as well as the minority in the Legislature. The Conservatives felt that some lawyer of high standing at the Charleston Bar should have been raised to the bench ; that judicial election should not be made a question of party politics. But they could not elect such a candidate as would have been their first choice ; and it was the part of wisdom to vote for the one candidate, of those who could be elected, who had most to recommend him. That was their plain duty to their constituents, and they did it. Governor Chamberlain, in public and in private, fought against the election of Baker and Whipper. Neither persuasion nor menace served to drive him from the position he had deliberately taken. The first fight which the Chamberlain Administration has made is won, and there is not an honest man in South Carolina who has not to-day a far better and a far higher opinion of Governor Chamberlain than he had a week ago. In one striking instance the word has ripened into action.

The effect of this action did not cease with the occasion. Not long afterwards there was a vacancy to be filled by the Legislature in the office of Judge of the Third Circuit. The notorious ex-Governor F. J. Moses presented himself as a candidate. He received the support of those who had supported Mr. Whipper; but the reform Republicans supported Mr. Northrop, whose qualifications and character were unobjectionable. The Democrats supported Major Shaw, a lawyer and soldier, who had served in the Confederate army. The fifth ballot stood: Northrop, 42 ; Shaw, 42 ; Moses, 36, and several scattering—79 being necessary to a choice. The Democrats in succeeding ballots transferred votes to Northrop until it appeared that he would be elected. Then the supporters of Moses, in revenge, transferred their votes to Shaw, and Shaw's original supporters returned, so that when the result was announced Shaw was elected. Thus again was an honest and capable man chosen, instead of one of the worst men in the State.

The first appropriation bill passed during Governor Chamberlain's Administration reached him on the 21st of December 1874, the day before the usual adjournment of the Legislature for the Christmas holidays. It was far from satisfactory to him ; but so many interests were affected by it, so much suffering would result from the necessary delay in passing another bill, that he reluctantly signed it, sending to the Legislature the following Message :

EXECUTIVE CHAMBER,
COLUMBIA, December 22, 1874.

Gentlemen of the Senate and House of Representatives :

I have this day approved the following Act :

"An Act to make appropriation for the payment of the salary and mileage of the members of the General Assembly and the salaries of the subordinate officers and employés and other expenses incidental thereto."

In affixing my official approval to this Act, I feel compelled to state to your honorable bodies that I have had grave doubts respecting my duty in the premises. The mode in which the Act was finally passed, under the operation of the joint rules of the two houses, is suggestive of more than one difficulty of a legal and constitutional nature. The Act in its present form has been distinctly and decisively disapproved by one house. Its final passage is due wholly to a joint rule of the General Assembly. I cannot at the present time enter upon a discussion of the legal effect of this fact, but it is easy to see how grave are the questions involved, and with what facility such a rule may be used to defeat the will of one or the other house of the General Assembly.

Again, whoever will inform himself upon the subject will be satisfied that the tax of one mill on the dollar, levied to meet appropriations for legislative expenses for the present fiscal year, cannot produce more than $110,000 or $115,000. The amount appropriated by the Act is, therefore, in excess of the means provided to meet the appropriation, and one of the prime requisites of good administration is thus early set aside.

Again, the old evil of appropriating a gross amount to meet contingent or incidental expenses re-appears. There are, so far as I am able to judge, no expenses of the General Assembly which are properly contingent. Every item of legitimate expenditures is capable of being ascertained in dollars and cents, and no occasion exists for making an appropriation in advance of a knowledge of the exact amount needed to meet such expenses.

Lastly, in the mode of payment provided in sections 2 and 3 of the Act, the proper safeguards, in my judgment, are omitted. What I deem these to be, I have indicated in my Inaugural Address before your honorable bodies. I greatly regret, in the interest of good administration, that your honorable bodies have not provided a mode of payment which is, in my judgment, conformable to a sound and safe practice.

Having thus briefly pointed out the features of this Act which seem to me objectionable, I acknowledge with gratitude the many features of the Act which stamp it with an honorable superiority over our recent Appropriation Acts. Called upon, as I am, to act in view of what is practicable and attainable, with only a brief time in which to reflect upon my duty, unless I subject the members of your honorable bodies to serious personal inconvenience, and especially in view of

the very great improvement in this Act upon former similar Acts, I
have reluctantly decided to give the Act my official sanction.

D. H. CHAMBERLAIN,

Governor.

The following graphic letter, written not long after the events
recorded in this chapter, and addressed to a friend in Augusta,
Ga., reveals how the Governor's course, thus far, had affected an
influential class of citizens not heretofore disposed to believe that
any Republican could possess the virtues held in honor by South
Carolinians. The writer, Col. Pelham, was formerly a professor
in the South Carolina University at Columbia, was for many years
a well-known editorial writer, and at the time of these events
was the editor of the Columbia *Daily Phœnix*. He was ever
an ardent South Carolinian and Democrat, and was distinguished
as a gentleman of fine tastes and high culture.

COLUMBIA, Feb. 3, 1875.

DEAR COLONEL :

. . . The old State is passing through a new phase of experience. I do not know where it will land us. . . . At any rate,
Chamberlain interests us all. I had no faith in him when he was
elected. He seemed to us capable of doing more injury than his "pals,"
and not really disposed to do more good. He made fair promises
when he took office. Some of our best people were quite taken by
his words and manner. Of course we always admitted his unusual
ability. He is in fact a remarkable man in this respect,—a fine orator,
scholar, and lawyer—leads an irreproachable private life, and has evidently, as he always has had, as little as possible to do with his party.
. . . I am compelled to say I have changed my views of him,
but I shall wait a good while yet before I *believe* in him. . . . One
incident I will relate. He went into office the first of December last.
Following right after his brave words, the "niggers and scalawags"
passed a legislative appropriation bill which was only a trifle better
than those of Scott's and Moses' days. Chamberlain approved it, but
sent in a message which virtually said that he ought to have vetoed it.
I believed, and so said at the time in the *Phœnix*, that this was due to
cowardice. Chamberlain said in private that it was not good policy to
make the fight on matters that were even a small improvement on the
past, but I gave him no credit for sincerity.

Last month [1] a judge was to be elected for the Charleston circuit.
Whipper, the blackest rascal and the most rascally black in the State,
set himself up as a candidate. The "nigger" Solons met in caucus to

---

[1] That the occasion seemed less distant than it was in fact evidences the vivid-
ness of the impression produced.

endorse Whipper. Following their custom, they invited Chamberlain as Governor to the caucus. I attended to see the fun. To the surprise of nearly all Chamberlain came, though Sam. Melton had told a few of us that he was going to come and oppose Whipper. Trescot and a knot of us were in the hall. Chamberlain came in quietly and sat down in the rear of the hall, quite out of sight. I watched him closely. Whipper was on the stage haranguing his followers, and espying Chamberlain, he launched into a fierce attack on him as a Cæsar who wished to break down the party etc., and elect a white man. The moment Chamberlain heard this, he rose coolly from his seat and walked down the aisle, in sight of all, and took a seat directly in front of Whipper, who went on with the bitterest denunciations, and wound up by daring him to come on the platform and face those who had elected him. For one I did not imagine Chamberlain would open his mouth. It looked like something worse than a "forlorn hope." Smalls, who presided, followed up Whipper by inviting "His Excellency," in tones meant to be sarcastic, to address the caucus. This looked like "rubbing it in"!

Chamberlain calmly arose and stepped upon the stage. The negroes were apparently stunned at his audacity. He began by speaking of the importance of the office of judge for Charleston and the proper qualifications of a candidate. He said there were three candidates, Whipper, Baker, and Reed. Whipper, he said, was totally unfit in character and attainments. These words fairly cowed his hearers. Whipper, however, rose pale, if blackness can be pale, with rage, and advancing towards the stage demanded to know on what ground the Governor attacked his character. "On the ground," replied Chamberlain, "that you have embezzled three thousand dollars of the sinking fund, for one thing." And then waving him off, he proceeded to go over Whipper's career without mercy. The burly carcass of Smalls shrank in his seat ; the negroes were dazed, but no one dared to interrupt him again, and an adjournment was carried as soon as he finished. I said then, as I say now, it was the finest specimen of intellectual, if not moral, courage and address I have ever seen. You know the result. It turned the scale. Whipper was defeated and Reed elected. Most of the negroes voted for Whipper, but the Governor held enough, with the Democrats, to carry the election. Our fear was that the speech had so maddened the negroes as to make Whipper's election certain. Trescot said to Chamberlain, after his speech, "*C'est magnifique, mais ce n'est pas la guerre*"; but it *was* war and victory too.

Since that night I have a different idea of Chamberlain, though I trust him yet only so far as he goes and does well. . . . But that he is not "afeard" I now admit. . . .

Yours truly,
C. P. PELHAM.

CHAPTER V.

THE reassembling of the Legislature after the recess was on January 3, 1875. A few days later, Governor Chamberlain sent to it a Message which embraced information in detail, presented with care and exactness, supplementary to his Inaugural Address. He recognized that in the work of reform he had set himself to attempt, the intelligent co-operation of the Legislature would be necessary. To secure such co-operation it was important that its members should be informed of the actual condition of the State's affairs, and of his understanding of the gravity of existing evils, as well as of the means of restoring soundness and honor.

It may appear to persons whose lives have been passed in communities where the citizens "from their youth up" are instructed in public affairs and the law-makers are fairly representative of the best intelligence, that Governor Chamberlain, in his communications to the Legislature, assumed somewhat the tone of a mentor; but if the circumstances are duly considered it will be recognized that he assumed in this regard no more than was justifiable and sagacious. The majority of those whose aid he hoped to win had but brief experience in the rights and obligations even of private citizenship, and had been advanced to the duties and responsibilities of public office while they were immature in freedom and untrained in civic virtues. Moreover, they had been misdirected at the start, their aims perverted and their motives debauched, by vicious examples. Therefore Governor Chamberlain's task was to instruct by exposition and pre-cept as well as by suggestion and example. He had to demonstrate the mistakes of the past to the apprehension of those who were in a degree responsible for them, and had made money by them. He had to create in his associates of his own party that ideal of patriotic duty which enables men to suppress the instincts of selfishness, and put aside the temptations of personal interest. It will hardly be disputed that the conditions demanded extraordinary wisdom and tact, thorough mastery of facts, high courage, and undespairing patience. The Message of January 12, 1875, is here given.

EXECUTIVE DEPARTMENT,
COLUMBIA, S. C., January 12, 1875.

Gentlemen of the Senate and House of Representatives :

In the Inaugural Address which I had the honor to deliver before the General Assembly, I stated that, "owing to the want of the information to be obtained from the Reports of the various officers in charge of the several departments of the Government and the public institutions," it would become my duty at a subsequent time to present to you some additional information and recommendations concerning several important interests of the State.

In accordance with that announcement, and in the discharge of the duty imposed upon the Governor by the Constitution, "from time to time to give to the General Assembly information of the condition of the State, and to recommend to their consideration such measures as he shall judge necessary or expedient," I call attention to the serious public inconvenience resulting from the delay on the part of the officers from whom annual Reports are required in furnishing the same. Even at this late day, nearly two months and a half after the close of the last fiscal year, and seven weeks after the annual meeting of the General Assembly, I have barely been able to obtain several of the most important Reports in time to make a brief and imperfect examination of their contents. My public duty will, perhaps, be discharged by calling your attention to the great detriment thereby occasioned to the public service. If such delays arise from causes beyond the control of our public officers, then, if possible, the General Assembly should remove those causes ; but if they arise from other causes, a remedy ought to be devised and applied.

STATE TREASURER'S REPORT.

The Report of the State Treasurer will, I think, be found to be a luminous and complete exhibit of the operations of that department. The observations of the State Treasurer upon the several matters discussed in his Report will likewise deserve your careful consideration.

APPROPRIATIONS AND RECEIPTS.

I desire especially to call attention to the prime importance, as urged by the State Treasurer, of keeping the appropriations within the receipts. This is manifest without argument. All proper deductions should be made from the gross amount of the taxes to be levied, and a rigid estimate, based upon the results of former levies, should be reached before the rate of taxation is fixed. After this has been done, the appropriations from the proceeds of the levies made should never be allowed to exceed, by a single dollar, the estimate of the amount of such proceeds. As the State Treasurer justly remarks : " This is absolutely essential to the restoration of the credit of the State . . . and the success and prosperity of our public institutions."

In this connection, I call attention to the statement on page 12 of the Comptroller General's Report of the total taxable property of the State under the recent assessment, and the amounts to be realized therefrom under the specific levies made by the "Act to raise supplies for the fiscal year commencing November 1, 1874." I am confident the estimates there made are the highest limits which will be reached under those levies. If this be so, it is absolutely necessary that the appropriations to be made at the present session should in no instance exceed the amounts there specified. One palpable departure from this rule has already occurred in the legislative appropriation bill passed at the present session, and I trust no other similar departures will receive the sanction of the General Assembly.

In this connection I call attention to the "estimate of supplies for the support of the State government," at page 101 of the Comptroller General's Report. The whole amount required, according to that estimate, for "salaries and contingent funds," is no less than $212,450 ; whereas at page 12, of the same report, the whole amount to be realized from the levy made for the same purpose is only $150,476.51. If this estimate, therefore, is made the basis of the appropriations, there will be a deficiency of $61,973.49. It is manifest that such a result must be avoided, and I point it out in order that it may receive the attention which it demands.

OVERDRAWN WARRANTS AND DRAFTS.

I concur especially in the views expressed by the State Treasurer upon the evil and unjust practice which has prevailed of drawing warrants or drafts on the State Treasurer in excess of the appropriations from which they are payable. I think this evil should be checked by immediate legislation. Towards those who, in good faith, accept such overdrafts in payment of dues from the State, such a practice may be properly denounced as fraudulent.

COMPTROLLER GENERAL'S REPORT.

The Report of the Comptroller General presents a well arranged mass of information, which will deserve the consideration of the General Assembly.

I call the attention of the General Assembly to two statements, at page 12, of "the total taxable property of the State," namely, $141,624,-952. The corresponding amount under the former assessment was $176,956,502.74. I also call attention, with approval, to the observations of the Comptroller General, at pages 13 and 14, respecting a change in the time of the year when property should be listed, the necessity of a revision of the present general tax Act, and additional legislation in regard to forfeited lands.

DELINQUENT COUNTY TREASURERS.

I call special attention to the fact, as stated by the Comptroller General at page 15, that the sum of $470,090.20 remains charged against County Treasurers on the books of his office ; that amount being about 15 per cent. of all State taxes collected since 1868. While only a part, possibly a small part, of that sum is actually due to the State, yet no reason of which I am aware exists why this entire sum should not at once be "accounted for." I therefore join with the Comptroller General in asking that " stringent laws providing severe and prompt punishment " be enacted to prevent such results in the future, and also that the Attorney General and solicitors be directed to use all existing legal means to compel an immediate settlement of all unsettled accounts of County Treasurers, and the recovery of the amounts found due, by suits, if necessary, against the sureties.

CLAIMS OF THOMAS W. PRICE COMPANY.

The Comptroller General has called the attention of the General Assembly to the character of the claims of the Thomas W. Price Company, of Philadelphia, for books and blanks furnished for the use of County Auditors and Treasurers for receiving the returns and assessing and collecting the State and county taxes. There is also an unpaid claim of the same Company on account of work done for the Superintendent of Education, as stated at page 24 of that officer's report for 1873, amounting to $4,539.35, which is equally meritorious. The work of this Company was superior in quality, was done at the lowest prices, and under circumstances which entitle the company to our grateful consideration. I transmit, herewith, copies of the correspondence relating to this matter, and I trust that the General Assembly will not fail to give it prompt attention.

BONDS OF COUNTY AUDITORS AND TREASURERS.

I transmit with this Message copies of a circular letter issued by the Comptroller General and approved by the Governor, fixing the amounts of the bonds of County Auditors, and also requiring all County Treasurers now in office to comply within thirty days with the requirements of law respecting their official bonds. The Governor is authorized to fix the amounts of the bonds of County Auditors, and I have endeavored to exercise this power in a manner which will secure the public interests.

OBSOLETE ACCOUNTS.

The Comptroller General, at page 18 of his Report, calls attention to the fact that the books of his office—and the same is true of the books of the Treasurer's office—are burdened with certain accounts which are really obsolete, representing values which do not now exist. These accounts must be annually carried forward until authority is given to the Comptroller General and the Treasurer to close them. For obvious reasons, as well as in accordance with numerous precedents in this State and elsewhere, I join with the Comptroller General in recommending that authority be given by the General Assembly to finally close all such accounts.

VACANCY IN THE OFFICE OF COMPTROLLER GENERAL.

The Comptroller General has called attention to the vacancy which will arise on the fourth of March next in the office of Comptroller General, occasioned by the election of the present incumbent as a member of the Forty-fourth Congress. I need not do more than to remind the General Assembly that it will be necessary to provide some mode of filling such a vacancy.

INSURANCE DEPOSITS.

In my Inaugural Address I ventured to say that, in my judgment, good policy dictated the repeal of the present laws requiring deposits from insurance companies not incorporated by this State. Further examination and reflection confirm me in that opinion. The supposed security to policy-holders from requiring such deposits is fallacious. If a company is sound, there is not the least difficulty in recovering any loss by process of law, and if it is unsound, the fact of a deposit being made in this State would afford very little protection to our policy-holders in case of disaster to the company. It is, moreover, a serious legal question whether these deposits can be so sequestrated from the general assets of a company as to prevent their becoming a part of the general fund applicable to the payment of all creditors in case of the insufficiency of other assets. The general effect of requiring such deposits is to exclude the best companies and admit the weakest, except in cases where the sacrifice of withdrawing from the State overbalances the injury to the company by scattering its funds in the manner required. I transmit herewith a letter addressed to me officially by an eminent insurance authority, in which the whole matter is discussed in a most clear and conclusive manner. I hereby renew my former recommendations of a repeal of the present laws on this subject, in order to allow free competition in this branch of business, under such restrictions only as have regard to the general character and strength of the several companies.

EXTENSION OF TIME FOR COLLECTION OF TAXES.

In connection with the Comptroller General's Report, I desire to correct a misapprehension now widely prevailing as to the power of the

Governor and Comptroller General in extending the time for the collection of taxes.

In the Tax Act of 1868, in Section 147, authority was given to the State Auditor, with the approval of the Governor, to extend the time for the performance of the duties required of any officer by that Act. It is more than doubtful whether this provision ever gave power to the Governor and State Auditor to extend the time for the collection of taxes. However that may be, that section was repealed by the Act of March 8, 1871 (vol. 14, Statutes at Large, p. 622). No similar power was again conferred on any officer until the passage of the Act of February 6, 1874 (Acts of 1873–4, p. 533). The latter Act was expressly limited in its application to the fiscal year commencing November 1, 1873, and its operation, of course, ceased with that year.

The result is that the only power now possessed by any executive officer or officers to extend the time for the collection of taxes is conferred by section 139 of the Act of March 19, 1874 (Acts 1873–4, p. 778), which is in the following words : " That whenever the General Assembly shall fail to make the annual levy of taxes, or the collection of the same may be in any way delayed, it shall be the duty of the Comptroller General to notify each County Treasurer that the penalty for non-payment shall not attach until after the expiration of sixty days from the date of his public announcement of his readiness to collect the said taxes."

Under this section the Governor has no power to act, and the power of the Comptroller General is limited to cases of delay in commencing the collection of taxes at the regular time. I call special attention to this statement of the law in order to relieve myself of the frequent and urgent applications made to me for my action in postponing the collection of taxes. If any further legislation on the subject is needed, it will be the duty of the General Assembly to provide it.

THE LUNATIC ASYLUM.

The Comptroller General's Report covers that of the Superintendent of the Lunatic Asylum. This institution deserves the generous support of the State. In many respects its present condition is very satisfactory. The buildings have been greatly improved, and the domestic economy of the institution and the professional treatment of the patients are believed to be worthy of high commendation.

It is, however, the financial condition of the institution which will require most serious attention. It appears that there was a debt owing by the institution of $55,295.55 at the close of the last fiscal year, October 31, 1874. This debt results from the excess of expenditures over receipts for several years past. From whatever motive expenditures beyond the means provided for meeting them are made, the practice is not to be approved. No public officer, under any thing less than very extraordinary circumstances, can be justified in assuming to incur obligations for the public without express authority of law.

It is proper to call attention at this point to the Act of March 17,

1874, "to regulate the manner in which public funds shall be disbursed by public officers." This Act makes it a felony "for any public officer (State or county) to enter into a contract, for any purpose whatsoever, in a sum in excess of the tax levied or the amount appropriated for the accomplishment of such purpose." Hereafter, therefore, no expenditures can be made in excess of the appropriation. The amount of tax for the support of penal, charitable, and educational institutions has already been fixed for the present fiscal year. This levy will not permit the appropriation of a single dollar for the payment of past indebtedness. By reference to page 12 of the Comptroller General's Report the amount to be realized from this levy will be about $150,000. By reference to the Act making appropriations for the last fiscal year it will be seen that the total appropriations under the same head were upwards of $190,000. It is clear, therefore, that no appropriations can be made for the present year in excess of those of last year. I cannot, therefore, consent to recommend an increased appropriation for the lunatic asylum for the present fiscal year, unless it can be shown from what sources funds can with certainty be obtained to meet such increased appropriations. I regret to reach such a conclusion, for no one can have a stronger sympathy with this institution than I have, or a more ardent wish to increase its efficiency and extend its blessings. But we must not, from sympathy or benevolence, repeat the financial mistakes of the past. It is far better for every public interest to keep our expenditures rigidly within our receipts, than to cripple our merchants and ruin our public credit by contracting debts which cannot be paid, except, possibly, at some indefinite future time.

I cannot give my consent to appropriations in excess of probable receipts, nor to expenditures in excess of appropriations. I shall approve of the most generous treatment of the lunatic asylum consistent with our ability to pay our obligations when they mature, but nothing more. I shall speak further of the action proper to be taken, in my judgment, in reference to the past indebtedness of the lunatic asylum, as well as that of the State penitentiary, at a later point in this message.

STATE PENITENTIARY.

The Comptroller General's Report covers also the Report of the Superintendent of the Penitentiary. Here, again, the feature of the Report which will arrest most attention is the statement of the indebtedness of this institution. The Superintendent states that the aggregate indebtedness of the institution on the 31st day of October, 1873, was $102,238.40. He further states that the present indebtedness is $87,918.39, of which $12,380 has arisen during that fiscal year. Another statement is, that there is due to the guards and employés of the institution $15,850.31. The appropriation for the penitentiary for the last fiscal year was $51,500.

These facts present a problem not easy to solve. The remarks already made concerning the financial condition of the lunatic asylum are applicable here. The levy of taxes for the present year will not permit an increased appropriation. One thing is evident, namely, that the expenditures of this institution must hereafter be kept within the appropriations. It is difficult to see how, without direct violation of the law of March 17, 1874, already referred to, an indebtedness of $12,-380, in excess of the appropriation, could have been contracted during the last fiscal year.

I strongly urge that the immediate attention of the General Assembly be directed to the question of making the labor of the penitentiary available for the support, in part, of the institution. I call attention to the remarks of the Superintendent on this point. If the labor of the convicts can be utilized within the walls of the penitentiary, this would be the wisest plan. Mechanical pursuits are conducted in similar institutions elsewhere with profit to the State. Such labor is advantageous in many ways—as a means of discipline during the imprisonment of the convicts ; as a means of encouraging habits of industry and the ability to earn an honest living when they return to freedom ; and as a means of reducing the public burden of their support while in confinement. If there are no opportunities for the utilization of this labor at present, I think the plan of letting out the convicts for hire, which is adopted in many other States, is worthy of immediate consideration. I am informed that such labor in other States can be leased at a net daily profit of at least twenty cents per day for each laborer. Out of an average number of two hundred convicts, at least one hundred able-bodied laborers could be constantly furnished, and from these laborers an income of several thousand dollars, above all expense for their maintenance, might be realized. Motives of economy, as well as the good of the convicts themselves, in my judgment, require that an effort be made to obtain employment of some kind for this class of laborers, and I earnestly recommend that the attention of the General Assembly be directed to this subject without delay.

NATIONAL PRISON ASSOCIATION.

I transmit herewith a letter addressed to me officially by the Secretary of the National Prison Association; and in this connection I respectfully invite attention to the truly noble work in which this Association is engaged. The Association proposes that the several State legislatures shall, if so disposed, make a small annual appropriation, which will entitle each State to 500 or 600 volumes of the annual " Transactions of the National Prison Congress." This would place the volume in the hands of each member of successive legislatures, officers of penal and reformatory institutions, public libraries and schools.

I do not hesitate to say that such a volume, so distributed, would rouse an interest among our people in one of the most humane and successful efforts to reduce the number of our criminal classes, and to restore them to the walks of useful industry.

The most distinguished statesmen, scholars, and philanthropists are officers and active promoters of the Association, and I recommend that the General Assembly, if possible, make the small appropriation of $1,000, which will entitle them to the benefit of the annual publications of this Association.

STATE ORPHAN ASYLUM.

The Report of the Trustees of the State Orphan Asylum has already been transmitted to the General Assembly. This institution is entitled to adequate support, and the report of the Trustees will furnish, I think, the necessary information for the action of the General Assembly.

EDUCATION OF THE DEAF, DUMB, AND BLIND.

The institution for the education of the deaf, dumb, and blind, formerly located at Cedar Springs, near Spartanburg Court-House, was closed in September, 1873. I regard the closing of this institution as a misfortune and reproach to our State. It was an act of educational retrogression, and a wrong to a class of our fellow-beings and fellow-citizens which has peculiar claims upon our aid and sympathy.

If the reopening and rehabilitation of this institution can be effected by any means within the control of the General Assembly, consistently with the present condition of our financial affairs, I unhesitatingly recommend that it be done without delay. If this cannot be done at once, I trust that such arrangements will be made as will secure that result during the next fiscal year.

QUARANTINE AT CHARLESTON.

The Report of the Health Officer of the Port of Charleston has heretofore been transmitted to the General Assembly.

I recommend to your consideration the various suggestions made in that report. The maintenance of an efficient quarantine department at the principal port of our State, and at our other seaports generally, is a duty of too obvious importance to need special enforcement.

REPORT OF THE SECRETARY OF STATE.

The Report of the Secretary of State presents information of great value, covering the matters connected with the ordinary duties of that office, and also the land commission department, and the improvements upon the State house and grounds during the past year. I call attention to the recommendations of the Secretary of State on page 6 of his Report.

REPORT OF THE ADJUTANT AND INSPECTOR GENERAL.

I herewith transmit the Annual Report of the Adjutant and Inspector General, with its accompanying documents and vouchers, and invite your attention to the information, as well as the various recommendations, therein contained.

REPORT OF STATE LIBRARIAN.

The Report of the Keeper of the State House and State Librarian has been heretofore transmitted to the General Assembly.

REPORT OF THE STATE SUPERINTENDENT OF EDUCATION.

The Report of the State Superintendent of Education is herewith transmitted to the General Assembly. I commend the entire Report to the earnest attention not only of the General Assembly, but of all our fellow-citizens who look to the welfare of the State. It presents the actual condition at this time of our common-school system, its progress during the past year, the causes that diminish the efficiency of the system, and also points out some remedies for present evils. It may be said, in general, that the Report shows a fair measure of progress during the last year. The school population of the State is 230,102 ; the total school attendance is 104,738, an increase of 19,144 over the school attendance of the preceding year. The number of free common schools in the State is now 2,353, an increase of 272 since the preceding report of the Superintendent. The total number of teachers employed is 2,627, an increase of 253 since the preceding report. The average number of months during which the schools were actually open was only five. The number of schoolhouses in the State is 2,228, an increase of 211 since the preceding report. The total amount of funds applicable to the common schools during the past year was $512,924.93, of which there remains as unpaid appropriations the sum of $29,779.71, leaving the sum of $483,145.22 as the net school revenue of the past year. The school expenditures for the year were $448,251.76.

I call attention to one or two facts, which appear from these statistics, and which show how far our school system still is from the standard which should be aimed at. First, the total school attendance falls considerably below one half of the total school population, being about seventeen thirty-eighths. Second, the average period during which our schools are in session is only five months. Our constant aim should be to increase the school attendance till it embraces all our school population, and to increase the length of time during which our schools should be in session to eight or nine months in the year. The State Superintendent calls especial attention to the incapacity of many of the teachers employed. I agree with him in the fact stated, and in his suggestion of the cause of that fact. The blame rests with the Boards of County School Examiners, whose duty it is to examine all teachers. These boards consist in each county of the County School Commissioner and two persons selected by the County School Commissioner. I recommend most earnestly that the appointment of the latter examiners be given to the State Superintendent of Education. I do not wish to be understood as reflecting upon all our County School Commissioners by this recommendation, but in view of undeniable facts as to the incapacity of some of these officers, I am persuaded that the mode of appointing the examiners should be immediately changed. That being done, I think this primary cause of inefficiency in our school system—the incompetency of teachers—will be almost entirely removed. I also renew the recommendation made in my Inaugural Address, that high schools be provided for in each county. The amount of money required by the State Superintendent, to carry on the school system for the present year, is based upon a school year of nine months, and is undoubtedly largely in excess of the means available for that purpose. I cannot recommend any appropriation under this head in excess of our means. The homely motto, "Pay as you go," is applicable here as elsewhere. Even in educational matters, we cannot afford to make expenditures until we have the means to pay. I do recommend, however, that the largest appropriation possible, with a due regard to our financial necessities, be made for all our educational institutions. But—what is quite as indispensable to the success of our school system—I trust that our fellow-citizens generally will take a more active personal interest in the practical working of the system. It is my purpose, during the coming season, to make some personal inspection of our schools in different parts of the State, and to seek, in some public and private ways, to call out and secure a greater interest in our people generally in this subject. In these efforts I know I shall be seconded by the State Superintendent of Education, as well as by all those who properly appreciate the relations of education and free government.

The State University, with its preparatory school, the State Normal School, and the Agricultural and Mechanical College at Orangeburg, will each, I trust, receive the attention which they require at the hands of the General Assembly.

REPORT OF THE ATTORNEY GENERAL.

I transmit herewith the Annual Report of the Attorney General. It will be found to present, with due fulness of detail, the labors of that office in respect to causes in the courts in which the State has been a party, or had an interest which required a legal representative. No one can examine the Report without being convinced of the importance and variety of the public interests to be represented by the Attorney General. I earnestly urge the perusal of this Report upon the members of the General Assembly. I think they will agree with me in the opinion that the litigation conducted through the Attorney General and those employed by him, has not only been extensive and most important, but that the manner in which it has been conducted, and the results attained, are such as to inspire confidence in the fidelity and professional skill with which the State has in this respect been served. The Report of the Attorney General shows the amount of litigation still unfinished. It is unnecessary to add that this unfinished business, together with that which will inevitably arise during the present year, will require that provision be made for the expenses necessarily connected with such litigation. I do not doubt that more than one private corporation in this State has expended a larger sum in litigation during the past year, than has been expended by the State. The professional fees paid to those who have represented the State have not equalled in amount those which are usually paid by private persons and corporations for like services. I call attention to the estimate of expenses for the present year, at page 103 of the Comptroller General's Report.

COUNTY FINANCES.

The financial condition of many, if not most, of the counties of the State is deplorable. The practice of making expenditures, incurring obligations, and issuing checks, warrants, and orders in excess of the funds provided to meet them, has prevailed to such an extent as to produce a state of affairs which calls for the action of the General Assembly. Under the present law, no part of the funds to be collected for county purposes during the present year can be applied to the payment of any obligations incurred prior to November 1, 1874. The result is, that no resource is open for the present payment of many of the most meritorious creditors of the counties. I instance here, as of that class, the jurors, sheriffs, and other officers, who have felt compelled, or actually been compelled, by their public duty, to give their time, or to use their personal credit, to maintain the public institutions of their counties. No juror could refuse to obey his summons to attend the courts; no sheriff could open his jail doors because the County Treasurers could not furnish funds to feed the prisoners. In this way it has happened, to my personal knowledge, that county officers have exhausted their personal means and credit, and are left without hope of present payment. To remove this injustice, authority should be given to the County Commissioners, under proper instructions, to levy taxes to gradually pay past indebtedness. This should not be done in one levy, but the tax should be distributed over two or more years. The next duty is to provide some effectual protection against such evils in the future. The only perfect protection is honesty and economy on the part of the County Commissioners; but in the absence of those qualities, something may be done, I think, by legislation. To this end, and as the result of my most careful examination of the subject, I recommend that the system of specific levies be applied to county taxes. I do not know that it will be expedient or practicable to make a specific levy for every class of county expenditures, but I do recommend that the levies be made specific for such objects as the pay of jurors, the dieting of prisoners, and other expenses which are of such a character as to be essential to the maintenance of public order and government. There is scarcely any subject which calls more loudly for redress than our county financial systems, and I trust the General Assembly will devise and apply the proper remedies.

FLOATING INDEBTEDNESS OF THE STATE.

The floating indebtedness of the State presents a subject so vast, undefined, and complicated, as to require the exercise of our best judgment, as well as great caution, in dealing with it. The total amount of the apparent indebtedness of this class is unascertained. The legal validity of a large part of it is more than doubtful, and the meritorious character of a still larger part may well be disputed. There is a certain view which may be taken of this whole class of indebtedness, which would treat it as a matter to be indefinitely postponed. In this view the present Administration and General Assembly might regard it as an indebtedness for which they are not responsible, and which they should not, therefore, permit to become a burden upon their management of public affairs. For my own part, I cannot altogether take this view of the subject ; I must regard so much of this indebtedness as has the character of legal and moral validity as a portion of the public burden which we, who are now called to conduct public affairs, must assume. On the other hand, I am inflexibly opposed to the hasty or present liquidation of any considerable portion of this indebtedness. The public interests, in my judgment, require, first, that we should provide for the payment promptly, and in full, of all expenditures made or to be made during the present year. Not until this is done should our attention be turned to the past floating indebtedness of the State.

Further than this, I am opposed to any plan which looks to the indiscriminate payment of all this indebtedness or its indiscriminate reduction or rejection. I think its amount, the various classes of which it consists, the time and circumstances under which and the objects for which it was incurred, should be ascertained. After this is done, I think such portions of this indebtedness as have the highest merit in point of general equity should be provided for, if it can be done without imposing too great a burden of taxation upon the people. Under this latter head, I think, would fall the existing indebtedness, in great part, at least, of the Lunatic Asylum and the State Penitentiary, and, perhaps, of other charitable and penal institutions. I know, for instance, from personal experience and information, that many of our merchants, bankers, and other citizens have come forward, from a sense of duty and not from ordinary business motives, on several occasions, to sustain our Lunatic Asylum and Penitentiary by furnishing supplies and by lending their money and credit. Such services create the highest possible obligation on the part of the State to repay such parties at the earliest practicable time.

I recommend, then, that, after due discrimination between the classes of our floating indebtedness has been made, such portions or classes of this indebtedness be selected as have the highest equitable claim to payment, and, then, that it be ascertained whether the people are able to bear the burden of any additional tax to pay them, in whole or in part. Whatever it may be found possible to do in this way, I trust will be done. Above all things, the General Assembly should make any such levy specific in all respects. The objects to which the tax is to be applied should be distinguished, beyond all doubt or question ; if any debts are to be paid in full, it should be so ordered ; and if a *pro rata* payment among several debts or classes of debts is to be made, the exact mode and percentage of payment should be specified. No opportunity should be given for any diversion of such funds from the precise objects for which they are designed by the General Assembly. With the expression of these views, I submit the matter to the wisdom of the General Assembly, with the hope that such action will be taken as will convince all honest public creditors of the readiness of this General Assembly to do all in their power to meet the just obligations of the State.

FISH CULTURE.

I have been requested by several citizens, for whom I have great respect, to call the attention of the General Assembly to the subject of the stocking of our streams and lakes with fish. It has been represented to me that a commissioner or commissioners might be authorized to be appointed by the Governor, to serve wholly without pay, who would enable the State, at a trifling expense—say about $1,000,—to procure from the United States and the other States the best varieties of fish with which to replenish our waters. I transmit herewith a copy of the annual report of the Commissioners of Fisheries of New York, and submit the subject to the consideration of the General Assembly.

MINORITY REPRESENTATION.

I commend to the consideration of the General Assembly the question of enacting a law applying the system of voting, known as "cumulative voting" or "minority representation," to the elections of incorporated cities and towns in the State. I do not feel prepared to do more than to recommend that the system be tried on a small scale at present. As a matter of theory, the system promises the best results, but I think our policy respecting it should be tentative at first. If its practical results are satisfactory when applied to our cities and towns, public sentiment will sustain its application to other elections. A bill introduced by Senator Cochran, of Anderson, is now before the Senate, which embraces this feature among its provisions, and I commend it to the favorable action of the General Assembly.

REVENUE RECOMMENDATIONS.

I renew, with increased confidence, the recommendations made in my Inaugural Address, and especially the recommendations for a reduction of all public expenditures to the lowest point consistent with the actual requirements of good government ; the discontinuance of contingent funds, except to a very limited extent ; the shortening of the sessions of the General Assembly ; the reduction of its expenses and the entire abolition of legislative contingent or incidental funds ; the removal of all abuses connected with the public printing ; the keeping of expenditures within receipts, and particularly the immediate adoption of a proper system of accountability in the disbursement of all public funds. The practical enforcement of the last recommendation I regard as absolutely essential to our success in avoiding the evils of the past, which now block our efforts at progress on every hand. Upon this subject my views are so decided that I shall feel obliged in future to place the responsibility for a failure to adopt some safer system than the one now prevailing entirely upon the General Assembly.

MODE OF SELECTING COUNTY AUDITORS AND TREASURERS.

In my Inaugural Address, I called attention to the question of the best mode of selecting the County Auditors and Treasurers. My re-

marks on that occasion have been understood as a positive recommendation of their election by the people. Such was not my intention,
nor does my language properly convey that meaning. I intended
simply to bring the question before the General Assembly. My relations to this question are such, at present, as possibly to give me an
unconscious bias in considering the subject. The importunity of
applicants, the difficulty of obtaining correct and unbiased information
as to the qualifications of applicants, and the personal dissatisfaction
certain to arise, whenever any selection is made from several candidates, may, I am aware, affect my present judgment upon this question,
and I therefore leave it, without recommendation, to the wisdom of
the General Assembly.

JUSTICES OF THE PEACE AND CONSTABLES.

In my Inaugural Address, I recommended that the provisions of the
State Constitution, which require the election by the people in each
county of "a competent number of Justices of the Peace and Constables," should be enforced without further delay. Considerable discussion has since taken place respecting the wisdom of that recommendation, and I now venture, in renewing that recommendation, to present
my reasons more fully. The one all-sufficing reason why those officers
should be elected by the people, a reason which should supersede the
necessity of further discussion, in my judgment, is that such is the
positive requirement of the Constitution. I do not think the general
policy or result of the system, nor especially any question of party
advantage or disadvantage, has any proper place in the consideration
of this question. I understand that constitutions are made to be
obeyed and executed. I understand that this principle applies to all
parts and provisions of the Constitution. I am aware that there is a
certain latitudinarian rule of construction, a sort of questionable
"judge-made law," which enable courts, at their discretion, to hold that
a statute which says "shall" only means "may"; but I know of no
respectable authority which permits such a rule to be applied to constitutions. All the requirements of a constitution are mandatory, and
if this particular requirement of our Constitution can be set aside,
then there is no such thing left, as far as I can see, as constitutional
obligation in our State. The whole question is, therefore, settled for
me by a simple reference to the Constitution. But if this were a
question of policy merely, my judgment and experience would lead me
to the same conclusion. It is a practical impossibility, in my judgment,
for any Governor to appoint three hundred and fifty Trial Justices, in
all parts of the State, so as to secure, to a proper degree, the interests
of the people affected by these appointments. This impossibility becomes more apparent when the Governor finds himself surrounded
and trammelled in the discharge of his duty in this respect, by what
are considered his obligations to the political party to which he owes
his election. The people of the several counties are certainly better
qualified to select these officers than any central appointing power can

be, and they are more certain to act in the spirit of a desire to secure the welfare of their local community than any Governor can be expected to be. Their knowledge is greater, their interest is greater, and hence their selections will be better. It is sometimes suggested that if these officers were elected by the people, their removal, if found unworthy, would be too difficult. The answer is that the fact of the difficulty in procuring their removal would, in the first place, produce that very caution in making the selection which is needed. But, in the second place, there need be no undue delay in procuring the removal of unworthy Justices of the Peace. They can, under the Constitution, be removed by the process of impeachment or address, and I see no difficulty in providing by statute that an indictment for any misconduct should work the suspension, and a conviction of such offence should work a forfeiture of the office. No officer ought certainly to hold his office by a weaker tenure than this. If the constitutional system shall, after fair trial, prove to be objectionable, the Constitution can be so amended as to put an end to the system and substitute a better system. My deliberate conclusion, after a careful consideration, is that the General Assembly is bound by the Constitution to provide for the election by the people of the several counties of Justices of the Peace and Constables, and I make that recommendation without hesitation.

REGISTRATION OF ELECTORS.

In my Inaugural Address, I recommended that the provision of the State Constitution which makes it the duty of the General Assembly "to provide, from time to time, for the registration of all electors," should be no longer disregarded. I have observed the discussion which this recommendation has occasioned, but I am unable to feel the force of any arguments drawn from considerations of political policy, when opposed to a plain requirement of the Constitution. If it were demonstrable that party advantage would arise from the neglect of this requirement of the Constitution, it would not have a feather's weight in deterring me from carrying into effect the Constitution which I have sworn to support. But it is idle to urge that a registration of electors will help or hurt any party which relies upon proper means to sustain its supremacy. A registration of electors is an obvious measure of justice. It will not prevent all election frauds, but it will go far towards that end, and will tend to give a degree of confidence in the result of our elections which has sometimes been wanting.

CONCLUSION.

In conclusion, I feel warranted in congratulating the General Assembly and our fellow-citizens generally, on the evidences already presented of a purpose on the part of all good citizens to aid the present Administration in its efforts to restore and enforce good government in our State. It is not too much to say that every substantial interest of our people has already revived, under the belief that our public trusts will be honestly administered. I acknowledge with gratitude, in the common interest of our whole people. the many proofs which I have received of the sincere purpose of those who did not support me in the late election, to sustain the measures and policy announced in my Inaugural Address. It betokens a practical unification, in its best sense, of our two races. So long as I can be the instrument by which such results are promoted, I shall not be disturbed by the unfriendly criticism of the few who may charge me with lack of partisan zeal. My political principles will never be concealed nor compromised, but whenever the necessities of any political party shall require me to disregard or abuse my public trusts, then my allegiance to that party will cease. All my recommendations now and heretofore made in the direction of public economy have been made in good faith ; nor shall I be satisfied, to borrow the language of another, with "that vague and verbal economy which public men are so ready to express with regard to public expenditures, but only with that earnest and inexorable economy which proclaims its existence by accomplished facts." The most auspicious day for our State will be the day which finds all our people so united in their regard for the public weal that the advent to power of any political party shall not endanger the liberties or the material interests of any class of our fellow-citizens.

D. H. CHAMBERLAIN,
Governor.

Among the comments upon the foregoing Message, the following, all from Democratic newspapers of the State, are indicative of the judgment of the people whose personal interests were most affected by public extravagance.

[From the Charleston News and Courier.]

We print to-day the special message sent by Governor Chamberlain to the General Assembly upon its reassembling yesterday. The message is warmly praised by both Conservatives and Republicans in Columbia ; and well it may be, for we can say of this message, what we could not say of any previous message, that it contains not a single recommendation which is not, in the main, wise, prudent, and just. And the tone of the message is as healthy as its policy is sound. Our Republican Governor tells the General Assembly, in plain words, that in South Carolina the Constitution shall be the highest law ; and he places on record, before the people, the manly declaration that whenever the necessities of any political party shall require him to disregard or abuse the public trusts, his allegiance to that party will cease. There is a world of cheer and comfort in these words. There is reason for hopefulness and for confidence. And we say, once more, to Governor Chamberlain, that so long as he maintains his present position, so long as he stands on the high plane of his inaugural address and special message, the honest people of all classes will sustain him and strengthen him, not as Conservatives or as Republicans, but as citizens of South Carolina, having one and the same interest in the present and the future of the State.

After a careful examination of Governor Chamberlain's message, of which we publish a part in this issue, we concede a very cordial approval. It deserves to be read and pondered by every citizen, for we think its counsel noble and its spirit earnest.— *Lexington Dispatch.*

The message of Governor Chamberlain on the reassembling of the General Assembly is just such a one as we were led to look for from him. It is, indeed, full of cheer, and the prospect which opens for the future of our State Government is hopeful indeed.—*Newberry Herald.*

Governor Chamberlain has addressed an extra message to the General Assembly, voluminous in text, strong and pointed in suggestions, has risen above mere party questions, and is every day fulfilling the pledges made alike to Conservatives and Republicans in his campaign.— *The Grange.*

The message is a fit complement of the inaugural address, which met with the hearty sanction of the State. All good citizens will labor with the Governor to hasten the coming of that auspicious day which shall find " all our people so united in the regard for the public weal, that the advent to power of any political party shall not endanger the liberties or the material interests of any class of our fellow-citizens."— *Chester Reporter.*

These words have the ring of the true metal, and in making good his promises Governor Chamberlain will be sustained by the good people of the State, irrespective of political ties or party affiliation. . . . It is gratifying to note that for the first time since reconstruction our State Government is honorably recognized abroad and commanding respectful mention.— *Yorkville Enquirer.*

We are happy to unite with others in the most hearty approval of the general contents of the message, and rejoice to see in it a fulfilment, so far, of the pledges made by the Governor in his inaugural, which were, in fact, only a vindication of those made during the canvass. We rejoice at the fine opportunity afforded by Governor Chamberlain to prove to the world that Southern gentlemen are not capable of the folly of proscription and oppression to men for mere opinions in politics. There is another illustration in this State of the real temper and feeling of Southern men. Governor Orr was a most pronounced Republican and a strong supporter, up to his death, of the administration of General Grant. Yet he never incurred the odium and dislike or general denunciation of old South Carolina, because the people who had known him were satisfied that all his aims were for his country's good, although they may have included his own personal promotion as well. In other words, they believed him honest. If Governor Chamberlain continues in the course he has set out in, he will earn the same position that was occupied formerly by Governor Orr.—*Enterprise and Mountaineer.*

We are sure that the good people of the State will hail the present message as a new proof of the good faith of the Governor, and will extend to him their cordial support—*Press and Banner.*

The Governor certainly has clear ideas of what ought to be done, and seems determined to have them carried into execution. A fine opportunity was afforded his Excellency to make a political speech and ventilate his views on outrages, "banditti," Sheridan and Grant ; but, with commendable good taste, he makes not the slightest allusion to these exciting topics. He addresses himself to the domestic economy of South Carolina, which he knows needs attention, and can furnish sufficient material for the patriotism and mental activity of the Legislature.—*Camden Journal.*

I think now it is generally conceded that Chamberlain will be a governor of the whole people, as to general justice and right, though he will confine his appointments chiefly to Republicans, where competent ones can be found. I have no objection to this, as it is natural and reasonable. Whenever, however, any unwise law or fraudulent measure seeks his approval, I think it will receive his official condemnation. His ability enables him to know the right, and his ambition and interest alike, apart from his moral sense of duty, prompt him to carry it out. The wisdom of his last message as to confining appropriations to the sum levied for the purpose, if heeded, will go farther to correct past evils than any thing else. In two years we hope and believe that his administration will be such as to render the white people of the State the strongest supporters of Governor Chamberlain. Our people only want a wise, just, and economical government, and this, I believe, he will endeavor to inaugurate.— *Cor. of Keowee Courier.*

CHAPTER VI

Message Regarding the Appointment of Trial Justices—Trouble in Edgefield County Settled by Disbanding the Colored Militia—Letter to the Chairman of the Senate Committee on Finance Presenting a Scheme for Retrenchment in Appropriations—Veto of an Act Validating Certain Payments by the Treasurer of Edgefield County—The *Union Herald* and the *News and Courier*—A Significant Article.

IN his Inaugural Address Governor Chamberlain had called the attention of the Legislature to the neglect to make provision for the election by the people, of Justices of the Peace and Constables, as authorized by the Constitution, and had sharply arraigned the evils of the existing system of Trial Justices, declaring that " the incumbents of these offices are to a great extent deficient in the qualities which make a useful magistrate," and pledging himself, while the system continued, " to use the power of appointment in such a way as to give to the people Trial Justices who will know the law, and will use their powers to preserve the rights and protect the interests of all." That the duty would be " onerous and difficult," he expressly recognized ; but he added, " I shall endeavor to discharge it without fear or favor." The Legislature paid no heed to his recommendation that the scheme sanctioned by the Constitution should be put in execution, and it soon became his duty to make certain nominations of Trial Justices. In what spirit he performed this duty and with what spirit he was met, appear in the following official papers :

SENATE CHAMBER,
COLUMBIA, January 25, 1875.

To the Editor of the Daily Union-Herald:
SIR—I am directed by the Senate to furnish to the press copies of the following communications.
Very respectfully, J. WOODRUFF,
Clerk of the Senate.

EXECUTIVE CHAMBER,
COLUMBIA, January 26, 1875.

Hon. R. H. Gleaves, President of the Senate :

SIR—I have the honor to acknowledge the receipt of your communication of the 25th inst., informing me that the Senate desires the removal of the usual secrecy observed with Executive communications in the case of any Message to the Senate, relative to the appointments of Trial Justices.

I cordially assent to such removal, and I beg leave to add that I have seen with great regret the erroneous statements made respecting this matter, and I feel that the publication of the Message will be the surest mode of doing full justice to the Senate as well as myself.

Nothing is more important to the public interests, or more desired by me, personally and officially, than the preservation of mutual confidence and respect between the Senate and the Executive. I am happy to believe that such are the sentiments of every member of the Senate.

Very respectfully,

D. H. CHAMBERLAIN,
Governor.

EXECUTIVE CHAMBER,
COLUMBIA, S. C., January 20, 1875.

To the Senate (in Executive Session) :

GENTLEMEN—I have addressed you a Message in executive session, in order that I may lay before you my views respecting the appointment of Trial Justices.

From all the information within my command, I am fully satisfied that there is no one feature of our administration of the State Government at the present time which demands change and reform more than the Trial Justices. The only reform practicable, so far as I can see, is the removal of unworthy Trial Justices, and the substitution of worthy men in their places. My determination in this respect has been fully announced in public. It is not to consent to the appointment of any man as Trial Justice whom I do not upon my conscience believe to be honest and capable. This I owe to myself, to my office, and to the people.

I am now endeavoring to discharge this duty, and I regret to find that there are, in many instances, irreconcilable differences, as to the proper men to be appointed between the Executive and those who represent the several counties in the General Assembly. I am anxious at all times to agree with those of my own political party in these appointments, but I can never purchase this harmony by disregarding my own judgment, founded upon the best information which I can obtain. I am not tenacious of any selections which I may make, if others equally competent and honest are presented to me, but I feel it due to the Senate and to myself to explicitly say that I cannot be expected to nominate men whom I do not believe to be duly qualified, even after the rejection by the Senate of those whom I may have first nominated. I think public duty will require me to make only such nominations as commend themselves to my judgment as fit to be made under all possible circumstances.

In regard to political qualifications, I recognize the rule that the dominant party is entitled to the greater part of these appointments ; provided always that that party can furnish men well qualified for such offices. I do not think that this rule requires me to refuse to appoint a political opponent as Trial Justice when, upon the whole, I judge that the good order and general welfare of a community will be better promoted by appointing occasionally one of the party now in the minority in this State.

On Saturday last I sent to the Senate a list of nominations as Trial Justices for Aiken County. All but one of those nominations were made upon the recommendation of the delegation from that county. The one exception was a most worthy, liberal-minded, and competent citizen, universally respected in his community, but belonging to the Conservative party. I have been notified of his rejection by the Senate. This I regard as a grave mistake, and a mistake which tends in a large degree to paralyze my efforts to rescue the administration of the law by our Trial Justices from the degradation into which it has fallen. If there were any charges of incompetency, bitterness of political or color prejudices, to be urged against the gentleman referred to, I would not have nominated him, but the only possible ground for his rejection was his political opposition to the dominant party.

I transmit herewith a list of nominations for Trial Justices in Chester County. These nominations are not wholly selected from the Republican party, because I have not been able to find men of that party in all the several localities who have seemed to me to be qualified. I present them to the Senate as the best result of my most careful inquiries, and I trust I shall be pardoned for expressing the hope that none of them will be rejected, except upon the ground that they are not qualified to fill these offices, or that others equally well qualified can be recommended to me in their places.

I am always ready upon suitable grounds to recall any nomination made by me, but I most earnestly urge Senators to consider these nominations from the high plane of the public welfare, and not to reject nominations made of worthy men merely because their political opinions are not in accord with those of a majority of the Senate, especially when their places cannot be supplied by equally competent men from the dominant political party. Very respectfully,

D. H. CHAMBERLAIN,
Governor.

Just at this time occurred an outbreak of race antagonism in Edgefield County of the kind that had been frequent hitherto. Commonly they had been suppressed by assuming that the colored people were being wickedly persecuted without cause, and calling upon the National Executive for troops to put down "domestic insurrection." The State militia, an irresponsible and undisciplined force, organized by Governor Scott more as a partisan weapon than a means of preserving the peace of the State, was under arms in the county, and already one or two lives had been lost in collisions between the militia and the white citizens, who, on their part, were organizing rifle clubs. The situation was serious. Governor Chamberlain resolved to deal with this trouble regardless of parties or races, and by establishing justice to restore peace and security, if possible, without an appeal to the President. To that end he took immediate steps to ascertain the real occasion of the trouble. He sent Judge Thomas J. Mackay, an able white Republican and a native of the State, to Edgefield County to make an investigation. Judge Mackay reported that the county authorities had been guilty of gross abuses and exactions which the people resisted, and, further, that the difficulties were aggravated by the lawless behavior of the colored militia, the officers being in the habit of calling out their men under arms to enforce arbitrary proceedings of petty officials and even to settle personal difficulties. He recommended that the militia be disarmed. Whereupon the Governor issued the following proclamation.

STATE OF SOUTH CAROLINA,
EXECUTIVE CHAMBER.

Whereas, information has reached me that grave disorders exist in the County of Edgefield, rendering insecure the lives and property of its citizens, and threatening still further to disturb the public peace of said county; and whereas, it appears that the arms of the State are now in the hands of the individual members of the State militia in said county, without authority of law or the orders of the Commander-in-Chief, and are used in a manner not consistent with the proper maintenance of the public peace; and whereas, it appears that other armed military organizations exist in said county, not authorized by the general militia law of the State, nor sanctioned by the Commander-in-Chief, which said military organizations are alleged to be an obstacle at the present time to the restoration of good order in said county; and whereas, it is further alleged that the said county is suffering from incompetent and dishonest county officials:

Now, therefore, I, Daniel H. Chamberlain, as Governor of the State and Commander-in-Chief of the military forces thereof, do make this, my Proclamation, whereby I command and require all arms and equipments belonging to the State, and now in the possession of the State militia in said county, to be forthwith delivered to the commanders of the several companies or militia organizations composing the State militia in said county, and by the said commanders to be delivered to the Colonel of the 9th Regiment of the State Militia, at Edgefield Court-House, there to be safely kept to await the further action of the Commander-in-Chief.

And I do further command and require all military organizations now existing in said county, not forming a part of the State militia, nor sanctioned by the Commander-in-Chief, to forthwith disband, and henceforth to cease from assembling, arming, drilling, parading, or otherwise engaging in any military exercises.

And I do further proclaim to all the citizens of said county, that the Constitution and laws of the State provide ample and convenient modes for the removal of any public officer, elected by the people, who shall be guilty of misconduct in office ; and that the Governor is ready, at all times, to listen to any complaints made against any officer who holds his office by Executive appointment, and upon reasonable proof of misconduct in office, to summarily remove or suspend such officer.

And I do hereby enjoin upon all good citizens of said county, to lay aside all passion, to refrain from all acts tending to produce excitement or ill-feeling between different parties or classes of citizens in said county, and to join in an earnest effort to restore that good-will towards each other, and that common regard for public order and reliance on the peaceful agencies of the law for the redress of wrongs, which are the chief safeguards of individual rights and the public welfare.

In testimony whereof, I have hereunto set my hand and caused the Great Seal of the State to be affixed, at Columbia, this [L. S.] twenty-eighth day of January, A.D., 1875, and in the ninety-ninth year of American Independence.

By the Governor : DANIEL H. CHAMBERLAIN.
H. E. HAYNE, Secretary of State.

This proclamation was obeyed, and order was restored in Edgefield. The course of the Governor was highly commended both within and without the State. It was something novel for a Republican magistrate in the South to exhibit self-reliance in such circumstances, and it was almost unheard of that one should be willing to concede that any blame for a local reign of violence could attach to the conduct of his political supporters. The New York *Tribune* gave significant expression to a general sentiment in the sentence: "Governor Chamberlain has manfully made issue with the disturbers of the peace, even in his own party ; something rare in the history of South Carolina since the war." How the action was regarded by the Conservative party of South Carolina is shown in the utterance of the Sumter *Watchman :*

> The State arms have been surrendered with alacrity, and the colored men who held them are said to be contracting freely for agricultural labor.   Rifle clubs, it is said, are also disbanding, and the prospect, so recently ominous, of a bloody war of races, seems to indicate a turning of swords into plowshares and spears into pruning hooks.   So mote it be throughout the whole South.   Then will the Southern " outrage mill " cease to grind, and an era of real reform, peace, and prosperity dawn upon the country.

But the Boston *Herald* was not mistaken when it said :

> For this, Governor Chamberlain will probably be commended by the Democratic press ; and we most heartily commend him also.   But if it had been a white league or Ku-Klux clan, we should have heard a terrible howl about the suppression of the liberties of the people.   It makes a tremendous difference whose ox is gored.

The Boston *Advertiser* of January 29th contained an article entitled " A Bold Example," in the course of which the following comments were made :

> South Carolina has a Governor now whose convictions of the justice of equal rights were acquired in the school of Wendell Phillips, who is, moreover, an honest man, who does not believe the right to plunder is one of the civil rights of anybody, and does believe that all the citizens of the State have a right to good government. He is putting these notions into practice to the extent of his power and influence, and we hear nothing more of the implacable hostility of the white race toward the blacks, nor any thing of the opposition of white men to Republican rule because it is Republican.   The people of all classes are hopeful and glad in tne prospect of better times under fair rulers. . . .   The trouble with most of the Southern States is that many of the new voters in them have been taught by unwise " friends " that they can, by the aid of the United States, compel justice to be done them by those to whom they constantly do injustice.   In South Carolina they are being taught that those who would have justice must themselves be just.   Such a lesson in Louisiana would do more to restore order and content than all the regiments in the army could.

The wasteful and profligate extravagance of the annual appropriation bills passed by previous Legislatures had been confessed and condemned by Governor Chamberlain in his speeches as a candidate, in his Inaugural Address, and in his special Message of April 12th, as has already appeared. The action of the Legislature in this particular during his term was naturally a matter of grave concern. In an important sense it would be the test of both his sincerity and his influence in the direction of reform.

In spite of all warnings and protests, the Legislature was preparing to pass an appropriation bill nearly as extravagant as those of previous sessions. In the hope of avoiding any occasion for a veto, the Governor determined to give further preliminary notice of his views; and when the objectionable purpose of the legislative majority became clear, he addressed the following official letter to the Committee on Finance, setting forth, in detail, his idea of what the annual appropriation bill should be, and how it might be framed to meet the imperative requirement of economical administration:

EXECUTIVE CHAMBER,
COLUMBIA, S. C., February 5, 1875.

Hon. W. B. Nash, Chairman Committee on Finance, State Senate:

DEAR SIR—I beg leave to lay before you and your committee some suggestions respecting the pending appropriation bill, now in the hands of your committee.

Before proceeding to speak specifically of this bill, I beg to call your attention to the views expressed by me in my Inaugural Address, on page 12 of the printed copies, and also in my special Message, at page 9 of the printed copies.[1]

The substance of those views was, that it was absolutely essential to good government to keep our appropriations within our receipts.

I am well aware of the increased difficulty of a strict observance of this rule at the present session, growing out of the want of any observance of it in the past. It is a hard and ungracious task to cut down appropriations when they have obtained the sanction of usage. It cuts off the means of support of many who depend upon them. But, as I understand our duty, yours as well as mine, it is to keep steadily in view the public good, and to disregard all personal considerations in the discharge of this duty.

Certain it is, that we can never reform the chief abuses of our past administration of this State Government until we pay heed to the rule of making our expenditures fall within our income.

Our embarrassment in this work arises from the fact that the present tax levy was made in view of an assessment of property aggregating the sum of $176,000,000, whereas the new assessment under which that levy is collected, aggregates only about $140,000,000. This falling off in the assessed value of the property of the State will doubtless make it impossible to keep the appropriations strictly within the receipts; but the duty of coming as near as possible to that result becomes only the more imperative.

In the case of salaries which are previously fixed by law I see no

[1] See p. 14 *et seq.*, also pp. 52, 59.

immediate mode of reducing the appropriations. It is probably the duty of the General Assembly to make the appropriation sufficient to cover the salaries now allowed by law.

I am glad to learn, however, that a bill is now pending which proposes to reduce all salaries to a limit which will bring them within the present resources for their payment. Until such reduction is made, we must, I think, let the appropriations stand as reported in all cases where the amount of salaries is fixed by law.

As the appropriation bill now stands, I find the amounts appropriated under the first section aggregate $234,205.75. The proceeds of the tax levied to meet these appropriations will amount to only $150,000—leaving a deficiency of $84,205.

The amounts appropriated under the second section aggregate $204,350. The proceeds of the tax levied to meet these appropriations will amount to only $150,000—leaving a deficiency of $54,350.

The appropriation made for public printing, under the third section, amounts to $50,000. The proceeds of the tax levied to meet this appropriation will amount to only $40,000—leaving a deficiency of $10,000.

The aggregate of deficiencies thus created is $148,555. Add to this amount the deficiency arising under the legislative appropriation bill, and we have an aggregate of deficiencies of $178,555.

No one will deny that it now becomes our duty to endeavor to bring our expenditures down to such an amount as will reduce this immense deficiency to the lowest possible limit. To this end I make the following suggestions :

1. Strike out the appropriation made in paragraph 13 of section 1, for additional compensation of County Auditors—$4,785.75.

2. Reduce the Governor's contingent fund to $3,000.

3. Reduce the Attorney General's contingent fund to $10,000, in paragraph 16 of section 1.

4. Reduce the appropriation for the Lunatic Asylum to $50,000.

5. Reduce the appropriation for the State Orphan Asylum to $10,000.

6. Reduce the appropriations for salaries of professors in South Carolina University to $18,000. This involves the abolition of the medical department, of which, under the circumstances, I approve.

7. Strike out the appropriation of $1,000 for demonstrator of anatomy in paragraph 5 of section 2.

8. Strike out in same section and paragraph the appropriation for apparatus—$1,000.

9. Reduce the appropriation for miscellaneous expenses of University to $1,500.

10. Reduce the appropriation for the preparatory school in South Carolina University to $2,000.

11. Reduce the appropriation for insurance and repairs on the University buildings to $4,000.

12. Reduce the appropriation for the State Agricultural College to $5,000.

13. Reduce the appropriation for the State Normal School to $5,000.

14. Reduce the appropriation for public printing to $40,000. About this I do not see how there can be any difference of opinion.

15. Strike out in section 1, paragraph 17, the appropriation for rebinding, etc., etc., in the office of the Secretary of State.

The reductions thus effected will amount to $76,530.75, which will reduce the entire deficiencies under this bill to $72,024.25.

I now recommend further that the proceeds of the phosphate royalty be entirely devoted to meeting the appropriations made in this bill. This fund will amount to at least $40,000, which will make a further reduction of deficiencies under this bill to $32,024.25.

To attain such a result ought to be not only the duty but the pride and joy of every man who seeks to serve the State.

No doubt the reductions suggested will produce hardship and temporary injury to some interests of the State ; but such evils will not be worthy of comparison with the vast gains to be derived from once more coming back to the true rule of expending only what we honestly have to expend. No injury can be so great as that which we now witness in our citizens who have worked for the State or lent their money or credit, and are now waiting and suffering, because the State made appropriations when she had no funds with which to redeem her promises.

I think the Government can be properly maintained during the coming year on the appropriations reduced as I have suggested.

I further recommend that in section 2, paragraph 1, there be inserted between the words "superintendent" and "approved," in line 10, the words " accompanied by bill of particulars " ; and after the word " directors," in the same line, there be added the words, "in respect to the prices paid and the quantity of commodities bought or work done."

I also recommend that the same changes be made in paragraph 2 of section 2, in respect to the lunatic asylum.

I commend these suggestions to your most earnest consideration, and remain your obedient servant,

D. H. CHAMBERLAIN,
Governor.

Upon this letter, the Charleston *News and Courier*, February 10, 1875, made the following comments :

. . . Talk about reform on the stump counts for nothing ; the fine words are forgotten almost as soon as uttered. Nor do we take it for granted that even the Governor of a State is fixed in the resolution to practise what he preaches. For this reason we did not accept the admirable recommendations contained in the Inaugural Address of Governor Chamberlain as proof conclusive that the Executive would act as well as speak—that he would put his shoulder to the wheel and keep it there. But Governor Chamberlain has proved that he can find the cure as well as describe the disease—that when he insists that the expenses of the Government shall be reduced, he is ready, also, to indicate clearly and decisively the precise places in which re-

trenchment shall begin.   This marks the difference between Governor Chamberlain
and his Republican predecessors.   They prated of economy and honesty, but when
they met their radical associates they smiled as the Augurs smiled.   Governor Chamberlain, on the contrary, shows the General Assembly what their duties are, and,
when they are stumbling in the morass, boldly tells them which way they must walk
if they would reach solid ground once more.

We have said that we demand for the letter of Governor Chamberlain the favorable consideration of the Legislature, and we mean the Republican members of the
Legislature.   The Conservatives have proved to the country that they were in earnest
when they declared that what they most desired was not the triumph of a political
party or faction, but the election of officers who would put a stop to stealing, and see
that no public money was wasted.   Since the election of Governor Chamberlain,
against whom they made a splendid fight, the Conservatives have unhesitatingly, but
firmly and consistently, supported every measure of reform which the Executive, or
any other Republican, recommended to be adopted.   We have a right, therefore, to
demand that the Republican majority—who denounce us as hypocrites, who swore
great oaths that they, and they only, were the reformers—shall do at least as much as
the minority have done, and prove to the nation, by their conduct in this emergency,
that they were and are sincere in their pledges, and that Republicanism in South
Carolina, as represented by the present General Assembly, is no longer rotten to the
core. . . .

The Legislature having passed a bill providing for increased
taxation of the county of Edgefield, for certain purposes, the
Governor returned it unsigned, with a message which exposes
the reckless business methods then prevalent.   The legislative
journals contain the following record:

COLUMBIA, S. C., February 24, 1875.

The Governor returned, without approval, an Act originating in the
Senate, entitled " An Act to amend an Act entitled ' An Act to validate
all payments made by the County Treasurer of Edgefield County
under and pursuant to the provisions of a joint resolution, entitled
' A joint resolution to authorize the County Commissioners of Edgefield County to levy a special tax of three mills, to be levied at the time
of the general tax'; and to declare the intent of said joint resolution."

My objections to this Act are as follows :

By a joint resolution approved December 22, 1873, entitled " Joint
resolution to authorize the County Commissioners of Edgefield County
to levy a special tax of three mills, to be levied at the time of the
general tax," authority was given to the County Commissioners of
Edgefield County to levy and collect a special tax of three mills on
the dollar for the year ending October 31, 1874, and to continue the
collection of the same tax for each succeeding year until the past indebtedness of that county should be fully paid.

By an Act passed at the same session of the General Assembly,
entitled " An Act to validate all payments made by the County Treas-

urer of Edgefield County, under and pursuant to the provisions of a joint resolution, entitled ' Joint resolution to authorize the County Commissioners of Edgefield County to levy a special tax of three mills, to be levied at the time of the general tax,' and to declare the intent of said joint resolution," the payments made by the County Treasurer of Edgefield County pursuant to the joint resolution of December 22, 1873, were validated and declared to have been duly and lawfully made in conformity with the true intent and meaning of the aforesaid joint resolution. It was further declared by the same Act to be the true intent and meaning of the said joint resolution, that all past-due claims which had been audited and allowed, and for which checks or orders had been issued prior to the passage of the said joint resolution—that is, December 22, 1873,—shall be paid in full out of the special tax levied under the said joint resolution, without requiring such past-due claims to be re-audited.

The scope and effect of the present Act is to extend the operation of the last-named Act so as to require the payment in full of all claims audited and allowed by the County Commissioners prior to October 31, 1874, without further audit.

The last-named Act gave no reason why it became necessary thus to validate payments made by the Treasurer of Edgefield County, nor why it became necessary to require the payment in full of all past-due claims without re-auditing.

If the payments made by the Treasurer were properly made, no enactment was necessary to establish their validity. If they were not properly made, there appears to be no good reason why they should have been made valid by the General Assembly.

The passage of the present Act cannot fail to create the impression that, but for such special enactment, the claims referred to will not be paid in full, or without some re-examination, or re-auditing. Such action does not commend itself to my favorable consideration. Grave and repeated complaints have been publicly made that the financial affairs of Edgefield County have not been correctly conducted. While the proofs of such charges have not been laid before me, and I am consequently unable to say whether they are well founded or not, yet the fact of such complaints may justly restrain me from consenting to any legislation which seems intended to summarily cut off all further opportunity for questioning the validity of any claims allowed by the County Commissioners prior to the close of the last fiscal year. These claims, so far as I can learn, have never been subjected to any examination, except such as they may have received at the hands of the County Commissioners. If, as has already been remarked, the action of the County Commissioners has been legal and just, the claims in question will not suffer from any examination to which they may be subjected. If, on the other hand, any injustice or wrong has been done by the Commissioners, it is not just that the people should be compelled to submit to such injustice or wrong without further opportunity for investigating such claims.

If no legal proceedings shall be instituted to test the validity of the claims in question, the Treasurer will need no special authority for paying them, and if such proceedings shall be instituted for testing their validity, I cannot consent to override such proceedings by legislation. The least that can justly be done in such a case is to leave the redress of any alleged wrongs done by the County Commissioners to the judicial tribunals.

The belief is general throughout the State that many, if not most, of our counties are now burdened with past indebtedness, which is due, in a great degree, to the improvidence or dishonesty of county officials. I share in this belief. I am confident that there is not one county in this State in which money enough has not been collected by taxation to pay every dollar of legitimate expense in maintaining the government of the county. It is right, therefore, that such past indebtedness should be most carefully scrutinized. No such scrutiny can be too severe or minute. To enact that such past indebtedness shall be paid in full and without further examination is to add to the burden of injustice under which the people of many counties are now groaning. Especially is this true of Edgefield County, where recent events should teach us that prudence and justice alike forbid any increase of the causes of dissatisfaction and disturbance which have hitherto existed.

The past indebtedness of that county should be most carefully examined, and, when duly examined, should be provided for in such a manner as to impose the least hardship on the taxpayers of the county. Certainly no such summary mode of payment and forbidding of further examination as is provided for in the present Act should be adopted.

But, in addition to the objections already stated, I find another weighty and conclusive objection to the present Act, in the fact that judicial proceedings are now instituted and pending in the Circuit Court for Edgefield County, which have for their object, as I am informed, the investigation of the claims which constitute the past-due indebtedness of Edgefield County. Such an investigation is the common right of all the people of that county, and it would, in my judgment, be unwise, and unjust, pending the conclusion of such judicial investigation, to direct the payment in full of all claims against the county.

The Cirucit Court can be safely trusted to do justice in the premises, and a due regard for the interest of the people of the county requires that the Court should be allowed to proceed to such conclusions as law and justice may dictate.

I am satisfied that the real object of the present Act is to make certain claims against the county, which are not now payable out of any funds, payable out of the proceeds of the special tax directed to be levied by the joint resolution of December 22, 1873. To that object I see no objections, but, unfortunately, the present Act has an effect far wider than simply to make such claims payable ; for as already shown, it makes such claims not only payable, but directs their payment *in full, and without any further examination.*

Very respectfully,   D. H. CHAMBERLAIN,
Governor.

This chapter will fitly close with an editorial article which appeared in the Charleston *News and Courier*, February 25, 1875. And here a word may be said regarding two South Carolina journals to which frequent allusion will be made.

The *Union-Herald*, published at the capital of the State, was the recognized organ of the Republican party It was the only Republican daily newspaper. But a small proportion of the members of the Republican party were able to read at all, and of those who possessed the accomplishment many were poor and regarded a newspaper as a luxury they could do without. Information was disseminated and opinion formed chiefly by oral communication and discussion. The *Union-Herald* was enabled to live by the official patronage given to it, and did valuable service in presenting and preserving much material of history regarding the reconstruction era in South Carolina which otherwise would have perished, or have been rescued only in the incomplete and distorted form which a bitterly hostile and contemptuous partisan press, without fear of permanently recorded correction, might vouchsafe. The weakness of the support of Republican journalism in South Carolina is shown by the circumstance that soon after the State government passed into the control of the Democratic party it ceased to exist. But even while it survived, the main dependence of Republican leaders for disseminating their ideas in their own party was not the press but the platform. During Governor Chamberlain's administration, the *Union-Herald*, edited by Mr. James G. Thompson, not only sustained him as a Republican, but cordially and earnestly supported his reform policy.

The Charleston *News and Courier* has long been recognized as one of the leading newspapers of the South and, in the ability of its discussion of public questions, among the foremost in the land. In South Carolina its influence has been almost autocratic. Intensely partisan and Southern in sentiment, it is capable at times of rising to a high plane of patriotism. In 1874 it was a fierce opponent of Governor Chamberlain's election, but after the delivery of his Inaugural Address it supported him, at first with cautious approbation, and later with confidence, zeal, and admiration, until the campaign of 1876, when, by a combination of circumstances, its counsel was overruled in the Democratic convention, and it again became an uncompromising party organ.

The article following was entitled " Governor Chamberlain," and pledges a support which must have been extremely gratifying in view of the conflicts pending.

· · · When Mr. Chamberlain accepted the nomination of the Republican State Convention last fall, the Conservatives asserted, in the words of the *Union Herald*, that he was "the reticent tool of this and that Ring." The event has proved that the Conservatives were both right and wrong. They judged Mr. Chamberlain by the company he had kept, and did not expect him to be bolder as Governor than he was as Attorney General. The *Union-Herald* confesses, at last, that the corruptionists accepted Mr. Chamberlain's nomination "with apparent heartiness, but with secret dread.". The promises of the Republican platform, and the speeches of the candidates, were, to many Republicans, "mere counters in the game of politics—never to be redeemed." This is what the Conservatives maintained. They formed a wrong estimate of Mr. Chamberlain's character, it is true. So did the men that supported him. When his own associates and companions misjudged him, it is not strange that his political opponents should have done the same thing. Both parties have discovered their error ; the Conservatives to their profound satisfaction, and the Radical Chadbands and Pecksniffs to their deep chagrin. The corrupt Republicans never dreamed, says the *Union-Herald*, that the wise legislation of last season would be obeyed or literally interpreted—the funding act, the disavowal of the fraudulent bonds, the specific tax levy, etc., were "only voted for by them for buncombe, or thrown as tubs to the whale of reform." The Conservatives, from the day when the brave, bright words of his inaugural address fell from his lips, have cordially supported Gov. Chamberlain's recommendations, and have not, in a single instance, failed to give him, by their votes in the Legislature, and by their voice in the public press, every possible help, comfort, and cheer. Especially has the conduct of the Conservative members of the General Assembly been distinguished for moderation, for consistency, for good faith. And this makes it incumbent upon us to put on record an emphatic denial that the Conservative citizens of the State will play the part for which the *Union-Herald* casts them.

We admit that the struggle between Governor Chamberlain and the more corrupt elements of his own party has "an immense political significance" for the Conservatives ; but it is unjust and untrue to say, as the *Union-Herald* does, that "they will not put a feather's weight in the way of the ruin of the political influence of any prominent Republican leader—especially if he be one whose ability makes him more than usually dangerous to them." The South Carolina Conservatives proved in 1870, and again in 1872, and once more in 1874, that their sole aim and purpose is to improve the character of the State Government, and that they will cheerfully co-operate with any body of Republicans who are honestly striving to reform abuses and reduce taxation. They cannot be twitted with neglecting to support the Bolters in 1872, particularly as Mr. Chamberlain and all the present Republican leaders of note supported the Regular candidate. As Judge Green, who was the candidate of the Bolters for the office of Attorney General in 1872, and the candidate of the Independents and Conservatives for Governor in 1874, said shortly before his death : " The success of the Bolters' movement, from which little real good could have come, would have made impossible the co-operation campaign of 1874." From this co-operative movement, as Judge Green saw, lasting benefits must arise. Nay ! we see them and feel them already. In his very first struggle with the knaves whom the *Union-Herald* holds up to scorn, Governor Chamberlain was saved from defeat by the solid vote of the Conservative members of the Legislature and by that alone. Had Whipper been elected Judge of the Charleston Circuit, in spite of Gov. Chamberlain's open opposition and public protest, the Administration would have been paralyzed, and the State would have fallen again into the hands of the plunderers. The Conservative vote, joined to the Independent Republican vote, enabled Gov. Chamberlain, and the better Regular Republicans, to break the Ring and defeat their chosen candidate. This should be answer enough to the charge that the Conservatives would not intervene to save Gov. Ghamberlain from ruin. They did intervene, at a time when their quiescence would have been fatal to the Executive and his supporters. What the Conservatives did at the time of the judicial election, they have continued to do upon every occasion. They have stood squarely by the Administration ; they have strengthened Gov. Chamberlain, and, in a measure, enabled Republicanism to lift itself from the slough into which it had fallen. And they have done this from no lust of office or hope of preferment. They have no expectation of reward, other than that which they will share with the citizens of the State when the rod of rascality shall be broken and cast aside. They are animated by a single desire to see the Government of the State in honest, capable, and faithful hands, so that they and theirs may live securely, and enjoy, in peace, what means the fortunes of war may have left them, or industry and energy may win. It is impossible to conceive, nor is there found in the history of American politics, a loftier and more generous position than that which is held by the Conservative citizens of South Carolina. They cling to their political faith and will not desert it ; but they look, first of all, to the interests of the State ; they recognize honesty and merit wherever they are found, and when they see a fearless and far-sighted man, in the ranks of the opposing party, making a gallant stand against the onslaught of thieves and rogues, they group themselves around him, and pledge to him, as they may, their steady and continuous support. Just as long as Gov. Chamberlain is faithful to his own words, so long will the Conservatives, quietly and unostentatiously, give him what aid they can. Their heartiest wish is that he may become what he aspires to be—the Governor, not of a party, but of a united and contented people.

CHAPTER VII.

The Attempt to Remove from Office Hon. F. L. Cardozo, the State Treasurer—Governor Chamberlain Condemns the Project, and Defends the Course of the Treasurer—Comments of the Press.

IN March, 1875, the Republican majority of the Legislature took proceedings for the removal from office of Francis L. Cardozo, State Treasurer. Mr. Cardozo had been elected in 1872 for a term of four years, and next to the Governor he was the most important State officer. He was an earnest advocate of the nomination and election of Governor Chamberlain, a strong supporter in all ways of his Administration, and, being a well-educated, able colored man, he possessed great and deserved influence. The motives which led to the attack upon him at this time, are fully stated in the documents which follow.

[Special Despatch to the Charleston *News and Courier*.]

COLUMBIA, March 10th.—The joint committee to-night submitted the address demanding the removal of State Treasurer Cardozo. The address prefers the following charges :

Charge First. Irregularity and misconduct in office.

Specification 1. In funding $978,500 of the hypothecated bonds, which were in the possession of persons not the actual owners thereof, which bonds were not lawfully issued, and were, therefore, not legal obligations of the State.

Specification 2. That the Treasurer did, between June, 1874, and February, 1875, fund $241,011 of detached coupons which matured before July 1, 1871, when he had the means of knowing, and should have known, that the whole of the interest due on the bonds of the State up to that date had been paid, and that said coupons were not entitled to be funded.

Specification 3. That the Treasurer funded $196,485 of coupons which matured between April, 1869, and October, 1871, and which were detached from bonds of the State before and during the period of the hypothecation of the said bonds, and that he should have known that said coupons were the property of the State.

Specification 4. That the Treasurer funded $6,960 of coupons detached from bonds, and which matured before the bonds themselves were issued from the State Treasury.

Specification 5. That the Treasurer funded $69,205 of detached coupons which

80

matured between January, 1870, and July, 1871, and the bonds from which they were detached having always been the property of the State, and still being in the possession of the State Treasury, marked cancelled and unused.

Specification 6. Diversion of the interest fund, thereby defeating the intent of the Funding Act, and endangering the security guaranteed to the creditors of the State.

Charge Second. Wilful neglect of duty, in failing to make monthly reports to the Comptroller General of the cash transactions of his office, which neglect of duty dates from October 31, 1874.

For these reasons the General Assembly, by a vote of two thirds of each house, respectfully address your Excellency and ask that the Hon. F. L. Cardozo be removed from the office of State Treasurer.

The committee recommend that a copy of the charges be served upon the Treasurer, and that he be required to appear before both houses in joint assembly on Tuesday, the 16th instant, to make answer to the same. The committee also promise to submit rules of procedure. The report was presented in both houses and adopted.

With this despatch the following report of a conversation with Governor Chamberlain on the subject was published:

COLUMBIA, S. C., March 10, 1875.—In obedience to instructions received from you by telegraph, I waited on Governor Chamberlain to-day, when the following conversation took place on the subject of the charges against State Treasurer Cardozo :

Reporter. There is a great public interest felt, Governor, to know your views of the case of Mr. Cardozo, and I have called to inquire if you are willing to make them known through *The News and Courier.*

Governor. Yes, sir ; I see no good reason why I should not answer your inquiries fully. The matter is one that interests me beyond any thing else which has occurred during my Administration, and I have not failed to read every word that has appeared in the various documents connected with it. Of course every fair-minded man holds himself open to the consideration of any new facts or evidence which may be added to the case, or any new arguments based on the facts already developed. Premising this, I do not hesitate to say that I have entire confidence in Mr. Cardozo. Men, many men, friends of mine, have come to me and said, " Don't mix yourself up in this fight. It is no affair of yours, and you ought to keep clear of it." Now, what sort of advice is this ? What do such men take me for ? Do they think I am going to sit by and see injustice done to a State officer without opening my mouth ? It would be damnable cowardice. If I knew to-day there was not another man in the world who would speak for Mr. Cardozo, I would all the more stand by him. I have n't come into this office expecting a bed of roses. I am not half so anxious to make friends or avoid enemies as I am to do right ; and until evidence, facts, compel me to lose faith in Mr. Cardozo, he shall have my confidence and my personal and moral support in every form. Well, sir, I have examined all the evidence yet adduced, and I find nothing to shake my faith in Mr. Cardozo's honesty.

Reporter. Let me ask you, at this point, Governor, what has been heretofore your estimate of Mr. Cardozo?

Governor. I have known Mr. Cardozo intimately since last summer. He was an early supporter of mine for my present position. I think I have known his aims and plans, and I say without qualification that I have never heard one word or seen one act of Mr. Cardozo's which did not confirm my confidence in his personal integrity and his political honor and zeal for the honest administration of the State Government. On every occasion, and under all circumstances, he has been against fraud and jobbery, and in favor of good measures and good men. The public do not know the pressure which has been brought to bear upon me in this office to make me yield my views of public duty. If I had known it myself beforehand, I would never have dared to take the office. But in the midst of it all, when I could count all the Republicans who *seemed* to sympathize with me on the fingers of one hand, there was one man who never faltered, who never failed to come unasked and stand at my side, and that man was Francis L. Cardozo. I tell you, sir, I should despise myself if I did not stand by such a man till the last gun was fired, unless I was driven to believe him a hypocrite and scoundrel.

Now, sir, I saw this storm gathering long ago. I knew that any man who did his duty as Treasurer, who lent himself to no jobbery, and had no private ends to serve, would make himself the most unpopular man in South Carolina. Cardozo knew it too. I confess I did not expect to see the elements which view the public service as a mere chance to make money, able to make such headway as they are now apparently making against Mr. Cardozo. I did hope for better things, but I also expected to find a howl and outcry against any man who did his duty by the Treasury. I do not wish to be understood as implying that all who are opposed to Mr. Cardozo are consciously striking down a faithful public officer; but every man here in Columbia knows that the real force which urges on this attack upon Mr. Cardozo is not a desire to guard the Treasury. I speak now what every man confesses to me when I ask him the question.

Reporter. But, Governor, what do you say of the attitude of the Conservatives toward Mr. Cardozo?

Governor. Well, sir, I think they intend to do justice to Mr. Cardozo in the end; and so I think of very many Republicans. I do not wonder at their voting for raising a committee to prepare an address. That is probably now the only way to bring the whole case to a point where justice can be done. I am bound to say that the Conservatives have acted with great political generosity and patriotism towards me and my Administration. I believe they will do what they think just by Mr. Cardozo, and their votes in this matter, so far, indicate no more, in my judgment, than a wish to have the case fully tried. I cannot believe their vote on appointing the committee represents their probable vote on the address of removal, unless new facts are developed.

Reporter. Will you be kind enough to give me your views of the case, as presented up to this time, against Mr. Cardozo?

Governor. Yes, sir, that is what I desire to do. The charges against Mr. Cardozo embrace two general points : *First*, the funding of certain bonds at one time hypothecated in New York, and the coupons attached to such bonds ; and *second*, the diversion of the interest fund.

Now, with regard to the bonds and coupons alleged to have been wrongfully funded, the Act to reduce the volume of the public debt makes no exception of any of these bonds or coupons. All are exchangeable under that Act. If these bonds and coupons were outstanding at the time of the passage of that act, then they were, by the terms of the Act, exchangeable. In funding them Mr. Cardozo simply followed the terms of the Act. If, however, any of these bonds or coupons were unlawfully outstanding, and knowledge of this were brought home to Mr. Cardozo, he might well have refused to fund them, as he did do in the case of some coupons. I do not think that Mr. Cardozo would have been guilty of any offence, if he had funded any and all coupons which were made fundable by the terms of the Act. A strict and literal compliance with the law would have been all that could have been strictly required of him. If he was in collusion with any parties presenting bonds or coupons illegally or fraudulently outstanding, then he is guilty. But I do not see any such evidence, nor any evidence pointing that way.

The attempt to hold Mr. Cardozo responsible for funding the bonds and coupons reported by the Dunn committee, last summer, as hypothecated without lawful authority is unjust to the last degree. All the information now in the possession of the public respecting these bonds was presented to the Treasurer and Attorney General last summer, and the Attorney General states in his last annual report that he did not consider it important enough to cause him to advise that those bonds should not be funded. On the contrary, he expressly defends the funding of all those bonds. Why, then, is it now attempted to punish Mr. Cardozo for doing what the law directed, and what the Attorney General advised ? This particular matter was likewise laid before me last summer, and I advised that there was no reason why those bonds should not be funded. And I say the same thing now.

Bring home to Mr. Cardozo any knowledge of any fraud, connect him in any way with any intention to do wrong to the State, convict him of a wilful neglect of duty or an unwarrantable refusal to act upon any evidence of illegality in the bonds or coupons presented to him, and you have a case against him. But I see nothing, nothing whatever, which gives color to any charge of fraud or evil intent on his part.

As to the diversion of the interest funds I see still less ground for the removal of Mr. Cardozo. Look at the general features of this charge. The State has n't lost a dollar. That the law is susceptible of the construction given to it by Mr. Cardozo is apparent, both from an examination of the Act and from Mr. Melton's letter to Mr. Cardozo. That Mr. Cardozo acted also from good motives is likewise evident. Where, then, is the ground for any charge involving moral turpitude, or rendering him worthy of removal ?

I personally know Mr. Cardozo's statements as to the reasons of his reducing the balance in the bank early in January to be the reasons which he then disclosed to me. His motive then met my approval, and I still approve it, though he acted at his own risk. That is, if he had failed to replace the funds he would have been liable on his bond and to the penalty prescribed in the Act. If the General Assembly, however, desire a strict and literal construction of that law, it can be secured without visiting any punishment upon an officer who erred, if he erred at all, because he sought to favor the General Assembly and to save the State funds from loss.

The position of the *News and Courier* on this question is a perfectly fair and just one. If Mr. Cardozo has falsified the records, or knowingly done any fraudulent act, or any wilful act resulting in injury to the State, then let him be duly punished. If not, let good men baffle those who have entered into a conspiracy to knock down one of the strongest pillars of the present reform Administration. At any rate, whether I stand alone or with many, that will be my course to the end. Consequences can take care of themselves.

The publication of the above despatch was followed by an editorial article, from which the following extract is made.

[From the Charleston *News and Courier*, March 12, 1875.]

The charges against State Treasurer Cardozo, as set forth in the address to the Governor, are (1) of irregularity and misconduct in office, and (2) of wilful neglect of duty. Under the first head he is accused of having funded certain bonds and coupons which, for different reasons, were not entitled to be funded, and of having diverted the interest fund ; and under the second head, he is accused of having failed to make monthly reports to the Comptroller General of the cash transactions of his office as required by law. This second charge will hardly be held sufficient to warrant the adoption of the address, if the defence on the first charge be found sufficient. Mr. Cardozo has already explained to the General Assembly that he had not the clerical force to enable him to make the reports in question, but his books have always been open to inspection by the Comptroller General, who has repeatedly been invited to examine them. The Treasury Department has been overburdened with work, and we see no reason to think that Mr. Cardozo has not done, in the making of the various reports, the best that he could. When half a dozen things were required to be done at the same time, and it was not possible to do them all, he appears to have applied himself to those which were most urgent in their nature. We assume that Mr. Cardozo will stand or fall by the specifications of the first charge, which are, in brief, the charges contained in the report of the Special Investigating Committee. As we have said before, we shall not express any final opinion as to the innocence or culpability of the Treasurer, until his full and final defence shall have been put in ; and the public may count on our saying exactly what we think of that defence, whether we concur or not with the two thirds of the General Assembly whose votes are required for adopting the address. Mr. Cardozo has, however, one witness who has cheerfully spoken in his behalf. That witness is Governor Chamberlain, and, in view of the boldness, persistency, and fidelity with which he has defended the public interests from the very day of his installation, the Governor's opinions, especially in a matter involving the honest management of the State finances, are entitled to great weight.

Governor Chamberlain said, in his conversation with the Columbia correspondent of the *News and Courier*, that he had read every word in the different documents connected with the case of Mr. Cardozo, and he " finds in them nothing to shake his faith in Mr. Cardozo's honesty." There is no mystery in the charges. The public know what the Investigating Committee know. Governor Chamberlain probably knows more than either the Committee or the public, and he unhesitatingly says that, while he holds himself open to the consideration of any new facts or evidence that may be brought out, he has entire confidence in Mr. Cardozo. Nor does the Governor content himself with glittering generalities. Governor Chamberlain, who was Attorney General from 1868 to 1872, and who is certainly familiar with the fiscal legislation of the State, says positively that "the bonds and coupons alleged to have been wrongfully funded" are all exchangeable under the Funding Act, if they were outstanding at the time of its passage ; and he does not think that Mr. Cardozo would have been guilty of any offence " if he had funded any and all coupons which were made fundable by the terms of the Act." This is a plain and sensible view of the case. So long as Mr. Cardozo was governed by the law, in its letter, he was not guilty of any official misconduct. If he was in collusion with any persons presenting bonds or coupons illegally outstanding, then he was guilty ; but Governor Chamberlain does not see " any such evidence, nor any evidence pointing that way." This is the deliberate opinion of a gentleman who ranks with the first of the foremost lawyers in the State, and who would be involved in personal and political ruin, with the Treasurer, if he sustained that officer in any unlawful act, or proclaimed him to be innocent when he had any reason to believe him to be guilty. It is, moreover, a strong point that the information now published about the bonds alleged to have been unlawfully hypothecated was before the public last summer. There is nothing new in it. The information was submitted to the Attorney General, who, in his Report to the Legislature, said that he did not consider it important enough to cause him to advise that these bonds should not be funded. On the contrary, the Attorney General " expressly defends the funding of all those bonds." Mr. Cardozo is blamed for doing " what the law directed, and what the Attorney General advised." Governor Chamberlain advised the Treasurer, last year, that there was no reason why those bonds should not be funded, and he " says the same thing now."

With reference to the diversion of the interest fund, Governor Chamberlain says that the law is susceptible of the construction given by Mr. Cardozo, that the State has not lost a dollar, and that it is evident that Mr. Cardozo acted from good motives. We think, nevertheless, that the construction put upon the law was not what the Legislature intended, and we think still that an Act declaring the exact meaning of the statutory provisions relative to the interest fund should be passed, so as to avoid any more complications in the future.

An important statement was made by Governor Chamberlain in explanation of the animus of most of those members who demand the removal of the Treasurer. We reproduce the Governor's own words :

" I saw this storm gathering long ago. I knew that any man that did his duty as Treasurer, who lent himself to no jobbery, and had no private ends to serve, would make himself *the most unpopular man in South Carolina*. Cardozo knew it too. I confess I did not expect to see the elements which view the public service as a mere chance to make money, able to make such headway as they are now apparently making against Mr. Cardozo. I did hope for better things, but I also *expected to find a howl and outcry against any man who did his duty by the Treasury*. I do not wish to be understood as implying that all who are opposed to Mr. Cardozo are consciously striking down a faithful public officer; but every man here in Columbia knows that *the real force* which urges on this attack upon Mr. Cardozo *is not a desire to guard the Treasury*. I speak now what every man confesses to me when I ask him the question."

This confirms us in the opinion we have frequently expressed. The Conservatives can have no other purpose than to see the case fairly tried; but the Radical members, with few exceptions, are only anxious for Mr. Cardozo's removal because he has been faithful and capable, and has jealously guarded the Treasury. Governor Chamberlain would not make this declaration unless he had ample warrant for so doing; and no honest man, Republican or Conservative, can hesitate to give full credit on this point to the Republican Governor, who, without counting the consequences and looking only to the public good, has stood like a wall of adamant between the public robbers and the honest and law-abiding people of the State. We are profoundly impressed, we frankly admit, by Governor Chamberlain's words. We believe that through him, and by the line of conduct which he pursues, can the Conservative citizens, as well as the Republicans, attain most quickly and easily that reform of abuses and the reduction of taxation which are vastly more important than any political victory. And we say to Governor Chamberlain what he says of Treasurer Cardozo: We are not half so anxious to make friends or avoid enemies as we are to do right, and until evidence, facts, compel us to lose faith in Governor Chamberlain, he shall have our confidence and our personal and moral support in every form.

The attempt to remove Mr. Cardozo was defeated by a union of the reform Republicans and the Democrats. The following extract makes still plainer the meaning of this incident, and its influence.

[From the Columbia *Union-Herald*, March 20th.]

The struggle is over. By an emphatic vote in both houses Mr. Cardozo has been sustained. . . . We entered into the fight earnestly, and we have put forth every energy to win success. We would be more or less than human not to exult over our opponents. To say that the result is a distinct triumph for Governor Chamberlain's Administration is to say only what every one knows. But the whole affair has been so significant in all its bearings from first to last that its lessons should once more be stated. We do not wish to stir up the passions which have been called out in this conflict; still less do we wish to pronounce every man as false or true, according to the side in which he placed himself in this conflict.

But, speaking generally, we express our conviction, based on what we call knowledge, that the struggle has been really and distinctly a struggle between honesty and corruption, between an effort to restore good government on the one hand, and an effort to perpetuate the disgraceful records of the Scott and Moses administrations on the other hand. It is now perfectly apparent that a large section of the Republican party regarded the platform and professions of the last campaign as mere baits to catch votes. All they wanted of Mr. Chamberlain was a respectable name to cover disreputable practices. They really wanted Frank Moses, *minus* his personal profligacy and debauchery. Official integrity, public duty, economy in expenditures, competency in officers, low taxes, all these things they neither desired nor intended to permit.

When, therefore, Governor Chamberlain showed his determination to stand upon the pledges of the campaign, these men marked for vengeance every man who stood by him. Conspicuous among these was Mr. Cardozo. To say that these men were moved to any degree by a desire to uphold official integrity is to mock the common knowledge of all men here. Plausible grounds existed for the attack. The utmost looseness of administration had grown up before Mr. Cardozo entered upon his office. Mr. Cardozo had not been able wholly to conduct his office on the highest plane of strict and undeviating adherence to the best methods. If he had done so, the storm would have come earlier and from opposite causes. These deviations from the strict letter of his duties were seized upon by those who desired to crush him for his fidelity. It was a perfect illustration of the folly of casting pearls before swine. Those who had demanded official looseness and favoritism turned to rend the man whose failings had come only from a desire to conciliate the favor of his present enemies by a too liberal construction of his duties.

The plot was well laid and enticing. Under the guise of punishing official misconduct, they sought really to introduce unbounded official profligacy. The cloak for a time concealed the assassin. The Conservatives were led to array themselves against the Treasurer and alongside of the Corruptionists ; but the alliance was accidental and short-lived ; and we say now, what we have not said in times before, that the Conservatives, in the final vote, have vindicated the purity of their motives, and deserve the unqualified approval of all who uphold public morality.

The blow aimed at Governor Chamberlain has been parried by a combination of the true friends of reform. His strength has been immeasurably increased by this very struggle. The cause of reform in South Carolina has been promoted by this most desperate attempt to crush it out. But the greatest gain of all will be found in the freedom with which Mr. Cardozo can now uphold the cause of official integrity. The plunderers have done their worst. He can now square accounts with them. He can now shake off their importunate demands and their dishonoring contact. Henceforth he will plant himself on the letter of the law. Henceforth he will have no favors to show to any man. The disgusting favoritism which these political traders have hitherto been able, in some measure, to enforce is forever ended. . . .

CHAPTER VIII.

WHEN the end of the session of the Legislature approached, the Governor's opponents marshalled their material and their forces for making what may be described as an attack upon his whole line of reform. Between the 4th of March and the 18th of the same month, the date of adjournment, four bills de signed to secure and continue the system of plundering extrava gance, which the Governor and both parties were pledged to reform, were passed in swift succession. They were all vetoed, the messages of disapproval constituting a body of sound doctrine and faithful instruction.

When Governor Chamberlain came into office he discovered that throughout the Administration of his predecessor the funds of the State had been kept in one depository, the Bank and Trust Company, at Columbia, commonly known as " Hardy Solomon's Bank." The State's deposit sometimes amounted to more than one million dollars. The capital of this bank was $125,000. Mr. Hardy Solomon, the principal owner and the manager of the institution, was a prosperous business man against whose financial credit there were no imputations. He was a Republican, and had ingratiated himself in the favor of officials by such accommodations as were much desired by State officers and others during the prevalence of the peculiar financial methods of the Moses Administration. One of the early acts of Governor Chamberlain was to take away the bulk of the State's deposit from Hardy Solomon's bank and distribute it among five other institutions, two in Columbia and three in Charleston, all having larger capital and the reputation of a more conservative management. In this ac-

tion he was heartily supported by the State Treasurer, while Judge
Hoge, then Comptroller General, and almost or quite every leading
Republican in the State, strongly opposed the proceeding. Of
course it was not relished by Mr. Solomon, who at that time had
great influence over a large proportion of members of the Legislature. The consequence was that the Legislature passed an Act
requiring all the public funds to be deposited in two designated
banks in Columbia, one of them Hardy Solomon's. This Act
the Governor vetoed, sending to the Legislature the following
message :

EXECUTIVE CHAMBER,
COLUMBIA, S. C., March 12, 1875.

Hon. R. H. Gleaves, President of the Senate :

SIR—I return herewith, without approval, an Act originating in the
Senate, entitled "An Act relative to the deposit of the moneys of the
State, and other provisions in relation thereto."

I have carefully considered the provisions of this Act. It is proper
to say that apparently no influence has been left untried to induce me
to approve the Act ; and, if personal considerations could be allowed
by me to influence my action upon such a matter, it would have given
me pleasure to sign the Act. But I have resolved, and I stand pledged,
not only to the people of the State, but to my own character and conscience, never to allow considerations personal to myself or to individual friends to have weight with me against my convictions of public
duty. I have accordingly examined this Act solely with reference to its
effects upon public interests, and under that rule am compelled to disapprove its general scope and its specific details.

The safe-keeping of the public funds should be made as absolute
and unquestionable as legislation can make it. Safety is the first requirement, and should never be made secondary to other considerations. If the present Act omits a single precaution or safeguard now
existing, it cannot command approval.

It will be useful to examine the present law regulating deposits of
public moneys, in order that we may compare that system with the one
now proposed in the present Act. The present law, as found in section 50, chapter 17, of the General Statutes, places upon a Board, composed of the Governor, Comptroller General, and the Treasurer, the
duty of selecting such banks for the deposit of State funds as the Board,
or only two of them, may judge, *first*, to be secure, and, *second*, shall
pay the highest rate of interest.

The Act now before me designates two banks, without qualification
or requirement regarding their safety, good management, or business
standing, and requires all State funds to be deposited in these two
banks.

The contrast between the two systems is too broad to escape atten--

tion or require designation. In the former system, the three highest
officers of the State, acting upon their official responsibility, and two of
them under very heavy bonds for the faithful discharge of their duties,
are required to select, from time to time, such banks of deposit for
State funds as they shall deem secure. Opportunity is here afforded
for the exercise of a reasonable discretion in the selection of the banks
of deposit, and the keeping in view of the strength and character of the
banks selected.

Further than this, and more important than any other consideration,
is the power given under this system, from time to time, to change the
banks of deposit whenever causes shall arise which may, in their judgment, warrant it.

Under the Act before me all this is changed. Not only are two
banks designated at the present time as the sole and exclusive depositories, but all power on the part of any one, except the General Assembly, to change the banks of deposit is taken away. The results to
which such a system leads are simply disastrous and unprecedented.
If disaster be impending to these two banks, if their officers are known
to be indulging in wild speculations, or even to be fraudulently squan-
dering the State funds, no public officer can intervene to arrest the disaster or to mitigate the loss. Nothing short of another Act of the
General Assembly, involving, perhaps, the assembling of the General
Assembly in extra session, could enable the State officers to withdraw
a dollar of money from either of these banks, except in regular payment of matured claims against the State. Once deposited, it must
remain without regard to the strength or conduct of the bank.

To sanction such a system is to deliberately trifle with the funds of
the State, and to tempt to the commission of wrongs which may, at any
moment, bring ruin upon every public interest of the State.

If the General Assembly, for any reasons satisfactory to them, shall
choose to place the duty and responsibility of designating the banks of
deposit for State funds in other hands than those of the present Board of
State officers, I shall not only not object to such a change, but, as I have
stated, I for one shall feel that a thankless and most embarrassing duty
is lifted from my shoulders. I care nothing for the prerogatives of
my office, except so far as they are essential to the protection of public
interests, and my short experience in my present office has been long
enough to cause me to welcome legislation which, without endangering
public interests, shall set me free from the nearly intolerable burden of
importunity from personal and political friends. But when I find
powers designed to be used for the constant protection of the State
funds, under any emergency or change of circumstances, not only taken
away, but these powers themselves abrogated, and an unchanging system, incapable of deviation, to meet the most imperious necessities that
may ever arise, adopted in their stead, it is no longer a question of
official prerogatives, but of a simple, ordinary, reasonable safe-keeping
of the funds. I cannot think of consenting to take away all power or
discretion in the State officers, and compelling the deposit of all State

funds in banks which the officers of the State may, at the moment of deposit, know to be insolvent.

But the system proposed in the present Act is not more dangerous and unreasonable in its general features than in its details.

The Act not only confines the deposits to two banks under all possible circumstances, but it proceeds to designate two banks which, if we concede all that can be claimed for them by their officers or patrons, have not sufficient pecuniary strength to render them safe depositories for all the State funds.

It is idle to say, in reply to this objection, that the State funds have been even more unsafely kept in the past, and no loss has yet occurred. What the State requires in such matters is not good luck under a system which daily exposes her to disaster, but the highest possible safety under a system which permits the exercise of the prudence and care suited to the exigencies which may arise. The State has now on hand nearly $1,000,000 in cash. This amount is distributed in three banks in Charleston and three in Columbia. The aggregate capital of these six banks is over $2,300,000, and yet I venture the opinion that no individual in this State, if possessing $1,000.000 in cash, would for one moment regard it as safe to place it as general deposits in six banks. I further venture the opinion that no man competent to care for his own funds would feel warranted in placing $100,000 as a general deposit in each of the two banks designated in the present Act. In saying this I do not question the character or management of either of these banks, but I simply call attention to the fact that it is proposed to do with the State funds what no prudent man would for an instant think of doing with his own funds.

It must be remembered, in considering this subject, that the State funds are not placed in the banks as special deposits. If the State funds were special deposits, we might calculate the strength of the vaults or safes of these banks, and the integrity of their officers, and thus reach a tolerably safe conclusion. But the State funds, when deposited in these banks, become general deposits, subject to loan and investment in the same manner as any other funds of the bank. The element of the financial wisdom and prudence in the management of the banks becomes, in view of this fact, a matter of prime importance. This element is a variable one. The officers and directors of the banks are constantly changing, and with such changes come changes in the financial standing of the banks and their safety as places of deposit.

Of all this the Act before me takes no note. The Act allows no discretion, and gives no heed to the inevitable changes which banks are constantly undergoing.

The experience of this community may be appealed to to show the utter folly of trusting too much to the skill or wisdom of banking institutions. In a single day this community has been aroused to the distressing fact that a bank holding the aggregate savings of thousands of families is hopelessly insolvent. Such events occur in every community, not necessarily from the dishonesty or unfaithfulness of those who manage these banks, but because the possession of large amounts of money tempts to hazardous ventures, in the midst of which the slightest general financial revulsion will cause suspension and bankruptcy.

For my part, I question most seriously, as an original policy, the wisdom or safety of placing our State funds in any banks. Why should the State encounter the risks always attendant upon banking operations? Is it for the little interest which accrues on her deposits? Even that is not exacted by the Act now before me. The effect of the Act is, that the State, without one dollar of gain to her funds, places them in two banks, to be used according to the discretion of those who control them. She runs all the risks attending general deposits in bank, and receives no reward or gain therefor. Certainly, if such a practice is to prevail, the State should have the highest assurance that her funds will be ready at her call, and this assurance must rest on the best guaranties that can be obtained.

The Act before me requires each bank to give a bond in the penal sum of $100,000, to be approved by the Judge of the Fifth Judicial Circuit, and this additional security was probably one of the inducements to the passage of the Act. If such a bond be given, the security afforded by the two banks named falls far below the proper security for general deposits aggregating at times $1,000,000 of State funds alone. Certainly the bonds here required fall far below the security afforded to the State by depositing its funds in six banks, the four banks not named in the Act having a pecuniary strength more than three times as great as that of the banks named, including the additional security afforded by the required bonds. What motive, I then ask, can the State have for putting all her funds in two banks in preference to six banks? Why should the State exchange the security afforded by the four banks not named in the present Act, whose pecuniary strength reaches nearly or quite $2,000,000, for that of two banks, whose capital stock hardly exceeds $400,000, and whose management is certainly not superior to that of the excluded banks? Why, especially, should this be done without even the paltry gain of one dollar of interest on all these vast deposits?

But, granting all that may be claimed for the feature of the present law requiring bonds to be given, there is no provision of the Act which affords any assurance that these bonds will be maintained so as to afford any real security to the State. No provision is anywhere made for any renewal of the bonds, or for keeping good the sureties of the bonds. The words are, "That this Act shall take effect so soon as a bond, etc., shall be given," etc. Under this provision, the bond may be approved and filed to-day, and become worthless to-morrow, and yet there would be no method of removing the deposits or requiring a new bond.

The examination now made of the general features of the Act before me persuades me, beyond doubt, first, that the designation by statute of two banks wherein shall be deposited all the funds of the State without provision for avoiding any disaster or loss which may be foreseen from the dishonesty of bank officials, or the pecuniary weakness of the banks, is utterly indefensible and hazardous to the limit of recklessness ; and secondly, that the designation of the Carolina National Bank of Columbia and the South Carolina Bank and Trust Company is likewise a policy which cannot be vindicated by the strength or standing of these particular banks, as compared with the vast amount of the deposits to be committed to them, or with the security now afforded by the six banks among which the State funds are now distributed.

But there are other features of this Act which do not meet my approval. I do not approve of that feature which forbids the banks to pay any checks of the State not drawn in a particular manner. If it is intended to require the State Treasurer to observe any additional regulations in the drawing of checks on State funds, it should be done directly by imposing that duty, with suitable penalties, upon that officer. To all such measures of safety I would gladly assent, but I do not consider it becoming in the State to place the power of refusing to honor the check of the State Treasurer in the hands of any bank. The bank is not amenable to the control of the State. No matter how arbitrarily, capriciously, or carelessly this power may be exercised by the banks, there is nothing short of a repeal of the Act that can control them. The enactment of such a provision is practically abdicating the proper powers of the State, and allowing them to be transferred to two corporations. It is a virtual confession that the execution of our laws must be transferred from our executive officers and vested in those who owe no duties to the general public, and are subject to no censure, punishment, or control of the State.

There is another provision of this Act to which I see grave objection.

Section 1 requires that all " the moneys to be drawn from the said banks shall be drawn therefrom equally." If this provision means what it says, it will be practically impossible to execute the law. A strict compliance with this provision will require the State Treasurer to divide every amount of money required to be drawn into two equal parts, and to draw a check upon each bank for one half of the amount required. He would not be at liberty at any time to permit the amount in one bank to exceed the amount in the other bank by a single dollar.

The same is true of depositing the funds. They must be deposited equally. The smallest sum received must be equally divided between the two banks.

Such provisions as these are serious hindrances to a proper administration of the duties of State Treasurer, and find no sanction in reason or necessity.

The reasons now stated compel me to withhold my approval from this Act, and to urge, with more than usual earnestness, upon the General Assembly the very grave dangers attending the proposed manner of keeping the State funds. No personal or political considerations

can have place in determining such a question. The safe-keeping of
the State funds is a matter of common interest to all our citizens. The
collection, safe-keeping, and disbursement of public funds constitute
the chief financial duties of the State Government. Each of these
functions must be exercised with prudence, wisdom, and integrity. If
either is permitted to free itself from all practicable restraints, the Government fails in its duty to the people, and disaster will sooner or later
follow.   Very respectfully,

D. H. CHAMBERLAIN,
Governor.

Perhaps the most important of all the vetoes of the session
was that of a bill for paying the floating debt of the State, commonly called in South Carolina the "bonanza bill," which had
passed both branches of the Legislature by large majorities, and,
for reasons that will be obvious, had a powerful and interested
support outside of the Legislature. It was a scheme to legalize
and liquidate the uncertain, vast, and, for the most part, corrupt
obligations which had been incurred and transmitted by the
previous Administration, and which were described in the Governor's Inaugural Address, and in his special Message of January
3, 1875.[1] The action of the Governor caused intense feeling
throughout the community. More than any thing that had
previously happened, it disappointed and vexed the corrupt factions in politics, while the citizens who desired reform were confirmed in their confidence that the chief magistrate was faithful
and courageous. The veto message is here given :

EXECUTIVE CHAMBER,
COLUMBIA, S. C., March 17, 1875.

Hon. R. B. Elliott, Speaker House of Representatives :

SIR—I return herewith, without approval, to the House of Representatives, in which it originated, an Act entitled "An Act to provide
for the settlement and redemption of certain claims against the State."

In refusing to approve this Act it is proper and necessary that I
should state certain facts connected with the history of the Act. When
I entered upon my present office it was my purpose to oppose any and
all plans for the present settlement of any of the various classes of
claims which constitute the so-called floating indebtedness of the State,
except the bills of the Bank of the State. This latter class of claims
having been judicially declared by the Supreme Court of the United
States to constitute a valid contract with the State, capable of enforce-

---

[1] See pages 19 and 57.

ment by the courts, and actually enforced in the cases before that court, I regarded it as dishonest and scandalous to delay longer to provide for meeting those obligations. This class of claims was likewise pressing by legal means upon the State, and seemed certain in the near future to produce disaster unless timely provision was made for their gradual payment. With reference to all other classes of claims, I was persuaded that the State had the right, and that her condition justly warranted her in postponing settlement until she could recover in some degree from the effects of a long course of extravagance and profligacy in the expenditure of public funds and the contracting of public obligations—at least until we should be able again to pay our current expenses during the year in which they arose. I was convinced that the people should not be taxed for the present year to an amount beyond the actual requirements of the public service, conducted on an honest and economical scale. My efforts were, therefore, mainly directed to the work and duty of stopping all unnecessary expenses, and restoring our Government to a cash basis in its transactions, leaving the past unsettled claims against the State to await the better times which the course indicated would surely hasten.

Especially did I regard this as the only admissible policy to be pursued towards those classes of indebtedness which are covered by the present Act, because they were believed to be largely tainted with illegality and frauds.

I was, however, strongly pressed to consent to some measure looking to the adjustment of the last-named classes of claims. Finally, being convinced by my own observation that some plan would be adopted, I turned my attention and efforts towards securing the adoption of a plan which would afford the best protection to the State and be least burdensome to the people. In modifying my policy in this respect I had the counsel and advice of the best men of both political parties, who agreed with me that, under all the circumstances, it was wise to endeavor to secure the best possible measure.

Acting with these aims and views, I gave my consent to a plan which embraced, first, the appointment by the Governor of a Commission of three, with power to audit all claims of the classes referred to, rejecting in whole or in part any claim presented upon any grounds satisfactory to them ; second, the reduction of all claims thus approved by the Commission to one half of their nominal value ; and third, the payment of the claims when thus reduced in four equal annual instalments.

Persuaded as I was that these claims were largely fraudulent, I regarded that feature of the measure which provided for the appointment of the Commission as by far the most vital one. Without a Commission whose character and ability would make the examination of the claims a work of searching vigilance and unquestionable honesty, the measure would be an atrocious and patent fraud. With a proper Commission the other features of the measure seemed to me to be reasonable.

Such a measure was introduced in the House of Representatives,

and was passed by that house.   In the Senate, for reasons which I have
not seen explicitly stated, the measure was changed by naming the three
members of the Commission.   The names inserted by the Senate were
changed by the House of Representatives, the changes were concurred
in by the Senate, and the Act as thus modified is substantially the Act
which is now before me.

Recurring now to the circumstances and motives which led me to
consent to the measure in its original form, I am compelled to say that
changes of circumstances have taken place since I was consulted concerning this measure, sufficient of themselves to warrant an entire
change of attitude on my part, apart from the complete change made
by the most essential feature of the measure.   The response given by
the General Assembly to my efforts to enforce a policy of rigid retrenchment and reform in our public expenditures has not met my expectations.   The passage of the Legislative Appropriation Act, the failure
to cut down appropriations to their lowest reasonable limit in the General Appropriation Act, the defeat of the bill reducing the salaries of
public officers, and the passage of a multitude of miscellaneous claims
have rendered it impossible for me to consent to add another dollar to
the weight of taxation which will now oppress the people of the State.
In addition to what has been specified, the passage already of Acts for
the levy of special taxes in no less than fourteen of the counties of the
State—these special taxes ranging from one and one half mills to three
mills on the dollar,—and the prospect of the passage of many more
similar Acts, is sufficient of itself to make my approval of the present
measure an act, in my judgment, of unpardonable injustice to all those
whose interests I am sworn to protect.

The supply bill for the present fiscal year has not yet reached me,
but as it passed the House of Representatives it provided for taxes
amounting to eleven and seven tenths mills on the dollar for general
State purposes.   Adding to this in most of the counties six mills for
regular and special county taxes, and from one to three mills for local
school taxes, we have an aggregate of taxation wholly without precedent, as it is without justification.   To all this are yet to be added the
taxes for town, village, and municipal purposes—in some instances
amounting to more than all the taxes for all other purposes.

Nothing will induce me to contribute to swell this already intolerable burden of taxation.   But if you look at the character of the claims
covered by this Act, there is nothing in general to commend to favor
and scarcely to toleration.   Included in the vast mass there are, doubtless, honest and just claims.   There is no doubt, moreover, that many
of the present holders of these claims are suffering by the delay in their
payment.   For all such I have profound sympathy, and would gladly
do any thing reasonable to relieve them.   But speaking generally of
the vast majority of these claims, what are they, and what do they represent?   They are, for the most part, the unpaid balance of the certificates issued during the last four years, under the guise of legislative
expenses of various kinds.   That certificates for legislative expenses

have been made the cover for vast frauds no man will dispute. They are universally regarded as the last culminating evidences of a prevailing system of corruption which has disgraced our State and offended the nation. The State has already paid on account of such claims an aggregate amount which, if we were not familiar with the facts, would pass the bounds of belief.

Since the regular session of the General Assembly for 1870–71, the State had paid, prior to the present session, on account of legislative expenses, the vast sum of $1,661,000. According to the registry already made by the clerks of the two houses, under a recent resolution of the General Assembly, there are still outstanding claims of the classes embraced by the present Act to the amount of $883,000, of which amount over $500,000 consists of claims for legislative expenses. Is there never to be an end to the payment of such expenses? Is the fact that such claims are outstanding to be successfully pleaded in justification for their payment without regard to the present ability of our people?

I speak, therefore, with accuracy as well as with justice when I say that these claims, as a whole, do not constitute an obligation which the State is bound to recognize or liquidate until her honest and valid indebtedness and the annual expenses of her government have been fully met. Certainly they cannot, with my consent, be made the occasion of a levy of taxes in addition to the unprecedented amount already levied for the present year.

But if I could overlook all other objections to the Act, there remains one objection which would, under any circumstances, forbid my approval of the Act. I mean the character, as a whole, of the Commission named in the Act. Upon this point I speak with a reluctance which all just men will appreciate ; but I am a public officer, bound to discharge an imperative public duty, and while I speak with reluctance, I must speak with perfect plainness. The Commission named does not, as a whole, command my confidence for the work assigned to it. I am equally confident it does not, as a whole, command the confidence of the public for that work. The duties required of the Commission demand the highest character for intelligence, honor, and incorruptibility which the State can furnish. By no fault or agency of mine I am forced to declare that, in my judgment, the Commission named in the Act does not meet that demand. The amounts involved are too great, the frauds believed to be involved in the claims to be examined are too widespread and pervading, the temptations to collusion and bribery are too powerful, to allow me to consent to placing these duties in the hands of any man whose circumstances and associations excite the faintest doubt of his inflexible determination to stand as an insurmountable barrier to the further advances of corruption and fraud.

The views now expressed compel me to withhold my approval of the present Act. I should be blind if I had not become fully aware that my action will give deep offence to many members of the General

Assembly.   I regret this, but I trust the lesson is nearly learned by all, that public duty is my only master.   It is not my nature to seek or enjoy conflicts, especially with those with whom I have had pleasant personal or political relations, but there is no loss or failure which I seriously dread, except the failure to see my duty and the loss of courage to do it.   Very respectfully,

D. H. CHAMBERLAIN,
Governor.

When this veto was received in the Legislature, there was a scene of wrath and confusion.   The *Union-Herald* of the next morning said :

The plunderers, led by Leslie, were full of wrath.   Green, Humbert, Hamilton, Thomas, Keith, Gantt, etc., were eager to exhibit the intense indignation which filled their righteous souls.   .   .   .   The opponents of the bill refrained from speaking, being convinced that they were strong enough to sustain the veto, with votes to spare. The debate came to an unexpected close on the point of order that the bill had been retained too long by the Governor, and that it, therefore, had become a law.

This point of order had reference to the constitutional provision that bills not returned to the Legislature within three days should become laws without the Governor's approval.   In this case the Legislature had not been in session on the third day, and therefore the bill was not returned until the fourth day.   The Speaker of the House ruled that the bill had become a law, and the ruling was promptly sustained by a vote of sixty-three to forty-six ; but, when passion had cooled, the Legislature voluntarily receded from this position, admitted the validity of the veto, and passed a second bill, omitting the objectionable features of the first one, and it was approved by the Governor.

One of the Commissioners named in the first bill for deciding upon the validity of the claims covered by it, was Mr. Hardy Solomon.   His name was inserted by an amendment made after the Legislature had passed the bill designating his bank as one of two in which all the State money should be deposited.   This is one of the facts which reveal the interdependence of the series of measures the Legislature was attempting to accomplish.

The Charleston *News and Courier*, commenting on the veto the next morning, said :

Governor Chamberlain has vetoed the bill to provide for the liquidation of the floating debt of the State. In vetoing it he will be, and must be, sustained by every honest citizen in and out of the Legislature. The public interests are safe so long as Governor Chamberlain continues in his present course. No job will be put upon the people so long as Governor Chamberlain's veto is sustained by the General Assembly. There will be wailing and gnashing of teeth in Columbia, of course. There will be more threats against the Governor. But the Conservatives and honest Republicans can see for themselves that the men who contrived the liquidation bill and their ring had no other desire than to plunder the people.

The Columbia *Phœnix*, the Democratic paper of which Col. Pelham was editor, said :

In this, as in many other instances since his inauguration, he has furnished unquestionable proof of the sincerity of his earnest desire for honesty and reform, so eloquently and forcibly presented by him during the campaign of last autumn.

Both parties pledged themselves in the election canvass of 1874 to abide by the adjustment of the public debt which had been reached, and to maintain it as a finality.[1] Nevertheless, the Legislature undertook to disturb it by establishing new conditions. The Act for that purpose, passed on the last day of the session, was immediately returned with a conclusive disapproval. "I, at least, must stand by my pledges," said the Governor,—a declaration which conveyed a merited rebuke to those who had acted as if they were under no obligation to keep faith with the public. The veto message is here given :

EXECUTIVE CHAMBER,
COLUMBIA, S. C., March 26th, 1875.
Hon. R. H. Gleaves, President of the Senate :

SIR—I return herewith, without approval, to the Senate in which it originated, an Act entitled "An Act to declare the true intent and meaning of certain provisions of an Act entitled ' An Act to reduce the volume of the public debt, and provide for the payment of the same.'"

The Act entitled "An Act to reduce the volume of the public debt, and provide for the payment of the same," has been regarded by the public, both within and without the State, as a final settlement of the public debt. Whatever differences of opinion may have existed respecting the Act as an original measure, the people of the State generally, as well as our public creditors, have now acquiesced in it, on the ground that it was the best attainable adjustment of the difficult and embarrassing questions involved.

So universal and deep-seated was this feeling, that both political parties in the last canvass for Governor and members of the General

[1] See sec. 7 of platform, p. 9.

Assembly pledged themselves in their platform of principles to especially maintain this settlement of the public debt.

These pledges are binding on me, and I understand them to require me to stand by that settlement *as it is*, without any change whatever in any of its important features and provisions.

I am compelled, therefore, to bring the present Act to this test : Is it in entire harmony with the present settlement of the public debt ?

By section 2 of the " Act to reduce the volume of the public debt, and provide for the payment of the same," the State Treasurer was authorized to exchange the coupons upon the bonds mentioned in section 1 of that Act, " which have accrued or will accrue *on the first of January,* 1874," for one half of their nominal value in " consolidation " bonds or stocks.

By section 5 of the same Act the " consolidation " bonds and stocks were to be made payable within twenty years from the passage of the Act, *to be dated January* 1, 1874, and the first coupon *to fall due July* 1, 1874.

It is clear, beyond question, to my mind that these provisions have absolutely and finally fixed the first day of January, 1874, as the period up to which the old bonds and stocks with their accrued interest are to be computed for exchange into the new bonds and stock. The holders of old bonds or stocks, by presenting them for surrender and exchange, became entitled to receive " consolidation " bonds or stock dated January 1, 1874, with a coupon maturing and falling due July 1, 1874. That was the leading feature of the "settlement"—the essential element in the offer made by the State to its public creditors.

Looking now to the Act before me, I find in its first section that all this is changed. Under this Act, *the first day of January,* 1874, is no longer the date up to which the computation is to be made prior to the reduction of one half in the nominal value of the bonds and stocks, and *the first day of July,* 1874, is no longer the date at which the first coupon shall fall due. On the contrary, the present Act provides that all coupons or interest orders which shall become due " *prior to the day on which such bonds or certificates of stock shall be tendered for funding,*" shall be funded or exchanged by the holder thereof.

I cannot well conceive of any more essential change in this " settlement." Instead of a fixed point of time, we have a constantly varying one. Instead of receiving bonds with the first coupons falling due July 1, 1874, the holder of outstanding bonds will receive bonds with the first coupons falling due according to the time when he presents his bonds.

In addition to the fact of this change, the influence of such a change on the particular execution of the " consolidation " Act must be considered. I cannot doubt that such a change will greatly retard, if not wholly arrest, the process of exchange now going forward with such gratifying rapidity. As time passes, and the holders of our unexchanged bonds and stocks perceive that no interest is received on their bonds while unexchanged, and that there is an accumulation of interest on the bonds and stocks to which they would be entitled under the

" consolidation " Act, it is manifest that a constantly increasing induce
ment is held out to them to exchange their bonds and stocks. When
the accumulation of interest shall have amounted to twelve or fifteen
cents on the dollar of the new bonds, the most reluctant of the holders
of the unchanged bonds will find himself compelled by regard to his
own advantage to make the exchange.

It should be borne in mind always, in considering this subject, that
those of our public creditors who bought our bonds at from seventy to
one hundred cents on the dollar do not look with favor upon a law
which takes from them one half of their debt, and substitutes for the
other half a security worth only from fifty to sixty cents on the dollar.
It will never be possible for the State to recover the confidence of
such men, or of the public generally, until a long course of undeviating
fidelity to our new promises shall convince them that we are seeking,
to the best of our ability, to repair the grievous wrongs of which they
are the victims.

I fear that there are some who feel that this subject of our public
credit is remote and unimportant in its relations to the interest of the
mass of our citizens. No mistake can be greater. There is not a man
in South Carolina whose pecuniary well-being is not largely bound up
with the condition of our public credit. Our vast natural advantages
of climate, soil, water power, minerals, are waiting for the coming in of
capital to develop them and enrich all our people. That capital must
come from abroad. Why does it tarry ? No one cause is so potent as
the utter wreck which has been made of our public credit. Men who
have surplus funds will allow them to lie idle rather than invest them
in a State whose public credit is the sport of the indifference or passion
which rules the hour. Public credit is like personal honor. It feels a
stain like a wound. It cannot be trifled with.

Therefore, while the " consolidation " Act was originally a measure
with which I had no concern, to-day it is the only method open to us
for recovering our public credit, and I must stand by it at all times
and in all its features, and the same obligation rests upon every member of the General Assembly.

I am aware that it is argued in support of the present Act that
there are matters of doubt connected with the " consolidation " Act
which the General Assembly ought to set at rest. It is true, perhaps,
that the view which I have presented of the intent of the Act may, if
carried out, prevent any surplus fund from arising with which to extin-
guish a part of the public debt. If this result were certain, it could
not change our duty to first pay all interest upon the " consolidation "
bonds and stocks accruing on and after the time specified in the Act,
namely, July 1, 1874. This is the first duty. If this exhausts the whole
fund, it will be a result for which we are not responsible, because it will
arise from a faithful adherence to the terms and meaning of the Act itself.

But if there are real doubts to be settled upon this point, the proper
place for their settlement is in the courts. The construction of statutes,

the interpretation of doubtful terms, the settlement of conflicting interests arising under legislative enactments, are properly judicial and not
legislative functions. The public creditor could not object to an appeal to the courts, for he holds his rights under his contracts with the
constant and understood reservation that the courts must, whenever
doubt arises, construe those contracts. The State could not object to
such a tribunal, for she professes herself to be bound by the pledge of
her faith and honor, and she has clothed her courts with the power to
interpret her duties and to fix her liabilities in all cases, which are properly subjects for judicial cognizance.

There are some changes made by the present Act to which, of themselves, I should make no objection, because they appear to promote the
general object for which the " consolidation " Act was passed, and could
not be regarded as impairing the contract established by that Act ; but
all such changes become absolutely unimportant compared with the
paramount duty and interest of standing by that Act in its integrity
and entirety as a final and complete settlement of our public debt. If
I could agree with the declarations made in the ·first section of the
present Act, I should still deprecate its passage, because the inevitable
effect of any change whatever in the " consolidation " Act will be to
unsettle the returning confidence felt by our creditors, and to seriously
retard the completion of the work of exchanging our public debt, which
is so essential to all our prosperity. When, however, the present Act
goes so far as to change the most essential feature of the " consolidation " Act, I have no alternative. I, at least, must stand by my pledges
and maintain the settlement as made by the Act of December 22, 1873.

Very respectfully,

D. H. CHAMBERLAIN,

Governor.

The annual Tax and Supply Bill as it passed the Legislature and
was presented to the Governor, not only disregarded his earnest
solicitations to economy and the reduction of expenses within
the limit of annual income, but it comprised cunning provisions
for accomplishing the objectionable purposes of several bills already vetoed, employing the artful device, not unknown in other
States and in Congress, for forcing an Executive ·to consent to
legislation to which he is inimical, by making it impossible for
him to prevent it without at the same time deranging the machinery of administration by a stoppage of supplies. It was a
serious situation, but the Governor did not flinch. Embarrassing
as the condition must become with no appropriations for the
whole year, the Governor, after much deliberation, determined
that he would not give his approval to the bill. By the Consti-

tution he was permitted, in case of the adjournment of the Legislature before the expiration of the three days within which bills might be returned unsigned, to hold such bills until the third day of the following session. The veto message, therefore, was not sent to the Legislature until it reassembled, and will be found in a subsequent chapter [1]; but the Governor's intention with respect to the bill soon became known, and was recognized by friends and foes as an additional proof of his consistency and inflexible resolution.

[1] Chapter XII.

CHAPTER IX.

THE three and a half months since the Legislature met and its members listened with surprise to Governor Chamberlain's Inaugural Address had been a period of strenuous and often bitter contest, of which only the salient and significant features have been presented. Upon the leader in the reform movement rested grave responsibilities, and it was neither by luck nor on account of the weakness of his opponents that he was able to frustrate their well-laid plans. The right does not win its victories over organized wrong except by superior force and skill in the fighting. The forces hostile to the Governor's policy were ably marshalled and led. Among his opponents were adepts in the arts of political organization, intrigue, manœuvre and attack ; politicians much better adapted by temperament, sympathy, and address to cozen the favor of the citizens who constituted the majority of officials and of voters in the Republican party, than was the serious, cultured, reflective gentleman, of dignified and refined manners, whose only apparent passion in public affairs was devotion to an ideal of public duty imposing severe labor, constant self-denial, and relentless thwarting of "good fellows" whose fault was a disposition to make politics profitable.

During this session Governor Chamberlain vetoed nineteen bills. Although several of them on their passage had a support indicating that a veto would be in vain, it is a remarkable fact that in no case did his opponents secure the two-thirds vote necessary to pass a bill notwithstanding the disapproval of the Executive. Every one of the measures was abandoned, or was revised and passed in a form that avoided the Governor's objections. As far as the consummated legislation of the session was a test, he had obtained conspicuous success in the development of his policy. In spite of a hostile intention, the Legislature had been compelled to serve the cause of reform. Throughout the country the " new departure " in South Carolina was regarded with a satisfaction hardly less than that of the relieved citizens of the State, and, almost without a discordant voice, the Governor's exemplary fidelity was confessed and praised, while unfavorable prejudices which had been fostered by partisan malice and misunderstanding were renounced, as his true character revealed itself under crucial tests. It did not escape the notice of men desiring to be just, that here was one whose conduct defied and taunted all the corrupt elements in politics to reveal any connivance with them that would humiliate or embarrass him, who yet bore himself as having a conscience void of such offence and unable to make him a coward in the performance of public duty. In truth, there had been wrought within the short space of four months, by the signal potential services of one hitherto misunderstood and unappreciated, a notable revolution in the affairs of South Carolina. Despair was succeeded by hope, distrust yielded to confidence, disparagement was turned to praise.

How general this happy revulsion of feeling was, will be clear from the quotations from representative journals that are given herewith. The concurring judgment of observers so variously situated and so independent of each other, having no common motive or interest except the instinctive respect of good citizens for things honorable and of good report in all public business, makes these contemporaneous expressions not only a valuable but an essential part of the record. With some which were published about the time of the adjournment of the Legislature, are given some that preceded that event and some that came later, but obviously all are founded upon the conditions already developed. Belonging to the latter class is the following article from the Charleston *News and Courier* of May 14, 1875:

GOV. CHAMBERLAIN.

Republican Governors in the South have so bad a character that it is difficult for the public to believe that any one of the number can be honest, capable, and fearless in the discharge of his duty.   Especially is this the case in South Carolina, where the Governor is a latter-day citizen, a native of New England, and an ex-officer of the Federal Army, and was an office-holder during four years when wholesale stealing by public officers was the rule and not the exception.   Nevertheless Governor Chamberlain has satisfied the masses of the people in this State that he is as true as steel, in the fight against public dishonesty which he began upon his installation and continues to this very day.

This newspaper, as the public know, was Mr. Chamberlain's stoutest opponent during the canvass of last fall.   It is due to the *News and Courier* that the movement against Mr. Chamberlain, which in the beginning had no life or force, swept like a wave over the hills and plains of South Carolina, and engulfed three fourths of the expected Republican majority.   We knew of what we spoke ! When, therefore, Mr. Chamberlain in his Inaugural Message promised a reduction of expenses, and declared, in substance, that he would have " two clean years " in South Carolina, we were not ready to jump to the conclusion that he would do what he said.   We remembered that for four years he was Attorney General ; that he was a member of the Financial Board, and the Sinking Fund Commission, and the like ; that he did not raise his voice in protest, if he knew the State was being robbed, that he must have been, as far as we could see, so weak as to sacrifice his convictions of right to personal friendship or party interest, or so blind and deaf, in public life, as to be unfitted to hold any high office of trust.   These things could not be forgotten ; but there was a ring of the true metal in Gov. Chamberlain's words, and faithful to the pledge that we would judge every man by his acts and according to his works no obstacle was placed in Gov. Chamberlain's path.   On the contrary, we said, and the public sustained us in saying it, that, as far as promises went, the Inaugural Address was all that could be desired, that the new Executive should have a fair field, and that the Conservatives would stand by him just as long as his acts squared with his words.

At the first opportunity, when the election of a judge for the Charleston Circuit took place, Governor Chamberlain broke away from the corrupt members of his own party, and accomplished the election of an unobjectionable Republican in place of the blatant and corrupt colored man who was the party candidate.   Only once did Governor Chamberlain make the slightest concession to the vicious element in the Legislature.   This was when he approved the first legislative appropriation bill.   Whenever any corrupt measure raised its head in the Legislature, Governor Chamberlain struck at it.   Whenever any stealing bill passed he vetoed it, and his veto was sustained.   The veto of the infamous bonanza bill was his last act, but the extravagant appropriation bill, passed just before the adjournment, has not been signed, and will not be.   In a word, it is due to Mr. Chamberlain that, for the first time in six years, there was no considerable stealing during the legislative session, and that not one swindling bill became a law.   The session of 1874–75 was far from being pure, but it was a vast improvement on any thing that the State has seen since Reconstruction. We do not speak of Governor Chamberlain's scholarly messages, of his patriotic utterances, of his unfailing tact and courtesy.   We speak only of his acts.   By them we judge him.   In the light of his acts, since he has been Governor, we say now that, however much appearances were against him, it is morally impossible that he should have been either facile or corrupt. Such a man as he is can never have been the man we did believe him to be. Governor Chamberlain, therefore, richly deserves the confidence of the people of this State. The people of South Carolina, who have all at stake, who see and hear what persons outside of the State cannot know, are satisfied of Governor Chamberlain's honesty. They believe in him, as well they may.

No one doubts that Governor Chamberlain is a man of ability and foresight. When he determined to oppose a square front to corruption in whatsoever guise, he knew that he must, on that, cut loose from the rogues who ruled the Republican party up to the time of his election, and that upon him would be poured out the seventy and seven vials of wrath. It would have been supreme folly to provoke their hate if there was any thing in his previous conduct that could expose him to ignominy and public shame. And he knew, also, that if the Conservatives did not stand by him, he would be ground to dust between the upper and nether stones of conservatism and rascality. This, to him, was a terrible risk ; for he could not have understood, as he now understands, the liberality and good faith and downright hard sense of the Conservative masses. By and with the aid of the Conservatives, Governor Chamberlain and the small band of honest Republicans defeated the thieves in every engagement. But the men whom he has thrown down, and who did not want or expect reform, are wild with rage and despair. They feel that only the first shock has been felt ; that a legislative session in which there was no considerable stealing will be followed by sessions in which economic and intelligent legislation will prevail ; that the condemnation of crime will be followed by the prosecution and conviction of criminals. Knowing that Governor Chamberlain stands well with the nation and not with this State alone, they strive to break him down by casting doubts upon his candor and integrity. Senator Patterson undertakes to disabuse the President of the idea that Mr. Chamberlain, in comparison with Scott and Moses, is as Hyperion to a Satyr, and vagabond newspaper correspondents fill such newspapers as will accept their letters with injurious untruths about the Governor and his supporters. One of these correspondents we have already exposed ; another has sprung up in Charleston to aid in the congenial work. The New York *Sun* believes what these correspondents say, and the Washington *Star* boldly asserts that ex-Treasurer Parker will never be prosecuted to conviction if Governor Chamberlain's influence can save him. The plain meaning of this is that Governor Chamberlain was a party to the frauds of 1868–72, and, therefore, dare not prosecute any of the officers who are accused of committing them.

We have endeavored to show that appearances were against Mr. Chamberlain up to the time of his election as Governor, and that the opposition to him, in the light we then had, was proper and necessary. We have weighed his conduct since November last with the care with which we weighed what we knew of his conduct in the first four years after Reconstruction ; and, against any positive or negative fault as Attorney General, we set the grand work he has done as Governor. We would be willing to condone any thing in his past conduct that fell short of actual criminality. But this is not necessary ! It is our fixed belief that Mr. Chamberlain has never, in great things or little, consented to, or aided in, any fraud upon this people.

We are confident that, whenever all the facts shall be known, the record of Attorney-General Chamberlain will be found to be every whit as clean as the record of

Governor Chamberlain. And there is only one way in which the facts can be made manifest. We say to the correspondents of the New York *Sun* and the whole tribe of slanderers, that if they will make their charges under their own name, and prove themselves to be trustworthy and unprejudiced, if they will give to their charges a shape in which they can be met, we will demand that the accusations shall be fairly met, as we know Governor Chamberlain can meet them. This is a challenge to the anonymous crew who cringe to Governor Chamberlain to-day, and lie about him to-morrow. It is a challenge that, if they are honest themselves, they must accept. And, until the challenge is accepted and the truth of the charges is proved, we have a right to expect that the press of the country will not, any of them, stab South Carolina in the back by lending their aid and influence to the persons who malign the only Republican officer of eminent ability, eminent culture, and eminent integrity, that the North has given to this people.

The following extract from an editorial article in the Kingstree (S. C.) *Star*, a Democratic weekly paper, is in the same vein; it was published April 21, 1875, nearly a month earlier than the article in the *News and Courier*.

It is well known we opposed Governor Chamberlain's election. We did not do so because he was a Republican, for his opponent, whose election we advocated, was also a Republican, but because his connection with the Scott Administrations, in the responsible positions of Attorney General and ex-officio member of various important boards, was such as to cause us to lack confidence in his integrity and honesty. We never doubted his ability, intellectually, to fill the gubernatorial chair. We confess we had no confidence in his high-sounding words of promised reform made in his campaign speeches and letters, for our people had so often been gulled by similar utterances on the part of his predecessors in the executive office, that we apprehended it was the same old story—reform, retrenchment, economy, and honesty—till the election was over, and then extravagance, corruption, plunder, and dishonesty afterwards. But we confess we have been agreeably disappointed. We have carefully watched Governor Chamberlain and his every public action and movement of which we could be informed and form a judgment at this distance from Columbia, and we cannot at this writing recall a single instance in which he has not made good, or attempted to make good as far as he could under the Constitution, the pledges made by him before his election. This is broad and sweeping language, but we think it is none too much so. Truth, consistency, and fair dealing demand it, and we make the statement cheerfully and without hesitation. . . .

But not all the conservative papers in South Carolina were so cordial in their treatment of the Governor's efforts; there were exceptions, two or three,—partisans reluctant to confess that any good could come out of the Republican party, or that any Republican could be honorable and sincere even when doing the best things for the State. Of these the Anderson *Intelligencer* was, perhaps, the most able and persistent. The character of this criticism and the manner in which it was met by the Republican supporters of Governor Chamberlain are fairly illustrated in the following article from the Columbia *Union-Herald.*

We print to-day an article from the Anderson *Intelligencer* which is so supercilious and impertinent in tone, and so illogical in its conclusions, that it seems to call for comment from us. It assumes an attitude toward Gov. Chamberlain and his friends entirely unwarranted by the condition of parties in this State. While pretending to great magnanimity of bearing, the intense partisanship of the writer is irrepressible. Gov. Chamberlain has not asked for the exhibition of any magnanimity, but has himself given a proof every day since his election that that admirable quality is a part of his character. He has paid back the virulent attacks of a long campaign by a calm and steadfast effort to show that his pledge that he would be a Governor of the people was not a mere political campaign promise. The admission that honesty and economy have not only been "the watchwords of his Administration," but that they have "borne fruits" in checking a shameful reign of official corruption, at the risk of losing the support of many powerful party supporters, is not one which he is called upon to be effusively thankful for. His acts speak for themselves, and will be the tests by which he will be tried before the great inquest of the people of the State, irrespective of party.

The *Intelligencer* refuses to "blindly pledge allegiance to his political fortunes," or trammel itself with "unbounded promises of support in the future." May we ask to whom it would be wise to pledge such allegiance, and whether it is ever safe to promise unbounded support in the future? We would not do it to any man. No man asks it of the *Intelligencer* or of us.

This patronizing tone must be offensive to the self-respect of any man, except a sycophant by nature. It is unworthy of those who assume it, and it is derogatory to the character of the man toward whom it is directed. Suppose Mr. Chamberlain were to say to the Conservatives : You are now behaving very well ; you are treating your Republican fellow-citizens with tolerable fairness ; you are creating no disturbances, are threatening no lives, have abandoned night-riding, whipping, and Ku-Kluxing for political opinions ; but I require more evidences of contrition for the outrages of 1870–71 before I will believe that your present attitude is not assumed from motives "not less selfish than those of the generality of ambitious and aspiring men in public life." Such an utterance would be resented, and properly, as insolent and uncalled for. But it would be just as much called for by the facts as is the tone habitual with certain Conservative newspapers when speaking of the Governor and his friends.

The *Intelligencer* says that "the brief history of his Administration clearly proves that political opponents saved him from inglorious defeat on more than one occasion." The way we read the history of the past six months, it appears equally fair for us to say that the Governor has, on more than one occasion, saved the Conservative, tax-paying citizens of the State from overwhelming disaster.

It says again : "We will never consent to ignore the fact that triumph over thieves was made possible only through the support of the Conservatives." Can we not say that the triumph of honest men was only possible because they had the aid of an able and upright Republican Governor? What could the seven Conservatives in the Senate and the thirty in the House have accomplished without him?

But we deprecate such eagerness to win for a man or a party political capital from acts of simple duty. We perceive nothing in the Governor's course or character to justify the insinuation that if he thought it to his political advantage he would play the rascal ; and we could be equally false to assert that the Conservative minority in the Legislature would be willing to reap political advantage by joining hands with corruptionists to oppress and plunder the people. We try to see in the future only the redemption of the State from misgovernment, to be attained by means of unity among all classes of good citizens to sustain what is right and to attack and defeat what is wrong. Party advantages we hope to make only an incidental question. We do not expect to abandon any political conviction, but long for the day when our citizens of each party may approach the polls and vote for candidates of their choice without feeling that the success of their opponents will be either destructive of the material interests of the State or perilous to the rights and liberties of any class of the people. We believe that Mr. Chamberlain is working to that end, and that neither the active attacks of the base men in his own party, nor the suspicions and detractions of the other, will cause him to falter in the course he has marked out.

The following extracts are all from South Carolina Democratic papers.

Governor Chamberlain has vetoed the bill lately passed by the Legislature for the settlement of the floating debt of the State. We publish this veto in full. It is a paper nobly conceived and nobly expressed. To say less would be simply churlish. . . . This bill proves that the thieves want our blood ; and this veto proves that Governor Chamberlain is our only hope.—*Edgefield Advertiser.*

From his Inaugural down to the present time the Governor has stood squarely and firmly upon the platform upon which his party placed him. But those who were to assist him, to stand by him and carry out the pledges of that platform and fulfil its promises—where are they to-day? Failing utterly in their legislative capacity to carry out the wholesome and needed reforms recommended so earnestly by the Administration—throwing every possible obstacle in the pathway of reformation—the language of *their* conduct plainly says we intended to deceive the people. The language of the Governor, so far, has been that his Administration shall not be a living lie. For this we honor and admire him. . . . The people of this county will give him united support in any and all efforts to make his Administration a success, in advancing the best interests of the State, and their full sympathy in the trying fight he is making against the thieves and practical traitors of his party.—*Spartan.*

Thus far the course pursued by Governor Chamberlain has met with the approval of all unprejudiced people in the State. He has shown the determination to put down fraud and corruption, and not to lend himself for an instant to schemes of robbery, wrong, and injustice. With the turbid waves of corruption seething all around him he stands, like a rock, firm and immovable.—*Darlington Southerner.*

We highly commend the boldness of the Governor in not hesitating to interpose his veto power whenever he deemed that interposition necessary for the public welfare. And at the close of this first session of the Legislature we take pleasure in saying to him : " Well done, good and faithful servant." And we are the more willing to say this because we had gloomy forebodings of the results of his election. We find, in him thus far one Republican who fulfils his promises.—*Winsboro News.*

We print to-day a batch of good news from Columbia. 1. Governor Chamberlain has decided not to sign the iniquitous thirteen-mill tax bill for 1875-76 . . . The General Assembly will, by the time that they re-assemble, understand the temper of the people better than they did when they adjourned last month. Low taxation must be had. Those who are opposed to it will do well to stand from under. 2. Dennis, of furniture fame, has been removed by Governor Chamberlain, and Col. Parmele appointed in his stead. The new Superintendent of the Penitentiary will have no fellow-feeling to make him wondrous kind with thieves or felons ; for he is, we are told, a highly respectable and thoroughly upright man, although a late arrival from the North. 3. The Bonanza men are desperate enough to seek for a mandamus to compel the Commissioners to act. Are they coy ? We doubt it. But when they have been constrained to serve, if they ever shall be, the work of plundering the State will only have begun. The United States Court has control over the bonanza bill, and that court is incorruptible. For the removal of Dennis and for the killing of the tax bill the public must thank Gov. Chamberlain, who also is at the bottom of the flank movement on the bonanza men in the United States Court. Two years of such noble work as this will cause him to be hailed as the savior of South Carolina. —*News and Courier.*

Well has Daniel H. Chamberlain redeemed the promise that he so eloquently and earnestly made—that if elected to be chief magistrate of South Carolina, he would be the Governor of the whole people, and for the strict performance of which he is entitled to the thanks of all.—*Marion Merchant and Farmer.*

The truth is, Gov. Chamberlain, like all reformers, has a hard fight before him. The difficulties of his position are manifold, requiring high courage and great sagacity. A Republican, he is fighting the frauds of his party within his party, and has to contend against all the plunderers of that party. It is very evident that the Republican party is split ; there are two distinct wings. One wing acts from principle and a desire to have an honest administration of public affairs, due respect being had to constitutional limitations and restrictions. The other wing is radical, and acts solely with a view to party success and for selfish purposes. Political principle and constitutional limitations are alike disregarded, if either or both stand in the way of party triumph or a pecuniary speculation. The Governor, in all his utterances since his inauguration, has given the highest proof of a determined purpose not to lend his aid to any scheme of fraud, peculation, or constitutional violation.—*Barnwell Sentinel.*

At the May session of the Circuit Court, in Fairfield County, the grand jury, composed equally of Democrats and Republicans, said in their report : " We congratulate the State upon the wise and just Administration of Gov. Chamberlain."

From the mass of encouraging comment in papers published in other States the following selections are made as being fairly representative of the prevailing sentiment :

We do not know how Governor Chamberlain's contest with these people will end, but we can assure him of the sympathy of honest people all over the Union, as one who is really defending civilization itself against barbarism in its worst form.—*New York Nation* (Ind.).

Before the election of Governor Chamberlain of South Carolina we avowed a want of confidence in his integrity. We take pleasure in saying now that his conduct in office has been such as to make us feel that we were wrong in distrusting him. He has set his face like a flint against the corruptionists of his party, thereby earning their hatred, and commending himself to the confidence of those who opposed his election. There has been a great improvement in the affairs of the State under his Administration, and if he goes on as he has begun, every honest man in the State will be in favor of his re-election.—*Christian Union* (Boston).

Governor Chamberlain, of South Carolina, by his honesty and boldness, is making a grand reputation for himself. He vetoes rascally measures, puts his foot upon corruptionists, and holds it down.—*Cincinnati Gazette* (Rep.).

Governor Chamberlain, of South Carolina, is winning golden opinions from all sorts of people for his just and able course in that State. Every thing seems to be going on well there under his management, and the conservative people are giving him their hearty support. This is the true road to reconstruction and peace after all.—*Richmond* (Va.) *Enquirer* (Dem.).

Having put his hand to the reform plough, Governor Chamberlain, of South Carolina, is driving a very straight furrow, and he shows no disposition, thus far, to look back.—*Springfield* (Mass.) *Republican* (Ind.).

The Republican Governor of South Carolina has been working wonders for the State he represents. His recent action in vetoing the tax bill has given a tremendous spur to South Carolina securities, no less than $10,000 worth having been purchased in Augusta yesterday on the strength of confidence restored. South Carolina stood foremost in the ranks of the South before the war in commercial credit. It would be a singular coincidence if a man whose party had plunged her into degradation should pull up her financial honor by its drowning locks.—*Augusta* (Ga.) *Constitutionalist* (Dem.).

. . . It is time that the negroes who have been disgracing their race, themselves, and American institutions by their reckless venality should learn that stealing must stop somewhere. The Republican party has done every thing it could for the

South Carolina people, and the latter have repaid this kindness by inflicting grave and lasting harm upon the party but for which they would now be things, not men, mere chattels, sold at the auction-block, without a right recognized by the law. If Governor Chamberlain's veto (of the bonanza bill) is not sustained, he can console himself by reflecting that adverse action by the South Carolina Legislature, as by the Chicago Common Council, is a proof of the merits of the thing condemned.—*Chicago Tribune* (Rep.).

It is worth while to note that this era of good feeling and charitable disposition has been brought about without any yielding of principle or firmness on the question of equal rights by Governor Chamberlain. But what is most significant is that, as soon as the white citizens of the State obtained their right to good government, there was an end of reports of outrages and calls upon the general government for interference to sustain the Republican State Government, such as were frequent under the corrupt *régime* of Moses. While the people of South Carolina were plundered and harassed by an Administration of scoundrels, they were as unreconciled and troublesome as the white people of Louisiana are now. When their just rights were respected, they forthwith respected the rights of others.—*Boston Advertiser* (Rep.).

Two valuable personal judgments upon Governor Chamberlain's course and the state of things in South Carolina are here given. The first is contained in a letter to the Boston *Commonwealth* by Richard T. Greener, a widely-known representative of the colored race graduated from Harvard College, whose sympathies, naturally, were all with his people.

. . . I was in the hall of the House of Representatives when the Governor-elect took the oath of office and delivered his Inaugural. . . . Officers of the army, Conservative editors and politicians, Grangers and Tax-Unionists, were all on hand to hear what this Governor that Massachusetts had sent to South Carolina had to say. They were sceptical and sullen at first, but I noticed that from careless interest there arose an intenser feeling ; and when some of the clean-cut sentences rang out unmistakably for reform the applause from the Democratic side was emphatic and hearty—much more so, perhaps, than from the side of the Radicals—myself among the number—who fear, somehow instinctively, that " reform," after all, means to take power from the hands of the negro, no matter how sincere its advocates may be. As I thought then, and many agreed, the message seemed to concede almost all the Conservatives had said, and resembled somewhat a Jeremiad. The course of events since has changed that opinion, and I now think that such a line did more to shut the mouths of the insincere Conservatives and assure the honest grumblers than any less pronounced advocacy of reform would have done. It certainly silenced the batteries which were ready, both in the Assembly and in the press of the State, to open upon the Republican party. Subsequent events have proved the honesty of the Governor and his fixedness of purpose in the resolution he has taken. Many say he is swayed only by a desire to ingratiate himself with the conservative element, and thus either be re-elected, go to the United States Senate, or look to higher honors on a broader field. In any event, his ability and well-known record render any such result not improbable, and not at all to be scouted at as a heinous offence, especially if the people so will it ; while those who are opposed to any such exaltation of a worthy Republican have the onus to show and prove that he is ambitious at the expense of principle. It makes little difference who gets honors or offices at the South, provided only impartial liberty, equal and exact justice, is preserved, and every man has a chance, without fear and without favor, to be in every sense a man in the land of his birth. Underneath all the questions of reform, good government, just taxation, negro supremacy, lie deeper and more fundamental issues. The minor ones are of trifling import if those upon which republican government rests are maintained. The latter are the Palais Royale which must be saved at all hazards.

Hon. Amasa Walker, of Massachusetts, a man whose conspicuous ability and high character give unusual value to his utterance, having, on account of his health, spent much time in South Carolina, wrote a letter (March 23, 1875,) to the Springfield (Mass.) *Republican*, from which the following passage is taken :

Governor Chamberlain was elected by the Republican party, has a majority in both branches of the Legislature, and it would seem, at the first blush, that his position was an eligible one and that he need find little difficult᷍ in conducting the affairs of the Government ; yet no man, in the whole history of the Reconstruction movement, has been surrounded by more embarrassing circumstances. This is owing to the character of the Administrations that have immediately preceded his own. They were corrupt to a most appalling extent, had wasted the revenues of the State, and plunged it into almost hopeless bankruptcy. And all this was done by his own party, and, to no small extent, by the ring men in concert with whom he must act in conducting its legislative and financial affairs. His enemies are those of his own household if he should undertake to stem the fearful tide of corruption, and be honest and just ; yet, if we may judge from what he has already accomplished, he has been determined from the outset that nothing should be done, so far as he could prevent it, injurious to the best interests of his adopted State.

Thus far he has succeeded admirably, and given assurance that his Administration is to be conducted for the benefit of the country rather than the advantage of official thieves. Should he be able, as it is confidently expected he will, to execute his intentions, it will be an important event, not only to South Carolina, but to other States that have, like her, suffered excessively from the faithlessness of their public servants. Governor Chamberlain offends a certain class, but, of course, gives high satisfaction to those who desire, above all things, the promotion of the best interests of the State, and we hear on all sides high and hearty commendations of the course he has thus far pursued. From present appearances he will, at the end of his two years' term, have the approbation and thanks of the great body of the citizens of both parties. Should this be the case, the moral and political effect upon the whole country will be very great. If a Yankee, born and bred in New England, should show himself, in the exalted station of Governor, an honest and fearless man, fully bent upon advancing in the highest degree the welfare of a Southern State, and successful in doing so, it need not be said that it would exert a very happy influence upon the entire nation.

CHAPTER X.

THE change wrought in the feeling toward the Governor of the
citizens who were not of his political party was manifested in
various expressions of respect and cordiality, often assuming the
form of an earnest solicitation to take a prominent part on public
occasions which had no direct connection with the business of the
State. The record of Governor Chamberlain's Administration
would lack not only completeness, but a quality of essential
justice, if it omitted becoming mention of his distinguished and
honorable performance of the non-administrative duties which are
imposed on a chief magistrate, in his character of representative
first citizen of the Commonwealth.

Until the end of the session of the Legislature he permitted
no inducement, however tempting, to divert his energy from the
work he had undertaken. Soon after his term began, he was invited to attend the meeting of the New England Society in
Charleston, in celebration of the anniversary of the landing of the
Pilgrims at Plymouth. In the reply which he made to the invitation to be present and respond to the sentiment " The State of
South Carolina," he confessed the pleasure and pride he would
feel in doing that service, if he were not compelled to remain at

his post of duty, and in the following passage, he indicated the thought which the occasion inspired in him :

If I had been permitted to respond for the State of South Carolina at your festival, I should have said that I, a son of the Pilgrims of New England and loyal in every fibre of my being to their memory, could look with pride, hardly less than if native-born, upon the high qualities which have marked the people of this State in all the varying fortunes through which they have passed—their early self-denial,their revolutionary patriotism, their brilliant record in the subsequent national councils, their devoted valor in the more recent struggle of arms, and their unwavering fortitude amidst the trials of misfortune and defeat. I should have said that from such elements of character, fixed and inspired by such a history, South Carolina, laying aside whatever was antagonistic to true progress in her former local institutions, and resting now on the broad foundation of perfect civil equality, will in the near future re-assert her supremacy in our great sisterhood of States. I know the sons of the Pilgrims of New England who are with us will not dishonor their sires by a weak succumbing before present discouragements. Faith in the invincibility of a good cause was the secret of our fathers' success. In that sign we may again conquer. In the restoration of good government to this State let us resolve to bear an honorable part, thereby proving our true descent from those who, two hundred and fifty years ago, gave to the world one of her most conspicuous examples of the spirit and methods by which Christian Commonwealths may be built up and perpetuated.

" The restoration of good government to this State "—that was the task he had set for himself ; and he neglected no proper opportunity of invoking the sympathy and aid of all citizens on the broad ground of common interest and obligation, well knowing that under our form of government the public welfare is never secure unless there can be established under all political organizations into which the people may be divided, a fundamental sympathy and co-operation of honest men in honorable aims.

In March, the same Society had its annual dinner, and the Governor was again invited to be present to respond to the same sentiment. Again he was compelled to decline. The brief letter of declination written two days before the adjournment of the Legislature, illustrated, as it was, by his public service, profoundly affected the assembly and the public, and was the occasion of a remarkable speech by an eminent citizen, for many successive years before the war the Speaker of the House of Representatives of the State. The Governor wrote :

COLUMBIA, March 16, 1875.

A. S. Trumbo, Esq., Charleston, S. C. :

DEAR SIR—Your very kind favor of the 12th inst. is received. It is a great disappointment to me not to be able to be present with you and to enjoy the high honor of responding to the sentiment which you have enclosed.

It fills the full measure of my ambition to win the approval of the good men of South Carolina of all parties in my efforts to have our State Government become a blessing and protection to all our people. My present position would afford me no compensation which I could value if I should fail to convince all that I am striving to be the servant of the whole people. Your kindness on this occasion is one valued proof of my success in this respect, and it shall nerve me to follow the same path in the future.

Yours, very gratefully,

D. H. CHAMBERLAIN.

What followed the reading of this letter was thus reported in the Charleston *News and Courier* :

After the reading of this communication, which was received with deafening applause, President O'Connor introduced General James Simons to respond to the following toast, which was to have been responded to by Governor Chamberlain :

"The State of South Carolina : There are signs which indicate the dawn of a new and better era, when, shaking the mildew of corruption from her garments, she will array herself again in the robes of honor and honesty."

General Simons, after alluding to the present condition of the State, asked who was to be the Cato who would restore her to her former greatness and glory. The office of Governor in South Carolina has been its most favored office. Its judiciary has always been favored and spotless, and, in my conception, South Carolina has been so catholic, so universal in her opinion and sentiment, that when she wanted a Cato she did not have to ballot for him. [Good ! good !] But whoever came to represent the people, whether he came from one portion of the Union or another, if he had honesty stamped upon his brow, he was welcomed and supported. I heard read just now the sentiment : "The compensation of my being Governor of South Carolina will be indifferent if I fail to convince all that I am the Governor of the whole people." Gentlemen, I have been accustomed to that sentiment in South Carolina amongst the Governors when I was no higher than this table. I have never heard them utter the sentiment, but I never saw the time when it was other than conceded that the Executive, the foreman of the grand jury of the Commonwealth, knew no difference between individual or party ; he was the Governor of the whole people. This I regard as a great sentiment, a noble conception ; it requires nobility of nature, elevation of spirit, power of self-respect, to carry it into execution.

You have a man ruling over your State who has the affections, the respect, the esteem, and the confidence of the people. Let him make good that exalted sentiment uttered in his letter which has just been read, and he will merit the "Well done, good and faithful servant," uttered with one accord by a grateful people. I do not expect miracles. I am of a profession which teaches me to find out what justice is. You must remember, gentlemen, that Governor Chamberlain is circumstanced as few of his predecessors have been. He is surrounded by difficulties. You cannot expect him to work a miracle, and tear off the corruption from the body politic in a few days or weeks. But he may take great strides towards it, and such is the power of virtue that a mere spark will illumine the whole. He has the opportunity to show himself fairly. He has started well, and he has made a profession this evening, not in a corner, not to me or any one else individually, but he has made it known to this society, composed of men who represent more than one fifth of the body politic of the metropolis of the State, and, in this letter which has been read, you hear his solemn declaration that you may publish to the world, that he intends to stand upon an apex above the miserable atmosphere of meanness and baseness ; to rise up as a man who says, I will put down corruption ; I will raise up honesty and uprightness. Then, my friends, let us unite in casting prejudice aside, and, whilst we hold him to a strict account of his stewardship, let us never forget the difficulties by which he is encompassed.

In the spring of 1875, the Washington Light Infantry of the city of Charleston held a fair for the benefit of the widows and orphans of its deceased members, of whom many fell in the civil war fighting for the consummation of secession. In Massachusetts, a number of citizens and ladies determined to aid the fair, intending thereby to indicate that they had ceased to foster personal animosity toward their countrymen in the South and were willing to join in benevolent action in behalf of widows and orphans of soldiers who had served in the rebellion. A large and influential committee in Boston sent out invitations for contributions. A copy of the Committee's circular having been sent to Governor Chamberlain, he at once addressed a letter to Mr. Richard Briggs, of Boston, Chairman of the Committee, which, when it became public, was most favorably regarded, North and South. Governor Chamberlain said :

I am delighted at this proof of good-will of the citizens of the capital of my native State toward those of the chief city of my adopted State. No patriotic duty is more commanding at this time than the restoration of fraternal feelings between Massachusetts and South Carolina, and the great sections of our country they represent, respectively. Every good interest in this State will take new strength from your exhibition of good-will to our people.

On the 19th of April, the towns of Lexington and Concord, in Massachusetts, celebrated the centennial of the first battles of the Revolutionary War. It was the beginning of a long series of patriotic celebrations which interested the whole people, and exerted a powerful influence, by the revival of memories of common sacrifices and triumphs, in healing the wounds of the recent civil war. Governor Chamberlain was invited to the celebration and attended. His presence in the double capacity of son of Massachusetts and Governor of South Carolina, two States between which there had been during the Revolution the strongest sympathy and comity, was one of the notable incidents of the occasion, and its significance was heightened by the eloquent address he delivered after the dinner. This address and that made to the same audience by another son of Massachusetts, then living in Virginia, General William F. Bartlett, were justly regarded as the oratorical gems of the day. They struck the chord of yearning for reconciliation and fraternity which was already tense and vibrant in hearts then, after long woe and bitterness, becoming responsive to the prophetic words of Lincoln: "We are not enemies, but friends. We must not be enemies. Though passion may have strained, it must not break our bonds of affection. The mystic cords of memory, stretching from every battlefield and patriot grave to every living heart and hearthstone all over this broad land, will yet swell the chorus of the Union, when again touched, as surely they will be, by the better angels of our nature."

The first sentiment proposed by Mr. Thomas Merriam Stetson, who presided at the dinner in the tent at Lexington, was, "The State of South Carolina. Never will Massachusetts forget the prompt response of South Carolina the very night she heard the war note from Lexington." Every one knew who would respond to this sentiment; but the introduction of the speaker and the applause which attended it showed how widely the fame of his recent actions had spread. "And Governor Chamberlain," said Mr. Stetson, "may veto any thing he wants to, except our earnest request for a response from the Palmetto to the Pine." Governor Chamberlain then spoke as follows:

To stand upon the spot where our fathers gave the last test of their devotion to civil freedom is a high and sacred privilege. If our hearts respond to the highest influences which human example and endeavor can afford ; if personal gratitude for blessings secured ; if honor for self-forgetting, single-eyed fidelity to duty ; if a sense of the far-reaching, limitless consequences which are sometimes wrapped up in

the actions of a few men ; if any or all of these considerations have
power to affect us, this place and this day must call up the tenderest
and proudest emotions.   Such emotions are too strong and deep to be
expressed in words.   The full inspiration of this occasion must be felt
in the heart.   The lips cannot utter it.

I confess, therefore, that I am loth to attempt to add to the tribute
of words which this occasion has already called forth.   The outward
scenes which were presented here a hundred years ago : the sequence
of causes and events which led up to that supreme hour which witnessed the opening in blood of this great chapter of American history ;
something, too, of the physical and moral lineaments of the actors in
those scenes ; the vast results already attained and the boundless future
still waiting ;—these have been presented before us with all the power
which eloquence and poetry can lend.   What remains, except that we
should fill our hearts with the lessons and sentiments and principles
which this day has taught us, and again take our places in the ranks of
that great army which on *all* days and on *all* fields must still carry forward the unending warfare of freedom against oppression, of justice
against wrong, of human progress against all efforts to circumscribe the
thoughts or fetter the actions of men except by the eternal laws of truth
itself ?

The men whose memory we seek to honor to-day were great because
they shrank from no dangers or sacrifices which were demanded of
them in order to vindicate and defend the rights which they claim by
virtue of their simple manhood.   That grand and imperishable declaration of the rights which man may claim as the inalienable endowment
of his Creator, which was made one year later, was but the echo of the
guns which disturbed the morning air of Lexington one hundred years
ago.   The grandeur of that hour was its absolute and unhesitating response to the call of duty.   Here stood our sires ; and here they fell.
They could do not otherwise.   They were British subjects.   No independence had yet been proclaimed.   No war had yet been declared.
And yet they resisted.   The thought of founding a new nation did not
fire their hearts.   And yet they dared to lift their hands against the
power of their lawful sovereign.   They counted no cost.   They knew
not that they were striking a chord which would vibrate through the
land and summon every colony to their side.   They stood alone, alone
with duty, face to face with an imperious necessity which their manhood laid upon them.

Ah, fellow-citizens, is not this their highest title to immortality ?
Not that they opened the vast drama of events which followed ; not
that they were founders of a new nation ; not that the American republic had its birth in that hour, but rather that in sublime fidelity to duty,
alone, unsupported, cheered by no voice save the still voice of duty
speaking within their hearts, they dared to be true to their convictions
and to strike a blow, however feeble, however hopeless, for their rights
as men.

If they had doubted, they must have despaired.   If they had shrunk from the perils and opportunities of that one hour, who does not see that the decisive moment would have been lost? To-day, seen in the ordinary historical perspective, the scenes which we are now recalling are covered with a halo which half conceals the heroism then witnessed. If we can for a moment dispel this false halo, we shall see more clearly than we are wont to see how simple, austere, and devoted was the sense of duty which animated the men who first resisted arbitrary power on this spot.

It is easy to imagine a great and proud nation pouring forth its wealth and strength to maintain its national supremacy. It is easy to imagine a people stung to desperate resistance by the merciless cruelties of the oppressor. No such scene was presented here on the 19th of April, 1775. No military pageant passing before their eyes aroused in the breast of those men the feeling of martial enthusiasm. Dramatic splendors, outward incitements, dreams of conquest, all were absent, and in their stead nothing presented itself but this simple, stern issue : Shall we, Englishmen, descendants of those who have gradually built up the great monuments and barriers of English liberty till that liberty has become the birthright of all Englishmen—shall we, a few weak, unprepared, unorganized colonists, assert in our own persons that great doctrine which lies at the foundation of English liberty—" Taxation without representation is tyranny "? The very simplicity of the issue discloses the grandeur of the event. These men were brave enough and true enough to accept the call of present duty, and to welcome whatever might befall in an effort to preserve their freedom. They had courage, and they had what, as Carlyle has said, is still better than courage—" no particular consciousness of courage, but a readiness in all simplicity to do and dare whatsoever is commanded by the inward voice of native manhood."

I come, therefore, first of all, as a devout pilgrim at this shrine of freedom. I come to refresh myself for coming duties by calling up in vivid recollection the images of that night of alarm, that morning of blood, the undaunted courage, the pure simplicity, the high and resolute daring, which will forever embalm the name of Lexington among the most priceless memories and inspirations of human history. But I come also in another character and for another purpose. I come to bring to this feast of patriotism the greetings of the descendants of a colony which, from the hour when Samuel Adams, speaking in the name of the town of Boston to its representatives, bade them, " Use your endeavors that the weight of the other North American colonies may be added to that of this province, that by united application all may happily obtain redress," till the long struggle was crowned with final success, never faltered in her devotion to the cause on whose first battlefield we now stand.

On the 30th of May, 1764, Virginia, under the impulse of Patrick Henry's eloquence, declared that " the people of Virginia are not bound to yield obedience to any laws designed to impose taxation upon them other than the laws of their own General Assembly."

On the 6th of June, 1764, the Legislature of Massachusetts, on the advice of James Otis, suggested the calling of an American Congress, to be composed of delegates from each of the thirteen colonies. On the 25th of June, 1764, the suggestion of Massachusetts was debated in the Assembly of South Carolina by the then youthful and eloquent John Rutledge, and adopted under the leadership of the intrepid and sagacious Christopher Gadsden. Thus Virginia sounded the alarm ; Massachusetts proposed the Union ; South Carolina responded with the pledge of her utmost support.

" Be it remembered," says Mr. Bancroft, " that the blessing of union is due to the warmheartedness of South Carolina. She was alive and felt at every pore. And when we count up those who, above others, contributed to the great result, we are to name the inspired ' madman,' James Otis, and the magnanimous, unwavering lover of his country, Christopher Gadsden."

As South Carolina was the first to respond to the call of Massachusetts for a Congress, so her delegates, Gadsden, Rutledge, and Lynch, were the first to arrive in New York, in October, 1764, to attend that Congress. The first question to be determined by that Congress was upon what grounds the colonists should rest their resistance to the impending usurpations of Parliament. Shall they stand on the royal grants or on grounds of original, unwritten, imprescriptible right ? Shall they plead their parchment charters, or their birthright as men and Englishmen ? Shall they claim under the grant of the King, or under the grant of God ? Who does not perceive that this was a vital question, on whose decision the distinctive character of American freedom and American self-government was to depend ? If at this moment of the first formulation of the claims of the colonists they had pleaded the royal grants as the source and ground of their rights, whence could Jefferson have drawn his immortal declaration of the inalienable rights of man ? That discussion in that first Congress was the harbinger not only of American independence, but of what, as I think, was more significant still to mankind, the *declaration* of American independence. Here again South Carolina spoke through Christopher Gadsden. "We must stand," said he, "upon the broad, common ground of those natural rights that we all feel and know as men, and as descendants of Englishmen. I wish the charters may not ensnare us at last by drawing different colonies to act differently in this great cause. Whenever that is the case all will be over with the whole. There ought to be no New England man, no New Yorker, known on the continent, but all of us Americans." These sentiments, so truthful, so generous, so comprehensive, were adopted by the Congress, and from them has sprung, it is not too much to say, the greatness of the American republic, the greatness of the principles on which it rests, and the greatness of its success as a practical example of government *of* the people, *by* the people, and *for* the people.

In all the deliberations of that first Congress, in framing the first formal declaration of the rights of the colonists, no influences were perhaps more powerful than the voices of South Carolina's delegates, Gadsden, Rutledge, and Lynch. It was due to the determined opposition of Rutledge that the right of Parliament to regulate the trade of the colonies was denied. It was Gadsden and Lynch who denied the propriety of even approaching Parliament by petition, the former declaring with impassioned earnestness : "We neither hold our rights from the House of Commons nor from the Lords." Animated by such sentiments, inspired by such leaders, Massachusetts and South Carolina, with the other colonies, on the 25th of October, 1764, bound themselves to the first formal and united proclamation of the rights which they claimed, of the grievances of which they complained, and of the relief which they demanded.

These, fellow-citizens, were the hours in which American freedom took its form. These were the prophetic voices announcing the future which we now see. Listen to them : Samuel Adams—" There are certain original, inherent rights belonging to the people which Parliament itself cannot deprive them of." John Adams—" You have rights antecedent to all earthly government ; rights that cannot be repealed or restrained by human laws ; rights derived from the great legislator of the universe." James Otis—" Freedom and equality. Death, with all its tortures, is preferable to slavery." Alexander Hamilton—" The sacred rights of mankind are written as with a sunbeam in the whole volume of human nature by the hand of divinity itself, and can never be erased or obscured by mortal power." Christopher Gadsden—" We neither hold our rights from the House of Commons nor from the Lords."

From 1764 to 1774, throughout the whole of the first epoch of the American Revolution, while events were hastening forward toward the final struggle of arms, South Carolina responded with earnest and unhesitating fidelity to the call of Massachusetts. The aggressions of Great Britain were hardly felt by her. Her commercial relations were almost wholly with England, but her proud and unconquerable spirit drew her to the side of her sister colonies. " Don't pay for an ounce of the damned tea," was the message of Christopher Gadsden to the people of Boston on the 14th of June, 1774.

When the Port Act fell with all its rigor in Boston, South Carolina was the first to testify her sympathy by a substantial contribution of rice for the support of the poor of that town. And when the call arose for another Congress, the planters of South Carolina again responded with Gadsden, Lynch, John Rutledge, Edward Rutledge, and Middleton as her representatives. When, in October of the same year, Congress resolved that if the grievances of the colonists were not redressed before the September following, no merchandise should be exported to Great Britain, Christopher Gadsden, against the protest of his colleagues, declared himself ready to adopt this measure though it brought ruin on his State.

. On the 11th of January, 1775, South Carolina again resolved to stand firmly by the demands of the colonies, and " if blood be spilt in Massachusetts, the Sons of South Carolina will rise in arms." Three months later the blood of Massachusetts was spilt on this spot. How truly, to the end, the sons of South Carolina kept that resolve history has recorded on her imperishable pages. It is a record which the sons of Massachusetts and South Carolina, which every true American, will recall with patriotic pride. Time forbids me to dwell on its incidents. It was a spirit which rose high above all personal and local interests and feelings, a spirit which bound together the men of Boston and the men of Charleston, Massachusetts, and South Carolina by the great bond of a common determination to maintain the freedom which they had inherited, and which belonged to them as men.

I come, fellow-citizens, to remind you, on this great day, of this early, unbroken friendship between Massachusetts and South Carolina throughout the whole revolutionary period. Differing however widely in lineage, in habits, in institutions, they were still bound together by a common love for civil freedom. Together they watched the beginnings of tyranny ; together they planned resistance ; together they declared their independence from Great Britain ; together, with their lives and fortunes, they maintained that declaration through the long war ; together they devised the fabric of government under which the republic has grown to its present proportions ; together they long labored to build up the strength, the prosperity, and the glory of America. Those precious memories of the past are secure. To-day, at least, we may recall them. At Lexington, surely, South Carolina may still claim a place to do honor to the common cause of American liberty and independence.

I know that I am commissioned here to-day to say for South Carolina that she joins with equal gratitude and reverence with all her sisters of the early days in honoring the 19th of April, 1775 ; that she claims her share in the glory of the struggle begun at Lexington ; that as of old she bade Massachusetts cheer in the struggle, so now she unites with her in these patriotic services.

It is not for me, it is not for any one, on this occasion, to speak of later events in which these two ancient allies stood face to face as enemies. Who that has an American heart does not rejoice that back of all the recent bitter struggle there lies the gracious heritage of those common labors and dangers and sacrifices in founding this common government? Who that looks with a just eye even on the recent struggle does not now see, on either side, the same high elements of character, the courage, the devotion to duty, the moral lineaments of the Adamses and Hancocks, the Gadsdens and Rutledges of a hundred years ago? Who that has faith in the destinies of America does not see in this early friendship—aye, and even in this later conflict—the potency and promise of that coming Union under whose protection liberty shall forever walk hand in hand with justice, wherein the North and the South, reunited in spirit and aims, shall again respond to every call of patriotic duty in the old tones of Samuel Adams and Christopher Gadsden, of James Otis and John Rutledge?

That spirit still lives, fellow-citizens, in South Carolina. If in

later days she has erred, forgive her, for even then she dared and suffered with a courage and patience not unworthy in its strength of the
days when Gadsden and Rutledge illustrated her civic wisdom, and
Sumter and Marion her martial prowess. "Magnanimity," says Mr.
Burke, "is not seldom the truest wisdom, and a great empire and little
minds go ill together."

Fellow-citizens, I offer you to-day the fraternal, patriotic greeting of
South Carolina—of all her people. She marches again to-day to the
music of that Union which a hundred years ago her wisdom helped to
devise and her blood to cement. There, in that hallowed Union, en-
deared and sanctified by so many blessed memories, and radiant with
so many proud hopes and promises, there, there she "must live or bear
no life." Oh, welcome her anew to-day to the old fellowship! The
monuments of marble and brass which we build to-day to the memory
of the fathers will crumble and corrode, but there is one monument
which we may erect in the hearts of all the American people, *ære
perennius*,—the monument of a re-united country, a free and just government, "an indestructible Union of indestructible States."

This address was widely published, and called forth expressions of cordial approval in both Northern and Southern journals.
There was an evident disposition in both sections to accept it as
truly representative of the desire and temper of the people of the
South. In South Carolina there was general and even enthusiastic approval of the manner in which the State had been represented on this occasion.

Soon after the Governor's return he was invited to a banquet
in Charleston in celebration of the centennial of the organization
of the German Fusiliers, a military company of the city which
numbered among its members many worthy and distinguished
citizens. Unable to accept the invitation, on account of the accumulation of urgent public business during his trip to the North,
he sent the following letter:

COLUMBIA, May 1, 1875.

A. MELCHERS, Esq., *President German Fusiliers, Charleston, S. C.:*

MY DEAR SIR—I have received, with peculiar pleasure, your invitation in behalf of the German Fusiliers of Charleston, to attend their
centennial celebration on the 3d inst., and to respond to the sentiment, "The State of South Carolina."

I appreciate this honor very highly, and I specially regret to find it
impossible for me to accept your invitation. I have feared that it
might seem a little inexplicable that I should be able to go to Lexington, but not to Charleston, to attend a centennial celebration; but

I know I ought not to doubt that you will accept my present assurance that public duties and labors which have accumulated during my recent absence are of such a nature as to make it unreasonable for me to leave Columbia at this time.

I trust, too, that you will, to no extent, attribute my absence from your celebration to a want of interest or sympathy in any celebration which specially concerns Charleston or South Carolina. It was a great privilege for me, on a recent occasion, to speak of our State in the presence of many thousands of our Northern brethren, and in some sense in the presence of the whole country. No native South Carolinian, however devoted to the traditions and fame of his State, could have failed to be deeply moved by the cordial manifestations seen on that occasion of the spirit of fraternal kindness, on the part of all who joined in those patriotic services, towards South Carolina. It would afford me the utmost pleasure to be able to testify in person to this great and increasing feeling of fraternity between the North and the South, on the occasion of your celebration.

I should rejoice, also, to do whatever I might, by my presence or words, to make a suitable expression of the feelings with which I know South Carolina responds to all sentiments and acts which tend to national harmony and repose. Others, who are better able than I to perform such a service, will be present with you, and will give voice to all the precious memories and hopes which your celebration will call up. I cannot regret my absence on your account, but only on my own, for I covet the honor of helping to open the series of centennial celebrations which South Carolina will institute in memory of her revolutionary heroes and history.

Above all things, my dear sir, I trust your celebration will speak and enforce the great present lesson and duty of political and social harmony between all the sections of our country, in the basis of the settlements which are now embodied in the Constitution and laws of the nation. Upon that basis let a new prosperity grow up which shall cheer and bless all races and conditions of men who dwell in South Carolina. Political differences ought to be significant and valued, only as they mark the greater or less fidelity of our parties to the common purpose of making our government and public service honest, patriotic, pure, and elevating.

Every man is my political friend whose purpose is to give peace and prosperity to South Carolina. Every man is my political foe who would, for any cause, stay or turn back the returning tide which is bearing these blessings to our people.

May your celebration give strength to our national feelings, to our honorable State pride, to our firm resolution to make South Carolina worthy to-day of the men who, a hundred years ago, with faith and courage, preserved her freedom and honor, and who transmitted to us blessings which still are greater than those enjoyed by any other nation.

Again expressing my profound regret at my necessary absence from your patriotic celebration, I give you this sentiment : " The German Fusiliers of Charleston—May their constant and highest aim be to perpetuate the spirit which made South Carolina in 1775 the heroic and unconquerable defender of American freedom and nationality."

Respectfully and gratefully, your fellow-citizen and servant,

D. H. CHAMBERLAIN.

The letter did not arrive in Charleston in time to be read at the dinner ; but it was published in the Charleston *News and Courier*, and was the immediate occasion of the following article in the same paper, which shows what impression the Governor's intellectual force and high culture were producing:

There is no doubt of that ! Governor Chamberlain is a master of the art of How to do it. This *Savoir faire* is possessed by few men in public life, and is totally different from the easy-going good-nature that makes a man hail fellow well met with the universal public. It is the knack, and the habit, of saying and doing the right thing, at the right time, and in the right way. Governor Chamberlain exhibited this quality in his Inaugural Message. Others might have declared, as boldly as he, a fixed purpose to purify the government, and have declared it with the curt brevity of a Grant or in the mixed metaphor of a Boyle Roche. To Governor Chamberlain it was left to announce his resolutions and purposes in faultless English, which serves as the silk glove on the hand of iron.

It is said to be exceedingly hard to make a first-rate after-dinner speech, Albert Edward, Prince of Wales, can do that, whatever else he cannot do ; while Charles Lamb was a complete failure on such occasions. But there is something harder than the post-prandial speech, and that is a post-prandial epistle. In this, likewise, Governor Chamberlain excells. There is found in every message or letter that he writes some phrase which lingers in the memory, some new and happy expression of what good folk at once recognize and receive as true. The letter to the German Fusiliers, published yesterday, is a case in point. Governor Chamberlain there says :

" Political differences ought to be significant and valued, only as they mark the greater or less fidelity of our parties to the common purpose of making our government and public service honest, patriotic, pure, and elevating. Every man is my political friend whose purpose is to give peace and prosperity to South Carolina. Every man is my political foe who would, for any cause, stay or turn back the returning tide which is bearing these blessings to our people."

These words, if we lived in the days of good Haroun Al Raschid, would be written in letters of gold and counted with the treasures of the kingdom. And on greater occasions, such as the centennial celebration at Lexington, where for the first time in our history, a New Englander, by birth and education, stood before the country as the Governor of South Carolina, Governor Chamberlain is equally happy. Indeed, from the messages, letters, and speeches of Governor Chamberlain, during the few months that he has been Governor, one might select just such examples of severe logic and polished declamation, just such stirring enunciations of eternal truths, as have made the names of the Fathers of the Republic honored and honorable. But it must not be thought that Governor Chamberlain does nothing but talk and write.

In act, in actual work, no man has been bolder or more decisive than he. This is the climax. To have a Governor who is honest in his purposes, and is inflexible in his determination to check extravagance and put down fraud, who is a man of force as well as culture, is more than South Carolina ever expected to have under Republican rule. Is there not a great deal in knowing How to do it?

Early in the month of May, the Governor was invited to deliver the address before the literary societies of Erskine College in South Carolina at the approaching commencement. He was obliged to decline because he had accepted a previous invitation to deliver an oration at the commencement of Yale College, his *alma mater,* at nearly the same date. In his letter (May 10, 1875) declining the invitation for this reason, he said : " I assure you it is not a merely formal regret which I now express in saying that if the two occasions had been presented at the same time, I should have accepted yours." The *Due West Presbyterian*, in which his letter was published " by request of the Committee of Correspondence," introduced it by a paragraph which in its apologetic suggestion shows how extraordinary this invitation seemed to some of the people.

The invitation, we are sure was prompted by the best of motives. Governor Chamberlain has belonged to a party that have not the sympathy of the white people of South Carolina ; but since his election to the Governor's chair he has shown himself to be above petty party influences, and has ruled to the satisfaction of the better classes of all colors in the State. He makes a good and acceptable Governor. He is acknowledged to be a gentleman of culture and a fine speaker. Hence our people would have welcomed him at commencement cordially. The reason assigned for declining the invitation is regarded here as a good one, and the whole letter shows the Governor in a good light. We publish it with pleasure.

On the 20th of May, 1875, was celebrated at Charlotte, in North Carolina, the Centennial of the daring and prophetic declaration of independence of Great Britain, resolved upon by the patriots of Mecklenburg County far in advance of similar action by the United Colonies. At this celebration, Governor Chamberlain was an honored guest. It was to the South what the celebration at Concord and Lexington a month before had been to the North, and was attended by a numerous company of distinguished citizens of other States, as well as by everybody of consequence in the old North State. On this occasion the Governor again spoke for South Carolina, presenting again, and to a Southern audience, the same high motives to union, reconciliation, and common national pride which he had lately urged in Massachusetts. He said :

Fellow-Citizens—I rise to offer to you and this assemblage the cordial response of the people of South Carolina to the sentiment which has just been announced, and to all the fadeless memories, the high inspirations, and the exalting hopes which this occasion commemorates and suggests. I know full well that I speak to-day for South Carolina, chiefly because it is my fortune to be her official representative. Older, abler, better voices than mine will, I cannot doubt, speak for her— voices of those who have sprung from this soil, who know as household words the traditions of the Carolinas, who will represent more adequately than I can hope to do the *genus loci* which has inspired, which still inspires, and which I know will continue to inspire and direct the eager, jealous, fervid, and constant patriotism of the men of Mecklenburg and Carolina.

. But what heart, if it be an American heart, whether it sprung to life beneath these sunny skies, or where nature presents herself in more rugged and repellent forms ; what heart, touched with one spark of the divine flame of love of country, does not bound and swell to greet and welcome this day and this occasion ?

If Marathon and Platæa, after two thousand years, still speak the lesson of devoted and valorous patriotism ; if Runnymede, after six centuries, is still a name for English patriots to conjure by ; if Marston Moor, though the heather and the daisy have covered the last traces of the shock and carnage of her battle for more than two hundred years, is still marked by reverent pilgrims as the spot where the long night of kingly prerogative was ended by the gray dawn of the new and glorious day of the people's rights ; with what measure of gratitude to God, of honor to our ancestors, of patriotic gratulation and gladness, should we, Americans, Carolinians, greet this spot, where, as we firmly and advisedly believe, only one hundred years ago, the first formal utterance of the great idea of American independence was heard.

To a man who believes in human progress, to one who sees and reverences the divine hand in human affairs, I care not in what section or country his sympathies may have been nurtured, the deed done in Charlotte town, in Mecklenburg County, May 20, 1775, will stand at once as a monument and an inspiration, a trophy and a prophecy, of the sure and pre-ordained coming of the day when the feeble light which flamed forth here a hundred years ago shall fill the whole world.

The declaration of Mecklenburg ! It was but a spoken word—an articulated breath of this universal air—yet it was a deed, a battle, a victory. No cannon thundered it, no telegraph flashed it ; yet it was "heard round the world."

> " That death-shot shook the feudal tower,
>   And shattered slavery's chain as well ;
>   On the sky's dome, as on a bell,
> Its echo struck the world's great hour."

The men of Mecklenburg! They were the plain farmers, physicians, lawyers, and ministers of this secluded canton, unambitious of fame, seeking nothing but their accustomed rights, the moral as well as lineal children of John Knox, resolute before men as they were reverent before God. Colonel Thomas Polk, a heart as pure and brave as Richard Cœur de Lion ; Dr. Ephraim Brevard, the gentle scholar and physician, the flame of whose devotion to liberty never flickered till it was quenched by the damps of a British prison-ship five years later ;—these, and such as they, were the men who alone, self-inspired, in advance of all others, at the time when Thomas Jefferson was writing to John Randolph : "I would rather be in dependence on Great Britain, properly limited, than on any nation on earth, or than on no nation," sounded the first signal note of absolute revolt and independence.

We tear no leaf to-day from the brow of any revolutionary patriot, who elsewhere, by pen or sword, upheld the same great cause. We seek only with the jealousy of filial reverence and love to guard the fame, to honor the memory, to proclaim the early, abounding, and impetuous patriotism of the men of Mecklenburg.

A few simple virtues constitute the sum and perfection of human greatness. Simplicity of character, singleness of aim, constancy of purpose, "readiness to do or dare whatsoever is commanded by the inward voice of native manhood,"—such qualities in due combination have made the true heroes of all ages. Of such stuff the heroes of Mecklenburg were made. I do not for a moment conjecture that they foresaw the vast consequences of their acts here a hundred years ago. The gift of prophecy was long since withdrawn from mortal men. These men caught no glimpses, I venture to say, of the America of thirty-seven States, of 40,000,000 of people, stretching from ocean to ocean, covering every sea with her commerce, and reaching every land with her influences. They loved their homes and their families ; they valued their home-born rights and privileges, the dear gifts of honored sires ; they reverenced the grand structure of English law :

> "A land of settled government,
> A land of just and old renown,
> Where freedom slowly broadens down
> From precedent to precedent."

These were their heritage, their wealth, their life. For these they were ready to live or die. And so they became heroes.

Napoleon has been thought to have uttered a great word when, standing within the shadow of the pyramids, he exclaimed : "Soldiers, from yonder heights forty centuries contemplate your actions." Vain and empty words ! The pyramids themselves were but the visible monuments of a slavery blacker than Egyptian darkness, and the voice which spoke from them was but a voice that mocked the unhallowed ambition of him who invoked it. The grand army long since melted away ; the fiery ambition of the great conqueror was quenched in ignoble bondage, and the last representative of the dynasty which he deluged

Europe in blood to found now challenges only our pity as he relieves his exile with the idle masquerades of his princely pretensions.

The men of Mecklenburg were surrounded by no dramatic splendors. Faith in the gracious and mighty power of the God of their fathers, the voice of duty, the spirit of manhood,—these were their strength and inspiration. *Their* work endures. Endures, did I say? It grows; it broadens; it deepens; it will yet cover the earth with the bounty, the grace, and the glory of enlightened freedom.

The declaration here made was a single, isolated act—the act of the representatives of the people of one county. But the spirit of independence was in the air. A year and forty-five days later the declaration of Mecklenburg was the declaration of the United States of America. From that hour the men of Mecklenburg made common cause with all Americans in the struggle which followed. Mecklenburg was thenceforth merged in the struggling, rising nation. Within a radius of forty miles from this centre a score of fields were wet with the blood which was the price of American independence.

It is a proud record. Let its voice be heard to-day above the estrangements of later times—above the differences which on other days may still divide us. The declaration of Mecklenburg was the quick response of this people to the first shedding of blood at Lexington. I stood the other day on the field of Lexington, amidst the wealth, the culture, the abounding population of Massachusetts, and I listened with proud and swelling heart to the cordial, heartfelt words of cheer and sympathy for the Carolinas and the South, which formed one of the most significant features of that great occasion. I thought I saw there the returning tide of fraternal feeling which will surely flow over the whole American people, making the men of Lexington and the men of Mecklenburg enemies no more, and rivals only, as of old, in the promptitude and constancy of their devotion to American freedom and nationality. Let a like voice be heard here to-day. The ear of Lexington is bent low to catch the welcome sound. Let it go forth—the voice of Mecklenburg—proclaiming the new Union more glorious even than the old, because tested by harder trials, planted on deeper foundations, and springing from a broader faith in the immortal principles of American freedom.

South Carolina bids me speak to-day her gratitude and reverence for the men of Mecklenburg of 1775, her fraternal feelings towards all who are assembled here, and her intense sympathy with the memories which lie behind us, and the hopes which stretch before us.

The addresses of the Governor, and the cordial spirit shown in the North, especially in Massachusetts, had kindled in South Carolina a lively interest in the historical anniversaries of the year. It was determined to send to represent the State at the celebration of the Centennial of the Battle of Bunker Hill a detachment of the Washington Light Infantry of Charleston, bearing the precious Eutaw flag, the one stand of colors preserved in America which had waved in a battle of the war for independence. The announcement of this intention was hailed with joyful anticipation throughout the land, and no feature of that brilliant and memorable occasion was more enthusiastically regarded. The company bore with them also a magnificent new State flag, presented before their departure by the Governor. Unable to leave Columbia to personally deliver the gift to the company, he requested the Hon. W. D. Porter, an eminent citizen of Charleston and senior ex-captain of the company, to perform this duty. In his letter to Mr. Porter (June 9, 1875) he said :

I have procured a flag with the emblems and legends of our State emblazoned thereon, which I wish placed in their hands to be borne by them on the patriotic mission which calls them from the State. I wish that its presence at Bunker Hill may signify the sincere veneration in which the people of South Carolina hold all who bore a part in founding the American nation. I wish that it may call to mind, wherever it may be seen, the early patriotism which gave to America and the world the example and memories of Eutaw and Bunker Hill, of Lexington and King's Mountain, and the hundred other battlefields where South Carolina and Massachusetts, the North and the South, mingled their best blood. If that early patriotism, if those costly sacrifices are to have full fruition, it will be when the North and the South shall again be united by the indissoluble bond of their love of country. If the recent bitter estrangements are to be succeeded by the sweet rewards of peace, it will be when, by the common efforts of the North and the South, a free and just national government shall command the love and honor of all sections and States. To hasten such results is the function of those memorial observances in which the Washington Light Infantry and this flag of South Carolina will bear a significant and honorable part. May Heaven prosper and protect them while absent, and may the Bunker Hill of to-day be to them and to us all a spot sacred from henceforth to national peace and fraternity.

In his reply, accepting the service the Governor had asked, Mr. Porter said :

Permit me to express my cordial concurrence in the sentiments so happily expressed by you. It seems to me as if there was something providential in the occurrence of these centennial celebrations so soon after our recent estrangement. If there be a common ground on which the people of the North and South can meet and look each other in the eyes and strike hands and renew their pledges of fidelity to liberty and union, without disparagement or loss of self-respect on either side, it is upon the grounds, the holy places, where their forefathers laid the foundations of independence and then cemented them with their precious blood. This is the way of all ways to bridge over the chasm.

The engagement of Governor Chamberlain to deliver an address before the Law School of Yale College has already been mentioned. His visit to New Haven for this purpose but thirteen years after he was graduated was an occasion of great interest, not only to himself and to the college but to the general public, for his recent addresses at Lexington and Charlotte had shown that the high-minded and resolute reforming Executive of South Carolina was an orator of mark. His theme, " Some of the Relations and Present Duties of the Legal Profession to our Public Life and Affairs," while strictly appropriate to the peculiar occasion, imposed a consideration of questions regarding which all thoughtful men were at the time concerned ; questions which have not yet lost their interest, although now they are presented under new conditions.

The relation of the State Governments to the National Government ; the wisdom of the policy of conferring the right to vote on the freedmen of the South ; the necessity of a sound and honest currency ;—these were the throbbing issues. The " carpet-bag " Governor of a Southern State, he insisted upon the conservative interpretation of the authority of the National Government to interfere with a State's autonomy. Representing a community which had suffered dreadful wrong through the ignorance and weakness of newly enfranchised citizens, and fresh from a desperate and determined struggle to rescue government from degradation by their assault, he asserted the substantial wisdom of the policy of which such happenings were a temporary consequence. Coming from the section where repudiation of public financial obligations had been most common, and the burden of the national debt was most onerous, he advocated vigorous adherence to severe standards of financial duty and honor. It was the voice of a studious and independent thinker, and, of all the orations of the commencement season of that year, none obtained more general attention and commendation. The Charleston *News and Courier*, while, of course, not agreeing with his views in some particulars, closed a long article with these words :

We hope that Governor Chamberlain's oration will be read everywhere in this State. We fancy that Governor Chamberlain is almost too philosophical, too much of the professor ; but, when we differ from him, we still admire the precision, polish, and symmetry, the thoughtfulness and thoroughness of what he says and writes.

On the 3d of July, Governor Chamberlain wrote a letter to the New York *Herald* in response to a request for information regarding any action by South Carolina in preparation for the representation of the State in the National Centennial Exhibition at Philadelphia. He said that while, practically, little had been done to secure a proper representative of the State, he had personally and officially a strong interest in the matter, and thought that there was a genuine interest felt by the people of the State. "With the revival of the spirit of hopefulness among our people, and the composing of the political bitterness of later days, and especially with the influence of the recent centennials at Lexington and Charlotte, there has appeared, as it seems to me, a new desire on the part of our citizens to join in the great reunion at Philadelphia." He promised to use his best efforts to encourage this disposition, but said he was persuaded that whatever might be done must be the result, largely if not wholly, of the recent awakening, and the voluntary action of the people in their representative social, industrial, and educational organizations. In conclusion he said that if the State failed to be properly represented at Philadelphia, it would not be due to indifference, sullenness, or hostility on the part of the people at large, but to " other causes which it is easier to understand here than to adequately state to the country." On the 25th of October he issued an address to the people of the State urging them to interest and action in this matter, and he appointed a State Board of Centennial Commissioners, consisting of Col. W. L. Trenholm, Captain Jacob Small, Hon. John R. Cockran, Col. D. Wyatt Aiken, Col. Thomas Taylor, Hon. Reuben Tominson, Col. C. W. Dudley, Professor F. S. Holmes, and Hon. D. R. Duncan, all influential and earnest men. Through their exertions South Carolina was not wholly unrepresented in the grand illustrative exhibition of American progress.

In the autumn the Governor yielded to several urgent invitations to be present at agricultural fairs to address the people. Since the campaign preceding his election he had made no tours in the State. These invitations were now pressed upon him by citizens who gave him no countenance then, and as an evidence of confidence and approval they were flattering. The Governor's addresses were not generally reported, but the local newspapers of the time afford abundant testimony that he received respectful and cordial welcome from every class, and that the practical, hopeful counsel he imparted gave general satisfaction. The following extracts, from a summary report in the Charleston *News and Courier*, of the address at Barnwell Court House before the County Agricultural Society, shows the spirit of these talks to the farmers of South Carolina by the son of a Massachusetts farmer, accustomed through all the years of boyhood to hard work on the land.

Look back just ten years and contrast the scene. The ashes of your houses and barns were then warm. Your stock was utterly gone. Your implements of labor were destroyed. The condition of the mass of laborers had suddenly been changed from slavery to freedom. Every feature of the farmer's situation seemed to be in sad and hopeless confusion or prostration. Now look on this scene! Here is cotton more than rivalling in quantity and quality the best days before the war. Here is stock, blooded and native, horses and neat stock, worthy of the reputation of any agricultural community. Here is contentment and peace between laborer and employer. Here are your wives and children, grace and beauty of the best type, all giving evidence of that unparalleled recuperation which Barnwell has witnessed. And yet, men are heard sometimes to despair of South Carolina! Some there are who gloomily dwell on the past, and think the proper attitude for our State is as a modern Niobe, in the dust and sackcloth of defeat and despair!

But the men of Barnwell, thank Heaven, have not thought so. They have fallen only to rise again. Like Antæus, they have touched the earth only to renew their strength and courage. Such a spirit will exorcise every evil that afflicts us. Never be despondent. "God is for us. Who, then, can be against us?" He was not here to discuss political issues even by allusion, but he might with propriety say that no influence is more efficient in removing bad government and uniting all the people in a firm purpose to have the blessings of good government than the industrial enterprise and success now so abundantly attained here and elsewhere in our State.

His first words, then, to the farmers and planters of Barnwell, the employer and employed alike, was: "Go on, and be of good cheer." The hardest fight has been won. No evils so great as those you have felt can ever come upon you again. Your progress now can be uninterrupted, even if slow. . . .

In conclusion, the Governor said that with these four things secured—faith in our future prosperity based upon the results of the past decade—pride in our occupation as tillers of the soil—broad and thorough education for our farmers—improved methods and appliances in farming, especially deep ploughing and improved stock—and added to all these a more diversified agriculture, the future of South Carolina would at once take on the roseate hues of its coming day of abundant prosperity. Discords of all kinds, which now retard her march, would pass away. "I have unbounded faith," said he, "in the future, the near future, of South Carolina. Evil is in its nature transient. Good is immortal. The bounteous hand of Nature has showered upon us the greatest advantages of soil, climate, and, I hesitatingly add, *people*. Our two races are, in truth, admirably adapted to each other. Each needs the other. Each will suffer without the other. All we need is a liberal, catholic spirit in all the affairs and relations of life to make the color and race line sink beneath notice, so far as the practical upbuilding of our State and her good government is concerned. Give us these, and we will secure the rest.

> " For sometimes flashes on my sight,
> Through present wrong, the eternal Right,
> And, step by step, since Time began,
> I see the steady gain of Man."

On the 16th of December, 1875, after the re-assembling of the Legislature, the Governor visited Greenville to present the prizes offered by Dr. William H. Whitsitt of that place to the successful contestants in an examination in Greek " open to any person in the State of South Carolina who is under eighteen years of age on the day of examination," and to deliver an address. This purpose to encourage excellence in classical studies appealed strongly to his desire to foster all educational progress, or he would not have accepted an invitation requiring even a brief absence from Columbia while the Legislature was in session. That his coming for that purpose was an appreciated service appears in the anticipatory remark of the Greenville *News* :

The people may be congratulated on having a Governor who appreciates learning, and they should reflect that he undertakes this duty at the very moment when his time and powers are engaged in official duties of a very arduous character. The fact that he takes on himself this additional task—for no man who values literary reputation can afford to make it less than a severe task—will show how high a place the higher education has in his regard.

What surprising advantage was taken of his absence from Columbia will appear hereafter.[1]

" On such an occasion there is but one theme for discourse," said the orator ; and his address was upon " The Value of Classical Studies." After its publication,[2] the Charleston *News and Courier*, speaking of the pleasure a perusal of it had afforded, said :

But there was an additional satisfaction involved in the realization of the fact that he whom we had been hitherto led to regard as but a lawyer and politician, albeit in the highest and truest sense in which the terms can be used, is, moreover, a scholar and a gentleman of broad culture and refined understanding. It was a pleasant surprise that we were thus enabled to discover a phase of the author's character, which,

---

[1] Chapter xiii.

[2] Published in the *New Englander* (New Haven, Conn.) for April, 1876.

in the noisy and turbulent surroundings of his political and public career, had never been disclosed—at least to us.   The man who has the brains and the heart to write such an address, has but to follow his natural instincts in order to make him a safe and trustworthy guardian of the public interests. . . .   It is itself the aptest illustration of the argument presented for a classical education.

With what sentiment and satisfaction Governor Chamberlain escaped for a day from the strenuous, anxious, harassing toil of state affairs to a retreat of scholarship, from the turbid strife of good and evil politics to the restful haunt of learning, appears in the exordium and peroration. A captain, long tossed on troubled seas, having won many hard battles and knowing that desperate conflicts with implacable foes are yet to be fought, does not more eagerly appreciate a brief recreation in a friendly haven. Resources of strength and content in the equipment of this earnest man of affairs, which have significance in explaining the spirit with which he attempted and executed his arduous work, are revealed in these passages :

We have met to-night to witness the award of two prizes offered by your liberal and learned townsman, Dr. Whitsitt, for excellence in Greek. This air is still and pure. No electric flashes of passion disturb it ; no murky vapors of prejudice poison it. Only the chaste ardors of a few expectant youths give it a healthful warmth, while the serene and approving countenances of these friends and exemplars of learning fill it with the spirit of sweetness and repose. I rejoice to be here. With my first word I welcome you all, the young and the old, the learned and the unlearned, to this restful scene, and this ennobling occasion. Sweet learning has here her hour ; culture spreads these viands ; the genius of aspiration for things pure and noble, a genius as ancient as man, as youthful as the child of to-day, a genius whose fires lighted up the Hellespont and the Ægean thirty centuries ago, and to-night, here in this secluded canton of a world not then dreamed of, burn with a warmth and radiance unsubdued, and

> " shall burn unquenchably,
> Until the eternal doom shall be,"

presides over this banquet.

How thankful should we be that such an occasion, so rare and precious, is permitted to us from out the still almost open jaws of a destruction which wasted the fields, swept away the material riches, burned up the very implements and supplies of learning, and soaked the earth with the life-blood of the bravest and best of this generation! How does the story which Æneas,

> " Quanquam animus meminisse horret, luctuque refugit,"

poured into the ear of the admiring Tyrian queen, come mended and heightened in its thrill and pathos by this later story of scenes fresh in the memories of us all ! How ought we to rejoice that our story may still be told around our own hearth-stones, in our own native land, and not like Virgil's immortal wanderer's tale, in a foreign realm, after cruel tossings by sea and land !

This occasion speaks a voice and has a significance which must appeal to the sensibilities of all who love learning. It is a pure tribute to the worth of classical culture. It is the evidence of the value set by this people on things that seem remote from their daily material wants. It is an effort to rekindle the fires, the cheering, unconsuming, enlightening fires of learning, in the places where the baleful, devouring flames of war so lately burned. Heaven's benediction be upon such occasions, such efforts ! They are worthy of any people. They are worthy of South Carolina, of her past, of her present. Let it be said now that our State has never wanted witnesses to the great truths of scholarship, exemplars of its spirit, patrons of its art, representatives of its high attainments. Though the statement may be challenged beyond our borders, yet I speak my sincere conviction when I say that nowhere in America has there been shown a more sincere devotion to classical culture on the part of those whose opportunities have permitted its cultivation, than in this State. The familiar line of our statesmen, orators, and divines proves it. The observation of one who even now shall observe the professional mind of the State proves it. If less widely diffused, if possessed by fewer, it has votaries as sincere, and its influence is as marked and constant in those who claim its companionship, as among any people to whom my acquaintance has extended.

*   *   *   *   *   *   *

My friends, the field which I sketched at the outset of this address has been traversed. By your most kind patience, my humble contribution to the interest of this occasion has now been presented. It has been wrought from opening to close amidst the unremitted pressure of labors and cares and anxieties, little suited, as I need not remind you, to the contemplative and studious mood which classical studies suggest. But the subject is one filled with so many delights of sentiment and memory that I rejoice to have been called to this service. My feelings for the classics are tinged, I know, by sweet and tender memories of youth and its struggles. As I look again on the pages of the old, worn books of school and college, by a kind of palimpsestic process the forms of the mother who guided me to the portals of the temple whose treasures I have sought to set before you to-night ; of the brother whose swifter and stronger though more youthful feet first followed, then accompanied, then outran mine [1] ; of the teachers whose instructions, more precious than refined gold, were less precious than the examples

---

[1] Rev. Leander T. Chamberlain, D.D., valedictorian of the class of 1863, Yale College.

of their character and life, all rise before me, and affection towards the studies of Greece and Rome rises into reverence, and "reverence melts back again into childish, tearful love." It is a subject, I confess, in which, like Macaulay, " I love to forget the accuracy of a judge in the veneration of a worshipper and the gratitude of a child."

But on this occasion I have hoped to present some of the elements of value for the purposes of education, which these studies offer to all. The review has impressed upon me not only the constant utility of classical studies in every age and under all conditions of life, but the permanence which belongs to the work of scholars. My closing words shall, therefore, be words of cheer to those whose liberal minds have devised the incentive of this occasion to good learning in our State. The torch of Athens and Rome, the torch whose light has never been quenched even in the midnights of ignorance and superstition which have sometimes overspread the world, is in your hands. O bear it aloft,—for light in darkness, for hope in discouragements, for courage in defeat, for wisdom in difficulties, for protection in dangers, for beauty and glory in every hour of success and victory ! It is the torch of learning, of principle, of morality. Beneath its illumination walk religion, law, and Christian civilization, while ignorance, and violence, and corruption glide away to haunts unvisited by its pure rays.

CHAPTER XI.

Politics and Administration during the Recess of the Legislature—Reply to a Memorial from Citizens of Barnwell County—Course of the New York *Sun*—Indignant Protest of South Carolina Journals—Failure of the South Carolina Bank and Trust Company—Prosecution of Niles G. Parker, a Former State Treasurer—His Attempt to Involve the Governor in his Wrong-doing—Report of a Conversation with the Governor—Comments of the Press of the State—The Governor Visits Charleston—Address upon State Affairs; His Policy and Aims Distinctly Avowed—Complimentary Reception by the Chamber of Commerce—Newspaper Comments Elicited by the Charleston Speech—Proclamation of a Thanksgiving Day.

A S there was no election in South Carolina in the year 1875, there was no occasion for special political activity or for drawing party lines strictly. The administration of State affairs went on without important open demonstrations of opposition in any quarter until after the meeting of the Legislature, although there were sundry incidents of a troublesome nature that provoked discussion among the people. The Governor steadily pursued his policy of reform upon the lines already distinctly marked out, exhibiting no sign of wavering. Owing to the failure of the appropriation bill the strictest economy of expenditure was enforced ; but this was not impracticable when it depended upon executive action alone. The effort to secure a better class of officials in the offices for which the Governor made the appointments, and to secure stricter responsibility by the requirement of safe and sufficient bonds, was not relaxed. A correspondent of the Cincinnati *Commercial*, who conversed with the Governor on his way from the Mecklenburg centennial celebration, made this report of his talk concerning the quality of one class of officers :

When I came into office there were, at least, two hundred Trial Justices in the State who could not read or write. The duties of a Trial Justice here are precisely the same as the duties of Justice of the Peace in other States. Yet previous Governors had appointed and commissioned over two hundred men to the important duties of this office who could not write or read a word of the English language. It was a farce and a fraud ; for how can men thus ignorant intelligently try causes, civil and criminal, brought before them ? The idea seems to hold that men must be rewarded for political service by giving them office, whether they are fit for the office or not. For instance, all the members, Senators and Representatives, from Edgefield County, united in an application to me to appoint a certain man there Notary Public. It requires a man who can at least write his name to fill that office, and I did not think but what the applicant was qualified, he was recommended so highly. I appointed him, and a few weeks after accidentally saw an official document from him, going to a distant State, to which he had made his mark, not being able to write his name. I revoked his commission.

In May a memorial from citizens of the town of Blackwell, in Barnwell County, was presented to the Governor, reciting the circumstances of the disappearance of the evidence (the ballots) of the result of the late election in that county, and calling upon him to officially condemn the act and adopt means and offer rewards for their recovery. In his reply (May 31, 1875) he expressed his condemnation of such acts, but reminded the memorialists that the duty of investigation and discovery belonged rather to the people of the county than to the State Government.

Your Trial Justices are believed to be efficient, your citizens are intelligent, your lawyers are able, and your Judge is one in whom we all have perfect confidence. . . . I have not a dollar at my disposal which can be used for the payment of rewards for detecting the authors of this crime, and I am not willing to offer a reward which I cannot pay. . . . My duty will be to see that the results of the efforts of your people and your county are not nullified by any action of mine— a duty which is more onerous and difficult than you probably imagine. But if the people of Barnwell County will do their duty I will do mine, and then the laws will be administered, crime punished, and the rights of all secured.

Early in the summer a series of articles attacking the character and record of the Governor and depreciating the motive, as well as the merit, of his Administration, appeared in the New York *Sun* in the form of anonymous correspondence from South Carolina. These letters rehearsed the inferential scandals which had been rife before the election and which, as already has been shown, had been openly and honorably abandoned by the fair-minded among the Governor's political opponents, in view of the clearer revelation of his character and aims which attended larger opportunities and more conclusive tests. An attempt was made to arouse prejudice and create alarm by insinuations of the existence of new rings formed for plunder. These attacks gratified the malice of two classes—the thieves in the Republican party whose designs the Governor had thwarted, and an element in the Democratic party which was angered rather than pleased by the demonstration of the possibility of honest administration by the Republican party, because this impeded the partisan ambitions of some, and tended to vitiate, in the State and the nation, the force of the representation that government by the Republican party in the Southern States was invariably corrupt and oppressive. But the attacks gave annoyance to candid and patriotic spirits in the ranks of the Democratic party, by whom they were met at first with expostulation and afterwards with spirited and contemptuous rebuke. The *News and Courier*, at different times, made the following comments on these slanders :

We do not know, and we do not care, who the present South Carolina correspondent of the New York *Sun* may be ; but his letters show plainly enough that, instead of being an honest reporter of facts as he finds them, he is simply a reckless scribbler, who is using the columns of the *Sun* to gratify his private spleen. Fact and falsehood are woven together in his letters too ingeniously for his mistatements to be the result of ignorance or carelessness. He evidently takes special delight in vilifying Governor Chamberlain. Now, whatever may be thought of Mr. Chamberlain's course before his election, the honest men of all parties look upon him to-day as a Governor whose administration has been bold, honest, and exceptionally able, and who is now the main bulwark that protects the State from further spoliation and fraud. Every well-wisher of South Carolina ought to sustain him in the war which he is waging with the public robbers.

The New York *Sun*, in an article published elsewhere, feels bound to say that " any alliance between the white taxpayers of South Carolina and the present Governor, founded upon a belief in the sincerity of the latter, must prove a fatal error " ; and adds that it has " the strongest reasons for supposing that the Governor has been instrumental in the formation of a new ' bond ring,' who, under the cover of Chamberlain's newly acquired reputation for honesty, expect to reap a rich harvest from the credulity of the creditors of the State." The South Carolina public would like to know what these " strongest reasons " are, before paying any heed to the *Sun's* advice. The Charleston correspondent of the *Sun* is conspicuously inexact in his assertions ; his letters are made up of a grain of truth and a bushel of misrepresentation or downright falsehood. Has the *Sun* any better authority than he for its statements ? If not, our New York contemporary has been sadly duped. We flatter ourselves in South Carolina that we can better judge of Governor Chamberlain's sincerity, and more surely gauge his worth, than any New York journalist can do ; and we know that the *Sun* is playing into the hands of the Elliott-Whittemore-Patterson ring, who are confident that they can impeach Governor Chamberlain next winter, if the Conservative members, misled by the *Sun*, can only be turned against him.

For some weeks past, the New York *Sun*, which takes delight in being on "the other side" of every question, has devoted to South Carolina the columns which had been monopolized by Deacon Smith, of Cincinnati, by Kemble, of "addition, division and silence" fame, and by the new *Tribune* building. In its Charleston and Columbia correspondence, the old tales of the transactions of the Financial Board, and of the Sinking Fund and Land Commission have been published in a score of different styles. Had the purpose been to hasten the prosecution and conviction of any public thieves, the people would have been grateful to the *Sun ;* but that paper had, and has, no other apparent purpose than to ruin Governor Chamberlain, and with him those citizens who see in him the mainstay of honesty and decency and ability in this State. This the *Sun* endeavors to do by placing forced constructions on simple words, and, in general, by declaring Governor Chamberlain guilty of every possible crime until he shall be proved to be innocent of each and every one of them. Even where his official acts have been most praiseworthy, the *Sun* asserts that he has a sinister purpose, as, for example, in his efforts to reduce the public expenditures. This, says the *Sun*, is only a part of the programme of a new "bond ring," of which Governor Chamberlain is the centre. Once, and only once, has the *Sun* printed any thing new or striking in connection with the charges against Governor Chamberlain, and this was in its issue of June 5th. It there prints a letter purporting to have been written by Mr. Chamberlain in 1870. The scheme discussed in that letter is described by the *Sun* as "a colossal scheme of plunder," and, on the strength of that letter, the *Sun* declares that "Chamberlain was the most guilty man in that notorious band of plunderers, and that his principles to-day are no better than when he was plotting to steal the whole railroad system of South Carolina." The letter, as published is as follows :

OFFICE OF THE ATTORNEY GENERAL,
COLUMBIA, S. C., Jan. 5, 1870.

MY DEAR KIMPTON—Parker arrived last evening, and spoke of the G. & C. matter, etc. I told him that I had just written you fully on that matter, and also about the old Bk. Bills.

Do you understand fully the plan of the G. & C. enterprise ? It is proposed to buy $350,000 worth of the G. & C. stock. This with the $433,000 of stock held by the State, will give entire control to us. The Laurens branch will be sold in February by decree of court, and will cost not more than $50,000, and probably not more than $40,000. The Spartanburg and Union can also be got without difficulty.

We shall then have in G. & C. 168 miles, in Laurens 31, and in S. & U. 70 miles —in all 269 miles—equipped and running—put a first mortgage of $20,000 a mile on this—sell the bonds at 85 or 90, and the balance, after paying all outlays for cost and repairs, is immense, over $2,000,000. There is a *mint* of money in this or I am a fool.

Then we will soon compel the S. C. R. R. to fall into our hands and complete the connection to Asheville, N. C.

There is an indefinite verge for expansion of power before us.

Write me fully and tell me of any thing you want done. My last letter was very full.

Harrison shall be attended to at once. I don't think Neagle will make any trouble. Parker hates Neagle, and magnifies his intentions.

Yours, truly,

D. H. CHAMBERLAIN.

This may be a forged letter. The Columbia correspondent of the *Sun* is an adept in such matters. But if the letter is genuine, it proves nothing criminal against Governor Chamberlain ; nor is there any thing in it that justifies the strictures of the *Sun*, unless upon the monstrous assumption that any project with which Governor Chamberlain was at any time connected must, because of that connection, have been a fraud and a cheat ! The South Carolina public will hardly follow the *Sun* so far ! Read without prejudice, the letter to Kimpton, if genuine, is evidence that a plan was afoot to obtain, by purchase, the control of the leading railroads in this State, with the purpose of putting them in thorough order, and of selling them again at a profit. It was, on the face of it, a legitimate business speculation, one very likely to command the support of any man who was not familiar with railroads, and did not know the difficulty of floating a mortgage of $20,000 a mile on such concerns as the Greenville & Columbia railroad, the Laurens railroad, and the Spartanburg & Union railroad then were. . . . It may prove to be the fact that he (Mr. Chamberlain) entered into an association of some kind, with a view to buy up railroads, as the members of the Southern Security Company did, and as Vanderbilt and Garrett and Scott do whenever they see an opportunity to make money. This is no crime ! Unless the *Sun* can prove that Mr. Chamberlain, as a member of such a syndicate, was guilty of corrupt practices, or helped others to be guilty of them, that he stole money or property himself, or knowingly took his share of what others stole—unless the *Sun* can do this, its vaunted letter proves nothing. . . . We wish there were in South Carolina an influential Republican newspaper of large circulation which could take up the cudgels for Governor Chamberlain whenever he is unjustly accused. There is no such paper in South Carolina, and we who have no esoteric information, and whose motives, because of our former opposition to the Governor, are always open to misconstruction, are forced, by a sense of duty, to say for the head of the Radical party in South Carolina, what no member of that party can effectively say for him. For the *Sun's* invectives in themselves we care very little. Our object is to set Governor Chamberlain right before the people of the State. At this very time, and in Charleston, Radical caucuses are held almost nightly to arrange the plans by which Governor Chamberlain shall be bound hand and foot by the Legislature next winter. There is only one difficulty—that is, the dreaded support of Governor Chamberlain by the Conservatives, in and out of the Legislature. But the Patterson-Whipper-Moses Ring are confident that the persistent attacks of the *Sun* will alienate the Conservatives from the Governor, who will then be powerless in face of the Ring. Eight Circuit Judges are to be elected by the Legislature next winter. The anti-Chamberlain Ring propose to drop Judges Reed, Maher, Townsend, and Shaw. Charleston is to be honored with the judicial presence of a Whipper or a Worthington. But their plans will come to naught if the good Republicans and the Conservatives give the Executive, as before, their united support. We have nothing to gain or lose by defending Governor Chamberlain. The loss or the gain is to the people of the State. Our purpose is to give them the facts, with our opinions, and leave them to judge and act for themselves.[1]

To these attacks Governor Chamberlain made no response. In the campaign preceding his election he had made full and unqualified public denials of wrong-doing,[2] and it was neither neces-

[1] See, also, in article from the *News and Courier*, Chapter IX., p. 107.

[2] See Appendix.

sary nor becoming for him to repeat them. The reference to the matter here is in order to put where it can be conveniently consulted, the most competent and influential judgment promptly expressed in South Carolina with regard to a treatment which is from time to time renewed, and may be most fitly characterized by a good old word, now unfortunately disused; it is, *dehonestation*.

The last article quoted is additionally interesting for the discovery it makes of what was at that time (June, 1875) going on in the camp of the Republicans hostile to the Governor. They were balked but not in despair. The mischief of their diligent plotting appeared in due time.

While the Governor was absent from the State on the occasion of his visit to New Haven, the South Carolina Bank and Trust Company, one of the two institutions in which, but for his veto of the bill requiring it, all the funds of the State would have been deposited, failed. During the previous Administration, this bank was the sole depositary of the public funds, having at times more than a million dollars in its keeping. The Governor had gradually reduced this amount; but at the time of the failure it had about $200,000. Although some of the Governor's opponents attempted to fix blame upon him for this catastrophe, most persons recognized that his action had been sagacious and protective of the State's interests. The *News and Courier* promptly said: "Any statements to the effect that, but for him, the State would have lost nothing are contrary to all the probabilities of the case, and must be classed with the numberless unreasonable rumors originating in the imaginations of excitable people, to which such an event as the failure of a bank always gives rise."

Another incident of this period was the prosecution of Niles G. Parker, ex-Treasurer of South Carolina, several civil suits having been brought against him by the Sinking-Fund Commissioners for the recovery of money alleged to have been wrongly taken from the State in the process of the conversion of the bonded debt. He was charged with stealing a large amount of coupons, and afterwards converting them into State bonds. The case was tried in June, and a verdict for $75,000 was obtained. By a *habeas-corpus* proceeding Parker was got out of jail and he left the State. In the trial a statement was made by one of the witnesses which afforded the enemies of the Governor much gratification for a little while ; but they soon discovered that nobody would give credence to it except those who had interested motives in aspersing him.   This testimony was one of the things which led to the publication of the following report of a talk with the Governor in which several matters of current public interest were considered :

[From the Charleston *News and Courier*, August 10, 1875.]

A representative of the *News and Courier* had a long conversation with Governor Chamberlain a few days ago at his office in Columbia. The conversation extended over all the recent topics of public interest in our State, and was so full and explicit as to lead to the request that we might present to our readers such parts of it as would in our judgment be of interest to the public.

The conversation opened with a reference to the recent absence of the Governor from the State, and the unfavorable comments, in some quarters, upon that absence.

Governor Chamberlain said that he went north on the 25th of June, primarily to meet his engagement before the Yale Law School, and next with a view to find rest from the uninterrupted strain of official cares and labors which he had borne since last December.   He stayed away, he said, no longer than was absolutely essential to his health.

After some further conversation of a general nature, our representative remarked that among the events occurring during the Governor's absence was the trial of ex-Treasurer Parker, and the testimony of Ladd that, in a conversation between Ladd and Parker, the latter had said that he understood that a part of the coupons ($50,000 worth) were set aside or apportioned to the Governor.   The Governor was asked if he proposed to make any public statement denying the truth of this testimony.   He replied with much warmth of manner and tone that he would never volunteer a denial of such a charge ; that self-respect required him to wait till such a charge was put in a form which would enable him to meet it.

It was suggested to the Governor that if he was willing to appear as a volunteer in denial of such matters, he might answer such questions as should be asked him.   To this he assented, and said : "Certainly I will answer questions to any extent ; but I will not appear before the public with a personal statement till somebody brings a direct charge against me."   He added : "I shall answer any question you may ask with pleasure."

The Governor was then asked if he recalled the testimony of Ladd in which allusion was made to himself.   He replied that he did ; and our representative then said : "Well, sir, is there any truth in the state ment or inference that you received any part of the coupons referred to in Parker's case?"

Governor. "None, whatever; it is a baseless falsehood, by whomsoever concocted, or repeated, or insinuated. It has not the slightest shadow of fact to rest upon."

Question. "Did you ever know of any division of coupons among any persons, such as was indicated in Parker's trial?"

Governor. "Never, sir. I never heard of such a thing, or of any transaction remotely resembling it till the public heard it on the trial of Parker."

Question. Did you ever hear that any coupons were set aside for you, or did you ever receive, or hear that you were to receive, any coupons or any thing else as part of a division of coupons?

Governor. "Never. But you need not multiply questions. I say to you that the statement to which you allude is false in every actual or conceivable phase, degree, sense, or meaning. I not only never had any part or lot in, or knowledge of, such a transaction, but I never in any way owned, held, or was in any manner interested in any coupons or any thing connected with coupons, and I never even owned or held a consolidation bond. If you can frame a broader or more explicit denial of every thing connected with the coupon business, I will adopt it. I have no knowledge of it whatever, except what the public have through the investigations of last winter and the recent trial. If any man living can connect me in any way whatever with these coupons, let him come forward. I defy the world to do it."

The Governor added that it was of course unpleasant and disgusting to have one's name connected with such transactions in any way, but that he could not be responsible for false and unfounded tales which might be told; and no fair-minded man ought to be affected by such tales till there was something like evidence to support them.

The Governor's attention was called to the subject of prosecutions generally against dishonest and unfaithful public officers, and he said with great emphasis: "I am in favor of holding every public officer to a rigid accountability, and if he violates the law I am in favor of his punishment. I shall do my whole duty in every such case. If I have any knowledge of dishonest transactions, I shall place it in the hands of those whose duty it is to prosecute offenders against the law. I will aid any man who is engaged in such a work in all possible ways. I confess, however, that I am not so interested in what is past and gone, as I am in what is present and coming. It will, I think, task all our energies to the utmost to stop up the open leaks and staunch the running wounds. Another thing; when prosecutions are started, if they are to command the public confidence, they must be so conducted as to give evidence that the motive actuating the State is the public good. The moment they seem to be used as political machines they will be worse than useless. Wherever I see or shall be shown an opportunity to aid in punishing crime or preventing crime, I shall do my duty; and I venture now to say that I shall not be the first to cry, 'Hold, enough!' Time will show whether I or others will find prudential reasons for dealing gently with public offenders. In the meantime malicious rumors and tales that fill the air will not disturb me."

The Governor continued the conversation by remarking that his powers and duties were greatly exaggerated in the public mind. In some States the Governor was authorized to direct suits and prosecutions to be brought in the interest of the State, but it is not so in this State. The public prosecuting officers are in no way made subject to his control. His powers are scarcely different from those of any citizen. If he discovers fraud he can only lay its evidences before the solicitors or the grand juries. In the actual prosecution of cases he has no voice or duty. He is bound to give all the facilities in his power, and to call attention to violations of law, but he cannot supersede or control or advise, except by courtesy, any prosecuting officer. If there is delay or failure to prosecute public causes, the responsibility is not with the Governor.

The Governor's attention was called to the failure of Solomon's bank, and a long conversation ensued respecting it. He said that the failure of this bank was a grievous blow to the State, affecting the work of consolidating the State debt, as well as embarrassing every department and interest of the State Government. Of its causes, he was not yet fully informed, nor what would be the probable amount realized from its assets. Referring to the State deposits in this bank at the time of its failure, the Governor said that if he had been as wise before as after the event, he should have tried to reduce the amount of the State deposits, but he now believed that any effort to draw out the State deposits at an earlier day would simply have hastened the failure of the bank. In regard to his own action, he said : "When I became Governor, one of the first and most unpleasant duties imposed upon me was that of providing other depositories than this bank for the public moneys. Mr. Solomon's bank had been the sole depository during the whole term of Governor Moses' administration and I think during the last term of Governor Scott's, and had had deposits amounting at times to one million of dollars. Still I felt that such a course was not safe. Mr. Cardozo heartily sustained me ; while Judge Hoge, then Comptroller General, and almost or quite every leading Republican in the State, warmly opposed my plan of appointing additional places of deposit. It must be remembered that this bank was very powerful with the party and in the Legislature. In discussing the subject with Mr. Solomon and the friends of the bank I invariably said that I did not discredit the bank, but I did insist that its capital and standing did not warrant its having more than a part of the State deposits, say $200,000, and that I was willing, in view of the strong sentiments of the friends of the bank, to allow this amount of deposit to remain in this bank longer than the ·deposits in other banks, as the money was drawn out for public use, but that the rest ought to be distributed among other banks. This course was adopted, and my action was aimed at keeping the deposits as low as $200,000. At times they were more and at times less, but did not, I believe, vary greatly during the winter from that amount.

"In the month of April, after Mr. Dunn became Comptroller General, I called a meeting of the Board of Deposit, informing the other members that I wished it determined how large an amount of deposits, and for how long, should be placed in the different banks. I explained to Mr. Dunn, the Comptroller General, my course towards this bank and my reasons, and that I especially wished his advice in settling the question then pending. The amount of deposits in the Bank and Trust Company (the Solomon bank) was then about $160,000, the amount having been reduced below the usual figures The Board voted to fix the amount in that bank at $200,000, and to allow it to remain until needed for the July payments. This action was in accordance with all my previous action, and was based upon the same reason and considerations. Nothing had occurred in the meantime to give any hint of any increased weakness of the bank ; and its standing in the community was then, I venture to assert, as high as ever.

"No change took place in the affairs of the bank, to my knowledge, from this time till its failure. I did perceive, late in June, that Mr. Solomon seemed embarrassed in raising the amount which he was notified would be needed on July 1st, but he gave no sign that it was more than a temporary embarrassment, and I left the State with no idea of his suspension or failure. I certainly sought to do my full duty by the State in this matter, and that, too, at great political expense to myself, as was well known by all who were in Columbia last winter. I was not all-wise or all-powerful. I did not foresee all that has come to pass. If others were wiser than I, I have no need to quarrel with them. I did all that I thought was my duty, and stood ready to do that at all times. The result has been unfortunate in the extreme, and, perhaps, no one man has so much cause to regret it as I have, but I do not reproach myself with any neglect or fault, so far as I can now see. If the result shall be to make it easier hereafter to banish all political and personal considerations from the determination of such questions, perhaps the gain will equal the present loss."

The conversation turned upon the political situation of affairs in the State, and the Governor expressed the hope that the cause of good government was making substantial progress in the State. He said he did not fear that any combinations aiming to restore the misrule of the last two years would succeed. He relied on the support of all the thinking Republicans, who must now be satisfied that reform was the only good policy, to take no higher view of it. Speaking of the Conservatives and their relations to him, he said : "I have never failed to give full credit to the Conservative press of the State, for their hearty support of my course. They have shown the best of spirit and have rendered effective and absolutely indispensable aid. I believe they will continue to do so. There are carpers, malcontents, reactionary politicians among the Conservatives and the Conservative press, who seem to think it wise to seek to discredit me and my work, but I am satisfied their influence is limited as their number is small. There are dozens of letters lying on this table from the best and most trusted men of this State deprecating such a course, and assuring me of their ardent and constant support. At any rate their course will not affect me. If I had been a man to take my public course from a desire to punish my enemies, *you* know no man ever had greater temptation to such a course than I had the day I took my seat as Governor. But the man does not live who ever heard me utter an unkind word to those who opposed me most bitterly in the political campaign. I bent all my efforts towards doing what I had promised to do, and I welcomed every opportunity, whether official or personal, to serve the people—all the people—impartially. Now, if any Conservatives see fit to renew their attacks upon me they can do so with safety. They will never drive me to do an act, even in revenge, which will harm them. Through good report and evil report I shall hold on to the end. This is a matter of principle with me, and it matters not who stands by me or who deserts me. I shall stand by the cause of reform with few or many to sustain me."

The Governor was asked what his relations were with the Administration at Washington, and he answered : "I understand that I am warmly sustained at Washington. I have not personally seen the President since I became Governor, but Senator Robertson assures me that the President is greatly gratified at the results of my Administration, and others tell me the same. I do know that every member of the Cabinet has expressed his most cordial approval of my course and the results already reached. They feel that a heavy load is removed from the Republican party, and that the prosperity of the State has in every way been promoted. In my visit to the North recently I heard but one voice, that of approval of my efforts and approval of the wise, prudent, statesmanlike attitude of the South Carolina Conservatives. I heard not one word of dissent anywhere from this view, and I met the ablest and best men of both parties. Their only anxiety was to know whether we had wisdom enough here to hold on as we had begun, and press forward to a practical union of all good citizens of all races in a determined effort to put down bad government and restore honesty and ability to public stations. If we can do this, we shall have the sympathy of good men, Republicans and Democrats, all over the Union."

The Governor's attention was called to the tax bill passed last session and not yet approved, and the question was asked if his views had undergone any change in regard to it. He replied that his views of that bill had not changed, that there were features of it which he could not conscientiously approve under any circumstances. He said that the failure of the Bank and Trust Company would make it necessary to modify the bill, and that he believed the Legislature would itself see the benefit of a new bill. He was anxious to have no difference between himself and the Legislature, and if that body, when they met, would devote themselves in good faith to the work of perfecting a tax levy, there need be no delay in passing such a bill as would satisfy all honest citizens.

This talk by its candor and boldness, not less than on account of its explicit declarations, was read with great interest, the evidence of which promptly appeared in the comments of the press of the State, a few of which are here presented.

We have not needed any disclaimers from the Governor to lead us to reject as untrue the insinuations of thieves. In spite of the sneers of scoundrels, character goes for something, and it takes more than the unsubstantiated hints of public plunderers and their sympathizers to break down the record of a pure life. There is a class of men in every community who profess to disbelieve in honor or patriotism. They are destitute themselves of such characteristics, and, as the prostitute laughs at the existence of virtue in other women, these political bawds habitually sneer at the idea of honesty in man. To such the attitude of Governor Chamberlain is at once an injury and a danger. Because he fails to smile when they laugh at reform, because he does not assent when they sneer at honesty, they hate him. His acts they might forgive if he were only a self-seeking hypocrite. But when they find him steadfastly abiding by his pledges, because they are pledges, they pursue the tactics of the street walker and attempt to drag him down to a level with themselves.—*Columbia Union Herald.*(Rep.).

———

Governor Chamberlain could not take a position more clearly than he has in this conversation. However dubious his conduct may appear, there is certainly no ambiguity in his language. He speaks with the boldness of innocence. . . . The course mapped out by Governor Chamberlain is a noble one, and will, if persisted in, be of the greatest benefit to the people. If he moves straight on he will have the hearty co-operation of the whole Conservative party.— *Winnsboro' News* (Dem.).

———

Governor Chamberlain's entire conversation was very outspoken and explicit. He made use of no ambiguities to serve as loopholes of escape. He has planted himself firmly upon his record, and defies his accusers. . . . No frauds have ever yet been proven against Governor Chamberlain. The suspicions attaching to his past career have arisen chiefly from the bad company he kept when Attorney General. Against these he pledges his solemn word of denial. . . . We are pleased to see that Governor Chamberlain proposes to pursue the line of policy he has begun. The Conservative party recognizes his ability and usefulness, and as it has labored with him for the past nine months, it will continue to support him strongly in any measure that is for the public good.—*Columbia Phœnix* (Dem.).

———

Mr. Chamberlain has spoken opportunely, and his words have the ring of the true metal. Many who have been disposed to question the sincerity of his professions will now cease to find fault and lend him their undivided support. Being the ablest and purest man in the dominant party, he has become a necessity to the welfare of the State, and it behooves all good citizens to stand by him while he seeks to secure for them good government.—*Camden Journal* (Dem.).

It is now acknowledged by the Governor that he is not much interested in un-earthing the pecadilloes of former Administrations with which he was connected, and this was exactly the reason for discrediting his pretences. It is our belief that genuine reform means a vigorous and unceasing pursuit of former thieves and plunderers, and acting upon this belief we have unhesitatingly demanded that no sham or pretence be palmed off upon the people of South Carolina, no matter whether it affected the high-est or the lowest. With Governor Chamberlain's efforts to staunch the wounds and stop the leaks in the hereafter, we shall not cavil or condemn unnecessarily, always holding tenaciously to the principle that it is the duty of the Conservatives to maintain an armed neutrality between the different factions of the Republican party, wresting from the present whatever is best calculated to advance the highest interests of the State, and not become the champions or adherents of any particular faction.—*Anderson Intelligencer* (Dem.).

Early in November Governor Chamberlain made a visit to Charleston, the first since he was elected Governor. The occa-sion was seized upon by citizens of all parties to testify their re-spect and confidence. On the evening of November 4th he was tendered a complimentary serenade by Republican party clubs, and in expectation of his response an immense audience, com-posed of citizens of all parties anxious to see and hear him, gathered in the open air. The Charleston *News and Courier* of the next morning said : " The serenade to Governor Chamberlain, last night, was eminently successful. At least five thousand per-sons were present who received the address of the Governor with hearty applause." The following report of the address delivered by him is from the same paper :

Fellow-Citizens of Charleston :—You do me great honor in calling me before you to-night by this demonstration. I accept it and value it as an evidence that, as a public officer, I have done some things which have met your approval. I rejoice to meet my fellow-citizens of Charleston, and to pay my respects, as it were, to the chief city of our State. This city has a great stake in the welfare of the State, her influence upon all our public interests is commanding, and her pre-eminence is the just result of the intelligence, enterprise, and liberality of her citizens. It is a special pleasure, therefore, to me, to feel to-night that I have the confidence of the people of Charleston in my efforts to do my duty as a public officer. It is a result which I have a right to believe comes from your actual observation of my public con-duct, for I do not forget that I did not have the honor of receiving a majority of the votes of this city one year ago. But I have never im-agined I was elected to be the servant or agent of my friends alone, or to be the servant or agent of any political party alone. Holding my

present office as simply a trust, I have constantly endeavored to keep
in mind that that trust was to be held and administered for the benefit
of all our people, without regard to race or party.

The only just basis for a political party is a certain view of
the manner in which the powers of the Government should be exercised, the principles and methods by which public affairs should be
conducted. It is not power or office merely which a party should seek,
but power and office must be sought as the means and opportunity of
increasing the purity, the efficiency, the beneficence of the Government.
Holding such views, I conceive that the just bounds of party obligation
are greatly transcended whenever public office is used to promote personal or party ends to the neglect of the best interests of the whole
people. [Cheers.]

I do not wish to disguise the fact that among the circumstances
which have given some significance to my administration, has been my
refusal to be a slave to the demands of party. In the course I have
pursued in this respect, I have simply done an unquestioned duty. I
never promised, and I was never asked to promise, and I never would
have promised, that I would approve a measure or make an appointment which I could not justify on its merits. And, let me add, if I had
done so, I should have struck the deepest possible blow at the strength
and permanency of the party which elected me.

No! fellow-citizens, I have been entrusted with the great office of
Governor of this State, and with many errors of judgment, no doubt,
with many shortcomings of ability, I know, I have, nevertheless, honestly labored to do that which would best promote the common welfare
of all the people. If any act done in the pursuit of such an aim has
hurt my political party, then all I can say is, that that party deserved
to be hurt. I offer no apology for putting the public welfare above all
other considerations in my official action. I should owe an apology if
I had done otherwise. [Prolonged cheering.]

I rejoice to be able to add that, in my judgment, the day is past in
South Carolina, never to return, when good will be rejected or wrong
accepted, because done in the name of any party. Here, as elsewhere,
throughout our country, men are more and more subordinating party
interests to public interests ; more and more regarding good government as an infinitely better thing than party power ; more and more
perceiving that, in the long run, that party will prevail which keeps
most steadily in view the faithful and impartial discharge of the great
functions of government in the interests of all the people. Well,
I for one welcome such a sentiment. I have valued my party because I thought it the best representative of freedom, of equality of
civil and political rights, of the ideas embodied in our Declaration of
Independence and our republican form of government ; but my attachment to my party does not extend one step beyond this. That is the
full measure of my party fealty. [Cheers.]

I value this expression of your confidence the more highly, therefore,
because having dared on some occasions to oppose the wishes of per-

haps a majority of my own party, I seem still, here in this centre of influence of the State, to have merited, in their judgment, the approval of my fellow-citizens of both parties.

Fellow-citizens, no man will dispute that our State needs reform in nearly every department of the public service. If something has already been done to stay the downward course of things, it is but a beginning of the work. The conditions of this problem are inherently adverse. The progress will be slow and gradual ; yet, I think all good citizens may now feel that the time for better things has begun.

And what, fellow-citizens, are those better things ? What are the changes in our present condition which are most needed ?

To my view, our first need is, what you have already largely secured here in Charleston, a cordial union, a harmonious working together, of both races in this State. The interests of our two races are identical. What injures the one, injures the other. What helps the one, helps the other. Granted, as a common platform, equal and impartial equality before the law, what is then to put a barrier of distrust or antagonism between the two races ? Absolutely nothing. Our commercial, agricultural, manufacturing, educational interests are the common concerns of every man. If the merchant of Charleston prospers under good government and low taxes, the clerk and the drayman who serve him prosper. The prosperity of the factor and the planter is the prosperity of the laborer who tills the field. The taxes that oppress our lands or merchandise, the extravagance or misrule which impoverishes the property-holders and drives away capital, reaches down and touches the humblest man, no matter what his pursuit, who earns his daily bread in the sweat of his face. There is, there can be, no separation of interest between classes or races, between rich and poor, landed or landless, in any of those matters which affect the general conditions of society. What is really good for the chief capitalists of this city in matters of government, is good for all, however poor or obscure. A recognition of this fact, and a complete union of all who do recognize it, is the first step in the march of this people towards true and lasting prosperity. [Applause.] Following such a union should come the determination to test all public measures and all public men by the invariable standard of their fitness and capacity to promote the common good. Let us have no more of the delusion that public office is valuable for its emoluments. Let us have no more of the other delusion, that measures which promote the interests of party only are the proper work of our legislators. In State, in county, and in city, we want a higher standard of public aim and service.

But, fellow-citizens, all other demands at the present moment are subordinate, merged in two great demands—*first*, for a great reduction of the burdens of taxation throughout the whole State ; and *second*, for an honest expenditure of the public moneys for public ends. [Loud cheers.] These constitute good government for South Carolina to-day. These are the planks of the platform of the party with which I propose to march hereafter. These are the things which will open the way to that restoration and reconstruction which South Carolina most needs.

One special word respecting the great subject of taxation. I undertake to say here to-night that no people in the Union pay their taxes with greater promptness and cheerfulness than the people of South Carolina. Such conduct entitles the tax-paying people of this State to have their voice heard on this vital question of taxation. They ought to be heard ; they must be heard.

I say here to-night that this people ought at once to be relieved of one third of the taxes which they have paid for the last six years. I say that this can be done without the least detriment to any public interest. I can sit down with any man or body of men who will look at the subject with a desire to do their duty, and I can point out in detail, specifically, item by item, the way in which this can be done.

If the Legislature at its next session will co-operate with me, I undertake to say that all our State taxation can be reduced below one per cent. And now, who is there bold enough to stand up here to-night and say that this ought not to be done ? No man, no man, dare avow such a purpose. [Long applause.]

While hard times are pressing upon us, while nearly every man who listens to me, or lives in the State, is practising economy, why should this public extravagance go on ? It is a wrong that should be prevented, without delay and without question. And what I say of the State expenditures applies, I believe, with equal truth to your county and city expenditures. The time has come when the public necessities should limit our public expenditures, and not the insatiate demands of individuals or combinations of individuals, who climb into power to grow rich from the public treasury.

The second great demand, I have said, is an honest and frugal expenditure of the funds which the people contribute for public purposes. If our taxes could not be reduced, the grievance would be far less if the people could feel that the taxes went to support public interests. If public improvements were the result of heavy taxation, if our public institutions showed the result of liberal and bountiful support, if our schools flourished under the generous bounty of the State, we should be able better to endure the burden. But what shall any honest man say of all these great public concerns ? Who will show me public improvements ? What is the condition of our public institutions of charity or correction ? What shall be said of our public schools ? Our public moneys are largely wasted, and that is worse even than the burden of taxation.

Fellow-citizens, these things must be reformed, and the public sentiment of Charleston can do much, very much, to make this demand heard and obeyed. I call upon every man, in whatsoever station, to emphasize and repeat these demands. They concern equally the moral and the material welfare of our State.

For myself, I stand ready to come up to the full measure of my duty, if I know what it is. I will keep abreast of the most advanced public sentiment on these subjects. I welcome aid from any and all quarters in this great work. I will regard him as better than a political friend, who, differing however widely from me in party associations, shall unite with me in securing these great results of good government. I will esteem him an enemy who, professing however loudly his party fealty, shall aid in adding to the burden of taxation or in using public funds for individual gain. The great results of good government are impartial administration of the law, an economical administration of public funds, moderate and reasonable taxation. All these blessings are within our reach, if we are united and determined in demanding them. They are our chief public concerns at the present time.

Whatever the changing fortunes of political parties in the nation at large, these things will remain for years to come the true aim of our people. It is a work worthy of our highest efforts. To found this State was the work of our fathers ; to rebuild it, to rescue it from the misfortunes of war, the waste of misgovernment,—this is our work. And, fellow-citizens, we have, aiding us in this good work, the auspicious era of our National Centennial. We do not know or feel, I think, how greatly the hearts of the American people of both sections will be drawn to each other as the great celebration of our national birth comes on. We have caught a little of its influence at Lexington and Bunker Hill, but the full tide will sweep over us at Philadelphia on the Fourth of July next.

Then let us hope that, under the full influences of those feelings which bound our fathers of the South and North to the great cause of American freedom and independence, we may find it easy to go forward to the completion of their great work, the accomplishment of their hopes and aims, the perpetuation for all coming generations of a nation wherein universal and impartial freedom shall show its perfect work.

With this hope, fellow-citizens, and with my thanks for your welcome, I bid you, Good-night. [Prolonged cheering.]

A special meeting of the Charleston Chamber of Commerce was held November 4th, at which, after the transaction of business relating to an application to Congress for an appropriation for the improvement of Charleston Harbor, the following action was taken :

The President announced that Gov. Chamberlain was in Charleston, and called attention to the marked courtesy and consideration he had always showed the Chamber. He thought it proper that the Governor should be invited to meet the members of the Chamber in this hall.

Col. W. L. Trenholm submitted the following resolutions, which were seconded by Mr. James T. Welsman, and unanimously adopted :

Resolved, That his Excellency, the Governor, be invited by the Chamber of Commerce to meet the members of the Chamber at such an hour to-morrow (Friday) as may be most agreeable to him.

Resolved, That the president be requested to convey this invitation, and to appoint a suitable committee for the purpose.

Resolved, That the president be requested to call a meeting of the Chamber to receive his Excellency.

The president appointed on this committee Messrs. James T. Welsman, F. W. Dawson, and J. Adger Smyth.

This commitee promptly waited upon the Governor to present the invitation, and it was arranged that he should visit the Chamber at 2 o'clock the next day. A special meeting was called for that hour. Of this meeting the Charleston *News and Courier* (November 6th) said : " The meeting was the largest and most influential that has been seen for a long time, and among those present were most of the oldest and most prominent merchants and business men in the city." When the Governor appeared, escorted by the committee, the President of the Chamber, S. Y. Tupper, Esq., made the following address :

Governor Chamberlain :—It affords us pleasure to receive you in our halls of commerce. This Chamber recognizes substantial benefits to our business community from your intelligent administration, and I gladly take this occasion to acknowledge repeated acts of courtesy on your part towards us in your prompt and considerate action upon all measures of reform which have been brought to your notice. This, sir, is not a political body. The rage and petulance of party never enter here. For nearly a century the efforts of this Chamber have been directed to a proper regulation of trade and the general interests of commerce in Charleston. Whatever tends to the promotion of these objects, and whoever aids us in the accomplishment of our wishes, must meet with our warmest sympathy and regard. We are happy to say to you that our city prospers. The industry and enterprise of our merchants have overcome great obstacles. We believe that there is yet a glorious future for Charleston. But, sir, the trammels of heavy taxation must be removed from our business men and public credit restored before a healthy confidence can exist and capital feel secure in coming hither. This can only be effected by the continued exposure and punishment of frauds upon the Treasury, and the destruction of those corrupt influences which have been to us the direful spring of all our woes—of disorder, prodigality, an unmanageable debt, crime, and repudiation. We are sensible of the efforts that your Excellency has been making, during a wise administration, for the remedy of these evils. Your courage in defence of the right and condemnation of what is wrong—rising superior to all faction or party—merits our hearty approbation and applause. We desire to encourage and strengthen your hands in the good work of reform, knowing that in these evil days malignity and disappointment will carp at and assail whoever attempts retrenchment and the exposure of fraud in our public affairs. We wish you all success in the further discharge of the responsible duties of your office, and again tender you a sincere welcome to the commercial metropolis of the State. [Applause.]

Gov. Chamberlain then said:

Mr. Tupper, and gentlemen of the Chamber of Commerce of Charleston:

This is, indeed, an unexpected pleasure and compliment. It has not been within the range of my hope and ambition, that if, at any time, I should be entitled to the support and gratitude of the people of Charleston, it would entitle me to the great honor you do me to-day. I accept it with the most sincere gratitude, and to you especially, Mr. President, for the very kind manner in which you have referred to my course of administration, as regards public measures. You do not expect me, gentlemen, to come here and say any thing instructive to you, upon those interests which you have peculiarly in charge. My duty is to protect all the interests of the State, so far as the faithful discharge of my public duties will affect them. I have already said to the citizens of Charleston that it is the sinking of party feeling, in the presence of the common concern, which is the fundamental principle of unity and prosperity, and *that*, I believe, the intelligent gentlemen who surround me have done and are ready to do. This demonstration of kindly feeling from the business men of Charleston strengthens me. I feel stronger to-day in the path of duty than I have felt since I entered upon the very arduous and thorny pathway of Governor of South Carolina. And I feel that you will have your reward, in the knowledge that you have strengthened me in my attempt to remedy some of the obstacles that lie in the way of prosperity to South Carolina. I believe, with all my heart, that there is in store for Charleston and South Carolina a very bright future, and I was greatly gratified this summer while at the North, in conversation with gentlemen of great financial experience and knowledge, to hear expressed the opinion that Charleston was the soundest commercial community south of Baltimore. These gentlemen remarked that immediately after the war Charleston seemed to display less enterprise, to embark in fewer hazardous transactions, than many other of her sister cities, and yet now she was acknowledged and recognized as the soundest Southern commercial community. All I can say is that I trust that Charleston will pursue the serene and even tenor of her way. Let her not be disturbed too much by political differences. Let us unite in strengthening each other's hands. If I have done any thing which meets with the approval of the people in South Carolina in the administration of her affairs, it was simply my duty, and you may rest assured that my best services shall be devoted to the commercial interests of Charleston. The utmost I can say is to heartily thank you for your thoughtfulness in recognizing the efforts I have made to serve you. I have been sincerely engaged in working for the welfare of South Carolina, and the most valued testimonial that I have received is the testimonial this day extended to me by the business men of Charleston. [Applause.]

The speech of the Governor to the people of Charleston on the occasion of the serenade was everywhere regarded as a notable utterance. The high ideal of public office as a trust to be held and administered for the benefit of all, without regard to race or party, appealed powerfully to a people who had suffered grievously by the absence of that motive in their officials. Some of the comments elicited are here given :

The address of Governor Chamberlain to the citizens of Charleston, last night, is admirable in every respect. Mr. Chamberlain is a Republican, but he asks for the aid of all good citizens, of all men who love South Carolina, in reducing taxation and securing an honest expenditure of the public money. And the aid he asks it is the duty, and the interest, of the Conservative Democracy of the State to extend to him, in his efforts to give the State a faithful and capable as well as an economical government. We have no right to expect Governor Chamberlain to abandon his party, but we have on the record his assurance that fealty to party shall never lead him to do any act which is injurious to the people of the State. To that pledge we hold him, by his fidelity to that pledge will he be judged, and by our conduct in upholding and sustaining him, in the fight that is before him, will our devotion to South Carolina be measured and determined.—*Charleston News and Courier.*

The views to which the Governor gives expression are very good, and if he will make them deeds instead of words he shall most certainly have the hearty support of all true Carolinians.—*Anderson Intelligencer* (Dem.).

The Governor strikes the key-note in this speech. It is not only truthful and patriotic, but a bold and manly declaration that he intends to rise above party and do his duty to the State at all hazards, relying upon the good men of both parties and races to sustain him. While the Governor does not abate one jot or tittle of his party fealty, he gives it to be distinctly understood that he is not the slave of party, and will not support any measure or party that does not tend to advance the interest of South Carolina. This is true statesmanship, and is all that we need to redeem the State.— *Barnwell Sentinel* (Dem.).

The Conservatives of this State have always avowed that an honest administration of public affairs, and not party supremacy, was the object for which they contended. Their record in the past has proven this to be true. If we have any hope then of improving our condition under a Republican Administration (and there is little likelihood of any other for several years to come), the present is the best opportunity we will have to make the effort. Mr. Chamberlain is the strongest man of his party in the State. No other could wield greater influence with it for good purposes.—*Greenville Enterprise* (Dem.).

Heretofore it has been the custom with our Republican rulers to put the success of party before the good of the State, and from this mistaken policy has flowed all

manner of evils.   Now the tide has changed, and we hope for better things.—*Abbe-*
ville Medium (Dem.).

Gov. Chamberlain, of South Carolina, is a man whose utterances excite our admi-
ration every time.   As old John Winthrop said of Roger Williams in good Old
Colony times, " he seems to have the root of the matter in him."—*Boston Herald*
(Ind.).

In response to a serenade at Charleston, Thursday evening, Governor Chamberlain made a speech which will do him good, and South Carolina good, and the country good.—*Springfield Republican* (Ind.)

The hearty reception given to Governor Chamberlain by the Chamber of Commerce of Charleston, and the congratulations he received upon the reforms of his
Administration and the increasing prosperity of South Carolina, ought to convey a
wholesome lesson to the Northern men whom accident has made Chief Executives of
Southern States.   Governor Chamberlain has apparently fulfilled his pledges in good
faith, and the result is that his labors in behalf of the State are fully appreciated by
the people.   The case of Governor Chamberlain forcibly illustrates the truth of the
proverb, " Honesty is the best policy," even in politics.—*Washington* (D. C.) *Star*
(Ind.).

We publish the chief portion of a recent address delivered at Charleston, S. C.,
by Governor Chamberlain, which will amply repay the most careful perusal.   The
address should be framed in gold and hung in the study of every Governor throughout the Union, and in the government offices at Washington.   Governor Chamberlain is a notable exception among the Republican rulers of the South, and his
address is a manly expression of sentiments truly honest and patriotic.   We commend
it to the earnest and careful study of Governor Kellogg, with the hope that he will
read, mark, and inwardly digest it.—*New Orleans Bulletin* (Dem.).

On the 8th of November Governor Chamberlain issued a proclamation appointing the 25th day of the same month to be
observed as a Day of Thanksgiving and Praise, and among other
reasons for gratitude to divine Providence he enumerated the
blessings " of increasing harmony and good-will among our people,
of progress towards good government, of a greater desire for
purity and integrity in public and private relations, and of a more
intelligent and earnest endeavor to make ourselves worthy of the
heritage of civil and religious freedom which we have received
from our fathers."

CHAPTER XII.

Meeting of the Legislature in its Second Session—Governor Chamberlain's Second Annual Message—Veto of the Tax and Supply Bill Passed at the Former Session —The Veto Unanimously Sustained—Comments on the Message and the Veto by the State Press.

WHEN the Legislature reassembled for the annual session of 1875–76, all the political elements of the State were once more in activity. While it was apparent that the Governor had greatly strengthened himself during the recess by the consistent development of his policy of administration, as well as by many public addresses that had created among the intelligent people of the State a genuine pride in his accomplishments and reputation, it was well known that his opponents in the Legislature had improved the time in devising means to make their opposition more effectual. There had been no sign of submission or conciliation, and the feeling was universal that the meeting of that body was the precursor of a fresh conflict, in which the Governor's resources and courage would be put to severer tests than had yet challenged his metal. In what shape the attack would be made did not clearly appear, although it was surmised.

On November 23d, the day of the meeting of the Legislature, Governor Chamberlain transmitted the Annual Message, setting forth the condition of the State's affairs, and making recommendations regarding the business that would come before the body, and he also communicated a Special Message vetoing the annual tax, or supply, bill, passed at the close of the preceding session. Both these messages are of peculiar importance in the formation of a judgment of the motives and measures of his Administration. They demonstrate, as certainly as official documents of this character may, the absolute and unyielding sincerity of Governor Chamberlain's reform policy. There is no suggestion of resting satisfied, no compromise of purpose, no slackening of devotion, no weariness in well doing.   His policy of reform was aspiring and progressive,—

> Built of futherance and pursuing,
> Not of spent deed but of doing.

It will be noted, also, that while the tone of both these messages is constant and firm, they contain no word of defiance or provocation.   The assumption throughout is that all who are responsible for the State's welfare will, with a willing purpose, strive to accomplish it, and to that end will act upon the best obtainable information and counsel.   His recommendations with regard to the contingent fund and the property designed for the Governor's residence, show how he exemplified in his own conduct the ideal of public responsibility he urged upon others. But these documents require no anticipatory reinforcement of their merit.   They are plain instructions.

The Annual Message follows.

———

EXECUTIVE CHAMBER,
COLUMBIA, S. C., November 23, 1875.

Gentlemen of the Senate and House of Representatives:

I welcome you on your return to the scenes of your public duties. The period since your separation has witnessed the death of but two of your number ; peace and health have prevailed throughout the State ; the labor of all classes of our citizens has been rewarded by a large degree of material prosperity ; the causes of discontent and hostility among our people have been greatly diminished ; and the feeling of respect and attachment to the Union, of which our State is a part, has been sensibly strengthened.   For these blessings we owe our sincere gratitude to the great Ruler of the world.

In presenting to you such information and views respecting public affairs as I deem important, I express the hope that we shall bring to the discharge of our present duties a deep and constant feeling that we are simply the servants and representatives of the whole people of the State.   The honors and emoluments of public office are merely incidental to its duties and responsibilities.   To seek the former and dis regard the latter is an offence against the first principles of moral and official obligation.   Those to whom we owe our present positions will justly measure us by the standard of our fidelity to the trusts confided to us.   I invoke, therefore, upon our deliberations and labors at this session the spirit of fidelity, of patriotism, of earnest co-operation in the measures best suited to advance the great interests of the State. I shall endeavor, for myself, to lend all my powers to the work of assisting the General Assembly in the proper discharge of its high duties. I shall be best content to follow you in the path of reform, economy, and good administration. That path I shall surely follow, whether with few or many, but I trust I shall hereafter find it made broad and clear before me by those who alone have the power to enact into laws the demands of the people

The amount of taxes levied and collected, the methods of their levy and collection, and the objects upon which they are expended, are the most important subjects with which the State Government has to deal. By the present assessment of real property, which was made in 1874, the total value of real property in the State is $90,095,407. While there are, no doubt, individual instances of error and hardship in the present valuation, yet, so far as my information extends, the general result is as fair as can reasonably be expected. If the individual taxpayer will avail himself of the means afforded by the present laws for his protection against unequal or excessive assessments, I think the instances will be very rare in which injustice will be finally done. At the last session of the General Assembly, the " taxation and assessment " Acts were carefully revised, and an additional Act relating to " forfeited " lands was passed. The tax laws of the State are now, in my judgment, well adapted to secure, in the language of the Constitution, " equality and uniformity " in the assessment of property for taxation. The total valuation of personal property under the assessment of 1875 is $46,791,006, in which is included a considerable amount of personal property which has hitherto escaped taxation.

I am happy to express my belief that the tax laws of the State are now administered with fairness and ability, and no instances are known to me in which complaints duly presented have not received due consideration. The results are highly creditable to the people, as well as to our tax officers. In an aggregate tax for the past year of $1,555,-201.68, only $12,519.47 have been returned as *nulla bona*, being less than four fifths of one per cent. In 1872 the returns of *nulla bona* amounted to $48,392.77, and in 1873 to $51,363.90.

During the past year, under the decision of the United States Supreme Court, the entire property of the Northeastern Railroad Company, and a large part of the property of the South Carolina Railroad Company, has been subjected to taxation. The question of the liability of the property of the Savannah and Charleston Railroad Company, and the Air Line Railroad Company, is still pending in the United States Courts ; and in the meantime the State authorities are enjoined from enforcing the collection of any taxes on their property. It is believed that during the present year final decisions favorable to the State will be reached in these cases, and thus several millions be added to the taxable property of the State.

I have no specific recommendation to make upon the subject of our tax laws, but I shall warmly favor any changes which may promise greater efficiency or fairness in the administration of this department of government.

In the matter of expenditures, I have the satisfaction of saying that great advances have been made during the past year towards a proper scale and measure.

The entire appropriation for legislative expenses for the fiscal year was $150,000. The appropriation under this head for the preceding fiscal year was $190,000, while the average cost of a regular session of the General Assembly from 1868 to 1873, inclusive, was $320,405.16, the cost of the regular session of 1871–72, reaching as high an amount as $617,234. In honorable contrast with former years, it should also be mentioned that no obligations have been issued or incurred by the officers of the General Assembly during the past year, in excess of the appropriations made.

The intolerable abuses of former years in connection with contingent funds have also been in a great degree removed. The entire amount appropriated during the past year for the contingent funds of all the Executive offices, including the contingent fund of the Supreme Court and the special litigation fund of the Attorney General of $7,500, was $15,250. The entire appropriation for legislative contingent expenses was $13,000. The corresponding appropriations for the fiscal year 1873–74 were, respectively, $47,100 and $32,500, showing a decrease in the aggregate of about sixty-five per cent. in favor of the last fiscal year.

But the gain to public morality and economy is still greater when we consider the fact that all Executive contingent funds have been drawn during the past year on vouchers appproved by and filed with the Comptroller General. Accountability and publicity, the two chief safeguards of official integrity, have thus been secured. For the last fiscal year the Governor's contingent fund was reduced from the previous annual average of $25,000 to $3,000, and at the end of the year the sum of $247.04 remained undrawn. I herewith transmit to the General Assembly a detailed statement of the disbursement of this fund, in accordance with the requirements of section 7 of the last general appropriation Act.

Provision having been made at the last session by an Act entitled " An Act relative to contracts for the Executive Departments of the State Government, and for the General Assembly " (Acts of 1874–75, page 958), for supplying the Executive Departments and the General Assembly with fuel and stationery, to be paid for by an appropriation from the phosphate royalties, it is obvious that the appropriations for contingent expenses to be made by the general appropriation Act of the present year should be greatly reduced.

I have already presented the favorable contrast between the appropriation of the last year for legislative expenses and those of former years. The pay of members of the General Assembly being provided for by an annual salary and mileage, the amount of money necessary for this purpose is determinate. The other items of legislative expenses are the pay of the subordinate officers and attachees, and the contingent accounts. The amount of these items will depend chiefly on the length of the session, and thus will afford full opportunity for the exercise of economy. With a session of from thirty to fifty days in length the entire amount of the appropriation necessary for legislative expenses for the present year can be brought within $120,000. The item of contingent legislative expenses will be nearly eliminated by the provision already made for fuel and stationery.

I most urgently urge upon your honorable bodies the propriety, in every view of the matter, of as brief a session as can be made compatible with the enactment of the necessary measures of legislation. Such a result would be of incalculable benefit to our State, not only in reducing the expenses of the legislative department, but in the wholesome and long-needed example it would furnish.

But there is one measure of legislative reform which I urge at this time as more vital and important than all others. I mean the mode of auditing and paying legislative expenses and claims passed by the General Assembly. In my Inaugural Address, one year ago, I presented my views upon this point, and I can do little more at the present time than to reiterate them, and to add that my present greater familiarity with the subject increases my conviction of their correctness.

It is a proposition which no one can dispute, that a permanent, public, accessible record should be kept of the disbursement of every dollar of the public funds. It is equally undeniable that all accounts calling for the expenditure of public funds should be audited by some officer who is officially responsible for the performance of this duty.

The present method of payment of legislative accounts does not meet these requirements of good administration. I therefore repeat my former recommendation, " that all payments to be made on account of legislative expenses, or claims passed by the General Assembly, be made by the State Treasurer, upon warrants drawn by the Comptroller General, for which the vouchers shall be filed with the Comptroller General."

In the payment of members, subordinate officers, attachees, etc., the only voucher requisite would be a duly certified list of all persons who hold these positions. The Comptroller General having satisfied himself of the correctness of the lists furnished by the officers of the General Assembly and the authority of law for their payment, would then draw his warrant upon the Treasurer for the proper sums of money.

In the payment of contingent expenses each branch of the General Assembly would, by committee or otherwise, make such audit as might be deemed necessary of such accounts and order their payments. The vouchers thus accepted by the General Assembly would be sent to the office of the Comptroller General, and there remain permanently exposed to the scrutiny of the public, and payment would be made only on the warrant of the Comptroller General.

In the case of claims passed by the General Assembly, the original accounts of such claims, and the certificates for their payment issued by the officers of the General Assembly, should likewise be filed with the Comptroller General, as vouchers to that officer for the issue of warrants. In this connection I may state that I have personal knowledge that in one instance, at least, a certificate for the payment of a claim passed by the General Assembly was issued at the last session, and both this certificate and the original claim were left in the hands of the person who presented the claim. Both these demands, the claim certificate and the original claim, were payable by the Treasurer without further examination, and thus this demand might have been twice paid without fault on the part of the Treasurer. I trust these considerations will render certain the adoption of such legislation upon this subject as will afford the proper securities.

The public printing has been reduced during the past year from the annual average of $181,209.95 during the three preceding years, to the sum of $50,000 per year. This branch of public work should hereafter be thrown open to the lowest bidder, under such regulations as will secure fair and genuine competition and the faithful performance of the proposals thus received.

In prosecuting the work of retrenchment, the number of salaried officers and the amounts of the salaries paid, will require strict examination. At the last session of the General Assembly a bill upon this subject was matured and passed by the House of Representatives, which was a long step in the right direction. This bill is now upon the calendar of the Senate, and I most heartily urge its immediate enactment into law.

Having in all practical ways brought the expenses of the government to the lowest limit compatible with the due support of our public interests, the next duty will be the levy of taxes sufficient, with other sources of revenue, to defray these expenses. This is not merely the plain dictate of common prudence and good administration, but it is a specific constitutional obligation. Section 3 of article IX of the Constitution is as follows : "The General Assembly shall provide an annual tax sufficient to defray the estimated expenses of the State for each year, and whenever it shall happen that such ordinary expenses of the State for any year shall exceed the income of the State for such year, the General Assembly shall provide for levying a tax for the ensuing year, sufficient, with other sources of income, to pay the deficiency of the preceding year, together with the estimated expenses of the ensuing year."

The first constitutional duty imposed and made imperative by this section is the levy of a tax sufficient to defray the estimated expenses of the State for the present year. The fact that the General Assembly cannot be compelled by any higher power to perform this duty, does not diminish the obligation to perform it. The practical evils of a neglect of this duty are oppressing nearly every branch of the public service at the present time. A vast floating debt and the loss of public credit, to say nothing of the hardship imposed upon thousands of individuals, are among these evils. I trust, therefore, that nothing will hereafter induce the General Assembly to neglect to provide by tax for all the estimated expenses of the current year.

The second constitutional duty imposed and made imperative by this section is the levy of a tax sufficient to pay the deficiency of the preceding year. This duty has likewise been neglected in former years. The total amount of deficiencies for the last fiscal year, including the loss in the South Carolina Bank and Trust Company, is $308,872.15, of which it should be said that $127,724.03 are the result of the failure of the South Carolina Bank and Trust Company. Of this amount the sum of $249,372.29 (as I have pointed out in detail in my Message of this date, returning the tax Act of the last session), should be provided for in the levy for the present year. If the General Assembly shall perform its duty in this respect we shall during the present year witness the prompt and regular payment of salaries and appropriations for public institutions, and a consequent restoration of our State credit, together with the increased efficiency of every branch of the public service. The ultimate burden of taxation will not thereby be increased, while in the absence of extraordinary causes the entire item of deficiencies will be eliminated from the next annual tax levy. Such results will follow the simple discharge of our constitutional obligations, and I do not permit myself to believe that the General Assembly will fail to secure them.

The most untoward event affecting our public interests during the past year has been the failure of the South Carolina Bank and Trust Company. At the time of its failure this Bank had $205,753.79 of money belonging to the State, of which amount $106,829.30 belonged to the funds for the payment of interest on the public debt, the remainder, $98,924.49, belonging to the general appropriations for the last fiscal year. This failure took place on the 2d day of July last, and immediately thereafter, on the motion of the Attorney General, the Court of Common Pleas of Richland County appointed Hon. T. C. Dunn the receiver of the assets and property of the bank. What amount the State will finally receive in the distribution of the property of the bank, on account of its deposit, it is now impossible to determine even approximately. The nominal amount of the liabilities of the bank is reported by the receiver to be $368,455.06, and the nominal assets $314,960.24. Of the assets of the bank, it may, in general, be said that they are to the last degree unsatisfactory and uncertain in value, as well as unavailable for present conversion into money. The evil effects of this failure have not been limited to the State, but the funds of several of the counties have also been lost.

The management of this bank, the causes of its failure, and the responsibility therefor, I do not deem it my province to discuss at this time. The property and assets of the bank being in the hands of the court, all legal questions involved in the failure must be determined by the court. The circumstances attending the deposit of the State funds in this bank, as well as the motives of the several members of the

Board having the selection of the banks of deposit for State funds, have already been made known to the public.[1] If the General Assembly shall desire further information respecting these matters, I shall be ready to furnish all information within my power ; or if it shall hereafter seem incumbent on me to discuss these matters further, I shall make a special communication to the General Assembly.

There is one subject conspicuously presented by this failure which I desire to bring to the immediate attention of the General Assembly : the question of the safest method of keeping our State deposits in the future. The law at present requires the Governor, the Treasurer, and the Comptroller General, acting together as a Board, to select the banks of deposit, having reference to the rate of interest which may be obtained upon the deposits and the security of the banks. It is obvious that the rate of interest paid on the State deposits is of little importance, compared with the security of the banks. With reference to the security of the banks, the Board of Deposit can do little more than to select such banks as stand well with the community generally and are trusted by private persons in the care of their private funds. This does not seem, in the light of recent events in this State, to afford sufficient protection to the public funds. I have been unable to arrive at a satisfactory conclusion on this subject, and I must therefore refer it, without specific recommendation, to the wisdom of the General Assembly. It is a subject demanding immediate consideration, and if I were to make any suggestion, it would be that the subject be referred by your honorable bodies for consideration and report to a joint special committee, selected with special reference to their financial and business experience and capacity.

Since November 1st, 1874, $2,624,706.80 of the bonds and stock authorized by the Consolidation Act of December 22, 1873, have been issued. The entire amount of this class of our public securities issued up to that date is $3,618,290.82. About seven tenths of all the bonds and stock made exchangeable under that Act have thus been exchanged. The great disaster of the failure of the South Carolina Bank and Trust Company has been most severely felt in its influence on this great public interest. It gave a shock to the growing confidence in the good faith of the State towards the public creditors, depressing the market value of the public securities, and checking for a time the process of exchange.

Since the 1st July, 1875, about $500,000 of consolidation bonds and stock have been issued, the coupons of which, from July 1, 1874, remain unpaid. I recommend that a tax be included in the annual levy now to be made for the deficiencies of the last fiscal year, to pay this amount of outstanding interest, amounting to $30,000.

The vital necessity of faithfully adhering to the contracts and obligations incurred by the present settlement of our public debt, I trust, needs no enforcement. It is as essential to the general prosperity of

---

[1] By newspaper reports. See the Governor's statement, p. 148.

the State as to the interests of her creditors. If good faith and un-flinching honesty shall be observed, the year on which we have entered will witness the complete exchange of the old debt of the State, a result which will be second to no other result of our efforts to restore the honor and welfare of the State. I recommend that such action be taken as will fully meet the just demands of the public creditors under the Consolidation Act, and remove all doubts respecting our intention to make that Act the point of departure for a new career of faith and honor, which shall help to hide the errors and failings of our recent history.

What is conveniently termed the floating indebtedness of the State presents a subject of great difficulty, but one which presses for decision. Under this head is included all the various evidences of indebtedness and claims against the State which have arisen between 1868 and 1874. Two reasons induce me to favor a settlement of this part of our debt, if a reasonable scheme can be adopted : first, justice to the many holders of these claims who have given the State valuable consideration therefor, in money, merchandise, or labor and services ; second, the removal from our current legislation of a disturbing and most unfavor-able influence. I shall not dwell upon this subject at the present time further than to say that any scheme to command my support must em-body these two provisions : First, the proper auditing of all forms of this indebtedness ; and, second, the gradual payment of the debts by such annual tax as will not be too burdensome to the people.

I am glad to express the belief that the financial condition of many of the counties of the State has been greatly improved during the past year. In general, I think the former habits of extravagance and fraud in county affairs have been corrected. A majority of the counties are, however, burdened, like the State, by floating indebtedness. The requi-sites of a proper scheme for the settlement of this indebtedness are the same, in my opinion, as those already stated ; first, the proper auditing of all claims, and, second, their gradual payment by taxation. Wher-ever these claims can be subjected to judicial scrutiny, such a course will furnish the best attainable mode of auditing the claims.

To guard against future evils of a similiar character, I recommend that County Commissioners be required to make specific levies for all the leading objects of expenditure, as is now done by the State. This will, to a great degree, prevent the diversion of funds from the objects which are most essential to the maintenance of county government, such as the pay of jurors, the dieting of prisoners, the ordinary expenses of the courts, and the support of the poor. County taxes are now extremely burdensome, and every effort should be made to reduce them.

It affords me very great satisfaction to state that I have received the Annual Reports of all the State officers and governing Boards and officers of all our public institutions in time to avail myself of their contents in the preparation of this Message. These reports are now in the hands of the public printer, and will, therefore, be laid before you in an available form in a very few days. I note this fact with pride, as an evidence that official responsibility is properly appreciated, and that a desire is felt by our public officers to facilitate the prompt discharge of its duties by the General Assembly. I am confident this fidelity will be fully appreciated by the General Assembly.

The Annual Report of the Comptroller General furnishes the grand source of information respecting nearly all the leading interests of the State. The present Report will be found a worthy example of fulness and convenience of tabular statements, as well as a valuable discussion of some special topics.

I have already, in presenting my views upon matters connected with the collection and expenditure of public funds, availed myself largely of this Report.

I concur in all the specific recommendations of the Comptroller General having reference to the good conduct of his office and the protection of public interests. His views of the mode of securing proper protection to policy holders in the various insurance companies doing business in this State seem to me correct, and the means suggested appear necessary and judicious.

The members of the General Assembly will find the entire Report a most valuable help, especially in dealing with the great subject of taxation.

In this Message, and in my Message of this date upon the Supply Act, I shall have presented so much of the information contained in the reports of the Comptroller General and the Treasurer, as will, I think, enable the General Assembly to proceed without delay to the practical work of the session.

The Annual Report of the State Treasurer contains the usual tabular statements showing the transactions of that office.

The Treasurer treats also of various subjects affecting the financial welfare of the State.

I call attention, especially, to his remarks upon the subject of specific levies.

The condition of the public debt is also presented in this Report in detail, and I trust this part of the Report will be carefully examined and considered.

The remarks of the Treasurer respecting the failure of the South Carolina Bank and Trust Company are worthy of careful examination, as presenting the actual relations of the State to that bank at the time of the failure, as well as his views of the nature of some of its leading transactions and the legal responsibility therefor.

The labor of this office is now greatly increased by the work of exchanging the public debt, and I discharge a duty merely when I bear official testimony to the ability and fidelity which the present State Treasurer brings to the discharge of all his duties.

The monthly statement of the transactions of this office mark a long advance in good administration. This practice will certainly demonstrate the truth that publicity is a protection to an honest officer and against a dishonest officer.

The Annual Report of the Secretary of State is herewith transmitted. This Report embraces a statement of the transactions connected with the ordinary duties of this office, and also with the department of the Land Commission, and the State census reports of 1875.

I call attention, with approval, to the remarks of the Secretary of State respecting the recent State census. It is a matter of deep regret that any results of this census should appear untrustworthy. But the total population of the State, according to the census, is put at 923,447, a reported increase over the result of the United States census of 1870 of 216,841, a result which will not bear examination. The Secretary of State having discussed this subject with so much candor and justice, I forbear to do more than to call attention to his remarks.

The industrial statistics furnished by this census may, so far as I am informed, be regarded as reasonably accurate, and these statistics will be found to be most interesting and valuable. I note a few of these statistics here, premising that, in giving the crops produced by the colored population, only the crops owned and produced by the colored population, independently and of their own right, are included ; all crops or parts of crops produced by colored laborers working for a share of the crops being credited entirely to the employer. Whole number of acres under cultivation, 2,070,441 ; by colored, 459,895 ; by white, 1,630,546. Whole number of acres of cotton planted, 818,197 ; by colored, 196,784 ; by white, 621,413. Whole number of pounds of long staple cotton produced, 1,821,989 ; by colored, 1,177,732 ; by white, 664,257. Whole number of pounds of short staple cotton produced, 139,939,459 ; by colored, 27,153,871 ; by white, 112,885,587. Whole number of acres of rice planted, 42,013 ; by colored, 10,459 ; by white, 30,554. Whole number of bushels of rice produced, 897,146 ; by colored, 176,194 ; by white, 720,952. Whole number of horses, 49,069 ; by colored, 10,431 ; by white, 38,638. Whole number of mules, 50,013 ; by colored, 10,244 ; by white, 39,769. Whole number of barrels of rosin produced, 343,146 ; by colored, 27,357 ; by white, 315,789. Whole number of gallons of turpentine produced, 3,421,262 ; by colored, 211,190 ; by white, 3,210,072.

The Annual Report of the Attorney General will be found a complete history of the causes in court in which the State has been a party, or had a legal interest. It will demand the attention of the General Assembly on many points. It is to be hoped that the greater part of the special litigation which has been imposed on the Attorney General during the past three years is now finally disposed of, and that the future will show a large reduction in the labors of the Attorney General and his assistants, in defending the State against special schemes for adding largely to our public burdens. All the duties of this office appear to have been performed with vigor and ability and with the best possible results to the State.

The Attorney General treats at length of the present condition of the suits which involve the question of the receivability for taxes of the bills of the Bank of the State.   It will be remembered that I called the special attention of the General Assembly to this subject in my Inaugural Address.   The Report of the Attorney General will present to your notice the changes in the relations of the State to these bills during the last year.   I content myself with remarking that this is a subject which forces itself on the' attention of the General Assembly, and will require a speedy solution.   What that solution shall be I leave to the General Assembly to determine.

The Seventh Annual Report of the Superintendent of Education will be found to convey important information concerning the common schools of the State.

The school population of the State, consisting of youths from 6 to 16 years of age, amounts to 239,264, of which, 85,566 are white, and 153,698 colored, showing an increase since 1873 of 9,162.

The present number of free common schools is 2,580, an increase since the last year of 227.   The present actual school attendance of both sexes is 110,416, of which, 47,001 are white, and 63,415 colored, an increase since the last year of 5,678.

The whole number of teachers employed is 2,855, of whom 1,876 are white, and 979 colored, an increase since the last year of 228. The average monthly wages of teachers is $31.64 for males, and $29.21 for females.   The average length of the last school year was four and a half months.

The number of common-school houses in the State is 2,347, an increase during the last year of 119.

The Superintendent of Education estimates the amount of money necessary to keep our free common schools open for a period of six months each year at $600,000, or $100,000 per month.

The foregoing statistics show a perceptible advance in the facilities for education afforded by our common schools during the last year. They also show that great advances must still be made before our common schools will reach our entire school population.   The length of the actual school year, now four and a half months, should be increased to at least six months.   Whether this can be done during the present year is doubtful, but it should be our aim to secure such a result at the earliest practicable time.

Three causes still retard the efficiency of our common schools : first the want of educational experience and capacity in many of our County School Commissioners ; second, the want of proper qualifications in many of our teachers ; third, the want of sufficient interest in the schools on the part of our people generally.   Remove these three hindrances and our advances would be rapid and certain.   How this can be done I have pointed out in a former message, and I again urge that your earnest attention be directed to these subjects.   The work of the State Superintendent,·it gives me pleasure to say, has been marked by intelligence and industry which are worthy of all commendation.   His report is full of instructive and vital information.

I renew the recommendation made in my Inaugural Address respecting the establishment of county high schools, by giving authority to the proper school officers to raise one or more of the most efficient and advanced common schools in each county, when deemed practicable, to the grade of high schools, with provision for an advanced course of study. No additional expense will thereby be incurred, but opportunity will be afforded to intelligent and ambitious youths to go beyond the ordinary common-school studies without leaving their counties—an opportunity now wanting and greatly needed. Such authority vested in the school officers need not be exercised unless such schools are required and the conditions are favorable for their establishment.

The condition of the State University has been improved during the past year. Owing to circumstances which are well understood, the University, under its present auspices, has been obliged virtually to begin a new life. An absolutely high standard of scholarship and discipline cannot be expected immediately. I do not hesitate, however, to say that I think the University is now doing a good work and deserves the support of the State. I regret that its benefits cannot be greater and more widely diffused, but I can never bring myself to regard with disfavor or neglect even the smallest beginnings of the educational interests of the State. During the past year the courses of study have been re-arranged and extended, and now comprise two quadrennial courses : an academical course, corresponding to the usual courses pursued in American colleges by candidates for the degree of Bachelor of Arts, and a course in which French and German are substituted for Greek and Latin. A special course is also provided for students who have not the time or means to spend four years in the University.

The whole number of students for the year ending October 31, 1875, was as follows : In the Preparatory Department, 102 ; in Law, 20 ; in Medicine, 2 ; in the Academical Schools, 107. Total, 233.

State scholarships have been awarded to 91 students, 15 of whom have since vacated their scholarships. The present Freshman Class contains 61 students, 22 of whom are pursuing the full classical course.

I think some changes in the present conduct of the University may be effected which will diminish its expenses and increase its efficiency. I therefore recommend that the attention of the General Assembly be directed to this subject, and I will lay before your proper committees my views in detail.

I take sincere satisfaction in stating that I regard the State Normal School, under the charge of Mr. M. A. Warren, as at present, perhaps the most entirely successful feature of our whole school work. I trust the members of the General Assembly will personally examine this school, and there learn how much a well-directed enthusiasm can do to solve successfully our hardest problems. In this school we have a source from which we shall obtain competent teachers for our common schools in the future. The school is divided into two departments, one called the "normal" and the other the "training." The former department, during the past year, had 10 students, the latter 25, making the whole number in attendance 35. In addition to this number, 21 have already left the school and are engaged in teaching—making the whole number of students since the organization of the school, 56. The school is in great need of additional facilities, all of which are fully set forth in the Annual Report of the Regents of the school. If the ordinary appropriation for this school can be obtained and made actually available during the present year, these wants can nearly all be met. The benefits of the school should be more widely enjoyed. All our counties are entitled to representation in the school, but at present only eleven counties are actually represented.

The State Agricultural College and Mechanical Institute, I regret to say, is in a condition far from flourishing. This is due, in great part, to the want of funds, which consist, under the law, of the interest on the bonds arising from the sale of the congressional gift of land scrip. If provision can be made to restore these funds I do not doubt that this institution can be made useful. I call attention to the subject without offering any recommendation.

In my Message at the last session I called attention to the suspension of the school for our deaf, dumb, and blind, at Spartanburg, and I characterized its suspension as "an act of educational retrogression." I cannot do less than again urge upon the General Assembly the duty of re-opening this institution. Humanity demands it. Our present reputation demands it. The buildings stand idle and empty, and our unfortunate children of this class are growing up in mental as well as physical darkness, for want of a small pittance of our public funds. This institution might literally be supported by the crumbs that fall from the tables of some of our other objects of expenditure. I trust the present year will not pass without seeing this school re-opened and adequately supported.

At the last session of the General Assembly, the Governor, Secretary of State, and Superintendent of Education, were directed to open negotiations for an exchange of the property of the State at Spartanburg for property suitable for the same purpose in Columbia. I regret to state that that Commission have been unable to effect an exchange. A Report of the Commission will be duly presented to the General Assembly. Meantime the buildings at Spartanburg can be used for the school until a removal can be effected to a more convenient location, if such a change is finally deemed advisable.

I transmit herewith the Annual Report of the Adjutant and Inspector General, with its accompanying papers. The condition of our military system is now deplorable. The original organization of the militia was exceedingly imperfect, and its present condition, for the most part, is not worthy the name of an organization. It is a subject worthy of candid and considerate treatment by the General Assembly. I call attention to the recommendations of the Adjutant and Inspector General, and I mention with approval his suggestion that the organization of the State militia be limited to large cities and towns of the State where arsenals and other indispensable facilities for the proper discipline and drill of the militia can be secured. In its present condition our militia is not a source of strength or an object of just pride. I will heartily aid in any efforts to elevate this department to a proper standard of efficiency and usefulness.

The Report of the State Librarian and Keeper of the State House, conveying much valuable information, is herewith transmitted. In this connection I desire to acknowledge the very faithful and valuable services rendered to the State by this officer in the care of the supplies of coal and wood purchased for the use of the State officers and General Assembly during the present year. The State has in this instance received full weight and measure, and the favorable result will be apparent during the year.

The Annual Report of the Board of Regents of the Lunatic Asylum, covering the Annual Report of the Examining Committee of that Board and the Fifty-third Annual Report of the Superintendent and Physician of the Asylum, fully presents the condition of that most important institution. I take pleasure in saying that, in my judgment, the officers of that institution have accomplished all that could be accomplished in its management, with the many disadvantages which continue to embarrass all our public institutions. Foremost among these disadvantages is the invariable deficiency in the funds available to meet the appropriation for its support, and consequent necessity of supporting the institution for a large part of the year upon credit.

A further direct consequence of this deficiency of funds has been the accumulation, since 1868, of an amount of past due indebtedness which now renders it nearly impossible to obtain any credit for the institution. The only remedy for these evils is the raising of funds sufficient to meet in full the appropriation, and the rigid limiting, as is now done, of all expenditures to the amount of the appropriation. Let the Asylum for one year be able to obtain its appropriation in full when due, and these evils will at once be remedied.

This institution affords a striking example of the evil effects of our practice of allowing deficiencies to arise year after year, and teaches a lesson which should not require further enforcement. I deem it simple justice to the present Superintendent to say that he has shown a rare degree of fidelity, ability, and patience in meeting these difficulties which have thrown upon him an amount of labor and anxiety of which the public have little conception. I implore the General Assembly, for the sake of that most afflicted class of our community thus committed to their care, to remove these burdens by providing an amount of funds which will enable the officers of the institution to conduct its affairs in a proper manner. Nothing is needed to effect this except a due regard to the most common business principles. Of course this institution has suffered, in common with all other public interests, from the failure of the South Carolina Bank and Trust Company, but, aside from this, the entire amount levied for the support of our penal and charitable institutions was greatly inadequate to meet the appropriations made.

With the funds at their command the officers of the Asylum have done more than could have been expected, and the results indicate how much more might be accomplished under favorable conditions.

A summary statement of the financial results of the year is as follows : Expenses for fiscal year 1874–75, $61,657.24 ; outstanding liabilities prior to last fiscal year, $57,641.85. Total, $119,299.09. Of this total $70,285 has been paid during the last fiscal year. Balance remaining unpaid, $49,014.09. Deduct from this sum $14,500 of Comptroller's warrants for the past year, now unpaid, and the entire indebtedness of the Asylum at the end of the last fiscal year was $34,-514.09, a reduction of the old debt by $23,127.76 in one year. I know no more gratifying result in any department of the public service. This result has been reached only by enforcing rigid economy to a degree which impairs the usefulness of the institution, but it furnishes an example which should command the thanks of all our people.

For the future the Asylum greatly needs a more liberal support ; the female department is now overcrowded ; improvements and repairs of various kinds are needed ; the roof of the male department, especially, is in need of immediate repairs ; and the new Asylum building should be greatly enlarged.

With proper retrenchment in other expenses of the State, I think all those wants could be met without increased taxation, but I am opposed, under all circumstances, to any appropriations in excess of the amount raised by taxation. The greatest degree of liberality compatible with the pecuniary condition of the State should be shown towards the institution.

I call attention to the practical recommendations made in the Report of the Board of Regents and the Superintendent, and especially concur in the recommendation of the Superintendent that the law should provide against the admission of patients afflicted with forms of chronic insanity (except violent cases), to the exclusion of acute and recent cases which present hope of successful treatment. The Asylum is now crowded with cases of hopeless chronic insanity. The entire report is extremely interesting, and should be read and considered by every legislator.

I concur fully in the views of the Board of Regents and the Superintendent respecting the past indebtedness of the Asylum. It is perhaps the most meritorious portion of our floating indebtedness, and should certainly be provided for without further delay.

The Annual Report of the Directors of the State Penitentiary, covering the Reports of the former Superintendent and the present Superintendent and other officers of that institution, are herewith transmitted.

From these Reports it appears that on the 31st day of October, 1874, the institution contained 168 convicts; that during the year ending October 31, 1875, additional convicts to the number of 312 were received ; that during the same period 9 escaped convicts were recaptured, making a total of 489 inmates during the year. Of this number it further appears that 46 were pardoned by my predecessor between the 1st November and the 1st December, 1874, and that 16 have been pardoned by me between the 1st December, 1874, and the 31st October, 1875, that 44 have been discharged by expiration of sentence, 4 by commutation of sentence, and 21 under the regulation allowing a reduction of one twelfth of the time of sentence as a reward for good behavior; that 24 have escaped, 4 have died, 1 was shot in altercation with a guard, and 1 was drowned ; 6 are designated as "trustees," who should, prior to May 1, 1875, have been dropped from the records as "escaped" ; making a total of 167 discharged during the year, and leaving 322 in confinement on the 31st of October, 1875, of which number 318 are males and 4 females.

I am gratified to state that great improvements have been made during the past year in the management of the Penitentiary, especially in the cost of maintaining the prisoners. On the 14th of April, 1875, Col. T. W. Parmele was appointed Superintendent, and on the 1st of May, 1875, he entered upon his duties. A proper system of accountability for all supplies furnished the Penitentiary was at once adopted and enforced. A set of books was opened in which the accounts have been entered, and written requisitions for supplies and vouchers for all expenditures are now on file for the verification of all accounts. All supplies received have been invariably weighed, measured, or otherwise taken account of. The results of these obvious measures of good management have been unmistakable. While the number of convicts has been greatly increased, the entire cost of maintaining this increased number has been greatly reduced. Thus for the month of April, 1875, with an average number of convicts of 243, the pay-roll of guards and employees was $1,426.78 ; while for the month of September, 1875, with an average number of convicts of 300, the pay-roll of guards and employees was $1,225.35. For the month of April, 1875, the cost of groceries and beef was $2,028.57 ; while for the month of September, 1875, the cost of the same items was $1,027.15 ; the *per capita* cost for the former month being $8.34, and for the latter month $3.42.

Notwithstanding many disadvantages, the financial condition of the Penitentiary, at the close of the year, was eminently satisfactory. The failure of the South Carolina Bank and Trust Company caused a loss of $493.92 in cash. Owing to the deficiency of the receipts under the levy of taxes made for penal and charitable institutions for the last year, together with the failure of the South Carolina Bank and Trust Company, the sum of $4,500 in unpaid warrants remain now on hand. These warrants, together with the income derived from the sale of bricks made by convict labor, will, however, fully meet all the outstanding indebtedness of the last fiscal year.

In the interior economy and discipline of the institution many wise changes have been made. The more youthful are now separated from the other inmates, and constitute what is known as the " Reformatory Department," in which they are regularly instructed each day by competent teachers, and their time occupied in such ways as to remove them from the demoralization of constant association with other and more confirmed criminals. In the employment of the convicts in labor all has been done that was possible under existing laws. An attempt was made to raise corn on lands near this city, but owing to the late period at which the work was begun, and the severe drought of the midsummer, comparatively little was realized from this labor, though enough was done to demonstrate that under ordinary favorable conditions such work can thus be made available in greatly reducing the cost of maintaining the institution. Besides this, between $3,000 and $4,000 worth of bricks has been made.

But the most advantageous use of this labor cannot be made while the present restrictions of law are in force, and I most earnestly recommend that authority be given, by a change of the present law, to the Directors to employ this labor in such ways as they may deem most advantageous, provided it does not come into competition with other labor. To a certain degree every man competes in labor with other men, but it will be easy to find employment for the able-bodied inmates of the Penitentiary, which will not sensibly affect the price or amount of the employment of other laborers. The cost of maintaining our convicts, now a heavy burden, will thereby be greatly reduced, and the welfare, physical and moral, of the convicts will be promoted.

I do not recommend an increased appropriation for the support of the Penitentiary for the present year. On the contrary, if authority is given to the Directors to employ the labor of the convicts, as above recommended, I shall recommend that the appropriation be reduced to $30,000. If such authority is not given, I shall recommend that the appropriation be continued at $40,000, and that $3,000 of this sum, if so much be necessary, be used in constructing a new roof for the south wing of the Penitentiary, and for putting a roof on the north wing, and for other permanent repairs.

The past indebtedness of the Penitentiary contracted prior to October 31, 1874, is, nominally, $87,918.39.

In connection with this subject I call attention to the Report of Pardons, Reprieves, and Commutations granted by me since December 1, 1874, which I herewith transmit, agreeably to the requirements of Section 11 of Article III of the Constitution. In discharging this most onerous and painful duty of my office I have endeavored faithfully to redeem the promise made in my Inaugural Address. The whole number of pardons and commutations granted by me up to November 1, 1875, was thirty-six. With scarcely an exception, all applications for pardon or commutation have been referred by me to the Judge who tried the case, and, as will be seen in nearly or quite every case, my action has had the sanction of the Courts and best citizens of the State.

At this point I also call attention to the matter of rewards for the capture of fugitive criminals. The custom of offering rewards through the Governor in such cases has been strongly established in this State. With one exception, which seemed to me to be justified by the circumstances, I have offered no such rewards, for the reason that I had no fund at my command for paying them. If the General Assembly desire to continue the custom, it will be necessary to set apart a fund for that purpose.

The Annual Report of the Trustees of the State Orphan Asylum is, with Reports of its officers annexed, herewith transmitted, and will be found to be elaborate and interesting.

During the past year this institution has been removed from Charleston to Columbia. The Asylum is now apparently beginning a new career, nearly all of its former officers and teachers, as well as the larger part of its inmates, having left during the past summer. The present number of inmates is eighty-four, of whom thirty-five are boys, and forty-nine are girls. The financial condition of the institution is fully presented in the Report of the Trustees.

The Annual Report of the Health Officer at Charleston, which is herewith transmitted, presents the operations of the quarantine departments at Charleston, Hilton Head, and Georgetown. The past year has demonstrated in a signal manner the benefits of a vigilant and skilful management of these departments. Our coast communities have not only been protected from epidemics of all kinds, but from the special scourge of yellow fever. As early as last March the yellow fever made its appearance at Havana and Key West. Our quarantine officers were in immediate communication with these points, and a system of rigid examination of all vessels from those ports was enforced, and never relaxed, under any pressure, during the entire summer. The result has been an entire exemption from that disease along our whole seaboard. The means adopted and the results thus secured reflect the greatest credit upon the Health Officer at Charleston, Robert Lebby, M. D., as well as S. B. Thompson, M. D., the Health Officer for Beaufort and Hilton Head. It is pleasant and proper to acknowledge the assistance rendered our Health Officers by the various United States officers on duty upon our coast, particularly Captain C. O. Boutelle, of the United States Coast Survey.

The Report of the Health Officer at Charleston embraces recommendations for certain changes in the quarantine law of the State which seem to me judicious, and which, I trust, will be adopted. Other recommendations contained in this Report, intended to increase the efficiency and completeness of our system of quarantine are approved by me and respectfully urged upon the consideration of the General Assembly.

I again urge that the provisions of Sections 1, 21, 22, 23, and 24 of Article IV of the Constitution relating to the election of "a competent number of Justices of the Peace and Constables in each county, by the qualified electors thereof, in such manner as the General Assembly may direct," be put into practice. The adoption of new consitutional provisions will give little confidence in our good intentions while important existing constitutional requirements are wholly and persistently disregarded. Though the General Assembly have the power, they have not the right to deprive the electors of the counties of the constitutional privilege of electing Justices of the Peace and Constables. If one constitutional requirement can be disregarded, all can be, so far, at least, as they depend on the positive action of the General Assembly. The results of the system of Trial Justices appointed by the Governor certainly cannot be considered so favorable as to justify the annulling of an important part of the Constitution. Let the Constitution be enforced in all its provisions, and a public sentiment will then be cultivated which will make the Constitution the shield for all classes of our people from the wrongs or excesses which the interests of any political party may prompt.

The Constitution, in Section 3, of Article VIII, declares that " it shall be the duty of the General Assembly to provide, from time to time, for the registration of all electors."

What has just been said of the election of Justices of the Peace and Constables applies equally to this provision of the Constitution. If it were a question of constitutional construction, there might be room for difference of opinion here. But it will not be questioned that the Constitution requires registration. It is equally plain that the phrase from " time to time " is intended to secure the constant observance of this safeguard of our elections. To my mind there is no place left for argument on this subject. In a political or party view I fear nothing more than the effect of a plain disregard of constitutional requirements. In the revolutions of political fortune which are always incident to a wide or universal suffrage, by a disregard of the Constitution

> " we but teach
> Instructions, which, being taught, return
> To plague the inventors."

I am confident, from various indications, that the principle of minority representation is growing in favor among all the people of the State. It offers in theory, certainly, and in practice, so far as yet tested, a mode of reaching that highest result of our representative system, the true proportional influence of each class or party into which our voting population may be divided. The rule of the majority is not thereby destroyed, while the voice and influence of the minority is not wholly suppressed. In this State its advantages in our counties and municipalities would be peculiarly great. Our voting population is now, in a great measure, divided upon lines which are not conducive to the best results in our public affairs. Minority representation will mitigate these evils without changing the basis of political power.

Practically, though not in name, this principle has already been applied in some of our counties and cities. Citizens of both parties or races have voluntarily agreed to share political power in approximate proportion to their numerical strength, respectively. The results of such a course have invariably been satisfactory, so far as I am informed, and I am sure that the example will be repeated more and more widely in the future. ✓ What is thus here and there secured by the voluntary concert of our citizens will be secured firmly and universally by the adoption into the law of the State of the principle of minority representation in all county and municipal elections. I cordially and earnestly urge this measure upon your consideration at the present session.

I call attention to the recommendations made in my Inaugural Address respecting a revision of the laws defining the powers of the Board of State Canvassers. Different opinions respecting the powers of the Board prevail among the present members of this Board, and expensive litigation is almost constantly in progress, growing out of this uncertainty. A few simple amendments of the present law will set at rest all doubts on this subject

The State Agricultural and Mechanical Society, through a committee of its members, has requested me to call your attention to the condition and wants of that Society, and to recommend an appropriation in its aid. The utility of societies of this character need not be argued. Our State is pre-eminently an agricultural State. Every practicable means should be employed to promote the interests of the planter and farmer, as well as the agricultural laborer, of whatever grade. The State Agricultural Society can be made a principal agent in this work. At the present time the condition of this Society seems to be one of extreme depression in some respects. I conclude, also, from many indications, that an opinion widely prevails that the Society has not in all respects been wisely managed hitherto. If the State shall contribute directly to the support of this Society I think it should, if practicable, make sure that the Society shall so manage its affairs as to enlist the support and confidence of all who regard the welfare of the State. How this can best be done I am not prepared to say. I do, however, cordially recommend that an appropriation be made in aid of this Society for the present year, to be drawn and expended under such restrictions and regulations as may be deemed best adapted to promote the general agricultural interests of the whole State. With economy in other expenditures, such an appropriation need not increase the burden of our taxation.

The very valuable property of the State on Arsenal Hill, in this city, formerly used as the Governor's residence, was placed in my charge at the beginning of the year, with the intimation that the rent derived from it might be regarded as applicable to my use. I have not felt willing to accept this offer, and inasmuch as the whole property was greatly in need of repairs, I have devoted the entire rent of the

year to that use. The residence has been repaired, the fences rebuilt,
and all the out-buildings put in good order. During the present year
this work can be extended and the value of the property greatly enhanced by judicious improvements. I transmit herewith a detailed
statement of all money received from rent, and all disbursements made
during the last year, the vouchers for all of which are on file for inspection in the Executive office.

The monument on the Capitol grounds, erected in memory of the
Palmetto Regiment, which achieved renown in the war with Mexico,
has been greatly injured by the tornado which visited this city during
the past year. The interest manifested by all classes of citizens in its
restoration is a strong tribute to the patriotic and martial spirit of our
people, and induces me to add an expression of my hope that the General Assembly may find it practicable to cause the monument to be
suitably repaired during the present year.

At the present session elections of Judges of the Courts of Common
Pleas and of the Supreme Court will take place. It cannot be deemed
improper for me to present to the General Assembly the paramount
importance of a wise discharge of this duty. The ancient fame of
South Carolina in this respect should be kept steadily in mind. The
standard of character and attainment once universally observed in this
State should never be lowered. Legal learning, a judicial spirit, and a
high, unblemished personal character, should mark every man who shall
be elected to sit in the seats of Harper and Dunkin, of O'Neall and
Wardlaw. If all these qualities are not attainable, let the one quality
of personal integrity never be lost sight of. That community may well
be pitied which is doomed to submit its great interests to the decision
of one whose judgments will reflect his own passions or interests.

On the 4th day of July, 1876, one hundred years will have passed
since the Declaration of American Independence was made. In obedience to the natural impulse, as well as the cultivated principle of
national pride, in grateful recognition, also, of the blessings communicated to us and to the whole world from the event of July 4, 1776, the
States of the American Union, the old and the new alike, will unite at
Philadelphia, on the spot where Adams and Jefferson, the North and
the South of a century ago, proclaimed the birth of the new nation, in
celebrating the most auspicious event of modern times. In that celebration South Carolina will have a place. Shall she occupy it or not?
I firmly believe that the true voice of South Carolina answers from all
her plains and mountains, by all her sons and daughters, "South Carolina *shall* fill her place in the centennial pageant."

In this confidence I now invite again the attention of the General
Assembly to this subject. At your last session, in response to a special
Executive communication, a Joint Special Committee was appointed
from your two Houses "to collect information of resources of the State
for representation at the Centennial Exposition at Philadelphia." Perceiving that the work was still progressing but slowly, if at all, and

being appealed to by many within and without the State to omit no effort to forward this object, and at the urgent invitation of the Centennial authorities at Philadelphia, I appointed, on the 25th October last, a commission of nine eminent and honorable citizens of the State, each of them a fair representative of some great branch of the resources and industries of the State, "to have in charge the perfecting of such arrangements as they may adopt for promoting and securing the proper representation of South Carolina—her resources, history, and industries—at the Centennial Celebration."

As my selection of the members of this Commission has occasioned unfavorable criticism in some quarters, I take this occasion to state that I was governed solely in my selection by a desire to secure the active co-operation of those of our fellow-citizens from whom a very large majority of all articles furnished for the Centennial celebration must necessarily come. I did not permit other considerations to influence my action. It was a duty voluntarily assumed by me, not imposed by law, and I recognized no other obligation in its discharge than the obligation to supply an indispensable element of success in this work, so far as it lay within my power. The functions and work of this Commission will in no respect supersede or embarrass any other agency previously or hereafter employed for the same purpose. The field of labor is open to all agencies, however appointed, and the only just rivalry should be a rivalry of zeal and efficiency in promoting the common end—an honorable representation of South Carolina at Philadelphia. The shortness of the remaining time for this work suggests earnest and prompt action on the part of all, and I urge upon your honorable bodies all such efforts as may be calculated to fulfil our duty in this respect to the State and Nation.

Gentlemen of the Senate and House of Representatives:

I have now discharged, so far as I have been able, the duty imposed upon the Governor by the Constitution, to "give to the General Assembly, from time to time, information of the condition of the State, and recommend to their consideration such measures as he shall judge necessary or expedient." The measures which I deem most essential to the present welfare of the State are: *First,* the prompt passage of a Supply Act which shall impose the lightest possible burden of taxation; *second,* the enactment of a law which shall require all disbursements of public funds, except the interest on the public debt, to be made upon warrants of the Comptroller General, issued upon vouchers approved by that officer, and permanently recorded in his office; *third,* the keeping of all appropriations within the limits of the funds actually provided for by taxation; *fourth,* the immediate and large reduction of the scale of all public expenditures; *fifth,* the equitable adjustment of the floating indebtedness of the State upon a plan embracing the rigid scrutiny, by impartial agencies, of all claims, and the gradual payment by taxation of the valid claims; *sixth,* the inflexible observance of exact good-faith respecting the public debt.

The work and spirit which I commended to you a year ago, I commend with increased earnestness to you now—the work of correcting abuses and restoring good administration—the spirit of integrity and fidelity towards those whose trusts we hold. Some gratifying results have been reached, but the future has heavier tasks than those already achieved. I might urge these things upon my political associates as essential to the life and success of their political party, for so they are; but I choose to urge them upon the common, unassailable ground of the public welfare. He will be a blind politician who is not also a patriot. The truly wise public man in this State to-day will labor and pray for the peace and honor of South Carolina; for the increase of official integrity; for the confirmation to every citizen of all civil and political rights; for the establishment of government which shall protect all and oppress none.

D. H. CHAMBERLAIN,

Governor.

The message communicating to the General Assembly his objections to the supply bill, passed at the previous session, was in the terms following:

EXECUTIVE DEPARTMENT,

COLUMBIA, S. C., November 23, 1875.

To Hon. Robert B. Elliott, Speaker House of Representatives:

SIR—I return herewith, without approval, to the House of Representatives, in which it originated, an Act entitled " An Act to raise supplies for the fiscal year commencing November 1, 1875." The fact that this Act, the most important of the year, did not reach me until the last hour of the last day of the session, deprived me of the opportunity of examining the Act with sufficient care to enable me to reach a conclusion as to my duty before the final adjournment of the General Assembly. When an examination had convinced me that official duty would not permit me to approve the Act, the unavoidable result was to postpone further action until the reassembling of the General Assembly at its next regular session. I appreciate fully the disadvantages arising from this state of facts, and I should be sorry to feel that I am responsible for them.

To the reasons which originally led me to withhold my approval from this Act have been added others, resulting from the failure of the South Carolina Bank and Trust Company, by which the sum of $205,-753.79 has been withdrawn from the use of the State, and a large part of that sum finally lost. Being compelled to withhold my approval from the Act, and to await the reassembling of the General Assembly, I feel bound to urge some objections which I might otherwise have waived for the sake of avoiding the disadvantages of the delay thus occasioned.

In framing a proper Supply Act the obvious dictate of prudence and good administration is to first ascertain how much money is needed, and then to provide for that amount. No deficiency should be permitted to arise except from causes which cannot be foreseen. The evils of a departure from this rule are most serious. Every person who looks to the State for salary or pay is now, and has been for years past, obliged to accept such part only of what is due him as may be realized from taxes which are levied, with a certainty that he will, at best, receive only a part. In the case of public institutions the evils are still greater. Supplies cannot be obtained at cash prices when there are no funds in the Treasury, and thus for a considerable part of the year the officers of public institutions are subjected to the greatest inconvenience, and the public to greatly increased expenses, with no compensating advantages whatever.

In examining the present Act, I propose, in the first place, to take the appropriations of the last fiscal year as the basis of calculation of the amount required to be raised for the present year ; and, in the second place, to take the actual needs of the public service as such basis, and present the results of each method.

In the first section of the present Act a tax of one and one half ($1\frac{1}{2}$) mills upon the dollar is levied to meet appropriations for the salaries of the executive and judicial officers of the State, and the clerks and contingent expenses of the executive and judicial departments, for the present fiscal year. The experience of the past year shows that this tax will raise $187,500. The appropriations for the last fiscal year under this head amounted to $224,105.75. The appropriations under this head for the present fiscal year can easily be reduced to the amount which will be raised by the levy. The following items in last year's appropriations will not be required for the present year :

1. Salary of Judge of Inferior Court of Charleston County, $ 625 00
2. For additional compensation to County Auditors . .   4,780 75
3. For portraits of Abraham Lincoln and Charles Sumner,   5,000 00
4. For expenses of general election, 1874 . . . . . .   15,000 00

Total $25,405 75

Deducting this amount from the total appropriations under this head, we have an aggregate amount of $198,700.

The contingent funds of the several executive offices can be still further reduced on account of the fact that all expenses for stationery, postage, and fuel are otherwise provided for by contracts payable from the phosphate royalties.

Upon the basis, therefore, of last year's appropriations, all the regular expenses falling within this section can be met by a levy of one and one half ($1\frac{1}{2}$) mills.

In the second section of the Act a levy of one and one half ($1\frac{1}{2}$) mills is made to meet appropriations for the penal and charitable institutions. This tax will raise $187,500. The appropriations under this head for the last year were $195,000. In this case it will be easy to bring the appropriations within the receipts for the present year.

In the third section of the Act a levy of two (2) mills is made to meet appropriations for the public schools. This tax will raise $250,-000. The appropriations under this head for the last year were $240,-000, and so much more as should be produced from the levy of two (2) mills, made in the Supply Act of 1874–75. Upon the basis of that appropriation no deficiency will occur.

In the fourth section of the Act a levy of one and one fourth (1¼) mills is made to meet appropriations for legislative expenses. This tax will raise $156,250.

It is evident that a reduction can be made under this head in the appropriations for the present year.

I find, by actual estimate, that the total cost, inclusive of contingent expenses, of a legislative session of one hundred days will be only $132,-000. Nearly all contingent expenses, except lights, are now provided for by contracts payable from the phosphate royalties. A tax for legislative expenses of one and one tenth (1 1/10) mills will raise $137,500, which will abundantly cover all expenses for a session of one hundred days.

By the fifth section of the Act a levy of one half (½) mill is made to meet appropriations for public printing for the fiscal year and the deficiency of the last fiscal year. I recommend that this levy be changed to two fifths (2/5) of a mill, which will raise $50,000, the full amount of the contract for last year, leaving the deficiency under this head to be provided for, as I shall hereafter show, in the levy for other deficiencies. There is no good reason why this deficiency should not be placed under the proper head of deficiencies.

By the fourteenth section of the Act a levy of one (1) mill is made to pay the deficiencies or unpaid appropriations of the last fiscal year. This tax will raise $125,000. The total appropriations for the last fiscal year amounted to $1,282,082.82. The total receipts for the same year applicable to the payment of the above appropriations amounted to $1,100.934.70. Of this amount there was lost by the failure of the South Carolina Bank and Trust Company $127,724.03, leaving the total available receipts $973,210.67. The deficiencies, therefore, with the loss in the bank, for the last fiscal year amount to $308,872.15.

The following items of deficiency require to be provided for:

1. Deficiency in salaries, contingents, etc. . . . . . . $ 90,445 31
2. Deficiency penal and charitable institutions 56,486 76
3. Deficiency public printing 11,875 25
4. Deficiency in January and July, 1875, interest . . . 30,000 00
5. Deficiency legislative expenses 7,860 12
6. Deficiency claims of T. W. Price & Co. 12,704 85
7. Deficiency census-takers 40,000 00

Total $149,372 20

The remaining items of deficiency are as follows :

Free schools $11,378 13
Deficiency free schools and School Commissioners prior
    to November 1, 1873 . . . . 13,497 72
Interest, July and January, 1875, on bonds not yet issued, 34,624 01

The deficiency for free schools represents the excess of the receipts over $240,000, the amount of the appropriation. As no liabilities, so far as I am aware, have been incurred for this excess, I think it will not be necessary to levy for that amount. The next item is not properly a deficiency, and should be provided for, if at all, with the floating indebtedness of the State. The item for interest represents the amount which would have been applicable to the payment of interest due in 1875, if bonds and stocks in sufficient amount had been exchanged. As, however, only $500,000 of consolidated bonds and stocks have been issued with coupons maturing in 1875, the levy for $30,000, as above recommended, will cover all outstanding coupons or interest orders falling due in 1875. To raise an amount of money sufficient to pay the above-named amount of deficiencies ($249,303.86) will require a levy of two (2) mills.

It is well known to the General Assembly that I am in favor of a large reduction of the current expenses of the State Government. I believe, on evidence which can be fully exhibited, that the appropriations provided for in the first five sections of the present Act can be reduced by one fourth without the least detriment to the public interests I consider it the duty of the General Assembly to do this ; but while the appropriations remain at their present limit I am in favor of raising money enough by taxation each year to fully meet the appropriations made for that year. Public interests constantly suffer and the public credit is constantly discredited by the practice of making appropriations and increasing expenditures largely in excess of the funds provided to meet them.

Having now considered the first five sections of the Act, together with the fourteenth section, I proceed to state my objections to the sixth section, as it now stands. The proviso of this section seeks to limit the use to be made of the proceeds of the levy therein directed to the payment, first, of the interest accruing during the present fiscal year, and requires the surplus to be expended in the purchase of the consolidated bonds and stocks of the State. My objection to this is that, in my judgment, it works an essential change in the Act of December 22, 1873, called the " Consolidation " Act.

It is clear to me beyond doubt that by that Act the State engages to provide for the interest on all bonds offered for exchange under that Act *from and after July* 1, 1874, and that any use of the proceeds of taxes raised in accordance with that Act which shall prevent the payment in cash of the interest due on and after July 1, 1874, is a violation of good faith and the compact entered into by the State with her public creditors under that Act. In my Annual Message, which will be laid before the General Assembly simultaneously with this Message, I shall present this matter more fully, and I content myself now with recommending that the entire proviso in the sixth section be omitted, leaving all questions connected with the public debt under the Consolidation Act to future legislation. To meet the interest outstanding on consolidation bonds and stocks for July, 1874, I recommend that by the concluding section of the Act these coupons be made receivable for taxes.

If the views now presented should be adopted, the first six sections and the fourteenth section would stand thus :

Section 1. For the salaries, etc., of executive officers, etc. . $1\frac{1}{2}$ mills.
" 2. For penal and charitable institutions, etc. . . . $1\frac{1}{2}$ "
" 3. For public schools . . . . 2 "
" 4. For expenses of General Assembly . . . . . $1\frac{1}{10}$ "
" 5. For public printing . . . . $\frac{2}{5}$ mill.
" 6. For interest on public debt . . . . 2 mills.
" 14. For deficiencies . . . . 2 "

Total . . . . $10\frac{1}{2}$ "

These are all the items in the present Act which make levies for regular annual expenses.

I desire now, most earnestly, to present to your honorable body the mode in which, in my deliberate judgment, the above aggregate of taxation may be largely reduced without in the least degree affecting unfavorably the public interests.

The House of Representatives, at its last session, matured and passed a bill by which a reduction of expenses for salaries is effected of about thirty thousand dollars annually. Deducting this amount from the aggregate amount of the regular appropriations under this head for the last year, the amount is reduced to $168,700.

It will be easy still further to reduce the appropriations to be provided for under this section by $14,000, which will reduce the total amount required under this head to $156,000, which will require a levy of only one and one fourth ($1\frac{1}{4}$) mills, a reduction from the above estimate of one fourth ($\frac{1}{4}$) of a mill.

As an illustration of the perfect compatibility with public interests of large reductions in our former expenditures, I may be permitted to refer to the appropriation made at the last session for the Governor's contingent fund. It is well known that for the past six years previous to the last year this fund has ranged from twenty to thirty thousand dollars annually. At the last session it was reduced by my recommendation to $3,000. This fund has been drawn by me on vouchers, which are now on file in the office of the Comptroller General, and at the end of the last fiscal year there remained an undrawn balance of $247.04. While it would on some accounts have been more agreeable to me to have responded somewhat more liberally to some calls upon this fund, yet I feel now that no public interest has really suffered thereby, while a much needed example of economy and strict accountability has, I trust, been furnished. Similar results will surely attend similar efforts to reduce public expenses under this head.

Passing now to the second section of the Act, the appropriations can readily be reduced to such an amount as to require the levy of not more than one and one fourth ($1\frac{1}{4}$) mills, a reduction of one fourth ($\frac{1}{4}$) of a mill.

In section 4 a large reduction is demanded. The estimate above made, of one and one fourth ($1\frac{1}{4}$) mills, will raise $156,000. The salaries of the members of the General Assembly, being fixed at $600 per annum, will require, together with mileage, an appropriation of $103,000. The other expenses of the General Assembly depend upon the length of the session. I have already shown that the cost of a session of one hundred days will not exceed $137,500. All expenses not otherwise provided for necessary to a session of reasonable length, say of fifty days, can readily be brought within such an amount as not to exceed, in connection with the salaries of members, the sum of $125,000, which will require a levy of but one (1) mill, a reduction of one tenth ($\frac{1}{10}$) of a mill.

In section 5 the levy for public printing should be reduced to one third ($\frac{1}{3}$) of a mill, which would raise about forty-two thousand dollars, a sufficient amount to provide for all necessary printing if the same should be fairly offered to competition. The result of these changes will be as follows :

Section 1.	For salaries, etc., of executive officers, etc.	$1\frac{1}{4}$ mills.
" 2.	Penal and charitable institutions, etc.	$1\frac{1}{4}$ "
" 3.	Public schools	2 "
" 4.	For expenses of General Assembly	1 mill.
" 5.	Public printing	$\frac{1}{3}$ "
" 6.	Interest on public debt	2 mills.
" 14.	Deficiencies	2 "
	Total	$9\frac{5}{8}$ "

I confidently assert that this estimate can be adopted without the smallest sacrifice of the public welfare. If so, no duty can be more imperative than to adopt it. At the present time the people of this State of all conditions of life demand the lowest possible taxes. It is our unquestionable duty to enforce the demand. It should be borne in mind that this estimate covers the entire deficiencies which require to be provided for, and provides for the payment in full of all appropriations necessary to be made. The entire item of deficiencies will, therefore, disappear from the next Supply Act, and thus reduce the entire levy for the next year to seven and five sixths ($7\frac{5}{6}$) mills, a result of more value to the people of the State, and to the political party which shall produce it, than any other result which it is now within our power to accomplish.

If, however, the General Assembly does not reduce the expenditures, I unhesitatingly recommend that the levies be made equal to the appropriations. There is no economy in raising less than is to be appropriated. The habit has already wrought the greatest mischiefs in this State, and should no longer be tolerated.

The remaining sections of the Act, from the seventh to the twelfth inclusive, make levies for objects which may be properly denominated the "floating indebtedness" of the State. With respect to these items generally, I think many of them are of questionable validity, and nearly all of them are the results of great extravagance in the past administration of the State. To press them to payment in one mass and in one year is a hardship which ought not to be imposed upon the State at this time. Without entering at this time into details, I recommend that all these claims now provided for in the sections of the present Act, from the seventh to the twelfth inclusive, be made the suject of a separate Act, and that the payment of these claims be distributed over a term of years, under such other precautions and regulations as may be best adapted to secure justice to the claimants and to the State. This will greatly simplify the Supply Act, as well as reduce the burden of immediate taxation.

In the fifteenth section of the Act I recommend that such changes be made as will impose all requisite duties upon the State Treasurer, without giving to any bank the power to withhold payment of checks drawn in due form by the State officers. The present provisions of this section are utterly unreasonable and impracticable.

The prompt passage of a just, moderate, and well considered Supply Act is demanded by the public interests, and I trust your honorable body will readily and wisely discharge this duty.

                                    D. H. CHAMBERLAIN,
                                                Governor.

By a remarkable conjuncture of influences this veto was unanimously sustained in the Legislature.

The following are examples of the general tone of the comments on these Messages by the newspapers of the State:

The Governor is resolute to carry on the good work of retrenchment and reform which began with his Administration, and his words will be hailed with satisfaction by every lover of honest and equal government, in and out of the State. . . . Nor does the Governor content himself with glittering generalities. Already he is pressing upon the attention of the Legislature facts and figures by which it is shown that the reforms upon which he is bent are as practicable as they are necessary. The public opinion of the whole State, and the whole country, sustains Governor Chamberlain in the noble task to which he has devoted his Administration. And now the men who were chosen as legislators upon the same platform upon which the Governor stands so firmly, will do well to have a care how they break their solemn pledges to stand by him!—*Charleston News and Courier* (Dem.).

The unanimous vote to sustain the Governor's veto of the tax bill of the last session is a gratifying evidence of the influence for good he has with his party, and a singular vindication of the wisdom of those conservative journals of the State which have sustained the Governor in the interest of good government in the face of fierce denunciations heaped upon them by their less conservative and more indiscreet contemporaries. O, that the State had more Chamberlains in this her hour of need—men who, though loyal to party, could rise above its trammels for the good of the whole people ; who could comprehend the situation and elevate the State Government to its requirements ! Let others say what they may, and seek to impress the popular judgment as they can, as for the intelligent, popular sentiment of Abbeville County, without reference to party, the endorsement of Governor Chamberlain is hearty and emphatic. This is our " declaration and testimony," without fear, favor, or affection (unless it be something of the latter), and so we pronounce for our readers.—*Abbeville Medium* (Dem.).

CHAPTER XIII.

THIS session of the Legislature is chiefly memorable for an offence against public honor and safety on the part of the legislative body more flagrant than any other which stained the era of Reconstruction in South Carolina, and perhaps the most alarming legislative action in any Southern State. It was the election of two infamous men as judges, W. J. Whipper for the First (Charleston) Circuit, and ex-Governor F. J. Moses, Jr., for the Third (Sumter) Circuit. Both of these men had been unsuccessful candidates for judicial office at the previous session, Governor Chamberlain actively opposing their pretensions.[1]

There had been much uneasiness and dread respecting the action of the Legislature in this matter, and in his Annual Message the Governor referred to the duty to be performed in these pointed words:

"At the present session elections of Judges of the Court of Common Pleas and of the Supreme Court will take place. It cannot be deemed improper for me to present to the General Assembly the paramount importance of a wise discharge of this duty. The ancient fame

---

[1] Chapter IV., pp. 38 *et seq.*

of South Carolina in this respect should be kept strictly in mind. The standard of character and attainments once universally observed in this State should never be lowered. Legal learning, a judicial spirit, and a high, and unblemished personal character should mark every man who shall be elected to sit in the seats of Harper and Dunkin, of O'Neall and Wardlaw. If all these qualities are not attainable, *let the one quality of personal integrity never be lost sight of.* That community may well be pitied which is doomed to submit its great interests to the decision of one whose judgments will reflect his own passions and interests."

On the 16th of December, 1875, as already recorded, the Governor went to Greenville to deliver an address upon the occasion of the awarding of the Whitsitt Prizes for excellence in Greek. His engagement for this day had been publicly known for several weeks. During this absence from Columbia of but one day, a conspiracy, secretly matured among the members of the Legislature, was developed in the election of the Circuit Judges, including Whipper and Moses. Whipper was chosen by 83 votes to 58 for all others; and Moses by 75 votes to 63 for all others. There can be no doubt that this date was selected in order that the Governor might not be at hand to interfere with the success of the plot. His immediate presence and influence might have thwarted the conspirators, as signally as during the previous session. By this action of the Legislature the whole State was stunned. Seldom has any community in modern times received such a shock. It was a moral earthquake by which the citadel of justice was violently shaken and left tottering. Demoralization appeared triumphant. But their was one man who did not quail or despair. Upon his firmness and courage all good citizens depended for their rescue. He promptly girded himself for the desperate struggle thus suddenly forced upon him, and the record shows with what spirit, tact, and might he opposed the consummation of the wrong and saved the altars of justice from profanation.

The evil deed was accomplished on a Thursday, which was straightway designated " Black Thursday," and is so known in South Carolina to this day. Governor Chamberlain's first public utterance regarding the situation was made on the Sunday following and published the next morning. It was in the form of an interview with the editor of the *News and Courier,* and is thus reported :

COLUMBIA, Sunday, December 19th.—Upon my arrival here to-day I sought an interview with Governor Chamberlain, and now give you an exact report of what passed.

Question.—Of course you are aware, Governor, of the result of the judicial election. Did you expect that election to take place on Thursday last?

Answer.—I did not, and I had the best reasons for not expecting it. On Tuesday, when the Senate passed the concurrent resolution to hold the election on Thursday, I spoke to both my Republican and Conservative friends, telling them that I had a very important engagement in Greenville on the evening of Thursday, which I was the more anxious to keep because it involved the convenience and interest of so many others. I stated that, if the election was to take place on Thursday, I must and should remain here ; but I earnestly appealed to them not to allow the election then to occur and thus disappoint my friends in Greenville. I also addressed a personal note to Mr. Speaker Elliott, in which I requested him, on personal as well as public grounds, to use his influence to stay the election, not only from occurring on Thursday, but to stay it until next week or after the holidays. In answer to this note, Speaker Elliott came to my office on Wednesday morning and said he regretted that he had not thought of my engagement in Greenville before he was asked to favor concurrence in the Senate resolution. However, he said, while he might vote for concurrence, owing to his previous committal, yet he would speak to his friends, and he thought there would be no difficulty in postponing the election until after my return from Greenville at the earliest. I accepted this assurance of the Speaker and the vote of the House, which was 72 to 31 on the motion to lay the Senate resolution on the table, as a sufficient guaranty, and left for Greenville on the morning of Thursday, without the slightest suspicion that the election would be brought on. It is true that I was told just before the train left that there was a bare possibility that the election might come off that day ; but it was deemed certain that the resolution could at least be fought off until Friday, and I contented myself with making arrangements for a special train to bring me back to Columbia by Friday morning if necessary. If I had really suspected the conspiracy which was developed on Thursday, nothing in the world could have induced me to leave Columbia.

Question.—Had you been present when the election took place, could you have changed the result?

Answer.—I see no reason to think I could. The conspiracy appears to have been carefully concocted. The color line, the party line, and the line of antagonism to my Administration, all were sharply drawn ; and the tone of the speeches made by the leading supporters of Whipper and Moses and Wiggins shows that it required a degree of boldness not possessed by many of our legislators to vote in opposition to the combination. Still it would have been a great satisfaction to me to have been on the spot and gone down fighting, if I must go down.

Question.—Was it not as a combination of the supporters of different candidates that the conspiracy of which you have spoken was so powerful ?

Answer.—Yes. The peculiar strength of the combination lay in uniting the interests of a large number of the candidates. This alone, I think, caused the defeat of Judge Maher. The opponents of this judge had a certain number of votes which they would cast for other candidates in other circuits only on condition that the friends of those candidates should pay them by voting against Maher. Mr. Wiggins, the successful candidate, had no strength, and was a mere leaf on the current ; but the combination that took him up was welded together by the force of a common purpose to rout an incorruptible judge who had been an insurmountable barrier in the way of those who have at last overthrown him.

Question.—How do you look upon the election of Wiggins, Whipper, and Moses?

Answer.—I look upon their election as a horrible disaster—a disaster equally great to the State and to the Republican party, and, greatest of all, to those communities which shall be doomed to feel the full effects of the presence of Moses and Whipper upon the bench. I did, a year ago, speak publicly of Whipper, who was then a candidate for the very position to which he has now been elected. Then I denounced him as incapable and utterly unfit for the office of judge. Of Moses, no honest men can have different opinions. Neither Whipper nor Moses has any qualities which approach to a qualification for judicial positions. The reputation of Moses is covered deep with charges, which are believed by all who are familiar with the facts, of corruption, bribery, and the utter prostitution of all his official powers to the worst possible purposes. *This calamity is infinitely greater, in my judgment, than any which has yet fallen on this State, or, I might add, upon any part of the South.* Moses as Governor is endurable compared with Moses as Judge.

Question.—What do you think of Wiggins ?

Answer.—He is not to be classed morally with Moses and Whipper ; but, in order to defeat Judge Maher, he has consented to be the tool of the same combination which elected Moses and Whipper, and, as such tool, he will be expected to, and doubtless will, do their work.

Question.—What, in your judgment, will be the effect of the election of these three men ?

Answer.—The gravest consequences of all kinds will follow. One immediate effect will obviously be the reorganization of the Democratic party within the State, as the only means left, in the judgment of its members, for opposing a solid and reliable front to this terrible crevasse of misgovernment and public debauchery. I could have wished, as a Republican, to have kept off such an issue ; but I have a profound belief in the logic of events, and a Providence, too, that shapes events ; and I do not allow myself to think that the good and honest men of South Carolina will find it impossible, because they are organized as Democrats, to give their help to whomsoever shall be best able to undo the terrible wrongs of last Thursday. I am free to say that my highest ambition as Governor has been to make the ascendancy of the Republican party in South Carolina compatible with the attainment and maintenance of as high and pure a tone in the administration of public affairs as can be exhibited in the proudest Democratic State of the South ; and it was also my fondest hope, by peaceful agencies, here in South Carolina, alone of all the Southern States, to have worked out, through the Republican party, the solution of the most difficult and one of the most interesting political and social problems which this century has presented. If these results shall not be reached, the responsibility for the failure will not rest upon me, nor upon the Conservative citizens of South Carolina, who have hitherto, with unvarying fidelity and generosity, stood by me in my work ; but upon those, and all like them, who dealt the cause of good government so deadly a blow on Thursday.[1]

Question.—Has your attention been called to the question of the right of the present Legislature to elect judges, where the incumbents had been elected to serve for unexpired terms ?

Answer.—Yes. I have read the discussions of this question in the newspapers, and have listened to the views of several members of the bar of the State ; but I cannot say that I have maturely studied the question. It is evidently a fair and open question, and involves most important consequences. If the judges who have, previous to the present session, been elected nominally to fill unexpired terms, are entitled under the Constitution to hold for a full term of four years, then it follows that this General Assembly had no right to elect their successors. This question covers the cases of Whipper, Moses, Judge Carpenter, and Judge Cooke ; but you will remember that both Judges Carpenter and Cooke are their own successors.

This ended the interview. F. W. D.

The hint is given at the conclusion of the interview, that there might be ground for declaring the election of Whipper and Moses illegal. The press had already raised the point; but the Governor was unprepared to give an opinion before making a thorough examination. This was accomplished with his habitual energy and promptness, and two days later his conclusion and decision were made known. The commissions of Judges Mackey and Northrop, elected at the same time, were signed on Saturday, before the conversation with the editor of the *News and Courier*. On the Monday following, the commissions of the six other judges elected were presented for his signature. Four of them were signed, but those of Whipper and Moses were not signed, and he placed on file and caused to be published the following

[1] The quotation on the title-page is from this paragraph.

statement of the grounds of his refusal to issue their commissions:

EXECUTIVE CHAMBER,
COLUMBIA, S. C., December 21, 1875.

I decline to sign the commissions of W. J. Whipper and F. J. Moses, Jr., elected as Judges of the Circuit Court of this State by the General Assembly, on the 16th inst., for terms to begin on the 26th day of August, 1876.

By the Constitution of the State the Judges of the Circuit Court are to be elected for terms of four years. By a series of adjudicated cases in the highest court of this State, extending from 1821 to 1872, it has, in my judgment, been determined that officers elected under provisions of law similar to this provision of the present Constitution are entitled to hold the offices for the full term prescribed by the Constitution or laws under which the election is held.

It follows that, as the terms of the present incumbents of the offices to which the above-named persons claim to have been elected on the 16th instant will not expire until after another general election of members of the General Assembly, the present General Assembly has not the right to elect their successors.

While in some cases, presenting similar legal questions, it might not be required of the Governor to decline to issue commissions, the circumstances of the present case compel me to this course.

D. H. CHAMBERLAIN,
Governor.

It has been often represented, and perhaps is generally believed, that this action of the Governor was a quibble, a makeshift without substantial foundation, which was seized upon merely as a pretext for keeping these two men off the bench. But the Governor's statement claims warrant for his action in a series of adjudicated cases in the highest court of the State extending over fifty years. If his judgment was sound, not he in refusing to issue the commissions, but the Legislature in its haste to elect judges, had transgressed the law and usurped authority. Afterwards this question, as presented in these cases, was again submitted to the courts of the State, and was decided in accordance with Governor Chamberlain's position, vindicating the rightfulness of his action.[1]

To exaggerate the sensation produced in the ranks of the conspirators by this course of the Governor, would be impossible. Their triumph was turned to ashes. All the hatred they had

[1] South Carolina Reports, vol. 9, p. 5.

nursed against him vented itself without measure or restraint. They threatened dire vengeance. The Legislature having suddenly undone, in great part, the work of pacification which his Administration so far had happily advanced, the prejudices and animosities of the white race toward the colored race as rulers were instantly revived in full vigor. The whole State boiled like a caldron, and in all parts of the Union there was an engrossing interest in this new phase of South Carolina affairs.

When Whipper was chosen, R. B. Elliott, Speaker of the House of Representatives, a colored carpet-bagger from Massachusetts, an ex-member of Congress, a person of considerable education, superior oratorical power, and unsurpassed influence as a politician among his people, seconded the nomination and declared that he should regard the vote on it as a test of fidelity to the Republican party. It was not strange, therefore, that the action of the Governor was followed by the denunciation of him by these men as a traitor to his party. They were outspoken in the assertion of their purpose to succeed in spite of him. Whipper declared that when the time came he should take the seat of Judge Reed and no power should prevent him. The impeachment of the Governor was strongly urged, and there is no doubt that it would have been attempted but for quailing before the storm of hostile sentiment. It was threatened to force the retirement of the judges in office by stopping their salaries; there was even wilder talk, which might have had serious results if the baffled conspirators had not felt assured of ultimate victory in the courts because the father of ex-Governor Moses was Chief-Justice of the State and might be expected to come to the rescue of his son.

While the Governor was thus scoffed at and repudiated by the majority of his own party in the State, he was strengthened and cheered by a great uprising in his behalf of citizens who appreciated the fundamental nature of the issue between virtue and vice which had been raised. The *News and Courier* spoke the general sentiment of gratitude in Charleston, saying:

Think, for a moment, of the complexion given to the election of Moses and Whipper by that refusal to sign their commissions, which has been read with grateful satisfaction, this morning, in every State of the Union! It is no longer possible to say that these two persons are stigmatized because of their politics or class; it is no longer possible to declare that the opposition to them is only the expression of Democratic hatred of every thing that is done by Republicans. Governor Chamberlain is a New Englander, a soldier of the Union, a Republican from his youth up. Upon his loyalty to the Union and the Republican cause there is no stain. President Grant declares him to be the best Governor in the South. And this Republican of the strictest sect, this Massachusetts Governor of South Carolina, is compelled to cast away from him this Whipper and this Moses as things so infamous and unclean that they cannot, and must not, stand before the American people as having any recognition whatsoever, save that which is found in their election by persons of their own character and calling. This will make the horrid story of Black Thursday plain to every American citizen. By the first bold blow the fight is half won !

Governor Chamberlain has done for the people of South Carolina what no other living man could have done. Great was his opportunity, and splendid is the use he has made of it. To him, thanks eternal for interposing the shield of the Executive authority between the chieftains of the robber band in Columbia and the people of the low country of South Carolina. But there is work now for the good people of South Carolina to do. Governor Chamberlain must be sustained, and promptly, in what he has done. It must be made manifest, and quickly, that the heart of South Carolina is touched and her brain convinced. Governor Chamberlain must be assured that what he has begun the people will finish. And this assurance can only be given by mass-meetings in every county in the State. Let Charleston begin the work ! To-morrow night, at latest, there should be an outpouring of the people of Charleston in vindication and approval of the conduct of Governor Chamberlain, and to express the unfaltering and immovable determination that the men whom the General Assembly had the audacity to elect, and whom a Republican Governor has refused to commission, shall never administer so-called justice in the courts of South Carolina.

Upon further consideration the proposed mass-meeting was postponed until Monday, the 27th of December, " in order that no undue haste should lessen its completeness and imposing character "; but the following despatch was forwarded to the Governor :

CHARLESTON, S. C., December 22d.

To His Excellency Governor Chamberlain, Columbia, S. C.:

Irrespective of parties, desiring peace and protection for persons and property, believing that a blow has been struck in the late judicial election, threatening ruin to the people of the State, we tender you, for this community and the State, our thanks for your action in refusing to sign the commissions. We thank you, and will do all we can to sustain you in what you have done.

ANDREW SIMONDS, President First National Bank.
E. H. FROST, President South Carolina Loan and Trust Company.
GEORGE E. GIBBON, President People's Bank of South Carolina.
CHARLES O. WITTE, President People's National Bank.
A. S. JOHNSTON, President Bank of Charleston.
L. D. MOWRY, President Union Bank of South Carolina.

Wm. C. Bee & Co.,
W. B. Smith & Co.,
Crane, Boylston, & Co.,
George W. Williams & Co.,
Geo. A. Trenholm & Son,
James Adger & Co.,
S. Y. Tupper, President Charleston Chamber of Commerce.

To this approbation the Governor made the following response :

Columbia, S. C., December 22d.

I thank you for your despatch. The issue rises higher than party, and I shall not fail of the full measure of my duty if I know what it is.

D. H. CHAMBERLAIN,
Governor.

The 22d of December was " Forefathers' Day," and it was celebrated in Charleston, as usual, by a banquet of the New England Society, to which the Governor had been invited. He was not present, but he sent a despatch which made a profound impression not only upon those to whom it was addressed, but upon the whole country, chiefly because its intense and kindling eloquence had been anticipated by deeds that heightened the value of every appropriate word. The following account of the reading of the despatch is taken from the *News and Courier's* report of the proceedings. The presiding officer who proposed the sentiment, in response to which the telegram was read, was Hon. James B. Campbell, a native of Oxford, Mass., but an old and venerated citizen of South Carolina.

" The State of South Carolina "—and I would take leave to add—" for better, for worse,—God bless her.!" [Tremendous applause.] Governor Chamberlain had been invited to respond, but public duties had prevented him. He (Mr. Campbell) was not going to answer for him ; he should be proud if he had the ability, the accomplishments, and, what ought to be valued even more highly than these, the pluck to answer for him. But he held in his hand a despatch in which Governor Chamberlain spoke for himself, and he was sure, when they heard his words, that every son of the *Mayflower* would be proud to feel that it was a son of New England who was presiding over the destinies of South Carolina. [Great applause.]

Mr. Campbell then read the Governor's telegram, as follows :

Columbia, S. C., December 22, 1875.

To the New England Society, care of Wm. S. Hastie, Jr., Charleston, S. C.:

I cannot attend your annual supper to-night ; but if there ever was an hour when the spirit of the Puritans, the spirit of undying, unconquerable enmity and defiance to wrong ought to animate their sons, it is this hour, here, in South Carolina.

The civilization of the Puritan and the Cavalier, of the Roundhead and the Huguenot, is in peril. Courage, Determination, Union, Victory, must be our watchwords. The grim Puritans never quailed under threat or blow. Let their sons now imitate their example!

God bless the New England Society!

D. H. CHAMBERLAIN.

The Governor's words were listened to with intense interest, and at the close of the reading there was a tremendous outburst of applause, lasting several minutes. The band played " Hail to the Chief ! "

The meeting held in Charleston on the following Monday (December 27th) was the first of numerous popular demonstrations held in most of the counties of the State. They were in their character and incidents significant of two thing which it is important to keep in mind : (1) the general confidence of the more intelligent citizens in Governor Chamberlain's fidelity to high ideals of government; and (2) the strong conviction of the same class that the majority of the Republican party, being obedient to corrupt leaders, could not be trusted to support him, and must be overcome and made impotent in public affairs. The following account of the Charleston meeting is abridged from the report in the *News and Courier.*

The Hibernian Hall was thronged last night with the white citizens of Charleston, who had assembled together to protest against the election of Whipper and Moses to the circuit bench, and to give expression to their hearty approval of the wise and patriotic conduct of Governor Chamberlain. It was the largest and most influential meeting of white citizens that has been held in Charleston these ten years. A marked feature of the meeting was the enthusiasm with which the declarations of the determination and power of the good citizens to redeem the State was received ; and the vociferous applause with which every word was hailed that pointed to a sustaining of Governor Chamberlain, to an exclusion, at any cost, of Whipper and Moses from the bench, and to the maintenance of the rights and privileges of the colored citizens under the law and the Constitution. The meeting was called to order by Colonel B. H. Rutledge, who said :

Fellow-citizens :—We are in the midst of a great crisis in our affairs. We have the safety of our property and our liberties, and, it may be, our lives, at stake. A blow has been aimed directly at the very centre of our civilization. Our honor has been trampled into the very dust. [Cheers.] Under these circumstances it becomes us to consult together, and, further, to promulgate the result of our deliberations calmly, seriously, earnestly, resolutely. It is for this purpose that we are met here to-night, and it is proposed that this meeting do organize immediately, without further preliminaries, under the following officers, taken from among the most respectable, the most influential and the most responsible of our fellow-citizens :

PRESIDENT—G. W. Williams.

VICE-PRESIDENTS.—C. T. Lowndes, W. D. Porter, Robert Adger, S. Y. Tupper, A. R. Taft, E. H. Frost, William Lebby, R. Tomlinson, John F. O'Neill, H. A. Middleton, A. B. Bose, B. Bollman, Thomas Miller, C. Irvine Walker, Hugh Ferguson, H. T. Williams, H. Bullwinkle, Wm. Bell Smith, Andrew Simonds, C. O. Witte, A. S. Johnston, L. D. Mowry, H. Gourdin, Alva Gage, W. C. Bee, Jacob Small, J. B. Bissell, J. M. Eason, F. J. Pelzer, J. L. Tobias, C. G. Ducker, J. J. Wescoat, D. A. Amme, Alex. McLoy, Louis Cohen, W. G. Whilden, W. W. Sale.

SECRETARIES.—G. D. Bryan, J. Ancrum Simons, A. C. Kaufman.

REMARKS OF MR. WILLIAMS.

Fellow-citizens :—While thanking my friends for the compliment in calling me to preside over this meeting, I would greatly prefer to see one of more experience in my place. I feel, however, that in a crisis like this, every citizen must do his duty. The objects of the meeting have my cordial sympathy. I hope an expression of approval from the good citizens of Charleston will go forth to-night, that will strengthen Governor Chamberlain in his manly and patriotic efforts for reform and for the preservation of law and order. At this trying peroid, caution must be united with firmness, to preserve the peace, honor, and integrity of our State.

It requires Roman firmness in Governor Chamberlain to stand, as he does, like a granite wall between an oppressed people and those who seek by foul means to rob them of their lives, liberties, and homes. For his fidelity and devotion, let a united voice go from the seaboard to the mountain top : " Well done, good and faithful servant."

REMARKS OF GEN. JAMES CONNER.

I had hoped never again to make a political speech. It is foreign to my disposition and pursuits ; but there are occasions when private inclination must yield to public duty, when every citizen must consider the State first and himself last ; and this, in my judgment, is such an occasion. [Cheers.] We are brought, by recent events, face to face with great issues. I am old enough to remember many eventful periods in the history of this State ; but I can recall not one more momentous than the present. [Cheers.]

The question is not, how you can live here, but *whether you can live here at all.* [Applause.] You have either to redeem the State or quit it. You must make a good government, or they will make a Hayti. For one I claim a heritage in the State, and I will not be driven from it. [Tremendous cheering.] Since 1868 the Republican party has ruled the State. No such government has ever before shocked the civilized world. No people have ever endured so much so patiently and so long. We have never even organized for resistance. We have sought relief through conciliation and compromise ; and I do not condemn it. I say it was well ; for had it not been tried, there are those who would have claimed that it was the true remedy and the sole panacea for all our ills. We have tried it, and have demonstrated by failure its utter inefficiency. [Loud cheering.]

When Governor Chamberlain stumped the State in his canvass for Governor, he pledged himself to Reform, and to lift from the Republican party of the nation and the State the odium and reproach of South Carolina politics. His party cheered him to the echo, and held him forth as their champion, and his speech as the expression of the will of the party to purify itself. But no sooner does he attempt to maintain his pledged faith and lift his party from the slough of corruption, than they repudiate his councils, defeat his plans, and crown their infamy by inflicting upon the people of this State a degradation greater than ever yet imposed. [Loud applause.] The election of Moses and Whipper was the legislative answer to his effort to reform the party from within.

All that stands now between us and the degradation of the bench is the wise and bold action of the Governor. He stands erect, bearing the wrath of his own party, to maintain unbroken his pledge of reform. As he is true to his duty, let us be true to ours and stand firmly and unitedly by him in support of the right. It is the path of duty ; it is the path of wisdom and of safety. [Loud cheers.]

There are two courses open : Abject submission to this and the worse yet to come, or a firm, determined resistance. [Cheers.] I would not be here to-night if I had not faith and hope in the future. [Loud cheers.] Just so strong as is my conviction of the moral government of the world, of the sure triumph of wisdom, truth, and right over ignorance, falsehood, and wrong, just so deep and settled is my conviction that the State can be saved. [Wild cheering.] But it cannot be saved by resolutions, by popular applause or popular assemblies. It can be saved only as every great and good thing is accomplished, by *work*—hard, earnest, persistent work ; work into which the whole heart and manhood are infused, work despite all obstacles and over obstacles, work that means to win and will not be defeated. [Tremendous cheering.] There must be organization, thorough, complete, over the whole State, to sweep from power those who have betrayed the trust which was confided to them. Every man, young and old, from the mountains to the seaboard, must be organized, ready and willing to meet every issue as it may arise, and to hold the next election as the paramount duty of the hour, that to which every interest must be subordinate, and every difference of opinion sacrificed. [Cheers.] Secure the election, and the rest will follow ! [Cheers.] Permit me now to submit, for your consideration, the following address and resolutions, which express, we believe, the feelings and the determination of this community :

THE ADDRESS.

We have assembled to confer upon a condition of affairs as grave as ever imperilled the peace and well-being of any community.

The foundation of society is a pure Judiciary, and its corruption, or perversion to evil purposes, destroys the last hope of securing to a people protection and liberty.

The action of the Legislature in electing, as judges, W. J. Whipper and F. J. Moses, Jr., men whose proper places in a courthouse is the criminal's dock, is an insult to every honest citizen and a violation of every safeguard which the law affords to life, liberty, and property.

But this action is not in itself the full measure of the evil that confronts us. Bad as it is, its graver aspect is in what it signifies.

We recognize in the recent judicial elections the ascendancy and control of the worst elements of the political party which governs the State. Actuated by a relentless hate based upon race, and stimulated by the prospect of "plunder and revenge," they have repudiated all restraint, and inaugurated a policy which inevitably leads to the destruction of decent government, ruins the material interests of the State, and imperils our very civilization. Under such a condition of things, Law ceases to protect, and Government itself becomes the oppressor.

What shall we do to avert the destruction which must surely result from the consummation of the policy thus inaugurated ?

Since 1868 the Conservative citizens of this State have put aside party obligations and the hopes of party ascendancy ; have put no party ticket in the field, but have sought and hoped for peace, stability, and pure government through the Republican party. They have striven not to antagonize, but to harmonize, conflicting races, interests, and opinions, patiently waiting to obtain, as the fruits of their forbearance, the blessings of good government.

In every form in which the effort could be made it has been tried, and when, through the wise, firm, and patriotic Administration of Governor Chamberlain, the end seemed about to be obtained, a Republican Legislature repudiates the honest efforts of a Republican Governor, impatiently resents his control, and with a recklessness born of ignorance and hate, commits the State to a career destructive of its peace and fatal to its prosperity. The failure to obtain relief through the agency of the Republican party of the State is utter and hopeless.

The responsibilities and obligations imposed upon us in this emergency must be fearlessly met.

It is our first duty as citizens, to whom the character and future of the State is dear, earnestly and solemnly to protest against the action of those who have not only brought reproach upon their own party, but have endangered the very foundations of our social fabric, and to use every means to wrest from them the power which they have so wantonly abused.

We deprecate all appeal to passion and prejudice, but it behooves us to speak plainly. The attempt to place infamy and corruption in the seat of Justice violates the primal instincts of civilized humanity, and to that we will not submit. The right to justice and good government is one which we dare not relinqnish.

With no hostility to the colored people of the State, mindful of the good conduct of those who have not been misled by evil counsels, we are determined to preserve to them every right and privilege guaranteed by the Constitution and laws of the country ; but the avowed purpose that there shall not be equality, but a domination of their race over the property and rights of the white people of the State, will be resisted to the last, and under no circumstances shall it prevail.

We appeal to the honest and intelligent portion of them, who bear their share of the political shame, but share no part of the political plunder, while there is yet time, to turn away from the evil counsels which are leading them to a contest which must end in their utter ruin.

We raise no political issue. "The issue rises higher than party," and seeks the end for which parties are organized.

We recognize the earnestness and fidelity with which a portion of the Republican party, under the leadership of Governor Chamberlain, has striven to establish a government which should respect the rights and protect the interests of all the people of the State. But they have failed. The worst elements of their party have defeated them. With confidence in their sincerity, we ask them to continue their efforts, and without the abandonment of political principles to aid us in the attainment of a common end, the establishment of pure and honest government. Be it therefore—

Resolved, That as citizens of this State we protest against the action of the General Assembly in electing, as judges, men so notoriously corrupt as W. J. Whipper and F. J. Moses, Jr., and avow our determination to resist it to the end.

2. That we protest against the continuance in office of legislators so regardless of duty and so reckless of the character, the peace, and the prosperity of the State, and we will use every effort to drive them from power.

3. That we cordially endorse the action of Governor Chamberlain in refusing to issue commissions as judges to W. J. Whipper and F. J. Moses, and pledge to him the full support of this community in his efforts to secure to the people of the State a faithful administration of the law.

4. That we tender to Governor Chamberlain our grateful thanks for the bold and statesmanlike struggle he has made in the cause of reform, in the economical administration of the government, in the preservation of the public faith, in the equal administration of justice, and in the maintenance of the public peace, and we pledge him our cordial support for the accomplishment of these ends.

REMARKS OF COL. B. C. PRESSLEY

Mr. President and Fellow-citizens :—We have occasion to learn now, as often before, the important lesson that the simplest and most natural method of accomplishing a laudable purpose is at last the easiest, the best, and by far the most effectual. In our greatest straits, our sore extremities, we are tempted to rush into desperate measures ; but, postponing that action, somehow, from a source unlooked for, a relief effectual and beneficial has come to us, and thus our cause has been saved, and we feel grateful that we have not been led to do that which might bring us in condemnation by our fellow-citizens. Such is one of the sore extremities through which we have lately seemed to pass, but are still passing. The partisans had laid well their plans for our final submission and subjugation. The conspirators had joined hand and hand ; the robbers had almost within their clutches the Treasury of the State ; and not only that, but the right and title to the property of every citizen within the State.

Now let us consider well the emergency in which we are placed. Remember, the Sinking Fund had already gone—gone, no one knows where, except, perhaps, the would-be judge, Whipper. The State by millions had been plunged into debt. Taxation upon taxation had been endured, until the people could not endure it longer. What was left for the plunderers, except that they should get possession of the bench, and by orders mandamuses, ejectments, etc., force the property from the people for division among themselves, so that you and I should be compelled to pay for justice on the bench or have injustice forced upon us. Well, indeed, did the robbers have their plans laid. Their forces were organized, drilled, and brought to battle, and the cry of victory had rung out in the halls of the Legislature. But not so ! They gloated over the visions of coming wealth, and with these bright images floating through their brains, they went to sleep. But before their dreams could be realized, before they could take possession of our property, they must get the deed signed and sealed. Just in the same way it was necessary that a signature should be put to the commissions of these robbers. They awakened in the morning to find their dream fade away, as the stars fade before the rising sun.

Sometimes, fellow-citizens, there are official acts done simply under the impulse of conscientious duty, done in a natural way, which burst upon us with all the blaze and glory and surprising power of a sudden successful revolution! Such a revolution did Governor Chamberlain achieve when he refused his signature to the commissions of these two judges. [Applause.] It was like one of those revelations of genius which disclose to us natural laws which, when put into operation, accomplish results which experienced minds had pronounced impossible. Thus men of intellect toil and climb, year by year, and one round after another, up the ladder to fame. They rise higher and higher until they come to that point which the world calls eminence. But genius united with will steps in, and rises at once, by its buoyancy, and mounts at once to the place where the great Webster says: "There's room enough. No crowding there." To such an eminence did Governor Chamberlain raise himself in a single night. [Applause.]

What would we have done if he had not acted for us? As I said, the plans of the conspirators were well laid, and had these commissions been signed, who among us could have considered life or property, or any thing he holds near and dear, safe and sacred? What reason had we to hope for redress from the Supreme Court? Governor Moses, the son of the Chief-Justice, used all his efforts to be elected. Can any of us doubt that the opinion of his father was, in some way, known to him, and that he had been satisfied, beforehand, that a decision would be rendered by the Supreme Court sustaining the ground that the terms of Judges Reed and Shaw had expired? Is it reasonable to suppose that Moses would have made the efforts he did unless he knew the opinion of his father on the subject? Wright (the colored associate justice), however disposed he may be to do right, could not have stood up against the issues of race which had been thrust upon him by the Legislature. Then, so far as the Supreme Court is concerned, we may regard it as settled that, if the question had gone before them, these commissions would have been sustained. Where was our hope? South Carolina has always been averse to Lynch law. The voice of our people is against it. But I will not undertake to say, in our sore necessity, what we would have done, when it came to the alternative of *no* law or *Lynch* law—between law administered by a corrupt judge, and law administered by an irregular jury drawn in the night-time. [Applause and cheering.] However we may have answered that question, and to whatever extremity we may be reduced in the future, does it not rejoice our hearts to know that we have been relieved, at least for the present, from the solution of that question, and that it is due to Governor Chamberlain? [Applause.]

And now we have come here to sustain him, and if we are to pledge to him our support, it is important for us to consider whether he be right, and whether it will be right to sustain him. After a very careful investigation of this question, as a legal question, and that before his decision was known, or before it was even known that he had it in contemplation, I and other members of the bar, after careful study of the matter, came to the conclusion that, without the shadow of a doubt, before any fair legal tribunal, Judges Shaw and Reed would be declared lawfully elected for a term of four years, and no Legislature had the power and the right to fill their places at this time. I say, fellow-citizens, that upon this point I have not the shadow of a doubt, nor do I know a single lawyer who has investigated the matter thoroughly who has not formed the same opinion. And if the Legislature, in searching for plunder, attempted to place others in the places of Judges Reed and Shaw, it was the duty of the Governor—it was his constitutional duty—to refuse them their commissions. Is the Governor the judge to determine whether the Legislature has done right or wrong? No; but he is the judge to determine his own duties. The two departments are separate, and, as it is the duty of the Governor to commission all officers duly elected, so it is his duty to refuse to commission these two officers whose places are already filled. He is to see that the laws are faithfully executed. So, in this case, when he is called upon to eject from office two judges whom he has already commissioned, he boldly and nobly refuses. [Applause and loud cheering.]

If the Supreme Court should decide that the elections were valid, would not that same court be apt to grant a mandamus against the Governor, and compel him to issue the commissions? Did you ever hear of such a thing before? Would any thing like that be talked of in a State where law was recognized? Who ever heard of mandamusing a Governor? Are not the Executive and the Judicial departments distinct? Or if the Supreme Court can travel out of its jurisdiction to grant mandamuses against anybody, why don't it mandamus the Legislature of the State? Is it not known that the Constitution of South Carolina expressly requires that the Legislature shall provide for the registration of voters? It is, in plain terms. Has the Legislature done it? No! Well, then, why don't the Supreme Court mandamus it? Why, simply because it is none of its business. If the Governor does an act, the Supreme Court can pass upon its legality; but no Legislature nor Supreme Court can mandamus him to do an act. So the action of the Governor is *a final checkmate*, in my opinion. [Cheers.] The only resort which this corrupt majority can have is by impeachment. Well, what will be the result of such action? Well, sufficient unto the day is the evil thereof. If Gen. Grant, the President of the United States, thinks that Governor Chamberlain ought to be impeached, then, if he will erect the United States flag over the Statehouse, and station his soldiery outside while that impeachment is going on, then it may be safely done. We never intend to fight against the United States again. [Cheers.] But if this Legislature, without that United States flag floating over them, attempt to impeach the Governor—Well! *I would n't like to be the insurance agent that held policies on their lives.* [Immense applause.]

I tell you that we have drunk the last drop of the bitter cup of that sort that we intend to drink, unless the United States army says so. I thought we had taken enough already before Whipper and Moses were elected to be our judges. So, fellow-citizens, Governor Chamberlain may go to sleep and sleep soundly, and wake up gloriously; for they don't dare to touch a hair of his head, because the people are awake, and they 're not going to sleep again. [Applause.] *The time has come for action !* There must be no mental reservations, when we say we will stand by Governor Chamberlain. We mean it as our fathers meant it when they pledged their lives, their fortunes, and their sacred honor; and I see by your responses and in your faces that this is what you all mean by it. Stand up for your civilization, your property, your lives, and your honor. [Prolonged applause.]

The adoption of the preamble and resolutions was seconded by Mr. J. Adger Smythe, who made an earnest speech in the same strain. Major Rudolph Siegling concluded a vigorous address, setting forth the magnitude of the peril of a corrupt judiciary and the necessity of " uniting all the elements of popu-

lar honesty and all the forces of self-preservation " for the
redemption of the State, with these words :

> Let ours, fellow-citizens, be the duty not only to resolve upon, but to effect this
> redemption. [Cheers.] It may be that in the discharge of that duty we shall have
> to pass through a dark valley overcast with lowering clouds. But in the vista there
> is a silver streak, in the person of the Chief Magistrate of South Carolina. In the
> position which Governor Chamberlain has assumed he has entitled himself not only to
> the support and gratitude of every honest citizen of whatever party, but has performed
> an act of statesmanship and of moral courage which has but few parallels in the his-
> tory of popular government. As it has been forcibly said elsewhere, he has made a
> manly effort to[ward] the improvement of the State by strictly confining himself to his
> legitimate duties, by leaving capital to find its most lucrative course, commodities
> their fair price, industry and intelligence their natural reward, idleness and folly their
> natural punishment, by maintaining peace, by defending property, by diminishing the
> price of law, and by observing strict economy in every department of the State.
> This has been the aim of his Administration. Let the virtuous citizens of the State
> organize and earnestly co-operate with him, and redemption will surely follow.
> [Applause.]

Major Theodore G. Barker said:

> I see no necessity that there should be a conflict of races. [Cheers.] The times
> are much changed since 1868 and 1870. The colored people have learned the lesson
> that the United States Government will not deprive the white people of this or any
> other State of any right or privilege guaranteed to them by the Constitution. That
> Constitution secures to us the right to bear arms, and until it is revoked we will
> bear arms in spite of them. [Loud cheers.] It is our right! But let no excitement
> precipitate you into any conflict with that race, the majority of whom are not, in full
> measure, responsible for this condition of things. In the next canvass I expect to
> see the white property-holders and the black, the white laborers and the black, the
> white mechanics and the black, united as never before, from the mountains to the sea-
> board, in one firm effort to rescue civilization from a corrupt Legislature. I have not
> thought out the contingencies of the programme. If these men (Whipper and Moses),
> who are mockeries of their race [cheers], should attempt to take their places on the
> bench, I expect to see a united and concerted effort to rescue power, at the ballot-
> box, from those who now hold and abuse it. I urge on those who have, and those
> who hope to have, property the necessity of contributing to that end. Secure that
> election, and we have the means of sustaining Governor Chamberlain, or any suc-
> cessor who may guarantee reform. The power of taxation, the power of legislation
> will then be ours, and these will relieve us, now and hereafter, from the dangers to
> which we are now exposed. [Loud cheers.]

The preamble and resolutions were adopted without a single
dissenting voice, as was the following resolution offered by Mr.
C. Richardson Miles :

> *Resolved*, That the chairman forward a copy of the preamble and resolutions just

adopted to Governor Chamberlain, in evidence of the esteem in which his labors, in the cause of good government, are held by this community.

The following resolution, introduced by Col. C. H. Simonton, was unanimously adopted, and the meeting then adjourned :

Resolved, That to carry into effect the objects declared in the preamble and resolutions just adopted, the chairman of this meeting do, at his leisure, appoint an executive committee of fifteen citizens, who shall thoroughly organize this county for the attainment of the ends proposed.

At a large meeting in Georgetown, Richard Dozier presided. Col. B. H. Wilson presented the resolutions, which were seconded by Alonzo Jackson, a colored man, and Parson Mosell, another colored man, made one of the effective speeches.

The following shows the action at Orangeburg :

ORANGEBURG, S. C., December 31, 1875.

To His Excellency, D. H. Chamberlain :

MY DEAR SIR—Enclosed find communication from the Bar of Orangeburg, which I have the honor to send you on behalf of my brethren.

We were unwilling to let an occasion pass whereon we could testify, for our county, our appreciation of your bold and manly stand, and to show you that we are prepared to support you in all your endeavors to put down the gross corruption existing in our State.

I will send you to-morrow a similar acknowledgment on behalf of our citizens generally. They have been rushing to sign, and all in town have signed. Still I preferred waiting for more signatures from the country.

With great respect, I am yours, etc.,

W. J. DE TREVILLE.

To His Excellency D. H. Chamberlain, Governor of the State of South Carolina :

The undersigned members of the Bar of Orangeburg, having read the resolutions adopted by the citizens and Bar of Charleston, on the 28th instant, beg leave to state to your Excellency our entire and sincere approval and endorsement of the same.

Thomas W. Glover, W. F. Hutson, W. M. Hutson, W. J. De Treville, Jas. F. Izlar, Mortimer Glover, C. B. Glover, Julius Glover, T. B. Whaley, S. Dibble, Malcolm I. Browning, James S. Heyward.

December 30, 1875.

The declaration of the citizens was in the same terms. To these expressions of approval the Governor made the following response :

EXECUTIVE CHAMBER,
COLUMBIA, S. C., January 2, 1876.

MY DEAR MR. DE TREVILLE :—I gratefully acknowledge the receipt from you of the endorsement of the Bar of Orangeburg County of the address and resolutions of the citizens of Charleston, adopted on the 28th ult. By the same mail I received the similar endorsement of the citizens at large of your town and county of the same address and resolutions.

Personally, I claim no merit for my recent action.   I did no more than any right-thinking man in my place *must* have done.   But I am deeply grateful for the proofs which every day reach me of the approval of my fellow-citizens.   The recent judicial elections in the First, Second, and Third Circuits cannot be tolerated.   They warn us that the hard-earned triumphs of long centuries are again in danger, that we must combine again to turn back the incoming tide of corruption and incompetency which will, unchecked, rise over our whole State.

In the presence of a common danger all true men must unite.   In this spirit I interpret all the support now given to me, and in that spirit I will use it.

Please make known to all my brethren of the Orangeburg Bar, and all my fellow-citizens who thus sustain my action, that I shall be inspired to continued fidelity to my trusts by the knowledge of their approval.

And so let me remain, my dear sir,

Your obliged fellow-citizen,

D. H, CHAMBERLAIN.

In Sumter, in the circuit for which Ex-Governor Moses had been chosen judge, a great meeting was held on the 3d of January.   The Music Hall was filled with the substantial citizens of the county. T. B. Frazer presided, and there were nineteen vice-presidents.   The president in his address said : " It is one of the purposes of this meeting to announce to F. J. Moses, Jr., that he shall never take his seat as judge in our courthouse, unless placed there by federal bayonets." Resolutions presented by Capt. E. W. Moise were unanimously adopted, among them the following :

1. That this meeting denounce the action of the Legislature in this matter as ruinous to the people and destructive of good government.

3. That we regard the action of the Governor in withholding commissions from these persons as patriotic, justifiable, and right.

4. That Governor D. H. Chamberlain has illustrated by his conduct the noble ends which may be achieved by a stranger, who differs from many of us in matters of political faith, but who unites with good men of all views in measures of earnest reform, and this people will sustain him to the end.

9. That, invoking the blessing of Divine Providence upon our resolutions, we now appeal to all patriotic citizens, white or colored, of all shades of political opinion, to assist us in an effort to restore good government to the State, by securing to all persons their full legal rights of person and property, without infringing the sacred privileges of others, and especially do we appeal to and rely upon the aid and assistance of those leading men of the country who control the national parties in this last struggle against degradation and disgrace.

Captain Moise, in supporting his resolutions, said:

We must have a leader, and I propose to you one who is eminently fitted for the position, a true Republican—a man of courage, learning, and ability. I refer to D. H. Chamberlain, our present Governor, who has shown even his worst foes the triumph of duty over party considerations—whose acts are epics, and whose words are "apples of gold in pictures of silver." Under his lead we cannot be accused of seeking Democratic ascendancy as an end, nor of a desire to abridge the rights of any as a means.

The other addresses were by J. S. Richardson, James D. Blanding, and Charles H. Moise, and their temper may be inferred from the concluding sentence of the last-named speaker:

Should F. J. Moses, Jr., by any legal trickery, attempt to ascend the steps of the courthouse to take his seat as judge, I, Charles H. Moise, forty-six years of age, with a wife and ten children to support, am ready to unite with a band of determined men, and with muskets on our shoulders, defend that temple of justice from such a desecration.

The voice of Barnwell, for which circuit Wiggins had been chosen, was spoken in an immense mass-meeting, over which General Johnson Hagood presided, also held on the 3d of January. Many leading men of the county took part, but the principal address was made by the venerable Judge A. P. Aldrich, who began with the remark that he thought he had attended his last political meeting and made his last political speech.

The following extracts from his speech indicate the spirit that animated all the speakers and was formally expressed in the resolutions:

I say to you, as I have said to Governor Chamberlain, I cannot withhold the grateful expression of my thanks for the patriotism and manhood he has displayed in the rebuke administered to the Legislature for their outrage against virtue, decency, and justice in the election of these judges. You all know Maher; he was born here in this village, of virtuous parents, raised in our midst, accepted this office at the solicitation of the Republican party who elected him, has been true to his education and instincts, made a judge of whom we and they are proud, and because he has administered the law without fear, favor, or partiality, his place has been supplied by Wiggins! You all know Wiggins so well that I need not increase your disgust by dwelling on his incompetency, and, I may add, venality. I say this reluctantly, for the creature has the good quality of amiability; but he proves, as every lawyer in this circuit knows, his utter unfitness for the office. I hope he will not make it necessary, before next August, to prove the official misconduct of which he has been guilty to confine him to a much narrower circuit than the Second. Why, fellow-citizens, I cannot contemplate this stupendous outrage without horror and dismay. Your executive department may be pure, your legislative department may be pure, but if the department of justice is corrupt, what security have you for life, liberty, or property ?

And see your condition to-day—a gallant Governor struggling against a Legislature who will elect such judges. Does it not awaken all your sympathies, arouse all your manhood, and reproach all your patriotism? It has required the courage of a Republican to arouse our manhood. I am stunned ; I cannot realize the abject degradation to which we have been reduced. We, who claim such a past, and see such a future for our children ! . . . The Governor has disposed of Moses and Whipper ; let us see that Wiggins makes a graceful retreat. We can't stand it. He knows his perfect inability to fill this office as well as we do, and I cannot conceive he will presume to thrust himself on a reluctant bar and a still more reluctant people. I am perfectly satisfied if these men attempt to preside in these three circuits, it will be a deliberate act of suicide.

And now, fellow-citizens, we must give Governor Chamberlain a generous, earnest, and united support. The political brigands and banditti have entrenched themselves in the State-house, and have raised the black flag. No white man, mulatto, or honest negro will be ever again countenanced by them. Their object is plunder, and they will grind the last dollar out of the taxpayer, white or colored, unless they are driven out. They trample the Constitution under foot by refusing to pass laws expressly commanded by that instrument. They pass thieving laws for, as their Senators and Representatives boldly and shamelessly avow, the pickings and stealings. They elect corrupt judges to uphold their infamous legislation. They tax you without stint or mercy, and make you pay for their aggrandizement and your own ruin. And now Governor Chamberlain has attacked them in their stronghold, his battle-cry rings out clear and shrill on the air ; he leads the attack, and calls on every honest man in the State, without regard to party, to follow him. These thieves must be driven out, or the State and our civilization is lost. Is there a man in South Carolina, white or colored, who loves his old mother, to stand back at such a call and such a time ? Some newspapers, in and out of the State, may speak cold words of approval, which have the sound of distrust ; but I tell you, when I read such sentiments and such utterances as he has lately given forth, I feel every confidence in the man increased. No man who did not have a clear head, a brave heart, and an honest purpose could give expression to such lofty words of patriotism and of duty, I can well imagine, as the grand words flashed across the wires : "I will not commission these men." "I have risen above party, and will do my duty." " The civilization of the Puritan and the Cavalier, of the Roundhead and the Huguenot, is in peril. Courage, Determination, Union, Victory, must be our watchwords. The grim Puritans never quailed under threat or blow. Let their sons now imitate their example." How the electric spark kindled enthusiasm in every bosom and scattered every doubt of the integrity and courage of the man who uttered them ! At that very moment the garb of the carpet-bagger dropped from his shoulders ; he was received with affection as an adopted son into the family of the children of the Palmetto State, and his name was enrolled with Blanding, and Nott, and Duncan, and the hundreds of New-Englanders who have adorned her society and illustrated her history. And the name of Chamberlain will stand high on the roll, for his burning words will go down to posterity and make a shining page in history, as Pinckney's " Millions for defence, not a cent for tribute " ; or the old Dictator's " By God, I will cut my right hand off before I sign the order"; or Patrick Henry's "Give me Liberty, or give me Death." I say, then, fellow-citizens, we must stand by him heart and hand. For God's sake listen to me now, and do not be deterred by the cry: "You are advising us to violate the law," in driving out these thieves, who have been violating Constitution, law, and virtue since 1868.

If we do not drive these brigands, this banditti, out at the next election, which we can do if we are united and work bravely, there is but one course left. Then we must go back to natural justice and form a committee of vigilance and safety from our best citizens, as they did in California, who will give them a fair trial and swift punishment.

This is my counsel. It is the Centennial year. We must redeem the State at the next election or sign another Declaration of Independence, not against the Union, but against these thieves and usurpers. And unless you do this you are a disgrace to your ancestry; you commit a crime against your posterity; your mothers will weep that you were born, and your sisters blush that you live. . . .

Mr. Alfred Aldrich offered a series of resolutions, and prefaced them with this remarkable speech:

A short time ago, in this house, I said, among other things, to the taxpayers, that I had "implicit confidence in the people of Barnwell County, but none in Governor Chamberlain." In the light of recent events, I desire to make the *amende honorable* to Governor Chamberlain, and here, with equal unreserve as when I made the declaration alluded to, I wish to submit the change in my opinion embodied in the following resolutions:

Resolved, That Governor Chamberlain, from his Inaugural Address to his last veto, has carried out every pledge of the platform on which he was elected, and if he does not receive the support of the leading men of his own party, is entitled to the confidence and will receive the cordial sympathy and merited aid of the honest and good men in South Carolina. . . .

Resolved, That the Governor, having taken care of the Charleston and Sumter Circuits by refusing to commission Whipper and Moses, and not being able to reach Wiggins in the same way, we of the Barnwell Circuit must see that he do not defile the bench and debauch the county now adorned by the virtue and the learning of the incorruptible Maher.

Resolved, That we recognize and appreciate the difficulties that the Governor has had to contend against to maintain his position as a political reformer; that we acknowledge his probity in redeeming the pledges contained in the platform on which he was elected to office, and admire his boldness in resisting the pressure of those who were not in earnest when they made them; that we are fully sensible of the opposition that he has encountered and the difficulties that have environed him in acting his arduous rôle, and that we take this occasion to assure him and the men of his party who endorse him, of our cordial support.

Two other series of resolutions were offered and adopted at this meeting, one series proposing a scheme for the reorganization of the Democratic party as the basis of opposition to the corrupt element of the Republican party, the other relating particularly to the case of Wiggins, and embodying an additional expression of obligation to the Governor.

Resolved, That we, the people of this section of the Second Circuit, not wishing to make an issue with any individual or party, and not being willing to risk our lives and property in the hands of the newly elected judge, P. L. Wiggins, for reasons obvious, do earnestly request the said P. L. Wiggins to tender his resignation to the Governor at once, and that the Governor do declare said office vacant, and that the said vacancy be filled by an election to take place before the close of the present session of the Legislature. . . .

Resolved, That a committee of two be appointed by the President of this meeting to communicate with Solicitor Wiggins, and to notify him of the action of this convention ; and that said committee be instructed to assure him that this convention is not prompted by any impure motives or personal animosity for him in taking this action, but alone for the interest of the country, and for the peace, harmony, and perfect satisfaction of all parties, irrespective of race, color, or political differences.

Resolved, That we heartily endorse Governor Chamberlain in his efforts to redeem the State from plunder and degradation, and while he has been faithful to his own party, he has also been faithful to ours, and we hereby pledge ourselves to stand by and support him promptly, faithfully, fearlessly, and defiantly.

Similar meetings were held in all sections of the State. That in Spartanburg adopted the following resolution :

That we cordially endorse the action of Governor Chamberlain in refusing to issue commissions as judges to W. J. Whipper and F. J. Moses, and pledge to him the full support of the community in his efforts to secure to the people of the State a faithful administration of the law.

That in Camden, where Gen. James Chesnut, ex-Senator of the United States, presided, Col. W. M. Shannon presented the resolutions and Gen. J. B. Kershaw seconded them, made these declarations :

Resolved, That we cordially endorse and approve the manly, patriotic, and statesmanlike course of Governor Chamberlain, in this behalf, as also in his general administration of his " great office."

Resolved, That while we recognize in him a pronounced Republican, we perceive in his course a devotion to " good government, well administered "—the first and vital need of South Carolina,—and we join hands and hearts with him in "rising above party," and give him assurance of earnest and admiring support.

That in Horry County adopted the following :

That we accord to Governor Chamberlain our highest meed of thanks and praise for the part he has taken, and for his efforts to stay the tide of evil which threatens to engulf the State.

In two or three instances, the reports of these meetings show

signs of the disposition of the men who supported the unrighteous action of the Legislature. Thus at Kingstree, according to
the report in the *News and Courier*, the following occurred after
the reading of the resolutions :

Just before the resolutions were put to the meeting, the question arose as to
whether the Republicans would participate in the meeting. Swails [a member of the
Legislature, a leader of the colored men] came in, and having said that he looked
upon the meeting as Democratic, retired himself, and every black man in the courthouse followed him.

The meeting at the courthouse in York County was nearly
captured by the Governor's enemies. The report says :

After the resolutions had been read, J. Hannibal White, colored, Senator from
York, opposed the resolutions. He said he had voted for W. J. Whipper and F. J.
Moses for judges in the late election, and was proud of it. In regard to Whipper,
charges of corruption in the management of the sinking fund had been made against
him, but he had never been tried for it. When he was tried and convicted it was
time enough to denounce him. There were other men, he said, on the Commission
besides Whipper, and the audience no doubt knew who they were without the speaker
telling them. Whipper had defied these men to prosecute him. As to Whipper
being a gambler, continued Senator White, that did not amount to much, as pretty
much all the judges and lawyers he had met were gamblers. He was ready to endorse the Governor when he was right, and to oppose him when wrong. The Governor was not his master, and he would permit no man to lead or dictate to him. He
would vote against the resolutions.

At the conclusion of Senator White's remarks, the question of adopting the resolution as the voice of the county being put, the chair was not able to determine the
result. A rising vote was then taken, and the resolutions were declared adopted, the
whites, with one exception only, voting in the affirmative, and nine tenths of the
colored people voting in the negative.

Notwithstanding the determined expression of public sentiment in these meetings, by the press of the State and of the country, and by the thorough political organization that followed,
both Whipper and Moses resolutely insisted that when the time
came they would take their seats in spite of all opposition. This
caused continued uneasiness and led to the following action
of the Charleston Bar, from which but two or three members
dissented :

CHARLESTON, April 25, 1876.

Hon. J. P. Reed, Judge of the First Circuit :

DEAR SIR—We, the undersigned, members of the Charleston bar, believe it to
be our professional duty to say to you that we regard the decision of Governor Chamberlain, that your term of office had not expired when W. J. Whipper was elected,
and would not expire until four years from the date of your election, and that there

was therefore no vacancy to be filled by the Legislature, as the decision of a co-ordinate branch of the government, which we intend to uphold.

We therefore earnestly request you to hold on to your office, and maintain your right to the whole term of four years from the day of your election, and pledge ourselves to sustain your claim in every way we can devise and you may require of us.

We further take occasion to say that we are fully determined not to recognize W. J. Whipper as Circuit Judge in this county, and will resist any attempt on his part to enforce his right to the office.

Very respectfully,

Edward McCrady,	S. Lord, Jr.,	John F. Ficken,
R. W. Seymour,	Theodore G. Barker,	C. C. Pinckney, Jr.,
C. G. Memminger,	Asher D. Cohen,	A. G. Magrath, Jr.
Alex. H. Brown,	Edward McCrady, Jr.,	W. M. Burns,
Henry D. Lesesne,	H. E. Young,	W. St. Julian Jervey,
James B. Campbell,	M. L. Wilkins,	Arthur Mazyck,
C. R. Brewster,	George R. Walker,	Wm. P. DeSaussure,
W. D. Porter,	G. L. Buist,	Joseph W. Barnwell,
A. G. Magrath,	Rudolph Siegling,	James P. Lesesne,
James Simons,	Julian Mitchell,	John C. Miller,
William Whaley,	Charles Inglesby,	Charles Boyle,
B. C. Pressley,	J. N. Nathans,	Charles S. Campbell,
E. Magrath,	James Simons, Jr.,	George S. Holmes,
W. G. DeSaussure,	Wm. J. Gayer,	Louis de B. McCrady,
Thos. M. Hanckel,	Robt. F. Touhey,	Henry A. M. Smith,
W. Alston Pringle,	W. James Whaley,	A. M. Huger,
John E. Rivers,	Augustine T. Smythe,	T. M. Mordecai,
B. G. Whaley,	Isaac Hayne,	T. W. Bacot,
Thos. Y. Simons,	D. T. Corbin,	William Seabrook,
V. J. Tobias,	W. D. Clancy,	Henry A. DeSaussure,
H. Buist,	Wm. H. Brawley,	Charles E. Carrere,
James Conner,	Robt. Chisolm, Jr.,	Alfred Hanckel,
Ch. Richardson Miles,	George D. Bryan,	Francis L. McHugh,
B. H. Rutledge,	G. Herbert Sass,	D. B. Gilliland,
Chas. H. Simonton,	J. E. Burke,	John C. Minott,
M. P. O'Connor,	W. M. Muckenfuss,	J. Bachman Chisolm,
G. W. Dingle,	C. O. Trumbo,	Jennings W. Perry.

The Orangeburg bar made a similar request. Judge Reed, in his response to the Charleston bar, set forth at length his opinion on the legal questions involved, and ended his letter with the following declaration :

Entertaining these views, and sustained by the learning, ability, and patriotism of the bar of the First Circuit, and, as I conceive, with very rare exceptions, those of the whole State, I consent " to hold on to my office " for the full constitutional term of four years, and will be ready at all times to co-operate with you in such measures as may be deemed necessary to maintain my position and authority, and to preserve the independence, dignity, and integrity of the judicial office.

Judge Shaw, of the third circuit, for which Moses had been chosen, gave similar assurances. But the commissions of these judges were written only for the unexpired terms of their predecessors, and to remedy this defect, the Governor determined to issue new commissions, as appears by the following official communication :

Executive Chamber,
Columbia, S. C., May 25, 1876.
Hon. H. E. Hayne, Secretary of State :

Dear Sir—On the 11th day of December, 1874, Hon. J. P. Reed was elected Judge of the Circuit Court of this State for the First Judicial Circuit, and on the 12th day of February, 1875, Hon. J. A. Shaw was elected Judge of the same court for the Third Judicial Circuit, and commissions were duly issued to the same persons in accordance with the certificates of the clerks of the two houses of the General Assembly for the unexpired terms of their predecessors in office. On the 21st day of December, 1875, I filed a statement of my reasons for refusing to issue commissions to W. J. Whipper and F. J. Moses, Jr., who claimed to have been elected on the 16th day of December, 1875, to the offices now held by Messrs. Reed and Shaw. I then announced my judgment, that Messrs. Whipper and Moses were not duly elected to said offices, and that the present incumbents, Messrs. Reed and Shaw, were entitled to hold for full terms of four years from their election.

In accordance with that judgment, I now deem it my duty to issue commissions covering the full periods of four years from the dates of their elections, respectively, to Hon. J. P. Reed and Hon. A. J. Shaw, Judges of the Circuit Court for the First and Third Circuits, and I respectfully request you to prepare such commissions for my signature.

Very respectfully, your obedient servant,
D. H. CHAMBERLAIN,
Governor.

Nevertheless, both Whipper and Moses, and especially the former, as the date (August 26th) approached when they claimed that they were entitled to assume office, threatened to possess themselves by force of the seats on the bench to which they aspired. In view of such a contingency, the Governor issued a proclamation of warning, and at once took measures, by the appointment of a special body of constables, upon whose fidelity he could depend, to prevent the accomplishment of this purpose. At the time of making this proclamation, other events, which will be brought into view in subsequent chapters,[1] had contributed to a

---

[1] The Hamburg massacre being one.

condition of affairs that would have relieved a mere partisan of any sense of obligation to persist in antagonizing the ambition of men willing to be his allies, in behalf of those who were plotting his political downfall. But Governor Chamberlain was not swerved from the right line of public duty. This was the proclamation :

Executive Chamber,
Columbia, S. C.

Whereas, the Honorable Jacob P. Reed, having been elected, was duly commissioned by me as Judge of the Circuit Court, for the First Circuit of this State, to hold the said office, according to the Constitution of the said State, for the term of four years beginning on the eleventh day of December, A.D., 1874, and under his said commission has been, and still is, in the actual peaceable possession and in the exercise of the duties of the said office ; and,

Whereas, satisfactory evidence has been brought before me that W. J. Whipper, who claims to be the Judge of the said Circuit, but who has neither any commission as Judge, nor has submitted the merits of his claim to the decision of any tribunal whatever, nevertheless, is making preparation, and intends, to enter by force upon the exercise of the duties of the said office, and in that character to resist, and to encourage, persuade, and conspire with other persons to resist, by force, the lawful authority and orders of Judge Reed ; and,

Whereas, a decent regard for the forms and principles adopted for the determination of conflicting claims to public offices requires that the claim of W. J. Whipper shall be submitted to, and be determined by, a competent legal tribunal, before any attempt is made by the said W. J. Whipper to take possession of, or exercise the functions or duties of, the said office :

Now, therefore, I, Daniel H. Chamberlain, Governor of the State of South Carolina, in performance of my duty to see that the laws of the State be faithfully executed, and, not only to repress vigorously and promptly all riotous and tumultuous disorder in the State, but also, by proper preparation and precaution, to prevent the same, do hereby proclaim that any such attempt as is hereinbefore stated, by W. J. Whipper, and those who may aid and abet him, will be regarded and treated by me, not only as an unlawful and riotous disturbance of the public peace, but also as an outrage upon judicial authority not to be tolerated in a civilized State. Such an attempt at the lawless and forcible usurpation of a judicial office,—wrong in itself, as an attempt to oust a judge in possession without any previous test of his right, wrong in its influences, as an example of lawless disregard of well-established forms of law by one aspiring to the judicial office,—is flagrantly and heinously wrong in its manifest tendency to create tumultuous riot, or a bloody conflict, and to exhibit a contagious example of disregard of law and right, and of violence, which will be likely to extend to other portions of the State now too greatly excited by passing events and issues.

I do, therefore, forewarn all citizens of this State against aiding or abetting W. J. Whipper in his said unlawful attempt, and I call upon all the officers of the law in said Circuit to exert their official powers promptly and vigorously, in sustaining the authority and executing the orders of Judge Reed, and in putting down all attempts in any manner to interfere with his discharge of the duties of his office.

I further call upon all citizens to frown upon and discountenance any and all attempts to usurp the authority of Judge Reed, and, when called upon, to assist in executing his orders ; and I further proclaim that, if the officers of the law in said Circuit shall fail to discharge their duties as hereinbefore laid down, I shall proceed, under the law of this State, to organize a sufficient force in the counties of Orangeburg and Charleston, under the command of the lawful deputy constables of those counties, under my own direction and control, to execute promptly and effectually such orders as may be issued by Judge Reed as Judge of the said Circuit, whenever such orders shall be resisted, and to arrest and commit all persons who may oppose or resist his authority, or who may, in contempt thereof, aid in the execution of any order which may be issued by W. J. Whipper, until his claim to be Judge of said Circuit shall have been established by some tribunal competent to pass final judgment thereon.

In testimony whereof, I have hereunto set my hand and caused the great seal of the State to be attached, at Columbia, this 21st of August, A.D., 1876, and in the one hundred and first year of American Independence.

By the Governor :

D. H. CHAMBERLAIN,
Governor of South Carolina.

H. E. HAYNE,
    Secretary of State.

The proclamation and the action taken to enforce it awed the conspirators, and no attempt was made to seize the coveted places. Thus the defeat of the infamous scheme sprung upon the State on " Black Thursday " was accomplished and sealed, and the " horrible calamity " averted. " Persons lightly dipped, not grained, in generous honesty," says Sir Thomas Browne, " are but pale in goodness." A magistrate pale in goodness would hardly have undertaken what Governor Chamberlain successfully accomplished.

CHAPTER XIV.

Influence of the Election of Whipper and Moses on the Politics of South Carolina—
Revival and Reorganization of the Democratic Party—Views of Governor Cham-
berlain and Dr. H. V. Redfield—The Political Situation in the State and the
Country—Letter of Governor Chamberlain to President Grant Setting Forth
the Nature of the Crisis—Letter of Governor Chamberlain to Senator Oliver P.
Morton on the Partisan Aspects of the Issue Made—Senator Morton protests
that He had been Misunderstood—Letter of Governor Chamberlain to Dr. H. B.
Blackwell—Comments of Newspapers in Other States on the Situation in South
Carolina—Hon. A. H. Stephens Corrects a Misrepresentation of His Opinion
Concerning Affairs in South Carolina.

TO complete the record of this dark crime of the Legislature,
it is necessary to exhibit its immediate malign influence upon
the *morale* and organization of the political parties. The corruption which obtained a riotous brief triumph in the State-house
at Columbia on the 16th of December, 1875, invited and prepared
for the colored race the doom of exclusion for a long period from
any controlling influence in public affairs. It was their Belshaz-
zar's feast.

No one apprehended the calamitous consequences more quickly
than the Governor. In his first utterance for the public, three
days after the mischief was done, he said: " I look upon their election as a horrible disaster—a disaster equally great to the State
and to the Republican party. The gravest consequences of all
kinds will follow. One immediate effect will obviously be the reorganization of the Democratic party within the State as the only
means left, in the judgment of its members, for opposing a solid
and reliable front to this terrible *crevasse* of misgovernment and
public debauchery. I could have wished, as a Republican, to have
kept off such an issue."

Dr. H. V. Redfield, a very intelligent and fair-minded correspondent of the Cincinnati *Commercial*, who had made the South-

ern States a field of special personal investigation, wrote to that journal from South Carolina, when the event was fresh, as follows:

A rumpus has begun in South Carolina which will end in the white people getting control of the State, as they now have control of Mississippi. The means to be adopted to overthrow negro rule in the Palmetto State may not be precisely the same as that which proved successful in Mississippi, but the result will be similar . . . Pick out two of the most notorious ward bummers in Cincinnati—men as ignorant of the science of law as a boy is of astronomy, men of no standing in the community, and no character save that of idleness, and elevate them to the bench in two of the most important Ohio circuits, Cincinnati and Cleveland, for instance. How would you feel about it ? . . . The whites are aroused ; the color line is drawn ; and before long you will hear of a " great Democratic victory " in South Carolina like unto that in Mississippi

The Governor has refused to sign the commissions of Moses and Whipper upon merely technical grounds—something that he would not have thought of doing, as he says himself, had these judges-elect been decent men. But how he is to carry out his point I fail to see. There seems no escape from Moses and Whipper on the bench but the complete overthrow of the so-called party which elected them. And that is what is coming. I say to the reader, and hope he will remember it hereafter, Look out for Democratic gains in South Carolina ! For a long time the whites have wanted a sufficient excuse to rise up and overthrow the African government under which they live ; and now they have it. Not a white Republican in the State, from the Governor down, nor a Republican journal, pretends to justify the election of these notorious men to the bench.

The campaign in South Carolina next year will be very bitter, if not bloody. The whites will now draw the " color line," and at the same time throw all the blame upon the blacks. We know what the color line means. If any there are who don't comprehend the term, they can have light by spending a few days in Mississippi.

The meetings that were held throughout the State to protest against the action of the Legislature and to sustain the action of the Governor, almost without exception, passed resolutions in favor of a thorough reorganization of the Democratic party, and appointed committees to effect it. While in some places, for example, Charleston, as already shown, the appeal was for an organization of all the friends of honest government, and not specifically for a reorganization of the Democratic party, in other places the latter course was considered the only safe reliance. This sentiment was clearly set forth in the resolutions adopted at the Barnwell meeting :

Resolved, That in view of our repeated failures to reform the State Government by the policy of co-operation with the Conservative element of the Republican party, who professed the same object, and of recent events, we recognize the absolute and immediate necessity of reorganizing the Democratic party to restore an honest and economical government.

Resolved, That the Democratic party of South Carolina will in the future, as it has in the past, support principles, not men, and we hereby extend a cordial invitation to all men in the State who desire honest government, to unite with us, at least until we have accomplished our purpose.

Resolved, That the co-operation now invited is not with the bad men who have heretofore deluded, deceived, and betrayed our colored fellow-citizens, but with the great mass of that class who, we believe, are willing to rescue the State from the grasp of these unprincipled adventurers.

A call was promptly issued for a meeting of the State Executive Committee of the Democratic party in Columbia on the 6th of January, and at the many mass-meetings held committees were appointed to co-operate in carrying into execution the plans that might then be resolved upon. Measures were also taken to perfect the party organization in every township and county. In this movement there was, at the time, no indication of hostility to the Governor. It was believed that the course he had taken had made an irreparable breach in the Republican party, that the portion of the party which sided with him was a weak minority that would be overwhelmed in the first convention, that the element, led by Elliott, Whipper, Moses, and their kind, would nominate the Republican candidates for the next election, and that the Governor would thus be forced, in obedience to his declared convictions, either to continue the combat for the salvation of the State as an independent candidate, or to give his support to a Democratic candidate. In either case the reorganization of the Democratic party for earnest and efficient service was deemed by its members a necessary condition of public safety. No well informed Democrat expected that the Governor would unite with their party. It was well known that, as to every other issue between parties in South Carolina except this of honesty and economy in the conduct of the State's business, and in regard to the issues which divided the national parties, he was a Republican. All the aid they could hope for from him was the aid of a Republican who believed it to be the primary duty of all government and all parties to establish justice and public prosperity by honorable methods and without wrong or oppression, and who in fidelity to this motive did not hesitate to rebuke and oppose the infidelity of his political associates.

While the spirit and the immediate aim of the majority of the Democratic party were such as have been indicated, there were ambitious leaders who had another purpose not yet plainly announced, and who joined in the general tribute to Governor Chamberlain's great public service with a sinister motive. They affected gratitude and honor; but they would have been better pleased if he had sinned with the rest. It exasperated them that any Republican should obtain credit for ability, wisdom, integrity, and honor, and they recognized in him the one man likely to be able to thwart their plot to overthrow the rule of the majority and seize by force and craft all the political honors of the State. Him alone they feared, as one having the sagacity to discover the unreality of their professed regard for the principle of equal rights, the power to cope with them in argument and organization, and the character to command respect for any report he might make to the people of the country of their machinations. They did not want South Carolina to be saved from misgovernment except by the Democratic party, and were incensed that he should have done any thing to deserve the praise of Democrats. By keeping his pledges with such fidelity, by bettering the promise in the performance, he had falsified their hopes built upon expectations of his failure.[1] The Anderson *Intelligencer* was almost the only newspaper which openly spoke the sentiments of this class. "His political course," it said, "has been outrageous in the past and deceptive in the present. Whenever any real reform has been accomplished by him it will be time to praise him. The mere prevention of Moses and Whipper taking their seats is something, to be sure, but he says he did it for the purpose of saving his party." Such expressions were then rare. Those who agreed with them were too discreet to talk much aloud. They preferred to be silent and to avail themselves of the opportunities which the reorganization of the Democratic party would afford, relying on their skill in political management to intensify party feeling and direct it to their advantage.

The chief promoters of this policy were men whose ambition

[1] By how much better than my word I am,
By so much shall I falsify men's hopes.
—*Henry IV.*, Part 1, I., ii., 234.

reached forward to participation in national politics. They were aspirants for seats in the national Congress and for the prizes that would follow the election of a President by the Democratic party. Belonging to the select circle of the South Carolina aristocracy, families which before the war had an acknowledged right to rule and represent the State, not so much because of their superior ability as because of their lineage and their wealth in land and negroes, they were impatient to resume their lordly sway. In their view, bred, as they had been, under the conditions and influences of a system of caste as unrighteous, unrepublican, undemocratic, as any under the sun, no man who *believed* in the equality of rights of all men was safe or tolerable in a place of authority. Since they could not prevent it, they submitted to the new constitution of government which formally asserted the equal political rights and opportunities of all, irrespective of race, color, or previous condition of servitude ; but they *believed* in the superior and substantially exclusive right of their caste to govern the State, whether they constituted the majority or the minority of the people. Understanding completely the prejudices which two centuries of slavery had fostered in those whites who, although free, had never been of the privileged caste, they counted upon their instinctive allegiance in all contests with the party which promulgated the doctrine that any black man could achieve by education and character a just claim to political influence and authority. Latent as these forces were for the time being, they were not dead, and the ebullition of gratitude to Governor Chamberlain on account of signal services, while it temporarily overflowed deep prejudices, did not wash them out. The brave slave that saved St. Michael's was gratefully emancipated ; but there was no conversion to the doctrine that a race able to produce brave men should be free.

The election of a President of the United States, that was to occur the next fall, cast its shadow before and clouded the vision of partisans on both sides. Leaders of the Democratic party in other States were even more anxious than those in South Carolina that the party organization should be revived there in anticipation of the national contest. More or less openly they deprecated the admission that a Republican in office in the South could deserve the favor and confidence of Democrats. The more noble and admirable Governor Chamberlain's conduct, so long as he abided in the Republican party the greater the necessity that he should be abandoned and overthrown. The example of a conspicuously wise and honorable Republican Governor in the South went far to nullify the force of the party argument that Republican administration, dependent upon the suffrages of the colored race, was inevitably oppressive, corrupt, and degrading. Throughout the North Democrats were hoping that by some means the minority in South Carolina would subjugate the majority, as had been done in other Southern States, notably in Mississippi, and secure the electoral votes of the State for their national candidates who would have small prospect of success without these votes. For this reason, the apparent willingness of South Carolina Democrats to honor Governor Chamberlain and sustain him, for the sake of good government at home, was not approved; and there is reason to believe it was severely frowned upon by the intimate and ambitious counsellors of the leading Democratic aspirants for the Presidency, who recognized that the support of a Republican for the Chief Magistracy of the State would make impossible such a campaign of intimidation of Republican voters there as would be necessary for preventing the unquestionable Republican majority, in a full and fair poll, from carrying the State. How much a hope that Governor Chamberlain, if circumstances should force him to oppose the nominee of his own party for Governor,—his own renomination seemed to be impossible,—might abjure the Republican party entirely, it is not necessary to conjecture. How little reason there was for such a hope will plainly appear.

The approaching national election made the leading politicians of the Republican party also sensitive concerning the effect of Governor Chamberlain's action. Many of them had never relished his open and defiant hostility to a section of his party in South Carolina. These were the men whose intense partisanship led them to deprecate whatever disturbed the harmony and coherence of the party forces. In their view honest administration might be commendable, but the conservation of the power of the Republican party and its continued domination in the nation were objects to be first sought, and whatever imperilled these was offensive. Men whose eloquence flamed over the North, and with good reason, on account of the unjust methods resorted to by Southern Democrats to carry elections, were willing to condone the flagrant corruption and monstrous stealing which characterized government by their allies in the Southern States. The partisan whose hopes of preferment depend upon party success, is apt to remodel the Scriptural injunction in its application to political duty, making it read " First successful, then pure." To whatever reforms may be accomplished without dividing the party, he may be induced to consent, but a virtue which cannot affiliate with, and make concessions to, rascals who are disposed to vote with " our side," seems to him incompatible with statesmanship or patriotism, and an obvious disqualification for public office. Governor Chamberlain had committed what this class deemed the worst of faults in a politician. He had confessed the truth of the indictment brought by the Democratic party against the character of the Republican government in South Carolina and, in effect, against all the Republican State governments in the South. That he did it regretfully, not as one hopeless of better things, or recreant, but as a faithful physician who had discovered alarming progress of a desperate disease, the nature and peril of which must be made known to the victim in order to secure his necessary co-operation in the restoration of health, was not appreciated by men whose ambition was focussed on the next election. It seemed to them that it was a party duty for every Republican to maintain, at least until after the next President was chosen, that the charges of incompetence and corruption made by Democrats against the Republican administrations in the South were the prejudiced and vindictive misrepresentations of men who were lately rebels.

Moreover, the Republican party at this time was much distracted regarding exposed misconduct elsewhere. The corruption that thrived and festered in official quarters during General Grant's second term,—not with his connivance, but sheltered by his fame and popularity,—had provoked a serious temper of revolt. General Grant had declared his disinclination to accept another nomination, and Senators Morton and Conkling were seeking and obtaining support for themselves upon the ground that his Administration had been wise and successful, especially in its Southern policy, and both these candidates were courting the support of the Southern Republicans by great zeal in arraigning the Southern Democrats for their misdeeds. The portion of the party which had sustained the Administration without criticism was inclined to one or the other of these senators, but Senator Morton was the best known by the colored race and most popular with the class designated " carpet-baggers." In the Northern States, the majority of those who, for any reason, were dissatisfied with the recent conduct of affairs were inclined to support Mr. Blaine ; but the brilliant career of Mr. Bristow in the Treasury Department, particularly his thorough exposure of revenue frauds and persistent prosecution of the guilty without respect to their political or social influence, was making him the preferred leader of those who thought the time was ripe for a purification of the administration of government. The work which Governor Chamberlain was doing in South Carolina and that which Secretary Bristow was doing in his department of the national government were similar in motive and aim, and both men were obnoxious to those who held that the duty of a true Republican is resolutely to shut his eyes and his ears to the wrongdoing of his own party and the rightdoing of the Democratic party. To this day the world is filled with politicians who have never comprehended the policy of Jehovah's requirement that the Jews should be righteous ; and his way of permitting his party, when it sinned, to be defeated by idolaters, shocks all their notions of able practical management.

Such, in brief, was the political situation when Governor Chamberlain wrote the letters following. Primarily they were written for the enlightenment of the party leaders to whom they were addressed. They were not made public for several weeks, not until it appeared that a mistaken notion of his motives and aims was being covertly disseminated to his injury, if not with the consent and aid, certainly without the disapproval and correction, of those whom he had been at pains to inform. The letter to the President was first published in the Washington despatches to the New York *Herald,* April 4, 1876, with this comment : " South Carolina Republicans complain that it has neither reply nor atten-

tion from the President, and that the Grant organs continue to
abuse Governor Chamberlain and misrepresent his political aims."
This letter, it will be observed, was written very soon after the
occurrences of " Black Thursday," with the sole purpose of fully
acquainting the President with the reasons for the course its author
had felt obliged to take.

EXECUTIVE CHAMBER,
COLUMBIA, January 4, 1876.

To His Excellency the President :
SIR—I am induced by recent extraordinary circumstances occurring
in this State to address you by this communication, as the head, in
a certain sense, of the Republican party. The General Assembly of this
State on the 16th inst. elected W. J. Whipper and F. J. Moses, Jr., as
Judges of the Circuit Court of this State, the former for the circuit
embracing the city of Charleston and constituting by far the most important circuit of the State in point of population, wealth, and business.
The character of F. J. Moses, Jr., is known to you and to the world.
Unless the entirely universal opinion of all who are familiar with his
career is mistaken, he is as infamous a character as ever in any age disgraced and prostituted public position. The character of W. J. Whipper, according to my belief and the belief of all good men in this State,
so far as I am informed, differs from that of Moses only in the extent to
which opportunity has allowed him to exhibit it. The election of these
two men to judicial offices sends a thrill of horror through the State. It
compels men of all parties who respect decency, virtue, or civilization
to utter their loudest protests against the outrage of their election.
They have not even the poor qualification of such a degree of legal
learning as to qualify them for the intelligent discharge of any judicial
duty. The least of all the evils inflicted on the people of this State by
their election is the fact that it compels all Republicans who love or
honor the principles of their party to refuse to countenance or tolerate
such representatives.

I am a Republican, of just as many years' standing as I have seen
years of discretion. I have been a strict party man, adhering to my
party here in South Carolina through good report and evil report, never
for once quitting its ranks amid the greatest discouragements arising
from the bad conduct and suicidal policy of many of its most prominent members ; but the time has now come when no self-respecting
Republican can tolerate the ascendancy of such men as, in this instance,
have been forced upon us. For you or me, as Republicans, to countenance the election of Moses and Whipper is as impossible as it would
be for Governor Tilden, as a Democrat, to countenance the election of
William M. Tweed and George G. Barnard to judicial positions in
New York. I cannot and will not do it, be the consequences what they
may politically. And yet I know there are men who will charge me
in this crisis, as they have charged me hitherto, with treachery to the Re-

publican party, because I cannot keep silent and still support a party loaded down with such men. The newspaper in Washington which has sometimes been called your organ, doubtless erroneously, will quite likely denounce me with renewed vigor for what simple self-respect will compel me to do in view of this outrage. I tell you, Mr. President, no act of mine, if I were the greatest living traitor to my party, could be so fatal to that party as the election of Whipper and Moses has been and will be. I want above all things to save South Carolina for the Republican party in the coming Presidential struggle, but I cannot save it, nobody can save it, if the party here or the party at Washington or in the North, do less than denounce this thing unsparingly, and join their efforts to those of the honest Republicans here in an effort to overthrow the power of such men as Whipper and Moses and their aiders and abettors.

Our only salvation is in cutting loose from all contamination with these men and requiring all who are amenable to our influence to do the same. To try to save the seven electoral votes of South Carolina at the price of silence under this infliction will cost us, in my judg-ment, many times that number of votes elsewhere. We want your moral and political support in this struggle with political iniquity in its worst forms. It is as suicidal to give countenance to Whipper and Moses here as it would be to give countenance to the whiskey thieves in St. Louis. The party fealty of such men is disastrous to the party. I have written earnestly. I cannot do otherwise. Let no man convince you that I am any thing but a Republican until common decency compels me to be something else. Give us your countenance as you have given it, as I believe, in the past, and if we cannot save South Carolina to the party, we can prevent our party here from becoming a thousand-fold greater burden to the national Republican party than it has ever been before. We propose to declare war against this Whipper-Moses gang. We propose to ask the national Republican party to sustain us, and we know that you and all true Republicans will bid us God-speed when you know the depths of degradation to which these men are plunging us. This letter is, of course, addressed only to you, but you can make any use of it you see fit, and I remain your sincere friend and fellow Republican, D. H. CHAMBERLAIN,

Governor of South Carolina.

The following letter, written to Senator Oliver P. Morton on the 13th of January, 1876, was given to the public by the New York *Herald* on the 25th of February. The name of the person to whom it was addressed was withheld by the *Herald*, he being designated only as " a prominent Republican member of Congress " :

To Hon. Oliver P. Morton :

DEAR SIR—I have to-day received a letter from a friend who has recently conversed with you, in which he writes : " Mr. Morton looks on your (my) attitude as in practical identification with the Democrats, and already gives up the State (South Carolina) to the opposition."

I am sure you would not willingly reach either of the above conclusions, and therefore I am forced to think that you are greatly misinformed in regard to the posture of political affairs in this State. I am aware, too, that you are greatly and sincerely interested in the fortunes of Southern Republicans, and I therefore conclude that you will listen to statements which may be laid before you, though they may not agree with the conclusions which you have already reached. I beg your indulgence while, as briefly as possible, I give you my views of the situation here.

Ex-Governor F. J. Moses, Jr., was my predecessor in office. During his term of office the conduct of public affairs by him and his followers was such that a vast majority of the Republican party became convinced that a thorough reform, or the promise of it, was the only way in which the success of the party could be secured in 1874. For some reason I was selected as the candidate for Governor of those who held such views. I had been Attorney General of the State from 1868 to 1872, and on account of my connection with public affairs here during that period I was distrusted by many Republicans, and my nomination was hotly contested, on the sole ground that I was not likely to carry out the promised reforms of our party. Upon my nomination, though I had pledged myself in every form to immediate and rigid reform, a bolt took place, embracing many of our best and most devoted Republicans, who refused to support me because I could not, in their judgment, be trusted to carry out practical reform. My election was fiercely contested by those Republicans on that ground alone, while my friends and I stoutly asserted, by our platform and speeches everywhere, that if I was elected thorough and complete reform should take place. I was elected by a majority of 11,000 votes, against a majority of 35,000 for Moses two years previous, and 40,000 for Scott four years previous, this reduced majority being solely due to the distrust of me and my supporters by a considerable wing of our party on the single issue of reform.

I took my seat as Governor, December 1, 1874, and I addressed myself earnestly to the work of keeping the pledges I had made and the pledges made for me by all my friends and by our platform in the campaign. I soon found that many of those who had supported me in the campaign and had talked reform did not want reform ; but I persevered, determined, as a matter of right and of good policy, to adhere to my party platform and pledges. Of course those who disliked practical reform cried out : " He is going over to the Democrats ! " " He wants social recognition from the rebels ! " and all the rest of those senseless cries such as you now hear about me. Still I persevered ; and when our Legislature met in November last there was apparent harmony between me and my party, and a complete acquiescence in the wisdom of the policy of reform as carried out by me. The result was that at that time the Democracy of this State was disarmed and had no hope, apparently, of even nominating a separate State ticket in opposition to the Republican party. Neither under the guise of " tax unions " or the " Conservative " party could they or did they maintain even an organization worthy the name. The leaders could not persuade the masses of the white people that they could secure any better government than they were enjoying under my Administration.

Now what had I done up to that time ?. I challenge contradiction from any source when I solemnly affirm that I had done nothing ; not one thing which was not pledged by me on every stump in the State when I was a candidate; nothing which our party platform did not demand ; nothing but what every man who now opposes me declared in that campaign to be indispensable ; nothing which you or any other honest Republican would not say was right and Republican. This is a broad statement, but I defy proof of any sort in contradiction of it in any particular. Suppose you talk with some one in Washington who is now denouncing me—and it certainly cannot be difficult, judging from what I hear, to find such. Ask him what Governor Chamberlain had done before these recent judicial elections, that indicated any infidelity to the Republican party ? Ask him if I had appointed Democrats to office ? If he tells you the truth, he will say no, for the fact is that never since 1868 were there so few Democrats in office in this State as since my Administration. I know whereof I affirm, and will prove it to you if you find it denied. Ask him further if I advocated or approved any measures of legislation which were in any possible sense un-Republican or opposed to the interests of the Republican party. He cannot name one, for there is not one. Ask him if I proclaimed any doctrines which were not held by the Republican party. He will not be able to point out one. Ask him if I ever in any way affiliated politically with the Democracy or had any thing to do with them politically, nearly or remotely. He will not be able to point out any such action or tendency of any kind or degree. What, then, is the matter with me ? Why was I disliked or denounced by some members of my own party ? Simply for this, I insisted on reasonable taxes, competent officers, honest expenditures, fair legislation, and no stealing, and the Democrats praised me for it.

The last two things are my offence. I did not sanction schemes of public plunder—such as our " printing ring," for instance, but the cost of public printing per year was cut down from $180,000 to $50,000, and contingent funds from $80,000 to $27,000, and, I repeat, the Democrats praised me.

Now, I make this offer : if any man will contradict a single statement of fact that I have thus far made, I will prove him a liar to your satisfaction. The extent of my guilt, for permitting the Democrats to praise me, I cannot precisely measure. Some men reason that I must be a traitor because Democrats praise me, but that will not quite do, I am sure, with you. Why should not the Democrats praise me ? Low taxes are popular, even with Democrats. Competent officers are preferred to incompetent ones, even by South Carolina Democrats. Honest expenditures of public moneys are acceptable to Democrats even, and " no stealing " is almost everywhere a popular slogan, to say nothing about its being right. I never asked their praise. If there had been any thing to ask of them, I would have earnestly asked them not to praise me, because their praise would give pretext to the Washington *Republican* and such sort of people to denounce me, as they are doing now, as fit only for .the penitentiary. But they did praise me, they do praise me ; and I confess I don't see how I can help it.

Seriously, sir, if I have told you the truth, ought I to be denounced by Republicans as a traitor ? Ought I to be considered by you as " in practical identification with the Democracy," because the taxpayers of South Carolina praise me for doing what every Republican who supported me in the last campaign said I would do, and asked the people to vote for me because I would do ? Such was the condition of affairs here on the 15th day of last December. The Democracy of South Carolina was in perfect collapse. No State issues could have given them life or activity. It is doubtful whether national issues would have had force enough to have even induced a canvass of the State for the Democratic candidates in the coming Presidential campaign, under the circumstances then existing.

On the 16th of December last the General Assembly, under influences which it is impossible now to state fully, elected F. J. Moses, Jr., and W. J. Whipper as Judges of the Circuit Court of this State, the latter for the circuit which embraces the city of Charleston, and constitutes the most important circuit of the State in point of population, wealth, and business. Are you aware who these men are ? Moses was my predecessor as Governor. Unless the universal belief among all classes of people in this State is mistaken, he is as infamous a character as ever in any age disgraced and prostituted public position. If there is anybody in Washington who shall happen to deny this, I will prove it to your abundant satisfaction. To mention nothing else out of the long roll of his offences, here is a specimen : Disappointed in not being renominated for Governor, he entered into a conspiracy with some of the leaders of the Democracy and independent Republicans to elect my opponent, and actually sold out the Commissioners of Election, of whom he had the sole appointment, to my opponents, for $30,-000, of which $15,000 was paid to him in cash, and the rest made contingent on the election of my opponent. Of Whipper it can be said that he seems to have lacked only opportunity to prove himself the equal of Moses in infamy. Ignorant of law, ignorant of morals, a gambler by open practice, an embezzler of public funds, he is as unfit for judicial position as any man whom by any possibility you could name. Neither of these men has even the poor qualification which the infamous Democratic judges of New York had, of such a degree of legal knowledge as to qualify them for the intelligent discharge of any judicial duty. What has been the result ! Their election has sent a thrill of horror through the whole State. It has split the Republicans in twain ; the moribund Democracy has awakened to new life and new hopes. No man who respects civilization and public decency can do less than denounce these elections without measure. No decent man can do less than oppose them, can do less than fight against those who elected them or who acquiesced in them. Do you expect us to do in South Carolina what you would sooner lose your right arm than do in Indiana? Such a test indeed could never arise in Indiana, but it has arisen here, and you err wholly if you imagine that you, living here, would, for one moment, think of tolerating these elections. You could not do it, and you would spurn as an insult the suggestion of supporting or acquiescing in them.

Well, what I have said and done respecting these elections is known to you, I presume. I have done what you would have done—refused to sanction, aid, or abet the carrying out of this great crime against society, and again—worst of all crimes, apparently—the Democrats praise me. Now, in the light of what I have stated, and I am responsible to truth and to anybody who questions or is aggrieved thereby for what I have stated, what would you have me do? At what points, in what particular have I "identified myself practically with the Democracy?" Is it treachery to the Republican party or "identification with the Democracy" to insist on decent men for judges of our courts? There is not a man in South Carolina who would trust Moses with $10. Is it treachery to my party to refuse to tolerate his elevation to the Bench, where he will have millions within the grasp of his thieving, bribed palm? Is it "identification with the Democracy" to oppose such a man by every influence to the bitter end? To doubt your answer is to doubt your moral perceptions.

Now, sir, I have a word to say about what you are reputed to have said to the effect that "you already give up the State to the opposition." That result rests very largely with you. You are influential, able; you hold a commanding position, and you have a commanding voice in our party affairs. If South Carolina is to be "given up to the opposition," it is because you and others whom you can influence fail to help me and my friends "unload"—to use a current phrase—the infamy of these judicial elections. And here let me speak plainly. To cry "Democrat" at me at this time is to support Moses and Whipper. I am a Republican of just as many years' standing as I have seen years of discretion. I have no tendency to any other party; no association, no sympathy with any other party. I want to see South Carolina remain a Republican State, but I tell you no party can rule this State that supports Whipper and Moses, and to denounce us who are to-day denouncing the election of these men is to support them. It is in vain, sir, to say, as the *National Republican* is saying, that you have no sympathy with those elections, that they are almost "an unpardonable blunder," and with the next breath declare that I am "practically identified with the Democracy." If I had done any thing but oppose bad government and especially to denounce and oppose these judicial elections, let it be pointed out. But, until that is done, to denounce me and my friends here as traitors to the Republican party is to "practi-

cally identify" yourself with Moses and Whipper. There is but one
way to save the Republican party in South Carolina, and that way is, I
repeat, to unload Moses and Whipper and all who go with them. It
will be difficult to restore confidence in a party whose members were
once capable of such an act as their election, but if our action is
prompt and decided, if you and the Republicans at Washington will
put your feet upon such things and stamp them out, we can yet make
South Carolina and keep her as safely Republican as Vermont and
Iowa. If this is not done we go down here as a party to hopeless and
deserved defeat and infamy. Neither the Administration at Washington, with all its appliances, civil and military, nor all the denunciations
of the world heaped upon me, can save the Republican party here from
overwhelming defeat during this year, unless we can persuade the people
of this State that such things as these judicial elections will be undone
and never by possibility be repeated.

I have written very earnestly, but with a spirit of perfect respect for
you, and of great admiration for your abilities and your devotion to
the Republican party. I could not forbear from making known to you
my views, and especially from stating to you the facts as they exist here
in South Carolina. I do not care so much to vindicate myself as to give
you a correct idea of the situation here, and the necessity of sustaining
those who are fighting against the suicide of the Republican party—
now nearly committed in South Carolina.

Make any use you see fit of this letter. Place me wherever you see
fit after you have read it ; but, I beseech you, help to save the Republican party here in the only way it can be saved—by a firm, uncompromising and instant denunciation of all such acts as those recent
elections, and by sustaining those who, at great cost to themselves, are
now trying to stay the mad waves of destruction put in motion by those
who find little else to do in such an emergency except to denounce me
as a " Democrat."

Yours respectfully,

D. H. CHAMBERLAIN.

Although Senator Morton had not taken the trouble to notify
Governor Chamberlain that he had been misinformed, or to give
him any assurance of sympathy, he made haste to avoid the force
of the storm of disapprobation which the publication of this letter
aroused against party leaders, who, for the sake of conciliating
the corrupt elements of the party in the South, were aspersing
Governor Chamberlain's party loyalty. It was quickly suspected,
and soon known, to whom the letter was addressed, and the following despatch from Washington appeared in the New York
Herald of February 27th :

The letter from Governor Chamberlain to a prominent Republican, which was
printed in Tuesday's *Herald*, was addressed to Senator Morton, who had been

wrongly reported as having expressed opinions derogatory to the Governor. Senator Morton does not profess to be sufficiently familiar with South Carolina affairs to entertain definite opinions upon them, and he does not, of course, mean to take or be put in the absurd position that he would support corrupt men, such as Governor Chamberlain describes in his letter. The publication of the letter without his name, in the *Herald*, left Mr. Morton unconnected with it ; but since then and in other journals his name has been connected with it, and this makes the statement proper that Mr. Morton did not know that the letter was to be published, and that the copy of it sent to the *Herald* was obtained from another quarter. The conversation reported to Governor Chamberlain, and on which he bases his letter, was a casual private conversation, which was reported without Senator Morton's knowledge and authority, and seems, he says, to have been imperfectly understood. The Chamberlain letter gets a good deal of attention here, especially since it is found that the western Republican journals notice it and him with approval, and demand that he shall be supported by the Administration, so far as it can, in this contest with the corruptionists.

The following letter, written to Dr. H. B. Blackwell, the well-known advocate of woman suffrage, was published in the *Woman's Journal*, February 19, 1876, with this introduction : " The following interesting letter from our faithful friend, Hon. D. H. Chamberlain, of South Carolina, was not written for publication, but is so largely of interest to all suffragists that we feel justified in making it public " :

DEAR MR. BLACKWELL—Your letter of August 26, 1875, was duly received and fully considered. At that time, and for a long time afterwards, I hoped to be able to make a strong effort towards testing the plan sketched by you in our Legislature. The great and constant pressure of duties less remote than this one in their immediate nature kept me from replying at length before the assembling of the Legislature. You know the rest. Disasters greater than you can conceive of in good old New England—wrongs which literally " stir a fever in the blood of age," and which, in Massachusetts, would, I firmly believe, excite violence and mob law—have fallen upon us. I have not an hour's time to look away from this fearful fight for civilization. I wish I could, for my heart goes out more than ever towards all good men and women engaged in any good cause. But my hands are more than full now, and I only write this word that you may know again of my unabated interest in your cause, and why I cannot help you at the present moment.

The most astounding views of our present struggle here seem to have possession of some minds at the North. Thus : I have just received a letter saying that Governor Claflin, like Senator Morton, fears I am straying from the *party fold*. Ah, if I were not too good a party man, such criticisms would make me quit the party forever. And I say now that no " party," however sacred its past, shall ever bind me to the work of helping to put over any people anywhere on earth, as Judges, men whom I know to be thieves, gamblers, and ignoramuses. I take no more counsel of consequences in such a crisis than I would if my wife's honor was at stake.

But I must not burden you with these things. Please give my warm regards to your wife, and believe me

Yours very truly,

D. H. CHAMBERLAIN.

It would be easy to fill the remaining pages of this volume with extracts from the press of the country in commendation of the Governor's prompt action in the exigency presented by the election of Whipper and Moses, and of his subsequent course in the matter. The only discordant voice among Republican newspapers was that of the *National Republican* in Washington, which affected to be, and, unfortunately for the Republican party, was regarded as, in some degree, the organ of the President's opinion. The public sentiment in South Carolina has already been clearly exhibited ; and a few brief extracts from leading journals in other States will sufficiently indicate the accord that existed. The future historian will find by an examination of the current newspaper files abundant amplification and confirmation of the judgment here given :

Many eloquent speeches were made at the banquets in various cities on Friday night, but to our thinking the most eloquent by long odds was that despatch of a dozen lines sent by telegraph from Columbia to Charleston by the Governor of South Carolina : "If there ever was an hour when the spirit of the Puritans—the spirit of undying, unconquerable enmity and defiance to wrong—ought to animate their sons, it is in this hour here in South Carolina." That was spoken like a son of Massachusetts filled with the grand courage of her early days. Unless we underrate the magnanimity of the descendants of the Huguenots in South Carolina, they will stand by this descendant of the Puritans, who, by force of circumstances, is fighting their battle against the deluded and enraged hosts of ignorance. To all appearance this is the crisis of affairs in that State, and whether honor and righteousness triumph depends for the time on the courage of one man who, in allegiance to his convictions of the supreme importance in a republic of an upright judiciary, has defied the organized corruption of the State. There is not at the present moment in the whole country a more splendid exhibition of Puritan character.—*Boston Advertiser* (Rep.).

There is to us something profoundly melancholy in that despatch of his in which he calls for a fresh display on the part of the New Englanders in South Carolina of the old Puritan " spirit of undying, unconquerable enmity and defiance to wrong " at this crisis in the history of the State. The old Puritans showed their mettle and formed their character in conflicts with what was highest and mightiest and most respectable in the civilization of their day. They contended on flood and field with "gallant men and cavaliers," with kings and priests and nobles, with the strongest faiths, the oldest prejudices, the loftiest pride, and the most revered customs the world had to show, and with a fortitude and heroism worthy in all ways of men who sought to establish the kingdom of God on earth. But the tracking of criminals, the work of bringing thieves and pickpockets and highwaymen to the gallows and the cart's-tail, the defence of the public treasury against forgers, and the exclusion of defaulters and embezzlers from the judicial bench, they never dreamed of as any part of their mission. When a man of Governor Chamberlain's standing has to appeal for the execution of tasks of this kind to the spirit which brought Bradford and Winthrop and Endicott over the sea, and closed the ranks behind Cromwell at Naseby, it must be confessed we have fallen on evil days. And yet the days are not so evil as they seem. American civilization may be threatened by many perils, but assuredly it is in no danger of being overthrown by jail-birds, and, bad as the condition of some parts of the South may seem, four years of a pure, high-toned, energetic, and conscientious Administration in Washington, with its face set like flint against peculation and corruption, with neither quarter nor protection for adventurers, jobbers, and intriguers, with cordial social and political relations with the best portion of American society—best, we mean, in regard to morality and intelligence,—would break up the corrupt elements in Southern politics without any difficulty, and if it did not turn the steps of the negro voters into the paths of honesty and economy, would at least fill them with the respect for character and ability through which, if the South is to be saved, its salvation must come.—*N. Y. Nation* (Ind.).

South Carolina is one of the two Southern States left to the Republicans, and, as a party they cannot evade the responsibility of the situation. If the corrupt and dangerous element controls the party there, if a Republican Legislature elects such a man as the country knows Moses to be, and such as Whipper is represented to be, the whole party must take the consequences. Even if the alternative be the restoration of the ex-rebel and negro-hating Democracy, honest men, however regretfully, must admit that such a result is preferable to the election of venal and unjust judges and a system of legislation which is virtual confiscation and robbery. It is in vain for some Republicans to declaim about negro outrages in Mississippi if other Republicans make Moses and Whipper judges in South Carolina without a Republican protest. The voice of the Republican press of the country should unite in such a chorus of condemnation of this act of the Legislature of South Carolina that that body and its abettors in such acts may know how the party abhors and repudiates its conduct. Here is an "outrage" which the simplest can understand, and which strikes at the root of civil society.—*Harper's Weekly* (Rep.).

The policy of Governor Chamberlain in South Carolina, so far as we are able to judge of it, is one which promises the possibility of a new state of things for the South. He has resolved to defeat misrule in the Republican party without ceasing to be a Republican. He has taken issue with the most powerful of the Republican managers, who at the same time include the most unprincipled. He has selected his position well, and it is so strong that it ought to be impregnable. The Governor's work is to begin in South Carolina the reorganization of the Republication party of the South in such a manner as to cast out its bad men, who are sources of incalculable weakness ; to retain all its present elements of enduring strength, and to attract to its ranks the progressive white voters of the section. The first blow has been well aimed. Whipper and Moses were not only bad men, but they were bad leaders, and conspicuous as such, and it was sought to place them where they could do more harm than in any other posts which, by any possibility, they could attain. . . . Governor Chamberlain has undertaken a task which honest and able Republicans in every State south of Virginia must prepare to undertake in their respective fields. The Republican party in the South, if it hopes to regain any of its former strength must be made a new party, as loyal as ever to the general ideas of the Republican national organization, but with more honest leaders, and with a State policy that will secure recruits from the native whites. Acute observers believe that such a reorganization is possible. We have no doubt of it. The old organization is badly shaken. It cannot count on a single Southern State with certainty. Nor can the means by which the power now lost was formerly obtained and kept be again employed. Nothing but a course suited to the times, having for its object the union of portions of both races for the promotion of the progress of the respective States can again give the Republican party the upper hand.—*N. Y. Times* (Rep.).

Governor Chamberlain has refused to commission these amazing judges. It is a bold thing to do, and we await with some anxiety the results. Meantime it is evident that this cannot be a lasting remedy. There is but one way of escape. The party which is responsible for the existing condition must do something for its cure, or at least its alleviation. The Democratic party was responsible for Tweed and his gang so long as it held them up and allowed them to carry on their robberies under its name. It flung them off, late, but at last, and they ceased to be dangerous. The oppressors of South Carolina are of the Republican party. In its name they have carried on their robberies. A Republican Administration has recognized them in the distribution of offices. Republican conventions have admitted them to their counsels. Republican newspapers have defended them. Republican leaders have affiliated with them and felt no shame. This has been one of the strongholds of the managing scamps upon the ignorant negroes, that they were all good Republicans. And the sign of Republicanism is the holding of a government office. The Administration can shake these fellows off if it will. Moses and Whipper and their kind would be hamstrung almost as completely by being stripped of their Republican name as were Tweed and his fellows when the Democracy disowned them. And would it not be better for the party, for the country, for right and justice, to say nothing of the benefit to the people of South Carolina, if a few leaders like Senator Morton should leave off for a little their unusual efforts to discover cases where negroes have been hindered from voting, and briefly consider the condition of the State in which they are having their own will and way ?—*N. Y. Tribune* (Rep.).

Governor Chamberlain, of South Carolina, has again struck a vigorous blow for reform. The Legislature of that State lately elected some notorious scamps as Cir-

cuit Judges—Whipper and ex-Governor Moses among them. The Governor has refused to issue commissions to these two, basing his refusal on some legal technicality.
It is hoped that this will save the State judiciary from the utter degradation prepared
for it by the Legislature. The corrupt judges were elected by a combination of all
the bad elements in the State. We rejoice that Governor Chamberlain has done all
in his power to prevent the consummation of the bargain. He deserves credit for
standing so well by his recent record of honesty and intelligence.—*Chicago Tribune*
(Rep.).

This action on the part of Chamberlain is promising, as it gives some hope that
South Carolina, the stronghold of the black and white carpet-baggers, will yet be
blessed with an honest government. The character of these men, Whipper and
Moses, is despicable beyond expression. It is encouraging to know that Governor
Chamberlain has determined to abate their recent triumph and free the judiciary from
such disgrace.—*Louisville Courier-Journal* (Dem.).

The whole proceeding was a disgrace to the State and degrading to the judiciary,
and will justly react against the dominant party. Such proceedings have a tendency
to make the people feel less indignant at such frauds as those by which the white people of Mississippi obtained control of the State. If the Senate sees fit to investigate
the Mississippi election, it should not overlook the judicial election in South Carolina.—*Hartford Courant* (Rep.).

For the escape, if it is an escape, for the reprieve, if it is only a reprieve, South
Carolina is indebted to her Yankee Governor. We are glad to see that the representative Conservative papers recognize the debt, and the obligation of standing by him
loyally and effectively in the coming campaigns against the public enemy. He has
gone too far to turn back, even if he had the faintest desire to do so, and they could
not ask, as they certainly cannot find, an abler leader.—*Springfield Republican* (Ind.).

At the annual dinner of the New England Society of Charleston, S. C., a telegram
from Governor Chamberlain "was read at midnight amid the wildest enthusiasm.
It contained this passage: "If ever there was an hour when the spirit of the
Puritans—the spirit of undying, unconquerable enmity and defiance to wrong—ought
to animate their sons, it is this hour, here in South Carolina." These earnest words
were what might have been expected from a brave and determined chief magistrate
engaged in a sharp conflict with a corrupt Legislature, whose choice of incompetent
and unprincipled judges he had just boldly hindered. Deaf to the entreaties of timid
friends, and undismayed by the bullying of influential partisans, he took the highest
ground, resolved to have no master but righteousness, and no leader but the truth.
If such a course injures a party, it must be because the party is rotten, and
not because the course is wrong; and Governor Chamberlain was wise in availing
himself of the best New England traditions in his eloquent appeal for sympathy and
help in the battle with iniquity.—*Christian Register* (Boston, Mass.).

Certainly the gratitude of the State of South Carolina is now due to her Governor,
the Hon. D. H. Chamberlain, for his last manly stand upon the side of intelligence

and virtue. In refusing to sign the commissions that would elevate Moses and Whipper to the judges' bench, he has probably saved that State from a future of misery and shame that no pen can describe. It requires considerable fortitude for a man to act in opposition to the majority of the party that elected him, but if in choosing Chamberlain as their Chief Executive they expected to make him a tool with which to rob and plunder the State, they were mistaken in the man, and by his wise and patriotic course he is fast gaining the admiration and esteem of the law-abiding and liberty-loving throughout the Union.—*Charlotte* (N. C.) *Observer* (Dem.).

The letter [to Senator Morton] of Governor Chamberlain of South Carolina, printed in yesterday's *Gazette*, is a manly, straightforward, and able document, and throws considerable light upon the difficulties the Republican party has had to contend with in the Southern States. Those States, most of them, have been lost to the party because rascals were elevated to office and thieves were suffered to plunder the people. The crimes committed honorable men were not able to defend, and to the indictments presented by Southern Democrats, those who were informed and had a regard for truth, were forced to plead guilty. As a consequence, nearly all of the Southern States are now in the hands of the Democratic party. South Carolina was moving steadily in the same direction until Governor Chamberlain was elected. He stepped in between the people and the thieves, and has manfully stood his ground. On this account many of his own party turned against him, and are now charging that he has left the Republican party ; but he says he has not, and we say that his course is the only one to preserve the South, or the North either. . . . If South Carolina cannot be saved to the Republican party by the course of Governor Chamberlain, it is not worth saving and had better be lost. That officer, therefore, deserves the thanks and moral support of the Republicans of the whole country, and it is only to be regretted that other Southern States have not men of equal ability and integrity to take the lead and guide the party to victory.—*Cincinnati Gazette* (Rep.).

The unique position of the *National Republican* has already been mentioned. Its temper is illustrated in the following sentences :

Governor Chamberlain has been inveigled into a path of political turpitude, which must eventually end in his personal political destruction. By a shrewd and carefully prepared scheme the Democracy have succeeded in making him a pseudo-apostate from his party constituency, and securing his gubernatorial influence to further their efforts in overthrowing the Republican power in the State.

The spirit of the Democratic papers, which were chiefly concerned, not for good government in South Carolina, but for party success there and in the nation, is shown by the following extracts, in which it is noticeable that the example of Mississippi, where, by a deliberately planned system of criminal terrorization, involving every brutal crime against persons and rights, supplemented by monstrous frauds in elections, the minority had obtained control of the State Government, is recommended to South Carolina. Governor Chamberlain stood for just administration in its broadest application, and the equal rights of all citizens without distinction of race or party. These cared only for securing the power of their party and caste, and did not hesitate to abuse, and to counsel abusing, law, rights, and humanity, in order to attain their end. The New York *World* indulged in appeals, of which this specimen will suffice :

Are the honest people of South Carolina less desirous of reform than were their brethren of Mississippi ? Is the necessity for revolution less urgent ? Are they less courageous and devoted ? If not, let them, by a similar course, achieve the same success. South Carolina dwells fondly upon the heroism of her sons during the Revolution of a century ago, and proposes to invite all who honor courage and patriotism to meet with her people at historic Moultrie. A better Centennial celebration than this will be the redemption of the State. The tyranny against which the free-born men of South Carolina rose in 1776 was far less oppressive, far less disgraceful, than that under which their descendants groan to-day.

Some Southern Democratic journals reiterated, and in less covert terms, the same advice.

In the emancipation of Mississippi from the dominion of corruption and barbarism the people of South Carolina have an exemplification of what can be accomplished by united, uncompromising, and determined effort. Let them then take courage, and casting aside all ideas of [an] unnatural, impossible alliance of intelligence and virtue with ignorance and villainy, let them resolve to protect themselves from threatened oppression, degradation, and confiscation. In the struggle that has been forced upon them they will have the sympathy and encouragement of true men of all parties and all sections of the Union. In such a struggle they will be sure to triumph.—*Savannah* (Ga.) *News.*

What has happened in Mississippi is inevitable in South Carolina. The whites must, by combination and enormous sacrifices of time and money in controlling this depraved suffrage, achieve for themselves a government under which honest industry can live, or they must abandon the State to African savagery, heathenism, and squalor. There is no use in disguising these plain facts. They are bound to be recognized and acknowledged as facts all over the American continent. Whether it will or no, Radicalism, in the enforcement of suffrage on the negro, is bound to stand convicted of high treason against good government and republican liberty. The fatal effects can be delayed or averted only by a management and address which shall overweigh the majority of voters against their own bias and in favor of a government which shall protect honest industry and civilization. That is Republicanism with a vengeance ; but it is the only condition and price of rescue from barbarism, and the salvation of the Anglo-Saxon existence in these States. All parties in South Carolina now see it. They have exhausted every other means to enlist the blacks in favor of public decency, honesty, and fair government, and met with total defeat at every turn. Now they have probably got to *buy* immunity from the black voters. They can do it cheaper from the original source of power than from its representatives. These last having the levying and appropriation of taxes, in the payment of which they are totally uninterested, can pay themselves as much as they choose to vote. But the ordinary black voter in South Carolina must be content with what i offered him. The bribe must be forthcoming either at one end or the other, and economy and security demand the earlier application.—*Macon* (Ga.) *Telegraph*.

The prime peril of South Carolinians at this moment, is being deceived by *a trumpery show of brave words* from the Governor and his organs, and so lulled into a security which may be at once false and deadly. It is certainly about time that some native of South Carolina, *who has not bowed the knee to Baal*, should come to the front and rally his people to such an effort as that of Mississippi. The civilization of the Carolinas, in *ante-bellum* days, produced great men. Since the irruption of Chamberlain and *his* civilization, *the fecundating power of the stock seems to have suspended operations.—Augusta* (Ga.) *Constitutionalist*.

To this slur the Charleston *News and Courier* replied :

The Augusta *Constitutionalist* does not advance the interests of the South Carolina Democracy by such words : . . . Governor Chamberlain has, by his acts, proved his sincerity as a reformer, and the Democracy of the State will stand by him and protect him, because he has proved his sincerity. Nobody asks Governor Chamberlain to leave his party or abandon his party. principles ; and in any other paper than the *Constitutionalist* it would be disgusting, as well as surprising, to set down one of the boldest executive acts of the decade as " a trumpery show of brave words." There is no false security in South Carolina, and the press of this State, in praising Governor Chamberlain, are the " organs " of the people, not of a man or a party.

Hon. Alex. H. Stephens, of Georgia, was a visitor to Columbia in the spring of 1876. After his departure a letter appeared in a North Carolina paper, the Charlotte *Observer*, professing to report a long conversation with Mr. Stephens, in which he was represented as denouncing Governor Chamberlain as a " carpetbagger," to whom it was a disgrace for the people of the State to submit. This report was so widely at variance with the sentiments he had expressed to the Governor and to others, that the editor of the *Union-Herald* addressed a letter to Mr. Stephens, inquiring whether he had been correctly reported. Mr. Stephens responded promptly and earnestly, saying :

The whole of this pretended report of a conversation with me is an entire fabrication from beginning to end. I never had any such conversation with anybody in Columbia or elsewhere. I uttered no opinion or sentiment about Governor Chamberlain while in Columbia or on my way home, except such as was expressive of gratification at the general satisfaction which his Administration seemed to be giving throughout the State—even to many intelligent citizens I had met with who had not favored his election. Of the merits or demerits of his official acts, however, I expressed no opinion of my own, for I was not sufficiently informed as to the facts to have any opinion upon the subject. I was nevertheless gratified to see those whose interests and welfare were most deeply affected so generally satisfied at his course. This feeling of gratification on my part I repeatedly expressed, but not a word of disparagement of Governor Chamberlain.

Unquestionably the purpose of the misrepresentation of the sentiments of this distinguished and influential Southern Democrat was to assist the efforts of those Democrats in South Carolina who were plotting for a partisan campaign, and fomenting hostility against the man whose fidelity in duty and courage in every exigency were commending him too much to the gratitude and confidence of voters whose suffrages they desired to command.

CHAPTER XV.

THE election of judges so overshadowed all other proceedings during this session of the Legislature that they
attracted comparatively little attention. In the whirlwind and
tumult following that event the members of the Legislature were
dizzied, and they recognized that so far as their political futures
were concerned, little depended on what they might do in addition to what they had done. Almost the only important business
transacted having special significance in illustration of Governor
Chamberlain's policy in administration related to appropriations
and taxation. The fact that the veto of the supply bill of the
last session was unanimously sustained has been stated. Much
as the Governor was engrossed with the affair of the judges and
its consequential incidents, he relaxed in no particular his personal attention and labors in the work of reforming the long-
standing evils of legislation and administration. In the task of
securing the passage of a fair tax bill and an economical appropriation bill' he exerted himself especially, and on the 27th of
January addressed the following letter to the Speaker of the
House of Representatives:

EXECUTIVE CHAMBER,
COLUMBIA, S. C., January 27, 1876.

Hon. R. B. Elliott, Speaker House of Representatives :

SIR—A copy of the annual appropriation bill, as reported by the Ways and Means Committee of the House of Representatives, has been laid before me for my consideration. It is suggestive of some considerations, which my sense of official duty leads me to present at once to the General Assembly.

Two striking facts appear from an examination of the first and second sections of the bill : First. That the appropriations made by the first section reach an aggregate amount of $190,800, while the tax levied by the supply act to meet these appropriations will produce not more than $130,000, leaving a deficiency of $60,800. Second. That the appropriations made by the second section reach an aggregate amount of $179,200, while the tax levied by the supply act to meet those appropriations will produce not more than $130,000, leaving a deficiency of $49,200. These two items of deficiency amount to $110,000.

It was foreseen when the supply act was matured, and passed early in the present session, that the reduction of the levies, so as to bring the entire amount to its present limit, would inevitably leave a deficiency, a result which I then greatly deplored, but which seemed necessary in the present impoverished condition of the people of the State.

An effort was made at the last session of the General Assembly to reduce the salaries of public officers, which resulted in the passage by the House of Representatives of a bill which would, in my judgment, have accomplished good results. That bill has been before the Senate during the present session, and has not yet been disposed of. That bill, or a bill which shall reduce the aggregate amount of salaries now paid to public officers, will furnish the chief means of preventing the immense deficiencies which I have pointed out. The delay of the Senate in acting upon this measure must embarrass all our efforts to properly adjust our tax levies and appropriations. If a bill reducing salaries shall pass, the present appropriations can, of course, be correspondingly reduced. If such a bill shall not pass, then the appropriations, so far as salaries are concerned, must remain as now reported, and our efforts to retrench expenses must be directed to other points. I therefore urge upon the General Assembly the great importance of prompt action upon the salary bill, in order that the amount of appropriations required may be known while the appropriation bill is under consideration.

Of the perfect practicability of a large reduction of salaries I have no doubt. I consider it compatible with the efficiency of our civil service generally, demanded by the wants of the people, as well as by their expectations when we were elected to our several offices, and especially by the present condition of the industries and sources of revenue in the State. And in making such reductions I say explicitly that I am in favor of large reductions, from the highest office to the lowest, wherever the salaries are not protected by the Constitution. I say, let there be no favoritism, no partiality, at any point ; and in the case of my own salary, though it is protected by the Constitution from reduction during my present term, I will voluntarily submit to as great a reduction as may be made generally in other salaries. A reduction by one third of the present salaries would not, in my judgment, be too great. Such a reduction would at once remove almost the entire amount of deficiency arising under the first section of the Appropriation Act, and would likewise reduce by nearly one third the deficiency arising under the second section.

In addition to this, there are points at which still larger reductions might be made without public injury. Upon this point I submit to the General Assembly whether the present salaries of the Circuit Solicitors might not be wholly abolished ; whether the salaries of County School Commissioners might not also be reduced by one half, and whether the pay of County Treasurers and County Auditors might not be so arranged as to increase the revenues of the State while at the same time reducing the pay of those officers. I know that if there is an earnest purpose on our part to serve the public exclusively in these matters, such reductions can be made as will nearly or quite remove the necessity of deficiencies in our appropriations for the present year.

I especially urge that the question of the reduction of salaries be brought to an early decision. No more light will be shed by delay upon the question, and if no reductions are to be made, it is better that the result be known, in order that the appropriations may be arranged accordingly.

I call special attention likewise to the propriety of a careful revision of the appropriations other than for salaries made in the second section of the appropriation bill as now reported. If our appropriations are brought within our receipts for taxes, the several appropriations will be promptly paid, and all our public institutions can be conducted upon a cash basis, which will of itself greatly reduce the expenses of these institutions.

By proper legislation the expenses of both the Lunatic Asylum and the State Penitentiary can be reduced, and the efficiency of both the institutions be increased. These are subjects which require careful and intelligent examination. I do not advise hasty or ill-considered reductions at these points, but I do express the opinion, founded on my own examination, that considerable reductions in the expenses of these institutions can be made by limiting the persons to be admitted to the Lunatic Asylum to those classes whose forms of lunacy require special medical treatment, and to those whose lunacy develops itself in violent or uncontrollable actions ; and in the case of the Penitentiary by employing the labor of the convicts in profitable occupations. I also urge that a careful inquiry be made as to the amounts actually required for the proper support of the State Orphan Asylum, the State Normal School, and the Agricultural College.

In the ways suggested and in many other ways it is possible, in my judgment, to bring the appropriations of the present year quite near to the amounts which will be derived from the levies already made. The work of retrenching expenses and removing abuses is always difficult, but it is always honorable, and at the present moment it is necessary. My own pledge when a candidate for my present office, and the pledges of the political party which elected me, require it, and, what should be even more binding in its obligations upon us all, the wants of the people of the State require it.

Very respectfully,
D. H. CHAMBERLAIN,
Governor.

On the 2d of February, the Committee of Ways and Means met to consider the tax bill that had been drafted; and, by invitation, the Governor was present to make suggestions. The following report of his part of the proceedings was published the next day in the Columbia *Union-Herald:*

The Governor, in addressing the Committee, said that he was glad to have been invited at a time when his recommendations would be most appropriate, that is, before any action had been taken by the Committee. He spoke not only as Governor, but as a citizen. He did not wish his views as now expressed to convey the impression that unless they were acceded to he would be bound to act strictly upon them when the bill should be perfected. He would urge his views as a citizen, as Governor, and as a member of a party which he desired to be strong because it was right.

A printed bill was before the Committee from which the Governor spoke when making his comparisons, it being one that had been proposed but not yet considered. He felt that it was necessary even in a party light to give token that the pledges of the last campaign had been in some measure fulfilled. He read the fifth plank, a resolution in the platform adopted when he was nominated. This pledges the party, if successful, to abate admitted extravagances, reduce salaries, dispense with unnecessary offices, and bring the expenses within reasonable appropriations and tax levies. This was a voice which should be heeded, but it was not the strongest one calling upon us. The voice of duty to a tax-burdened and impoverished people demanded that we should practise that economy which the hard times had enforced upon them. He felt bound, as Governor and as a citizen, to insist upon carrying out these pledges by practical reforms. This is the last year of the two for which we are elected, and it is our last chance to do that which ought to have been done before.

In vindicating his views on the tax levy he was necessitated to refer largely to the appropriation bill, and a reduced levy means also reduced appropriations.

The first section of the proposed tax bill levies $1\frac{1}{4}$ mills. This should be reduced to $\frac{9}{10}$ of a mill. In order to do this, a reduction of salaries should be made. The Governor's salary should be made $2,500; private secretary, $1,200; messenger, $300. The Lieutenant Governor's salary should be struck out entirely, and he should receive the pay and emoluments of a Senator, he having no duties except that of presiding officer. In speaking of the State officers he said that they should no longer be considered as "heads of departments," whose sole duty is to sign papers prepared by clerks. They should be required to do the work themselves for which the State pays them, with an allowance for clerk hire when it was necessary. He recommended the following as a fair basis: For Secretary of State, $2,000, with $500 for clerk hire; Comptroller General, $2,000, clerk hire, $2,000; Treasurer, the same; Superintendent of Education, $2,000, clerk hire, $500; Attorney General, $2,000, clerk hire, $500; Adjutant General, $500, with no clerk, there being almost nothing to do in that office.

No change was recommended in the salaries of Judges. They are not only protected by the Constitution, but they are prohibited from engaging in their professions. The Clerk of the Supreme Court should be allowed but $1,000, and the salary of the Reporter struck out altogether; the reports can be not only made, but published, by contract, without expense to the State. The salary of Solicitors should be struck out altogether. Good lawyers can easily be found now, as in the past, to take the office for the fees. Such men as C. D. Melton, Mr. Youmans, and Judge Reed, were Solicitors without any salaries. He would not say that some of our present Solicitors could live on the fees, but the better the lawyer the more easily he could live upon them.

Reductions were recommended, also, as follows: Keeper of Statehouse, to $600; watchmen to $300; Superintendent of Lunatic Asylum to $2,000; Physician of Penitentiary to $300.

The County Auditors are aggregated to receive $32,200; they should be reduced so as to bring the aggregate to $25,000, and the salary of a clerk for the Auditor of Charleston County should be stricken out. School commissioners should not be elected to live upon the office. Such men were generally unfit to be school commissioners. What a travesty upon a school system it was to elect men to examine and employ teachers who themselves, in many cases, were too ignorant to more than sign their names.

The health officers, who are employed but six months in the year, should be reduced to half their present salaries. Competent physicians in Beaufort, Charleston, and Georgetown could add such duties to their regular professions.

The Governor's contingent would be sufficient at $2,000, and the system of offering rewards by the State for murderers should be discontinued. The counties should act in such matters. The proposed contingents for other officers were reasonable, except that of the Adjutant General, who needed none.

He recommended that no fund be provided to carry on litigation. If occasion demanded, the best lawyers in the State could be had to aid the Attorney General and get their pay when the service was performed, through the action of the Legislature.

The Comptroller General and School Commissioner could doubtless get on with $2,000 and $500 respectively for blanks. The funding expenses and the publication of statements of the Treasurer can be done for $2,000 and $1,000 respectively. These items are all in the first section, and if the recommendations are adopted, the tax levy can be brought down to $\frac{9}{10}$ of a mill.

The second section can be reduced to $\frac{1\frac{1}{3}}{13}$ of a mill. This is for penal and charitable institutions. The Governor suggests the letting out by contract of the labor of the convicts. If this is done, he thinks that $20,000 will be sufficient for the Penitentiary.

The Lunatic Asylum, if those now in it who are only weak-minded, idiotic, and harmlessly insane were sent to the county poorhouses, leaving those who are curable and those who are too violent to be left unrestrained, can be carried on for $40,000.

The State Orphan Asylum has only seventy-five children, and should be allowed $6,000, instead of $10,000.

The University should be reduced to an expenditure of only $30,000. The keeping up of the hollow shell of an ancient institution should give place to a useful and practical high school. As at present conducted, it was a waste of money and a waste of effort. We do not need the name of a university, but the reality of a practical education.

The Normal School and the Agricultural College should be voted no more than $5,000 each.

These reductions would amount to $68,000, and would be sufficiently provided for in a levy of $\frac{11}{13}$ of a mill.

The printing contract will expire with this year, and all the printing needed by the State can easily be contracted for by responsible parties for $25,000. One fifth of a mill will be enough for this, instead of one third.

Legislative expenses could by a proper law be brought into one half of the present expense. Six dollars a day for fifty days for 157 members would be $47,100 ; mileage, $9,000 ; attachés, $5,000 ; contingents, $3,000. This would call for one half mill, instead of one mill.

The two mills for schools could as well as not be made one and a half mills. He was not certain but that, instead of being injured, the schools would be benefited by reducing State aid and relying more upon local aid. Our space forbids an attempt to give the Governor's very interesting remarks upon this subject.

The deficiency tax, as at present advised, could not be less than $\frac{4}{5}$ mill, but if the Senate passed the salary bill now before it $\frac{1}{2}$ mill might be enough.

The above, with two mills for interest, and $1\frac{1}{2}$ mills for the two "bonanza" Acts, will foot up $8\frac{1}{4}$ mills. The Governor urged that an effort be made to bring it to 8 mills, expressing the belief that it could be done.

Some discussion took place upon the subject of taking care of the bills of the Bank of the State. The Governor refused to advise the Committee on the subject. His advice given heretofore had been misunderstood and disregarded. That there would be a great deal of trouble experienced this year from this source he now knew and all knew. If they were to be taken care of, the tax levy would not fail to be high, let the reductions made be ever so sweeping. The duty, in view of this, was the more imperative that the suggestions made to-night be carefully considered.

The Columbia correspondent of the Charleston *News and Courier*, in his despatch that evening, after mentioning the items of retrenchment recommended by the Governor, said :

His estimate reduces the appropriations as follows : Salaries, from $190,600 to

$118,000. Public institutions, from $179,200 to $110,800. Legislative expenses, from $128,000 to $64,000. The public printing, from $50,000 to $25,000.

His speech was long and earnest, and was carefully listened to, the reporters being allowed to be present. The Committee decided at once to come down to the Governor's figures, adopted his recommendations, and will to-morrow report the bill in that form. In addition to this, the Senate Finance Committee to-day reported the House bill to reduce salaries, with amendments making reductions aggregating $60,000.

The same journal, commenting editorially on these facts in a subsequent issue, said :

This is the direct work of Governor Chamblerlain, and we value it for the proof it gives that he has the determination and the power to bring the Legislature to terms, and for the hope it raises of still better things next year, more than for the amount of money actually saved to the people, important as that is. The tax bills had become a test question with the public. Both Governor Chamberlain and the Legislature were pledged to reduce the taxes to the lowest possible figure. The public were determined to hold both departments of the Government to their voluntary engagements, and to allow neither the Executive nor the Legislature to excuse its own shortcomings by pleading the perversity of the other. The result is a most auspicious one. Governor Chamberlain has done what no Democrat could, with such radical materials, have hoped to accomplish ; and if, by his conduct, he has strengthened himself with his own party, as he doubtless has done, we need not deplore that fact so long as he exerts his influence for the benefit of the whole people.

As a further testimony to the energy and success of the Governor, an editorial article from the *News and Courier* (February 5, 1876), which bore the title "A Week's Work," is here given.

The rapidity with which defeat follows defeat must stun the thieves in Columbia, and certainly takes away the breath of the public. Here is one week's work :

1. The Radical rascals, in caucus, are unable to agree to take a recess, so as to bring the General Assembly together again in the summer.

2. The resolution of Jones to inquire whether the Governor had done his duty, in relation to the official bonds of certain State officers, is laid on the table in the Senate, and the irascible Nash admits that he has had enough of fighting Mr. Chamberlain.

3. The Committee of Democrats, appointed on Leslie's motion to investigate the charges of fraud against him as Land Commissioner, ask to be discharged, because Leslie will not consent to a thorough investigation, and Mr. Speaker Elliott decides that the Committee already have full power to inquire into all the transactions of the Commission ; the Committee will, therefore, give Leslie more than he bargained for.

4. Governor Chamberlain meets the Committee of Ways and Means, shows them how to cut down expenses for 1876–77, and tells them they can, and must, reduce the State tax from 10 mills, as proposed, to $8\frac{1}{4}$ mills ; the Committee agree, and report accordingly.

5. Governor Chamberlain notifies the Ways and Means Committee that they can further reduce the State tax, for 1876–77, from 8¼ mills to 8 mills ; the Committee agree.

6. The new election bill, putting the appointment of Managers of Election in the hands of the Legislature, and creating a Canvassing Board of the Louisiana sort,—a deliberate plan of the thieves to count in their candidates next November,—is defeated in the House, on the first division, by a handsome majority, Speaker Elliott and Whipper voting with the minority.

7. J. D. Robertson, Text-book Commissioner, is reported by the Committee of Privileges and Elections as having made corrupt proposals to Northern publishing houses, and will probably be expelled from the Legislature.

8. A motion prevails to expunge from the House journals the infamous harangue in which Whipper poured out his abuse on Governor Chamberlain and his praise on F. J. Moses, Jr.; in the course of the debate Whipper attacks Elliott, and Elliott, in return, denounces Whipper as an ingrate, a falsifier, and a knave ; it was Elliott who secured Whipper's election as a Judge, and who told the colored members of the House that, by their vote for Whipper, he would measure their Republicanism.

Governor Chamberlain has cowed these people. They are on the run, and he keeps them running. To him, not to them, the honor and praise ! They are not changed in heart or purpose. They are as corrupt, as malicious, and as ignorant as on Black Thursday. The people know it, and will not be deceived.

The tax bills and appropriation bills, as passed by the Legislature and approved by the Governor, were the lightest for many years, and in all particulars substantially in accordance with the Governor's earnest recommendations. The Legislature also passed two "bonanza" bills which were framed to his satisfaction and thus avoided the objections made to the similar bills of the previous session. These things were not accomplished without hot and bitter conflicts, and the abuse poured out upon their "ugly honest" chief magistrate by the leaders of a faction in the Legislature was as virulent as can be conceived. They were enraged beyond all control because they discovered that they were growing weaker while he was growing stronger. Having failed in their attempted *coup* of the 13th of December, their followers had lost confidence, and were beginning to hedge.

The Worcester (Mass.) *Spy*, commenting on Governor Chamberlain's struggle with the Legislature over the supply bills, made these suggestive remarks :

Considered in connection with the history of supply bills, and the analogy between our political institutions and those of Great Britain, the fate of the bill above referred to is especially curious. English sovereigns had quarrels with their parliaments on various occasions, and the parliament could only bring the monarch to terms by refusing the supplies he asked for. The king often complained of the meagreness of the parliamentary grants, and to obtain even much less than he asked had often to submit to what he considered humiliating concessions, but he never complained that the supplies were too great. But in South Carolina we have the novel spectacle of a prolonged contest between the Executive and the Legislature, in which the cause of quarrel is that the latter persists in raising from the people by taxation more money for executive uses than the Governor thinks the people ought to pay or the executive branch of the government ought to spend.

On the 21st of January the Governor removed Mr. Thomas S. Cavender from two offices held by his appointment, one that of Auditor of Chesterfield County, the other that of a Commissioner under the Act for the settlement and payment of claims against the State. By charges brought to the attention of the Governor, and to which the defence, to say the least, was not conclusive, it appeared probable that in the latter office Mr. Cavender had abused the confidence reposed in him, to the injury of the State and his personal profit. The Governor made public a full statement of the circumstances, reviewing all the evidence, and concluding as follows:

No duty could well be more painful than that of reaching a conclusion unfavorable to Mr. Cavender. The matter has, however, passed beyond my control, and I am compelled to take my action under my responsibility as a public officer. During the passage of the Act in question, I insisted, as a condition precedent to my approval of the Act, that the Comptroller General, or some other competent and responsible officer, should have the power, and be charged with the duty, of auditing all claims under the Act ; and if now, in view of the facts which at the very least raise a very grave suspicion that Mr. Cavender has sought to abuse that power, I should fail to act with promptness and decision, I should justly expose myself to suspicion equally grave respecting myself. I shall therefore require the immediate resignation by Mr. Cavender of both the offices he now holds under my appointment. Whatever further steps may be taken, either to vindicate or condemn any parties connected with those transactions, will be properly conducted by other tribunals having greater powers and better facilities than I have for reaching the exact truth.

In his Inaugural Address Governor Chamberlain spoke with much emphasis on the subject of Executive pardons of persons duly convicted of crimes. Probably no form of the misrule of the State under Scott and Moses was more degrading and intolerable than the system of wholesale pardons for political, personal, or pecuniary considerations. The sale of pardons was open and notorious under Moses, and the last hour of his official life was spent in signing and issuing pardons, to the number of fifty-seven. Governor Chamberlain, in his Inaugural Address, said :

I think it proper that I should state on this occasion, that in the exercise of the power conferred on the Governor by the Constitution "to grant reprieves and pardons after conviction," I shall endeavor to keep in view the end for which our criminal laws are framed—the repression of crime and the protection of society. The occasions will be rare and attended by peculiar circumstances, in which I shall feel justified in setting aside the judgments of our courts and the verdicts of our juries.

How he maintained this standard and performed the most painful duty of a chief executive officer, the records afford most satisfactory evidence During his term the majesty and authority of the law were not made contemptible by the Chief Magistrate. His scrupulous care and firmness in this particular a few examples will serve to illustrate conclusively. The following letter was addressed to citizens of both political parties in Colleton County who had petitioned for the pardon of a man convicted of manslaughter :

EXECUTIVE CHAMBER,
COLUMBIA, S. C., August 27, 1875.

GENTLEMEN :—I have received your petition for the pardon of Joseph Corley, convicted at the last February term of court in your county. I have referred the same, according to my invariable rule, to His Honor Judge Maher for his report and advice. I now have his reply, accompanied by his notes of evidence at the trial. I have carefully read all the evidence, and I fully concur in the following extract, which I make from Judge Maher's letter : "It will be seen," says the Judge (from the evidence), "that the dying declarations (of the deceased) were proved by other witnesses besides relations of the deceased ; that they were corroborated to some extent by the confession of the prisoner himself ; that the notion of self-defence is supported by the prisoner's statement alone, and that the verdict of manslaughter was the most charitable view that could have been taken of the case by a conscientious jury."

I cannot reconcile the testimony with the position set forth in the petition. On the contrary, it seems to me that the evidence fully warranted the verdict, and if so, how can I grant a pardon within less than six months after the trial?

I am aware it may be said that you, gentlemen, who have signed the petition have more interest in the welfare of your county than I can possibly have, and that you would not ask the pardon if it were incompatible with the public good. Still I feel that I ought not to act against the evidence presented to me, and that something ought to be shown which impairs the moral validity of the verdict or shows that justice does not require the enforcement of the sentence before I should intervene. I am struggling hard to restore the laws to their proper force by abstaining from the use of the pardoning power, except in cases when I can see sufficient reason for believing that the law will not be weakened by the Executive clemency. It would be vastly easier to yield to such appeals as the present case makes to me, but I submit to you whether in so doing I should not be responsible for an improper interference with the course of justice.

As now advised, I must decline to grant a pardon in this case, or to modify the sentence at present.

Very respectfully your obedient servant,
D. H. CHAMBERLAIN,
Governor.

It was Governor Chamberlain's invariable custom in acting upon applications for commutations of sentence, or for pardons, to prepare and give to the public, through the press, a statement of the reasons for his actions. The following examples of this practice exhibit the feelings of a merciful man, who recognizes that he is bound by public duty to execute the laws. The closing paragraphs of the first paper are worthy of special attention. In the second it is noticeable that the Governor refused to grant a pardon even upon the recommendation of the judge who tried the accused, being convinced of his guilt and fair trial.

THE STATE vs. DENIS R. BUNCH—MURDER.

Denis R. Bunch was tried and convicted upon an indictment for murder before His Honor Judge Reed, at the February term of the General Sessions for Charleston County, and sentenced to be hung on the 16th day of April, 1875.

On the day previous to the execution of the sentence I was induced to grant a respite of one week, and before the expiration of this respite an order was granted by the Lieutenant Governor postponing further the execution of the sentence until the 28th of May, 1875.

It appears from the papers submitted to the Lieutenant Governor, and subsequently placed in my hands, that the action of the Lieutenant Governor was mainly influenced by the statements contained in affidavits of A. F. Farrar and Julius M. Bing, to the effect that they were in possession of information and facts which would show extenuating circumstances sufficient to induce Executive clemency, which information and facts they were prevented from laying before me by my temporary absence from the State.

Subsequently the friends of Bunch laid before me the papers, which were considered by the Lieutenant Governor sufficient to justify his action, and, by the friends of Bunch, to warrant me in at least commuting the sentence from death to imprisonment for life. Official copies of one or two papers which were deemed essential, and which were to have been furnished me, have not been received, owing to sufficient causes, but I have been able to obtain, in a reliable form, all the information which those missing papers could have contained.

I have now patiently heard and read all that is claimed by any one can bear upon the question that I am to decide.

Having previously considered the whole case, with the exception of such information and statements as have been laid before me since the order of the Lieutenant Governor was made, it is not necessary for me to repeat that I am forced to concur in the verdict of the jury and the sentence of the Court, so far as they depend upon the facts developed on the trial.

The additional circumstances which are now relied upon as furnishing grounds for a change of the sentence are these : That upon the trial one F. A. Michell testified, among other things, that about nine o'clock on the morning after the homicide, Bunch, in reply to an inquiry why he shot Donahue, said " that he had killed the Irish son of a ――, and he was not sorry, and he intended to kill two more sons of ―― if he got out " ; that upon the trial subsequently of the case of the State *vs.* F. W. Dawson, in the same court, Michell being a witness, his testimony was disproved, and his general character for veracity was successfully impeached. It is urged that these facts are sufficient to justify me in concluding that the statements made by Michell on the trial of Bunch are unworthy of credence, and that when his testimony is rejected an essential part of the evidence upon which the verdict and sentence rest is eliminated. My attention was also called to the reference made by Judge Reed in passing sentence upon Bunch to the testimony of Michell, and it is urged that this testimony must have been essential in establishing in the minds of the jury and the Court the malice of Bunch in committing the homicide.

It is clear that it is now impossible to determine with certainty what weight was given by the jury to the testimony of Michell ; but I cannot think that it follows from this that, admitting the falsity of Michell's testimony, the conclusion should be reached that the jury would have rendered a different verdict, or that the present verdict is not fully supported by the other testimony in the case. On the contrary, the question before me is whether the testimony of Michell can reasonably be regarded as an essential part of the testimony necessary to fully sustain the verdict rendered. If, after rejecting the testimony of Michell, there manifestly remains sufficient evidence to support the verdict, I cannot feel myself at liberty for this reason to disregard it. I have carefully re-examined the testimony in the case other than that of Michell, and am fully convinced that the verdict of the jury was correct, and the sentence of the Court such as the law prescribes.

I find, indeed, that Judge Reed, in passing sentence and reciting the leading features of the evidence, used the following language : " Next morning, when you (Bunch) had had time to cool, you repeated your declaration that you had shot ' one Irishman, and, thank God, he was not a native, and when you got the chance again you would shoot others." Bunch at this point shook his head, and, the judge observing him, continued : " This may not be true ; but, after a fair trial, and a defence by able and zealous counsel, after a fair hearing, the jury have pronounced you guilty of the murder of that unfortunate man, John Donahue."

This seems to show clearly that the judge did not regard the testimony of Michell as essential to sustain the verdict of murder.

The other testimony in the case seems to me to show affirmatively that the deed was done with malice as well as excessive brutality.

The testimony tending to show that Bunch was at the time of the homicide under the influence of intoxicating drink was before the jury, and must be presumed to have been fully weighed by them.

The unusual interest manifested in urging Executive clemency for this unfortunate man has excited my deepest personal sympathies in his behalf, and I have been more than willing to find a ground upon which I could avert his fate. The power lodged in the Governor in such cases brings a fearful responsibility, which nothing but experience can enable one to fully appreciate.

Doubts and misgivings thicken around me whenever I am called upon to pass upon the life or death of a fellow-being. The only clear light which I can see is the light of my official duty. I am appointed and sworn to "take care that the laws are faithfully executed, in mercy," but still that they are executed. The fact that the duty which I feel I am now discharging has been so often imposed upon me is due, I cannot refrain from saying here, to the failure on the part of those who have preceded me to discharge their duty.

I am fully persuaded that public duty forbids me from interfering to any extent with the execution of the sentence imposed upon Bunch.

D. H. CHAMBERLAIN,
Governor.

THE STATE *vs.* GEORGE HARDEE—MURDER.

George Hardee was tried and convicted of murder in the same court and at the same term with Denis R. Bunch. The execution of the sentence of death was likewise postponed in the same manner until the 28th of May, 1875. Upon the urgent appeals of his friends I have again carefully examined his case. It is due, perhaps, to Judge Reed, as well as to myself, that I should state that Judge Reed, in a communication to me, dated April 5, 1875, recommended that the punishment of George Hardee should be commuted to imprisonment for life. This recommendation was entitled to the greatest weight with me, and has induced me again and again to examine the testimony taken at the coroner's inquest, as well as in the general sessions. I cannot discover any evidence or circumstances which reduce the crime of George Hardee below murder. If the law of the State as it now stands is to be executed in any case, it should, in my judgment, be executed in this case. There are, no doubt, degrees of atrocity in murder, and the case of George Hardee does not present those revolting features which sometimes attend the commission of this crime, but, as I remarked in a former statement of this case, "I see no evidence that he was under the influence of passion arising from the quarrel to such a degree as to reduce his offence below murder, nor do I see any evidence under which his action can be regarded as self-defence."

D. H. CHAMBERLAIN,
Governor.

In this place the following letter may properly be quoted, although it has reference to the correction of an abuse of power in the matter of pardons rather than to its legitimate exercise. It also shows how some of the Governor's associates in administration were lying in wait to take advantage of any opportunity to assert their authority in opposition to him.

EXECUTIVE CHAMBER,
COLUMBIA, S. C., August 13, 1875.

Hon. J. P. Reed, Judge First Judicial Circuit, Charleston, S. C. :

DEAR SIR—At the June term, 1875, of the Court of General Sessions for Charleston County, Joseph Gibbes and John Smith were convicted of the crime of murder and sentenced to be hanged on the 30th June, 1875. I now learn that, during my recent temporary absence from the State, the Lieutenant Governor, Hon. R. H. Gleaves, has assumed the authority to commute the sentence of Joseph Gibbes, as above stated, to imprisonment in the penitentiary for twenty years, and that in consequence of this action of the Lieutenant Governor the execution of Joseph Gibbes did not take place on the day fixed by you, and has not yet taken place. I have no information of any kind in regard to this matter, except what I have observed in the newspapers, no order, or copy or notice of the order, of the Lieutenant Governor having been sent to this office. Joseph Gibbes, I assume, in the absence of official information, is still in the jail at Charleston.

The action of the Lieutenant Governor as above stated is, in my judgment, wholly without authority of law, and hence null and void ; and my purpose in addressing you at this time is to call your attention to what I consider the necessity of action on your part, if you agree with me in regarding the action of the Lieutenant Governor as unauthorized and void.

It is proper to add that at the time of leaving the State I informed the Lieutenant Governor by letter of my proposed absence, and that I should be in direct communication with my office in case any necessity for the official action of the Governor should arise.

You will remember, also, that the question of the right of the Lieutenant Governor to act as Governor during the temporary absence of the Governor was directly involved in the recent cases of Hardee and Bunch, in Charleston.[1] In those cases, however, the action of the Lieutenant Governor extended only to the postponement of the execution of the sentence. In the present case it extends to the change of the sentence, and involves the right to exercise all the powers of the Governor. It presents a case, therefore, which compels me to seek a judicial determination of the question involved, and to this end I beg to call your attention to the case, and to say that, in my judgment, your Honor should regard the action of the Lieutenant Governor as null and void, and proceed to enforce upon the said Joseph Gibbes the sentence of your court, subject to such action by the Executive as he may take whenever the case may be submitted to him for his action.

Very respectfully your Honor's obedient servant,

D. H. CHAMBERLAIN,

Governor.

Judge Reed took no action in line of this suggestion, and the Lieutenant Governor's interference with the course of justice could not be undone.

[1] See the Governor's statement in the case of Denis R. Bunch, p. 254.

CHAPTER XVI.

I N April, before the adjournment of the Legislature, a Republican State Convention met in Columbia for the purpose of choosing the party's representatives in the National Convention to be held in Cincinnati in June. This presented the first occasion since his inauguration for a judgment of his party on his course, and the Governor challenged a judgment by allowing it to be known that he desired such an expression of approbation and confidence as would be implied by his selection as one of the delegates at large to the Cincinnati Convention. He knew, and all knew, that the fate of reform in South Carolina, so far as it depended on the Republican party, was involved in his ability to maintain his leadership. The convention to be held later in the year for the nomination of candidates for State offices would be greatly influenced by the action of the earlier convention. The Governor's enemies were alive to the significance of the occasion. It was their opportunity. They determined to rebuke him decisively and "read him out" of the party. The Republicans in the Legislature, whom he had thwarted and exposed, and whose wrath was hot, had powerful allies. United States Senator John J. Patterson came from Washington to South Carolina, avowedly in the interest of Senator Morton and to secure the defeat of

Governor Chamberlain. For active helpers he had most of the Federal office-holders in the State, with Gen. Worthington, Collector of the Port of Charleston, at their head. Associated with Patterson were also the Speaker of the House of Representatives, ex-Congressman R. B. Elliott, whose influence over his own race was almost despotic, and C. C. Bowen, the white Sheriff of Charleston County.

With these professional politicians was associated R. B. Carpenter, the Judge of the Fifth (Columbia) Circuit, who had been elected a delegate from Edgefield County,[1] and who had once been a candidate for Governor, supported by the Democrats. Hatred of Governor Chamberlain's reform policy had taken him from his judicial duties to join in this assault.

When the Convention met, April 12th, the combination appeared to have been wholly successful. Governor Chamberlain, who was himself a member, chosen by the Republicans of Horry County, seemed to have no chance whatever. There were rival delegations from several counties, but in every instance the State Executive Committee had enrolled only the delegates hostile to him. A strongly supported effort to admit contestants, without prejudice, until the Convention should decide who were entitled to seats, was promptly voted down. The strength of the majority and their bitterness towards the Governor were shown by an early incident. He was nominated for temporary chairman ; but S. A. Swails, a colored Senator of no particular distinction or ability, was chosen instead by a vote of 80 to 40. The Convention held a day and evening session on the 12th, and a day and evening session on the 13th, the last session beginning at 9 o'clock, after a brief recess, and continuing until after 7 o'clock the next morning. From beginning to end the sessions were scenes of noisy excitement and angry struggle. At one time, owing to the indiscreet language of a delegate, there was peril of bloodshed. Confusion reigned for a quarter of an hour, and most of the spectators, with many delegates, having regard for their personal safety, left the hall. It was reported that a chair was raised over the head of the Governor, as if to strike him down. Progress under these conditions was slow.

[1] Edgefield County, as will appear hereafter, was the headquarters of the plotting to prevent the Democratic party from giving any support to the Governor.

The report of the Committee on Credentials was not made until the third session, and the permanent organization was not effected until just before the brief recess preceding the final all-night session, when the real business of the Convention was transacted. During all this time, the combination headed by Senator Patterson held solidly together. Every proposal of the minority was voted down, and every case of contest for seats was decided against the Governor's friends. The proceedings culminated in an oratorical duel between Judge Carpenter and Governor Chamberlain, which is still referred to as a notable triumph of character and eloquence over ignorance, prejudice, and personal animosity. Howard Carroll, Esq., then a special correspondent of the New York *Times*, was present on this occasion, and sent to that paper a graphic description of the scene. Having reviewed the circumstances and course of the Convention, and the repeated defeats of the Governor's party, some of them of a character to make them seem like wanton affronts, the report proceeds as follows:

So Chamberlain was left almost unaided in the Convention. State Treasurer Cardozo, a most intelligent colored man, was his strongest supporter, and the only man upon whom he could depend. He fought gallantly against overwhelming odds, however, and it was not until late last night that a permanent organization was reached. Then a great deal of discussion ensued as to the election of district delegates, and it was 2 o'clock this morning when the business of electing delegates at large was reached. At this time Chamberlain's stock was at its lowest, and it was an open secret that he intended to leave the Convention, and, claiming that it did not represent the honest Republican element in South Carolina, call an independent meeting, and send a contesting delegation to the National Convention. Elliott was the first delegate at large elected ; then United States Senator Patterson was nominated, and against him was named Governor Chamberlain. His nomination was greeted with shouts of derisive laughter, and if the call had then been made, he would not have received twenty-five votes. The scene at this point was an exceedingly interesting one. It was past 3 o'clock in the morning, yet the grand old Assembly chamber, intended for the use of the Southern Confederacy, was filled to the doors with black and white spectators who had been present and attentive through the night. On the floor the delegates— they had been in session fourteen hours—were reclining upon their desks or upon the Speaker's platform, completely worn out in mind and body. As the name of D. H. Chamberlain was put in nomination, however, many of them started to their feet, and all gave the closest attention to the proceedings. Then, amid a breathless silence, Judge Carpenter, one of the most effective speakers in the country, arose and said : "Gentlemen of the Convention, I rise to oppose the nomination of Governor Chamberlain, and I am sure that I will convince you that my opposition is just." Then for nearly an hour the Judge heaped reproach after reproach upon the head of

Chamberlain. He was not true to his party ; he was playing into the hands of the Democrats ; he had betrayed his official trusts ; he cried reform, but gave none ; he had been Attorney General under Scott and Moses [1] ; he must have been aware of their crimes ; and in short he was in every way unqualified to represent the State of South Carolina in a National Convention of Republicans. It was just five minutes after four o'clock, and daylight was coming in through the window, as Gov. Daniel H. Chamberlain, "the most eloquent man in the South," rose to defend himself against his accusers. His slight frame trembled, and great drops of sweat hung on his forehead as he commenced the speech which would bring to him political life or death in South Carolina. Then for an hour and a half he spoke, delivering one of the grandest orations ever listened to in America. He not only denied, but clearly disproved, every charge which Carpenter had brought against him ; and then turning to attack the man by whom he had been so terribly assailed, he accused him of complicity with Ku-Klux, and proved that all through the bitter campaign of 1870 he had worked for and with the Democrats. As the speech progressed, the colored delegates gathered around the speaker ; then they stood on chairs and desks to get a better view of him. Those who were nearest to him sat on the floor, looking up into his face with open-mouthed wonder at his terrible denunciation of his foes and his grand vindication of himself. Some of the negroes were entirely carried away by his oration ; they shouted with delight at the conclusion of some of the most effective passages ; and as the Governor took his seat, pale and exhausted from over-exertion, all the enthusiasm of their fiery nature broke into one long-continued cry, and the name of "Chamberlain, Chamberlain, *our* Chamberlain," was echoed from every part of the Capitol. Carpenter tried to reply, but they would not listen to him. The roll was then called, and Chamberlain was elected over Patterson by a vote of 89 to 32.[2] He had won by his eloquence.

That Mr. Carroll's report, enthusiastic as it seems, was not extravagant appears from the testimony of others present. J. F. Keegan, who represented the Washington (D. C.) *Chronicle*, in a letter written from Charleston three days after the adjournment of the Convention, said :

I will not attempt to do his eloquent apppeal even simple justice, as I feel confident that a miserable failure would attend my efforts. Whang ! bang ! went the solid shot of argument, whizzing through the air into the Edgefield camp. "Ooh ! ooh ! ooh !" exclaimed the colored brethren, when the Governor referred to Judge Carpenter's former Ku-Klux affinities ; "now, now ; he 's got him, shoo !" For two long hours the "Little Giant" proceeded uninterrupted, except every now and then by the warm and enthusiastic applause of the assemblage, but a few hours ago his bitterest foes, and now his adorers. I have often been favored with an opportunity of listening to some of the very best orators in the Senate and House of Representa-

[1] This is obviously an error. Governor Chamberlain held no office during the administration of Governor Moses.

[2] The Columbia *Union-Herald* reported the vote as being 73 to 39. The whole number of delegates was 124. Of the votes for Patterson it was said that 27 were cast by the delegates whom the earlier majority had admitted in cases of contest.

tives, but never, since the days of the late lamented Stephen A. Douglas, did I ever
enjoy such a magnificently polished oration.   Senator Patterson sat in front of the
Governor during the delivery of his response to Judge Carpenter, and at its conclusion
pronounced it as being simply superb.

The correspondent of the Charleston *News and Courier* telegraphed from Columbia at 6:45 A.M. of the 13th:

No words could describe the effect of the reply of Governor Chamberlain in a
speech as graceful and finished as it was bold, cutting, and at times even pathetic.

The Columbia *Sunday Sun*, a Democratic journal, said:

It was a master production, and whether it be considered from a rhetorical standpoint or from its wonderful effect upon the audience who listened to it, will rank our
Governor with the leading forensic orators of the land.

It is much to be regretted that these speeches were but imperfectly reported.   The *Union-Herald*, in publishing them, said:

The report is necessarily imperfect.   Reporters, tired out by a session of fourteen
consecutive hours, were incapable of doing justice to the occasion.

From this unsatisfactory report the passages to be here given
will indicate at least the vigor and temper of the combatants.
Judge Carpenter, a man of fine ability, imposing mien, and high
repute as an orator, claiming to be Governor Chamberlain's personal friend, and his ardent supporter whenever he had been a
a candidate for office, thus defined the issue he now made with
him :

Governor Chamberlain was elected by the Republican party, and I propose to
state this evening what I consider to be the real issue between him and the other wing
of that party.   It has been flashed over the wires and published day after day in the
public prints.   It has been stated by the Governor, or rather by his organ or organs,
day after day, that the issue is between Governor Chamberlain and honesty and the
Republican party, and a den of thieves.   I deny that this is the issue.   I say that the
issue is whether he has kept fealty with that band of men who by their suffrages
placed him in power.   You remember that election.   Too vile for me to repeat were
the maledictions, curses, and denunciations that were showered upon his head by the
Democratic press of the country ; but we stood around him and took the pelting
storm, and hurled back their cries of thieves and robbers, and bore him triumphantly
into the gubernatorial chair.   I state, without fear of contradiction, that from the day
he entered the office of Chief Magistrate of this State he turned his back upon the
men who fought for him and with him, and has sought only to advance himself at the
cost of his allegiance to his party.   [Cheers.]

After asserting that all the corruption developed in the State
Government had developed during the administration of Governor

Scott, when Chamberlain was Attorney General, he asserted that all the reforms for which Chamberlain claimed the credit were initiated during the administration of Governor Moses. "We have heard," he exclaimed, "a great deal about the reforms effected by Governor Chamberlain. What are they? The saving of $27,000 of the contingent fund, nothing else!" Then resuming his argument on the issue he had made, he continued as follows:

Well, sir, the Governor was elected after a bitter contest, and the moment that he was elected he turned around with a spirit of forgiveness that excelled that displayed in the Sermon on the Mount—forgave his enemies, blessed them that cursed him, and prayed for those that despitefully used him and persecuted him. You are asked to say that this Governor has represented the Republican party properly. He can't say that for me. I won't let him say it. He has said that the men who have voted for two certain judges in this State are a gang of thieves. I did not vote for them, so this epithet does not apply to me. But one hundred gentlemen in this hall did vote for them. Are they willing to say that it applies to them? How were these men elected judges? The Governor, instead of talking to his friends, remonstrating with and advising them, saw fit to use the goad and lash upon the party from the time he came into power until now, and he used that goad once too often, and that is the reason why they were elected.

Judge Carpenter charged that the Governor had refused to counsel with his party friends, but had acted dictatorily and arbitrarily in all matters, and this was the reason why they had revolted from his leadership.

He is no ordinary man. You, who see him in his calm, quiet moods, do not know him as I know him. He is a man of splendid ability, as brave as Cæsar, as ambitious as Napoleon. He is bold, daring, and ambitious. If he were in France there would be a *coup d'etat*, and he would be king, just as he has tried to be king of the Republican party here. [Applause.] Under and over all that apparent control he has deliberately planned this campaign, and he is deliberately carrying it out, and I observe here that some of these men, cowed and lashed by his arbitrary assertions of power, are even now crouching at his feet. I was born free, and, by Heaven, I will die free! I call no one master but my God, and when the political, lash is applied I lay no claim to the lofty forgiveness of my friend. I cannot kiss the hand that smites me, nor turn the other cheek to him who smites,—I strike back! [Applause.] In my judgment Daniel H. Chamberlain has been murdering the Republican party from the hour he became Governor of South Carolina. As he is my friend I shall spare him; but when he meets me in the conflict, there shall be no quarter.

Well, sir, I may be asked where is the proof of these charges? I will answer that it is to be found in the vetoes, interviews with newspaper reporters, and in various discourses delivered at various times and places all over this country. It was he who sent that famous despatch to the New-Englanders at their dinner in Charleston, in which he announced that the civilization of the Roundhead and Cavalier, of the Puritan and Huguenot, was in danger. My friend is so overpowered with the classics that he has failed to see the broad view of civilization which flows through the land. The Puritan and the Cavalier have not been in danger in South Carolina since freedom came within her bounds. Thank God, that civilization has been dead since that freedom came into the land. The freedom of the Cavalier and the Puritan was the civilization of the master and the slave. It was the civilization of the tyrant and the crouching slave. In its stead has come the bright sun of liberty, shining through her fields all blossoming with the blooms of liberty. Thank God that the civilization of the Puritan and Cavalier is gone never to be reinstated. Freedom has come, not only to four millions of slaves, but to millions of whites also. Slavery did not pertain alone to the negro. When freedom came it came to the whites as well as to the blacks. I have no tears to shed over the graves of the civilization of the Puritan and Cavalier.

Now, Mr. President, if the gentlemen in this Convention, a large number of them members of the Legislature, who cast their votes for these judges, are ready to place their hands upon their mouths and cry " guilty " before Governor Chamberlain, it is their funeral, not mine. So far as I know this Legislature, it is not to be bought on those terms. The Legislature and not the Governor is the judge of the judges they elect. It is neither his business nor mine ; and when they attempt to say that because the Governor says that a man is not moral or learned enough for a judge that he can withhold his commission and enforce his arbitrary imperial power to a tyrannical extent, they take a ground that I cannot endorse.

Thus Judge Carpenter fulfilled his formal announcement at an earlier stage of the Convention that at the proper time he intended to show that there was " an irrepressible conflict between the Governor's policy and the principles of Republicanism." He denied that the Governor deserved any credit for accomplishing reforms in the State Government, and maintained that the existing schism in the party was not on account of the Governor's fidelity to the pledges made by the party and himself when he was a candidate, but to an unnecessary, arbitrary, selfish, and treacherous course on the Governor's part. How monstrously unjust such an arraignment was, need not be argued to those who have perused the foregoing record. Nor does it seem worth while to quote from that part of the Governor's speech in which he set forth the results of his Administration in reply to the amazing statement that there were no reforms except a small saving of the contingent fund. No one will be likely to doubt that he marshalled the statistics bearing on this point with forceful and conclusive logic. But how did he meet the imputations of infidelity to his party, of courting his traducers, of disregarding his friends, of seeking his own advancement through treachery? And how did he overcome the reiterated appeal to the animosity of the members of the Convention, also members of the Legislature, whose intended action he had many times defeated and denounced? To these inquiries of a legitimate curiosity the following passages from the speech will give answer :

Mr. Chairman :—Frequent allusion has been made to my coolness. I sometimes feel that nothing could be further from the truth than that statement respecting me, but I am happy to say that as I stand here to-night amongst the Republicans of South Carolina, the touch of whose elbows I have never failed to feel since 1868, I feel as calm and cool as a May morning, and as ready to meet the charges that have been brought against me as I shall be to meet the sweet kisses of my wife and children this morning. It has been announced here that the issue is that of party fealty, and the charge is brought by one whose lips ought forever to be sealed against making the charge concerning party fealty against any other man that lives in South Carolina. [Cheers.]

I am reminded to-night of the only other occasion when I had the pleasure of measuring swords with him who assails me to-night. I remember that in 1870, when the Republican party's life was assailed and a strong and vigorous hand clutched at the throat of the Republican party, I was commissioned by that party to go to Chester, in this State, and see if I, with my friends, could unloose the death-grip which he had fastened upon it. [Loud cheering.] [A voice : That 's it, give it to the traitor of 1870.] Sir, I went to Chester. I met there, as the chosen leader of the Democracy in South Carolina, this man who now assails me with the charge of a want of fealty to the Republican party, covering with words such as never yet sullied my lips, with invective and obloquy which no reporter has ever been able to take down, covering the Republican party, I say, with reproaches and curses too deep to be repeated here. Performing that task for the Republican party of South Carolina, I say I found there the gentleman who now comes into a Republican convention for the first time in his life, and calls me to account for my want of party fealty.

Well, Mr. President, there are other incidents that should have taught the gentleman from Edgefield to make his attack upon me at some other point than party fealty. He went through the Democratic campaign of 1870, and what was the result of that campaign? The Republican party triumphed ; but what was the condition of the upper counties? Was it not true that York, Lancaster, Fairfield, Union, and Spartanburg were in a state of rebellion against the laws? Was it not true that the gentleman from Edgefield sowed in that campaign those dragon teeth that afterwards sprung up into the masked Ku-Klux at night? [Cheers.] Well, Mr. President, for eight long months succeeding that campaign the tardy arm of government waited to bring help to the people whose burning cabins lit up the face of heaven for miles at midnight, and whose cold bodies weltered in that light under the bloody stab of the Ku-Klux ; and when at last relief came, and when in this very building the perpetrators of those deeds stood face to face with justice, it was my duty as the law officer of the State to stand for the government against these malefactors who had sprung up from the teaching of the gentleman from Edgefield. I well remember that when we were in one of the most critical of those trials, the first, that was to establish the question whether we could proceed far enough to bring these red-handed assassins to justice, among witnesses called from afar and brought here to give testimony that should shield the Ku-Klux, was the Hon. R. B. Carpenter. [Loud cheers and intense excitement.] And this, fellow-Republicans—men of South Carolina,—is the record of the man who tells us here to-night, if we trust those that have never yet betrayed us, "God help us !" God help us, indeed, fellow-Republicans, if we are not yet sufficiently grown to manhood and the estate of man, to be able to understand that nothing of the motives which have solely to do with the prosperity of the Republican party animates the breast of him who addresses such teachings here to-night.

Talk about party fealty ! I have sometimes felt, Mr. President, that I was the greatest slave on earth. I have felt so because brought up at my father's knee, at my mother's side, all my life long I have worn the great bonds of principle that bind me forever and ever to the principles of the Republican party. If I have ever erred in the matter of party duty, it is that I have shrank from sometimes asserting my manhood, even above the dictates of any earthly party. Well, I wear those fetters, as others in the party, yet. Why ? Because we love her principles. Because neither in '68 nor '72 nor '76 is there earthly inducement strong enough to lead us one step beyond the great circle that holds and protects the Republicans of South Carolina and the United States. Here I stand, and I might borrow Luther's great words and say : " Here I stand, I can do no other, within this sacred circle of the Republican party. God help me ! " I scorn—I put the foot of my uttermost contempt upon any charge from mortal lips that I have swerved from my allegiance to the Republican party, or that the thought has ever lodged in my breast that did not breathe fidelity, honor, and allegiance forever to the principles and organization of the Republican party.

Now, sir, as to my Administration. I wish, Mr. President, that I might clothe myself always in the beautiful garments of modesty and humility. I trust that I have some of that spirit that says : " He that would be greatest among you, let him be the servant of all." I wish to speak with becoming modesty of that which I must call, for the sake of brevity, " my Administration." To go back to the last campaign. I stood then, after a long and fierce struggle, on the same ground upon which you now, Mr. President, stand—the recipient of the suffrages of the people for the highest position in the State. I call to mind, when I stepped down from that platform I remember so well, that I was met on the last step by the gentleman whom I now have in my eye, the gentleman from Charleston, who is now the Comptroller General of the State, and who said to me : " Mr. Chamberlain, I congratulate you personally, but nothing more. I cannot make myself the champion of any man who is surrounded by such men as those to whom I now point (C. C. Bowen and John J. Patterson). [Loud laughter.]

* * * * * * *

Let me go back to the moment when I was standing where you, Mr. President, now stand, and heard my language applauded to the echo (as I shall not probably be applauded to-night) by every Republican, man, woman, and child, within these walls ; where I said first, last, and all the time, that the steps of the Republican party must be steadily upward and forward towards reform and better government. You placed that banner in my hand, and I grasped it with an ardent though all too feeble grasp, and I bore it through a conflict which was headed by the gentleman from Charleston whom I now have in my eye. He had denied me his support, but I bore your banner at last to victory. Beneath my feet you put your platform, and above my head you spread the magic and glorious words : " Political Reform." We went to victory, and when that victory was won, I stood again where you now stand, Mr. President, and I spoke again words that met the approval of the community, and of the Republican party, when I said that I was pledged in honor, in character, and pledged in language, to be steadfast and immovable in my efforts to lift up the Republican party above the crimes of the campaign of 1870, and above the crimes of 1874. [Immense cheering.]

It has been said that I have used the whip and spur from that day till now. I wish I was " as brave as Julius Cæsar," but I know that I am an arrant coward ; and I can tell you, gentlemen, that there have been times in my Administration when, had it not been for the tender counsels and support of the wife of my love, I should have faltered on the way, and stained the record that I would lay down my life for, rather than tarnish, for the sake of the dear children that now lie sleeping at home. As weary as I am, I must come here to take up this new cross and hear myself assailed and taunted by one who covers with a gloss of praise the dagger that he would plunge to my heart. I have done things, no doubt, that have seemed to others to have been done in wantonness of power towards them. I know that ; and I also know that before the combination led by the delegate from Edgefield was formed, he said : " Chamberlain, I am with you at every step you take, but I wish you would be a little more communicative to your friends." I accepted it as the advice of a friend. I am willing to plead guilty to so much of the indictment. I sometimes wish my nature was such that I could make known more easily my purposes and intentions. I say it sincerely, that if a lighted window had been placed in this bosom, and you could have seen the purposes I have had towards the Republican party, you would know that a kind and helpful word from any man, entitled to respect, would have been received gratefully by me, and would have made me a greater and a better man than I am.

* * * * * * *

Oh, I wish, in this night of turmoil, that I could seek refuge in the quiet calm of the civil courts, where I love to practise, and where I could hide myself away from one who comes here to stab me as a friend. I would borrow from these courts the Latin phrase and apply it to his case,—*Falsus in uno, falsus in omnibus.* False in one statement, false in all. I know not how long I could take the time of this Convention, by proving that this Administration, notwithstanding the taunts of the gentleman from Edgefield, has advanced good government in South Carolina. Ask that distinguished gentleman there (pointing to Chancellor Johnston), once an honored incumbent of the bench, whether or not this Administration has husbanded the resources of the people and protected the taxes of the people. I wish I had been " as brave as Julius Cæsar," that I might have led this people, black and white, up to the summit of peace to which we climb so slowly. I could not do it, and now that my weary steps have just ascended to the first table-ground, this assailant comes and clutches me in the rear, as he clutched you by the throat in 1868. He is the same Democratic warrior, this gentleman from Edgefield. God helping me and the Republicans of South Carolina, we are going to shake off this burden that is now hung on us, and we are going to ascend that mount together, and our feet shall never tire until the sunlight of victory bathes our brows on its peaceful summit.

* * * * * * *

I go for the protection of every man. The meanest man who assails me because he is my political enemy, shall have my protection with the rest. Democrats and Republicans alike shall have my protection, and when South Carolina can't protect the lives and liberties of her citizens, I conceive it to be the highest duty of the United States to protect them, and my highest duty, I conceive, is to invoke that aid in time of need. But, Mr. President, I am charged with possessing something more than human or divine forgiveness towards my enemies. I am growing weary, and I must not detain you longer. If, there is one sweet drop that I drink to-night, it is this,—that though my enemies have hunted me like a partridge on the mountain, yet never since my feet stood there where you stand now, Mr. President, on the 1st of December, 1874, have I ever uttered one word of reproach against those who had so bitterly opposed me. Blot out the whole record, fellow-Republicans, if I have betrayed you ; blot out every thing else, but let it stand there as my recompense, that never against all my enemies have I ever raised one harsh or vituperative word. Let it be written somewhere that Chamberlain never said an unkind word against those who abused him and looked upon his coming almost as a thief in the night. Tear down the scaffolding that I have erected, condemn my whole record, cast me off if I have betrayed you ; yet to me comes the sweet word, like silver bells, "forgiveness!" If I don't get the blessing of the gentleman from Edgefield and the people of South Carolina, I will get the blessings of my wife and children and the blessings of my God. [Loud and prolonged applause.]

I am getting weary and shall say only one word more. I will not again defend myself. Let me say that the only sin that I can lay to my door is that I have not stood still firmer in this pathway of political reform. I shall fix my eye more steadily upon the polar star of political reform, and I shall strain myself more zealously at the oars that shall waft that bark with its freight of hopes and aspirations and blessings into the calm sea of political equality and administrative reform. If it has been supposed by setting on this cry and attack upon me to-night, if it has been imagined, that my cheeks would blanch with fear, let it be set down once for all as a dead mistake and failure. *Nulla vestigia retrorsum.* Never a step backward.

Do you imagine invectives have any terrors for me? I have been told, I don't know how many times, that, if I would cut loose from one or two of my friends, the majority would stand by me. Thank God, I have one or two friends who have stood by me. Let me tell you, that if I knew that your suffrages would sink me so deep that no bubble would rise to tell where I went down, I would stand by F. L. Cardozo. [Immense cheering.] If you think that I am to be bought by going to Cincinnati to go back on a man who, to my knowledge, has never done a dishonest act, and who has always stood by me, you are mistaken, that's all. Do with me as you please. If you dismiss me to the shades of private life, be it so. You called me. I am your servant always, and I bow to your commands. [Loud and long cheering and intense excitement.]

The most significant feature of this triumph is that it was obtained, not only without suggestion of concession or compromise, but by courageous and defiant insistance on the course which had provoked all the hostility confronting him. The only promise he had made for the future was that he would be more faithful to reform, more antagonistic to corruption, than he had been in the past. No shorn Samson, this! Before the multitude of his foes he rejoiced in and renewed "the pledge of his unviolated vow." In the hour when they were exulting over their bound victim, he burst their withes and stood forth victor. What but a heart of truth, an absolute, dauntless sincerity,—

> "That heat of inward evidence
> By which he doubts against the sense,"—

could have inspired him so to meet and so to subdue the majority enlisted and arrayed to destroy him? Have we not here a fresh

illustration of the genuine, the prevailing, the nigh irresistible
eloquence which is apt to be kindled, even on unready lips, in the
exigency of a cause esteemed higher and dearer than any personal fortune? The man, the subject, and the occasion, which
Webster declared to be the three constituents of eloquence, were
all present together in Columbia on that April morning.

The further proceedings of this Convention were of little im-
'portance, comparatively. A resolution approving of Governor
Chamberlain's Administration was, after brief debate, laid on the
table, for the avowed reason that it expressly condemned the
conduct of so many who were in the Convention. A resolution,
highly complimentary to Senator Morton, although not instruct-
ing the delegation to Cincinnati to support him, was passed ; but
the effect of it was countervailed by the adoption of the following
resolution immediately offered by the Governor :

Resolved, That this Convention leaves the delegates of South Carolina to the Cincinnati Convention wholly uninstructed and untrammelled in their choice of individual candidates for President and Vice-
President of the United States ; but requires them, and each of them,
to vote and work earnestly and always for those candidates whose
characters and careers have shown them to be most faithful to the
cardinal doctrines of the Republican party, namely, equal civil
and political rights for all men ; instant and complete reformation of
the existing abuses in the administration of the government ; purity,
ability, and integrity in all public appointments ; and an unflinching
determination to make the public service, in all its departments and
branches, as honorable and benignant as when the unsullied Washington wielded the executive power of the republic.

Thus it happened that he not only headed the delegation to
Cincinnati, from which he was to have been excluded, but he
dictated the instruction imposed upon all.

Governor Chamberlain went to the National Convention in
Cincinnati, where he was received with marked respect and honor.
He was a member of the Committee on Resolutions, and to him
was assigned the duty of drawing the resolution defining the
policy of the party regarding affairs in the Southern States. It
was in the following terms :

The permanent pacification of the Southern section of the Union,
and the complete protection of all its citizens in the free enjoyment of

all their rights, is a duty to which the Republican party stands sacredly pledged. The power to provide for the enforcement of the principles embodied in the recent constitutional amendments is vested by these amendments in the Congress of the United States, and we declare it to be the solemn obligation of the legislative and executive departments of the government to put into immediate and vigorous exercise all their constitutional powers for removing any just causes of discontent on the part of any class, and for securing to every American citizen complete liberty and exact equality in the exercise of all civil, political, and public rights. To this end we imperatively demand a Congress and a Chief Executive, whose courage and fidelity to these duties shall not falter until these results are placed beyond dispute or recall.

In the first four votings for a candidate for President, Governor Chamberlain, of the South Carolina delegation, voted for General Bristow, the other thirteen members voting for Senator Morton. On the fifth trial two joined him in voting for General Bristow, five voted for Mr. Blaine, one for Governor Hayes, and five refrained from voting. On the sixth trial the Governor was again alone in supporting General Bristow, seven voted for Mr. Blaine, one for Governor Hayes, and two for Senator Morton. General Bristow and Senator Morton were then withdrawn from the list of candidates, and on the final trial, which resulted in the nomination of Governor Hayes, the votes of South Carolina were equally divided, the Governor and six besides voting for Governor Hayes, the other seven for Mr. Blaine.

CHAPTER XVII.

THE effect upon the Democrats of the State of Governor Chamberlain's victory in the April Convention was to confirm the judgment of those who believed that his intention and his ability to secure good government were superior to those of any other citizen whom it was possible to elect in his place. These Democrats soon came to be known as " Coöperationists." The other class of Democrats, those who wanted the offices for themselves at any desperate hazard, were deprived of an argument of which they had made much use. It was not so apparent as they had previously represented, that the Governor would be driven out of the Republican party, and have no refuge but in the Democratic party, or in uninfluential private station, leaving the former party in the control of the representatives of its ignorance and corruption, and so establishing their own claim that the Democratic party must be regarded as the only hope of good citizens. Nevertheless they labored with no abatement of zeal for their ends, and it soon became evident that the struggle of the Democratic factions would be a fierce and angry one.

Early in January, at the height of the agitation following the election of judges, the Democratic State Executive Committee had been called together in Columbia, and their deliberation resulted in the following address :

To the People of South Carolina:

The State Central Executive Committee of the Democratic party do not deem it necessary to publish any lengthy statement of the reasons which induced them to meet at this time. It is sufficient to say that events with which the people of the State are painfully familiar, made it indispensable that the organization of the Democratic party in South Carolina should be revived as the speediest and most practical means of bringing together our hitherto scattered forces, and of concentrating them in the struggle into which we are forced for the maintenance of liberty and law in the State. Thus it has become the duty of the State Committee to take such steps as will enable the people of the State to begin the work of party reorganization at once, and make it thorough and complete.

In the contest in which we are about to engage we must win. Defeat cannot be borne. Success, however, cannot be expected to crown our labors unless there be absolute unity in the Democratic party, together with such discipline as will insure the prompt and efficient execution of its policy when declared. From our adversaries must we learn, at last, the lesson of organization and activity. When the agencies on which society relies for the conservation of its varied interests menace those interests with destruction, and threaten a whole people with ruin, politics are no longer a matter of sentiment in which the citizen is free to engage or not, according to his tastes. Upon the management of our political affairs depends the security of property, as well as the safety of person. By political movements alone can the purification of the State Government be accomplished. Only through political instrumentalities can honesty, fidelity, and capability regain a preponderating influence in the councils of the State. To politics, then, for their own salvation, must the people of South Carolina now address themselves with the vigor, the persistency, and the systematic endeavor which mark their conduct in business life. It would not be wise to declare a policy before the party which shall give effect to it is ready for both deliberation and action. The officers must not be chosen until the rank and file of the political army shall have been mustered in and trained. There should be, in fine, such organization in each ward, township, and county, that when the State Convention shall assemble, it shall represent, by its delegates, the known wishes, opinions, and purposes of the organized Democracy of the State. Then will its voice be the voice of the people ; its determination theirs ; its fight their battle. To such organization, searching and far-reaching, should the people of the State without delay address themselves. Without it the State cannot be saved !

The State Convention, when it shall assemble, will determine authoritatively the policy of the party ; and by the decision of that Convention shall we all be bound. As, however, the Democratic party, as such, has had no active existence in South Carolina for some years, the State Committee desire to say emphatically that in recommending its instant and comprehensive organization, their sole purpose is to obtain an honest and economical government in South Carolina which shall maintain, without abridgment or change, the public rights and liberties of the whole people, and guarantee to all classes of citizens the blessings of freedom, justice, and peace. And in this crisis in the constitutional life of the State, when civilization itself is in peril, we look for and confidently expect to receive the sympathy and aid of every citizen whose aims and desires are like unto our own.

In common with their fellow-citizens, the Democratic State Committee have watched with anxious solicitude and growing confidence the course of the present Governor of the State. They recognize and appreciate the value of what he has done in promoting reform and retrenchment during the past year. They applaud his wise and patriotic conduct in exerting his whole official power and personal influence for the undoing of the infamous judicial election. And they declare their belief that the Democracy of the State, rising above party as he has done, will give an unfaltering support to his efforts, as Governor, for the redress of wrongs, for the reduction of taxation, to obtain a just administration of the law, and to make the State Government a faithful guardian of the public and private interests of the people.

Therefore, the State Executive Committee earnestly advise the people of the State to reorganize thoroughly the Democratic party, in preparation for the State Democratic Convention, which will meet at a time and place to be hereafter designated by this Committee. The following gentlemen are charged with this organization of the party in every precinct, ward, and township in their respective counties.

*   *   *   *   *   *   *   *   *   *

This address formulated no policy except the policy of thorough organization. Public sentiment was then running too strongly in the Governor's favor to be tolerant of any open opposition to him. For six months the debate between the "Straight-outers," so called, and the "Coöperationists" was vigorously conducted, and the latter faction appeared to be gaining ground. The *News and Courier* was the able and unwavering advocate of their policy, and it was earnestly supported by many other influential journals. The hostile faction, the "Straight-outers," were numerous and demonstrative, especially in the upper counties, where the colored men were numerically weakest, and in a partisan contest, in which race issues could be made to play a conspicuous part, would be practically overwhelmed. The following editorial article from the Charleston *News and Courier*, of May 8, 1876, defines the attitude of the "Coöperationists" towards the Governor, and the ground of their objection to the scheme of the "Straight-outers." The parts here printed in italics were so printed originally :

The Lancaster *Ledger* says that "the frequent expressions of *The News and Courier* favorable to D. H. Chamberlain have led the Democrats in the up-country to believe that it favors the nomination of Governor Chamberlain by the Democratic Convention." We give "the Democrats in the up-country" credit for more sense than the *Ledger* would seem to do. But if they believe what the *Ledger* says, it will be their own fault, and the *Ledger's*, if they believe it any longer. *We do not favor, nor have we ever favored, the nomination of Mr. Chamberlain by the Democratic Convention.* That, we hope, is clear and positive. What we do favor, under certain circumstances, is something widely different.

Whether the colored voting majority in South Carolina be twenty thousand or thirty thousand, it is certainly large and exceedingly difficult to overcome. The difficulty is increased by the fact that the colored population is massed in the lower counties, where the whites are few, and the Radical majority can be made whatever the Commissioners and Managers of Election choose to make it. The courage and energy of the white Democrats in the upper and middle counties avail us nothing in the lower counties. These lower counties, in unscrupulous hands, can overcome any possible majority that the rest of the State can give. Charleston County alone, on the straight-out plan which the Radical Democracy demand, can give from five to ten thousand majority for the Radical Republican State ticket. . . .

Mr. Chamberlain will probably be the candidate of the Republican party for re-election. The wilder the talk of the Radical Democracy the greater is his strength, as a commanding necessity to his party. In case that he be nominated he will have the undivided support of the Radicals. *There will be no bolt.* Judge Carpenter, his stoutest opponent, admits that. Add to the solid Republican vote, the power to obtain Federal troops as they may be needed, the Executive appointment of Commissioners of Election, the broad and undefined powers of the Board of State Canvassers, and what prospect is there that he could be defeated? It could be done in only one way : *by armed force.* For that the people are not ready, and if they were ready such a course would end in disaster and ruin.

These reasons, and others like them, force us, as they force thousands of Conservatives Democrats, to the conclusion that it would be folly to run a Democratic candidate for Governor against Mr. Chamberlain. It would force the Executive to exert his whole influence for the election of the whole Radical ticket, and the Democrats, losing the State officers, as well as the county officers and the members of the Legislature in the low-country, would find no compensation in the thirty or forty members of the Legislature who, *if no protests prevail,* can be elected in the up-country. What we advise, then, is, not to make Mr. Chamberlain, under any circumstances, a Democratic candidate, but to waive a nomination for Governor *if the Regular Republicans nominate him,* and to concentrate our efforts on the other State officers and the members of the Legislature. With Mr. Chamberlain as Governor, and a Conservative Democratic majority, or thereabouts, in the lower House, the State, in every sense of the word, would be safe. In attempting to gain more we might lose every thing.

We grant that there may be a change in the situation ere the time comes for a Democratic nomination. It is possible that the action of the Republican Convention will be such as to make it wise and proper that a full Democratic ticket shall be nominated. But unless there be a radical change, unless Mr. Chamberlain fail to receive the Republican nomination, we must, for the public good, as we understand it, oppose the nomination of a Democratic candidate for Governor. There is not a Democrat in South Carolina who would not prefer to run a full ticket, and who would not rather vote for such a Democrat as Kershaw than for any Republican who ever trod the soil of South Carolina, but it is not just or wise to slaughter our friends, or make them the Cardigans of a new Balaklava, which, however magnificent, is not war. . . .

The admission is here made that the normal colored (Republican) majority in South Carolina was between twenty thousand

and thirty thousand votes, and that it could be overcome " *in only
one way :* BY ARMED FORCE." It is an admission that has
peculiar significance with reference to future events. A month
later (June 5th) the following article appeared in the same
journal :

Abstract political propositions are of no service to the people of South Carolina.
It is idle to tell them what ought to be. Their concern is with what is. It is folly
to tantalize them with descriptions of what others, differently circumstanced, have
done. Their desire is to know what, in their actual condition, they can do. This,
therefore, is the guiding principle we have in whatever we advise or propose—to
avoid what is hazardous and impracticable, and seek the public good by such ways as
are, however long and devious, accessible and safe. For South Carolina cannot
afford to lose one whit of what has been gained during the past two years. True
political wisdom lies in retaining what we have, and in adding to it, year by year,
until the political fortunes of the people are assured. This is the *raison d'être* of the
policy of political coöperation.

The Democrats in South Carolina are in the minority, else they could and would,
as a party, obtain control of the State by their own efforts. The Democrats pay the
bulk of the taxes, and, more than their political opponents, feel the grievous burden of
extravagant and corrupt government. For eight years the Republicans have held
possession of the State ; and in that time they have destroyed its credit, and squandered its substance—making the Democratic minority poor indeed, without enriching
the rank and file of their own party. As a party, the Democrats have, and can have,
no higher aim than to drive out incapable and venal officials, and place in power
men of integrity, capability, and honor. The Republicans as a party, in South
Carolina, have no loftier object than to enjoy what Senator Patterson describes as
" five years of good stealing." Nevertheless, in the Republican party there are
persons who loathe rascality and love honesty as devoutly as the most pronounced
Democrat can do, and on two several occasions, as we have shown in a previous
article, about twenty thousand Republicans have refused to vote for party candidates
who were believed to be unworthy, and supported other Republican candidates whose
platform was opposition to profligacy and fraud. Only by working together can the
Democratic Reformers and the Republican Reformers out-vote and overcome the
eighty or ninety thousand colored Republicans who are too ignorant to understand
that every individual suffers by public rascality, or who deem the perpetual re-election
of their unscrupulous leaders requisite to their personal security and freedom.
Neither sixty thousand Democrats nor twenty thousand Republicans are powerful
enough to do this. The two bodies together can, and will, if the people think before
they act and look before they leap.

The Reform Republicans have, at present, no active existence as a party ; although
there is a nucleus of organization which can be developed and ramified when necessary. They have given to Governor Chamberlain their unflagging support ; for they
know that in him they have unexpectedly found the fearless reformer whom they
sought. Because his single object as Governor is to correct abuses, they have stood
by him. The Democrats, in and out of office, have done the same thing for the

same reason. Both Democrats and Republicans opposed Mr. Chamberlain until he had shown that no Democrat or Republican, in his position, could go farther than he would go in advocating and working for economy, purity, and low taxation. Then they ranged themselves by his side. Never was there a more splendid example of devotion to principle, never did South Carolina Democrats give nobler evidence that the end they aimed at was their country's good. As the Democrats and Reform Republicans went over to Mr. Chamberlain, the princes of wrong-doing placed themselves in opposition to him. The qualities which attracted honest citizens drove the knaves away.

Because of his strenuous labors in the cause of good government, because of his denunciation of roguery, because of his personal dignity and culture, Governor Chamberlain is proscribed to-day by the radical politicians who, until his advent, held the State in the palm of their hands, and emptied its treasury into their pockets. Mr. Chamberlain will accept a nomination for re-election ; not because of the emoluments of the office, which are pitiful, nor for the love of politics, which are not to his taste, but because in two years more, with a sound, intelligent, and upright Legislature, he can, with the knowledge he has of our condition and wants, complete the work now begun, and make South Carolina as contented and progressively prosperous as any State in the South. The probabilities are that the very rogues who hate him most will be forced to consent to his renomination. Our reasons for believing that no Democratic candidate can defeat Mr. Chamberlain have already been given. If nominated by the Republican Convention, Mr. Chamberlain will be Governor for a second term. But, as events have proved, a Governor, whatever his ability, is hampered and thwarted at every turn, unless the legislative branch of the government be in sympathy with him. A hostile Senate can prevent the filling of public offices with fit persons ; a factious and greedy House of Representatives can frustrate any economic scheme, by voting down every measure that lessens its own profits and diminishes its opportunity of robbing the people. Governor Chamberlain, therefore, cannot, in 1877, any more than in 1876, have an affirmative power in shaping legislation, unless a majority of the members of the General Assembly be honest, sober, and patriotic men who will give effect to his recommendations, and will reinforce and supplement them by their own prudent counsel. In the Legislature of 1874-75 and 1875-76, Governor Chamberlain, although sustained by the Democrats and better Republicans, had only a negative power. As a rule he could prevent the passage of measures that were conspicuously bad ; but he could not secure the passage of measures which were eminently necessary as well as proper.

The Radicals who elected Mr. Chamberlain, who now abuse him as a renegade and the like, will probably be forced, as we have said, to abandon the attempt to nominate a man of their own stamp in his stead. They intend, however, to elect such local officers and such a Legislature as will make them masters of the situation, although the Governor be against them. And they know they can do this, if the party lines be drawn and the Democrats run a straight-out party ticket. It is certain that the solid Republican vote is larger, by many thousands, than the solid Democratic vote ; and the defeat of the Democrats, in a bitter " straight-out " contest, will give the State, in spite of the Executive, the worst government we have yet had.

With these facts before the people they can see, at a glance, how united effort can be made practical and beneficial. The first step, and the indispensable one, is to nominate no Democratic candidate in opposition to Mr. Chamberlain, if he shall receive the Republican nomination.   This is put on the broad ground that Mr. Chamberlain has earned the gratitude and deserves the confidence of the whole people.   The next step is, to make such Democratic nominations for State offices, from Lieutenant-Governor down, as may be rendered necessary by the character of the Republican nominees—the opposition and nomination in every case to be based upon the dishonesty or incapacity of the Republican candidate.   The next step is to elect the largest possible number of members of the Legislature and county officers. The white counties will send solid Democratic delegations to the Legislature, but they cannot elect members enough to do any real good, if the colored counties elect none but their Elliotts, Whippers, and Leslies.   The object then must be to strive to elect such Democrats and Republicans, in the colored counties as, with the up-county members, will form a Legislature the majority of whose members shall be capable and upright men.   In so working the Democrats will command the aid of the Reform Republicans everywhere ; they will command the sympathy and moral support of the whole country ; they will secure, without a revolution, a government in every way satisfactory, and have solved, without bloodshed or violence of any kind, a momentous social problem.

This is a bare sketch of the way in which Democrats and Republicans can advantageously work together in South Carolina.   It is a general application to our present condition of the principle that a party is truest to the objects for which it was formed when it makes the public welfare its first and most serious consideration.

Unquestionably the policy indicated in these articles was wise, just, and eminently patriotic.   Equally unquestionable are the premises upon which it was based : *" It is certain that the solid Republican vote is larger, by many thousands, than the solid Democratic vote "* ; and that a Democratic candidate could defeat Governor Chamberlain *" in only one way*—BY ARMED FORCE."

CHAPTER XVIII.

The Record of Governor Chamberlain—A Series of Editorial Articles from the Charleston *News and Courier*, July 5–18, 1876.

EARLY in July, 1876, the *News and Courier*, still devoted to the purpose of combining all good citizens for the security of the State's highest interests by sure and peaceful means, began the publication of a series of elaborate editorial articles, entitled "THE RECORD OF GOVERNOR CHAMBERLAIN." This series extended through the daily issues of nearly two weeks. The candid and judicial temper in which the articles were conceived, and the fulness of their information, produced a great effect. So well was the work done that it now seems worthy of reproduction here in its entireness, being both a concise and just *résumé* of so much of the history of Governor Chamberlain's Administration as has been already set forth in these pages, and also an evidence of the light and reason against which the " straight-out " Democrats were then acting, and upon which the *News and Courier* itself, a few weeks later, turned its back, yielding its own intelligent judgment and submitting to a party behest entailing wrongs and evils, from which the Commonwealth still suffers. The way by which South Carolina might escape the woes of misgovernment without resort to bloody crimes or denial of equal rights was open and apparent. But that way did not immediately gratify the impatient ambition of men determined to advance their political fortunes by means as offensive to the principles of republican government as to the fundamental rights of humanity. Incompetent and corrupt officials are a great evil in a State, no doubt ; but an evil less harmful and more readily corrected than the wrongful usurpation of political power either by armed force or by systematic fraud.

The series of articles referred to is given in this chapter.

Since they relate mainly to subjects already presented, they have, in some degree, the quality of repetition ; but they bring to light so many new facts and conditions and set forth all so distinctly with reference to the public welfare and the peculiar interests of the white citizens of the State that they constitute a testimony which may not be ignored or garbled.   The articles were prefaced by an introduction as follows :

INTRODUCTION.

The tendency naturally is to shape the policy of the Democratic party in South Carolina, this summer, according to the opinion entertained of the value of the services of Mr. Chamberlain as Governor of the State.   In this way Mr. Chamberlain has become an important element in the canvass ; for if he were not a candidate for re-election, or if he could be eliminated altogether from political calculations, there would be absolutely no differences in the Democratic ranks.   As it is, the only question open is, whether the Democrats, in the event that Mr. Chamberlain receive the Republican nomination, shall, or shall not, waive the nomination for Governor, and allow Mr. Chamberlain to walk over the course.   In our judgment this should be done ; but if it can be shown that Mr. Chamberlain has been false to his pledges as Governor, if he has failed to do his duty in any important particular, then, we concede, the objections to waiving the Democratic nomination for Governor are increased, and the objections to a " Straight-out " nomination are correspondingly diminished.

Several of our Democratic contemporaries contend that Mr. Chamberlain is no more entitled to public confidence now than he was at the time of his nomination ; that he has done nothing of any value, except what he was obliged to do ; that he is bent on solidifying and strengthening the Republican party, rather than upon reforming the Government of the State.   Such newspapers have short memories, or they would not rail at the *News and Courier* for its high appreciation of Governor Chamberlain's work, or blame us for maintaining the inexpediency of making war upon a Governor whose political power is enormous, and who has won the confidence of an important part of the taxpaying citizens.   Under these circumstances we think it proper, for public guidance and information, as an answer to scores of questions, and in justification of our own course, to scrutinize and explain the record of Mr. Chamberlain, from the moment of his nomination down to this day ; and we shall hope to conduct this inquiry with the impartiality, and certainly with the high motives, which animated us, two years ago, when examining the record of Mr. Chamberlain as Attorney General of the State.   We are as much in earnest as we then were ; and we are confident that we have as good reason to praise as we then had to condemn.

It will be necessary to make the proposed scrutiny of considerable length ; but by taking up successively the different branches of the subject, we shall hope to avoid confusion and to retain the attention of our readers.   Our purpose is to begin with a brief description of the condition of the State at the close of the term of office of Governor Moses.   We shall then show what are the pledges given to the public by

'Governor Chamberlain, in his speech accepting the Republican nomination, and in his inaugural and other addresses. This being done, we shall take up, in turn, the following subjects, which cover, without exception, we think, the promises and recommendations by which Governor Chamberlain, upon taking office, was bound : 1. Minority representation. 2. The election of Justices of the Peace and Constables by the people. 3. The registration of voters. 4. The pardoning power. 5. Executive appointments. 6. The Consolidation Act. 7. The veto power. 8. The Solomon Bank failure. 9. The Bonanza bills. 10. The tax laws. 11. Contingent funds. 12. Legislative expenses. 13. Contingent legislative expenses. 14. The public printing. 15. The salaries of public officers. 16. Taxation. 17. Deficiencies. 18. County finances.

The list is a long one ; but we cannot well make it shorter, and when the work shall be done we can argue our case by the record, instead of relying, as most of us are prone to do, upon gossip or rumor. We shall, in these articles, confine ourselves as closely as possible to a recital of the facts, and give our readers the opportunity to verify, by reference to the original documents, the material statements we shall make. We propose to give time, place, and amount, wherever it is practicable, and we shall be quite willing then to leave the public to decide whether Governor Chamberlain has, or has not, done whatever any man in his position could do for the correction of abuses and the institution of just and equal legislation in the State.

[First Article—July 5, 1876.]

CONDITION OF THE STATE—GOVERNOR CHAMBERLAIN'S PLEDGES TO THE PUBLIC.

In order that the public may understand the nature of the difficulties which beset Governor Chamberlain at the time of his installation, it is necessary to describe the general condition of affairs in South Carolina at the close of the term of his predecessor.

South Carolina was then known throughout the Union as the " Prostrate State," and Moses as her " Robber Governor." Thanks to the efforts of the public press and the conventions of taxpayers, the infamies of Radical rule were already understood, and President Grant, while doing nothing to arrest the progress of the plundering crew, sententiously announced that it was time for the Republican party "to unload South Carolina." The principal departments of the State Government were utterly disorganized. Offices of honor and trust were bartered and sold with shameless effrontery. Moses appeared to regard the appointing power as a perquisite of his office, and regardless of that honor which is said to exist among such as he and his fellows, removed the officers he had profitably appointed so soon as there was an opportunity to resell the same place at a higher price. Money entrusted to him for public purposes paid the hire of his procurers, and gilded the shame of the victims of his lust. Warrants were duplicated, with shameless haste, when the regular appropriations were exhausted, and thus the State or the creditor was doubly defrauded.

Free from any restraint, the legislative branch of the government revelled at the public expense in every luxury that money could purchase. In the concoction and passage of corrupt measures a complete understanding existed between the Legislature and the Executive. Nothing out of which money could be squeezed escaped a most vigorous squeezing. Upon the statute-book were placed, it is true, Acts which laid the foundation of subsequent reforms ; but they were enacted either because their purpose was not understood, or because Moses and his fellows were confident that they could repeal or evade them whenever it should be necessary.   The chagrin of the robber band when they found that they had, by the "specific tax levies," surrendered the key of the treasury, was too marked to escape notice.

The criminal courts were almost a useless expense to the State, as they were no protection to the people.   Money and favor opened wide the doors of the penitentiary for the most hardened and depraved criminals.   Judges on the bench knew that conviction and sentence was a farce while the Executive, the depository of the pardoning power, "combined the corruption of a Tweed with all the vices of a Sardanapalus."   The credit of the State was buried with her departed public honor. Capital shunned our shores.   Public indignation grew hoarse in denouncing Moses and his radical allies.   Blind as were the ignorant masses, the shrewder leaders, the Pattersons and Whittemores and Bowens saw that the choice lay between Reform and Revolution.

Such was the position of public affairs when the Republican State Convention met in Columbia in September, 1874.   The Conservative citizens were resting on their arms.   They had announced that, if an unobjectionable candidate were nominated by the Republicans, they would not oppose his election ; and that, if the Republican candidate should be unworthy of their support, they would vote for any unobjectionable candidate who might be nominated by Republicans who seceded from the regular party convention.   The candidate selected by the radicals was Mr. Chamberlain. There was nothing in his record up to that time, as the public knew it, that warranted the belief that he would be other than a willing instrument of the men who procured his nomination.   These were the very thieves who had increased the State debt from $6,000,000 to $16,000,000, and had shared the profits and crimes of the Moses *régime*.   After a severe canvass, in which the Radical majority was cut down from 30,000 to 10,000, Mr. Chamberlain was elected.   Then for the first time was any heed given to the fair promises which had been made by the successful Radicals and their candidate.   It was as certain then as it is now that those promises were made for show, and as a means of turning the sharp edge of public opinion.   The public now looked anxiously to see what the promises were, and, with little hope or confidence, awaited the meeting of the Legislature which should show whether the Governor-elect was indeed the tool of his party associates and supporters.

We pass to an enumeration of the reforms which the Republican party generally, and Mr. Chamberlain specially, were pledged to carry into effect.   In 1872 the Republican party, after nominating Moses, solemnly declared "that the public expenses shall be reduced within the public revenue to be derived from a moderate system of taxation, based upon a fair and equitable assessment of all property liable to taxation," and insisted that "there shall be an immediate reduction in the salaries of all public officers, from the highest to the lowest," and that "there shall be a judicious reduction in the number of public offices themselves."   No attempt was made by Governor or Legislature to redeem these pledges.   They had answered their purpose. And the Convention of 1874, with equal sincerity, reaffirmed them, pledging the Republican party "to reduce the public expenses within the public revenue, derivable from a moderate assessment and tax rate," and "to advocate such a modification of our present system of taxation as shall prove of the largest advantage to our agricultural interests," and " to pass such laws as will tend most speedily to develop the resources and build up the manufacturing and industrial prosperity of the State." In accepting the nomination for Governor (September 8, 1874), Mr. Chamberlain said to the Convention :

" I cannot forbear to now say to you that no platform which does not commit us irrevocably and solemnly to the duty of reducing public expenditures to their lowest limits ; of administering the public funds honestly in the public interests ; of electing competent public officers ; of filling the local offices of our counties and townships with honest and faithful incumbents ; of guarding our language and our action so as to allay rather than rekindle the flames of past controversies ; of directing the attention of our fellow-citizens to the hopes of the future rather than to the memories of the past, can bring to us party success or political honor."

And he warned the Convention that their platform would be " empty words," their nominations would bring no honor to their party, and their political success would be less than worthless, unless they placed behind their candidate for Governor the evidence of their wisdom and truth " in the nomination and election of your best citizens for members of the Legislature." In this strain Mr. Chamberlain spoke throughout the canvass, pledging himself personally to carry out, in sincerity and truth, the promises of the platform. Nor did he underrate the obstacles in his way, for in a conversation with a correspondent of the New York *Tribune* (September 15, 1874), he said : " The work of reform will be a constant struggle. It will require time to put things right here. If in my two years as Governor I can even ' turn the tide,' I shall be more than rewarded."

It remained to be seen whether Governor Chamberlain, after the election, would renew the promises he had made while " under fire," and before the fight was won. He was sworn in on December 1, 1874, and immediately delivered his Inaugural Address. In this address he recommended a revision of the tax laws, so as to secure the assessment of property at its true value ; the limitation of the amount of taxes to the actual requirements of the government ; the abolition of contingent funds ; the reduction of legislative expenses ; the establishment of proper accountability in the payment of legislative expenses ; the extermination of the existing system of public printing, the reduction of salaries ; the keeping of public expenditures within the receipts ; the election of Justices of the Peace and Constables by the people ; the registration of electors, minority representation, and other measures looking to an application of the principles of administrative reform laid down in the party platform and in his addresses on the stump. As the first step we see, therefore, that Mr. Chamberlain, as Governor, went further than he had done as a candidate ; for as Governor he had not only reiterated the salutary recommendations previously made, but showed how they could be taken out of the domain of theory and made substantial facts.

We shall next inquire what was done by Governor Chamberlain in support of his recommendations, and point out what was accomplished and what remains undone. According to the plan of these articles, the first topic will be Minority Representation.

[Second Article—July 6, 1876.]
1. MINORITY REPRESENTATION. 2. JUSTICES OF THE PEACE AND CONSTABLES.
3. THE REGISTRATION OF ELECTORS.

1. Minority representation is no longer under discussion by the people in this State, although in such counties as Charleston, by voluntary arrangement, its principles

have been successfully applied at popular elections. We only notice it here as one of the reform measures advocated by Governor Chamberlain.

Mr. Chamberlain was a member of the Taxpayers' Convention of 1871, and in that body urged the passage of resolutions in favor of the adoption of the system of proportional representation in South Carolina. In the course of his remarks he said : "Do you believe, for a moment, that when you put into an ignorant Assembly, many of whom can neither read nor write, forty-seven gentlemen, whom I might select in this body, that you would not shame them into decency, or frighten them from crime?" Again : "From the moment you place in the lower House forty-seven of your ablest citizens, bad legislation will cease and good legislation will begin." The resolutions passed, and Governor Scott promised to recommend the measure in his next message to the General Assembly. This he did, but in such a way as to ensure the inaction of the Legislature. Mr. Chamberlain, however, still saw in minority representation a means of relieving the State from its worst troubles, by checking the power of the majority ; and, in his first Annual Message of January 12, 1875, he recommended that the system be tried by applying it, in the first place, to the elections of incorporated cities and towns. A bill applying this principle to the elections in the town of Anderson became a law ; and, confirmed in his views by a practical test of the plan, Governor Chamberlain, in his message of November 23, 1875, renewed his previous recommendations on the subject, and cordially and earnestly urged the General Assembly to frame and enact the necessary legislation. The General Assembly took no steps to inquire into or consider the question, and adjourned without taking any notice of it whatever.

For the failure to engraft the system of minority representation upon our political system Governor Chamberlain clearly is not responsible. It is true that, in this State, such representation may not have as much protective force as in States where the average intelligence of both majority and minority is about equal. It is apparently a necessity in South Carolina that the voting minority should have a majority in the Legislature. Nevertheless, with forty-seven Democrats in the lower House last session, and the independent vote, the Radical majority could have been checked at every turn. What the thirty-three Democrats did succeed in doing is evidence enough of the value of the additional votes that minority representation would have given them.

2. The State Constitution provides for the election, by the people of the several counties, of Justices of the Peace and Constables. From 1868 to 1874 these provisions remained wholly dormant and nugatory. The Radicals were unwilling to lose the control of these offices in counties where they were in a minority ; the Senate and House were unwilling to give up the opportunities they had of helping their friends, by pushing them forward as candidates for Executive appointments ; the Executive was loth to surrender that patronage which strengthened a Scott with his party and filled the pockets of a Moses.

Governor Chamberlain, however, in his Inaugural Address, called the attention of the Legislature to the requirements of the organic law. "The General Assembly," he said, "is responsible, at all times, for the failure to enforce the constitutional system." The Trial-Justice system, he declared, "was costly, inefficient, and oppressive" ; the number of the Trial Justices "should be reduced immediately by at least one third" ; the incumbents of these offices "are, to a great extent, deficient in the qualities which make a useful magistrate." As usual, no heed was given his salutary recommendations, and, in his first Annual Message, he again called attention to the matter, saying that the one sufficient reason why Justices of the Peace and Constables should be elected by the people is, that " such is the positive requirement of the Constitution." Governor Chamberlain also explained that provision could be made, by statute, that an indictment for any misconduct should work the suspension of such officers, and a conviction work the forfeiture of the office. This would meet the objection that magistrates and constables, if elected, could, if found unworthy, be with difficulty removed. No action on the subject was taken by the General Assembly during the session of 1874-75, and Governor Chamberlain, in his second Annual Message of November 22, 1875, again urged the Legislature to comply with the mandates of the Constitution. " The adoption of new constitutional provisions," he pointedly said, " will give little confidence in our good intentions, while important existing constitutional requirements are wholly and persistently disregarded." Frankly admitting the defects of the existing method, he said : " The results of the system of Trial Justices appointed by the Governor certainly cannot be considered so favorable as to justify the annulling of an important part of the Constitution."

At the session of 1875-76 several bills were introduced in the General Assembly providing for the election of Justices of the Peace, or Trial Justices, and Constables. None of them, however, passed. The only gain was the passage of some local bills, limiting the number of such officers and the expenses of their courts. No general measure was enacted.

Upon this subject the record of Governor Chamberlain is absolutely clear. The defects of the existing plan were obvious to him, the requirements of the Constitution could not be mistaken. Caring nothing for the patronage he would lose, looking only to the law and the public good, he exhausted argument and censure in the vain attempt to make a debauched and malignant Legislature discharge an imperative obligation under the Constitution which every member of the House and Senate is sworn to obey.

3. Year after year the frauds at elections in South Carolina had grown more and more barefaced, reaching their height in 1870 and 1872. The State Constitution makes it " the duty of the General Assembly to provide, from time to time, for the registration of all electors." Such a registration, while not ensuring fair elections, would certainly tend to prevent the wholesale repeating, the voting under age, and the ballot-box stuffing in which the Radical managers and rallyers regularly engage. The absence of registration was, therefore, one of the principal means whereby the dominant party retained, and expected to continue to retain, control of the State. This well known fact did not prevent Governor Chamberlain from reminding the Legislature, in his Inaugural Address, that " no registration of electors has been made or provided for, since the adoption of the Constitution in 1868." He recommended that the constitutional requirements be no longer disregarded. " The obvious justice," he said, " of a registration of electors, aside from the positive mandate of the Constitution, renders any argument in its favor needless." The Legislature and the press discussed this recommendation ; the Radicals opposing it and the Democrats supporting it. In his Annual Message of January 12, 1875, Governor Chamberlain renewed his exhortations. This time, defying the sentiment of the corrupt members of his own party, he said :

" If it were demonstrable that party advantage would arise from the neglect of this requirement of the Constitution, it would not have a feather's weight in deterring me from carrying into effect the Constitution which I have sworn to support. But it is idle to urge that a registration of electors will help, or hurt, any party which relies upon proper means to sustain its supremacy. It will not prevent all election frauds, but it will go far towards that end, and will tend to give a degree of confidence in the result of our elections which has sometimes been wanting."

The session of 1874–75 having passed without action, Governor Chamberlain, in his Annual Message of November 23, 1875, told the General Assembly that "the Constitution requires registration," and "the phrase from ' time to time' is intended to secure the constant observance of this safeguard of our elections." " To my mind," he said, " there is no place left for argument on this subject. In a political or party view I fear nothing more than the effect of a plain disregard of constitutional requirements." The General Assembly was not moved by the cogent reasoning of the Governor, or by the mandate of the Constitution, and adjourned without taking the slightest notice of the grave question which had thrice been submitted to them.

We have seen that in the matter of minority representation, of the election of Justices of the Peace and Constables by the people, and of the registration of electors, Governor Chamberlain not only recommended restrictive and anti-Radical measures which his predecessors had not condescended to notice, but recommended them, and urged them, in the teeth of the well understood wishes of the Radical leaders, who depend, for their continued authority, upon the exclusive rule of majorities, the saddling of Democratic counties with Radical officials, and false voting, and fraudulent counting at elections. It may be said, and it has been said, that Governor Chamberlain made these recommendations knowing that they would be disregarded, and that otherwise he would not have made them. But it must be remembered that the Executive has no affirmative power in matters of legislation. It is his duty to recommend to the consideration of the General Assembly " such measures as he shall judge necessary or expedient " ; but no responsibility attaches to him for their failure to adopt his recommendations. On the other hand, he is entrusted with the power of vetoing such measures as do not meet with his approval, and for the exercise of that power, promptly and fearlessly, he is responsible to the people, for whose protection that power is conferred upon him. Governor Chamberlain used the veto, as will be shown, with unexampled frequency and boldness ; and it is tasking even political credulity too far to argue that he would make insincere recommendations, to gain the praise of his political opponents, while he was unhesitatingly killing by his veto, the pet projects of the leaders of his own party. In view of what he recommended where he had only the power to recommend, and what he did, where he had the power to act, the irresistible conclusion is, that he was as much in earnest in recommendation as in action, and that in both cases, with equal earnestness, he exerted the whole power and influence of his office to promote the public good.

[Third Article—July 7, 1876.]

4. THE PARDONING POWER—5. EXECUTIVE APPOINTMENTS.

4. No power entrusted to the Governor of a State calls for more wisdom and caution, in its exercise, than that of granting reprieves and pardons to criminals. In the stern words of the Constitution of South Carolina, the Governor shall " take care that the laws be faithfully executed in mercy " ; but any misuse of the pardoning power,

either through the weakness or viciousness of the Executive, strips the law of its terrors, and impairs, if it does not destroy, the security of property and person. To what degree, and with what effect, the Executive prerogative can be perverted and abused is read in the history of the Moses Administration. Such was his recklessness and his cupidity that judges announced, from the bench, their unwillingness to put the State to the expense of convicting criminals for the Executive to pardon. In the closing hours of his term of office Moses wellnigh emptied the cells of the penitentiary. Justice was bound hand and foot in her own temple! Crime was rampant in the State! Any offender who had strong friends, or whose purse pleaded his cause, could count on being set free, after a short detention, to prey anew upon the public. It was this deplorable condition of things that caused Governor Chamberlain, in his Inaugural Address, to say:

"In the exercise of the power conferred on the Governor by the Constitution, to grant reprieves and pardons after conviction, I shall endeavor to keep in view the end for which our criminal laws are framed—the repression of crime and the protection of society. The occasions will be rare, and attended by peculiar circumstances, in which I shall feel justified in setting aside the judgment of our Courts and the verdict of our juries."

The Constitution requires the Governor to make a report to the General Assembly of the pardons, reprieves, and commutations granted by him. This requirement had been conveniently disregarded, but is faithfully complied with by Governor Chamberlain. In explanation of the report of pardons, reprieves, and commutations, in his second Annual Message, he said:

"In discharging this most onerous and painful duty of my office I have endeavored faithfully to redeem the promise made in my Inaugural Address. The whole number of pardons and commutations granted by me, up to November 1, 1875, was thirty-six. With scarcely an exception, all applications for pardon or commutation have been referred by me to the Judge who tried the case, and, as will be seen, in nearly or quite every case, my action has had the sanction of the Courts and best citizens of the State."

This is clear and positive enough; but a comparison of the number of pardons granted by Governors Scott and Moses with the number granted by Governor Chamberlain, gives a still better idea of the steadfastness with which the latter kept in view "the end for which our criminal laws are framed":

Pardons Issued by Governor Scott.

| 1868 to 1870 | . | . | . | . | . | . | . | 332 |
| 1870 to 1872 | . | . | . | . | . | . | . | 247 |

Pardons Issued by Moses.

| 1872 to 1874 | . | . | . | . | . | . | . | 457 |

From December 1, 1874, to May 31, 1876, Governor Chamberlain pardoned only *seventy-three* convicts. Sixty-six of these were recommended to be pardoned by the Judges before whom they were tried; and in the case of the remaining seven the Judges, while not advising the pardons, made no objection. In every case where a pardon has been granted, the petition therefor was signed by a number of citizens of the locality where the applicant had lived. In nearly every instance a considerable part of the sentence had been served out, and the ends of justice, in the opinion of the Governor, fully met, before a pardon was granted. The whole number of applications for pardon up to May 31, 1876, was 147. Seventy-four, more than a half, were refused. During the same period the whole number of persons confined in the penitentiary was 723 ; the number pardoned bearing to the number confined the relation of 1 to 10. When Governor Chamberlain entered upon the duties of his office in December, 1874, there were 124 convicts in the penitentiary. On the 31st May, 1874, the number was 400. This increase is due mainly, if not entirely, to the wise moderation with which pardons are granted. Society has been weeded of hundreds of criminals over whom a Scott or a Moses, as the records show, would have thrown the shield of ill-judged or mercenary clemency.

We have been particular in giving the exact number of pardons granted by Governor Chamberlain, because it has been asserted that the " pardon-mill " is running as merrily as in the piping times of his predecessor. Such assertions, innocently made, are best met by the hard facts. No Governor, however careful and conscientious, can hope to escape error ; but when pardons are recommended by judges who try a prisoner, and by citizens who know his character, when the number of pardons is reduced by one half, and when a statement of the reasons for granting a petition is exposed to public scrutiny at the time that the pardon is announced, the Executive, it seems to us, must, in the absence of proof to the contrary, be considered to have discharged a most painful and onerous duty with a scrupulous regard for the interests of the people.

5. In noticing the earnest endeavors of Governor Chamberlain to induce the General Assembly to give effect to the constitutional requirement that Justices of the Peace and Constables be elected by the people, we incidentally mentioned that he frankly admitted that the results of the appointment of Trial Justices by the Governor could not be considered favorable. From the moment of his installation one of his greatest difficulties was to find, and procure the confirmation of, suitable and worthy persons to fill the various offices within the gift of the Executive. Before he had been a month in office he saw (S. J. 1874–75, p. 208) '' that the importunity of applicants, the difficulty of obtaining correct and unbiased information as to the qualifications of applicants, and the personal dissatisfaction certain to arise whenever any selection is made from several candidates," would seriously embarrass him in restoring good government and harmonizing the various antagonistic elements of the body politic. In his first Annual Message he said .

" It is a practical impossibility, in my judgment, for any Governor to appoint three hundred and fifty Trial Justices, in all parts of the State, so as to secure, to a proper degree, the interests of the people affected by these appointments. This impossibility becomes more apparent when the Governor finds himself surrounded and trammelled, in the discharge of his duty, in this respect, by what are considered his obligations to the political party to which he owes his election."

No sooner did Governor Chamberlain begin to make nominations than the factious Radical majority in the Senate began to reject them. So annoying did this opposition become that Governor Chamberlain addressed an Executive Message to the Senate on June 20, 1876, in which he said :

" I regret to find that there are, in many instances, irreconcilable differences, as to the proper men to be appointed, between the Executive and those who represent the several counties in the General Assembly. I am anxious at all times to agree with those of my own political party ; but I can never purchase this harmony by disregarding my own judgment, founded upon the best information which I can obtain.

. . . I recognize the rule that the dominant party is entitled to the greater part of these appointments ; provided, always, that that party can furnish men well qualified for such offices. I do not think that this rule requires me to refuse to appoint a political opponent, as Trial Justice, when upon the whole I judge that the good order and general welfare of a community will be better promoted by appointing occasionally one of the party now in the minority in this State."

The embarrassments of which Governor Chamberlain speaks, in connection with the appointment of Trial Justices, were far greater when the more important offices of County Auditor and County Treasurer were to be filled. One precaution could, however, be taken. The sureties upon the bonds of all public officers have been required to make affidavit of their ability to fully meet the liabilities they have assumed. Under previous administrations most public officers gave " straw-bonds " ; but under the present rule the State is secured, up to the full amount of the bond required by law to be given, unless the sureties shall swear falsely, which they cannot be prevented from doing if they are willing to take the chance of detection and punishment.

In the exercise of the appointing power Governor Chamberlain was always confronted by a majority in the Senate hostile to whosoever should attempt to fill the public offices with any other than their own creatures. Only those familiar with the proceedings of the Senate in executive session can realize the bitterness with which the " Senatorial group " fought against the confirmation of any person not of their selection and under their control. The words we have quoted show that Governor Chamberlain understood both the dangers and the duties of his position, and it is shown besides that he did his utmost to divest himself of the power of appointing no less than 350 public officers, and to give their choice to the people. That he did persevere in nominating the best men who stood any chance of confirmation, the roll of public officers proves. In some instances objectionable persons were appointed, but, as a whole, the character of the public officers is far higher than under Scott or Moses. This was the best that could be done.

It must be remembered likewise that not one in ten of those who are recommended for public office are personally known to the Governor, who relies, perforce, upon the representations of third persons. How easy it is to be deceived, how hard it is to form a correct judgment, need not be explained to those who have had experience of the difficulty of making proper selections, under the most favorable circumstances, in civil or military life. Governor Chamberlain had, it is true, the power to remove, for cause, officers of his appointment ; but his action is subject to review by the Senate, which can replace the removed officer. This has been done. Again, the Governor cannot act upon rumor. Charges capable of proof must be made before he can justly remove a public officer, and unless such proof of incapacity or dishonesty be furnished, the officer must keep his place. It is annoying, we grant, that every public officer should not be a person of high respectability and intelligence ; but when a Governor has improved the general character of the public service, and has nominated the best of the available candidates who could be confirmed, he has done as much as can be expected of him. For the shortcomings of any who were confirmed, the perverse Senate, rather than the Executive, must be held accountable. The course of Governor Chamberlain, up to this time, is in itself a guaranty that whenever the Senate will act favorably, and without imposing conditions, upon his free nominations, the public officers of his appointment will be as capable and upright as the people can desire.

[Fourth Article—July 8, 1876.]

6. THE CONSOLIDATION ACT—7. THE VETO POWER.

When the Radical majority in the General Assembly had succeeded, as they supposed, in electing an ignorant gambler and a mendacious debauchee to the Circuit Bench, their exultation found fit expression in the cry, " Chamberlain can't veto that ! " They could not, in few words, have manifested more defiantly their sense of the effect with which the Executive veto had been used to set aside, or put down, schemes just as infamous as that which culminated in the election of Whipper and Moses. They laughed too soon. Governor Chamberlain did veto the action of the General Assembly, on that Black Thursday, by refusing to issue commissions to the would-be Judges, and the claimants are no nearer their coveted seats than they were six months ago. In the hands of a Governor who is vigilant and bold, the veto is an almost insurmountable barrier to vicious and venal legislators. What use of it Governor Chamberlain has made we shall now show ; taking up the proposed amendment of the Consolidation Act, before running through the general list of measures which were returned to the House in which they originated, without the Executive approval.

6. The Act to reduce the volume of the public debt, commonly called the Consolidation Act, provides for the funding of the recognized debt of the State at one half its nominal value, in consolidation bonds and stocks The interest on the old debt, up to January 1, 1874, was to be funded in like manner. The consolidation bonds and stocks, whenever issued, drew interest from January 1, 1874, the first interest being payable July 1, 1874. At the legislative session of 1874–75, an Act to declare the true intent and meaning of the Consolidation Act was passed. This Act amended the Consolidation Act so that the interest on the fundable debt should be funded up to the time of the funding, instead of up to January 1, 1874 ; and so that the consolidation bonds should bear interest from the time of their issue, instead of from January 1, 1874. Governor Chamberlain vetoed the Act, in conformity with the declaration made in his Inaugural Message, that as the people of the State were apparently united in support of the settlement of the public debt which had been effected, " it must be regarded, so far as legislation and popular influence can go, as a final settlement." Governor Chamberlain, in his Veto Message (S. J. 1874–75, p. 77), took the broad ground that " the inevitable effect of any change whatever in the Consolidation Act will be to unsettle the returning confidence of our creditors, and to seriously retard the completion of exchanging our public debt, which is so essential to all our prosperity." In declaring the Consolidation Act to be a final settlement, Governor Chamberlain, it must be noted, binds himself to maintain the rejection of the $5,965,000 of conversion bonds which, in the words of that Act, " were put upon the market without any authority of law, and are hereby declared to be absolutely null and void." The veto was sustained by a vote of 15 to 14 (less than two thirds in favor of passing the bill), and the Consolidation Act was not again disturbed. Of the fourteen Senators who voted to sustain the veto five were Democrats.

7. During his term of office Governor Chamberlain has returned to the General Assembly, without his approval, seventeen Acts and Joint Resolutions. Twelve of these related to matters of a local or personal nature, and five were of such character as to affect the whole State. In every instance the veto of the Governor was sus-

tained by the requisite vote, and this vote was cast by the Democrats and the better class of Republicans.

Three of the local or personal measures were returned without approval because they were in conflict with the State Constitution ; two were returned on account of verbal inaccuracies : one was returned because it would accomplish no practicable object whatever ; one was returned under a misapprehension caused by an imperfect examination of the legislative precedents in this State ; two were returned in deference to the wishes of nine tenths of the citizens of the towns affected ; one (the Barnwell-Blackville bill) because it sought to settle the vexed question of the location of the county seat of Barnwell, then pending in the Supreme Court, and, by an appeal to the General Assembly, to deprive the people of the right to decide by local action their local controversies ; one was returned because the language of the Act defeated the intention of its framers, by preventing the levy of a tax which it sought to continue ; one was returned because it proposed to require the payment in full of all claims against the County of Edgefield, audited and allowed by the County Commissioners prior to October 31, 1874, without further audit, the Governor contending that " to enact that such past indebtedness shall be paid in full, and without further examination, is to add to the burden of injustice under which the people of many counties are now groaning." This brief statement, by the way, will give the outside public some idea of the intelligence and wisdom of the South Carolina Legislature. The majority of the members of that body are, however, acute enough when there is money to be made by selling their votes, or when a reasonable and well-considered proposition, coming from a Democratic source, is ordered to be voted down.

The vetoes of a general character were : 1. Of the Act relative to the deposit of the moneys of the State. 2. Of the Act to provide for the settlement and redemption of certain claims against the State. 3. Of the Act to declare the true intent and meaning of the Consolidation Act. 4. Of the Act to raise supplies for the fiscal year commencing November 1, 1875. 5. Of an Act to appropriate $30,000 of the phosphate royalty to certain purposes.

These five vetoes (excepting that relating to the Consolidation Act, which is noticed above) will be considered successively and in connection with the general subjects of the Solomon Bank failure, the Bonanza bills, and State taxation, to which they relate. They are cited here as evidence that Governor Chamberlain, not content with recommending reformatory legislation, unhesitatingly exerted the whole power of his office to defeat unwise or injurious legislation. Nor can the value of his services, in this respect, be determined by the bare enumeration of the bills and joint resolutions which he returned with his objections. Many a corrupt scheme died still-born because its projectors knew that, when it had passed the turbulent House and loquacious Senate, it would encounter an irresistible veto. The Legislature of 1874–76 was fully as corrupt and demagogical as any of its predecessors. It did less injury to the body politic than was done by the Legislatures of Scott and Moses, only because, for the first time since Reconstruction, the Governor of the State could be relied on to strike down with his veto whatever rascally jobs the two Houses might pass, and because at the back of the Executive was a body of patriotic Democrats and staunch Republicans strong enough to prevent the overriding of a veto, although, unhappily, not powerful enough to secure the passage of the judicious, economic measures which they framed and introduced.

[Fifth Article—July 9, 1876.]

8. THE SOLOMON BANK.

8. The loss of money to the people of the State by the failure of the South Carolina Bank and Trust Company (the Solomon Bank) on July 2, 1875, was over two hundred thousand dollars—equal to the proceeds of a tax of *one and a half per cent.*[1] upon the value of the taxable property in the State   It is natural, therefore, that the failure should have attracted unwonted attention, especially as the Solomon Bank was regarded as a semi-political concern, organized and carried on in the interest of the Radical officials.   Somebody was certainly to blame, inside or outside the bank, and that person, in the opinion of many excellent Democrats, is Governor Chamberlain.   We shall see what the record shows.

The General Assembly in March, 1875, passed a bill "relative to the deposit of the moneys of the State."   This bill was intended to repeal the existing law, which imposed upon a Board of Deposit, composed of the Governor, the Comptroller General, and the State Treasurer, the duty of selecting such banks for the deposit of State funds as shall be secure and pay the highest rate of interest.   The new bill provided that all State funds should be deposited in the Solomon Bank and the Carolina National Bank of Columbia.   These two banks were made the exclusive depositories ; and no officer was authorized, for any reason, to change them.   Even if the banks were obviously unsound or on the brink of bankruptcy, the public funds could not be removed, except by authority of the General Assembly.   The disadvantages and dangers of such a bill were only too plain.   It was, as was afterwards admitted, a job put up for the benefit of the Solomon Bank.   Governor Chamberlain vetoed the bill, and in his message (S. J. 1874-75, p. 609) said that the State had in hand nearly one million dollars in cash, distributed in three banks in Charleston and three in Columbia, with an aggregate capital of $2,300,000, and he ventured the opinion that "no man competent to care for his own funds would feel warranted in placing one hundred thousand dollars in each of the two banks designated in the present Act."   Governor Chamberlain distinctly disclaimed any intention to reflect upon the character or management of the designated banks, and his objections were specifically directed to the system proposed.   On the question of passing the bill, notwithstanding the objections of the Governor, the vote in the Senate was, Yeas 18, Nays 12 ; and the bill, failing to receive the necessary two-thirds vote, was lost.   Of the twelve votes sustaining the veto, five were cast by Democrats.

In less than three months after the rejection of the bill, which would have placed in its coffers half a million of money, the Solomon Bank closed its doors.   Governor Chamberlain was absent from the State, but in the following December, in response to a resolution of the House, he gave that body (H. J. 1875-76, p. 234) such information as he had concerning the bank.   In this report or message Governor Chamberlain says that soon after his installation he became satisfied that the State deposits ought not to be kept in any one bank in Columbia or elsewhere ; that since 1870 the Solomon Bank had virtually been the sole depository, and had had on hand at one time as much as $1,400,000 ; that Treasurer Cardozo, and no other person connected with the State Government, agreed with him in his unwillingness to continue the Solomon Bank as the sole depository.   He called, he said, a meeting of the Board of De-

---

[1] Evidently an error for *one and a half mills.*

posit, and laid before them his views. The friends of the Solomon Bank vehemently opposed the proposed change, giving assurance that the bank was strong, and showing that it had not suspended payment in the panic of 1873, and that in four years the State had not lost a dollar that had been entrusted to its keeping. Governor Chamberlain, as he shows, insisted that the deposits in the Solomon Bank should not exceed $200,000. Treasurer Cardozo made no opposition to this. Judge Hoge, then Comptroller General, unequivocally opposed any change unfavorable to the Solomon Bank. This was in the winter of 1874–75. Subsequently the Board met again, and three banks in Charleston and one additional bank in Columbia, making, with the Solomon Bank and the Carolina National Bank, six banks in all, were designated as depositories. This was the condition of affairs when the bill to make the Solomon Bank and the Carolina National Bank the sole depositories was vetoed. At the time of the veto, Governor Chamberlain had, he says, no knowledge of the affairs of the Solomon Bank in addition to that upon which he had acted in January, when he insisted on increasing the number of the depositories ; and that from that time up to the failure of the bank, no proposition or advice was tendered to him, from any source, for any change of the State deposits.

It is evident that Governor Chamberlain was right in insisting, in the winter of 1874–75, that the number of depositories should be increased, and that his objections to the bill to make two banks the exclusive depositories were sound and conclusive. But in April, 1875, after the veto of the new bill, the deposits in the Solomon Bank were increased to $200,000, and Governor Chamberlain's consent to this increase blotted out, for a time at least, the recollection of the prudent action of the winter and early spring. We find in this action nothing inconsistent with Governor Chamberlain's previous conclusions. It is true that he was not disposed to put more than $100,000 in the Solomon Bank ; but it showed large assets, and was apparently sound, and there was no reason to believe that $200,000 would not be safe. In his sworn testimony before the Legislative Committee (R. and R. 1875–76, p. 921) he said that he understood and believed, in the January before the failure, that the bank had from $200,000 to $300,000 surplus, and that at the time he left the State (June 25th), he had no doubts as to the solvency of the bank, or fears as to the State deposits. Treasurer Cardozo, the arch-opponent of the Solomon Bank, testified before the same committee that he was surprised at the failure and at the amount the bank failed for. Comptroller General Dunn testified that at the April meeting of the Board of Deposit he "was willing to vote for $250,000 being left in the bank " (R. and R. 1875–76, p. 915) and that he had no reason to doubt the solvency of the bank. And the Legislative Committee, in the majority report, which is signed by Senators Duncan and Ward, say that there "was $163,000 on deposit in the Solomon Bank in April, 1875, when the action of the Board was taken, so that the *actual authorized increase* was $37,000," and they report that "there is nothing in the facts discovered which necessarily shows that the Board or any members thereof had any knowledge of the instability of the bank, or is censurable for not having determined its true condition." Again they say : "In the light of subsequent events it would have been better if a scrutiny had been instituted into the standing of the bank ; but no facts had at that time been developed which would fairly prove the absence of such investigation to have been culpable." Join to this the fact that if the sworn statement of its affairs made in January was correct, $156,000 of money was made away with, under the name of legislative expenses and stock retired, by the Solomon Bank between January and July, 1875, and the failure of the concern is easily accounted for. Indeed, the Legislative Committee say that "during the ten days immediately preceding the failure, Mr. Solomon was studiously and skilfully at work in so manipulating the affairs of the bank as that he might reap the largest practicable harvest, while the impending catastrophe was being made correspondingly disastrous to the creditors."

The weight of evidence is clearly in favor of Governor Chamberlain. We have seen that he would not allow the Solomon Bank to continue to be the sole depository, as it had been for four years ; that he vetoed and defeated the bill to make two banks, including the Solomon Bank, the exclusive depositories ; that he caused six banks, instead of one or two, to be designated as public depositories. This is indisputable ; and half a million at least, instead of $200,000, would have been exposed to loss, had Governor Chamberlain remained quiescent, or failed to veto the amendatory bill. Such conduct as his is irreconcilable with any other hypothesis than that he was unwilling to leave with the bank a dollar more than appeared to be perfectly safe. Comptroller Dunn would have consented to a deposit of $250,000, and Treasurer Cardozo did not fear an early failure or for a large amount. This suffices to show that if there was an error, it was purely an error of judgment, which Governor Chamberlain shared with his colleagues in the Board, and which cannot, in the light of his previous action, be turned to his disadvantage. Governor Chamberlain is not by any means the only officer who has consented in good faith to the deposit of money in an institution which proved to be rotten to the core ; and in every such case there must be proof of wanton negligence, or the officer cannot be held even morally responsible for the loss that follows. Such proof, as is shown, is conspicuously absent in the record of the dealings of Governor Chamberlain with the Solomon Bank.

[Sixth Article—July 12, 1876.]

THE BONANZA BILL—10. THE TAX LAWS.

9. One of the most embarrassing legacies of the Administrations of Scott and Moses was what Governor Chamberlain describes as "the unpaid balance of the certificates issued, during the last four years, under the guise of legislative expenses of various kinds." He said :

"That certificates for legislative expenses have been made the cover for vast frauds, no man will dispute. They are universally regarded as the last culminating evidences of a prevailing system of corruption which has disgraced our State and offended the nation. Since the regular session of the General Assembly for 1870–71 the State had paid, prior to the present session, on account of legislative expenses, the vast sum of $1,661,000. According to the registry already made by the Clerks of the two Houses, under a recent resolution of the General Assembly, there are still outstanding claims to the amount of $883,000, of which amount over $500,000 consists of claims for legislative expenses."

In this wise, in his message of March 17, 1875 (H. J. 1874–75, page 663), Governor Chamberlain speaks of the floating indebtedness of the State, made up of legislative pay certificates, treasurer's due bills, and bills payable and claims passed by the General Assembly. The members of the Legislature were largely interested in these claims, for themselves or their friends ; it was certain that they would, as in previous sessions, be ordered for payment, if the proper inducements were furnished the legislative branch of the government. Between the holders and the treasury stood the Executive and the Executive veto ! No other protection, short of revolution, could the taxpayers hope to find.

In his first Annual Message (S. J. 1874-75, page 206) Governor Chamberlain warned the General Assembly that the legal validity of a large part of the floating indebtedness was "more than doubtful, and the meritorious character of a still larger part may be well disputed." So much of the indebtedness "as had the character of legal and moral validity" he regarded as a part of the public burden which must be assumed ; but he declared himself "inflexibly opposed to the hasty or present liquidation of any considerable portion of this indebtedness." This decisive language had a perceptible effect upon the claim holders ; and Governor Chamberlain, as the easiest and safest mode of settlement that could be devised, consented to a plan which embraced (1) the appointment by the Governor of a Commission of three, with power to audit all claims, and to reject any claim in whole or in part ; (2) the reduction of all approved claims to one half of their nominal value ; (3) the payment of the claims, when thus reduced, in four equal instalments. Such a measure was accordingly framed by the House, but the Senate amended it by inserting the names of the three Commissioners. The House, when the bill was returned to it, changed the Commission, and the Senate concurred in the change. The bill was sent to the Governor, and was vetoed by him on March 17, 1875. In this Veto Message, from which we have already quoted, Governor Chamberlain explains the character of the floating indebtedness and the necessity of protecting the people against the payment of fraudulent claims. Apart from other objections, a fatal objection to the bill was that the Commission named in it did not, "as a whole," command the confidence of the Governor or the public. The Governor said : "The duties required of the Commission demand the highest character for intelligence, honor, and capability which the State can furnish. By no fault or agency of mine, I am forced to declare that, in my judgment, the Commission named in the Act does not meet that demand."

Speaker Elliott ruled that the Act had become a law without the Executive approval, not having been returned to the House in which it originated within the time prescribed by the Constitution. This ruling was sustained by the Supreme Court, and the Legislature were jubilant at having defeated the Governor. They were ready, with the Commission of their own choosing, to make the Act a true "Bonanza," the suggestive name by which the bill was commonly known. Governor Chamberlain, however, took the case up on appeal to the Supreme Court of the United States, and the "Bonanza" men, appalled by the prospect of waiting two or three years for a decision as likely as not to be unfavorable, passed, at the session of 1875-76, a new "Bonanza" bill, giving the appointment of the Commission to the Governor, and free from the objections urged against the former Act. This "Bonanza" bill (the "big Bonanza") was approved by the Governor, and, the Commission having been appointed, is in successful operation. The Commission appointed came fully up to the standard insisted on in the Veto Message. They are men "whose circumstances and associations do not excite the faintest doubt of their inflexible determination to stand as an insurmountable barrier to the further advance of corruption and fraud." They are "a Commission whose character and ability make the examination of the claims a work of searching vigilance and unquestionable honesty."

Thus, after a year of constant effort, Governor Chamberlain succeeded in saving to the people over $400,000, by scaling the floating indebtedness to one half its nominal value, besides the huge saving which will result from the rejection of illegal claims. Every claim which has the "character of legal and moral validity," will undoubtedly be allowed by the Commission ; but the mass of tainted claims will be branded on their face as fraudulent. Already many of the larger claim holders, fearing the scrutiny to which their certificates will be subjected, seek to evade the law and to set aside the rules of the Commission. Than this no better evidence can be had of the character of their claims, and of the wisdom of the law that subjects them, before payment, to a sifting which quickly separates the valid debt, for services rendered, from the fictitious certificates which, in the days of Moses, filled the pocketbooks of every hanger-on or favorite of the junta who ruled this State.

10. In his Inaugural Address (H. J. 1874–75, page 51) Governor Chamberlain, discussing the character of the laws under which property is assessed for taxation, declared that "the people demand, and have a right to demand, that property shall be valued for taxation at its true money value, as nearly as the imperfection of the human judgment will permit." He said : "My examination of the Act of the General Assembly of March 17, 1874, commonly called the Assessment and Taxation Act, leads me to recommend that a full revision of that Act be made by some appropriate means by the General Assembly, at this session, in conjunction with the Comptroller General, in order to remove inconsistencies and supply defects now apparent in the law." This recommendation, for a wonder, was acted on, and in his Annual Message of November 23, 1875, Governor Chamberlain says :

"The tax laws of the State are now, in my judgment, well adapted to secure, in the language of the Constitution, 'equality and uniformity' in the assessment of property for taxation." Further, he said : "While there are, no doubt, individual instances of error and harship in the present valuation, yet, so far as my information extends, the general result is as fair as can reasonably be expected. If the individual taxpayer will avail himself of the means afforded by the present laws for his protection against unequal or excessive assessments, I think the instances will be very rare in which injustice will be finally done."

The assessment of property for taxation at far more than its market value had been a crying evil in the State. Instances were known where property which had rather declined than advanced in value since the purchase, was assessed at twice or thrice what it cost the taxpayer, and in every quarter of the State there was an outcry against the assessments. This wrong has in general been remedied, and, besides, ample and liberal provision has been made for the redemption of lands forfeited to the State at delinquent tax sales. The extent of the reduction of the assessed value of real and personal property, for purposes of taxation, in this State, is shown in the subjoined memorandum, which gives the total valuation in each year, together with the amount of a tax of one per cent. on the total valuation in each year :

	Valuation.	One per cent. tax.
1869	$168,434,553	$1,684,345
1870	183,913,367	1,839,133
1872	145,585,428	1,455,854
1873	166,234,869	1,662,348
1874	131,738,375	1,317,383
1875	134,968,224	1,349,682

Such has been, in the past five years, the reduction in the assessed value of property that a tax of one per cent. takes from the people, at the present valuation.

less than a tax of *three quarters* per cent. would take, on the basis of the valuation of 1870. In the past two years the gain, by the revision and reduction of the assessment, is equal to a saving of twenty per cent. Even if the rate of taxation were the same, the actual burden upon the taxpayers, at the reduced valuation, would be one fifth less than in 1873.

[Seventh Article—July 13, 1876.]

11. CONTINGENT FUNDS—12. LEGISLATIVE EXPENCES—13. CONTINGENT LEGISLATIVE EXPENCES.

11. Secret funds, otherwise known as contingent funds, played an important part in South Carolina politics during the six years succeeding the adoption of the Constitution of 1868. They were believed to be applied, in great part, to the personal uses of the officers entrusted with their disbursement, and the system of creating such funds undoubtedly encouraged improvidence and waste where it did not end in downright stealing. With this abuse Governor Chamberlain grappled in his Inaugural Address (H. J. 1874–75, page 52), saying : "I do not hesitate to characterize the whole system of contingent funds which has recently sprung up, as wrong in principle and mischievous and demoralizing in effect." During six years there had been appropriated and paid for contingent funds the "astounding sum of $376,832 74," and Governor Chamberlain ventured the opinion that "the State would have received equal benefit from one fifth of that sum, if expended with economy upon proper objects."

"Some governments [he said] deem it necessary to entrust certain officers with a fund commonly called the 'secret service,' which may be expended for objects which might be defeated by publicity. I confess I am wholly unable to imagine any such objects in South Carolina. I think the people of the State should be able to trace every dollar of the public funds to the precise object on which it is expended. This cannot be done under our present system of contingent funds."

He recommended, therefore, that the appropriation of contingent funds be wholly discontinued ; that distinct appropriations be made for all public objects which can be anticipated or enumerated ; that $10,000 or $12,000 be appropriated for contingent expenses, to be paid upon the warrant of the Comptroller General, drawn upon vouchers to be filed by the officers obtaining the warrant. In this way the records of the expenditure of the fund would be open always to examination and publication.

In his second Annual Message (H. J. 1875–76, page 7) Governor Chamberlain said : "The intolerable abuses of former years in connection with contingent funds have been in a great degree removed. But the gain to public morality and economy is still greater, when we consider the fact that all Executive contingent funds have been drawn during the past year on vouchers approved by, and filed with, the Comptroller General. Accountability and publicity, the two chief safeguards of official integrity, have thus been secured."

Well might the Executive congratulate the people ! For the year 1875–76 the entire appropriations for the contingent funds of Executive officers, including the expenses of the Supreme Court and the litigation fund of $3,000 for the Attorney General, were $9,100. We will compare this with similar appropriations in previous years :

For the fiscal year 1872–73 (Acts 1872–73, page 409), the appropriations were $47,000
For the fiscal year 1873–74 (Acts 1873–74, page 612) . . 41,100

For two years $88,100

Annual average $44,050
For the contingent expenses of the Executive Departments for the fiscal year 1874–75 (Acts 1874–75, page 885) the appropriations were $15,250
For the fiscal year 1875–76 (Acts 1875–76, page 98) the appropriations were 9,100

For two years $24,350

Annual average $12,175

The saving in two years, therefore, amounted to $63,750. This was directly and individually the work of Governor Chamberlain ; and when we remember that Moses applied his contingent fund to the purchase of a controlling interest in a party organ, and that equally disreputable uses of the fund were suspected, if not established, we can well see that, while the reduction of public expenses is not inconsiderable, " the gain to official morality, by the removal of opportunity for questionable uses of public funds, will be great."

12. The pay of the members of the South Carolina Legislature was formerly six dollars a day and mileage ; it now is $600 a year and mileage—not an inconsiderable sum considering that the upright and sagacious gentlemen who served the State, in the same capacity, before the war, did not receive, on an average, more than $100 a session. But the payments for salary and mileage form only a small part of the cost of the South Carolina Legislature in post-Reconstruction days. The host of attachés, or "snatchees" as they call themselves, the numerous committees with their hired rooms and luxurious furniture, and a thousand and one other expenses, large and small, swell the total expenses to an almost incredible amount. In his Inaugural Address, Governor Chamberlain called attention to the urgent necessity of reducing legislative expenses.

"Since 1868 [he said] six regular and two special sessions of the General eral Assembly have been held. The total cost of these sessions has been $2,147,-430 97. The average cost of each regular session has been $320,405 10. The lowest cost of any regular session was that of the regular session of 1868–69, amounting to $169,005 79 ; and the highest cost was that of the regular session of 1871–72, amounting to about $617,234 10. Besides the amounts now specified there are outstanding of bills payable, issued on account of legislative expenses, during the same period, $192,275 15. . . . The public, within and without the State, have united in pronouncing the expenditures heretofore made, for legislative expenses, an intolerable abuse."

The General Assembly, lashed by public opinion, relinquished a part of the spoils. In his second Annual Message (H. J. 1875–76, page 7) the Governor said :

" I have the satisfaction of saying that great advances have been made during the past year. The entire appropriation for legislative expenses for the fiscal year was $150,000. The appropriation under this head for the preceding year was $190,000. . . . In honorable contrast with former years, it should also be mentioned that no obligations have been issued or incurred by the officers of the General Assembly, during the past year, in excess of the appropriations made."

The concrete value of the "great advances" noticed by Governor Chamberlain will now be shown. For the fiscal year 1875–76 (Acts 1875–76, p. 5) the entire appropriation for legislative expenses was $140,000, being $10,000 less than in 1874–75, $50,000 less than in 1873–74, and $180,000 less than the annual average of the six preceding years.

The following appropriations for legislative expenses were made during the term of office of Governor Moses :

Acts 1872–73, page 307	$ 75,000
Acts 1872–73, page 321	135,000
Acts 1873–74, page 491	75,000
Acts 1873–74, page 613	190,000
Total	$475,000

The following appropriations, for the same purposes, were made during the term of Governor Chamberlain :

Acts 1874–75, page 821	$150,000
Acts 1875–76, page 5	140,000
Total	$290,000

Being a saving to the public, in two years, of $185,000, or a reduction from an annual average cost of $237,500, under Moses, to $145,000 under Chamberlain. These figures need no comment.

13. The next reform insisted on by Governor Chamberlain was a reduction of the legislative contingent expenses, and a change in their manner of payment. Not less than $190,000 had been expended for legislative contingent expenses at each regular session. The payments were made upon the bare certificate of officers of the two Houses, and no sufficient scrutiny or audit was had. As one remedy for the grievance Governor Chamberlain recommended that all payments be made upon duly audited and accepted vouchers, filed with the Comptroller General, and forever exposed in his office to the examination of the public. In this, as in the matter of Executive contingent funds and ordinary legislative expenses, the object of the Governor was to enforce "a proper system of accountability." More than a year later, in his second Annual Message, Governor Chamberlain renewed his recommendations. In this Message he avowed his conviction of the correctness of the views expressed in his Inaugural Address, and said :

" It is a proposition which no one can dispute, that a permanent public, accessible record should be kept of the disbursement of every dollar of the public funds. It is equally undeniable that all accounts calling for the expenditure of public funds should be audited by some officer who is officially responsible for the performance of this duty. The present method of payment of legislative accounts does not meet these requirements of good administration."

In illustration of the evil opportunities of the existing plan, he said :

" I have personal knowledge that in one instance, at least, a certificate for the payment of a claim passed by the General Assembly was issued at the last session, and both this certificate and the original claim were left in the hands of the person who presented the claim. Both these demands, the claim certificate and the original claim, were payable by the Treasurer without further examination, and thus this demand might have been twice paid, without fault on the part of the Treasurer."

The General Assembly were prevailed upon to pass " An Act to provide the manner of proving claims against the State (Acts 1875–76, p. 157), which fully embodies the suggestions of the Governor as to the passage and payment of claims ; and an Act was passed (Acts 1875–76, p. 91) which covered the Governor's recommendations as to the payment of legislative expenses.   On the second reading of the bill an attempt was made so to amend it as to exclude from its operation all legislative accounts ; but this move was only partly successful, as an examination of the Act shows that the payment of all legislative contingent accounts must be made, as recommended, on the warrants of the Comptroller General.   Nor was this the only positive reform accomplished.   The appropriations for legislative contingent expenses for the year 1875–76 (Acts 1875–76, p. 8) were $12,000 ; and for the year 1874–75 (Acts 1874–75, p. 823) were $13,000, making a total of $25,000, or $12,500 a year, being a saving, as compared with the average appropriations of the preceding six years, of $178,500 a year.

Gov. Chamberlain earnestly urged the Legislature to reduce the length of the session, contending that a session of thirty days was sufficient for every proper purpose. The Legislature took no notice whatever of this recommendation, and the last session was the longest ever known in the history of the State, having continued for one hundred and forty-four days.   It is demonstrated, however, that, apart from the salutary legislation regulating the passage of claims and the payment of contingent funds and contingent legislative expenses, an astonishing reduction was made in the expenses of the government under the three classes of appropriations just examined.   Taking the average annual cost for the six years ending in 1874 as : Contingent funds $62,805, Legislative expenses $320,405, Legislative contingent expenses $190,000, we find that the reduction, in the two years of the present administration, is as follows :

Contingent funds	$101,260
Legislative expenses	350,810
Legislative contingent	355,000
Retrenchment in two years	$807,070

This enormous saving is unquestionably due to the exertions and influence of Governor Chamberlain, for the recommendations came from him, and no such retrenchment was accomplished or attempted by his predecessors.

[Eighth Article—July 14, 1876.]

XIV. PUBLIC PRINTING—XV. SALARIES OF PUBLIC OFFICERS.

14. Very few persons in South Carolina have any idea of the extent of the plundering that has been done by State officials since 1868 under the cover of public printing.   The extent of the "gratifications" so supplied to members of the State Government will probably never be known, and the public must content themselves with the assurance that all the profits of the printing contracts did not go into the coffers of the Republican Printing Company.   A "gratification" to a Governor was, at times, as necessary as a "gratification" to a Comptroller who drew the warrants, or a Treasurer who paid out the money.   The Republican Printing Company is the very centre of legislative intrigue, and its sole stockholders, the Clerks of the two Houses, have more power and influence than a group of Senators or a crowd of Representatives.

A few statistics (H. J. 1874–75, p. 55) will show what public printing cost the State prior to the installation of Governor Chamberlain. From 1868 to 1874 the cost of the permanent and current printing was $843,073. The cost of advertising the statistics for the same period was $261,496, making a total cost of $1,104,569. There was, indeed, a steady increase in the demands of the public printers. Of the $1,104,569 spent in the six years ending in 1874, no less than $918,629 were absorbed in 1872, 1873, and 1874. For these three years the average cost of printing and advertising was $306,209 a year ! These figures are appalling.

Governor Chamberlain, in his Inaugural Address, offered no comments upon such statistics as we have given. " The only appropriate inquiry is," he said, "how shall such results be prevented hereafter ? I answer by exterminating the present system, root and branch, and substituting a safe and economical system." The Governor recommended that the necessary public printing be done by contract, for a fixed price, the most advantageous offer to the State being accepted. The Act of 1873–74, "to regulate the public printing," could not, he said, accomplish any good result, since the amount of work required to be done could not be estimated by the bidder. When the Act was passed the *News and Courier* pointed out that any bidder who was not in the ring could, if he received the contract, be ruined by the requirement that he do more work than he had calculated on, the Act requiring that all the printing of the General Assembly, the quantity not stated, should be done for a fixed price.

The first effect of these recommendations was the reduction of the appropriation for public printing to $50,000 a year, and in his second Annual Message of November 23, 1875, Governor Chamberlain, commending the reduction that had been made, again urged that the work " be thrown open to the lowest bidder, under such regulations as will secure fair and open competition, and the faithful performance of the proposals thus received." And on February 2, 1876, Governor Chamberlain appeared before the Committee of Ways and Means of the House, and, among other things, said : " The printing contract will expire with this year, and all the printing needed by the State can easily be contracted for by responsible parties for $25,000." A bill embodying the suggestions as to advertising for proposals was subsequently introduced in the House. It was referred to the Committee on Printing, who reported back, as might have been expected, a substitute in which the most important provisions of the original bill was modified. It was an improvement, however, on the present law. The House passed the substitute, and it went to the Senate, which struck out the provisions which made its passage desirable. Owing to the sudden adjournment of the General Assembly, the bill failed to become a law, and it is assumed that the public printing will cost the State, for the next two years, $50,000 a year, under the old law.

The reduction in the cost of public printing during Governor Chamberlain's term is from an annual average of $306,209 to $50,000 a year. Net saving in two years, $512,418.

15. No matter of reform has been advocated by Governor Chamberlain more earnestly and persistently than the reduction of the salaries of public officers. In his messages to the General Assembly, in conferences, speeches, and conversations, he has urged this reduction as a measure of vital importance to which the Republican party was solemnly pledged. In his Inaugural Address he said he would give his hearty support to any plan that would reduce expenses by abolishing offices or cutting down salaries. The subject received his personal attention as soon as he was installed, and a bill embodying in many respects the result of his investigations was introduced in

the House (H. J. 1874-75, p. 284), and passed in a modified form.   When it reached the Senate it was referred to the Committee on Finance, and pigeon-holed by that body for the rest of the session.   In a letter to Senator Nash, Chairman of the Finance Committee, dated February 5, 1875, he pointed out specifically what reductions could be made in the salaries of public officers without the slightest detriment to the public service.   Both the Finance Committee and the Senate disregarded these recommendations, passed the appropriation bill without any important reduction, and took no action upon the salary bill.   The bill which thus hung fire in the Senate effected a reduction in salaries of about $30,000 a year, and in his second Annual Message Governor Chamberlain once more advised the Senate to pass it.   In his message vetoing the supply bill of 1875-76 (H. J. 1875-76, p. 35), he showed how the expenditures for salaries and contingent expenses could be still further reduced, citing the fact that of an appropriation of $3,000 for the contingent expenses of the Executive office, $247 remained unexpended at the end of the year, while under former administrations an appropriation of $25,000 for the same purpose was considered wholly insufficient. Again, in a Message to the General Assembly, dated January 27, 1876, he urged, in the most forcible language, the passage of the salary bill, as a means of preventing the immense deficiencies that were imminent.   He showed that a large reduction was compatible with the efficiency of the public service ; that it was demanded by the wants of the people, as well as by their expectations, and declared that, although his own salary is protected by the Constitution, he would submit to as great a reduction as might be made in other salaries.   " A reduction of one third of the present salaries," he said, " would not, in my judgment, be too great."   At the same time he suggested that the salaries of Circuit Solicitors be abolished ; that the salaries of School Commissioners be reduced one half, and that the pay of County Treasurers and Auditors be so arranged as to increase the resources of the State, while reducing the pay of those officers.   The appropriation bill was under consideration by the General Assembly when this Message of the Governor was presented.   The further discussion of this bill was postponed for a day or two, and it was then taken up and passed without the slighest change of the character recommended.

After weeks and months of delay the Finance Committee of the Senate reported back the salary bill, with the recommendation that the salaries of every public officer be reduced according to a fixed percentage, without reference to the duties performed by such officers or to the public necessities.   The bill, as amended, passed the Senate, and became a law ; but the only feature that gave it immediate value, viz., that the bill should take effect from the beginning of the fiscal year 1875-76, was carefully stricken out.   As passed, the bill will go into operation next November.

Having failed, after resorting to every means within his power to effect an immediate reduction of the salaries of public officers, Governor Chamberlain now directed his efforts to securing greater reductions of salaries than were provided for in the salary bill, as it finally passed.   He accordingly went before the Committee of Ways and Means of the House, on February 2, 1876, and reminded them that the Republican party was pledged, by its platform, to reduce salaries and dispense with unnecessary offices.   He said that " the voice of duty to a tax-burdened and impoverished people demanded that we should practise that economy which the hard times had forced upon them," and he insisted, as Governor, that the pledges of practical reform be carried out.   The Governor then read an itemized statement of the reductions that, in his judgment, were imperative, and advised prompt action upon them. A bill covering these reductions was at once introduced in the House, and passed that body, and was sent to the Senate. There it received its first reading, and remains upon the calendar awaiting the accidents of the coming session. Thus, after all his efforts, the only tangible result accomplished was a saving of about $30,000 in the salaries to be paid in the next fiscal year. The General Assembly heard, but did not heed, the counsel of the Executive. Alternately the Senate and the House gave the cold shoulder to his recommendations, and, between the two, every important proposition looking to a reduction of salaries fell quickly to the ground.

[Ninth Article—July 15, 1876.]

16. TAXATION—17. DEFICIENCIES—18. COUNTY FINANCES.

16. The bill to raise supplies for the fiscal year commencing November 1, 1875, was passed in the last hours of the session of 1874-75. This bill levied for State purposes the enormous tax of thirteen mills. Unexampled political and personal pressure was put upon Governor Chamberlain, but he declined to approve the bill, and at the beginning of the session of 1875-76 returned it with his veto. In the veto message Governor Chamberlain (H. J. 1875-76, p. 31) recommended that the taxes for current expenses, and for claims against the State and other indebtedness, be raised by separate Acts. Insisting that the entire tax for the current expenses should be reduced below one per cent., Governor Chamberlain showed how this could be done. Among other things he advised that the payment of past indebtedness be distributed over a term of years, the object being, in view of the poverty of the people, to reduce the rate of immediate taxation.

The veto of the thirteen-mill tax bill was unanimously sustained by the House of Representatives. A bill was then passed levying a tax of nine and a half mills for current expenses, and a bill (the " little Bonanza ") was passed levying a tax of one mill for the payment of deficiencies of the preceding fiscal year. These levies, with a levy of one half mill in the Act to provide for the payment of claims against the State (the " big Bonanza "), made the total tax for State purposes eleven mills. On a basis of $120,000,000 of taxable property, this levy would raise $1,320,000. Upon the same basis the tax levied by the bill which was vetoed, and by the big Bonanza bill, would have raised $1,620,000. By the veto of the thirteen-mill tax bill, therefore, Governor Chamberlain relieved the taxpayers this year of a burden of $300,000, which, in the absence of that veto, they would, at any cost, have been forced to pay.

This gratifying result was reached, as we have shown, by enforcing the reduction of the tax levy. There will be heavy deficiencies this year, as is known, but these deficiencies are caused by the persistent refusal of the General Assembly to reduce the expenditures to the level of the known and fixed revenue of the State, and by the failure of the Legislature to provide any mode of absorbing the bills of the Bank of the State, the receivability of which for taxes is established and cannot be evaded. For these shortcomings Governor Chamberlain cannot be held responsible ; and it should be borne in mind that, whatever the deficiencies may be, the taxpayers are, to the full amount of those deficiencies, the gainers in the present year, and that they have a positive and lasting benefit in such reductions of expenses as were, as shown in previous articles, actually secured.

17. Upon the subject of deficiencies, already alluded to, the record of Governor Chamberlain is clear and unmistakable. In all of his official communications to the General Assembly, relating to the State finances, the Governor has denounced deficiencies as an intolerable abuse, and has vehemently urged their abolition by keeping the expenditures within the income. In his Inaugural Address he showed that the deficiencies for 1874 were $472,619, and for 1873 were $540,328, and advised that "the amount of money should first be ascertained, and then a levy should be made, adequate to raise that amount." In his first Annual Message he said : "The appropriations from the proceeds of the levies made should never be allowed to exceed, by a single dollar, the estimate of the amount of such proceeds." Again, on February 5, 1875, in a letter to the Finance Committee of the Senate, he said : "We can never reform the chief abuses of our past administration of this State Government, unless we pay heed to the rule of making our expenditures fall within our income." What effect did these exhortations have ?

The tax levy for 1874–75 was made at the session of 1873–74, and the General Assembly were in possession of an accurate estimate of what that levy would realize. Nevertheless, appropriations were made for the fiscal year which were $180,000 in excess of the possible receipts. To this deficiency must be added the loss by the Solomon Bank failure which (H. J. 1875–76, p. 33) made the total deficiency for 1874–75 (H. J. 1875–76, p. 33) no less than $308,872. The General Assembly (H. J. 1874–75, p. 34) were called upon to levy a tax to pay $249,303 of this deficiency. Notwithstanding, however, the loss by the Solomon Bank, which could not have been anticipated, the deficiencies for 1874–75 were $291,024 less than the deficiencies of 1872–73, and $223,315 less than the deficiencies of 1873–74. This is some improvement, but there would have been no deficiency, except that arising from the failure of the Solomon Bank, had the advice of the Governor been followed. That advice, in brief, was : 1. Reduce expenses to the lowest possible point. 2. Levy a tax sufficient to pay the expenses.

18. In his Annual Message of January, 1875, Governor Chamberlain exposed the condition of the county finances, urged that the passed indebtedness of the counties be gradually paid by tax levies distributed over two or more years, and, to prevent future deficiencies, recommended that the system of specific levies be applied to county taxes. He advised also (H. J. 1875–76, p. 13) that claims against the counties be properly audited before payment, and be submitted, where practicable, to judicial scrutiny. That the improvement in the fiscal condition of the counties is less than was desired is not the fault of the Executive.

We have now scrutinized, as we undertook to do, the several promises and recommendations contained in the addresses and messages of Governor Chamberlain. It remains only to summarize the results of the investigation.

[Tenth Article—July 18, 1876.]

A SUMMARY.

We have scrutinized, one by one, the most important pledges and recommendations contained in the addresses and messages of Governor Chamberlain since his election, and we now briefly sum up the result of the investigations we have made.

We find that many, if not most, of the urgent and repeated recommendations of the

Governor were disregarded by the Radical Legislature. That body refused to test, even in cities and towns, the wise and beneficent system of minority representation ; it refused to provide, as required by the Constitution, for the election of Justices of the Peace and Constables by the people, and for the registration of Electors ; it failed to shorten the length of the sessions ; it declined to provide a mode of gradually absorbing the bills of the Bank of the State, and did not reduce the public expenditures to the level of the known revenue of the State. Bills covering these different measures of reform were submitted to the Legislature, and were pigeon-holed in committee-rooms, or squarely voted down. The blunders thus committed were, in a party sense, worse than crimes. Out of the folly and neglect of the Legislature, combined with its rascality and ignorance, grew the deficiencies which this year embarrass every department of the State Government.

What was accomplished in spite of the passive or active opposition of the Radical majority in the General Assembly is now set forth :

The abuse of the pardoning power has been corrected.

The character of the officers of the government, appointed by the Executive, has been improved, and the sureties upon the bonds of public officers have been required to make affidavit of their ability to meet the liability they assume.

The settlement of the public debt has been maintained unchanged, and faith with the public creditor, so far as depended on executive and legislative action, has been fully kept.

The effort to place the whole of the public funds in two banks of small capital was frustrated, and the State so saved from the danger of far greater loss than was sustained by the failure of the Solomon Bank.

The floating indebtedness of the State has been provided for in such a way that the recognized and valid claims are scaled to one half the amount, and their payment is distributed over a term of four years, resulting in a saving to the State of at least $4,000,000.

The tax laws have been amended so as to secure substantial uniformity and equality in the assessment of property for taxation.

The contingent funds of the Executive Department have been so reduced in amount that the savings in two years, upon the basis of the average of six previous years, is $101,260.

Legislative expenses, in like manner and upon a similar basis, have been so reduced as to save the people, in two years, $350,810.

Legislative contingent expenses, in the same way, have been so reduced as to save to the State $355,000.

In the expenditure of contingent funds accountability and publicity have been secured.

The cost of public printing has been reduced from an annual average of $306,209 to $50,000, saving in two years $512,418.

The salaries of public officers have been reduced $30,000 a year.

The tax levy for the current year for State purposes has been reduced from 13$\frac{1}{2}$ mills to 11 mills, a saving to the people of $300,000.

The deficiencies (including the losses by the Solomon Bank) are, for the year 1874–75, $308,872, which is $291,024 less than the deficiencies of 1872–73, and $233,-315 less than the deficiencies of 1873–74.

Under the several heads the savings that have actually been made are :

In the Bonanza bill	$400,000 00
In the executive contingent fund	101,260 00
In legislative expenses	350,810 00
In contingent expenses	355,000 00
In public printing	512,418 00
Total	$1,719,488 00

To realize this amount would require a tax of nearly one and a half per cent. Had the appropriations of the past two years been so inordinate as the average of the appropriations aud expenditures of the preceding years, the State taxes of the past two years would have been three fourths per cent. a year more than the outrageous rate actually levied.

This is the record of Governor Chamberlain as shown by hard figures and unmistakable facts. We have strained or exaggerated nothing. The plain truth, as we know it, has been faithfully given. And we maintain that the record, as it stands, is one which Governor Chamberlain has cause to be proud of, that it justifies the support which has been given him, and is a complete answer to those of our friends who think that no act of Governor Chamberlain deserves public commendation but his refusal to issue the commissions to Whipper and Moses. That last act, applauded everywhere in South Carolina, has not been mentioned in these articles. Without it, omitting all notice of the many occasions on which he has defied and overcome the rascally Radical leaders, the record of Governor Chamberlain, in what he did, is an evidence of his own earnestness and sincerity, and, in what he failed to do, is a proof of the obstinacy and venality of the majority of his party.

CHAPTER XIX.

THE county of Edgefield, the hot-bed of uncompromising
"Straight-out" sentiment, was a constant occasion of anxiety
to the Governor. Lawlessness was its normal condition ; and the
vicious example of the whites was not without evil influence upon
the freedmen. The following documents narrate with sufficient
fulness the circumstances of an affair disgraceful to the State
and, in its brutality, significant of the temper which was even
more horribly shown a few months later at Hamburg. The first
is a Proclamation issued in June :

STATE OF SOUTH CAROLINA,
EXECUTIVE CHAMBER.

Official information has reached me that on the 23d day of May last
six persons, named Austin Davis, Stephen Lake, Larkin Holloway, Jesse
Lake, Jefferson Settles, and Marshall Perrin, charged with the murder
of John L. Harmon and Catharine A. Harmon, his wife, at a place
called Winter Seat, in the County of Edgefield, were forcibly taken
from the Sheriff of Edgefield County by a body of men numbering
several hundreds, and immediately shot to death.

The murder of Mr. and Mrs. Harmon, so far as the evidence produced at the coroner's inquest shows, was cold-blooded and fiendish ;
but the subsequent killing of those charged with this crime by others
than officers of the law, and in a manner not authorized by the law,
renders every person engaged in the killing a murderer in the eye of

the law. No plea of provocation, or of the necessity for protection and example can for a moment be admitted to justify such an act.

This State is not a new or imperfectly organized community in which concerted violence must sometimes supplement or supersede the laws. The laws of this State take notice of all crimes and provide punishment for all criminals. The Courts are everywhere accessible and frequent.

Nor were there special circumstances attending this affair which could give occasion or excuse for this defiance and overthrow of the law and its officers. The persons charged with the crime were in the custody of the officers of the law. Escape was impossible. If the county jail was deemed insecure the citizens could have guarded it. A term of the Court of General Sessions was close at hand, a Court in which the presiding Judge and juries could not possibly be charged with lenity towards such crimes. No ground whatever existed for fearing Executive clemency after due conviction. During the term of office of the present Executive, no person capitally convicted has been pardoned, and the sentence of no person so convicted has been changed by the Executive except upon the urgent and combined recommendation of Court, jury, and citizens.

And yet, in the face of such facts, six citizens covered by the ægis of our laws, their persons inviolable from touch or hurt, except by the hands of the ministers of the law, have been summarily, deliberately, openly, and ruthlessly slain, without legal trial, without proper legal scrutiny of the evidences of their guilt, and without the smallest chance of legal defence. To the horror inspired by the original crime is now added the horror which such lawless vengeance should everywhere inspire. The peace of society was broken by the first crime ; but the supremacy of law was overthrown by the second crime.

As the Chief Magistrate of the State, it is my duty to warn my fellow-citizens of the nature and effects of such resort to violence for the punishment of crime, and to call upon all the officers and agents of the law to bring to just account those who have dared to usurp the awful prerogatives with which the lawfully constituted representatives of public justice are alone invested.

In testimony whereof, I have hereunto set my hand and caused the seal of the State to be affixed, this third day of June, A.D. 1876, [L. S.] and of the independence of the United States the one hundredth.

D. H. CHAMBERLAIN,
Governor.

By the Governor :

H. E. HAYNE,
    Secretary of State.

The following official letter was given to the public at the time of the publication of this Proclamation :

EXECUTIVE CHAMBER,
COLUMBIA, S. C., June 3, 1876.

Hon. R. B. Carpenter, Judge Fifth Judicial Circuit:

DEAR SIR—I enclose for your examination a copy of an Executive Proclamation having reference to the recent killing of six persons in Edgefield County, charged by the verdict of a coroner's jury with the murder of John L. Harmon and his wife, in said county.

It is my duty to do all in my power to cause the execution of the laws in all cases of their violation. The Courts and their officers and agents are, of course, the chief means for the execution of the laws and the punishment of crimes. Over the Courts I have no control, but in the present instance I deem it my duty to call your official attention to the matter embraced in the enclosed Proclamation, and to suggest to you, with proper deference, that the attention of the Grand Jury of Edgefield County be directed to a full examination of the matter referred to, to the end that such judicial action may be taken as the due execution of the laws may require and the facts of the case may warrant.

It having been brought to my attention that two women, named Matilda Holloway and Bettie Perrin, who were charged by the coroner's jury as accessories to the murder, are still at large, and that other persons still living were probably connected with the crime to a greater or less degree, I beg leave to suggest that measures should be adopted to bring these persons before the Court to be dealt with according to law.

In all possible ways it will be my duty to assist your Honor in the enforcement of the laws in this most extraordinary and painful affair.

Very respectfully, your obedient servant,

D. H. CHAMBERLAIN,
Governor.

The comments of the Charleston *News and Courier* on this Proclamation have peculiar interest, for the reason that, besides fully approving of the action and sentiment of the Governor, while presenting the mitigating circumstances in the case, they acknowledge the fact, and the pernicious influence, of "the brutal deeds by the Ku-Klux in South Carolina."

The most captious critic will scarcely find fault with the tone and temper of Governor Chamberlain's Proclamation on the subject of the lynching of the Harmon murderers, for the whole purpose of it is to point out the danger to society of such acts, however provoked, and to remind the public, in their own interest, of the inexorable need of maintaining the law's supremacy. As the Chief Magistrate of the State, Governor Chamberlain could say no less than he has said, nor could it be said with more kindly dignity.

We have not pretended to justify the killing of the Harmon murderers. What we could not do when the horrors of the deed for which the murderers died were fresh in our recollection, we cannot do at this later day. But Governor Chamberlain must remember that confidence is a plant of slow growth, and that for years past the people have had reason to doubt the efficiency of the Courts in this State as a means of punishing criminals. The records of the Courts are covered deep with mis-trials and acquittals, through the instrumentality of ingenious lawyers or ignorant juries, and for two years, in common opinion, pardons could always be had by those able and willing to pay for them. It was the fear that the Harmon murderers would escape, as other criminals had escaped, which provoked the Edgefield lynching. The better course would have been to try the law once again, and resort to Judge Lynch only when the constituted tribunals of justice had failed to mete out to the murderers the doom they deserved.

In reading the accounts of the lynching, it will doubtless have been noticed that a number of influential gentlemen strove hard to persuade the lynching party from carrying their determination into effect. And we remind the public that in such inability to control bodies of men whose passions are excited, lies the danger of mob law of any kind and under any circumstances. The brutal deeds of the Ku-Klux in South Carolina grew out of the organization of a society for strictly defined defensive purposes. Its objects, in its original form, were eminently proper ; but it soon changed in character, and was made the means of wreaking private vengeance on poor wretches who were guiltless of the acts for which they suffered. And so will it be, if experience is any guide, whenever private citizens usurp the functions of the law's appointed officers. The temptation to make a quick ending of red-handed criminals is often, we admit, almost too strong to be resisted ; but it is best for the State, best for every man, woman, and child in it, that such deeds as the Edgefield lynching should never be committed. The whites cannot expect the negroes to respect the law, if they give them a ruinous example by setting the law at defiance.

Later in the same month the Governor addressed another official letter to Judge Carpenter, which also was made public. It discloses the reality of his concern for the public welfare, his anxious foreboding, and his readiness to do every thing in his power to secure order and prosperity.

EXECUTIVE DEPARTMENT,
COLUMBIA, S. C., June 24, 1875.

Hon. R. B. Carpenter, Judge Fifth Circuit, Columbia, S. C. :

DEAR SIR—Referring to our conversation respecting affairs in Edgefield County of day before yesterday, I think it best for me to address you officially upon the subject in addition to our conversation. Complaints have come to me so frequent and strong of late that I ought to lay their substance before you for such official action as you may be able to take, if, in your judgment, any is needed. I am the more bound to do this because when I was seeking last winter to restore peace and order to that county I especially advised the people that the Courts were open, and all their wrongs could there be redressed, and I am sure this admonition had a happy effect. The present complaints are, in general, as follows :

1. They complain that the funds of the county are now being squandered on the poor, while the roads, bridges, and other great interests of the county are almost wholly neglected.

2. They complain that the school fund is so managed and administered as to do little good, incompetent teachers being employed at excessive rates of pay.

3. They complain that the office of the Probate Judge is in a condition of disgraceful neglect, and that large parts of the records are gone, and that the Probate Judge is himself totally incompetent to discharge his duties.

4. They complain that the Sheriff has, from incapacity or inability of some kind, totally failed to fill the office, or perform its ordinary duties, his incapacity or inability culminating recently in the escape of several prisoners under sentence of your Honor to the penitentiary.

5. They complain that the past indebtedness of the county is still unadjusted, and the large fund of some $13,000 is still undistributed, though many of the claimants are worthy men and holders of just claims, and that this fund has been for a long time in Court, and a referee appointed to audit the claims.

6. They complain that indictments now pending and presentments made against public officers in that county have not been duly pressed by the Solicitor, and that the result has been a feeling of discouragement in the work of holding officials to their proper accountability.

7. They complain generally of great incapacity on the part of many of the county officers elected by the people, resulting in a deplorable state of things in all public interests of the county.

These matters embrace the main substantial complaints. You will, of course, understand that I do no more than state these complaints. They are *ex parte*, but they come from sources which seem entitled to respect.

I must say that I fear not a little for the peace of that county during the present summer, in the present state of feeling there ; and if any thing occurs to you as a preventive or remedy for any evils existing there, I most earnestly urge you to apply such preventive or remedy. If, from your superior knowledge of the affairs of that county, you regard the complaints now stated as unfounded in fact, or if, being founded in fact, you have no power to apply a remedy, then the results will not be chargeable to you. If, on your part, you see any official or personal action on my part which will, in any degree, tend to the advantage of good citizens of that county, I beg that you will inform me, and I will act with promptness. If the complaints made have sufficient foundation to warrant it, I venture to suggest the calling of an extra term of Court for that county, at some time not far distant, at which many of these matters could be fully and finally investigated. Of the possibility of such action I cannot judge, but I think, if practicable, it would tend to the peace and welfare of the county. I am, very respectfully, your Honor's obedient servant,

D. H. CHAMBERLAIN,
Governor.

Following close on these efforts to establish peace on the basis of justice, and while the publications reproduced in the preceding chapter were in progress, there occurred, on the 8th of July, 1876, at Hamburg, a village in Aiken County (formerly Edgefield), just across the Savannah River from Augusta, Ga., what has passed into history as the " Hamburg Massacre." Undoubtedly this event was the turning point in the course of political affairs in South Carolina, although it did not immediately divert from Governor Chamberlain the favor of all Democrats who were well-disposed to him. It was the first demonstration of the revival of the spirit of violent persecution of the colored race which had characterized the period of the Ku-Klux outrages, and which thus far during the Governor's Administration, owing to the rigid and zealous enforcement by him of impartial law protecting the rights of all, had been inactive. For Governor Chamberlain to treat this occurrence with forbearance was impossible. A crime of deepest dye had been committed, and he would have been as false to his magisterial duty as to the dictates of justice and humanity.if he had hesitated to denounce it, or to use every power in him vested to bring the guilty to punishment. It was probably equally impossible for the majority of the white people of South Carolina, bred to the system of slavery, and habituated to consider any resistance of black men to the will of white men as intolerable, meriting stripes, or sale, or death, in the white man's discretion, without intervention of process of law, to join the Governor in condemnation of their fellow-citizens who had, for any reason, engaged in a conflict with negroes. In this event the " barbarism of slavery " asserted itself once more in revolt against the new condition of equal rights under equal laws. Governor Chamberlain had been trained where no man, however high his station, has privilege to murder without answering to the State. By a moral necessity, Governor Chamberlain and his Republican supporters parted company at this point with the " white man's party" of South Carolina. But until their Convention had acted, many Democrats continued to advocate that no nomination should be made in opposition to him ; after that date the conduct of the campaign was adapted to the condition of the race war initiated at Hamburg.

The story of this dark and horrible crime is given succinctly in official documents. These show the care taken by the Governor to ascertain the exact facts without partisan motive or bias. In his speech in the April Convention, referring to his course when he had suppressed a negro riot in Edgefield and Laurens counties which threatened the property and lives of white men, action which brought upon him much criticism from his own party, he said: " I go for the protection of every man. The meanest man who assails me because he is my political enemy shall have my protection with the rest. Democrats and Republicans alike shall have my protection, and when South Carolina cannot protect the lives and liberties of her citizens, I conceive it to be the highest duty of the United States to protect them, and my highest duty, I conceive, is to invoke that aid in time of need." And he then made known that, at the time referred to, he had requested the intervention of the Federal authorities in case the negro rioters became too powerful to be dealt with by the civil authorities of the State. The Democrats of South Carolina had only praise and gratitude for his course on that occasion ; but when they, in turn, and in a vastly aggravated form, became offenders against the law and the public peace, his firm application of the same principles brought upon him their angry condemnation. Unswerved by any praise or blame, he kept a true course with courageous heart, guided by voiceless beacons of duty that shone over his troubled way like stars above the trackless sea.

As soon as possible after the affair, the Governor sent the Attorney General of the State to Hamburg to investigate the circumstances. He made the following report :

COLUMBIA, S. C., July 12, 1876.

SIR :—According to your request of Monday last, I have visited Hamburg for the purpose of ascertaining the facts connected with the killing of several men there on the night of the 8th of July.

My information has been derived chiefly from Trial-Justice Rivers, and from the testimony of persons who have been examined before the coroner's jury now in session, and from those who received wounds from the armed body of white men who had taken them prisoners. From this information the following facts seem to be clearly established :

During the administration of Governor Scott a company of State militia was organized at Hamburg, of which Prince Rivers was captain. This company was known as Company A, Ninth Regiment National Guard of the State of South Carolina.   Arms were at that time furnished to it, and some ammunition.

This company, previous to May, 1876, had for some time but few names on its rolls, drilled rarely, and scarcely kept alive its organization.   But in May, of this year, the number of members increased to about eighty, and one Doc Adams was chosen captain.

On the 4th of July the company drilled on one of the public streets in the town of Hamburg.   The street on which they drilled was between one hundred and one hundred and fifty feet wide ; but it was little used, and was overgrown with grass, except in that portion which was used as a carriage-road.   While the company was thus drilling, Thomas Butler and Henry Getzen, his brother-in-law, came along in a carriage, and demanded that the company should make way for them. Adams halted the company, remonstrated with Butler and Getzen for thus seeking to interfere with the company, and called their attention to the fact that there was plenty of room on each side of the company to pass.

Finding them unwilling to turn out of their course, Adams finally opened ranks and allowed them to drive through.

This incident seems to have angered Butler and Getzen, who made complaint before Trial-Justice Rivers against the militia company for obstructing the highway.   The Trial Justice on the following day issued a warrant against Adams, as he was the captain of the company, and had him brought before him for trial.   During the progress of the trial, Adams was arrested by the Trial Justice for contempt of court, and subsequently the case was continued until four o'clock Saturday afternoon, July 8th.

At that time Butler and Getzen, with General M. C. Butler, who had been employed by Robert I. Butler, father of the former, as their attorney, repaired to the office of the Trial Justice, but Adams did not appear.

General Butler inquired as to the nature of the charges against Adams, and asked if the Trial Justice was to hear the case as trial justice or in his official capacity of major general of militia.   To this the Trial Justice replied that he was to hear the case as a trial justice, but if the facts showed that a military offence had been committed, Adams would have to be tried by a court-martial.   General Butler then stated that he thought the case might be arranged, and, at his suggestion, time was given him to see the parties.   After this, the Trial Justice did not see General Butler at his office, but learned that he had gone over to Augusta.   In the meantime the Trial Justice had been informed that some two or three hundred armed white men were in Hamburg, and that a demand had been made by them that the militia should surrender their arms.   After a consultation with Messrs. Jefferson and Spencer, Rivers sent for General Butler.   He rode up to the back gate of Rivers' house ; the two had a conversation, in which General Butler said that he had given orders to have the guns given up in half an hour, and the time was nearly up.   Rivers asked if some other arrangement could not be made, to which General Butler replied in the negative.

Rivers then asked if he would not consent to have him receive the arms, box them up, and send them to the Governor, to which General Butler replied that he would box them up and send them to the Governor, and if he (the Governor) should return them to the company it would be at his own risk. Rivers then asked if they would give a bond for the arms, to which General Butler said that he would stand the bond, and turning to another person—I think R. J. Butler—asked if he would n't go on a bond also, to which he replied that he would. Rivers then asked for time before fire should be opened on the militia, so that he might have a conference with the militia officers. This was acceded to, and Rivers then went to the building known as the Sibley building, in the second story of which the company had its armory and drill-room, and where it was then assembled, and told Captain Adams what might be expected if he should refuse to give up the arms. To this Adams replied that General Butler had no right to the guns ; that the company held them, and he proposed to hold them unless General Butler showed some authority to take them. After this interview, Rivers returned to General Butler, with whom was Robert J. Butler. He told them the decision to which the company had come. Then Robert J. Butler said that General Butler was his attorney ; that he had come to settle the matter. If the company would apologize for the insult to his son and son-in-law, he would do nothing more, but the whole matter was in General Butler's hands. General Butler said that, as the men would not meet him, he would have no more to do with them. General Butler was asked by Rivers if he would guarantee the safety of the town should the militia surrender their arms. He said that would depend on how the men behaved themselves afterward. This statement is confirmed by S. P. Pixley.

While these negotiations were going on, the armed body of white men in the town were concentrated on the bank of the river near the Sibley building. Soon after they were broken off firing began. Men who were in the building say that it was commenced by the whites firing upon the building. Adams gave his orders not to shoot until he directed them to. The company had very little ammunition, and all they had was a portion of that issued to the company when it was first organized.

After the firing had begun, it was returned by the militia, and one of the attacking party, McKee Merriwether, was shot through the head, and instantly killed. After this a piece of artillery, said to belong to the Washington Artillery of Augusta, was brought over from Augusta, and four charges of canister were fired from it upon the armory, but without injuring any one. The persons in the armory escaped from the rear by means of ladders, and hid under floors of adjacent buildings, or wherever else they could find shelter.

The first man killed by the whites was James Cook, town marshal. He had been in the armory, but was not a member of the company. He had gone into the street from the rear of the Sibley building, and was at once fired on, and fell dead instantly, pierced by five or six bullets. Afterward the whites began their search for the members of the company. They succeeded in getting about twenty-five colored men as prisoners, some of whom were never members of the company. As fast as they were captured they were taken to a place near the South Carolina Railroad, where a large party of armed men stood guard over them. None of those thus captured had arms in their hands.

Subsequently, and at about two o'clock A.M., six men took A. T. Attaway out of the "ring." He and his mother begged for his life, but in vain. He was told to turn round, and was then shot to death by the crowd. David Phillips was next taken out, and was similarly killed. Pompey Curry was next called out. He recognized among the bystanders Henry Getzen and Dr. Pierce Butler, and called on them to keep the other men from killing him. He ran, and was shot at as he ran, one bullet striking him in the right leg, below the knee.

Afterward, Albert Myniart, Moses Parks, and Hampton Stephens were killed. Stephens did not belong to the company. Nelder John Parker, who has been commonly referred to in the newspaper reports as John Thomas, was corporal in the company. When he was arrested and taken to the spot where the other prisoners were, he recognized among the party two gentlemen of Augusta, named Twiggs and Chaffee. He appealed to them for protection. They said he should not be hurt. He states that General M. C. Butler asked if he was one of the d——d rascals. The reply was in the affirmative. He was then shot in the back. Messrs. Twiggs and Chaffee then said if he was shot again they would shoot the ones who did it. They took him off, and had him taken to Augusta. He was shot before Attaway was killed. He may recover from his wounds.

One Butler Edwards was taken as a prisoner. He says he was taken before General Butler, who at the time was in the street near the Sibley building. This was about twelve o'clock.

Threats were made to shoot him. General Butler directed that he be taken to the others. He recognized among the crowd one Captain Carnile and —— Dunbar, of Augusta ; said he had a long talk with the former. He was among the prisoners who were let loose and told to run ; as they ran they were fired at, and he was shot in the head. He was not a member of the company.

Willis Davis, one of the members of the company, was taken to the place where were the other prisoners. The men stated that John Swaringen, of Edgefield County, had charge of the prisoners. He states that he saw General Butler before the men were killed, who asked him what he was doing, and told him he would have enough of it before he got through. He was shot in the arm near the elbow when about twenty paces distant from the crowd. The ball is still in his arm, and he suffers much pain. He also states that some of the young men from Georgia remonstrated against shooting the prisoners, but in vain.

Besides the killing and wounding of the men herein named, the party broke open several stores and houses, and, in some instances, robbed the inmates. They took from Mr. Charles Roll, the postmaster, and a very respectable white citizen, a gun which he had in his store, and his private property. From an old colored man named Jacob Samuels, in his employ, they took a watch, and set fire to his house. They broke open the house of Trial-Justice Rivers, and did much damage, as well as robbed him of clothing. They obtained kerosene oil and attempted to set fire to the house, but were prevented by Col. A. P. Butler from doing so. The ropes of the public wells were cut, and some fences were torn down.

So far as I can learn, the primary object of the whites was to take away from the militia their arms.

The man Parker, who was wounded, states that on Friday, the 7th instant, he had a long talk with one Harrison Butler (white) on Broad Street, Augusta. Butler told him that if Rivers did not give orders for the militia to give up their arms they would take them any way on the next day.

On Saturday rumors were abroad in Hamburg that there were armed parties coming in to take the guns, but little credit was attached to them.

One of the white citizens of Hamburg heard a conversation between David Phillips and General Butler in the afternoon. Phillips talked very "big," as the gentleman said, and General Butler told him that they wanted those guns and were bound to have them.

In the afternoon Col. A. P. Butler went to the various stores in town and told the proprietors that they must not sell any liquor to his men. In spite of this, however, some of the men compelled one of the storekeepers to furnish them liquor. From the same person they obtained kerosene oil to use in setting fire to a house.

The whites were armed with guns and small arms of various kinds, and many of them had axes and hatchets.

It is proper to state that the intendant of Hamburg, Mr. Gardner, was informed by General Butler, in an interview with him, that the arms of the company must be given up.

Trial-Justice Rivers is now holding an inquest, and taking the testimony of witnesses. Until their verdict is rendered it will be impossible to tell who were engaged in the attack on the militia, and the subsequent killing and wounding of the colored men.

It may be possible that a careful judicial investigation may show some slight errors in some of the minor details stated in this report. But making due allowance for such errors, the facts show the demand on the militia to give up their arms was made by persons without lawful authority to enforce such demand or to receive the arms had they been surrendered ; that the attack on the militia to compel a compliance with this demand was without lawful excuse or justification ; and that after there had been some twenty or twenty-five prisoners captured and completely in the power of their captors, and without means of making further resistance, five of them were deliberately shot to death and three more severely wounded. It further appears that not content with thus satisfying their vengeance, many of the crowd added to their guilt the crime of robbery of defenceless people, and were only prevented from arson by the efforts of their own leaders.

Yours, very respectfully,

WILLIAM STONE,
Attorney General of South Carolina.

Hon. D. H. CHAMBERLAIN,
Governor.

Upon receipt of this report and other trustworthy evidence, Governor Chamberlain addressed the following letter to Senator Robertson at Washington, where, naturally, the newspaper reports of the affair had excited serious concern:

EXECUTIVE CHAMBER,
COLUMBIA, S. C., July 13, 1876.

Hon. T. J. Robertson, United States Senator, Washington, D. C.:

DEAR SIR—Your request for a statement from me of the recent bloody affair at Hamburg in this State was duly received. I have waited before replying until official reports and statements should be received. There are now before me the official reports of the Attorney General and the Adjutant and Inspector General, the testimony taken at the coroner's inquest, and the written statement of several other persons who were present and witnessed the whole or parts of the affair. I will present to you the leading facts as they appear from the evidence to which I have referred.

On the 4th of July inst. a company of the State militia (colored) were marching along one of the streets of Hamburg. The street was over one hundred feet wide, and the company was marching in columns of four. While so marching they were met by two young white men in a buggy, who insisted in keeping their course in the street without regard to the movements of the militia, and drove against the head of the column, which thereupon halted. Some parleying took place, which resulted in the company yielding and opening their ranks, and allowing the young men to proceed on their course. On the following day the young men referred to took out warrants of arrest against some of the officers of the militia company, who were brought before a Trial Justice for trial. The trial was afterwards adjourned till 4 P.M. of Saturday, the 8th. Before that hour arrived, on Saturday, many white citizens from the country around Hamburg began to gather in the town, and armed themselves with guns and pistols.

The militia company in the meanwhile had assembled in the armory in the village, and at the hour set for trial the defendants did not appear. At this point it has been stated in despatches and newspapers that the militia officers, having defied the authority of the Trial Justice, the citizens were called in to assist the Trial Justice by acting as his posse. Nothing of the kind in fact occurred ; the militia failed to appear because of their fear of injury at the hands of the armed white men, and the Trial Justice, after formally calling them, took no further steps to cause their presence in his Court, on account of the excitement and the evidences of an impending conflict.

While affairs were in this condition, there being, according to all accounts, from two hundred to three hundred armed white men from the surrounding country in the town, a demand was made by the whites for the surrender to them of the arms of the militia. An hour or two passed in negotiations concerning this demand, the whites informing the militia company that if the arms were not given up in a short time (most of the witnesses say in a half hour) the whites would open fire on the militia. The militia refused to deliver up their arms, saying that the demand was wholly unwarranted and illegal, and that they had reason to fear for their lives if they gave up their arms. A brisk fire was then opened by the whites on the building in which the militia were assembled, and soon after one of the attacking party was killed by a shot from the militia in the building. A piece of artillery was thereupon brought across the bridge from Augusta, loaded with canister, and fired several times at the building in which were the militia. This had the effect to cause the militia to endeavor to make their escape from the rear of the building.

The Town Marshal of Hamburg, a colored man, who was living in the building, was instantly shot by the attacking party while thus endeavoring to escape from the building. Twenty or twenty-five of the militia were captured by the attacking party and kept under guard several hours. Finally about 2 o'clock on the morning of the 9th of July (Sunday), after consultation among their captors, and with complete apparent deliberation, five of the captured militiamen were called out, one by one, and shot to death in the presence of a large body of their captors. The rest of the captured party were either turned loose or broke loose and ran. They were fired upon as they ran, and three of them were severely wounded, one of them probably mortally. Attorney General Stone thus succinctly reports this part of the affair.[1]

. . . Such was the affair at Hamburg; if you can find words to characterize its atrocity and barbarism, the triviality of the causes, and the murderous and inhuman spirit which marked it in all its stages, your power of language exceeds mine. It presents a darker picture of human cruelty than the slaughter of Custer and his soldiers, as they were shot in open battle. The victims at Hamburg were murdered in cold blood after they had surrendered, and were utterly defenceless. No occasion existed for causing the presence of a single armed citizen at Hamburg the day of the massacre. No violence was offered or threatened to any one. It is indeed said, as usual, that "the niggers were impudent," but the evidence shows that all the actual physical aggression was on the part of the whites; that they made a demand which they had no right to make, and when that demand was refused, as it should have been, they proceeded to enforce it by

[1] The quotations from the Attorney General's report, already given in full, are here omitted.

arms, and crowned their success in enforcing their demands by brutal murders. Shame and disgust must fill the breast of every man who respects his race or human nature as he reads the tale.

To me, in my official capacity, wherein, as you will testify, I have done my utmost, at no little risk of personal and political detraction from my political friends, to remove abuses and restore good government and harmony to our people, the occurrence of such an appalling example of human passion and depravity comes as a deep mortification and discouragement. What hopes can we have when such a cruel, bloodthirsty spirit waits in our midst for its hour of gratification? Is our civilization so shallow? Is our race so wantonly cruel? Such acts call for condemnation and punishment, for condemnation as a bloody blot in the record of your race and mine, as a cruel affront to a race whose long-suffering and patient forbearance challenges the admiration of the world, as a shameful dishonor to the name of South Carolina; for punishment as a violation of the laws and a wanton blow at the peace and happiness of our State.

I am glad to testify to the horror which this event has excited among many here who have not been wont to heartily condemn many of the past bloody occurrences at the South. Nothing, however, short of condign and ample punishment can discharge the obligation of society and our State toward the authors of this causeless and cruel massacre.

Very respectfully, your obedient servant,
D. H. CHAMBERLAIN,
Governor.

This letter was published in despatches from Washington, August 18th. The sober judgment of the Northern press regarding the affair and its significance is fairly, but not extravagantly, exemplified by the following comments of the New York *Nation:*

. . . From Governor Chamberlain's account it appears that there was no excuse for these horrible brutalities, the whites having murdered their unoffending victims while begging for their lives. This account, based as it is on the report by the State Attorney General, and practically vouched for by the *News and Courier*—a newspaper which would naturally seek to give as favorable a view of the behavior of the whites as possible—is no doubt correct. The massacre does not seem to be disputed by anybody, and the Charleston *Journal of Commerce*, which is an out-and-out white man's paper, does not scruple to declare that no one can expect ruffianly negroes to "be treated as prisoners of honorable warfare according to the laws of nations,"—a sentence which, by the way, shows in a curious manner how the semi-military habits engendered in the South by long years of war and misgovernment have blotted out all the ideas of law and justice common to people living under a peaceful rule. The town of Hamburg is almost entirely filled with negroes, while it is close by the State of Georgia, now fully in the possession of the whites, and near by the white populations of Aiken and Edgefield counties, in the latter of which bad blood was not long ago created by the performance of a company of negroes under a man named Tennent, who were disarmed by the State authorities and the United States troops to prevent a suspected attack on the whites. Politics are, just now, in a very unsettled condition in South Carolina, as the Democratic Convention, which meets on the 15th of next month, will have to choose between a straight-out nomination of some such Democrat as Wade Hampton and a combination with the Reform Republicans under Chamberlain, and the straight-out Democrats are now, of course, accusing Chamberlain of using the Hamburg massacre for political purposes, and as a means of getting troops for the election. There can be little doubt that a union of all the respectable portions of society under Chamberlain would now do more to restore harmony and prosperity in South Carolina than any other possible course. Whatever views were taken of his connection with Scott and Parker in the early carpet-bag days, there is no doubt that since he has been Governor he has given the most substantial proof of his determination to root out corruption and give the State good government. There is no better test in a community like South Carolina, where there is a close connection between politics and crime, of a Governor's intentions than his exercise of the pardoning power. Scott, for instance, between 1868 and 1870 pardoned 332 convicts, and, between 1870 and 1872, 247 more. Moses, between 1872 and 1874, pardoned 457; while from December 1, 1874, to May 31, 1876, the total number of Chamberlain's pardons were 73, 66 of these being recommended by the judges, and in the other 7 cases the judges making no objection. Mr. Chamberlain has in this and in all other ways ever since his election stood between the community and the ruffians who governed it before his time, and the Democrats will make a fatal mistake now if they throw him overboard. . . .

The effect of the massacre upon the public order of the State, especially upon the colored race, and Governor Chamberlain's foreboding of its consequences, were set forth in the following letter to the President :

EXECUTIVE CHAMBER,
COLUMBIA, S. C., July 22, 1876.

SIR:—The recent massacre at Hamburg, in this State, is a matter so closely connected with the public peace of this State that I desire to call your attention to it, for the purpose of laying before you my views of its effect and the measures which it may become necessary to adopt to prevent the recurrence of similar events.

It is, in the first place, manifestly impossible to determine with absolute certainty the motives of those who were engaged in perpetrating the massacre at Hamburg. The demand which was made by the mob upon the militia company for the surrender of their arms, taken in connection with the fact that the militia are not shown to have committed or threatened any injury to any persons in that community, would seem to indicate a purpose to deprive the militia of their rights on account of their race or political opinions. It seems impossible to find a rational or adequate cause for such a demand, except in the fact that the militia company was composed of negroes, or in the additional fact that they were, besides being negroes, members of the Republican party. Those who made the demand were, on the other hand, white

men, and members of the Democratic party. The lines of race and
political party were the lines which marked the respective parties to
the affair at Hamburg. I mention this as a fact, and as, apparently,
the most trustworthy index of the motives and aims which inspired
those who brought on this conflict.

As affecting the public peace, however, the effect of this massacre
is more important than the motives which prompted it. Upon this
point I can speak with more confidence. It is not to be doubted that
the effect of this massacre has been to cause widespread terror and
apprehension among the colored race and the Republicans of this
State. There is as little doubt, on the other hand, that a feeling of
triumph and political elation has been caused by this massacre in the
minds of many of the white people and Democrats. The fears of the
one side correspond with the hopes of the other side.

I do not intend to overstate any matters connected with this affair,
nor to omit any statement which seems to me essential to a full understanding of its significance. It is certainly true that the most, though
not all, of those who have spoken through the newspapers or otherwise
here, on the white or Democratic side, upon this matter, have condemned the massacre. Their opposition to such conduct has not, however, sufficed to prevent this massacre ; nor do I see any greater reason
for believing that it will do so in the future. That class which now
engage in this cruel work certainly disregard the expressed sentiments
of those who assume to speak, for the most part, for their communities, and go forward without fear of public opinion or punishment.

It is sometimes asked : Why do not the colored race return this
violence with violence ? Why do they suffer themselves to be thus terrorized, when their numbers greatly exceed those of their enemies in
the localities where many of these outrages occur ? The answer is not
difficult. The long habit of command and self-assertion on the part
of the whites of these Southern States, their superior intelligence as
compared with the colored race, the fact that at least four fifths of the
property of these States are in their hands, are causes which contribute
to give them an easy physical superiority thus far over the recently
emancipated race, who still exhibit the effects of their long slavery in
their habit of yielding to the more imperious and resolute will and the
superior intelligence and material resources of the white men.

Add to this that in almost every Southern community there may be
found a considerable number of daring, lawless, reckless white men, accustomed to arms and deeds of violence, over whom the restraint of
the sentiments of the better and more conservative classes of society
have little if any power, who are inspired by an intense and brutal
hatred of the negro as a free man, and more particularly as a voter
and a Republican, and you have the elements which would naturally
give rise to, and in point of fact do give rise to, nearly all the scenes
of bloody violence which occur in the Southern States. Besides all
this, another fact must be noted here, a fact which, in my judgment,
marks and explains the world-wide difference between the effects of

such occurrences as this at Hamburg upon the mass of the white people here, and the effects of deeds of blood and violence upon the people of other sections of the country, namely, that such occurrences as this at Hamburg have generally resulted in what is thought to be political advantage to the Democratic party here. From this fact it results that the white people here are induced, to a considerable extent, to overlook the naked brutality of the occurrence and seek to find some excuse or explanation of conduct which ought to receive only unqualified abhorrence and condemnation, followed by speedy and adequate punishment. In this way it often happens that a few reckless men are permitted or encouraged to terrorize a whole community and destroy all freedom of action on the part of those who differ from them in political opinions. The more respectable portion of the white people here content themselves with verbal perfunctory denunciations, and never adopt such measures or arouse such a public sentiment as would here, as well as elsewhere, put a stop to such occurrences.

In respect to the Hamburg massacre, as I have said, the fact is unquestionable that it has resulted in great immediate alarm among the colored people and all Republicans in that section of the State. Judging from past experience, they see in this occurrence a new evidence of a purpose to subject the majority of the voters of that vicinity to such a degree of fear as to keep them from the polls on election day, and thus reverse or stifle the true political voice of the majority of the people.

But the Hamburg massacre has produced another effect. It has as a matter of course caused a firm belief on the part of most Republicans here that this affair at Hamburg is only the beginning of a series of similar race and party collisions in our State, the deliberate aim of which is believed by them to be the political subjugation and control of the State. They see, therefore, in this event what foreshadows a campaign of blood and violence, such a campaign as is popularly known as a campaign conducted on the "Mississippi plan."

From what I have now said, it will not be difficult to understand the feeling of a majority of the citizens in a considerable part of this State. It is one of intense solicitude for their lives and liberties. It is one of fear that, in the passion and excitement of the current political campaign, physical violence is to be used to overcome the political will of the people. I confine myself here to a statement of what I believe to be the facts of the present situation in this case as connected with the public peace and order, without any expression of my individual feelings and opinions. My first duty is to seek to restore and preserve public peace and order, to the end that every man in South Carolina may freely and safely enjoy all his civil rights and privileges, including the right to vote. It is to this end that I now call your attention to these matters. I shall go forward to do all in my power as Governor to accomplish the ends above indicated, but I deem it important to advise you of the facts now stated, and to solicit from you some indication of your views upon the questions presented. To be more specific, will the General Government exert itself vigorously to repress violence in this State during the present political campaign on the part of persons belonging to either political party, whenever that violence shall be beyond the control of the State authorities? Will the General Government take such precautions as may be suitable, in view of the feeling of alarm already referred to, to restore confidence to the poor people of both races and political parties in this State, by such a distribution of the military forces now here as will render the intervention of the General Government prompt and effective, if it shall become necessary, in restoring peace and order?

It seems proper to add that I am moved to make this communication to you by no motive or feeling save such as should animate me as the Chief Executive of this State, bound to do justice to all, and to oppress none. I venture to say that I have given sufficient evidence by my whole conduct in this office that, as Governor, I am guided by my oath of office and my duty to all the people. I challenge any proof or indication, from any word or act of mine as Governor, that I am capable of doing injustice or denying justice to any citizen of this State. But I do deem it my solemn duty to do my utmost to secure a fair and free election in this State; to protect every man in the free enjoyment of his political rights, and to see to it that no man or combination of men, of any political party, shall overawe or put in fear or danger any citizen of South Carolina in the exercise of his civil rights. In accomplishing these results I now recognize, with deep regret, that there are many indications that it will be necessary for me to invoke the aid which, under the Constitution and laws, the authorities of the General Government may extend under certain circumstances.

And I trust you will permit me to add that I know no official duty more binding, in my judgment, on the Chief Executive of the United States than that of exercising the powers with which he is invested for the protection of the States against domestic violence, and for the protection of the individual citizen in the exercise of his political rights, whenever a proper call is made upon him. I understand that an American citizen has a right to vote as he pleases; to vote one ticket as freely and safely as another; to vote wrong as freely and safely as to vote right; and I know that whenever, upon whatsoever pretext, large bodies of citizens can be coerced by force or fear into absenting themselves from the polls, or voting in a way contrary to their judgment or inclination, the foundation of every man's civil freedom is deeply, if not fatally, shaken.

I inclose, for your information respecting the Hamburg massacre, the following documents: The report of Hon. William Stone, Attorney General of this State; the report of General H. W. Purvis, Adjutant and Inspector General; a copy of all the evidence taken before the coroner's jury; a copy of the printed statement of General M. C. Butler; a copy of a letter addressed by me to Hon. T. J. Robertson; an Address to the American people by the colored people of Charleston; and a similar Address by a Committee appointed at a convention of leading representatives of the colored people of this State, in Columbia, on the 20th inst. I have the honor to be, your obedient servant,

D. H. CHAMBERLAIN,

Governor of South Carolina.

To the Governor's letter the President made the following reply:

EXECUTIVE MANSION,

WASHINGTON, D. C., July 26th.

DEAR SIR :—I am in receipt of your letter of the 22d of July, and all the inclosures enumerated therein, giving an account of the late barbarous massacre at the town of Hamburg, S. C. The views which you express as to the duty you owe to your oath of office and to citizens to secure to all their civil rights, including the right to vote according to the dictates of their own consciences, and the further duty of the Executive of the nation to give all needful aid, when properly called on to do so, to enable you to ensure this inalienable right, I fully concur in. The scene at Hamburg, as cruel, blood-thirsty, wanton, unprovoked, and uncalled for, as it was, is only a repetition of the course which has been pursued in other Southern States within the last few years, notably in Mississippi and Louisiana. Mississippi is governed to-day by officials chosen through fraud and violence, such as would scarcely be accredited to savages, much less to a civilized and Christian people. How long these things are to continue, or what is to be the final remedy, the Great Ruler of the universe only knows ; but I have an abiding faith that the remedy will come, and come speedily, and I earnestly hope that it will come peacefully. There has never been a desire on the part of the North to humiliate the South. Nothing is claimed for one State that is not fully accorded to all others, unless it may be the right to kill negroes and Republicans without fear of punishment and without loss of caste or reputation. This has seemed to be a privilege claimed by a few States. I repeat again, that I fully agree with you as to the measure of your duties in the present emergency, and as to my duties. Go on—and let every Governor where the same dangers threaten the peace of his State go on—in the conscientious discharge of his duties to the humblest as well as the proudest citizen, and I will give every aid for which I can find law or constitutional power. A government that cannot give protection to life, property, and all guaranteed civil rights (in this country the greatest is an untrammelled ballot) to the citizen is, in so far, a failure, and every energy of the oppressed should be exerted, always within the law and by constitutional means, to regain lost privileges and protection. Too long denial of guaranteed rights is sure to lead to revolution— bloody revolution, where suffering must fall upon the innocent as well as the guilty.

Expressing the hope that the better judgment and co-operation of citizens of the State over which you have presided so ably may enable you to secure a fair trial and punishment of all offenders, without distinction of race or color or previous condition of servitude, and without aid from the Federal Government, but with the promise of such aid on the conditions named in the foregoing, I subscribe myself, very respectfully, your obedient servant,

U. S. GRANT.

To the Hon. D. H. Chamberlain,
Governor of South Carolina.

In his letter to Senator Robertson, the Governor bore witness to the fact that many who had not been wont to condemn heartily past bloody occurrences in the South, were horrified by the startling brutality of this case. The Charleston *News and Courier* was outspoken in denunciation of it. The following extract from an article in that paper exhibits its sentiments regarding the Governor's letter to the President :

. . . This is not, in the usual sense of the words, "a call for troops"; it is rather the natural inquiry of a public officer who, at a critical time, desires to know what outside aid he can rely on, when his own resources shall have been exhausted. No attempt is made to attach to one race or party, more than another, the responsibility for the apprehended disorder ; and no action on the part of the General Government is contemplated, unless the violence in question shall be " beyond the control of the State authorities." The State really has very little active power. In case that a band of negroes were engaged in a riot, the white rifle clubs could be called on by the Executive to repress the disorder ; but there are no negro militia who could be, or dare be, moved against the whites, if they were riotous, and the white rifle clubs again would be the only reliance. Governor Chamberlain appears to think that a company of United States soldiers will have a more sedative effect than rifle clubs or civil *posses*. This was the position taken a few weeks ago by the newspapers that berate Governor Chamberlain for "calling for troops." These very journals, at the time of the Combahee troubles, were clamorous for troops, and were furious in their denunciation of Governor Chamberlain because he would not call for them. We object to military garrisons, at election times, on principle. The presence of soldiers at a polling place is an indirect menace, and, as such, is an interference with the freedom of elections. We insist that the State, in every case, shall manage its own affairs in its own way, and we disapprove of the interference of soldiers, whether to put down a strike or to guard ballotboxes. This is a political principle with us, or we should not object to the sending of a company of United States soldiers to every courthouse in the State. The whites have no thought of killing anybody, or abusing anybody. The sympathies of the soldiers are with the whites, not with the blacks. And the quietest election we ever had in Charleston was when every polling place, at the request of Democrats, was guarded by troops. . . .

General M. C. Butler's statement, referred to by Governor Chamberlain as among the documents forwarded by him to the President, is in two parts, one a communication to the Columbia *Register*, the other a communication to the Charleston *Journal of*

Commerce. The first is an explanation of his personal connection with the affair, the second a defence and justification of it. In the former he claims that he was in Hamburg on professional business solely,—namely, as counsel for the two white men against whom charges had been preferred. He acknowledges that he was informed before entering the town of the excitement prevailing. He narrates what he did toward allaying it, his efforts being wholly of the nature of advice to the colored men to surrender their arms, which of course they were reluctant to do while the town was filling up with armed white men breathing vengeance. He drove to Augusta, also on professional business, but in response to inquiries he notified the people there that he " thought a collision between the whites and blacks imminent and likely to take place." He remained until " after the firing of the negroes had ceased." His narrative continues : " I left the crowd arresting the negroes. How many were killed, or how they were killed, I do not know. This collision was the culmination of the system of insulting and outraging of white people which the negroes had adopted there for several years."

In the second communication he defends the murders by the following reasoning : "The town had a negro Intendant, negro Aldermen, negro Marshals. . . . They had harbored thieves and criminals from every direction. They had arrested and fined some of the best and most peaceable citizens for the most trivial offences against their ordinances." He alleges that the guns they had were taken without authority from the custody of the person to whom they had been committed by the Governor. He then proceeds to justify the conduct of the mob thus :

The negroes had assembled riotously, were in a state of armed resistance to the laws, and any citizen, or number of citizens, had the right to disperse the rioters and suppress the riot, and to use just so much force as was necessary to accomplish it, and if every negro engaged in the riot had been killed in the suppression, it would have been excusable if not justifiable. . . . Delay would have been fatal to the safety of the lives, families, and property of unoffending, peaceable citizens. Prompt, short, sharp, and decisive action was necessary under the dictates of that unwritten inalienable law known as self-preservation, the first of all laws. Some there may have been who were glad of an opportunity to punish those who had accumulated wrongs, insults, and umbrages upon them such as I have enumerated. I can sympathize with them if I cannot approve such a means of vindication.

Such was the apology for, and justification of, the Hamburg massacre by a leading Democratic politician of the State, one whose wish was law to the citizens of his county, a foremost man in the "Straight-out" movement, who was chosen a United States Senator immediately after the Democrats organized a Legislature, and while he was yet unrelieved by any legal exculpation from such guilt of participation in the affair as was alleged in the finding of the coroner's inquest.

The nature of that finding is set forth in the following despatch published in the Charleston *News and Courier* of August 2, 1876:

AUGUSTA (GA.), Tuesday Night, August 1st.

Prince Rivers has not yet filed the verdict of the coroner's inquest, held at Hamburg. He returned to Hamburg this morning. Parties in Aiken obtained a copy of the names embraced in the verdict. The following is a verbatim copy:

Aiken men—R. J. Butler, Dr. Shaw, Rev. John Mealy, Thomas Butler, Harrison Butler [and thirty-five other men].

Edgefield men—M. C. Butler, Benjamin Tilman, Charles Glover, Frank Settles, Joseph Merriwether [and eight other men].

Georgia men—Thomas W. Carwile, Wm. Robertson, James Clark, Dish Ramey, John Smith, Garland A. Sneed, [and twenty-four other men].

Of these, seven, Messrs. R. J. Butler, Henry Getsen, Thomas Butler, Harrison Butler, John Lamar, Thomas Oliver, and John Oliver, are charged with murder in the first degree. All the others are charged with being accessories before the fact. The penalty, upon conviction, is the same in each case, but the accused may be bailed in the discretion of the presiding Judge.

It is charged in the verdict that Moses Parks was killed by R. J. Butler; James Cook by Henry Getsen, Thomas Butler, and Harrison Butler; A. T. Attaway, Daniel Phillips, Hamp Stevens, and Alfred Minyard, by John Lamar, Thomas Oliver, and John Oliver.

Warrants for the arrest of all the parties above named were issued by Prince Rivers, Trial Justice, and placed in the hands of Sheriff Jordan, of Aiken County. All these warrants charge the accused with having committed the crime of murder. The warrants against the parties living in South Carolina will be served at once. The accused will offer bail in any amount, which it is expected will be accepted by Judge Maher. The warrants against the parties on this side of the river cannot be served without a requisition upon Governor Smith, which, it is said, will be made. The entire bar of Aiken has volunteered to defend the accused.

Another telegram published the next day announced that those named in the finding had come in and delivered themselves up, and would go before Judge Maher on a motion for bail. The fact that persons thus accused of guilty participation in such a crime as the massacre at Hamburg, the revolting circumstances of which were undisputed, felt in no peril, voluntarily surrendered themselves, and commanded the volunteered support of "the entire bar," that is to say, all the white lawyers of the vicinage, in their defence, needs no enforcement of its significance as a revelation of the existing social conditions there ; and the degree of fear of the law which was entertained by the white race when the matter was one of killing negroes, needs no other enforcement than is supplied by the following official paper :

COLUMBIA, S. C., September 6, 1876.
Hon. D. H. Chamberlain, Governor, Columbia, S. C.:

DEAR SIR—It is due to you, as well as myself, that I should state why no action has been taken by me at the present term of the Court of General Sessions for Aiken County, in the matter of bringing to trial the persons accused of complicity in the murder of colored men at Hamburg on the night of the eighth of July last.

I had been called North but a few days before the Court was to meet, by a family bereavement, but returned here expecting to go to Aiken to lay before the Grand Jury bills of indictment against such persons as seemed to have been engaged in these murders.

On the day of my arrival here, I received a telegram from Judge Wiggins, [1] then holding the Court at Aiken, in which he stated that he thought it best to have all of these cases continued without giving out bills.

I had, before going North, determined, after full conference with Hon. D. T. Corbin, who had been employed to aid in the prosecution of these cases, that it would be neither practicable nor advisable to try them at the present term of the Court, even though bills should be found ; but that they ought to be continued until the next term of Court. Various reasons influenced us in coming to this conclusion.

The witnesses on the part of the State are chiefly colored persons resident in Aiken County. This class of persons has become greatly alarmed and intimidated during the past few weeks by the presence of armed bodies of white men who attend meetings in their neighborhood. Whether they have reason to apprehend injury from these men or not it is needless to inquire, so long as it is apparent that they are alarmed and intimidated.

While these witnesses continue to feel in this way, their attendance at Court could not be depended on ; and, even were they present, they would testify with reluctance and fear, and the value of their testimony would be greatly weakened. On this ground alone it would have been my duty to have moved to continue the cases.

Again, since the time when many of the accused parties surrendered themselves and were admitted to bail, an exciting political contest has

[1] Judge Wiggins, one of those chosen on Black Thursday, had superseded Judge Maher.

opened in this State, and the events connected with the Hamburg riot have been discussed by men of both parties and from different standpoints. The cases have thus come to have, to some extent, a political bearing, and the real issue, as to who are the guilty parties, has been overlooked.

The attempt to try the cases while this political conflict rages would, in my opinion, have been equivalent to a trial by the passions and prejudices of juries, and not a trial by their calm, unbiassed judgments. This would be true whether the juries were composed of men of either or both political parties.

As I concluded to move for a continuance of the cases until the next term of Court, had bills been found, I thought it advisable, in view of Judge Wiggins' telegram, to defer to his opinion and take no action at all at this term of Court.

I was more inclined to do this because of the fact that a case is now pending in the Supreme Court of this State, in which the question is directly raised as to the legality of the present Grand Jury of Aiken County. Should the Court decide that the present Grand Jury is not a legal one, all bills found by it would be void, and new ones would have to be given out to another jury.

Still, I should have taken the risk of a decision adverse to the State upon this question, had there been no other grounds for continuing the cases.

In view, then, of all the facts surrounding these cases, I am confident that the course I have taken is the one which it was best to follow, and that the interests of public justice will be better secured at the next term of the Court, when it is fair to suppose that the present political excitement will have subsided and the attendance of all the witnesses can be secured, than it can be now.

Very respectfully, your obedient servant,
WILLIAM STONE,
Attorney General, S. C.

Events of subsequent occurrence enabled the guilty agents and abettors of the bloody work at Hamburg to escape all punishment for their crime at the hands of human justice. The race hatred, signalled into activity by the " Straight-outers " of Edgefield and Aiken, wreaked itself by many a grumous stain on the soil and fame of the State before November. What the Governor dreadingly foreboded in his letter to the President, when this affair loomed in the murky sky of South Carolina politics, " a vast, tremendous, unformed spectre," became a terrible experience.

CHAPTER XX.

THE publication by the Charleston *News and Courier* of the series of articles in vindication of Governor Chamberlain, and the Hamburg affair, which forced the Governor to proclaim his uncompromising hostility to the violence sanctioned by many Democrats and not effectually condemned by any, were concurrent events that promoted and intensified the conflict within the Democratic party. The passions and prejudices aroused by the revival of bloody race persecutions were unfavorable to a just consideration of the argument addressed to reason and patriotic interest. While the excitement so fomented was at its height, the Democratic State Executive Committee issued a call for a State Convention at Columbia on the 15th of August. The apparent motive of this action was to force the Democratic party to determine upon its course before the meeting of the Republican Convention, and thus forestall the influence which the renomination of Governor Chamberlain, then daily becoming probable, might exert upon Democrats more concerned to secure honest administration of the State Government than to strive for a doubtful partisan victory. The "Coöperationists" were taken by surprise, but at once they began an agitation to induce the Committee to reconsider its action and postpone the date of the Democratic Convention until after the Republican Convention.

Failing in this, they sought to secure an expression in the county Conventions, when choosing delegates to the State Convention, which would compel the latter body to postpone the nomination of candidates until the Republicans had shown their hand.

In this effort they obtained a degree of success which, until the meeting of the Convention, appeared to be decisive. While it was no secret that the favorite candidate of the "Straight-outs" was General Wade Hampton, they flattered the "Coöperation-ists" by bringing into prominence as candidates men whose sym-pathies were known to be with that party. One of these was Judge Maher, a leading citizen and lawyer, a life-long Democrat, and the Judge who was superseded by Wiggins through the ac-tion of the Legislature on "Black Thursday." But Judge Maher, by means of an interview published in the *News and Courier*, pub-licly repudiated the seductive proposal. His judgment regarding Governor Chamberlain's Administration and the proper course of the Democratic party was emphatically expressed.

Reporter. Judge Maher, you have been nominated, or at least you have been suggested, as the Democratic candidate for Governor of South Carolina. Would you mind stating your views upon the subject—I mean whether you would accept such a nomination.

Judge Maher. I could not, and would not, under any circumstances accept the nomination for Governor, not if I could be assured of the vote of every man, woman, and child in the State. In the first place, I could not afford it; and again, as you know, politics are not congenial to me. I am a fireside man, and prefer the enjoy-ments of home to public life.

In the second place I do not think that any Conservative or Democratic Governor could accomplish any thing in the Executive chair, unless we could change the char-acter and complexion of the Legislature of the State. This, in my opinion, can hardly be effected. A large number of honest men may be elected, but scarcely a majority, and even with a strong minority of Democrats, I do not think that a Demo-cratic Governor could effect any material reforms, because he could not control a suffi-cient number of Republican votes. Under existing circumstances, and with the Legis-lature constituted as it is, Governor Chamberlain could do the most good for the State, and could effect the most reforms.

If Gen. Kershaw or Gen. Hampton had been Governor for the past two years, neither of them could have effected as much reform or benefited the State as much as Governor Chamberlain has done. It would not have been in their power. Governor Chamberlain has been true to his pledges, and I believe that under any circumstances he will continue the same course of reform that has marked his Administration. It is to his interest and that of his party to do so. I don't believe that he pursued his policy of reform for the purpose of pleasing the Democrats, but because he believed it to be right, and because it was to his own interest and that of his party to do so.

Reporter. What are your views as to the "Straight-out" policy?

Judge Maher. Well, as I have before stated, I don't think that my views are of much consequence. But it seems to me that it would be just as easy to reform the Legislature as to elect a Governor, and it would accomplish more practical benefits. If it were in our power to elect a Governor we should be under no obligations to the Republicans, as we could then secure a majority in the Legislature. But, as I said before, I have bestowed very little thought on politics. I have been pressed with the duties of my office, and have always made it a point not to mingle in politics.

Reporter. What are your views as to the expediency of making nominations on the 15th?

Judge Maher. I am decidedly opposed to any nominations on the 15th. It would be premature, and the Convention was evidently called at that date with the intention of forcing "Straight-out" nominations. I am at a loss to see the good of it. It can answer no purpose except to commit the Democrats to the "Straight-out" policy, an exceedingly unwise measure, at this time at least.

Reporter. Do you think that a majority of the counties can be carried by the "Straight-outs"?

Judge Maher. I can't, of course, undertake to speak for the other counties. In Barnwell the Democrats seem to be very much enthused, and, although the Radicals have a majority of about 2,000, the people seem to think that they had better run the risk of a total defeat than to make any compromise on a county ticket. The real truth is that, in this county, the Radicals have never offered a man fit to vote for.

Reporter. Do you think, Judge, that Mr. Chamberlain will get the Republican nomination?

Judge Maher. Judging from his victory in the State Convention, some time ago, I think that he will get it. If he does, I think that the Democrats had better hang on to him, as I see no chance of defeating him, unless there is a bolt, which is exceedingly doubtful. Governor Chamberlain could probably do more good to the taxpayers than anybody else, because he could control Republican votes in the Legislature. As to the counties, the leading men must know best what to do. In Barnwell County there is scarcely any use to make a compromise, as the other side never offer such a man as Governor Chamberlain, nor do they ever offer anybody that a respectable man could vote for, and I think, therefore, that we had better run the risk and nominate county officers.

Another of these gentlemen was Hon. George W. Williams, an old Charleston merchant, very wealthy, and highly esteemed throughout the State. Knowledge of this use of his name coming to him in his summer retreat, he sent the following communication to the *News and Courier :*

MOUNTAIN HOME, NACOOCHEE, GA.,
July 28, 1876.

To the Editor of the News and Courier :

Having received numerous inquiries desiring to know whether I would accept a nomination for Governor of South Carolina, I beg leave to say to my friends that

I have no political aspirations, and would not exchange the independent life of a civilian for the office of Chief Magistrate of the United States. In my judgment the Democratic party ought not to make a nomination for Governor. We are not in a condition to enter into an excited political contest. I honestly believe that Governor Chamberlain can do more for South Carolina, in and out of the State, than any other man.

Yours very respectfully,
GEO. W. WILLIAMS.

In publishing this letter the *News and Courier* said :

No citizen of South Carolina has more at stake than Mr. Williams has ; nor will any one citizen gain as much as he by the completion of the work of administration reform in South Carolina. . . . The most influential bankers and merchants in Charleston hold substantially the same opinions as Mr. Williams. They have no axes to grind. They are not officeholders or officeseekers.

The following passage from a public letter written to the Charleston *News and Courier* by the Hon. B. O. Duncan, exhibits the feeling of a native South Carolinian of high education, character, and social position, who in national politics had acted with the Republican party. He was appointed Consul at Naples in 1869, and still held that office :

Governor Chamberlain can, as I believe, and in this many of the most enlightened Democrats agree with me, do more for the good of the State in the present crisis than any other man, Republican or Democrat, could do. Were it even possible to elect a Democratic Governor, I presume the blindest " Straight-outer " will not pretend that it will be possible to elect also a Democratic Legislature. If not, their Governor would have his hands tied hard and fast. But with Governor Chamberlain it would be quite different. If the Democrats will do as the *News and Courier* advocates, *i. e.*, make no nomination for Governor, but support Chamberlain, and then throughout the State spare no effort to send honest, moderate, and able men to the Legislature, they may, together with the Chamberlain Republicans, get a majority. In counties where they have a majority of voters, let them send their own men of course. But it would be good policy even there to send as moderate, sagacious men as possible. In counties where the majority is on the other side, every advantage of any division should be taken, and every effort be made to compromise and form fusion tickets with the better elements of the Radicals. With the example of the fusion delegation from Charleston in the recent Legislature, I need not recall the advantages to be gained by such a course. Not only would the honesty and the capacity of the Legislature be increased, but better and more friendly relations between the two races would be established thereby in every county where it succeeded or even where it was undertaken. I have conversed as freely as I could with the colored people wherever I have met them, and I am of the decided opinion that they are ripe for such a movement if undertaken in good faith and with fairness.

"WATCH AND WAIT" was the counsel of the "Coöperation-ists," and the phrase became a watchword. When the county conventions met it plainly appeared that the course of the Demo-cratic Executive Committee was disapproved. In but a few coun-ties was it specifically commended; others elected delegates with-out instructions, leaving them to exercise their own discretion at the State Convention; but in many counties express and empha-tic opposition to the policy of making nominations before the Republicans had developed their policy was expressed in resolu-tions adopted. Such resolutions, however, were accompanied by a pledge to support the action of the Convention. On the 8th of August the *News and Courier* said:

> The telegraphic despatches from thirteen counties, in eleven of which the county Democratic Conventions assembled yesterday, bring the welcome news of a hearty popular endorsement of the recommendation to postpone the nominations for State officers until the plans and purposes of the Radicals shall be known. Only two coun-ties took decided ground in favor of immediate action, while in eight counties there was a positive expression in favor of the "watch and wait" policy. The State Con-vention will be composed of 158 delegates, and over 70 of the delegates can already be set down as in favor of adjournment without making nominations. Other counties yet to be heard from will swell the roll.

The Democratic Convention met in Columbia on the 15th of August and did not adjourn until the 17th. The issue between the two factions was at once raised in the choice of a presiding officer. The Charleston *News and Courier* of the 16th reported the vote as 65 for Col. C. H. Simonton, of Charleston, and 78 for Gen. W. W. Harllee, of Marion; the latter representing the policy of making nominations immediately. The debate with regard to the policy to be pursued was carried on in secret session. On the 17th the *News and Courier* gave the following brief account of the proceedings and their result:

> It was half-past eleven o'clock when the convention went into secret session, and the doors remained closed until half-past six with a recess of about one hour for dinner. The debate is said to have been long and exciting, but was conducted in the best spirit. Speeches were made by Gen. Butler, Gen. Gary, Capt. De Pass, and Capt. Lipscomb in favor of immediate nomination, and by Maj. E. W. Moise, of Sumter, Gen. Connor, and others, in favor of postponement. At about half-past six the doors were thrown open, and the following resolution was announced as adopted by a vote of 88 yeas, 64 nays.

Resolved, That this Convention do now proceed to nominate candidates for Governor and other State officers.

Reports were current at the time that the debate was heated and bitter, and the division much closer than these figures indicate. Whether or not any other vote was taken, the statement of the *News and Courier* with reference to the final action is doubtless entitled to full credit. General Wade Hampton was selected to head the Democratic ticket. It is not true, as has sometimes been said, that Governor Chamberlain was voted for as a candidate in the Convention. He neither sought, nor did anybody seek for him, a Democratic nomination. When it was determined not to wait to see whether he would be nominated by the Republicans, it was determined to nominate a Democrat.

The two causes that brought about this decision have already been referred to. They were, first, the Hamburg massacre, and, second, the influence of the presidential election. Mr. Tilden had been nominated for President by the Democratic National Convention held in St. Louis in June. The hope of his election lay in securing a "solid South," and he was encouraged by the "Straight-outers" to believe that they could secure to him the electoral vote of the State if a party nomination for Governor was made. The promoters of this policy adroitly got letters written by prominent Democrats of the North advising a separate nomination, and leading Democrats from other Southern States which had been "reclaimed" to the Democratic party by a policy of intimidation and fraud, were present to counsel and instruct the members of the Convention regarding the methods of overcoming Republican majorities. That which the *News and Courier* had said could be accomplished "only by armed force," it was resolved to attempt,—a resolution which had brutal and bloody consequences in the ensuing campaign, subverted the rule of the majority, and entailed a continuing wrong by which the political life of the State is still degraded and debauched.

How this action was contemporaneously regarded by leaders of conservative sentiment in the North will be apparent from the following expressions of two journals, one Republican and one Independent, and both disposed to regard Mr. Tilden's nomination as a sign that the Democratic party was facing toward reform.

[From the New York *Evening Post.*]

It is impossible to regard the course of the Democrats in South Carolina as any thing but reactionary. What is needed in that State more than anywhere else is the restoration of peace and order. If the Democrats had thought more of this end than of partisan success they would have done one of three things. They would have united to strengthen the hands of Governor Chamberlain, who, if he has not absolutely succeeded, has done more than anybody else since the war to restore tranquillity. This, we believe, would have been their wisest course. Or they would have nominated an independent Republican whom they could trust. This would have shown more plainly than any words could do their sincere acceptance of political changes. Or, if they must choose a Democrat, they would have nominated the one who had been least identified with the old order. This would have shown that they were resolved not to take a step backward. Instead of doing any one of these three things, they have nominated a candidate who, however worthy personally, represents the past more exactly than any other citizen of the State. The name of Wade Hampton, not only in South Carolina, but throughout the country, stands for the old order. The nomination of no man mentioned for Governor would do more to revive questions which ought to be obsolete, and to restore party lines which ought to be obliterated. It is not likely that Hampton will be elected, but his coming to the front is in harmony with many other proceedings of the reactionary Democrats. They seem to be straining every nerve to consolidate the voters of the country into the old-time divisions, although it is plain that, if they are so consolidated, the Democratic canvass is a hopeless one.

[From the New York *Nation.*[1]]

The South Carolina Democrats, in the nomination of General Wade Hampton for the governorship, have shown that they possess their full share of the party 'capacity for blundering. This step will make it comparatively easy for the Radicals not to renominate Governor Chamberlain, and it is plain as possible that there is no man who can be elected who can render the State, and especially the property-holders of the State, so much service as Governor Chamberlain. The corrupt element among the Radicals hate him, and will prevent his renomination if they can, but would probably have been forced to submit to it if the Conservatives had been wise and put off their nomination until the Radicals had made theirs. The platform on which General Hampton has been nominated contains all the things that proper platforms have to contain in these days—acceptance of the Constitutional Amendments and other results of the war, devotion to equal rights, love of peace and order, immeasurable hatred of theft, fraud, and other forms of villany, so that the only thing the Republican organs can say against it is that it is " hypocritical." General Hampton's letter of acceptance is equally unexceptionable, but then no letter or platform can make the General himself unexceptionable. No matter what views he may now hold as to expediency, he is neither a statesman nor a politician, nor a man of conciliatory disposition, nor any thing but a soldier and Southern gentleman of the old school, to whom niggers, Yankees, schools, roads, free labor, and free speech are naturally almost as hateful as to the Pope himself. To put him up as a candidate, this of all

---

[1] At this time the *Evening Post* and the *Nation* were quite distinct journals.

years, on the eve of a Presidential election and close after the Hamburg massacre, seems to indicate a constitutional love of mischief.

That this action was an open departure from the plain course of a true and sure reform policy for the sake of a doubtful partisan advantage, no argument is needed to show; or if any were needed, it is furnished in the clear logic, conclusive as a demonstration in geometry, of the following extract from the Charleston *News and Courier*, when replying (July 6, 1876) to the charge that support of Chamberlain was support of the worst element of the "corrupt constituency" which elected him.

Now the corrupt leaders of the ignorant negroes nominated Mr. Chamberlain for Governor, and if they continued to support him, if he had remained at peace with them, it could be truthfully said that to support him is to support them, and through them their ignorant, not corrupt, constituency. But the fact is that these leaders are the bitterest foes that Governor Chamberlain has, and they have been so ever since his election. There is not one of the gang who has not fought him to the death. In the Legislature and in convention, on the streets and in such sheets as the *National Republican*, the Whittemores, Pattersons, Swailses, Bowens, Whippers, Maxwells, Worthingtons, and Carpenters have been, and are, the relentless opponents of the Executive. We do not recall one conspicuous rascal in South Carolina who is not as savage in his denunciation of Mr. Chamberlain as the Democratic party are in their denunciation of Radical misrule in South Carolina. Now, it is evident to us, and it should be evident to every thoughtful man, that whatever Democratic support is given Governor Chamberlain, instead of being a support of the infamous Radical leaders, is really the most effective opposition to them. In supporting Mr. Chamberlain we oppose his enemies, who are likewise the enemies of the public. If we desire to support the corrupt Radicals we can do it at present in but one way, and that is by opposing Mr. Chamberlain.

In this lies the reason for advocating the waiving of Democratic opposition to Mr. Chamberlain's election. Should the Democracy run a Democratic candidate for Governor the fight will be strictly a party one, and in every county the worst of the Radicals, who have most popular strength, will be set against the Democratic candidates. Mr. Chamberlain, when elected, will be surrounded by the same gang of plunderers who obstinately opposed every reform measure in the last General Assembly, and these plunderers will be stronger than ever before. If Mr. Chamberlain's nomination be not opposed by the Democrats he can, *and will*, use all his influence to improve the character of the Legislature ; but he will have no influence in that direction if the contest be "Straight-out," for then the leaders in the several counties, no matter what he may say or do, will feel that they are fighting for political existence, and will stop at nothing that may be necessary to carry the election. There is, it seems to us, no plan of action that will as certainly give aid and comfort to the public enemy, and as surely perpetuate the rule of ignorance and vice in South Carolina, as opposition to Mr. Chamberlain.

Yet when the Democratic Convention had decided to thus "give aid and comfort to the public enemy," the *News and Courier* wheeled into line, and from that date labored with tremendous zeal to refute the arguments and counteract the influence of its wiser and nobler judgment. What Washington in his Farewell Address fitly called "the baleful influence of party spirit" never had an apter illustration.

CHAPTER XXI.

BEFORE resuming the narrative of the development of that desperate political conflict which is the theme of most of the following chapters, certain happenings antedating the Democratic State Convention, and having importance with reference to the subsequent record, claim attention.

The events of the summer of 1876 tested in various ways and in an extraordinary degree the firmness of the Governor's motive to deal fairly with all classes of citizens. In May there was an alarming strike of agricultural laborers in Colleton County, the negroes on certain plantations quitting their work and organizing to force the hands on other plantations to join them in a demand for higher wages. The planters feared the loss of their crops, the destruction of their property, and possible personal injury, if the excitement was not allayed. Fortunately the civil authorities, by energetic pacific means, prevented any serious conflict. On the 26th of May the Sheriff of the county telegraphed to the Governor: "Many are disposed to work, but are prevented by the others. They have a large meeting to-morrow. I will attend and try to persuade them to resume work at the old prices. The whites have not been molested." To him the Governor immediately sent the following despatch:

Exert all your powers to restore peace. Speak for me to the meeting to-morrow, and say to them that they have a right to refuse to work for low wages, but they have no right to make others join them against their will ; that if they molest those who are willing to work they violate the law, and will be arrested and punished. I am willing to overlook all that has been done thus far, but they must stop all disorder and all interference with those who are willing to work, or I shall be compelled to adopt whatever measures are necessary to enforce the law. I sympathize deeply with all who are struggling for a bare subsistence ; but wrong never brings right, and it is wrong to trouble any man who is willing to work, no matter how low the wages. Advise the planters from me to act with all possible liberality towards the laborers. I cannot of course dictate terms, but let them be fair and just and it will be advantageous to all. Keep me informed often and fully.

These counsels and warnings were potent for the time being ; but late in August a more serious difficulty occurred in Beaufort County, the laborers on the rice plantations along the Combahee River striking for an advance of fifty per cent. in wages, at a time when the immediate gathering of the crop was necessary in order to secure it at all. The strike began in the abandonment of work on one of the plantations by about two hundred negroes, who forthwith, armed with clubs and horsewhips, proceeded to other plantations and forced the hands to join them. Some who refused were imprisoned in outbuildings under guard. The Sheriff and a *posse* made a few arrests, but were overpowered, and the prisoners were released. When the Governor was notified of the condition of affairs, he at once gave orders to Robert Smalls, who had command of a company of militia, to assist the Sheriff. But many members of Small's company were among the strikers. Thirteen of the ringleaders, acting under advice, gave themselves up, but they were discharged the next morning by the Justice before whom they were taken. The whites then began collecting for safety. The assistance of volunteers was offered from Charleston, and the Governor said he would accept it unless another effort on the part of the constituted authorities should be effectual. On the 24th of August the Governor telegraphed to the *News and Courier* that he was advised that " the mob is completely dispersed, the ringleaders arrested, and all is quiet," adding, " I have directed that the law be fully enforced at all hazards. I trust that all trouble is over, but if not, the law shall be enforced."

Neither the brutal outrage upon negroes at Hamburg, then a fresh embarrassment, nor the action of the Democratic State Convention, depriving him of expectation of political support from the whites, affected in any degree his resolute insistance that the colored race should refrain from all unlawful acts.

The Governor was present in Charleston at the observance of the centennial of the heroic defence of Fort Moultrie. Much preparation had been made for a suitable celebration of this famous incident of the revolutionary war, and intervening estrangements and hostilities added a peculiar significance to an occasion which would revive on Southern soil memories of the time when South Carolina and Massachusetts were united in a common patriotic purpose. By a Proclamation issued on the 27th of May the people of the State were invited " to consider the day a public holiday on which ordinary business shall be suspended." Governor Chamberlain's presence and addresses at the Lexington and Mecklenburg celebrations had given the State an honorable prominence, which was proudly appreciated, and there was an earnest desire on the part of South Carolinians to show forth their cordial sympathy with the citizens of other States of the " old thirteen " by proper commemoration of the events within her own borders which were a distinguished part of the national glory. Delegations came from all parts of the country to testify their gladness and friendship, and especially welcome were the Northern military companies, the " Tigers," from Boston, and the "Old Guard," from New York.

During this festival of exalted sentiment Governor Chamberlain was conspicuously honored, although he took no other than an official and incidental part in the proceedings. At a banquet given to the guests of the State in Hibernian Hall, Charleston, Major G. L. Buist presided, with General Wade Hampton seated on his right, and Governor Chamberlain on his left. Governor Chamberlain responded to a toast to the State of South Carolina. This extract from his brief speech, with the indications of its favorable reception, is from the report in the *News and Courier :*

South Carolina welcomes you to-night because there is in the hearts of all her sons a desire for concord and union. [Applause.] Though not a native, I know what feelings have been subdued in their breasts, and I know enough to assure you that when South Carolina pledges you welcome, in the interest of unity and peace, she means what she says. [Prolonged applause.] Whatever sacrifices have been made ; whatever prejudices have been crushed out ; whatever memories have been forgotten, she recognizes herself a factor in our nationality, and she is determined to do her duty. [Applause.] In conclusion I need only say : "South Carolina, let her future only be worthy of her past." [Loud and continued applause.]

General Wade Hampton in his speech on this occasion, said:

Misconstruction has been the great source of mistrust between the North and South, and we wish you, gentlemen of New York and Massachusetts, to correct it. We believed we had the right to secede, and we did it ; but I declare to you to-night, on the honor of a soldier and gentleman, in good faith and sincerity, that we consider the decision of war as final, and we accept the Constitution as it is. Go back and tell your people what you have seen, and not what you may have heard. I have spoken to you frankly on this subject, because between men who have been enemies there can be no perfect peace which is not based on perfect candor and sincerity.

There were many other speeches, and the report of the affair says, in conclusion : " Loud calls were made to bring out Governor Chamberlain again, but to no purpose."

On Sullivan's Island, where the formal ceremonies of the occasion took place (June 28th), Governor Chamberlain ; General J. B. Kershaw, the orator of the day ; General Hunt, of the United States Army ; General W. G. De Saussure, of Charleston ; William Gilmore Sims, and other distinguished citizens and guests were entertained by Major Gayer, the Intendant of the town. At the close of the dinner the Charleston Riflemen, a select company of volunteer militia, marched to the door of the dining-room, and gave " three cheers and a tiger " for Governor Chamberlain. The Governor, in acknowledging the compliment, said that since his election he had been cheered and upheld in the performance of duty by the support and encouragement received from good people of all classes in the community, and especially from those belonging to a different political party. 'This compliment," he added, " from the citizen soldiery of South Carolina to a man who is not a South Carolinian nerves me to say that I pledge myself to support that candidate for Governor of the State who will carry the banner of reform." The crowd had by this time been increased by members of the visiting companies from New York and Boston. General Kershaw was next called out, and in his remarks said : " As a Carolinian I appreciate the efforts that have been made by Governor Chamberlain to effect reforms in the administration of the State Government, and no one will give him a more cordial and hearty support than myself."

In the formal ceremonies, the President of the day, Major G. L. Buist, called upon the Governor to make the introductory address. His few words were charged with the significance of the occasion as a symbol of national Union.

Fellow-Citizens :—We have assembled to-day and here to commemorate an event of high significance to South Carolina and the American Union—an event which illustrated American valor and patriotism, and gave hope and confidence to the men who were then entering upon their momentous struggle for civil freedom and national independence. This spot is consecrated to valor and freedom. This air is redolent of self-sacrifice and patriotic devotion. In the name of South Carolina, and of all South Carolinians, I welcome you to the fellowship of this hour, to the fraternity of this memorial of national unity. We stand, indeed, on the soil of South Carolina ; but this occasion, its spirit, its lesson, its voice, is confined to no State. It is a part of the common heritage of all Americans, aye, it belongs to all men everywhere who feel the thrill of martial ardor or are touched by the story of heroic devotion. Moultrie and Jasper are no longer local heroes ; they have been admitted to the great Pantheon of the heroes of all ages and nations.

A welcome, deep, earnest, overflowing, then, to all who are with us to-day : to you of Massachusetts, who bring to us cheer from the soil of Lexington and Concord and Bunker Hill ; to you of New York, whose patriotic pride boasts of your Fort Ticonderoga and Saratoga ; to you of Georgia, and you of whatever State beneath the broad folds of our national flag, and within the sacred bond of our undivided and indivisible Union. You come not on an errand of war. Sweet peace smiles upon all to-day. You come not to aid a struggling cause. You come to honor the martyrs of a cause which has long since triumphed over all its foes—the cause of American independence.

We desire that this celebration shall promote peace, fraternity, good-will among all Americans. The valor of our fathers made the event which we celebrate one hundred years ago " the bright morning star and harbinger of American independence." We desire that this day shall unite us all in new bonds of devotion to the nation which a century of time has now built up and perfected.

While with reverent and grateful hearts we assemble to honor this event, to recall its story, to cherish all its memories and lessons, let us never forget that the struggle which opened here one hundred years ago was the struggle for *American* independence and *National* freedom. This event, this day, belongs to all Americans. Massachusetts and New York, Virginia and Georgia, the oldest and the youngest, the greatest and the humblest in our sisterhood of States, share in the glory of this battlefield and the renown of this day.

Let, then, this day be honored by a deep and sincere spirit of American patriotism. I invoke the genius of that unselfish valor and self-sacrifice which gave victory to our fathers here, to fill all our hearts. "Peace hath her victories not less renowned than war." Let this day record a victory of peace, not less auspicious for the cause of American freedom than the victory won on this spot one hundred years ago by the arms of Jasper and Moultrie.

An incident that followed the delivery of the oration by General Kershaw vividly illustrates the esteem in which the Governor was then held. The account of it was given in the *News and Courier* as follows :

The oration was received with repeated rounds of applause, and at its conclusion the speaker stepped forward and said : " Since concluding my remarks to you, gentlemen, it has struck me that a certain portion of them, in which I alluded to the sad political condition of our State, might have been misunderstood and accepted as a reflection upon my honored friend who sits here to-day (pointing to Governor Chamberlain). Let me assure him and you that my language is carefully worded, and, if it is closely examined, it will be seen that my remarks refer to the condition of the State prior to the time that Governor Chamberlain assumed the charge of her interests." [Great applause.]

Governor Chamberlain smilingly arose from his chair, advanced two or three feet to the front of the stage, and said : " Gentlemen, it is needless for me to say that I have detected nothing in the words of General Kershaw that I do not recognize as the sincere utterance of a true heart. I could not expect, indeed it is impossible, that General Kershaw, so brave upon the battlefield of war, could be unjust upon the peaceful field of this day." [Immense cheering.]

In July, Governor Chamberlain began an extended tour of the State, making addresses to large and deeply interested assemblies of Republicans in support of the principles and candidates of the National Republican Party, and in defence of his Administration in South Carolina as a Republican Administration. In the first of this series of addresses, delivered at Beaufort, July 16th, he discussed the history, relations, and tendencies of the two great parties in a broad and thorough manner, enforcing the consideration that the Republican party was the party of freedom, the party which from its birth had been opposed to slavery, which had accomplished the destruction of that wrong, and which, if continued in power, would "cure the evils of the present hour." While courteous throughout to the Democratic party and its

leaders, he was unequivocal in his profession of belief in, and
fidelity to, the Republican party, and in the assertion that its
success in the nation and the State was the safest guaranty of
freedom, equal rights, and good government. One or two brief
extracts will sufficiently exhibit the spirit and tenor of this portion
of the address.

I am a Republican, and I am a Republican only because I believe
the principles of the Republican party, if honestly and faithfully carried
out in our State and National Government, will give the greatest degree
of prosperity, happiness, and good-will to the people of South Carolina
and the country at large: If I believed there was any thing in the creed
of the Republican party which added a feather's weight to the burden
of man, woman, or child, I would not be a Republican, for it is no part
of the creed of an honest man that wishes well to his fellow-men to seek
to build himself up on the wrongs of others. I am free to say to every
man who listens to me here, that although his condition in life may
have been and is widely different to mine; although some of you may
never have read the books that I have, or had the privileges or the
opportunity for culture that I have had from my youth, yet I can say
to you, it has never been in my heart, nor never will be, to say that I
should have a single right, privilege, or immunity under the government of my State which the humblest and poorest man should not have
also. [Cheers.] This is Republicanism—freedom, justice, and equality; civil and political privileges for all men ; chains and fetters for
no man. . . . I am calling your attention to these facts because I
want you to know why I am still a Republican, and why you should
stand by the party which gave you freedom, that will build you up into
the stature of true civil freedom and manhood. But having your physical fetters that bound you struck off is not half of freedom. I sometimes
think my fellow-citizens have escaped from physical slavery only to
plunge into a slavery more hopeless. I want you to understand why
you are Republicans. I do not want you to be Republicans because
Abraham Lincoln was a Republican, but because you believe in the
principles of the party as Abraham Lincoln understood and believed in
them. We talk about the dangers of an ignorant ballot, but to-day, in
presence of the world, if I had to choose between an ignorant ballot
and an educated ballot controlled by prejudice, I would say give me
the free ballot and I can make it an intelligent ballot. The only way
to work out of the difficulties that now surround you is to accept freedom for every man in all its length and breadth, and trust that freedom
will build up and lead the people into intelligence, frugality, and all the
civil virtues.

The larger part of the speech was devoted to advocacy of the
principles and policy of the National Republican Party, the remainder to the aspect of State affairs, and in this speech he an-

nounced for the first time that he would be a candidate for renomination. It was early and defiant notice to the politicians who had antagonized him, and who, as he well knew, were conspiring to humiliate him and cast him out of the party, that he accepted the issue made by them, and intended, if possible, to defeat their schemes and secure an approval of his Administration from the party that elected him. He was speaking in Beaufort, a city he had never before visited. A large majority of its population belonged to the colored race, and the same Whipper whose election to the bench he had twice thwarted was their acknowledged leader. These are circumstances to be borne in mind while reading what he said regarding State politics.

. . . I have already alluded to the fact that I have been charged with the duties of Chief Executive for almost two years. You voted for me in Beaufort, and my election was as much due to you as to any people in the State, and I therefore come here to submit to your judgment my conduct. I am here to listen to any charges and complaints, and to answer them, not in a spirit of defiance, not in a spirit of rebuke, but in a spirit of one who understands that what the people have given me, the people have the right to take away, and for the trust placed in my hands they have the right to call me to account. Two years ago your convention nominated me at Columbia for Governor ; put me upon a platform upon which was written from beginning to end, reform. We admitted that in the six years which preceded that time, corruption and intolerable abuses had grown up, and we resolved that they should be removed, and that good government should be restored in the place of bad government ; that the laws should be administered without favor, that the public treasure should be honestly used ; that the taxes should be reduced to the lowest possible point. You placed that duty on me, and I have borne it always in mind, and I believe I have carried those pledges, which you laid down in the platform, into execution. I have labored with but comparative success, I admit, but I am not here to discuss the causes of that failure. I have labored with only partial success to reduce taxes, to expend the money with honesty and economy, and to fill the offices with honest men. Something has been done, however. The Republican party to-day, instead of struggling under a weight of shame and disgrace that covered it two years ago, is looked upon by the country, by impartial men, as a party that is endeavoring to administer its functions with honesty. I have been subjected to a great amount of criticism by prominent men in my own party. I say to you it is the wish closest to my heart, and has been, to keep the Republican party united and harmonious—the harmony of honesty, freedom, peace, and good government. You remember that the great reformer, the Saviour himself, said his doctrine was first the sword, and not until the sword had done its work would peace come.

You let any man undertake to do his duty, and many of his fellow-men will point at him as a traitor to his party. . . .

I am here to-day to say that I am a candidate for renomination for Governor of this State. I say this to you because I desire to be perfectly frank, and if you cannot say any thing else of me when I leave the stand, I would not have you say that I was not man enough to tell you the truth on this point. If I could conscientiously lay down my position as Governor to-day I would gladly do it, on account of the difficulties that gain upon me every day. Just now the heart of every decent man in the State and in other States is rankled and filled with indignation and disgust at the horrible massacre that has disgraced the country at Hamburg.

I have told you that you cannot trust your liberties and your future to other than Republican hands. I do not love to allude to such things as this at Hamburg. They ought to be wrested out of the domain of politics and be held in scorn of every man, woman, and child that fears God and loves man. What is the trouble? Out of a trifling and insignificant affront against two white men, the town of Hamburg has been made, by white men, the scene of a most foul and bloody massacre, in which five helpless, disarmed colored men have been shot down with more than Indian barbarity and cruelty.

Let me pause long enough to say that if the office of Governor carries with it force enough to bring these men to justice, I shall not rest until all my official power is exhausted, I shall not slumber until punishment shall overtake the men who have reddened the streets of Hamburg with the blood of their fellow-men. Let me say further that you must not be impatient at the least delay that may arise. It is necessary, in the first place, to ascertain the exact facts and put the Government in such an attitude that it can enforce the law; and in this I may say that the United States and the State are as one in their purpose to prevent such massacres, and when they do occur they will see to it that proper punishment shall follow them as speedily as possible.

I was saying, when I turned aside to speak of the Hamburg matter, that this great work of reform must be carried forward, and, as I have begun, those who stood by me say it is my duty to stand by the cause in the same capacity; and I have accepted their judgment, and if the Republican party shall place me again upon a platform of reform, and say to me, go forward for two years more and perfect the reform you have begun, with an honest Legislature and a pure Judiciary, I say I will do it, but I will not purchase a renomination by the relinquishing of a tithe of the work I have done, nor of the principles I have proclaimed. I will not, for any official station, insult my manhood by taking back any thing. . . .

In the spirit of this speech the Governor made a tour of the State, speaking nearly every day in the hot summer months to large meetings. It was a task of extreme labor, hardship, and anxiety, but it was the only course that gave promise of rescuing the Republican party from the domination and control of the local politicians who were hostile to his reform policy. The anxiety and difficulty of the canvass were greatly enhanced by the course of the Democrats, instigated by the leaders of the "Straight-out" faction. Fully organized in a semi-military fashion, uniformed in red shirts, they appeared at Republican meetings, officered and bravely armed, demanding "a division of time." To refuse it was to run the risk of an immediate violent breaking up of the meeting and the greater risk of murderous outrages upon the negro Republicans afterwards. Again and again the Governor spoke to the faithful members of his party while they were surrounded by a cordon of armed enemies who had their representatives on and about the platform, when an injudicious word, when a hasty or indignant resentment of a studied insult, would have been made the occasion of more cruel deeds of the kind for which the capacity, as well as the disposition, had been often demonstrated. Of some of these meetings the Governor's own report appears in a subsequent chapter.[1] It is only necessary to say here that no man of either party has impugned the courage and fairness of his bearing through this ordeal. Neither the heat of a summer almost without precedent, nor the hostility of foes who were inflamed with the cruel instincts of the middle ages untinctured by the grace of knightly courtesy, made him quail. He confronted the one as he endured the other, with a spirit and fortitude that compelled admiration.

It was not until after the Democratic Convention that the Republican Executive Committee issued the call for the Republican State Convention to meet in Columbia on the 12th of September, nearly a month after the nomination of Wade Hampton. During the interval the peculiar campaign by which the Democratic party hoped to win was thoroughly organized and put in operation. Rifle clubs, artillery companies, and various other military organizations were recruited all over the State. To be a Democrat and not to belong to one of these organizations—all outside the law and in violation of law,—or to disapprove of them, was to incur odium. The motive, the method, and the spirit of this display of force are succinctly exposed in a brief

[1] Chapter XXIII.

paragraph of a letter by Dr. H. V. Redfield to the Cincinnati *Commercial*, which was republished in the Charleston *News and Courier :*

The outsider is apt to be puzzled by accounts of affairs here. He may not understand the formation of "rifle clubs," "rifle teams," "artillery companies," among the whites. What are they afraid of? They are not afraid of any thing. Why, then, this arming? They intend to carry this election, if it is possible to do so. The programme to have "rifle clubs" all over the State, and, while avoiding actual bloodshed as much as possible, to so impress the blacks that they, or a number of them, will feel impelled to vote with the whites out of actual fear. The blacks are timid by nature, timid by habit, timid by education. A display of force unnerves them. The whites understand this, and an immense marching about at night, and appearance at any Republican meeting to "divide time," is with a view to impress the blacks with the sense of danger of longer holding out against white rule. Add to the number they can scare, the number they can buy, and they hope to have enough, united with the solid white vote, to gain the day, elect Hampton, and secure the Legislature.

It was under the *surveillance* of such an enemy and in the face of such demonstrations that the Republicans prosecuted their campaign before their State Convention met. They could hold no announced meeting that was not liable to invasion by a terrorizing mob. Premonitions of the character of the campaign in prospect were abundant on every hand, and it was apparent that voters of the Republican party in many sections of the State would exercise their right of suffrage, as they already exercised their right of assembly, in imminent peril. But the Governor pursued a steady course, avoiding with wise discretion any occasion of just offence, and taking care that no man or party should have reason to complain of a lack of fairness on his part. Within ten days after the nomination of General Hampton, and three weeks before his own nomination, he issued the following public statement as an earnest of the spirit in which he proposed to act:

EXECUTIVE CHAMBER,
COLUMBIA, S. C., August 25, 1876.

It will be my duty to appoint, on or before the 7th proximo, three Commissioners of Election in each county in the State.

It is just and proper, in my judgment, that each political party should be fairly represented in these several Boards, and I therefore purpose to appoint, as a general rule, on each Board two representatives of the Republican party and one of the Democratic party. In all cases I intend to appoint only fair-minded and just men.

I, therefore, invite suggestions and recommendations as to these appointments from both political parties.

I shall decline to appoint candidates for office as Commissioners of Election, and if those first appointed shall thereafter become candidates I shall expect their resignations as Commissioners of Election, and I shall feel warranted in making removals for this cause.

D. H. CHAMBERLAIN,

Governor of South Carolina.

On the night of the 6th of September there occurred in Charleston a riot lasting several hours, which threatened to be a serious matter, but fortunately was subdued by the prepared and prompt action of the State authorities. The occasion was a Democratic political demonstration, and party feeling ran so high that all conservative and order-loving citizens dreaded the event. Although there was much promiscuous firing, but one life was lost, that of a white man; and one policeman was seriously wounded, both being Democrats, and both suffering through misdirected shots of their party friends. The Governor, in referring to the affair in a public letter, several weeks afterwards, said : " It was inexcusable and disgraceful, but it was subdued by the Republican authorities; it was attended by no slaughter, it was followed by no butchery. . . . The riot was the result of high political excitement, and was an exhibition of the dastardly spirit of political intolerance. It has fastened a bloody blot on the party that caused it." These plain words were the accompaniment of a declaration that, according to the best information he had, the fray was begun by a Republican. Again he showed that he held his own party to as rigid a rule of conduct as he applied to its opponents, the plain rule of tolerant liberty subject to law.

CHAPTER XXII.

The Republican State Convention—A Three Days' Session—The Party Committed to an Approval of Governor Chamberlain's Policy of Reform, and Pledged to its Completion—Failure of the Opposition to the Governor—He is Nominated for a Second Term—His Speech Accepting the Nomination—The State Ticket Completed—Elements of Weakness—Governor Chamberlain's Answer to a Call upon Him by the *News and Courier* to Withdraw from the Republican Party and Support the Ticket Headed by Wade Hampton—Comments of the New York *Times* on the Work of the Republican Convention.

THE Republican State Convention assembled on the 13th of September, and did not conclude its work until the morning of the 15th. A large part of the time was taken up in making speeches, and the affairs of the party were abundantly debated. The opponents of the Governor exerted all their influence to compass his defeat, but they were unable. His own addresses to the people had greatly strengthened him, and many county delegations came to the Convention instructed to support him. The contest did not culminate until the final session. On the second day the following statement of party faith and policy was adopted :

I. The Republican party of the State of South Carolina, in Convention assembled, believing that the principles of equal civil and political rights are vital to the interests of good government, and that they can only be enforced by the party which has engrafted them upon the State and National Constitutions, hereby reaffirms its confidence in the National Republican Party by pledging firm adherence to the platform adopted by the Cincinnati Convention in this the one hundredth year of American independence.

II. We hereby pledge our undivided support to the standard-bearers of that party, Rutherford B. Hayes and William A. Wheeler, whose unblemished and statesmanlike record in the past is sufficient assurance that all reforms lying within the province of their respective offices will be earnestly prosecuted, and the National Government wisely and economically administered, with due regard to the rights and interests of the whole American people.

III. We heartily endorse the Administration of President Grant, so honestly and economically conducted as to exalt the nation in the estimation of the world and advance its faith and credit. We recognize in the soldier statesman and President a firm, devoted lover of American liberty, a stern, unflinching champion and protector of the rights of American citizens at home and abroad, and we will ever hold in grateful remembrance his deeds in war, in peace, in all that makes our country great—though the youngest of the nations, yet the equal of all.

IV. That in presenting to the people of South Carolina our nominees for the high offices of the State for the coming two years, we believe we should make plain and unmistakable the aims and principles to which we stand pledged, in the event of their election, not in glittering generalities of reform, but in specific and substantial articles.

V. We declare our abhorrence and repudiation of all forms of violence, intimidation, or fraud in the conduct of elections, or for political purposes, and denounce the same as crime against the liberty of American citizens as well as the common rights of humanity ; and, while we insist upon and will jealously guard the right of every citizen freely to choose his political party, and deny the unfounded charge that the Republican party countenances any interference with colored voters who may choose to vote the Democratic ticket ; we protest against and denounce the practice now inaugurated by the Democratic party in this State of attending Republican meetings and by show of force and other forms of intimidation disturbing such meetings or taking part therein without the consent or invitation of the party calling them.

VI. We pledge ourselves to thorough reform in all departments of the State Government where abuses shall be found to exist, and, as an earnest of the same, declare our purpose of submitting to the qualified voters of the State the following specific reforms as amendments to the State Constitution :

1. That the present adjustment of the bonded debt of the State shall be inviolable.

2. That the General Assembly shall meet only once in every two years, and that the length of no session thereof shall exceed seventy days.

3. That the number of sessions of Courts of General Sessions and Common Pleas shall be reduced to two annually in each county, with power reserved to the Judges to call special sessions when necessary.

4. That the veto power of the Governor shall be so modified as to allow of the disapproval of a part without effect upon the rest of an Act.

5. That agricultural interests shall be relieved from burdensome taxation by a more equitable distribution of taxes and by the inauguration of a system of license fixed upon fair principles.

6. That no public funds shall ever be used for the support of sectarian institutions.

7. That the enormous evil of local and special legislation shall be prohibited whenever private interests can be protected under general laws.

8. And inasmuch as the system of free schools was created in the State by the Republican party, and should be especially fostered and protected by it, we pledge ourselves to the support of the amendment to the State Constitution, now before the people, establishing a permanent tax for the support of free schools, and preventing the removal of school funds from the counties where raised.

VII. We pledge ourselves and the nominees of the Republican party of this State to the securing of the following purposes by legislative enactment :

1. The further and lowest reduction of salaries of all public servants consistent with the necessities of government.

2. The reduction of fees and costs, especially of attorneys in civil cases, and the amendment of the laws governing the settlement of estates in such manner as to secure a more economical administration and settlement of small estates.

3. The immediate repeal of the agricultural lien law.

4. Public printing to be reduced at least one third of the present appropriation.

5. Convict labor to be utilized under such laws as shall secure humane treatment and the support of convicts without needless expense to the State.

6. The annual appropriations for public institutions to be economically made and properly expended.

7. The number of Trial Justices to be reduced throughout the State, and each Justice to be assigned to specific territory ; with moderate salaries to cover costs of criminal business, adjusted in proportion to populations.

VIII. Recognizing the enormous expense of fencing farms, and the scarcity of timber in some sections of the State, we feel it to be necessary that practical relief be afforded to the people of the State, and we pledge ourselves to secure such legislation upon the subject as will give to the electors of each county the right to regulate this question for themselves.

IX. That whereas in some of the upper counties of the State certain evil-disposed persons have induced many citizens to disregard and violate the revenue laws of the United States, by representing them to be oppressive and in violation of the rights of the citizen, and it is apparent from the action of the National Democratic House of Representatives that the revenue tax will be continued, we therefore earnestly recommend that His Excellency, the President of the United States, do grant a general amnesty and pardon for all violations previous to this time. And the Senators are hereby instructed, and the Representatives in Congress are requested, to urge this action without delay.

X. We charge the Democratic party with perversion of all truth and history ; with opposition to all the interests of the masses ; with fostering class preferences and discriminations ; with a denial of rights to those who do not accept their political dogmas ; with constant and persistent antagonism to the principles of justice and humanity ; with a resistance to the manifest will of the people and the spirit of the age ; with a determination to make slavery national and liberty sectional ; with a purpose to rend the Union in twain to perpetuate human bondage ; with plunging the nation into a fratricidal war ; with deluging the land in blood and filling it with sorrow and distress ; with burdening the people with a debt that makes a higher taxation necessary and continuous ; with opposition to the reconstruction of the States they had violently forced into a confederacy ; with resistance to the passage and ratification of the amendments to the Constitution of the United States made necessary by the results of the war, which clothed the humblest in the nation with citizenship and placed in his hands the power of protecting it ; with a purpose to reopen sectional prejudices and animosities, to make "the war a failure," reconstruction "void," and the amendments to the Constitution nullities ; with deception, misrepresentation, extravagance in the conduct of government, dishonesty in the disbursement of the public funds, and an abuse of the public confidence ; with fraud in the management of elections ; with intimidations of electors ; with atrocities during political campaigns unheard of in civilized communities ; with assassinations and murders of those whose only offending was a steadfast adherence to the principles of the Republican party ; with threatenings of violence and death against those who advocate the perpetuity of the Republican party ; with armed preparation and hostile intent in the States of the South, intending by such a formidable array to frighten or force Republicans into a support of their party and partisans, or to remain away from the polls ; with dissembling to the North, by assurances of an acceptance of the results of the war, a desire for reconciliation and brotherly relations, when they are only thirsting for the opportunity to secure what they have lost by the ascendancy of the National Democratic Party to power, and thus inflict upon the nation further evils and embarrassments ; with nominating national and State officers known for their antagonism to all the Republican party has accomplished.

XI. Reiterating our reliance in the justice of our cause and the truth of the principles underlying our national platform, and of the Thirteenth, Fourteenth, and Fifteenth Amendments to the Constitution of the United States, pointing with gratification to the many important reforms established by the Republican party of our State during the last few years, we invoke the guidance and blessing of divine Providence upon our standard-bearers and upon the whole people of South Carolina. And we the members of the Republican party, in Convention assembled, do hereby earnestly pledge ourselves to an uncompromising support of its nominees, with the firm hope and the solemn determination to guard our rights, protect our friends, and elect our candidates.

In spirit and terms this was an unqualified committal of the party to the continuance of the policy pursued by the Governor. The specific declarations regarding reform in administration he formulated and insisted upon. They marked out a course which was obviously advantageous, and, in the interest of good government, necessary ; and they did it so definitely that it would not be easy for any Republican to avoid the duties thus assumed.

A large part of the subsequent sessions was occupied with speeches advocating and opposing the renomination of the Governor. The opposition was marshalled and led by R. B. Elliott, Speaker of the House of Representatives, C. C. Bowen, Sheriff of Charleston, B. F. Whittemore, an ex-Congressman, and others of like fame as politicians. The discussion continued from noon of the second day more than fourteen hours without cessation, Mr. Elliott making the last speech in opposition, to whom the Governor himself replied. The reporter of the Charleston *News and Courier* in his despatch said : " The scene in the April Convention was repeated. The Governor took up each point that had been made against him, and answered it amid the cheers of his supporters." His victory was not less complete. He was immediately nominated, receiving eighty-eight out of a total of one hundred and twenty-three votes, thirty-one being cast for T. C. Dunn, then Comptroller General of the State.

By this result it was shown that the Governor was able to command the support of his party in the course upon which he had entered. Respecting the differences between himself and the legislative faction that had attempted to thwart him, he had yielded nothing and apologized for nothing; but he had often publicly expressed his regret that he had not power to prosecute the reform work more vigorously. All the threatenings and all the efforts to secure his humiliation, made by those whose mistaken and corrupt schemes he had frustrated, had been fruitless. By plain, frank, earnest appeal to the good-sense and the better sentiment of the voters who constituted the controlling majority of the Republican party in South Carolina, without concealment or degradation of his aims, without pandering to their prejudices, without resort to any charlatanry or delusive tricks, he had measured forces with those who thought that influence over ignorant and untutored minds could more certainly be gained by other arts than those of honesty and straightforwardness, and he had achieved a notable triumph. The lesson is one that may be remembered for encouragement and strengthening whenever political leaders are tempted to believe that the way to contend successfully with demagogues and unscrupulous rivals is to overmatch them in cajolery. Unless it be true that in a fair and clear presentation of an issue the great body of the people, the uncultured and the unfortunate as well as the learned and the rich, may be depended upon to prefer what is honest to what is dishonest, what is honorable to what is shameful, the warrant for confidence in the permanence of Republican institutions has little value. The consistent integrity of the Governor's speech and action made no confusion in any mind. They were mutually illustrative; and they made the issue between him and his enemies so definite and complete that the humblest Republican could understand and estimate it; and because he could do that, he had no option without wronging his own sense of right.

In the speech which the Governor made accepting the nomination, he said:

This victory is doubly joyful to me because I know it has not been obtained by any of those processes or influences which have been said at times to control the Republican party in South Carolina. The men who have supported me are no band of mercenaries, but a gallant, devoted, patriotic company of Republicans of South Carolina, who have believed that I represented certain principles, certain aspirations, and certain purposes of the great Republican party in this State, which could be carried into practice through my agency better than that of other men offered for your consideration as candidates.

He spoke for some time regarding the issues of national politics as they affected the people of South Carolina, then turning to subjects of immediate concern, he proceded in a strain which reveals, with eloquent distinctness, both his aspirations and his anxieties. If he had left nothing else on record, the following passages from this address, in consideration of the circumstances of their delivery, would infallibly indicate the motive and spirit of his acceptance of official responsibilities.

But I accept this nomination as significant of another thing. I accept it as significant of the desire of the Republican party of South Carolina for the continuance, for a higher degree, for a more complete carrying out of the reforms demanded by the present condition of our public affairs. I accept it in this sense with peculiar joy, because it has been my fortune for two years to have been conspicuous in the contest which has gone on here in behalf of what we may call administrative reform and good government.

Fellow-citizens, I have always had a profound confidence in the desire of the common people of South Carolina for good government. I have seen occasions when those who have been reared as Republicans, taught to believe that universal suffrage was safe because it was right, have faltered in their confidence in the success of this people in bringing about good government in South Carolina. But I can say for myself that my confidence in their capacity has never been lost, and I have believed, through all the mismanagement, corruption, and wrongs of their leaders, that the colored people, the colored masses of South Carolina, were as loyal as any people in this country to the demands and necessity of good government in South Carolina. [Cheers.] It is in that spirit that I have occupied the last two months in visiting the counties of this State in order that I might speak to the people, not only in behalf of the principles of Republicanism, but especially in behalf of the principles and policy of reform in South Carolina.

And, let me say here, on no occasion have I found the people failing in their real and sincere desire that good government should be restored and made permanent and effective in South Carolina. The result of this Convention, in my judgment, in selecting me as the nominee for Governor is due to the spirit of the people of South Carolina more than to the leaders of the Republican party. The people of South

Carolina have believed that in the contest of the last two years I have represented faithfully the principles and the idea of reform, and their voice has been heard in this Convention, and without any of the appliances or influences which have characterized former conventions, they have stood under the fire of the most vigorous assaults, and have declared their purpose that through me, and those you associate with me on this ticket, the great cause of reform should go forward until every burden that oppresses this people should be put away forever. I accept this nomination, therefore, as an endorsement of my conduct upon the subject of reform. If I could not regard it as an endorsement of my Administration I could not accept it, because I have no purpose in occupying public position in South Carolina, except that I may be instrumental in putting the Republican party upon a platform that will cause it to command the respect and confidence of the nation. [Loud cheering.]

You know how little, comparatively, has yet been done in this great work of reform in the last two years, but enough has been done to point the way and to encourage us to future efforts. Taxes have been reduced ; a higher tone among public officials has been introduced ; the judicial bench has been saved from pollution ; public moneys have been honestly disbursed ; official accountability has been established ; and now, upon the basis of what has been done, it remains for us, in the spirit of the platform now adopted, to go forward, devoted to the idea of reform as something that is due to all the people of the State, and devoted to it because it is the only hope and only possibility of success, permanently or presently, for any political party in South Carolina. [Cheers.]

Mr. President and gentlemen, I might pause here, but I think it is due to the position which I hold towards the coming campaign that I should seek to impress upon you the necessity of completing your work in the spirit in which it has been begun. If you have nominated me to represent the reforms which have been inaugurated during the last two years ; if your nomination is an endorsement to any extent of my Administration, then you are bound to see to it that the ticket that is to be associated with me shall be a ticket in harmony with those principles and those purposes. [Cheers.] I confess to you frankly that it will be a difficult question for me to determine, if I am not surrounded by those whose sympathy and support I can enjoy, whether it will be worth while for me to enter upon this campaign. I am not willing to admit, and do not, that you will fail to carry out the work you have begun in the spirit in which you have begun it. Put upon this ticket none but honorable, honest, and competent Republicans. Fill every office upon this ticket in a manner that shall strengthen the nomination which you have already made. [Cheers.]

I cannot, of course, enter into details, but you cannot mistake, in the issues which will come before you, the meaning of my words when I say that if this ticket, at the head of which you have placed me, is to win, it must be made up of those who are in harmony with the principles and policy which I represent ; and not only that, but hereafter, when the other local conventions of the Republican party shall be assembled, and especially when you come to make up your legislative tickets, above all things don't place before me again the task which I have borne during the last two years, of standing for the cause of reform against a Legislature the majority of whom were not in sympathy with me. [Cheers.]

It is a thankless task, an almost fruitless task, for the Executive to undertake to carry out the platform of a party unless he is supported by the Legislature. If I am not mistaken, therefore, in my interpretation of your purpose in selecting me, I am certainly justified in calling upon you in all your subsequent nominations to select those who represent the cause of reform, who have opinions which they will stand up for, even at the expense of immediate popularity ; men who are willing to give advice or take action which may not be agreeable even to their own party. I have but little respect for political life or political men if we have not arrived at such a position that we are able to go forward in the path of duty without immediate success.

I confess I have never counted the cost of these struggles. If I had I should never have entered on them. But my gratitude to God is constant that in the trials that have come upon me during the past two years I have been enabled to do my duty without regard to consequences. [Cheers.]

In that spirit I stand here to-day for the Republican party and for reform, for the complete and entire carrying out of governmental reforms in South Carolina. I am for shaking off all the remaining abuses that now hinder our progress and success. I am for marching forward in the same line which the party as a whole has taken during the last two years. I propose to take no step backwards, but to take up the cause of reform and carry it forward, and I don't know why I am selected to lead in this canvass if that is not the spirit of the majority of this Convention and the Republican party of South Carolina. [Loud cheers.]

It is needless for me to say that we are entering upon a most arduous and difficult campaign. No campaign which the Republican party has seen in South Carolina can compare with this in the intensity of spirit already evoked, in the importance of the contest in the estimation of both parties. We must enter upon it upheld and inspired by our political principles, and not by the mere desire for political power. I shall enter it in that spirit. I propose to advocate throughout the State of South Carolina, wherever the people shall desire me to address them, without fear of consequences, with such protection as the State and United States can give me, in all their length and breadth, the principles of the Republican party and Republican reform. [Cheers.] But we need to cheer ourselves with a constant appreciation of the cause in which we are engaged ; that our liberties, our progress, our happiness, not only as a party, but as a people, are wrapped up in the issues of this campaign. No matter what dangers threaten, let us go forward as honest and sincere Republicans. For myself, I dare now appropriate the consecrating words of one whose devotion to freedom and equal rights I early learned to reverence : " I boast no courage. I fear sometimes that I may turn out to be no better than a timid man. But I do trust still that every drop of blood in these veins of mine would be freely given to stain the scaffold or boil and bubble at the stake before by any act of mine," the principles of the Republican party shall be betrayed or its great record dishonored. [Great applause.]

But the Convention to which this brilliant appeal was made was not able wisely to justify it. Like many other conventions of all parties, North and South, national as well as State, it felt bound to promote harmony and good feeling by giving the faction beaten in the superior contest a salve for their hurt. The ticket was completed by the following nominations: For Lieutenant Governor, Richard H. Gleaves ; for Secretary of State, Henry E. Hayne; for Comptroller General, T. C. Dunn ; for State Treasurer, F. L. Cardozo ; for Attorney General, R. B. Elliott; for Superintendent of Education, John B. Tolbert ; for Adjutant General, James Kennedy. Probably nothing did more to perfect the consolidation of the Democratic party and destroy all hope of support for Governor Chamberlain from that quarter than the nomination of R. B. Elliott for Attorney General, and the renomination of Comptroller-General Dunn. Both of these men had been pronounced and bitter enemies of reform and of Governor Chamberlain's policy. How keen was his disappointment and how thoroughly he appreciated the mischief, will appear in the sequel.[1]

A few days after the Convention had finished its work, the Charleston *News and Courier* formally called upon Governor Chamberlain, in view of the action of the Convention in giving sanction and honor to Elliott, to redeem his profession of devotion to a reform policy by withdrawing from the Republican State ticket and giving support to the candidates of the Democratic party for State officers. To that call the following response, understood to have been written by Governor Chamberlain himself, appeared in the Columbia *Union-Herald* of September 22d. No doubt it was intended as a reply to all criticism of his course in accepting the nomination.

[1] See Appendix. Letter to William Lloyd Garrison.

The editorial article in the Charleston *News and Courier* of the 19th instant, deserves further notice. Aside from its direct personal reference to Governor Chamberlain as an individual, its authorship entitles it to reply. The relations of the *News and Courier* to Governor Chamberlain during the past two years—relations of cordial and honorable coöperation in the cause of reform in our State affairs—give a peculiar signification to the attitude of these parties to-day, and make it important to present Governor Chamberlain s views of his present position and duty in contrast and opposition to those of the *News and Courier.*

We shall undertake to present Governor Chamberlain's views, but we shall write in a spirit of respect towards the gentlemen who conduct the *News and Courier*, and of regret that a deep and radical difference must now take the place of former harmony and coöperation.

The attitude and policy of the Democratic party under its present leadership should first be considered. That policy is the "Edgefield" policy. The men who dictated it were the Butlers and Garys and Lipscombs and Tillmans and Aikens. No man will deny this. A clear majority of that party, including conspicuously the editors of the *News and Courier*, are to-day enlisted under leaders and seeking to carry out a policy which does not command the approval of either their heads or hearts. This policy has been forced on them by the most unwise, impracticable, reactionary, and aggressive men of their party. The essence of that policy is intimidation. The only hope of its success is intimidation. The editors of the *News and Courier* know this. Every intelligent man in this State knows that Dr. Redfield, the careful correspondent of the *Cincinnati Commercial,* states the truth when he says in his letter, reprinted in the *News and Courier* of the 19th instant, that "nine hundred and ninety-nine out of a thousand of the blacks will, when left to an untrammelled choice, vote the straight Republican ticket."

This is the party and policy which the *News and Courier,* contrary to its judgment and conscience, in defiance of all its protests and warnings and entreaties, finds itself forced to adopt and advocate at this moment. The editors of the *News and Courier* are the galley-slaves of the Butlers and Garys, whom, personally and politically, they detest. But we find them equal to the emergency. Not only have they consented to abdicate every opinion they have expressed for the last two years, but, under the eye of their taskmasters, they seek to wipe out, by superserviceable zeal, the remembrance of their former opposition to the policy they now find themselves compelled to advocate.

Such is the position of the Democratic party and of the *News and Courier.* Is it not, then, a most marvellous example of assurance when we find this paper, with apparent seriousness, calling upon Governor Chamberlain, a Republican, to assist in securing the success of a ticket and policy which three months ago the *News and Courier* itself openly and earnestly denounced? We tell the editors of the *News and Courier* that Governor Chamberlain is a free man no matter who else are slaves.

He will never, by word or act, by doing or failing to do, contribute in any degree to the success in this State of a party led by the Edgefield crew. The *News and Courier* is to-day dishonoring itself, not only in the eyes of the world, but in its own eyes, by yielding to what it deems a necessity. Does the *News and Courier* flatter itself that it will have influence with the Democratic party if it succeeds in this campaign? It has already been notified by the Chairman of the State Committee that its former liberality cannot and will not be forgiven. The spirit of Edgefield will rule the State. That spirit is simply brutal, blood-thirsty, revengeful, devilish.

We will consider next the position of the Republican party. Governor Chamberlain has been nominated on a platform which is wholly unexceptionable, a platform vastly more satisfactory than that of the Democratic party. The platform of the Democracy lacks a single specific pledge or promise. It commits the party to no single practical measure of reform. The Republican platform, on the other hand, presents a practical programme of reform. All its pledges are specific and defined. They cover the entire demands of reform at this time in South Carolina.

Upon this platform Governor Chamberlain has been nominated as the deliberate, well-considered, determined choice of more than two thirds of the Convention. So far, certainly, a great advance has been made. Two years ago, as the *News and Courier* itself points out, he was nominated by many of those who supported him under the belief that reform with him was a mere cover and pretence. To-day, after his two years of constant and conspicuous fidelity to practical reform, in all its features, he is again nominated with the full knowledge of his purposes and character as an executive officer. The gain here for reform is simply immense.

We come, now, to the pretence upon which the *News and Courier*, and one or two who have called themselves Republicans, have seized to demand of Governor Chamberlain that he shall assist in the election of Hampton. It is that the remainder of the Republican ticket is of such a character as to demand of Governor Chamberlain his refusal to remain at its head. In answer to this, it is to be said, first, that the ticket is, except in one particular, as good, and, perhaps, on the whole, better than any ticket heretofore placed in nomination by the Republican party. The two most important officers, the Treasurer and the Comptroller General remain the same. The nominees for Superintendent of Education and Adjutant General are generally held to be equal if not superior, to the present incumbents. It is only in reference to the nomination for Attorney General that the claim can be made that Governor Chamberlain should withdraw. Admitting, for argument's sake, that the objections to General Elliott are well founded, and that he will be opposed to Governor Chamberlain and reform during the next two years, it is still manifest that General Elliott will occupy a far less important position in relation to Governor Chamberlain and reform than he has held during the past two years as Speaker of the

House of Representatives. In this respect there is no loss, but a gain. But there is no warrant for the assumption that General Elliott will oppose any reform measure laid down in the present platform of the party. On the contrary, he is pledged and bound, as a man and as a politician, to stand by that platform and Governor Chamberlain.

There is, then, a positive gain, both in the platform and ticket of the Republican party, for reform and good government. Governor Chamberlain has distinctly triumphed over his enemies within the party, and he is to-day its leader in a sense in which he has never been before. Every indication, moreover, points to better nominations by the Republican party for members of the General Assembly and for the county offices.

Such is the position of the Republican party towards Governor Chamberlain and the cause of reform. A substantial gain and advance has been made. In every respect the party is to-day more thoroughly committed than ever before to Governor Chamberlain's leadership and policy.

We are now in a position to ask what reasons are there to induce Governor Chamberlain to heed the call of the *News and Courier* and withdraw from the ticket? We answer, none whatever. Every consideration which has heretofore governed his course upon the question of reform dictates to him the necessity of standing firmly and cordially by the Republican party and its platform and ticket. He will do so. He will do so in full loyalty to the cause of reform, in full consistency with his own record as Governor, with all his convictions of duty, with all his past utterances and professions as a public man and a citizen. If he turns to the Democracy, he finds it the party of violence, proscription, and fraud. He finds it in the hands of men who are the worst foes South Carolina now holds to her peace and welfare; men whose characters and careers are the abhorrence of the country, and whose policy, at least, is abhorrent to every honest conviction of the editors of the *News and Courier*. If, on the other hand, he turns to the Republican party, he finds the prospect for reform brightening on every side.

Governor Chamberlain will, therefore, stand earnestly and unreservedly by the Republican party in this campaign. It is his mission again to rescue the people of this State who oppose him from their own madness and folly. He will be elected, and, as Governor, he will continue to command the confidence of the editors of the *News and Courier*, who will again have reason to wish to forget the craze of partisanship or the bondage of political necessity, which alone could have led them to write the article to which we have now replied.

The New York *Times* (September 4th), in an editorial article on the renomination of Governor Chamberlain, said:

The renomination of Governor Chamberlain by the Republican Convention of South Carolina is a grateful act, and one that is eminently politic. It upsets calculations that have been built upon an expectation of Republican dissensions, and identifies the party in the State with the reform purposes and plans which are really the secret of the hostility the Governor has encountered. The condition of the State at the time he entered office was bad enough. The public money was squandered. Gross corruption prevailed everywhere. Most of the offices were unworthily filled. The whole system might have been set down as a travesty of self-government had the practical consequences been less disastrous.   .   .   .

Governor Chamberlain is entitled to the credit of having exerted the influence of his office to stem the tide of political demoralization, to root out abuses and wrong, and to wrest the controlling power, legislative and judicial, from hands that were perverting and disgracing it. In the performance of this task he ran many risks and made many enemies. The demagogues whose plans he thwarted, misrepresented his motives to the ignorant electors, and threw all possible obstacles in the way of his plans. His efforts to promote Republican reform were assailed as treason to Republican principles. His avowed determination to drive into oblivion the adventurers who had traded upon the credulity of their followers, was denounced as evidence that he had gone over to the Democracy. He persevered, nevertheless. He did what he could to improve the credit of the State. He marked for extinction abuses that were rank in the State administration. He urged economy upon the Legislature. He stripped rascally leaders of their claims to partisan support. And with a moral courage which at this distance is not easily appreciated, he interposed his authority to prevent the further degradation of the judiciary by keeping off the bench a notoriously unfit man. At one time a split in the Republican ranks seemed to be an inevitable consequence of this fearless devotion to the right. The Democrats were disposed to coquette with the Governor, and, by affecting friendship, precipitate the break between him and the party that had elected him. They wooed in vain. The Governor kept on his course. He confronted his accusers at Republican meetings, and vanquished them. He remained steadfast in the work of reform, but insisted that it should be reform within the party, by agencies of its own creation.

We have the result in last Friday's action of the Republican Convention   .   .   . The Convention has not only sustained the Governor by placing him once more at the head of the State ticket, but has adopted and bound itself to carry forward the reforms he has persistently advocated. The fact is encouraging, both for the State and the Republican party. It shows that among the freedmen of South Carolina, whom the Democrats are accustomed to deride as unfit for political power, educating forces are at work which will deliver the State from the bondage of misgovernment, and render the Republican organization the means of effecting all needed reforms.

CHAPTER XXIII.

ON the day succeeding the renomination of Governor Chamberlain, there broke out at Ellenton, in Aiken County, a riot which was continued with vindictive passion by horrible murders for several days. It was as revolting in circumstances of wanton barbarity as the Hamburg massacre, and multiplied by many fold the victims of that bloody affair. The story is told with studied reserve and caution by Governor Chamberlain in a letter written three weeks afterwards to A. C. Haskell, Esq., Chairman of the Democratic State Committee, who on the 28th of September had addressed a letter to Governor Chamberlain, the extraordinary purport of which is fairly set forth by the Governor in his elaborate response made October 4th. From this letter liberal extracts are given. They reveal a state of things of which only a glimpse has been had hitherto, and make plain the conditions of the contest then fairly begun.

COLUMBIA, S. C., October 4, 1876.

A. C. Haskell, Esq., Chairman Democratic State Executive Committee, Columbia. S. C.:

SIR—I have received your communication of the 28th ultimo, covering several matters connected with the political canvass now in progress in this State and the general condition of our public affairs. You first invite me and the nominees upon the Republican State ticket "to attend the Democratic mass-meetings which are being held in succession in each county in the State." This part of your communication would have been addressed more naturally—and I trust you will permit me to add, more properly—to the Chairman of the Republican State Committee, whose function it is, as the organ of that Committee, to consider and determine the methods and order of the canvass on the part of the Republican party. In answer, therefore, to your invitation, I am unable to say more than that I have informed the Chairman of the Republican State Committee that as soon as the duties of my office, which now imperatively require my presence at the capital, shall permit it, I shall be ready to meet General Hampton at any suitable points in the State, not in "Democratic mass-meetings," but in mass-meetings to be called by both parties for the purpose of joint discussions, upon terms of perfect equality in all respects, of the political issues now before our people. You will doubtless receive at an early day a proposition of such a nature from the Republican State Committee, with such suggestions regarding details as will commend themselves to your sense of fairness and secure the objects which you profess to seek in your invitation—the removal of "the bitterness of race feeling, which we (you) attribute to the prejudices and erroneous views which have been instilled into the colored race," and a "peaceful and untrammelled discussion, that the people may become enlightened on the issues of the day." In saying this, I am confident I faithfully represent also the wishes and purposes of all my associates on the Republican State ticket.

The remainder of your communication is occupied with statements of what you claim to be the spirit and conduct and purposes of the Democratic party in the State, with a special call upon me "as Governor and candidate," to contradict certain alleged statements respecting the present condition of the State and the action of men who belong to the Democratic party, which you call "slanderous charges," or to "look into them by going in person to ascertain the truth." You say that "my appearance before the Democracy throughout the State will be to me as Governor a most pleasing refutation to the slanderous charges which constantly are published against your party in some newspapers which claim to be my political organs, and also in the Northern papers, backed by the name of Senator Patterson or some other person who claims to be my political friend and exponent." You say that I am, "as Governor and candidate, bound by my gubernatorial pledge and honor to prevent my followers using the sanction of my official silence to sustain these charges against my opponents, when these charges allege the overthrow of the peace and dignity of the State which I am sworn to defend." You present three examples of the charges to which you refer, taken from the Washington correspondence, respectively, of the New York *Sun*, New York *World*, and New York *Tribune*. You say that "these utterances, in the instances above cited, are totally false, and affect the character of the State," and that if I "believe them to be true it is my duty to restore peace and order, and to do so it is my sworn duty to call upon the citizens to sustain me and enforce the law."

You proceed further to say that "I, and no one better, know that the white people of South Carolina are struggling as few people ever have done to cast off a burthen of corruption and wrong, such as yet fewer people have ever borne so long," and you proceed to make extended quotations from former remarks of mine respecting our public affairs, and to say that the men who committed the wrongs which I denounced "are the same men who control the ticket upon which my name stands, who devised my party platform, and are to-day my political exponents." You say that I "know that it is against all this that our unfortunate people are struggling, and yet that I know full well that their efforts, although in the warmth of canvass, are orderly and within the law." You say that my "manhood compels me to approve your course," and finally you declare that "as Governor of the State I am called upon to either contradict the assertion that the law is overthrown, and that terrorism prevails, or to suppress this lawlessness," and that "it is your right that I call upon you before I appeal to the Government of the United States."

I am pleased to observe and acknowledge the respectful terms in which your statements and charges are framed, so far as they affect me. These statements and charges cover in substance the whole field of our present political controversy, together with the matters growing out of that controversy, and affecting the public peace and the common civil rights of our citizens. In addition to your direct call upon me, in your character as the official representative of the Democratic party, to express my views upon the matters presented by you, the nature of your communication and the statements and charges which you make seem to compel me to speak. I do this with profound reluctance. Not only will the expression of my views disclose how widely you and I stand apart upon all the questions involved, but it will, in my sober judgment, disclose to the world a condition of things inexpressibly disgraceful to the good name of our State. Though General Hampton is reported to have said substantially, in recent public speeches, that I could not, by reason of my nativity, feel such an interest and pride in the fame of South Carolina as becomes her Governor, and, though you may share in this opinion, I still venture to say to you that I have regretted deeply the receipt of your communication, because it forces me, while I hold my present high office, to present views and convictions which, if correct, reflect infinite discredit upon a large portion of the people of this State. It is, however, as portions of your communication show, no new experience to me to find myself compelled by a sense of duty to pursue a course which has subjected me, not only, as in the present instance, to the increased hostility of political opponents, but to the suspicion and denunciation of political friends. But I profess to put my duty to the State above all other present considerations, and that duty, as I understand it, requires me to reply to your communication fully, plainly, and fearlessly.

SLANDEROUS CHARGES.

With respect to the specific instances of "slanderous charges," which you cite from the New York papers, let me first say that the statements respecting me made in the *Sun* and the *World* are wholly untrue and unfounded. Nothing remotely resembling what is there stated was ever said or done by me.[1] The extract from the *Tribune* professes to give the views and statements of Senator Patterson, for which I am not responsible. How far my views coincide with or differ from those attributed to Senator Patterson will best appear in what I shall hereafter say. I shall now proceed to present my views upon the several matters relating to our present political condition which are covered by your communication.

THE ISSUE STATED.

Your claim in substance is that I am the head of a party and ticket which represents and is responsible for a burden of corruption and wrongs grievously oppressive to the State ; that the success of that party and ticket would be disastrous to the interests of the State ; that my position upon that ticket is inconsistent with my public record ; that the Democracy, on the other hand, are engaged in a political struggle with the sole aim of freeing the State from this burden of corruption and wrongs, and that all your methods and actions are peaceful and within the law. In support of your view of my present position, you refer to my public denunciations of past acts of the Republican party or its members. You thus challenge not only my political integrity and honor, but my personal consistency as a public man. In order properly to meet your challenge, especially as to my personal consistency, I must refer to the course of events in this State during the last two years.

A REVIEW.

I was nominated and elected in 1874 as the candidate of the Republican party, under pledges, both personal and party, to reform the abuses which then existed. In my Inaugural Address I developed in detail my plans of reform—plans which met the earnest approval of the general public of the State without regard to party. That I pursued the course there marked out earnestly and faithfully is a claim which cannot be successfully or even plausibly disputed. I found a

---

[1] These statements were in special despatches from Washington, and alleged that Governor Chamberlain had violently abused the Democratic leaders ; had declared that he was " done with reform talk, and henceforth the Legislature would find no barrier in him "; and had arranged to have 20,000 stands of arms shipped from New York to South Carolina to be put in the hands of the blacks.

considerable part of my own party opposed to my course, and thus my fidelity to my pledges and to the cause of reform, as I understood it, was put to severe and unexpected tests. It is not egotism but truth which leads me to affirm that I bore those tests in a manner which commanded the praise of the friends of reform throughout the State. The press of this State, the public utterances of its leading citizens, every organ of public opinion, will furnish the proof of this assertion. My record as Governor was elaborately reviewed in July last by the Charleston *News and Courier*—beyond comparison the ablest, and, in a normal condition of affairs, the most liberal, Democratic newspaper in this State or in the South—in a series of editorial articles founded on official and indisputable records. From the closing article of this series, entitled " The Record of Governor Chamberlain—A Summary," I make the following extracts [1] : . . .

This is the record of Governor Chamberlain as shown by hard figures and un-mistakable facts. We have strained or exaggerated nothing. The plain truth as we know it has been faithfully given. And we maintain that the record as it stands is one of which Governor Chamberlain has cause to be proud, that it justifies the sup-port which has been given him, and is a complete answer to those of our friends who think that no act of Governor Chamberlain deserves public commendation but his refusal to issue the commissions to Whipper and Moses. That bold act applauded everywhere in South Carolina has not been mentioned in these articles. . . .

No act or word of mine since the publication of those articles, and up to my renomination as Governor during the past month, can be pointed to which is inconsistent with the record thus presented. I was a candidate for renomination by the Republican party upon my record as a Republican reformer. Every man and every newspaper speaking for me or representing me, placed his advocacy of my renomination upon the distinct ground of my fidelity and success in the work of reform in this State. I myself during the months of July and August last made an extensive canvass of the State, addressing mass-meetings in over twenty counties, and on every occasion when I addressed the people without hindrance or restraint (the exceptional occasions I shall refer to hereafter), I announced in clear and aggressive terms my determina-tion to push forward the work of reform, declared that I stood upon my record as Governor, and had become again a candidate solely for the purpose of completing the work I had already begun. The issue involved in my candidacy for renomination was everywhere proclaimed by my friends and admitted by my enemies to be the endorsement or rejection, by the Republican party, of my work and policy of reform. Upon the assembling of the Republican nominating Convention during the past month it appeared that fully two thirds of its members were immovably determined upon my renomination. I have never heard of a suspicion or hint that any motives were presented to any members of that Convention to influence their action, except the single considera-

---

[1] As this article is given complete in chapter XVIII., pp. 304–306, all but the final paragraph quoted is here omitted.

tion of my merits or demerits as presented in my record of the past two years. My renomination was earnestly, not to say violently, opposed by a minority of the Convention, but this opposition was placed wholly upon charges of my want of fidelity to strictly partisan interests of the Republican party or a failure to sufficiently regard the interests and wishes of some members of the party.

THE REPUBLICAN PLATFORM.

In preparing the platform of our party I was invited by the Committee having the work in charge to meet the Committee and to present my views. I accepted this invitation, and I here present those portions of the platform adopted by the Convention to which my efforts were especially directed.[1] . . .

I make no comment on this platform further than to invite its comparison with the platform of the Democratic party, and its examination as a statement of the practical reforms and changes now demanded by the best interests of the State.

RESULTS ACCOMPLISHED.

Two results accomplished by the Republican Convention have now been presented. First, my renomination by more than a two-thirds vote upon the sole and distinct issue of my reform record ; second, the adoption by the Convention of a platform which binds the Republican party to reform in general and to reform in detail,—a platform which must meet the approval of every man who is familiar with the present practical wants of the State. I now present these two results as a complete refutation of your charge of personal inconsistency on my part in accepting my present position on the Republican ticket, as well as a vindication and proof of the determination of the Republican party to carry forward and complete the work of reform. So far as these two results are concerned, I do not know how my policy and record as Governor—which has commanded, as I have shown, in its relations to reform, the cordial praise and approval of almost every man in your party—could have received a more signal or satisfactory endorsement by my own party. Looking at these results my position is one of complete, fairly earned, honorable triumph. It is far better than that—it is an ample and remarkable triumph of the great cause of governmental reform in this State.

NOMINATION OF MR. ELLIOTT.

But there are expressions in your communication which indicate that in your view the alleged inconsistency and dishonor of my present position lie in my association upon the Republican ticket with certain other nominees, and especially with Mr. Elliott, the nominee for Attorney General. Of my associates upon the State ticket, other than Mr. Elliott, I know of no alleged public cause of complaint or dissatisfac-

---

[1] The portions of the platform here quoted are sections IV., VI., and VII., with the specifications embraced in the last two. See Chap. XXII., pp. 353, 354.

tion, except that two of them have disapproved of my course as Governor on certain party grounds, while I ought not to omit to add that in the renomination of Mr. Cardozo as Treasurer, a gentleman who has been my conspicuous and devoted friend and supporter in every feature of my Administration, the cause of reform has achieved another most notable triumph. With reference to the nomination of Mr. Elliott, I am charged with individual inconsistency and want of fidelity to reform because Mr. Elliott has opposed my course as Governor in some important features and was strenuously opposed to my renomination. It is true that Mr. Elliott has differed from me widely in some instances, and particularly in respect to the election of Whipper as Circuit Judge and my refusal to sign his commission. If it be inconsistent and dishonorable for me to remain upon the ticket for this cause I think I can point you to similar instances of dishonor among those who still command your support.

Governor Tilden was nominated by the Democratic party as a professed hard-money candidate on a professed hard-money platform. He is associated on the same ticket with Governor Hendricks, his most prominent opponent for the nomination of President, and the leading champion of soft money and inflation. No more pronounced antagonism of views upon the leading political issue, prior to their nomination, could have existed; yet we now see Governor Tilden and Governor Hendricks adjusting themselves, with a skill and success greatly satisfactory to your party, at least, upon the same ticket and the same platform, and I hear no charge of inconsistency or dishonor against Governor Tilden from the Democratic party.

But I do not choose to answer your charge with this retort alone. While it is true—and I think it due to myself to state the fact—that I did not approve of or aid in or consent to the nomination of Mr. Elliott, it is also true that Mr. Elliott, at the time of his nomination and since, has declared his full and cordial acceptance of the work of the Convention in renominating me and in adopting the platform which pledges the party and its nominees to thorough and specific reforms. The causes of his nomination were not his opposition to me or to reform, but his admitted ability for the position, his long record of political service to his party, and a desire, as in the case of Governor Hendricks, to conciliate an element of the party which had been defeated in my renomination. I am, therefore, in no sense compromised or dishonored in my character as a reformer by my association upon the same ticket with Mr. Elliott. On the contrary, I am entitled to all the confidence ever bestowed upon me in that respect, so far as my individual or personal position is concerned, and I am entitled to all the increase of confidence which comes from my success in bringing my own party to endorse me and the entire policy of reform which I have inaugurated and carried on, and the consequent increase of my ability to serve that cause.

Whenever you or others present the record of my denunciations of past wrongs done by the Republican party in this State, you present that portion ot my record of which I am most proud ; for, while it is very easy to float with the tide of party sentiment and action, it is some test of one's fidelity to duty to denounce the actions of one's party associates and defy their opposition and hatred.   I stand by every word and syllable of that record.   I wish the record were longer and louder, though, as it stands, I challenge its comparison with that of any man in this State who now opposes me.

WHIPPER AND MOSES.

Your communication lays special emphasis, as supporting your position, upon the election of Whipper and Moses, and you quote conspicuously my denunciations of those elections.   I reaffirm every word you quote, and I further declare that what I then asserted to be the only path of duty or safety for the Republican party has been done. Whipper and Moses and all who go with them have been repudiated and "unloaded."   Their elections have been defeated and their threatened elevation to the bench of South Carolina has been prevented. Moses has resigned, and Whipper has been compelled to seek the courts, wherein ninety-nine out of every hundred of the lawyers of this State regard his claim as destined to sure defeat.   And this has been accomplished by the Republican party ; for whatever I have done is chargeable to the credit of the Republican party, which has now endorsed and renominated me.   "Courage, determination, union, victory," have been "our watchwords," and in that sign we have conquered.

Such, sir, is my answer to your charge of personal inconsistency and dishonor in accepting my present position on the Republican State ticket, and to your further charge that the success of that ticket would be disastrous to the interests of our people.   I occupy individually to-day a greatly advanced position on the line of the great battle of reform, and I have behind me, following my lead, the united Republican party of this State.

THE "CONSERVATIVE" POLICY.

I must now examine your claim that the Democratic party is engaged in the present canvass in a simple struggle to throw off the burden of misgovernment, and that all your methods and agencies are legitimate and peaceful.

You are aware that the present policy of the Democratic party in this State was earnestly opposed, and its adoption deeply deplored, by a portion of that party amounting to nearly a majority, and I am aware that that policy is still deeply deplored by many of the members of that party.   The opponents of that policy embraced the leading and only widely circulated newspaper in the State, the Charleston *News and Courier,* as well as a great number of our most honored and experienced citizens, in all ranks and occupations of our society.   If I were to call the roll of those names I think it would be found to embrace and represent a vast preponderance of the talent, property, political experience, and breadth of sentiment and view in our State.   The grounds of their opposition to the policy, popularly called the "straight-out" policy, were clearly defined, and had exclusive reference to the advancement of the cause of practical reform in the State. They knew and recognized the fact that the Republican party embraced a majority of at least twenty-five thousand of the voters of the State. They knew and recognized the fact that the colored race, who constitute the larger part of the Republican voters, were attached to that party by ties the strongest which ever govern men's political actions—the profound conviction, whether mistaken or not, that the great boons so recently conferred on them—freedom and suffrage—were safe only, in their full breadth and beneficence, under the protection of the party which had conferred them. They believed, upon evidence too clear to leave room for doubt, that for this cause no number of these voters, sufficient to change the relations of our parties, could be detached from the Republican party by argument or legitimate persuasion, or other lawful methods of influencing their political action. They recognize in me one whose Republicanism was original and radical, but whose course in the practical conduct of public affairs gave assurance that I had the true interests of all the people of the State as my guiding principle in public life. Upon these grounds the men to whom I refer counselled a policy which subordinated the interests of party to the good of the State. Their policy contemplated, first, the acquiescence of the Democratic party in my nomination by the Republican party, if that should take place, and such other of the nominees upon the Republican State ticket as should be unexceptionable ; and, second, an effort by all conciliatory and legitimate means to secure a large minority of representation for the Democratic party in both Houses of the Legislature, and in all local or county offices. In the May convention of the Democratic party this policy apparently received the support of a majority of the Convention. That it offered the only prospect of the removal of the present race and party lines, and the establishment of relations of confidence and co-operation in public affairs between the two races, was clear then and is clearer now.

THE "STRAIGHT-OUT" POLICY.

Opposed to this policy was the "straight-out" policy—the nomination of entire Democratic State and county tickets and the inauguration of a purely party struggle. This policy was advocated by a class of men, the most conspicuous of whom are well known as men of extreme views, with strong proclivities towards violent methods and measures. it was openly advocated as the "Mississippi plan," and at the convention which adopted it General Ferguson, of Mississippi, appeared as an honored guest and filled the office of drill-master in the Mississippi tactics. This policy is properly termed in this State the "Edgefield" policy, and was also called by the editor of the Charleston *News and Courier* the "shotgun" policy. Of the practical details of this policy I shall speak hereafter.

This policy was adopted in the Democratic State Convention in August, and was followed by the nomination of a full Democratic State

ticket. It was adopted under influences and auspices, it was advocated by arguments, it has been carried out by methods and measures
so exclusively and entirely partisan as to deprive the present Democratic canvass of all just claims to be what you claim for it—"the struggle of the white people of South Carolina to cast off a burthen of corruption and wrong," and to warrant me in declaring it to be a struggle by
the Democratic party of South Carolina to gain political control of the
State for the sake of partisan power and advantage. The men who
looked exclusively to reform, the arguments which promised the attainment of practical reform, the methods which are warranted by a desire
for the public good, all were opposed to this policy. In saying this I
am regarding the facts of the case without any reference to myself.
The Democratic party of South Carolina were under no political obligation to me, but if they wished to have their present claim respected
—that they are moved by non-partisan motives in their present course
—they were under obligation to adopt a policy which did not, as does
their present policy, array race against race and party against party in
a fierce struggle for political mastery.

DEMOCRATIC "PEACEFUL" AGENCIES.

I come now to your claim that in the present canvass all the methods
and agencies employed by the Democratic party are peaceful, orderly,
and within the law. In your communication you especially assure me
that if I accept your invitation " my appearance before the Democracy
throughout the State will be to me as Governor a most pleasing refutation of the slanderous charges which are constantly published against
your party." My knowledge of the serious cast of your character forbids me to think that you are indulging in conscious satire or badinage
in giving me this assurance. Without expressing any doubt of the
good faith of your present assurance, I fear that your experience in
attending Republican meetings has been widely different from mine in
Republican meetings where your party have attended and demanded an
equal hearing. I shall, therefore, first call your attention to my personal experience in this respect.

As I have already stated, during the months of July and August I
made a convass of a number of the counties of the State. The object
of this canvass, which was conducted almost wholly under my own
auspices, was, first, the advocacy of the election of Hayes and Wheeler,
and, second, and more especially, a defence of my own course as Governor, and an appeal to the Republican party to stand by the cause of
reform in the coming State Convention. It was not a general party
canvass under party auspices. The meetings were called at my request
or suggestion and for the purpose of hearing me upon the question
chiefly of reform in the State.

THE MEETING AT EDGEFIELD.

Under these circumstances I went, on the 12th of August, to address
a Republican meeting at Edgefie'd courthouse. This meeting had

been called by the Chairman of the Republican party of that county, at my instance, and as rumors had repeatedly reached me that the meeting was to be in some way interrupted by the Democrats, I invited one or two Republican speakers to accompany me. Hon. Robert Smalls, Member of Congress from that District, also accompanied me. We reached the courthouse at 9 o'clock in the forenoon. Almost immediately upon my arrival I found the town rapidly filling with mounted white men, who signalized their arrival in town by riding rapidly through the streets and uttering almost continuously the shout or cry which you must pardon me for describing by its familiar name as the "rebel yell"—a sound to which my ears were well accustomed in Virginia twelve years ago. By 11 o'clock this crowd of mounted white men numbered, I judged, five or six hundred at least. Command of these men was apparently formally assumed at the public square by General M. C. Butler and General M. W. Gary, and they proceeded to the grove where a stand had been erected by the Republican Committee for the speakers. I should mention that at about 10 o'clock several white gentlemen had called at my hotel and asked that Democratic speakers should be heard at our meeting. I answered that we had several Republican speakers present who would require the whole day if they all spoke, but I suggested that these gentlemen should see the Republican County Chairman, and stated that I would personally consent to any arrangement they might make with him. The chairman being engaged in preparations for the meeting did not meet these gentlemen and no arrangement was made.

At 11 o'clock I left the hotel and proceeded to the grove. On arriving I found the mounted white men who had assembled in town, with a large number of other white men, occupying one entire half of the space around the stand, and one end of the stand already broken down by the white men who had crowded upon it. I stepped upon the stand in company with Judge Mackey and Senator Cain, the Republican County Chairman. Simultaneously General Butler and General Gary mounted the stand with a number of their followers. The white men vociferously cheered General Butler and General Gary as they appeared upon the stand, and the speaking was actually opened by General Butler, who returned his thanks to his followers for their presence and their tribute to him. He was followed, in response to deafening calls from his party, by General Gary, who announced in emphatic and plain terms that they—he and his party—had come there to be heard, and that they should be heard ; that the Radical leaders had failed to make any arrangement for a division of the time in speaking, but that he and his friends should be heard, with or without our consent, and he added, with great significance of tone and manner, that " if any trouble took place in consequence the responsibility and consequences would be upon the Radical leaders." During all this time no Republican had been allowed to speak. A glance at the crowd of white men who by this time covered the stand and swarmed around nearly three sides of it, besides climbing into the trees above our heads, all, so far as I could observe, heavily armed with pistols, displayed in many instances on the front of their persons, and even held in their hands, convinced me that any attempt to refuse the demand made, or even to abandon the meeting, would result in collision and bloodshed between the parties.   I therefore advised Senator Cain that we had no alternative but to yield to the demand, and after a moment's consultation I announced that we would divide the time, giving a half hour each to three speakers from each party.   Senator Cain then proposed to call the meeting to order and to announce the speakers, but General Gary declared that they wanted no chairman, and accordingly I stepped forward, under these circumstances, to address the meeting.   From the beginning to the end of my half hour I was interrupted by the crowd of white men with jeers and insults of every kind.   Twice during my remarks the confusion and interruption was so complete that after vainly appealing to the crowd to allow me to be heard, General Butler had the decency to come forward and so far restore order as to barely permit me to resume my remarks.   Of the whole half hour allotted to me I certainly was not permitted to occupy over twenty minutes with any remarks such as I should naturally have made on such an occasion. In truth I spoke under great constraint and a consciousness that any word might precipitate a bloody collision, which I had no means of preventing or controlling.   I was denounced by voices from the crowd as a companion thief with McDevitt ; was told I would never come to Edgefield again ; was charged with getting up the Hamburg riot to kill the white people, excite the North, and get United States troops to carry the election, and with a variety of other crimes of which these are but specimens.

I was followed by General Butler, who occupied his time without interruption.   His speech was exceedingly violent and bitterly personal towards me, on account principally of my report of the Hamburg massacre.   Judge Mackey followed General Butler, and he in turn was followed by General Gary.   Nearly the whole of Ceneral Gary's speech was directed against me.   In bitterness and violence of personal abuse, I have certainly never heard or known its parallel.   Nothing short of a verbatim report could give an idea of its character.   His attacks were not confined to my official character, but extended to my personal life and affairs, with frequent threats against me personally in various contingencies.

Judge Mackey next occupied about fifteen or twenty minutes in replying to some of General Gary's personal charges against me, and he was followed by General Butler.

What I have now described occupied the time from a little after eleven until half-past three—a fact which will give an idea of the time consumed by the interruptions of which I have spoken.   At half-past three I left the grove in order to reach the Columbia train, at Pine House, the same evening, amid a torrent of jeers and yells which continued to reach my ears without cessation until I had passed beyond the limits of the town.   The meeting, though called and arranged for in every particular by the Republicans, was at no time and in no sense under our control; only two of the six Republican speakers from abroad who were present were permitted to speak at all, and under the pressure of the white men who crowded upon it the entire platform was brought to the ground before I left the scene. At this meeting the Republicans were told in the most emphatic terms that the Democrats had made up their minds to carry Edgefield County and that they would carry it; that their leaders would be held to account personally; that the white people must and should rule the county. The whole meeting may be justly described as a torrent of abuse of me personally, and an exhibition of force and threats designed to intimidate the colored voters and their leaders. After we had reached the train, at the several railroad stations in Edgefield County a number of the armed and mounted men who had attended the meeting at the courthouse entered the car in which we sat, and, with rude and threatening manners, addressed their jeers and insults to General Smalls and myself, especially, warning us not to come to Edgefield again.

I will add that the foregoing account of the meeting at Edgefield has been made from written memoranda made by me while on my way to Columbia and after my arrival at home the same evening. Nothing has been overstated, though much that was disgraceful has necessarily been omitted in this description.

THE MEETING AT NEWBERRY.

On the 18th of August I visited Newberry courthouse, to address a Republican mass-meeting, called for the same purpose and under the same circumstances as the meeting at Edgefield courthouse, which I have described. I was accompanied by two Republican speakers, Hon. S. L. Hoge, Member of Congress for that District, and Hon. J. K. Jillson, Superintendent of Education. On our arrival at the depot at Newberry, we were met by the Republican County Committee who informed us that the Democrats were assembled in large force, mounted and armed in the Edgefield fashion, and had called for a "division of time" at our meeting. I conferred with the Republican Committee who were firmly convinced that if we refused the demand our meeting would be attended and probably interrupted by the Democrats, with imminent danger of bloodshed if any misadventure should occur. As the Republicans were wholly unorganized for any purpose of resistance to physical aggression, we deemed it our duty either to abandon our meeting or consent to a division of time. We chose the latter alternative and proceeded to the place of meeting. At the stand we found the Republicans occupying mainly the space in front and at one side nearest the platform, while the mounted white men deployed themselves in a continuous line, completely enveloping the Republicans and the platform on all sides. The usual accompaniment of yells was not omitted. I addressed the meeting for an hour, and was followed by Colonel J. N. Lipscomb. His speech was bitterly personal in its character towards me and my friends who were present, and offensive in matter and manner. He constantly alluded and pointed to me and my friends as we sat upon the platform as " you fellows " or " them fellows " ; declared in violent tones that we white leaders were to be individually held responsible hereafter ; and by way of illustration of his meaning, referred to the lynching of six colored men in May last, charged with the murder of the Harmons in Edgefield County, and declared that, " if he had been present he would have taken Dr. Barker, the white Coroner, and Mr. Richardson, the white Sheriff, tied them between the niggers, and given them the same fate." Judge Hoge spoke next, and was followed by Colonel D. Wyatt Aiken, the Democratic candidate for Congress in that District. I did not hear Colonel Aiken's speech, but all the reports of it which I received agreed in stating that it was of a similar tone to that of Colonel Lipscomb, though exceeding it in violence of personal denunciation and threats. I left the ground at 3 o'clock in order to take the Columbia train, and I may mention as my last experience at this meeting, that as I left the stand and reached the outer margin of the crowd, I met a cordon of mounted white men, so closely " dressed," in military phrase, in ranks of two or three deep, that I was forced to request to be allowed to pass through, and to wait until the ranks could be broken for my exit. Every mounted white man whom I observed was armed with one or two pistols.

THE MEETING AT ABBEVILLE.

At the date of the Newberry meeting I was under engagement to address a similar Republican meeting at Abbeville courthouse on the 22d of August. On the return of Judge Hoge and Mr. Jillson from Newberry on the 19th of August, they strongly advised the abandonment of the meeting at Abbeville, in view of their experience at Newberry, and especially on account of a violent and threatening harangue made at the depot at Newberry, on the morning of the 19th, to a band of his partisans, by Colonel D. Wyatt Aiken. I replied that I should keep my engagement at Abbeville from a sense of imperative duty to my Republican friends there. Unwilling to allow me to go alone, these gentlemen gallantly consented to accompany me on the 21st to Abbeville courthouse. On arriving at Abbeville I found our Republican friends, as at Newberry, firmly convinced that if we held our meeting, prudence would compel us to allow the Democrats to occupy half the time, and even then they were greatly apprehensive of trouble. An arrangement was accordingly entered into by which three speakers from each party were to take part in the meeting. At the hour appointed we proceeded to the place of meeting, where we found the Republicans assembled, after the manner of ordinary political meetings. As soon, however, as the Republicans were assembled, companies of mounted white men, marching in martial order, and under the command of officers or persons who gave orders which were obeyed, began to pour over the hill in front of the stand, and to take their places at the meeting. At this time I sat beside General McGowan, and we agreed in our estimate that there were from eight hundred to one thousand mounted white men present. They came, as I know, from Edgefield County, and, as I was informed, from Newberry, Anderson, and Laurens counties, as well as from Abbeville County. When fully assembled, they covered more than one half the space around the stand, besides entirely encircling the whole meeting with mounted men. I spoke first. In the course of my speech, in response to loud and repeated cries from the white men, "How about Hamburg?" "Tell us about Hamburg," I replied, "Yes, I will tell you about Hamburg," whereupon I saw a sudden crowding towards the stand by the mounted white men on my right, and heard distinctly the click of a considerable number of pistols. I was followed by Colonel D. Wyatt Aiken in a speech filled to overflowing with the spirit of intolerance and violence. With his thousand mounted and armed partisans cheering him on, he shouted to the five or six hundred colored Republicans : "If you want war you can have it—yes, war to the knife, and the knife to the hilt." With a thousand armed white men drinking in his words, he singled out one colored man in the crowd for special personal denunciation. Turning to me, he charged me personally with complicity in sending arms clandestinely to Newberry to arm the blacks against the whites, with absolute falsehoods in relation to the Hamburg massacre and the calling for United States troops, and declared over and over that the white leaders must be held personally responsible for all future misgovernment by the Republican party. Later in the day Mr. Jillson, while speaking, was so greatly interrupted by the white men that he was unable to make a connected speech or to pursue his intended line of argument. After the meeting was closed, and while the colored Republicans were carrying a United States flag past the public square in the village, an effort was made by a party of mounted white men to snatch it from them, fifteen or twenty pistols were discharged in the air, and a general riot was thereby made imminent.

THE MEETING AT MIDWAY.

I attended a similar meeting at Midway, in Barnwell County, on the 24th of August, called by Republicans, but attended by a large body of white Democrats, who marched into the village on horseback, but who, on this occasion, dismounted before they reached the place of meeting. This meeting was addressed by two Democratic speakers, both of whom alluded to and described me and the other Republican speakers present as "buzzards," "plunderers," "adventurers," and "carrion crows." Major G. D. Tillman, the Democratic candidate for Congress in that District, made a speech rivalling in some respects the speech of General Gary at Edgefield. He charged that I shared the plunder with McDevitt ; that I sought to shield him from arrest by giving information to him of the fact that I had issued requisitions for his return from Florida and Louisiana ; that I pardoned Walker because I had shared with him in legislative "steals"; and finally assured his friends that within a few months I would either be "a fugitive from justice or wearing the striped suit of a convict in the penitentiary." These are but a few specimens from his speech. During the speech of Judge Hoge, who spoke later in the day, in consequence of a retort by the speaker to a white man who had repeatedly interrupted all the Republican speakers with insulting remarks and questions, several pistols were drawn, violent threats were made against Judge Hoge, and a Trial Justice who was present rushed upon the stand to inform me that he could no longer restrain the white men, and for full twenty minutes the speaking was completely interrupted.

THE MEETING AT LANCASTER.

I went on the 30th of August to Lancaster courthouse to address a Republican meeting similar in all respects to those I have already named. The same scene was repeated, several hundreds of mounted and armed white men, their leaders having previously demanded, and been granted, a division of the time for speaking, surrounding the entire Republican audience. After two Republican and two Democratic speakers had been heard, Hon. A. S. Wallace, Member of Congress from that District, took the platform ; but after vainly endeavoring to obtain a hearing, he was obliged to leave the stand without making a speech.

Nearly every fact and incident stated in the foregoing account of these meetings fell within my own personal knowledge. I have omitted many facts vouched for by perfectly trustworthy eye-witnesses, such as the repeated drawing of pistols on me behind my back and the threats against my life uttered by persons at too great a distance to be heard by me. At none of these meetings did I witness or know of a single disorderly act on the part of any Republican, nor did I hear a word spoken by a Republican speaker personally disrespectful to a Democratic speaker. At each of these meetings the coolest and best-informed Republicans felt that the only alternatives were to abandon the meeting or to yield to the demands made by the Democrats, unless we were willing to run the imminent hazards of violence and bloodshed. These meetings were, moreover, as you have observed, held at points widely asunder in our State, and thus were evidently the result of a matured and well understood plan.

I now present these to you as an answer to your claim that all the methods of the Democratic canvass are peaceful, orderly, and within the law. I pronounce such a course of conduct as I have now described as an outrage upon free discussion, a mocking travesty of free speech, and a plain, palpable, systematic attempt to deter Republicans from canvassing the State, and to overawe and put in physical fear peaceful citizens assembled to discuss political questions ; and I submit the justness of this verdict to the candid judgment of all who respect individual rights or public order and peace. . . .

The Governor next set forth by quotations from the newspaper press and the resolutions of Democratic meetings, the evidence that a concerted and determined effort was being made to intimidate Republican voters by proclamation and threats that no person who refused to enroll himself in a Democratic club, or who voted for the Republican candidates, would hereafter obtain employment by Democrats. The *News and Courier*, in urging this policy, had said: " Once convince the masses of the voters that the Democracy in town and country are in earnest about this, and the fight is surely won. . . . The more general the practice the greater will be the Democratic majority. With a fair election we need at least fifty thousand. Employers of Republican labor can get them and more." With a grim irony this monstrous policy was labelled " Preference, not Proscription." Another feature of this scheme, advocated by the press and resolved upon by the Democratic clubs, was " to rent neither lands nor houses to any one who votes the Radical ticket." The following is a sample series of these resolutions, one which was adopted *in toto,* and without variation by many clubs in Orangeburg and Barnwell counties.

1. *Resolved*, That we will not rent land to any Radical leader, or any member of his family, or furnish a home, or give employment to any such leader or any member of his family.

2. That we will not furnish any such leader, or any member of his family, any supplies, such as provisions, farm implements, stock, etc., except so far as contracts for the present year are concerned.

3. That we will not purchase any thing any Radical leader or any member of his family may offer for sale, or sell any such leader or any member of his family any thing whatever.

4. That the names of such persons, who may be considered leaders, be furnished to this Club at the earliest date, and that a list of the same be furnished each member of the Club.

5. That whenever any person or persons who shall be denominated Radical leaders by a vote of this Club shall cease as such, these resolutions shall become null and void so far as such leader or leaders, or any member of his or their families, are concerned.

6. That we will protect all persons in the right to vote for the candidates of their choice.

7. That these resolutions be published, and that all the Democratic clubs in the county and throughout the State are hereby requested to adopt them.

The following appeared in the Columbia *Register* (September 28, 1876), as having been unanimously adopted by the Democratic Club of Ward 3 in that city.

Resolved, That rumors being current in the city that certain merchants in this ward are going to show their preference for the present Administration on the 7th of November next, that the President of this Club do appoint a Committee of three or five, the duty of this Committee being to present the roll to every man in the ward for signatures, thereby giving to each one the opportunity of vindicating himself, and at the same time enabling the honest laborers for reform to discriminate between friends and foes, and that they report at the earliest possible time.

Resolved, That this resolution shall apply equally forcible to porters about stores and offices, carpenters, mechanics, barbers, butchers, hack drivers, and, in fact, to every one who receives wages from the honest citizens of this ward.

Many more similar examples were quoted by the Governor, who continued, saying :

The foregoing examples, selected from a vast mass of similar evidences, are presented here as proof of the fact already alleged—that the Democratic party has adopted and is carrying out a systematic plan of social and political proscription with the set and avowed purpose of forcing men to vote contrary to their convictions and wishes. It is within the knowledge of every man who is acquainted with the present condition of the State, that the written and formal statements of the plans of political coercion convey a very faint idea of the actual practice of your party. Prudence and good policy in a majority of instances dictate the concealment of such plans, and the instances now cited of open avowals of the purpose of political coercion are for that reason the more startling proofs of the spirit in which the system has its origin. The advertising columns of the Charleston *News and Courier,* and the local columns of other Democratic newspapers in this State, furnish constant examples that the published evidences which I have cited fall far short of representing the extent of the system which they disclose.

He then quoted several sections from the Statutes applicable to this state of affairs, among them the following :

Whoever shall assault or intimidate any citizen because of political opinions or the exercise of political rights and privileges guaranteed to every citizen of the United States by the Constitution and laws thereof, or by the Constitution and laws of this State, or for such reason discharge such citizen from employment or occupation, or eject such citizen from rented house or land or other property, such person shall be deemed guilty of a misdemeanor.—Chapter 131, section 26, page 728.

This portion of the letter closed as follows:

I am now prepared to pronounce the system which I have set forth, and which constitutes a prominent part of the Democratic canvass, a plain infringement of moral and social right, and a clear violation, in its most prominent features, of the laws of the State.

RIFLE CLUBS.

He continued :

I next call your attention to another state of facts bearing upon your claim that the present Democratic canvass is conducted by agencies which are peaceful and within the law. I refer now to the armed organizations which go under the names of "Rifle Clubs." "Sabre Clubs," and "Artillery Clubs." Of the exact extent of these organizations your information is doubtless much more ample than mine ; but I think I am warranted in saying that such organizations exist in every county in the State, and that in many, if not most, of the counties they embrace a large majority of the white men between the ordinary limits of age for military duty, as well as a large number both below and above such limits. That these organizations are armed, officered, drilled, to a considerable extent at least, in the manual and military movements appropriate to the character of their arms and organizations, and obey the orders of their officers, is clear in many cases, and is probably true in all cases. That they have appeared in public on a number of occasions in different parts of the State, and recently here in Columbia, with their arms and under command of their officers, is well known. That they serve as the basis of political organization, and under the command and control of their officers engage in political duties and work, is equally clear. In fact a leading feature of the present Democratic State canvass is the constant attendances upon the Democratic meetings of these Clubs, acting in their organized character and capacity. In no instance of such Clubs organized since December 1, 1874, has authority for their formation or existence been given by the Governor, nor are any such organizations reported to him officially, or in any manner authorized or recognized by him as forming any part of the military force of the State. The existence of a few military Clubs, organized for professedly social purposes, many months since, was made known to the Governor, but, aside from these cases, the whole system of military organizations now referred to has no official sanction or recognition from the Governor of the State. So long as these organizations retained their character as social clubs, little importance was naturally attached to the question of their legality. Recent and present events, however, and the use now made of these organizations as a prominent agency in the Democratic canvass, give public importance to their character.

The Governor quoted the section of the Revised Statutes regarding the organization of the militia, in which was this explicit proviso :

Provided, That there shall be no military organizations or formations for the purpose of arming, drilling, exercising the manual of arms, or military manœuvres, not authorized under this Chapter and by the Commander-in-Chief, and any neglect or violation of the provisions of this Section shall, upon conviction, be punished by imprisonment at hard labor in the State penitentiary for a term not less than one year, nor more than three years, at the discretion of a competent Court.

Pressing home the conclusion with unrelenting logic, he declared :

The organizations to which I call your attention are now seen to be organizations not only not authorized by the law, but forbidden by the law. But their organization is not more illegal than their objects. Those objects are disclosed by their conduct, and are no more doubtful than the fact of their existence. The incidents of the present canvass which I have already stated, and others which I shall hereafter state, show the use which is made of these organizations. . . . In organization, in object, in conduct, they are neither peaceful nor orderly, nor within the law. And yet they are perhaps the most prominent method and agency employed by your party in this canvass.

The next topic related to occurrences that showed still more glaringly the falsity of the claim that all the methods of the Democratic party were " peaceful, orderly, and within the law." The facts and circumstances of the Hamburg massacre have been given so fully in a preceding chapter, that the force of his comment will be appreciated. It is based wholly on the undisputed facts in the case which were set forth :

THE HAMBURG MASSACRE.

Those who committed the massacre were white Democrats ; those who were massacred were colored Republicans. Passing over what occurred before the time when all resistance, or show of resistance, to the white Democrats had ceased, it is a fact as well authenticated and undeniable as the assassination of President Lincoln, that five unarmed Republicans, while held as captives by a large body of armed white Democrats, were deliberately and wantonly shot to death by their white Democratic captors. If the facts of the riot were admitted to show that both parties were equally responsible for its origin, and equally engaged in its progress from beginning to end, the unimpeachable fact would remain that five colored Republicans, after the riot was ended, were butchered by a band of white Democrats. Intention and motive, when not expressed in language, must be judged by acts and circumstances. Applying this test to the Hamburg massacre, the conclusion seems to be that color and political party had much to do in prompting the massacre. It is sufficient, too, that the massacre occurred in a section of our State in which the present " Straight-out " Democratic canvass took its rise, and where were found its most efficient promoters in all its earlier stages. . . . One of your Democratic orators has sought to cover this vast crime with the plea of Mr. Burke for the American colonists ; " I pardon something to the spirit of liberty."

But the American colonists needed no advocate to acquit them of wholesale murder, nor did Mr. Burke sully his lips with the atrocious plea that wanton butchery of unresisting prisoners could be condoned when committed in the name of liberty.

Of the Governor's remarks on the Charleston riot of December 6th and subsequent days, something was quoted in another place.[1] Passing this we come to the account of occurrences yet more hideous and brutal, if that may be thought possible.

THE ELLENTON RIOT.

And now, contrasting the methods and circumstances and results of this riot [in Charleston] with the Hamburg riot, I ask your attention to a more recent occurrence which is called the Ellenton riot. Though this riot occurred chiefly on the 16th of September and the three or four days following, it has been impossible up to the present time to obtain a full and connected report of its origin and course. Certain general facts and some specific details are, however, known. Its origin was an assault upon a white woman in the course of an attempted robbery of her house by two negroes.[2] One of the alleged robbers was arrested, and, while in the custody of his captors, was shot. Out of these occurrences grew the riot. Of the conduct of the colored people engaged in or connected with the riot I will not speak with confidence, lest my present information should be found to give a too favorable account. It is certain that a force of armed white men was speedily assembled from the surrounding country from a distance of thirty miles and more.

On the 18th and 19th this force amounted to not less than six or eight hundred men, all armed, under officers, company and general, but assembled by no lawful authority, and acting under no lawful orders. On the morning of the 19th the arrival upon the scene of a company of United States troops caused the dispersing of these rioters. The results of this riot are stated by General Johnson Hagood, one of the nominees on your State ticket, to be two white men and about thirty colored men killed. My other information reduces the white men killed to one, and increases the number of colored men killed to forty or fifty. That nearly all the colored men killed were not killed while resisting the execution of the law or any legal process, or while violating the peace or threatening or attempting any violence, is a fact established by clear proof. They were shot down wherever found ; in fields and woods, on highways and in cabins, along the railroad track and at the railroad stations.

I give you an account of the murder of Simon P. Coker, a member of the present Legislature and a delegate to the recent Republican Convention in Columbia, as related to me by an intelligent and trustworthy eye-witness of the same, a person well known to me personally. While

---

[1] See Chapter XXI., p. 351.   [2] An error. See p. 414.

sitting in the car of the railroad train at Ellenton, on the 19th ultimo, my informant saw Coker walking unarmed in company with several armed white men. Coker's manner indicated that he did not consider himself a prisoner or in danger, as he was talking freely with the white men who accompanied him. Coker and those who accompanied him proceeded to a piazza in front of a store at Ellenton station and sat down for a few moments, but soon proceeded to a large tree standing about thirty rods from the spot where my informant stood, Coker still appearing unconcerned. While standing under this tree the white men suddenly stepped away from Coker about six paces, and, turning, fired a volley into his body. He instantly fell, whereupon several of the party advanced towards his body and fired upon it a second time. My informant also mentions as a fact that he saw N. A. Patterson, a Democratic Trial Justice of Barnwell County, walking in company with Coker at Ellenton station at the time first above stated. Coker, it now appears, had been enticed from his home to Ellenton upon some false pretence of a summons to answer a criminal charge.

The killing of colored people in connection with the Ellenton riot extended far and wide, and was kept up for several days. In truth, my information leads me to believe that it cannot be said to have ceased now. Persons living in the vicinities named vouch to me personally for the truth of these, among many other, instances of murders of colored men in Barnwell County, growing out of the Ellenton riot.

On the 24th of September several colored men were picking cotton near Elko, among whom were two refugees from the vicinity of Ellenton. Eight or ten white men rode into the field and fired upon these refugees, killing one and wounding the other. The dead body was carried and thrown into a swamp, where it was found on the 25th by Trial-Justice Black, of Blackville, and Captain Kenzie, of the United States garrison at Blackville.

On the night of the 24th, a party of white men visited the house of a colored man about seven miles from Blackville, and took out a colored man who was a refugee from near Ellenton. This refugee has not been seen or heard of since.

On Sunday, September 24th, two colored men escaping from the vicinity of Ellenton, passed a church near Allendale while the white people were at church. They were pursued by white men from the church, and overtaken at the cabin of a colored man at early evening. One was shot and died of his wounds at 9 o'clock that night, and the other, though wounded, escaped.

These are but a few of the outrages which I fully believe have been committed by white Democrats, members of Democratic Rifle Clubs, upon colored Republicans in Barnwell County alone. More than forty colored and white refugees are reported to me as under the protection of the United States troops in their camp at Blackville at this time.

I present these facts to you as a portion of the evidence now in my hands and within my knowledge, which refutes your claim that the methods and agencies now employed by the Democratic party are peaceful, orderly, and within the law.

The present armed organizations which constitute the effective force of the Democratic party, as well as its chief agency in its canvass, are manifestly a menace to the peace of the State and the rights of the members of the Republican party, because those organizations are unlawful in their origin, unlawful in their aims, and aggressive and lawbreaking in their conduct.

This vigorous letter closed with a statement of the reasons why the Governor did not call upon the white citizens of the the State to suppress the disorders which were alleged to exist:

WOLVES TO GUARD SHEEP.

I come now to your demand that if I believe that lawlessness and terrorism prevail in the State I should call upon you and your party to suppress it, before I appeal to the Government of the United States. I am familiar with this demand. I have heard it here and have heard it abroad. It is made the occasion of constant reproach that I am Governor of the State, and yet cannot and do not preserve the public peace. General Hampton and his followers are seeking to profit politically by uttering this reproach and declaring their easy ability to maintain the peace of the State. I shall answer your demand with perfect plainness of speech. The reason I cannot and do not maintain the peace of the State and suppress lawlessness and prevent terrorism, is solely because the Democratic party are the authors of the disturbances of the peace, the lawlessness and terrorism which they now reproach me with, and demand that I shall allow or invite them to suppress. *Quis custodes custodiet ?* To entrust the protection of those who are today endangered by the present disturbances to the armed, mounted, unlawful, Democratic Rifle Clubs would, in my sober judgment, be as unnatural and unfaithful in me as to set kites to watch doves, or wolves to guard sheep.

Actual lawlessness is, in my judgment, and upon the evidence before me, prevalent to-day in several counties and sections of the State, and I believe, upon the best attainable evidence, that it has already resulted in the killing of from forty to fifty defenceless and unresisting Republican voters. Terrorism, resulting from lawlessness and violence, extends far more widely ; and in support of this statement, I repeat here the remark made to me two days since by a white Democrat who had crossed the country from the vicinity of Robbins' Station, through Barnwell County to Blackville, that "he did not see a 'nigger' man anywhere." But when, in view of this lawlessness and terrorism, you and your associates mock me with the demand to put it down by calling on the white, armed Democrats who are the authors of it, I answer that you are welcome to the political advantage such a demand may give you, but I shall yield to no such demand as long as I hold the office of Governor.

You know, as I know, that the Republican voters of this State are not organized for successful resistance to the aggressions of the

Democratic Rifle Clubs. You know, as I know, that to call upon the colored Republicans alone to suppress this lawlessness and terrorism would be to invite or precipitate a conflict, the result of which would be to increase, rather than suppress, the lawlessness and terrorism which now exist.

THE ONLY RELIANCE.

In such an emergency my only reliance for effective physical force must be upon the United States troops. I have struggled long and hard to avoid a resort to this agency. I have hoped against hope that a sober second thought would come to those who govern the Democratic party strong enough and just enough to relieve me from the necessity of action which must inflict great temporary injury upon the material interests of the State. But I am invested with large and extraordinary powers by the laws of the State to meet extraordinary emergencies. The Executive of the United States will do his duty, and I shall do mine ; and it shall be seen by the world whether the right to a peaceful and free ballot by the citizens of this State, conferred and made inviolable by the Constitution and laws of State and Nation alike can be trampled underfoot by any combination or party of men in this State. The people of this State know that I am not a rash or unjust man ; that I am tender of every private and public interest and right ; but they know, also, that I am accustomed to doing my duty, without haste, but without fear.

I have doubtless wearied you, sir—I certainly have wearied myself —in setting forth the various matters which were essential to my reply to your communication. The statements of facts herein made all rest upon actual evidence now before me, the sources of which I should have here stated if I had not been compelled, in order to secure the evidence, to give a solemn promise, in many instances, not to make known the sources.

In conclusion, I have only to renew my acknowledgments for the respectful form of your communication, and to express the hope that I have followed your example in that regard, and that the peace and prosperity of South Carolina may be speedily restored and perpetually maintained.

I have the honor to be, very respectfully, your obedient servant,

DANIEL H. CHAMBERLAIN,
Governor of South Carolina.

Such a document, clear and accurate in its statement of the actual condition of affairs, reserved and candid regarding all matters of doubt ; dignified, forceful, earnest, and bold, being widely published in the press of the country, arrested attention in an extraordinary degree. *Harper's Weekly* (November 4th) referred to it in the following terms:

The letter of Governor Chamberlain of South Carolina to the Democratic Committee of that State is a plain and conclusive representation of the actual situation. The attempt to stigmatize him as a schemer bent only upon his own success is ridiculous. . . . Its quiet and firm tone shows a man who, under extreme difficulties, is master of the situation. In the course of the letter Governor Chamberlain had proved the entire illegality of the armed Democratic organizations, and had recited incontestable evidence of their purpose. . . .

There is no man in the Southern States since the war who has done so much for a true pacification as Governor Chamberlain. His Democratic competitor, Wade Hampton, has been a mere firebrand. For ten years Hampton and other Democratic leaders like him have remained passive and sullen. His nomination now is due solely to the expectation of a Democratic restoration, and the rifle clubs and the terror are a part of the system by which the Republican vote of South Carolina is to be intimidated, and an apparent Democratic majority obtained. Governor Chamberlain, in the interests of good government, had earned the opposition of the Republican bummers in the North as well as in the South. The fact that his efforts were applauded and sustained by sensible Democrats was one of the reasons that he was opposed by corrupt Republicans. And had the Democratic party of South Carolina sincerely wished peace and good order, they would have sustained Chamberlain with all the best Republicans in the State. . . .

We bespeak for Governor Chamberlain among all intelligent and patriotic citizens of the country a most patient consideration. There is no man who has graver responsibilities, and no one who meets them more courageously. He would not deny that the presence of United States troops is not a final solution of the question. But that is not a reason that he should submit to the despotism of Democratic rifle clubs and the order that reigned at Warsaw. He stands for civilization, for the country, and the principles that have amended the Constitution, and all good citizens in every State should stand by him.

Violence and public disorder continuing in the counties of Aiken and Barnwell, the Governor, three days after the publication of the foregoing letter, issued a Proclamation which gave distinct warning of his purpose to call on the President for the assistance of national troops in preserving order unless the illegal armed forces violating the public peace should disband and disperse.

STATE OF SOUTH CAROLINA,
EXECUTIVE CHAMBER,
COLUMBIA, S. C., Oct. 7, 1876.

Whereas, it has been made known to me by written and sworn evidence that there exists such unlawful obstructions, combinations, and assemblages of persons in the counties of Aiken and Barnwell that it has become impracticable, in my judgment as Governor of the State, to enforce, by the ruling course of judicial proceedings, the laws of the State within said counties, by reason whereof it has become necessary, in my judgment as Governor, to call forth and employ the military force of the State to enforce the faithful execution of the law ; and whereas, it has been made known to me as Governor that certain organizations and combinations of men exist in all the counties of the State, commonly known as " Rifle Clubs " ; and whereas, such organizations and combinations of men are illegal and strictly forbidden by the laws of this State ; and whereas, such organizations and combinations of men are engaged in promoting illegal objects and in committing open acts of lawlessness and violence ;

Now, therefore, I, Daniel H. Chamberlain, Governor of said State, do issue this, my Proclamation, as required by the 13th section of chapter 132 of the General Statutes of the State, commanding the said unlawful combinations and assemblages of persons in the counties of Aiken and Barnwell to disperse and return peaceably to their homes within three days from the date of this Proclamation, and henceforth to abstain from all unlawful interference with the rights of citizens, and from all violations of the public peace. And I do further, by this Proclamation, forbid the existence of all said organizations or combinations of men commonly known as " Rifle Clubs," and all other organizations or combinations of men, or formations not forming a part of the organized militia of the State, which are armed with firearms or other weapons of war, or which engage, or are formed for the purpose of engaging, in drilling or exercising the manual of arms or military manœuvres, or which appear, or are formed for the purpose of appearing, under arms, or under the command of officers, bearing titles or assuming the functions of ordinary military officers, or in any other manner acting or proposing to act as organized and armed bodies of men ; and I do command all such organizations, combinations, formations, or bodies of men forthwith to disband and cease to exist in any place and under any circumstances in the State.

And I do further declare and make known by this Proclamation to all the people of this State that in case this Proclamation shall be disregarded for the space of three days from the date thereof, I shall proceed to put into active use all the powers with which, as Governor, I am invested by the Constitution and laws of the State for the enforcement of the laws and the protection of the rights of the citizens, and particularly the powers conferred on me by Chapter 132 of the General Statutes of the State, as well as by the Constitution of the United States.

In witness whereof I have hereunto set my hand and caused the great seal of the State to be affixed, at Columbia, this 7th day of October, A.D 1876, and in the one hundred and first year of American independence.

D. H. CHAMBERLAIN.

By the Governor :
H. E. HAYNE,
  Secretary of State.

The Democratic State Executive Committee issued an address to the country disputing the statements in the Governor's letter to Col. Haskell and denouncing the Governor's Proclamation as being unwarranted by law and facts and issued to furnish a pretext for asking for troops. To this address, Governor Chamberlain made a prompt response, as follows:

COLUMBIA, S. C., October 9, 1876.

To the People of the United States :

An effort having been made by the official representatives of the Democratic party of this State to deny the facts and condition of affairs which were set forth in my recent letter to the Chairman of the Democratic State Executive Committee, and upon which my Proclamation of the 7th instant rests, I deem it my duty to say, upon my full official responsibility, that I am at this moment in possession of authentic legal evidence to substantiate every fact and statement made by me in the documents above referred to. And I further assert, upon my full official and personal responsibility, that the lawlessness, terrorism, and violence to which I have referred far exceed in extent and atrocity any statements yet made public. This latter statement rests upon the evidence in my hands of persons who have officially investigated the facts at the places where they occurred, and upon the affidavits of United States army officers who were present at the scenes of violence and murder.

Hon. D. T. Corbin, United States District Attorney for this State, who has personally made a separate and independent investigation of the Ellenton riot, furnishes me with the following statement of the results reached by him, a statement, as will be seen, more than verifying my statements and vindicating my action. Of the four Judges whose statements are presented by the official representatives of the Democratic party as impeaching my statements, not one professes to have any knowledge of the facts stated by me, and of the two Republican Judges, Judge Moses disclaims any such knowledge, and Judge Willard states that he has been absent from the State for the past three months.

All the evidence in my hands, and in the hands of the United States District Attorney, will be made public so soon as the interests of public justice will permit it. I pledge myself to the country to prove a condition of affairs in this State, produced by the Democratic party, more disgraceful than any statement yet made by me, and I shall not stay my hand until punishment overtakes its guilty authors. My only offence is too great caution in obtaining evidence, and too great delay in exercising my utmost powers to protect our citizens.

DANIEL H. CHAMBERLAIN,
Governor of South Carolina.

COLUMBIA, S. C., October 9, 1876.

Governor D. H. Chamberlain :

DEAR SIR—You having asked of me a statement of the general condition of affairs in Aiken County as I found them to be on my visit there during the past week, have the honor to state :

That I spent three days in Aiken and had before me and took the affidavits of a considerable number of citizens from different parts of the county. I find that rifle clubs or regular military organizations, organized substantially after the manner of military companies in the United States army, exist throughout the county. The officers of these companies are called captains and lieutenants, and the subordinate officers are called sergeants and corporals. They are all armed with weapons of various patents, but many of them of the latest and most improved kinds. Rifles and sixteen-shooters are most common. Pistols are universal. These companies meet at stated intervals for drill in the various military manœuvres. They are also subject to be called out on occasion by their commanding officers.

These clubs have created and are causing a perfect reign of terror. The colored men are, many of them, lying out-of-doors and away from their homes at night. Many of them have been killed, and many have been taken from their beds at night and mercilessly whipped, and others have been hunted with threats of murder and whipping, who thus far, by constant watchfulness and activity, have escaped. The white men of these clubs are riding day and night, and the colored men are informed that their only safety from death or whipping lies in their signing an agreement pledging themselves to vote the Democratic ticket in the coming election. From the best information I could obtain in the time I was in Aiken, I fix the number of colored men killed in this county alone by white men of these clubs, during the past three weeks, at thirteen certainly and at probably twenty-five or thirty. The civil arm of the government in this county is as powerless as the wind to prevent these atrocities. The Sheriff of the county, if disposed, dare not attempt to arrest the perpetrators of these crimes for fear of his own life being taken. He did not, as I am credibly informed, go within seven miles of the eight hundred men (so estimated by United States army officers who saw them) assembled under the command of A. P. Butler, near Rouse's Bridge, and marching upon a crowd of colored men there, whom they had surrounded and intended, as scores of them allege, to kill.

In conclusion I have only to say that the condition of affairs in Aiken County rivals the worst demonstrations of the Ku-Klux Klan in 1870 and 1871.

In my judgment you owe it to yourself as Governor and to the people of the State to exercise, and at once, all the powers vested in you as Governor of the State, to put down this deplorable state of affairs. Very respectfully,

D. T. CORBIN,

United States District Attorney for South Carolina.

The proposition of the Chairman of the Democratic State Committee relative to holding joint discussions with General Hampton, having been referred by Governor Chamberlain to the Republican State Committee, a correspondence followed, which is herewith given. Its significance is obvious:

COLUMBIA, S. C., October 5, 1876.

A. C. Haskell, Esq., Chairman Democratic State Executive Committee, Columbia, S.C.

SIR—Governor Chamberlain has referred to the Republican State Executive Committe, of which I am Chairman, for answer, so much of your letter to him of the 28th ult. as relates to your invitation to him and to his associates on the Republican State ticket to meet General Hampton in public meetings for the purpose of joint discussions. In reply I am authorized by Governor Chamberlain, and the other nominees on the Republican State ticket, to make to you the following proposition, which will enable the candidates of both parties to appear before the people upon terms of equality and secure the purposes of joint discussion, namely :

Governor Chamberlain will meet General Hampton at ten places, five to be selected in what is called the low country and five in the up country, the places to be selected by mutual conference between the Executive Committees of the two parties, or such representatives as they may appoint, or, in case of disagreement, five places shall be selected absolutely by one committee and five by the other. Inasmuch as General Hampton is now under apppointments mainly in the low country, I am authorized to say that Governor Chamberlain and his associates will agree absolutely upon five places now named among his appointments in the low country. At the places agreed upon, the meetings shall be called by the proper representatives of each party in such manner as each shall deem proper. When the meetings are assembled they shall be called to order and presided over by a chairman from each party, who shall, each for his own party, introduce the speakers. The speakers shall occupy equal spaces of time, and be in all respects upon a perfect equality in all rights and privileges pertaining to the discussion.

This proposition is made to apply to General Hampton and Governor Chamberlain alone, or to other or all the nominees on the State tickets. If the discussion is limited to General Hampton and Governor Chamberlain, then the usual arrangements respecting the opening and the close, and the alternations in the order of speakers on successive days, shall be made. If other speakers are allowed, they shall come in equal numbers for each party, and have equal time for speaking, and all the usual rules of joint discussion shall be applied.

No speakers shall be allowed at any meetings called for joint discussions except such as shall be agreed upon under this proposition, or their substitutes or representatives.

At all meetings assembled under this proposition, the space around the speaker's stand shall be equally divided between the two parties, in all respects, and this division shall be observed throughout all the meetings, from their opening to their close. The Chairmen of the respective State Executive Committees shall stipulate with each other for respectful and courteous treatment of opposing speakers, and for the orderly and quiet conduct of their respective parties at the meetings, and at all times during the assembling and dispersing of the meetings.

This proposition, with all its details, is made solely with a view to secure joint discussions in which both parties shall meet upon fair and equal terms. If any of the details are objectionable for any cause to you, or those whom you represent, I shall be glad to hear such objections and to accept any modification which will secure the object which we sincerely and earnestly seek—" a free and untrammelled discussion, that the people may become enlightened on the issues of the day."

Very respectfully,

ROBERT B. ELLIOTT,

President Executive Committee, Union Republican Party of South Carolina.

COLUMBIA, S. C., October 9, 1876.

To R. B. Elliott, Esq., President Executive Committee U. R. P., Columbia, S. C. :

SIR—Your letter of 5th instant was received. We have no objection to the manner you propose for the holding or conducting of the joint meetings. You have ac-

cepted the five appointments in the low country as they stand upon the list already
published. We cannot deviate from the order in which our appointments have been
made in the other counties ; but we see no reason why you cannot commence the
joint meetings at Yorkville on the 13th instant, and continuing thence at Chester on
the 14th, Winnsboro, in Fairfield, on the 16th, Lexington on the 17th, and Edgefield
on the 18th. These will constitute the five up-country meetings. The meetings in
the low country will be in Beaufort, at Early Branch, on the 23d, in Colleton, at
Walterboro, on the 27th, in Charleston on the 30th, in Georgetown on November 1st
and in Orangeburg on November 3d. The counties of Aiken and Barnwell are pre
cluded by Governor Chamberlain's Proclamation. The number of speakers we pro
pose will be four, subject to change by agreement.

Very respectfully, your obedient servant,

A. C. HASKELL,
Chairman Democratic Executive Committee.

COLUMBIA, October 9, 1876.

*Colonel A. C. Haskell, Chairman State Executive Committee of the Democratic Party
of South Carolina, Columbia, S. C. :*

SIR—I am instructed by my colleagues of the State Executive Committee of the
Union Republican Party to acknowledge the receipt of your communication of this
date, and to express our gratification at its general purport. We shall be glad to
proceed, as soon as practical, to arrange such details as may be necessary in connec
tion with the proposed joint discussions, and to this end we would like to be informed
whether your Committee prefer to agree upon the requisite details through the agency
of correspondence or by personal interviews between committees from each party.

If the latter mode be agreeable to you, Messrs. F. L. Cardozo, T. C. Dunn, and
R. B. Elliott, representing our Committee, will be pleased to meet any similar Com
mittee which you may designate, in the Library of the Supreme Court to-morrow, at
such hour as may be found most convenient to them.

Very respectfully, your obedient servant,

ROBERT B. ELLIOTT,
President State Executive Committee Union Republican Party.

Memorandum of agreement entered into this 11th day of October, A.D. 1876, be
tween Colonel A. C. Haskell, Chairman State Executive Committee of the Demo
cratic party of South Carolina, of the first part, and R. B. Elliott, President State
Executive Committee of the Union Republican party of South Carolina, of the other
part, witnesseth : That it is herein and hereby stipulated and agreed between the
parties aforesaid, for and in the behalf of the political parties represented by them :

First. That joint discussions of the political issues involved in the present cam
paign in this State shall be held between representatives of the two parties at ten
different places in the State, five of these to be in the upper, and five in the
low country, to wit :

At Greenville C. H. . . . ——————	At Gillisonville . . . . October 25t
" Union C. H. . . . . ——————	" Walterboro . . . . " 27t
" Winnsboro . . . . . ——————	" Charleston . . . . " 30t
" Abbeville C. H. . . . ——————	" Georgetown . . . . November 1
" Cheraw . . . . . . ——————	" Orangeburg . . . " 3

Second. That at the times and places above mentioned Governor D. H. Chamberlain and General Wade Hampton, and two others from each side, shall participate in the discussions contemplated by the memorandum : Provided, That if, from any cause, one or more of the speakers on either side shall be unable to be present, their places may be filled by an equal number of speakers to be substituted for them by the political parties to which the absentees may belong.

Third. That notice of each of the several meetings above enumerated shall be given to the voters of each political party by their proper representatives, in such manner as they may deem proper—said meetings, in all cases, to commence at 12 M.

Fourth. Each of the meetings shall be presided over by a chairman from each political party, who shall each, for his party, introduce its speakers.

Fifth. That the order of speaking, with reference to the representatives of each party, shall be alternated at successive meetings, and each speaker, on each side, shall be entitled to one hour of time ; provided that it shall be optional with the speakers of that party which opens the discussion either to consume, individually, all of their time, or to reserve a portion of it for the purposes of reply ; their opponents in all cases, however, to confine themselves to one uninterrupted space of time. In no case shall any speaker be allowed to transfer any portion of his time to another.

Sixth. That at all the meetings provided for in this memorandum the space on and around the speakers' stand shall be equally divided between the two political parties from the commencement to the closing of such meetings.

Seventh. That at all meetings the speakers shall treat their opponents with decorum and courtesy, and the representatives of each party shall stand pledged for the maintenance of peace and good order by their constituents, respectively, as well during the assembling and dispersing of the audiences as during the progress of the discussion.

COLUMBIA, October 12, 1876.

Colonel A. C. Haskell, Chairman State Executive Committee of the Democratic Party of South Carolina, Columbia, S. C. :

SIR—I have recited to my colleagues of the Executive Committee of the Union Republican Party the matters discussed in the interview which I had the honor to hold with you yesterday in reference to the details of the proposed joint discussions, and they reluctantly conclude that our negotiations for that purpose cannot be conducted further upon a basis that involves additional concessions on our part.

You will remember that our original proposition was to hold ten meetings—five in the up and five in the low country. At the latter we consented to meet all your appointments of places and days, with the understanding that you were to conform to ours, in these particulars, at the up-country meetings. Upon finding that you would be inconvenienced by a strict adherence to this part of the programme, we consented to regard your appointment for Columbia as embraced in the up-country list, and subsequently went further and agreed to reduce the number of the meetings to eight, reserving the right to name the two places, in the up country, not previously agreed upon, but conceding to you the designation of the days upon which these two meetings should be held.

So, in brief, we have yielded to the reduction of the number of the joint discussions from ten to eight ; to your designation of six out of the eight places at which they should be held, and to the selection of such days, in every instance, as would observe your convenience.

Now, upon conference, we find that we can concede nothing more without infringing gravely upon the programme agreed upon for our own appointments, previous to our negotiations for joint discussions, and consequently prejudicing our canvass by the change of our appointments at this late day, and the confusion which might incidentally follow such a course.

We present these facts in the hope that your Committee may find it convenient to recede from the position which I understood you to take, in the course of my interview with you yesterday, and, by consenting to the places to be suggested by us for the two up-country meetings, enable us to consummate our arrangements without further delay.

Requesting an early reply, I have the honor to be, very respectfully,

ROBERT B. ELLIOTT,
President State Executive Committee Union Republican Party.

COLUMBIA, S. C., October 16, 1876.

SIR :—Your communication of the 12th instant received. The committee assembled to-day, and considered your propositions. We cannot go further than in our previous letters. We desire joint discussion, and we offer now, as we did from the first, to arrange on your terms for joint discussion at the places named in the list of Democratic appointments. These appointments were made long prior to the opening of this negotiation, and, as I early told you, cannot be departed from. Very respectfully, your obedient servant,

A. C. HASKELL,
Chairman State Democratic Executive Committee.

COLUMBIA, October 17, 1876.

Colonel A. C. Haskell, Chairman State Executive Committee Democratic Party, Columbia, S. C. :

SIR—Your communication of the 16th instant has been submitted to my colleagues of the Executive Committee, who concur with me in the propriety of ceasing all further efforts to consummate arrangements for the joint discussions contemplated by our correspondence with your Committee.

We reach this conclusion with unaffected reluctance, because we have always been anxious to agree upon such preliminaries as would enable us to meet you before the people of the State in a fair and full discussion of the issues of the day. Finding now that despite all the concessions which we have made to bring about this result, and which are summarized in my note of the 12th instant, it is no longer possible to secure at your hands such a corresponding relinquishment of previous engagements as would place us on equal terms in the canvass, we are reduced to the necessity of closing negotiations for that purpose.

Very respectfully, your obedient servant,

ROBERT B. ELLIOTT,
President State Executive Committee Union Republican Party.

ROOMS STATE DEMOCRATIC EXECUTIVE COMMITTEE,
COLUMBIA, October 17, 1876.

SIR :—The Executive Committee submits another proposition in the hope that it may bring about joint discussion :

General Hampton, personally, cannot depart from his line of previous appointments, but he agrees to send a substitute to meet Mr. Chamberlain at any points he may designate in the up country ; provided Mr. Chamberlain comes to the low-country appointments and meets General Hampton in discussion there.

If you will accept this proposition, and send a list of your speakers at each meeting, I will return to you the names of those who will speak on our side.

Reply at your earliest convenience is respectfully requested. We mean that General Hampton will meet Mr. Chamberlain at any of our regular appointments, and will have Mr. Chamberlain or any of his speakers met at any appointments that they may make.

Very respectfully, your obedient servant,
A. C. HASKELL,
Chairman State Democratic Executive Committee.

To R. B. ELLIOTT, ESQ., President Union Republican Executive Committee.

COLUMBIA, S. C., October 18, 1876.

SIR.—Your note of the 17th instant is received, proposing that Governor Chamberlain shall meet Mr. Hampton in the low country and that Mr. Hampton shall send a substitute to meet Governor Chamberlain in the up country.

In the absence of General Elliott, and as acting President of the Republican State Executive Committee, and in their behalf, I have to say in reply, that such a proposition is wholly inadmissible. It departs entirely from the prime purpose of joint discussions, as contemplated by our previous negotiations. While substitutes were allowed under the terms of our first proposition, they were only to be allowed in exceptional cases, when the principals, for some special cause, could not be present. Your present proposition contemplates at the outset, and as the basis of your offer, the absence of Mr. Hampton from one half of the joint discussions.

It will require no further assignment of reasons to justify the Republican State Executive Committee in declining your proposition.

Very respectfully, your obedient servant,
F. L. CARDOZO,
Acting President Republican State Executive Committee.

To A. C. HASKELL, ESQ., Chairman State Democratic Executive Committee. ⌉

CHAPTER XXIV.

THE campaign from this time forth was a series of conflicts and disturbances, the responsibility for which no attempt will here be made to fix or apportion. The published documents of the time will be allowed to tell their own tale and to have such credit as they may appear to deserve in view of the character of their authors and their own character, and the conditions of the contest already so fully presented.

In October, the New York *Tribune* published a series of letters descriptive of the campaign which attracted much attention. They were written by a native and resident of the State. Extracts from the first of these letters are here given as affording a graphic and intelligent review of the situation. It was printed in the *Tribune*, on October 14, 1876, as a letter "from a white native of the State who is not a Republican '—a description known to be correct in both particulars.

    *   *   *   *   *   *   *

Governor Chamberlain's Administration for a year and a half was the golden era of South Carolina politics. The negroes were free, enfranchised, and undisturbed in their rights, and yet the whites were conscientiously protected from plunder and high taxes. But Governor Chamberlain had not been in power a year when the XLIVth

Congress assembled at Washington. The great tidal wave of 1874 had sent a large Democratic majority to the House of Representatives, and prominent among that majority were many ex-Confederate generals. From the very moment it met I noticed an unusual, though carefully concealed, agitation among the fire-eating aristocracy of this State. For years their occupation had been gone. Discarded in politics, out of office, they had been compelled to keep the noiseless tenor of their way along the cool, sequestered vale of private life. But their pride, it seems, had not fallen with their fortunes. They had been compelled to keep quiet ; they complied against their wills, and held to their old opinions. They bitterly reflected that they had seen better days, and nursed their wrath to keep it warm. But now a ray of hope dawned on them. They heard of Ben Hill defending Andersonville and Jefferson Davis in the Congress of the United States. They saw Southerners once more holding up their heads in the national capital. They could hardly trust their senses. And then they looked around them ; all the Southern States were once more Democratic except South Carolina and Louisiana. These States alone had Republican Governors and negro Legislatures. They alone had not their Stephenses, Gordons, Lamars, Hills, and Proctor Knotts in Congress. Then they reflected on Mississippi—how her 30,000 negro majority had been transformed into 30,000 Democratic majority by the use of the shotgun and revolver. It was true that they had been relieved from oppression ; that their confessed debt to their reform Governor was yet unpaid, and that while they supported him, as in the past, there was no danger of misgovernment. But should they rest content with this ? Why not get the upper hand at home, and then make a desperate attempt to seize on the reins of power at Washington ?

The fruits of such thoughts soon began to appear. A violent Democratic daily was established in Greenville—a section of the State where the whites outnumber the colored people. It began a series of the most outrageous onslaughts against Governor Chamberlain, and accompanying these were the most vehement exhortations for the whites to arouse and shake off their lethargy, and follow in the wake of Alabama and Mississippi. Very soon in several of the adjacent counties—the old Ku-Klux counties where the negroes are in the minority—the whites became, during the spring of this year, estranged from Governor Chamberlain and opposed to the compromise policy. But despite its efforts the majority of the whites (all those living in counties where the negroes predominate) remained content with things as they were. And this, too, although a Columbia daily joined in the advocacy of the blood-and-thunder policy. The influence of the Charleston *News and Courier* had much to do with this. It was then the only daily published in Charleston, was by all odds the leading journal of the State, perhaps of the South, and had a circulation ten times as great as that of the Straight-out organs combined. It was found necessary to establish a fire-eating daily in Charleston ; so *The Journal of Commerce* appeared in May. It was intemperate past all expression in advocating its views ; and, as soon as possible, the duellist, R. Barnwell Rhett, Jr., formerly editor of the Charleston *Mercury* and New Orleans *Picayune*, was installed as editor. He is the son of the famous R. Barnwell Rhett, Sr., lately deceased, ex-Senator of the United States from South Carolina, the most ultra Southerner that ever breathed, the man to whose efforts above all others is to be attributed the passage of the Ordinance of Secession, the rival of Jefferson Davis for the Presidency of the Confederate States.

The State Democratic Convention was called unusually early by the Central Committee, composed largely of fire-eaters, and the election of delegate after delegate pledged to Straight-outism in the compromise counties indicated the success of these tremendous efforts. The Convention finally met on the 15th of August. The Straight-outs were in the majority. But so strong was the confidence of the whites in Gov. Chamberlain that notwithstanding all the exertions that had been made, this majority was only a few votes. But it was sufficient. The Convention resolved to nominate a Straight-out, Bourbon Democratic ticket, and to make a desperate attempt to carry the State on the Mississippi plan. The ticket was nominated. Every man on it is an ex-Confederate officer, and bears wounds received while fighting against the Union. And at the head of it, nominated for Governor, stands Wade Hampton, the aristocrat of the aristocrats, the fire-eater of the fire-eaters, a famous General in the Confederate army, the incarnation of Calhounism, Jeff. Davisism, anti-North-ism, and Southern intolerance. After the measure was once resolved upon the delegates acted in concert, Butler, the hero of Hamburg, placed Hampton in nomination before the Convention. The whites once more resolved to trust them and surrendered at discretion. The Convention gave sentence for open war. After a torchlight procession and a mammoth ratification meeting the delegates went home with a full understanding of the methods to be employed.

*   *   *   *   *   *

But this is not all. The air is filled with reports of outrages and murders which never appear in print. No prominent Republican of either color can safely leave a town. Let a hint that he intends to ride out into the country get wind and he is sure to be ambuscaded. But more than this. The whites regard a Republican of their color with tenfold the vindictiveness with which they look upon the negro. Scores of white Republicans are hurrying in alarm to the newspaper offices to insert cards in which they renounce their party and profess conversion to Democracy. If these men hang back and refuse or neglect to join the precinct club or the nearest military company, their conduct is reported to the township meeting. A committee is appointed to request an explanation. They call on the suspected man at their earliest convenience. If he be sensible, he will submit profuse apologies and regrets, and hurriedly take up his rifle and follow them to the drill-room. Three or four white Circuit Judges have been dragooned into conformity, and the crowd of lesser lights threatens to absorb every white Republican in the State, except Governor Chamberlain and the United States Senators.

*   *   *   *   *   *

If a white man refuses to join the precinct club ; if a white man's loyalty to the party is suspected ; if a white Republican persists in his opinions, he is spotted, marked, doomed. He is scowled at if he walks abroad. If he passes a crowd of loitering whites at a street corner, an ominous silence falls on them till he is out of hearing. No warning is given him. No midnight visits are now paid, or Ku-Klux missives despatched. The whites have found by bitter experience that such things are boomerangs, which return with tenfold force to injure the thrower. They manage the matter better now. They wait till an obnoxious man whom they have doomed as a victim chances to stand, or pass near them, say on the public square, at the post-office, in a bar-room, on the street. A crowd of white desperadoes will cluster near him or follow him. They appear to be drunk, and begin to quarrel over some silly matter having nothing to do with politics. Several bystanders come up and take sides. Finally blows are exchanged, pistols drawn, and a regular free fight occurs. Shots are fired by all the party. Yet, strange to say, when order is restored, it is found that not one of the combatants is injured, while the poor Republican has been struck by several random shots and killed. An account of the affray appears in the press (the press is almost wholly Democratic) under the heading, " Street Row—One Man Killed." Not only are single men picked off in this way, but sham fights are arranged by white ruffians on some non-political pretence, which swell to the proportion of riots, and in which several Republican bystanders are killed by chance shots, while none of the combatants are hurt. Of course the authors of these deeds go unpunished. In the first place, it is impossible to tell who fired the shot. Then it is unsafe for any one to indict anybody about it, or for the officials to be too zealous in investigating or prosecuting. But if an assassin does get into trouble by imprudence, his comrades, who of course compose most of the bystanders, are called as witnesses, and swear him out safely by giving in doctored testimony.

*   *   *   *   *   *   *

I now find myself carried back to the time of secession. Then no Southerner dared to avow Union sentiments. There were thousands of them in the South, but they were ruthlessly subjected to a system of terrorism, and had to choose between conformity and almost certain death ; and with hardly an exception they conformed. To-day there are thousands of whites forced into this Confederate revival against their judgment and inclination ; but they must conform or take the consequences. They conform, and then, to avoid the imputation of lukewarmness, they endeavor to prove their sincerity by outdoing their comrades in violence. The same men head this movement who led the State into secession. They have thoroughly revived the policy of intimidation. Talk of the blacks being intimidated ! It is through the intimidation of the whites that the intimidation of the blacks is rendered possible. The election is to be carried on the Mississippi plan ; and a part of that plan, be it remembered, was the intimidation of the whites. Wade Hampton is as much a Mississippian as a South Carolinian. It is true that he is descended from Carolinians famous in the Revolution, that his ancestors have always lived in this State, that he himself is a citizen of this State, and that the family homestead is in the city of Columbia. But besides the immense estates he owned in South Carolina before the war, he had vast demesnes in Mississippi and other Southern States. This will not seem surprising when I mention the fact that he possessed 90,000 acres of land in fee simple, and owned 4,000 slaves. Now the war took from him the bulk of his property. But so much remained after all his losses that he is at this day the wealthiest man in the Southern States. Most of his property now, however, is in Mississippi. He has abandoned by far the larger part of his ancestral estates in South Carolina. Though his home is in Columbia, he spends half his time on his plantations in Mississippi. He has one plantation there on which 800 of his former slaves are employed—so well has he been able to keep up this old plantation plan while the small-farm system has been becoming wellnigh universal. The fact I desire to call attention to is this : Hampton was in Mississippi prior to the last election there, which the Democrats carried by the shot-gun policy. The similarity of the methods employed by the Democrats in the canvass going on here now, with Hampton as their leader, forces me to the conclusion that the experiment is to be repeated here.

*   *   *   *   *   *   *

The truth of this startling exposure of the terrific pressure brought upon all white South Carolinians to force them to conform to the scheme of tyrannous electioneering instituted by the rifle clubs, is emphasized by the fact that before the end of the canvass the author of the letter to the *Tribune* himself succumbed to it.

The following open letter, by William Lloyd Garrison, addressed to Governor Chamberlain, was published simultaneously in the Boston *Journal* and New York *Times*, October 16, 1876.

BOSTON, Oct. 13, 1876.

DEAR GOVERNOR CHAMBERLAIN :—Our acquaintance and friendship are not of to-day. Years ago, when you were completing your collegiate course at Yale, I knew how clear, just, and decided were your convictions in regard to the anti-slavery struggle, and how steadfast was your adhesion to them, under circumstances requiring rare moral courage and a noble disregard of consequences to yourself. Ever since, I have watched your career with deep interest ; especially from the time you became a citizen of South Carolina, and more particularly since your elevation to the Governorship of that State ; and, whether acting in your private or public capacity, your conduct has been marked by such circumspection and wisdom, such gentlemanly courtesy and refinement, such patriotic devotion to the cause of the whole country, such fidelity to principle in ferreting out and exposing judicial corruption and official mal-administration even under Republican rule, such disinterested zeal and sleepless vigilance in seeking to promote the best interests of all the people of South Carolina without distinction of caste or party, and such heroism in unflinchingly confronting trials and dangers of the most formidable nature, as to excite my highest admiration, and to secure for yourself the sympathy, respect, confidence, and hearty approval of every true friend of freedom throughout the land.

I hailed, as a cheering sign of the times, your nomination for the office which you now so meritoriously hold ; and, eminently deserving as you are of the support of all classes, for the signal services you have rendered the State in the expulsion of untrustworthy officials, saving to the treasury millions of dollars as compared with previous Administrations, and assiduously endeavoring to effect a general reconciliation of disastrous conflictive elements on the basis of equal and exact justice, I cherished the hope that, however candidates for subordinate positions might be regarded, you at least would receive such a concurrent approval as would indicate a common desire to retain "the right man in the right place." It cannot be pretended that, with all your sympathy for a race so long " peeled, meted out, and trodden under foot," you have shown any undue leaning toward them in administering the laws, or dealing with official incompetency or corruption. On the contrary, you have spared no delinquent on account of his complexion ; but, as in the notable cases of Moses and Whipper, have nobly demonstrated that you have been " no respecter of persons," and have lifted yourself far above all partisan and caste considerations. *Transeat in exemplum !*

But, it seems, you are to be as bitterly scorned, denounced, run down, and ostracised as though you had been guilty of the worst crimes, and had prostituted all the powers committed to your trust for the most venal purposes. Against the opposition now so fiercely combined for your overthrow,—including as it does the great body of those who madly rose in arms for the destruction of the Federal Government, and who reveal themselves to be in a state of chronic sedition,—neither freedom of speech or of the press, nor the unquestionable right to assemble peaceably *ad libitum* for the adoption of legal political measures, can be exercised without imminent personal danger, or the risk of a bloody catastrophe. The laws of the State for the protection of equal rights among the citizens are openly and successfully set at defiance. The reign of terror is in the ascendant ; the reign of law is in the dust. As Governor of the State, without the prompt and vigorous interposition of the National Executive, you are as powerless to enforce order and afford security to the imperilled (whether white or black), in the discharge of their constitutional duties as the feeblest occupant of the soil.

Standing before the country unimpeached and unimpeachable, you are certainly entitled to decent treatment and fair play by virtue of your official position ; but, instead of this, you can make no attempt to address your constituents, *viva voce*, without being assailed with the coarsest epithets, hissed and howled at, and overpowered by the ominous " rebel yell." This—as you have calmly set forth in your cogent, dignified, and irrefutable reply to the preposterous letter of the Chairman of the State Democratic Executive Committee—was your experience at the Republican gathering at Edgefield, at Newberry, at Abbeville, at Midway, and at Lancaster. Each of those gatherings was ruthlessly invaded by hundreds of mounted white miscreants, armed with shotguns and pistols (the " Reform " supporters of Tilden and Hendricks), lawlessly demanding one half of the time for their side of the question, and virtually taking the whole—their object being not to argue but to menace, not to compare candidates but to find a pretext for slaughtering the defenceless colored victims of their hatred and oppression. None but dastards and assassins behave in this manner ; and that you escaped from them with your life was owing, doubtless, to your admirable self-control, and to the consciousness that you were walking among scorpions and along the perilous edge of a precipice, the slightest deviation threatening a fatal result—so that no possible incitement to murder could be found in your speech or demeanor. Their portraiture was drawn to the life ages ago (see Isaiah, 69th chapter) with prophetic skill and foresight—" Their lips have spoken lies, their tongue hath muttered perverseness ; their works are works of iniquity, and the act of violence is in their hands. Their feet run to evil, and they make haste to shed innocent blood ; wasting and destruction are in their paths. The way of peace they know not, and there is no judgment in their goings. Yea, truth faileth ; and he that departeth from evil maketh himself a prey." Shuddering earth and indignant heaven cry out against them in thunder tones.

But, primarily, this controversy is not with you, nor with the Republican party, nor with those who have been so marvellously brought out of the house of bondage ; it is directly, flagrantly, and defiantly with the Ever Living God, whose laws are not to be violated with impunity ; whose edict is, that the reaping shall be as the sowing ; who was never yet evaded, duped, or circumvented ; and who, in the sequel, " according to their deeds, accordingly he will repay." They are their own deadly enemies ;

enemies to the character, repose, development, and prosperity of the State ; enemies of the Republic in all that makes it great, free, and independent ; enemies of the human race. And they are such by no special depravity of their own. They simply reveal how terrible has been the demoralization wrought by one class of the people reducing another class to brutal servitude, from generation to generation ; and the curse still cleaves to them like leprosy. Yes, negro slavery has cursed them in the city and in the field ; in their basket and in their store ; in the fruit of their body, the fruit of their cattle, and the fruit of their land ; in their manners and morals, their pursuits and aspirations, their understandings and hearts ; yet they are precisely what any other portion of the inhabitants of the land would be, placed under the same debasing circumstances. Truly, " They grope at noonday, as the blind gropeth in darkness, and they shall not prosper in their ways," for they are smitten with madness. Bedlam has no form of insanity more desperate, more deplorable, or more hopeless than that moral insanity which persistently calls good evil, and evil good ; which puts darkness for light, and light for darkness ; which regards chaos as order, and declares :

> " To reign is worth ambition, though in hell ;
> Better to reign in hell than serve in heaven."

Such, alas ! is the spirit, such the condition, and such the determination of a large majority of those at the South, who, in order to establish a vast slaveholding empire, rose in rebellion to effect a bloody dismemberment of the Union, never doubting of success ; and who, defeated in their evil design, are still strongly under the influence of lunacy. Hence their loss of all moral discernment, of all power of reasoning, of all sense of justice, of all self-control, when it is a question as to the enjoyment of equal rights and privileges with themselves on the part of those whom they once " yoked with the brute and fettered to the soil," whose chains are now severed, and on whom has been conferred the title of American citizenship by the Constitution and laws of the land. Hence their equipment with the bowie-knife, the revolver, and the shot-gun, in order to control by murderous violence where they have no legal right to rule ; and hence, too, the many horrible atrocities they have committed upon white and black Republicans alike.

When charged with these, they have three modes of defence. First, they boldly declare that no such atrocities have been committed ; that it is only a base device to " wave the bloody shirt " for political ends ; and that the exercise of the franchise is as free and unconstrained for all classes at the South as at the North. Second, they unblushingly maintain that the entire responsibility for their occurrence lies at the doors of the colored people, and especially their leaders, who have sought to bring on a bloody strife, so as to invoke the interposition of the Federal arm to place them in the ascendency. Third, when unable to outface the facts presented, they meanly attempt to screen themselves from merited condemnation by alleging that the outrages complained of were perpetrated either by a few hot-headed young men or by a low class of whites, and that no countenance is given to them by the respectable members of society.

These pleas, it will be seen, are utterly incoherent and irreconcilable. The last one, however, though most untruthful, has served to deceive a very considerable number of persons at the North, and thus to allay that alarm and indignation which would surely be awakened if they were correctly informed. No such state of things could exist if the intelligence, respectability, and wealth of the city, county, or State did not give at least a passive sanction to it.

In some cases, no doubt, "hot-headed young men and low-born whites" have been particularly active in driving the terrified negroes into the bushes, or burning their dwellings, or subjecting their persons to horrible torture, or shooting them down like game at sight ; but never against the prevailing sentiment of the dominant class, upon whom a righteous God will affix the dread responsibility, and in due time bring a fearful retribution. " Were they ashamed when they had committed abomination ? Nay, they were not at all ashamed, neither could they blush : therefore they shall fall among them that fall : at the time I visit them, they shall be cast down, saith the Lord."

Who were they that instituted and upheld the accursed slave system, that dehumanized its victims, that provided its fetters and thumb-screws, that employed its slave-drivers and slave-hunters, that kept its bloodhounds ready to take the scent of the fugitives at a moment's warning, that enacted its barbarous code, that pronounced it a patriarchal and divinely sanctioned institution, that subjected to lynch law or banishment all who dared in its immediate locality to question its rectitude, that gathered their wealth from the unpaid labor of their lash-driven chattels, that trampled upon all the dearest relations of life, that abolished the marriage institution, that sold the husband from his wife and the mother from her babe, that made it a flagitious crime to teach a slave the alphabet, that denied the Bible to the millions deprived of it, that extended the domains of the slave power, that plotted rebellion against the government they had sworn to uphold, that for four years waged deadly war to consummate their treasonable purposes, that saddled the nation with a debt of thousands of millions of dollars, that sent to bloody graves a mighty host ?

Were they the poor " white trash " that are everywhere seen at the South, ignorant, degraded, vicious, and only a slight remove from the lowest barbarians ; or were they those who stood recognized as highly respectable, intelligent, cultivated, wealthy, pious, and (save the mark) "chivalric " ?

So it is now. The same class rule to-day in essentially the same spirit, and must be held responsible for whatever additional sufferings have been inflicted upon their former bondmen.

And how palpably they indicate their unchanged spirit by the nomination of the leading slaveholder and rebel in the State, General Wade Hampton, as their standard-bearer and candidate for Governor of South Carolina ! In what attitude he stands to the cause of liberty and equal rights, what are his avowals and designs, no room is left for doubt.

If fraud, intimidation, violence, and the shedding of innocent blood can effect it, he will be your successor, Governor Chamberlain ! But of your triumphant re-election (so well deserved at the hand of every voter) there can be no uncertainty, provided these methods are not resorted to, to the driving of thousands of your warm and grateful friends from the polls. You can be defeated only in this manner, thus rendering a legal choice impossible. Whatever may be the result, you have the proud consciousness of having acted well your part, and faithfully discharged every official duty and obligation. Yours is a position as sublime as it is critical. Faithful and fearless to the end, you shall take your place in American history by the side of the foremost champions of Liberty and Justice. Fraternally yours,

WM. LLOYD GARRISON.

The disturbances of the public peace continuing and increasing, Governor Chamberlain, in the early part of October, applied to the President for aid in suppressing domestic violence in the State. The following documents exhibit the official action on this application:

PROCLAMATION

By the President of the United States of America.

Whereas, It has been satisfactorily shown to me that insurrection and domestic violence exist in several counties of the State of South Carolina, and that certain combinations of men against law exist in many counties of said State known as "Rifle Clubs," who ride up and down by day and night in arms, murdering some peaceable citizens and intimidating others, which combinations, though forbidden by the laws of the State, cannot be controlled or suppressed by the ordinary course of justice ; and

Whereas, It is provided in the Constitution of the United States that the United States shall protect every State in this Union on application of the Legislature, or the Governor when the Legislature cannot be convened, against domestic violence ; and

Whereas, By laws in pursuance of the above it is provided in the laws of the United States that in all cases of insurrection in any State, or of obstruction to the laws thereof, it shall be lawful for the President of the United States, on application of the Legislature of such State, or of the Executive when the Legislature cannot be convened, to call for the militia of any other State or States, or to employ such part of the land and naval forces as shall be judged necessary for the purpose of suppressing such insurrection or causing the laws to be duly executed ; and

Whereas, The Legislature of said State is not now in session, and cannot be convened in time to meet the present emergency, and the Executive of the State, under Section 4 of Article IV. of the Constitution of the United States, and the laws passed in pursuance thereof, has therefore made due application to me in the premises for such part of the military force of the United States as may be necessary and adequate to protect said State and the citizens thereof against domestic violence, and to enforce the due execution of the laws ; and

Whereas, It is required that whenever it may be necessary in the judgment of the President to use the military force for the purpose aforesaid, he shall forthwith, by proclamation, command such insurgents to disperse and retire peaceably to their respective homes within a limited time.

Now, therefore, I, Ulysses S. Grant, President of the United States, do hereby make Proclamation, and command all persons engaged in said unlawful and insurrectionary proceedings to disperse and retire peaceably to their respective abodes within three days from this date, and hereafter abandon said combinations and submit themselves to the laws and constituted authorities of said State.

In witness whereof I have hereunto set my hand and caused the seal of the United States to be affixed. Done at the City of Washington, this 17th day of October, in the year of our Lord 1876, and of the independence of the United States one hundred and one.

U. S. GRANT.

By the President :
JOHN L. CADWALADER, Acting Secretary of State.

WAR DEPARTMENT,
WASHINGTON, D. C., October 17, 1876.

To General W. T. Sherman, Commanding U. S. A.

SIR—In view of the existing condition of affairs in South Carolina, there is a possibility that the Proclamation of the President of this date may be disregarded. To provide against such a contingency you will immediately order all the available force in the military division of the Atlantic to report to Gen. Ruger, commanding at Columbia, S. C., and instruct that officer to station his troops in such localities that they may be most speedily and effectually used, in case of resistance to the authority of the United States. It is hoped that a collision may thus be avoided ; but you will instruct Gen. Ruger to let it be known that it is the fixed purpose of the government to carry out fully the spirit of the Proclamation, and to sustain it by the military force of the General Government, supplemented, if necessary, by the militia of the various States.   Very respectfully, your obedient servant,

J. D. CAMERON,
Secretary of War.

In reply to urgent requests from many quarters, Governor Chamberlain sent to the New York *Tribune* the following telegraphic letter in reference to, and explanatory of, his course in appealing to the President for aid :

[From the New York *Tribune*, October 25, 1876.]

To the Editor of the Tribune :

SIR—The condition of South Carolina justly attracts the attention of the country. The gravest questions are here presented ; questions of constitutional power and right, of Executive prudence and duty, of political discretion, and, unhappily, of partisan and individual interests. To be at once clear-sighted and impartial among the excitements and animosities which now envelop all parties here, is exceedingly difficult. I should claim more than will be conceded to me if I were to assert my own entire exemption from disturbing influences. The fact that I am myself a candidate will be set down to discredit me as a witness or judge.   On the other hand, those who denounce my action and deny my statements would seem to be exposed, in any fair estimate, to equal discredit.   When I assert upon my personal and official responsibility that domestic violence exists here of such kind and degree as to be beyond the restraints of ordinary civil and judicial agencies ; and when Wade Hampton, upon his personal responsibility, denies it, the country must look to the character and information of the opposing witnesses, and to the evidence which each presents to inform its judgment.   I do not perceive that the exposure to bias is greater in my case than in that of my opponent.   Sir James Mackintosh says : " Official responsibility composes the mind and sobers the judgment."   I certainly feel the truth of the remark, and I venture to think that I am under heavier bonds at this moment to speak the truth and to act with all the impartiality I can command than any other man in South Carolina.

The statement I now make is called forth by the special efforts made by my opponents here to set the sentiment of the country against the cause which I have the fortune to represent, and against the President of the United States, who has responded to my call upon him for aid in suppressing domestic violence.   The press despatches present only the views of my opponents.   I do not expect to affect partisans greatly on either side.   Without doubt, many, if not most, Republicans will sustain my action, and that of the President, because we are of their party, while, for a similar reason, Democrats will denounce it. Fortunately there is a considerable reserve force of men not blinded or perverted by mere partisanship.   By such men a statement from me will be candidly considered ; and to such men I especially address it.

NO TIME TO ASSEMBLE THE LEGISLATURE.

The provision that "the United States shall protect each State of this Union on application of the Legislature or of the Executive (when the Legislature cannot be convened) against domestic violence," is a part of the Constitution of the United States.   It was intended to meet a foreseen necessity.   It imposes a high duty upon the General Government.   The only inquiry at present needful is, has a case occurred here which warrants the exercise of the power thus conferred and the discharge of a duty thus imposed ?   The answer depends mainly upon the facts.   The President of the United States, upon my application conformably to the terms of this constitutional provision has decided to grant the protection demanded.   It has been suggested that the Legislature might have been convened in this State.   Certainly this suggestion can have no foundation except in the desire for delay.   It does not go to the merits of the case.   If a case has now arisen which would warrant the Legislature in calling for protection against domestic violence, then the Legislature could not be convened in time to secure protection before the domestic violence would have accomplished its purpose.   Besides this, there are no funds available, or which can be made available, within the next sixty days for the expenses inseparable from a session, however short, of the Legislature.

THE FACT OF DOMESTIC VIOLENCE.

As to the fact of domestic violence in this State, what kind and measure of proof should be required? It is well to notice that the Constitution does not prescribe the kind or extent of domestic violence which will warrant either the Legislature or the Executive in applying for protection or the United States in granting it. The United States Revised Statutes give power to the President " in case of an insurrection in any State against the Government thereof," to give military aid on application of the Executive, when the Legislature cannot be convened. Whatever may be the exact legal definition of the term " domestic violence," as used in the Constitution, or "insurrection," as used in the statutes, it will be conceded by all that the occasions here contemplated are such as present so formidable a resistance or obstruction to the discharge of the functions of the Government of the State, the enforcement of its laws, and the protection of its citizens, as to require greater force than the Government of the State possesses for that purpose. Neither by the Constitution nor the statutes is it made a condition of the exercise of the power in question, that the domestic violence or insurrection shall have overthrown the Courts or actually resisted their officers or processes. The occasions for its exercise seem to rest in the official discretion of the Executives of the State and United States. Their official responsibility is the safeguard against its abuse. This is the doctrine laid down by Chief-Justice Taney, in Luther against Borden. There is, therefore, no specific infallible test by which it may be known when the proper moment or occasion has arrived.

Those who assert that such an occasion does not now exist in South Carolina, declare that the civil officers have not been resisted in the execution of the laws. But domestic violence may arise and utterly paralyze the arm of the civil authority, without actual physical resistance to any officer of the law. Insurrection may exist in complete proportions before a blow has been struck against any civil officer. To send a constable or sheriff to arrest a thousand armed and mounted men, assembled in violation of law, and engaged in riotous acts and murders, is not necessary to establish the fact of the existence of domestic violence or insurrection. To send a colored constable or a treacherous white sheriff with a colored posse to arrest or disperse a thousand armed, mounted, disciplined white men, organized in military companies and acting under the command of military officers, in the midst of a violent political campaign in this State would be an act of criminal folly.

THE RIFLE CLUBS.

I now proceed to present a statement of the facts upon which the present call upon the President for aid in suppressing domestic violence in this State has been made. I shall make no statement which does not rest on official information now in my possession.

First: As to the rifle clubs. These clubs are organizations having every distinctive feature of military companies. They exist, unless disbanded since my proclamation of the 7th inst., of which I have no evidence, in every county in the State. I have the evidence of the existence of 213 rifle clubs, with the names of some or all of their officers. These clubs have an average membership of 60 men. The evidence shows that the members of this force of nearly 13,000 men are armed with not less than 8,000 improved breech-loading rifles. My estimate of the whole number of men enrolled in the rifle clubs and armed with effective weapons is not less than 16,000 or 18,000, while the estimates of my informants vary from 20,000 to 30,000, besides company officers. The evidence shows that these clubs are organized into regiments. I have before me at this moment an authentic printed copy of the " general orders " issued by the colonel of one of these regiments, countersigned by the adjutant, in which instructions are specifically given to the lieutenant-colonel, major, and commanding officers of companies. The evidence points also to the existence of general officers having control of other formations composed of regiments and brigades. There is much evidence from independent sources showing that fully 10,000 improved breech-loading rifles have been purchased by rifle clubs in this State within the last four months.

These organizations are not only outside the law, but they are strictly prohibited by the laws of the State. The evidence is overwhelming that these clubs were formed and have been constantly used as the chief basis of organization of the Democratic party. During the month of August I attended Republican meetings, among others, in the counties of Edgefield, Newberry, Abbeville, Barnwell, and Lancaster, at each of which these clubs were present in numbers varying from 400 to 1,000. They were heavily armed with pistols, and were commanded by persons bearing the titles of military officers. They marched and manœuvred as ordinary military companies. They attended these meetings as Democrats, took control of them in some instances, and in all instances enforced their demand for participation in Republican meetings by their presence as armed, organized bodies.

In their several localities these clubs have operated openly and ostensibly as Democratic campaign organizations. Far and wide in the State they have ridden by day and by night as a menace to the members of the Republican party, especially its colored members, uttering threats, and not seldom executing them. Prior to the recent instances of widespread violence which occasioned my Proclamation and call upon the President, these clubs, or those who were members thereof, had killed, exclusive of the Hamburg and Ellenton massacres, not less than fifteen members of the Republican party ; had whipped and outraged hundreds, and had individually threatened thousands. They had for the most part evaded punishment by reason of their numbers and the terror inspired both in their victims and in the officers of the law. Constituting or representing as they did almost the entire body of white men in their localities, no efficient way of enforcing the law was left. A constable or sheriff with a colored posse would have been massacred in an attempt to execute the law. If I were to pass through the same scenes again, I should never order, advise, or permit the effort to be made to overcome such obstructions to the law by any force then at my command. It would be not less idle than cruel.

These clubs constituted a vast conspiracy against the State Government. A conspiracy is defined to be a confederation of two or more persons to do unlawful acts, or to do lawful acts by unlawful means. This conspiracy was a confederation to do unlawful acts by unlawful means. It rose to proportions and exhibited itself in ways which made all ordinary civil agencies impotent to cope with it. It aimed, by the commission of crimes ranging from threats of personal injury to murder, to destroy the freedom of a majority of the people in the present election, and thus to overthrow the lawful Government of the State.

THE ASSASSINATIONS AT ELLENTON.

I come now to the transaction which is known here as " the Ellenton massacre," and which was the immediate cause of my call upon the President for military aid. The country is already familiar with the Hamburg massacre, which was at the time of its occurrence, in July, declared by my opponents here to be sporadic and unpremeditated in its character. Ellenton, the centre of the scene of the latter and more extensive massacre, is situated in the same county with Hamburg (Aiken), and about twenty miles distant. The counties adjoining Aiken on the north and south are Edgefield and Barnwell. The riot and massacre continued from the 16th to the 24th of September. The affair was so carefully planned, all truthful reports of its character were so successfully suppressed, and the terror inspired in all the local officers of the county was so great, that I was unable to obtain my first official report through special officers sent from Columbia until the 8th of October. Even then the report was very imperfect on account of the fact that the colored people who were the witnesses and objects of the violence were absent from their homes through fear, and, when accessible, were in many instances unwilling to give their testimony until further protection could be guaranteed to them. An elaborate investigation has now been made, and the following statement is made up from the written testimony of more than one hundred sworn witnesses who have been carefully examined. It will be seen that all the discrepancies between the present statement and that made in my letter of October 4th to the Chairman of the Democratic State Executive Committee simply add features of deeper horror to the affair.

In the county of Aiken and the adjoining counties of Edgefield and Barnwell the white Democrats began as early as last July systematically to inform the colored Republicans that the Democrats had resolved to carry the coming election, and that the colored Republicans would have to vote with them. In August and the early part of September these threats took a more definite form. The colored Republicans were told far and wide that if they did not vote the Democratic ticket they would be killed. Scarcely a colored man can now be found to whom these threats were not personally made. They were ordered to discontinue their political meetings, and were told that a list of all their leaders had been made out, and that these leaders would be killed. Silverton, Rouse's Bridge, Chavis' Store, Matlock's Church, and Union Bridge are points in the vicinity of Ellenton. In this section is a large colored population, constituting perhaps the strongest Republican section of Aiken County.

During the week preceding the 16th of September word was sent to the colored Republicans, by the members of white rifle clubs, that the Republican club at Chavis' Store would be broken up on Saturday the 16th. The rifle clubs in that section, contrary to their custom, assembled on Friday the 15th, instead of on Saturday, at Matlock's Church. The Republican club met on the 16th according to the custom ; but, owing to the threats referred to, only twenty-three persons were present. On the 16th throughout the day the rifle clubs were assembling at Matlock's Church, five or six clubs being present numbering not less than 300 men, a part of the men being from Augusta, Ga. A little before sunset of the 16th these clubs formed as military companies, and marched upon a run down to Chavis' Store, where the Republican club was supposed to be assembled. They found only about ten Republicans present. The rifle club leaders demanded to see the leader of the Republican club. Columbus Rountree, the Chairman of the Republican club, being absent, Samuel Darby acted as spokesman. The chief spokesman of the rifle clubs then told the colored members of the Republican club that they must not meet again ; "that they would be all killed off if they did." Seeing one colored man with a shotgun, they took it from him ; but, finding it worthless, they retained his ammunition, and gave back the gun. The colored men were then informed that "there had got to be a fight between the whites and the blacks," and the rifle clubs then demanded that the colored men present should step out in line and "fight it out." This offer was naturally declined. Finally, with yellings and threats of vengeance, the rifle clubs marched off, declaring that they were going to kill Gloster Holland and. Simon Coker (two colored members of the Legislature) that night. During the night of the 16th several colored men were killed in this section.

On the morning of the 17th the rifle clubs appeared in large numbers at Rouse's Bridge, near which, on the edge of a swamp, the colored people, men, women, and children, panic-stricken by the murders of the previous night, had gathered. About nine o'clock on the morning of the 17th (Sunday) the rifle clubs formed across a field in front of Rouse's Bridge, threw out pickets, and assumed the position of a hostile army. Before moving forward they sent a messenger to the leading colored men, who had now concealed themselves as much as possible in the swamp. This messenger called for the leading colored men, and asked if they would compromise. The colored men replied that they had no quarrel, and did not know what compromise meant. The representative of the rifle clubs then said that the clubs had a warrant for the arrest of Alexander Pope, and they wanted him. The colored men answered that Pope was not with them, but that if the rifle clubs had a warrant for any one they could come and search for him.

The representative of the rifle clubs then proposed a conference of five men from each side. Such a conference took place, and it was agreed that both parties should disperse and go to their homes. The white men who attended the conference, on their way back to the lines of the rifle clubs, chanced to meet three colored men retiring to their homes in pursuance of the agreement now stated. They instantly fired upon them, and killed Henry Campbell, and wounded Abram Overstreet in the head and Nelson Bush in the thigh. This demonstration convinced the colored people that the conference was a mere trick, and that the purpose of the rifle clubs was to kill them in detail after drawing them out of the swamp, as well as to learn their numbers, and whether they were armed. During the conference the colored men had freely stated that they had only a few shotguns, and not a round of fixed ammunition of any kind.

During the 17th a large part of the rifle clubs moved off from Rouse's Bridge toward Union Bridge and Ellenton, on the Port Royal Railroad, and during the day shot and killed a considerable number of colored men, probably as many as twelve. At one cabin they found six colored men, who had crawled out of the swamp to get something to eat. The rifle clubs surprised them, killed two of them in the yard, two more while running toward the swamp, and wounded the remaining two.

Early on the morning of the 18th the rifle clubs appeared in great force on the Port Royal Railroad, having been reënforced by white men from Augusta. They moved up and down the railroad, killing all colored men whom they chanced to find. Among their victims was an old man, of ninety years, and a harmless deaf-and-dumb boy.

About ten o'clock the report was received that the colored men had assembled at Robbins' Station, about fifteen miles below Ellenton. Thereupon about twenty-five men from the rifle clubs got into a box-car, and were taken down to Robbins' Station. Here they found Simon Coker, already named, an honest, peaceful man, well known to me personally as a member of the Legislature from Barnwell County, sitting on the railroad platform with his wife and a colored female schoolteacher. Coker was then awaiting the train from Ellenton in order to go to Yemmassee, where he could telegraph me the condition of things in his vicinity. The rifle club men forced him into the box-car, took him back to Ellenton, and, after a brief parley, shot him in an open field in full presence of the passengers on the train and of the rifle clubs, robbing his dead body of his watch, money, shirt-studs, and ring. A number of colored men were also killed at and near Robbins' Station by another detachment of the rifle clubs on the same day, but the number cannot yet be fixed.

Late in the day, on Monday, the 18th, the main body of the rifle clubs, with large reënforcements, returned to Rouse's Bridge, and during Monday night completely surrounded the swamp in which the crowd of colored persons were hiding to the number of about eighty or ninety, throwing out a line of pickets armed with breech-loading rifles. Early on the morning of Tuesday, the 19th, one of the leaders of the rifle clubs, a prominent white man living in this vicinity, told his confidential colored servant that "they had got the niggers in a bunch at Rouse's Bridge, and got them surrounded, and, by God, they intended to kill the last one of them."

About eight o'clock the officers of the rifle clubs gave orders to their force to advance, and they had actually advanced to within one hundred yards of the spot where the colored people were huddled together in the swamp awaiting their doom, one or two of them having been actually shot by the skirmishers, when Captain Lloyd, of the Eighteenth United States Infantry, appeared on the scene with a small command of United States soldiers. The guns of the rifle clubs were levelled at his command, under the belief, as the rifle clubs informed him, that a black militia company was coming to relieve the colored people in the swamp. On discovering that they were United States troops a messenger was despatched to inquire of Captain Lloyd what he proposed to do. The officer responded that he had no orders, except to keep the peace. A consultation then took place between the chief of the rifle clubs and Captain Lloyd, in which it was agreed that the rifle clubs would disperse. Thereupon, under the protection of the United States troops, the colored people came out from their hiding-place, and clustered around the soldiers with expressions of gratitude not to be described.

The rifle-club men did not affect to conceal their chagrin at the intervention of the United States troops, and loudly and repeatedly declared in the presence of the troops that they had intended to "kill the last one of the niggers." The rifle clubs now broke camp, and apparently started homeward, but their tracks could be followed and distinguished by the bodies of dead negroes whom they chanced to meet, or whom they succeeded in hunting down. The rifle clubs which had assembled at Rouse's Bridge for this final slaughter were estimated by the army officers present to number, at least, eight hundred men, fully armed and equipped for war, and collected from the counties of Edgefield, Aiken, and Barnwell. Before leaving Rouse's Bridge the leaders of the rifle clubs informed the colored people that "the Yankees had saved them this time, but they would get them the next time." At the same time the rifle clubs declared that "they intended to carry the election and kill every colored Republican who would not vote the Democratic ticket."

The testimony before me clearly shows that the pretext heretofore assigned by the rifle clubs for their assembling—the assault of the two colored robbers upon Miss Harley, a fact which I assigned in my former letter, already referred to, as the cause or occasion of the riot—is utterly unfounded. The rifle clubs assembled in pursuance of a well-matured plan, known and published in the three counties, to "put down the niggers" by inflicting such violence upon them and by such demonstrations of force as to cause the leaders to flee and the mass of the followers to forego voting or vote the Democratic ticket.

I have now merely described in outline the domestic violence and insurrection as it was actually developed at Ellenton and within a radius of fifteen miles therefrom. But in truth this was only one phase or centre of the violence and insurrection. It virtually overspread the counties of Aiken and Barnwell, producing a reign of terror which depopulated large sections of those counties of all colored males. Investigations now in progress indicate unmistakably that the actual murders committed exceed the estimates heretofore formed by me or by those most familiar with the facts. Scores of colored men are still missing in addition to those already known to have been killed.

These are some of the leading evidences of the domestic violence and insurrection which were the occasion of my call upon the President for military aid. The facts presented are clearly proved, and the conclusions reached are, I think, sustained by the facts. They make a case amply warranting my call and the President's response. To have done less would have been to abandon the chief functions of government, and to have permitted domestic violence and insurrection to accomplish results against which the Constitution of the United States was designed to guard effectually.

FALSE REPRESENTATIONS. There is one pretext somewhat widely suggested in excuse or mitigation of the offences which I have described, namely, that those who engaged in this conspiracy were crushed by an insupportable burden of misgovernment. In answer to this I assert that by the statements of a vast majority of the leading men and organs of public opinion in this State among the present supporters of Wade Hampton, prior to his nomination, my administration of public affairs for the past two years has been honorable and successful; and that at no time since 1868 were the public evils in this State so far abated or the prospect of complete good government so bright. The utterances of Democratic newspapers and Democratic speakers and leaders on this point would fill volumes. No man who knows or seeks to know the truth will question this assertion.

The charge that I have been influenced by the desertion of Republicans to the Democratic party would receive no consideration from those acquainted with the political situation here. A free vote to-day in this State will elect the Republican candidates by fully 20,000 majority. Besides this I declare, and I challenge any shadow of proof to the contrary, that no party interest, however great or pressing, could ever have induced me so much as to contemplate the use of my official position for asking the military aid of the United States to carry an election. It is only as an incident inseparable from the case at this time that I have considered or alluded to facts or results affecting political parties.

I have acted as the Chief Magistrate of the State. I have sought to protect the lives and rights of the people without regard to party. No man in South Carolina, by reason of any act of mine or of the President of the United States, will be hindered or dissuaded from voting the Democratic ticket if his free judgment shall so incline him. Right-minded men would have judged us recreant to our trusts if, in a proper case, we had failed to exert the powers intrusted to us for the restoration of public peace and the preservation of the State Government. Upon a calm review I am convinced that such a case has arisen and that such a condition of affairs now exists in this State as warrants my action and that of the President of the United States.

D. H. CHAMBERLAIN,

Governor.

COLUMBIA, S. C., Oct. 24, 1876.

The following official reports of officers of the army confirm statements in the foregoing letter and throw additional light on one dark incident of this strange campaign :

AIKEN, S. C., Sept. 21, 1876.

Assistant Adjutant General, Department of the South, Louisville, Ky., Through Commanding Officer United States Troops, Aiken, S. C.:

SIR—I have the honor to report that, in compliance with the telegram of Brevet Brigadier General Commanding the Department, dated Louisville, Ky., September 18, 1876, directing me to proceed immediately with the bulk of my force to Silverton, S. C., and report the condition of things and facts as to any trouble at that place, received at 9 P.M., on the 18th inst., I left this camp at or about 10:30 P.M. of the same date with Lieut. C. B. Hinton and thirty-three men of Companies F and I, Eighteenth Infantry, with three days' rations, and marched about twenty miles to Rouse's Bridge, S. C., arriving there about 9:30 o'clock on the morning of the 19th inst. About seven miles from Aiken we were challenged by a detachment of some fifteen or twenty men on the road, mounted and armed, and apparently organized as a regular company of cavalry. There were other men secreted in a barn near the road. In questioning the man who had charge of the party, he stated that he had been within a few miles of Rouse's Bridge and found the road picketted, and that there had been some skirmishing, and that he had orders to report there in the morning. On arriving at Rouse's Bridge, we found a body of about one hundred negroes, some of them armed with old-patterned muskets and shotguns. They were very much excited, and seemed to possess no organization. We had scarcely arrived at our camping ground, when we heard shots fired, and the negroes running up the road crying that one of their number had been shot, and that the white men were arming. They afterward acknowledged that nobody had been shot, and that the shots had been fired by themselves. A short time after a body of some 320 white men, all mounted and well armed, and under command of one A. P. Butler, were seen coming up the road from the direction in which the negroes had been fired upon. Lieut. Hinton and myself went down the road to meet them, and on approaching the party found that they had thrown out a skirmish line in the woods, almost surrounding the negroes, while the main body marched up the road. As soon as we were recognized as United States officers, we heard the command given the skirmishers to halt, by a man who rode in the woods, evidently to give the skirmish line information of our presence. There was undoubted evidence of a well-digested plan of attack which, if carried out, would have resulted in the slaughter of nearly all the negroes in the place. This man Butler has a regularly organized body of men known throughout this country as " Butler Cavalry," a well-drilled and organized company. Besides this force there were other men from this vicinity and some from Augusta, Ga., under the command of Butler.

From what I can learn the party which I intercepted at Rouse's Bridge was the largest that had got together and included almost all those which had been raiding through the country for two or three days previous. After finding that there were United States troops on the ground, these men proposed to disband and go home, provided the negroes would do likewise. An agreement to that effect was easily made as the negroes were already much frightened, and both parties left the vicinity.

On the morning of the 25th inst. we marched from Rouse's Bridge to Ellenton, a distance of five or six miles. On the road I saw at the house where we stopped for water the bodies of three negroes who had been killed, two of whom had been dead since Sunday. The negroes were afraid to bury them, as they said the white men who were there on Monday had ordered them not to. I saw two negroes at Rouse's Bridge who had been wounded, and have positive information of five others who were killed in the vicinity of Ellenton. As far as I can learn, only one white man has been killed during the four days' rioting.

On our arrival at Ellenton we found a party of twenty-five or thirty mounted, white men, who left town soon after our arrival with the avowed intention of going to their homes. I sent a small detail in a light wagon back to the bridge, which returned in the evening and reported all quiet there, and no armed parties on any of the roads in the vicinity. It was reported to me in the afternoon that there were disturbances down on the Garnwell road. I was requested to send down to inform the people in that vicinity of the agreement which had been made at Rouse's Bridge. Lieut. Hinton, with one of the citizens rode down to Robbins, about six miles, and found there a body of twenty or thirty white men, who stated that they were a detachment from Gen. Hagood's command, who were at Steel Creek. They stated that Hagood had authority from Judge Wiggins to make arrests and disarm the negroes, and that they had been sent there to protect the negroes while burying the body of Simon Coker, a colored member of the Legislature, who had been shot near Ellenton, on Tuesday morning.

Just Anton saw Esker's body. This man was brought from his home at Robbins to Ellenton and deliberately shot. I estimate the total number of white men engaged in the riot as not less than eight hundred, coming from Edgefield, Aiken, and Barnwell, S. C. The negroes at and about Ellenton were completely cowed. Many of them came in from hiding-places in the woods while we were there. They were afraid to go to work, saying they were afraid of being shot down in the cotton fields.

The Port Royal Railroad was torn up about ten miles above Ellenton during the riot. The General Superintendent said that his men were afraid to work on the road, and requested me to leave him a small guard. Six men were left at Ellenton for that purpose, and were withdrawn and joined their companies next day. The road was almost entirely repaired when the detachment returned. The detachment left Ellenton at 12:30 P.M., Sept. 21st, on an extra car and engine connecting with the 2:20 o'clock train from Augusta and arrived at Aiken at 4 P.M.

Very respectfully, your obedient servant,

THOMAS J. LLOYD,

Capt. Eighteenth Infantry, Commanding Detachment.

POST OF AIKEN, S. C., Sept. 23, 1876.

Respectfully forwarded to the Assistant Adjutant General of the Department of the South.

From what I have learned since my arrival here, I am satisfied that Capt. Lloyd's arrival at Rouse's Bridge was just in time to prevent a massacre of the negroes.

WILLIAM MILLS,

Captain Second Infantry, Commanding Post.

HEAD-QUARTERS DEPARTMENT OF THE SOUTH,

ATLANTA, GA., Oct. 5, 1876.

Respectfully forwarded to the Adjutant General United States Army, through head-quarters, division of the Atlantic.

The order from the head-quarters for Capt. Lloyd to proceed to the place of disturbances was based on an application by telegraph from the Governor of South Carolina, stating that a serious conflict was in progress, and that he had no adequate means for its suppression. The presence of troops, it appears by the within report, averted serious consequences. An investigation of the facts and circumstances connected with these riots is, I am informed, now being made by the civil authorities of South Carolina.

THOMAS H. RUGER,

Col. Eighteenth Infantry,

Brevet Brigadier General, U. S. A. Commanding.

The following editorial article appeared in *Harper's Weekly*, October 28, 1876. It fairly exhibits the prevailing sentiment of the time among the conservative Republicans of the North regarding the condition in South Carolina, and the action of President Grant in response to Governor Chamberlain's call for aid :

SHOTGUN REFORM.

The Democratic effort to arouse indignation against the President's South Carolina proclamation has signally and ludicrously failed. For why should the country be angry that the President, under the law, proposes to protect all citizens of South Carolina in their rights ? There is no doubt that the Democrats in that State mean to carry it for " Tilden and Reform " by means of the shotgun. We have no more doubt of it than we have that the Tilden reform is a fraudulent pretence. The Governor of the State is conscious of his inability, in the peculiar situation, to keep the peace. There is no time for delay, for the mischief is designed for a particular day, and if it is to be prevented, the means must be made ready. The protest against the Governor's action and the President's response is a demand that the Democratic Derringer shall control the election. Every good citizen regrets that there should be any armed force near the polls. But it is altogether better that, if there must be such a force, it should be that of the United States to protect every voter of all parties, rather than that of a Democratic rifle club to prevent Republicans from voting.

The danger will be denied, and the law-respecting character of the South Carolina Democracy will be asserted, and the words of Wade Hampton quoted. The facts meanwhile remain unchanged. There is no more doubt of the existence and purpose of the rifle clubs than there was of the Ku-Klux and the White League. There is no more doubt that it is the purpose of Wade Hampton and his associates practically to suppress and destroy the colored vote than there was of their intention formerly to carry slavery into the Territories. The rifle club and Ku-Klux are simply suckers from the root of slavery. When they become so formidable as to threaten the honesty of the election, it would be merely idiocy to intrust the protection of the voters to those who are armed to overawe them. Does anybody pretend that Democratic voters are threatened in South Carolina, or that they are in any danger of being driven from the polls or prevented from voting? If anybody should assert it, he would be laughed into silence. It is only Republicans in that State who are threatened by Democrats, and it is only Democrats elsewhere who rage at the protection guaranteed by the President under the law.

The practical terrorism over the colored vote is shown in Georgia. The Democrats have lately carried the State by 80,000, or more, majority. They might as well have carried it unanimously, and by the same general means. In 1870 Georgia had 237,627 legal voters. There was a white majority of but a little more than 21,000. A certain number of these are fairly to be called Republicans, and the colored vote is naturally chiefly Republican. In 1872 the Democrats carried the State by less than 19,000 majority. Where are the Republican voters this year? "Why is it," asks the Buffalo *Commercial Advertiser*, "that in a State with 240,000 legal voters, the Democrats can win a majority of about 80,000 on a vote of only 100,000?" The answer is very short and simple: the shotgun. The colored Republican voter in Georgia is terrorized. Georgia will give perhaps 100,000 majority for "Tilden and Reform." When the same result is accomplished in every Southern State, when the Southern vote is solid and its Congressional representation is solid, if the Administration should be Democratic also, the work of the war would be virtually undone.

The following letter, from Hon. B. Odell Duncan, United States Consul in Naples, Italy, was also published in the latter part of October. Being a South Carolinian, he understood accurately the motives and influences that were controlling, and the methods to which resort would be had:

NAPLES, October 8, 1876.

MY DEAR GOVERNOR :—Affairs in South Carolina have not taken the conciliatory turn you and I hoped for when we parted. The Democratic Convention did not show that moderation and wisdom which the situation so manifestly required, and which the better elements of both parties wished for. On the contrary, it took the very course that its own most sagacious leaders both publicly and privately condemned. In the nomination of Hampton, the most violent element of the party triumphed over those who were in favor of moderation and prudence. The Butlers and Garys, and all those under indictment for riot and murder come to the front, and the George W. Williamses, the Judge Mahers, the Campbells, the McGowans, the Kershaws, etc., etc., the better and more substantial elements of the party, are pushed into the background. The *News and Courier* makes another of its "lofty tumbles" and vibrates from the extreme of moderation and good sense to the extreme of violence and madness. It cannot find language strong enough to condemn the Republicans for going armed to public meetings of their own ; but it is all right for Democrats to go mounted and armed, cap-a-pie, not to their own, but to trespass on Republican meetings, and not for the purpose of free and fair discussion, but to enable them to indulge in bitter personal abuse of their opponents. I refer specially to Gary's attack on you at Edgefield.

The natural, indeed the inevitable consequence of the action of the Democratic party we are now witnessing. A state of uneasiness exists all over the State. Violence and riot and bloodshed are of frequent occurrence. The moderate men of six weeks ago are forced along with the current to avoid snspicion and social ostracism, if not actual danger.

Extreme men and extreme measures on the one side have, as was to be expected, caused the same on the other. So we are not surprised to hear of the supremacy of the worse elements of the Radical party at its conventions.

But the one redeeming feature of the Convention was your renomination, and for that it cannot claim any special credit, as it was forced to do so by public opinion of the North and to have any hope of success. But, nevertheless, I congratulate you on your success, and especially do I congratulate the State on the prospect of having you for Governor another term.

Of the chances of your election of course I cannot judge so well at this distance. Were I to credit the *News and Courier*, I could entertain no hope. But I know too well the character of our papers to trust all they say about elections. These numerous colored clubs, I take it, are rather myths than realities. A course of conciliation on the part of the Democrats towards the colored people would, in my judgment, be much more successful then these mounted and armed parades all over the State, and such a policy I could heartily endorse. But of course their policy is to intimidate, and not to conciliate. That was the prime object of the Hamburg massacre, and that is the object of all this semi-military display. In this they may possibly be successful, the colored people being in general a timid race. Here there arises the necessity for what I must strongly deprecate in principle, that is the presence of the United States troops, and if they should be used at all I hope it will be simply to preserve order and to enable every one, white and colored, to vote freely and as he desires, not to intimidate either side. If we can have a fair and orderly election, I entertain no doubt you will be re-elected, and with a handsome majority. Nor do I believe that you will only get Radical votes, for, notwithstanding the excitement, and pressure, and social ostracism, I still believe that some Democrats, who assured me they would vote for you if a candidate in preference to anybody else, will have the courage and manliness to do so. Your success I should regard as the triumph of law, order, moderation, conciliation; Hampton's as the triumph of violence, of oppression, and the virtual disfranchisement of a race. I also hope the Legislature elected will be such that a good working majority of Democrats and honest Republicans may be formed to support you in your reform measures. . . .

Hoping that no very serious disturbance may occur during the campaign in South Carolina, I remain, very truly yours,

B. O. DUNCAN.

The incident of the campaign narrated in the following extract from the Columbia *Union-Herald* has peculiar interest

Hon. A. G. Magrath and General W. F. De Saussure called yesterday upon Governor Chamberlain to represent the necessity for the presence of some United States troops at certain points in Charleston County. They asked his coöperation in an application to be made to General Ruger to that end. The delegation told the Governor that the white population outside of the city were alarmed at certain reports of ill-feeling towards them manifested by the negroes who are in such an immense preponderance at many points. Many families had already removed to the city, and those unable to do so were in much anxiety and dread.

To this representative delegation of Charleston Democrats the Governor addressed the following letter:

EXECUTIVE CHAMBER,
COLUMBIA, S. C., October 25th.
Hon. A. G. Magrath and General W. F. De Saussure, Charleston S. C.

GENTLEMEN—I had hoped after our interview this morning to have met you again, as I then intimated to you, in company with General Ruger, in order that we might confer more fully upon the matters which you brought to my attention.

My views and purposes were stated to you with entire frankness in our interview, but I desire again to present them in writing. I am glad of an opportunity practically to prove that in all my relations to the present canvass, and especially in seeking the aid of the military force of the United States, I am acting in the interest of all our people, and for the protection in all their rights of the Democrats as well as the Republicans. I expect no favor—and hardly justice—in the judgments pronounced upon me by political opponents in the heat of this campaign; but you, gentlemen, know me well. You have in times past honored me with your confidence, and I know you will believe me when I say that I am as solicitous that you and your political friends shall be protected by the United States troops now in the State as I am that my political friends shall be protected. I deplore the fears which have called you here. If the anxieties and distress which now afflict the white people of Charleston are the effect of the mad policy inaugurated by Democratic leaders in this State, we will not pause to discuss it.

Our common and only present duty is to strive to say peace and to secure peace to all our fellow-citizens. I will conferfully and promptly with General Ruger, as I have already promised you, and I have no doubt he will take such measures as will fully insure a peaceful election in Charleston County and ample protection to all whom you are here to protect.

I beg to express my sincere gratification at the confidence you have manifested in bringing these matters personally to my attention, and to again assure you that I am, as truly now as in any other and more peaceful days, your friend and servant,

D. H. CHAMBERLAIN,
Governor of South Carolina.

The following telegraphic letter, published in the New York *Tribune* of November 2, 1876, was called out by a statement made public by United States Senator T. F. Randolph of New Jersey, who visited South Carolina as one of the managers of the Democratic party's national campaign:

To the Editor of the Tribune:

SIR—Ex-Governor Randolph of New Jersey appears as the latest apologist of the "shotgun" Democracy of South Carolina. If I were to follow his example, especially if I were to speak the exact truth, I should pronounce his letter to the Chairman of the Democratic National Committee the result of gross ignorance, bitter partisanship, and wilful falsehood. It is difficult to deal with such a vast, chaotic mass of untruths. I shall single out a few only as specimens. Governor Randolph writes as follows:

> The Constiution of the State requires the registration of every voter. Governor Chamberlain has been earnestly urged to execute this constitutional provision. He has omitted to do so, and in many districts, especially in those where the colored voters are in absolute control—there is no limit to fraud. Because of this persistent refusal the confidence of the better class of citizens has been lost to him.

Now mark the facts: The only constitutional provision respecting registration in this State is in these words:

> It shall be the duty of the General Assembly to provide from time to time for the registration of all electors. Section 3, Article VIII.

The Governor has no power to " execute this constitutional provision." He has therefore not " omitted " to execute it. His only power or duty is to recommend and urge its execution. In my Inaugural Address, December 1, 1874, in a Special Message to the General Assembly, January 12, 1875, and in my Annual Message, November 23, 1875, I urged in the most earnest terms the execution of this constitutional provision. In each instance I urged this in unqualified terms, and enforced it by special argument. These Messages are public documents within the easy reach of Governor Randolph and his informants, if he or they had wished to state the truth. This is not all. There being no registration, all parts of the State (those where the whites predominate equally with the others) are exposed to all the evils, if any, following from the absence of registration. The statement that I have "lost the confidence of the better class of citizens by my persistent refusal to enforce registration," of course now falls to the ground. The Charleston *News and Courier*, the Democratic organ of the State, referring in July last to my record on this subject, declared :

> In view of what Governor Chamberlain recommended where he had only the power to recommend, and what he did where he had the power to act, the irresistible conclusion is that he was as much in earnest in recommendation as in action ; and that in both cases, with equal earnestness, he exerted the whole power and influence of his office to promote the public good.

Governor Randolph states that the three Supreme Court Judges and ten of the Circuit Court Judges have testified "that they are acquainted with no cause that warranted the issuance of the Governor's Proclamation, or that of the President of the United States." I pronounce this statement to be absolutely false. No such statement has been made by the persons whom he names, and Governor Randolph has seen no such statement which was made by them. Further than this, I assert that in no one of the several statements made by the Judges of this State in respect to these matters is there one fact stated of their own knowledge or observation which traverses or qualifies any statement made by me in my Proclamation or other public statements, or in that of the President of the United States. This is a broad statement, but is true in every detail.

Not one of these Judges denies my statement that I have proof of the existence of two hundred and thirteen rifle clubs (I now have the proof of the existence of more than two hundred and forty), with their localities and officers. Not one of them denies the facts as stated by me in regard to the Ellenton riot and massacre, or the assembling and conduct of the rifle clubs at Rouse's Bridge. Not one of them denies my statement that more than thirty, and probably fifty, colored Republicans were massacred, wantonly and murderously killed, between the 16th and 24th of September, in the immediate vicinity of Ellenton, by the rifle clubs. Not one of them denies my statement that this horrible. Indian-like butchery was committed solely for political purposes. Not one of them denies my statement that these facts are now proved by the sworn testimony, carefully taken by the United States District Attorney and the Attorney General of the State, at Aiken and vicinity, before the United States Commissioners, of one hundred and thirty witnesses who saw the transactions to which they testify. Not one of the Judges denies my statement that this violence and insurrection far exceeded the power of the State Government to suppress.

Equally infamous and false are the statements made by Governor

Randolph that I have obtained my information " alone through my own creatures," and that " I refuse to show the evidence on which my statements are made." Is Mr. Corbin, the United States District Attorney, my creature? Are the United States Commissioners my creatures? Are Capt. Mills, Capt. Lloyd, Lieut. Hinton, and other army officers at Aiken, my creatures? Are the one hundred and thirty witnesses, whom I never saw and do not know, my creatures? Governor Randolph did not apply to me for information. He spent his time exclusively with those who knew no facts respecting these matters, or who were, like him, determined to suppress and deny them. His mission here was doubtless well stated to me to-day by a Democrat of this city: " Randolph came here to keep the bit in our mouths till election day."

Look also at Governor Randolph's statements respecting my action in appointing the Boards of Election Commissioners of the several counties. He asserts that " by public proclamation I invited the two political Committees to designate their choice " ; that I " announced that no candidate for office would be appointed by me " ; that " the persons named by the Democratic Committee were not generally appointed " ; and that " of the Republican Commissioners selected by the Governor, in nearly every instance the appointee is a Republican officeholder or a candidate for office at the coming election."

Having plenary power to appoint whomsoever I choose, I publicly announced that " as a general rule," I should appoint one Democrat and two Republicans on each of these boards, and I invited " suggestions and recommendations as to these appointments from both political parties." I also announced that if any of the persons appointed by me in the first instance should thereafter become candidates for office, I should " feel warranted in making removals for this cause." Now what have I done? I have appointed an unquestionable Democrat, a supporter of Wade Hampton, on every Board of Election Commissioners throughout the State. I have never appointed from my own party a candidate for office, and whenever any Commissioner appointed by me has subsequently become a candidate for office, I have appointed in his place one who is not a candidate. Thus, while no justice, mercy, or decency has been shown to me by my opponents in this campaign, I challenge the naming of a single official act of mine connected with the canvass or election which has not been fair and impartial.

The statements of Governor Randolph respecting Mr. Hagood, the Clerk of the United States Circuit Court, and Mr. Poinier, the United States Chief Supervisor of Elections, are bald misrepresentations and travesties of their views and statements. Both these gentlemen are my warm political supporters, and both unequivocally commend and applaud my recent action in suppressing domestic violence and insurrection in the State.

Governor Randolph's statement to the effect that all Republican Judges and many other leading Republicans have deserted me in the canvass are likewise false. Of the ten Republican Judges in the

State, six are now my supporters ; and of the remainder, only two are opposing me. Of other leading and conscientious Republicans, I assert that I know of no one who does not now support me or who does not especially approve my recent conduct. Conspicuous among these latter are the Hon. Reuben Tomlinson, the Hon. D. T. Corbin, W. E. Earle, and the Hon. William Stone, all gentlemen of the highest reputation and character here and abroad.

Governor Randolph is equally unfortunate in his efforts to ascribe my recent action to aspirations for the United States Senatorship. If he had sought the truth he would have known that at the outset of my candidacy for the Governorship I publicly announced that if elected I should under no circumstances be a candidate for Senator, an announcement published conspicuously by the Charleston *News and Courier* and used by that Democratic organ as a ground for advocating my support by the Democratic party of the State.

Enough has now been presented to show the character of Governor Randolph's letter. Many of the matters referred to have no interest to the public outside of South Carolina, except as they affect the great question of the necessity of my recent action in respect to the domestic violence and insurrection which I have declared to exist here. Upon that question evidences accumulate each day and hour which would appal the stoutest and hardest heart. New murders come to light. New atrocities are revealed. The evidences of a conspiracy to disfranchise a race and crush by brute force a whole people multiply with each step of investigation. Governor Randolph consigns me to a " wretched fate, whether elected or defeated." I accept the full responsibility of all my acts, and I await with confidence the verdict which just men will render upon my efforts to discharge duties as difficult and trying as have fallen to the lot of any American Governor. I certainly do not envy the fate which will overtake the man who has come here for purely partisan ends to gather slanders to heap upon me and the people whom I am struggling to protect and defend.

D. H. CHAMBERLAIN,
Governor of South Carolina.

COLUMBIA, S. C., Nov. 1, 1876.

In a political speech at Massillon, Ohio, Hon. Carl Schurz made the following reference to the condition of things in South Carolina :

That there is a Republican Administration in South Carolina nobody doubts. At the head of the Republican Administration stands now a true reform Governor, Mr. Chamberlain, who has already accomplished much to relieve the people of that State of the evils they justly complained of. If it was reform the white people of that State wanted for its own sake, the best course of the better class naturally suggested itself. It was to stand by Governor Chamberlain, and thus to effect the desired reform without subverting or endangering the rights of any one, by means of a most peaceful character, without any resort to force of arms. Instead of that they have opposed to him an extreme partisan nomination. We learn, not through the usual channel of sensational reports, but from reliable authority,—and I may say that I have never been the most credulous of men when Southern outrages are spoken of,—that all sorts of threatening demonstrations are resorted to to overawe and interrupt the discussion of public affairs in Republican meetings, or to make it wholly impossible, and also to impress Republican voters with a sense of personal danger in case they vote the Republican ticket. When such things occur—and unfortunately we can no longer doubt that they do occur—nobody must be surprised if in the North the cry for free speech rises up again, which never fails to make an impression upon the popular mind.

The following proclamation, issued a week before the election, is a part of the record of this extraordinary campaign.

PROCLAMATION.

STATE OF SOUTH CAROLINA,
EXECUTIVE CHAMBER.

In pursuance of Chapter 8 of the General Statutes of the State of South Carolina, amended by an Act approved March 12, 1872, an Act approved March 19, 1874, an election will be held in the several counties in this State on Tuesday, the 7th day of November, eighteen hundred and seventy-six, for the following State, Legislative, Circuit, County, and Congressional officers, and for the next two and four years, as provided by the State Constitution, the Statutes of the State, and the Acts of the Congress of the United States, to wit : Governor, Lieutenant-Governor, Secretary of State, Comptroller General, State Treasurer, Attorney General, State Superintendent of Education, Adjutant and Inspector General, Circuit Solicitors, members of the General Assembly, Sheriffs, Clerks of Court, Judges of Probate, School Commissioners, County Commissioners, Coroners in the several counties, together with one Representative to the Forty-Fourth Congress from the Second Congressional District, and one Representative to the Forty-Fifth Congress from each Congressional District in the State.

At the said election the following Amendment to the State Constitution will be submitted to the voters of the State, for ratification or rejection, to wit :

That Section 5, Article 10, be amended so as to read as follows :

SECTION 5. The Boards of County Commissioners of the several counties shall levy an annual tax of not less than two mills on the dollar upon all taxable property in their respective counties, which levy shall not be increased, unless by special enactment of the General Assembly, for the support of public schools in their respective counties, which tax shall be collected at the same time and by the same officers as the other taxes for the same year, and shall be held in the county treasuries of the respective counties, and paid out exclusively for the support of public schools as provided by law. There shall be assessed on all taxable polls in the State an annual tax of one dollar on each poll, the proceeds of which tax shall be applied solely to educational purposes : Provided, That no person shall ever be deprived of the right of suffrage for non-payment of said tax. No other poll or capitation tax shall be levied in the State, nor shall the amount assessed on each poll exceed the limit given in this section. The school tax shall be distributed among the several school districts in the counties in proportion to the respective number of pupils attending the public schools. No religious sect or sects shall have exclusive right to, or control of, any part of the school fund of the State, nor shall sectarian principles be taught in the school.

The manner of voting on this Amendment shall be as follows : Those in favor of the Amendment shall deposit a ballot with the following words written or printed thereon : "Constitutional Amendment—Yes." Those opposed to said Amendment shall cast a ballot with the words thereon : "Constitutional Amendment—No."

All barrooms and drinking saloons shall be closed on the day of election, and any person who shall sell any intoxicating drinks on that day shall be, under the law, deemed guilty of a misdemeanor, and on conviction thereof will be fined in a sum not less than one hundred dollars, or be imprisoned for a period not less than one nor more than six months.

The Commissioners and Managers of Election, all and each of them, are hereby required, with strict regard to the provisions of the Constitution and laws of the State, touching their duty in such cases, to cause such elections to be held in their respective counties on the day aforesaid, and to take all necessary steps for holding of such elections, and for the ascertaining and determining of the persons who shall have been duly elected thereat, according to the rules, principles, and provisions prescribed by the Act and the Amendment to the Act aforesaid.

In testimony whereof I have hereunto set my hand and caused the Great Seal of the State to be affixed, at Columbia, this first day [L. S.] of November, A.D. 1876, and in the one hundred and first year of American Independence.

D. H. CHAMBERLAIN.

By the Governor :
H. E. HAYNE, Secretary of State.

CHAPTER XXV.

THE election of President of the United States and that of State officers occurred on the same day, November 7, 1876. Fortunately the day passed without any serious outbreak of violence, a result to which the presence of the United States troops undoubtedly contributed, if it did not alone secure it. No troops were at or near the polls anywhere, but by Colonel Ruger, the officer in command, the small force was so disposed as to be available for the suppression of a riot in the sections where an outbreak was most feared. Moreover the consciousness that actual violence would certainly provoke, in the judgment of the nation, unfavorable prejudices against the party responsible for it, may be presumed to have had a restraining influence. Reliance was placed by the Democrats on the efficiency of the work of intimidation and proscription which had been done, and on the effect of repeating and other fraudulent voting. But the voting itself was accomplished without bloodshed. At every voting place there were, by Governor Chamberlain's appointment, two Republicans and one Democrat as Inspectors, and no question was ever raised regarding the accuracy of the return of the vote actually cast, where the return was certified by all the Inspectors.

By law, the returns from the whole State were required to be canvassed, and the result disclosed, by a Board of State Canvassers, composed of the State Treasurer, the Comptroller, the Secretary of State, the Adjutant General, and the Attorney General. It had judicial powers to hear protests and determine the legality of the election in respect of all candidates except Governor and Lieutenant Governor, the vote for whom was required to be canvassed by the General Assembly after its organization. The Board of State Canvassers was required by law to meet on the third day after the election and to conclude its work within ten days.

The returns came in slowly. Meantime the concern and excitement, both within the State and without, increased to an alarming degree. The whole country was agitated on account of the doubtful issue of the contest for President, making the vote of South Carolina of great moment; but the leaders of the Democratic party in the State were comparatively indifferent to this matter, being so much more concerned regarding their personal fortunes and the success of the plan of campaign they had prosecuted by such lawless and desperate expedients. The city of Columbia straightway became a camp of rifle clubs, marched there from all sections of the State to make sure of the results they desired. There is no reason to doubt that, but for the presence of the United States troops they would have taken possession of the State Government by violence.

Constrained to act within the forms of law, proceedings were instituted by them in the Supreme Court of the State to prevent the Board of State Canvassers from performing the duty imposed by the Constitution and the law, which, without question of their right, its members had always heretofore performed. The Chief Justice of the Supreme Court, F. J. Moses, father of the Governor of that name, whose aspirations for the bench were thwarted by Governor Chamberlain, had been an active sympathizer with, and supporter of, the aims of the politicians striving to compass Governor Chamberlain's defeat, as had his notorious son. The other members were Justice Willard, a white man who was elevated to the place by a Republican Legislature, and had been an avowed supporter of Hampton in the campaign; and Justice Wright, a negro of some ability, but of little or no moral courage.

The proceedings in Court were begun before the Board of Canvassers entered upon their work. The following report of the course and issue of this action is reproduced from a carefully prepared summary of the proceedings from authentic sources, that appeared in the New York *Times*, in the latter part of November previous to the meeting of the South Carolina Legislature, in which all the essential facts are clearly and dispassionately presented.

The action of the Board of State Canvassers and of the Supreme Court of South Carolina seems to be so much misunderstood, that it would be well to state briefly, from authentic sources, what were the actual proceedings in the Supreme Court and of the Board of State Canvassers.

The duties and powers of the Board are those usually residing in such Boards. Sections 26 and 27 of an Act approved March 1, 1870, are as follows :

SECTION 26. The Board, when thus formed, shall, upon the certified copies of the statements made by the Board of County Canvassers, proceed to make a statement of the whole number of votes given at such election for the various officers, and for each of them voted for, distinguishing the several counties in which they are given. They shall certify such statement to be correct, and subscribe the same with their proper names.

SECTION 27. Upon such statements they shall then proceed to determine and declare what persons have been, by the greatest number of votes, duly elected to such offices, or either of them : *they shall have power, and it is made their duty, to decide all cases under protest or contest that may arise, when the power to do so does not, by the Constitution, reside in some other body.*

The exception here refers to the offices of Governor and Lieutenant Governor, decision on which, in case of contest, is with the Legislature.

On the 14th of November Mr. Youmans, for the Democrats, asked the Supreme Court for two writs—one of mandamus to compel the Board to perform the purely ministerial function "of ascertaining from the managers' [County Canvassers'] returns what persons have the highest number of votes, and certifying the statements thereof to the Secretary of State "; and one of prohibition " from hearing any protest or contest, and from exercising any judicial functions whatever touching the elections."

The Court adjourned to the 16th to give the counsel of the Board time to answer.

On the 16th of November the motions were argued and the Court adjourned,

On the 17th the Court again sat, and the Chief Justice [Moses] said that "the Court had examined the suggestions of mandamus and those in prohibition, and before it proceeds to final judgment it desires to save time, . . . and that the Court requires an order to be drawn that the Board of State Canvassers forthwith proceed to count and compare the returns, and make a report of the result to the Court, and certify their action in the premises to the Court.

Counsel on both sides then consulted as to such an order, but failing to agree as to the terms, such an order was thereupon *issued by the Court itself*—Associate Justice

Wright dissenting from so much of the order as required the Board to certify their action in the premises to the Court.

The order did not extend to the offices of Governor and Lieutenant-Governor, which, it was understood, were left by law to the decision of the General Assembly.

It will be observed that this is, so far, the only order issued, that it was understood to be intermediary, and that it leaves the original motions still undecided.

On the 18th, the Board not being ready to report, further arguments were heard by the Court on the motions for mandamus and prohibition, and the Court adjourned without expressing any opinion, giving counsel on either side privilege of submitting written arguments before 10 A.M. Monday, if they should so desire.

Monday, November 20th, the Board not yet reporting, affidavits were presented to the Court by the Democratic counsel, on which they asked an order from the Court requiring the Board of Canvassers in reporting their action under the order of November 17th, to report to the Court at the same time all errors and irregularities in the statements of the County Canvassers, "*and to annex to their reports all official documents and papers in their possession showing the nature and character of such errors and irregularities.*"

The Democratic counsel said : " No notice had been given, and he did not suppose the other side would object."

The order was so outrageous in its requirements, that Chief Justice Moses said : "It seems to me to be a very irregular mode of proceeding." Associate Judge Willard said : "What responsibility are the Board under in virtue of that order? They are not Commissioners in equity nor Referees at law. *They are not in performance of a power conferred upon them by this Court.* It seems to me you have mistaken your right." The order asked for was not granted, and the Court adjourned to await the report of the Board.

November 21st, on the opening of the Court, Mr. D. T. Corbin, counsel for the Board of State Canvassers, moved that the order of November 17th be rescinded, arguing that it was an interlocutory order, and always subject to the discretion of the Court ; that it was in the nature of mandamus, and that it could not be issued at that stage of the proceedings. During the arguments which followed, Judge Willard said : "*I cannot see the object of asking the Court to pass upon the abstract question*" [that of the exercise of judicial powers by the Board] "*with its eyes shut ; we want to know who received the highest number of votes.*" And again, later, he said: "*We do not want to decide the abstract question of law and then have you come before us on the application of those questions to the facts.*"

It thus appears that the relative position of the Supreme Court and of the Board was this : The Supreme Court, *before* it would decide an abstract question of law, wanted to know what facts (whose election) would be affected by its decision.

The Board wanted to know by what construction of the law it was to decide questions of fact.

Associate Judge Wright probed the matter to the quick when he said : " I take an entirely different view of the proceedings before the Court," and later on he said, referring to his dissent from that part of the order of the 17th of November requiring the Board to certify their action to the Court : " I dissented for the reason that I did not consider it necessary that the Court should know whether A, B, or C was elected, and the only question before the Court was one of law, whether the Board had the power to hear and determine protests and contests. To pass that part of the order I thought would be to turn the Court into a political machine to elect parties."

Later in the day Mr. Corbin submitted the report of the Board of State Canvassers, reading only its conclusion, part of which was as follows : " This statement is made to the Court in obedience to its order of November 17, 1876, but it is respectfully submitted that, under the present proceedings in this Court, this Board is not, by law, compelled to report any of its actions to the Court." The statement then recites certain errors, and the results from correcting the same, and further, that allegations and evidences of fraud had been filed with the Board as to the elections in Edgefield, Barnwell, and Laurens counties. The body of the report of the Board showed that on the face of the returns two Democratic members of Congress would be elected, a part of the Democratic State officers, and such Democratic members of the General Assembly as would give them a majority of one on joint ballot ; but it also showed that, on the face of the same returns, the Republican Electors of President and Vice-President were elected, and also some of the State officers—Elliott, Cardozo, and Hayne.

This simple statement furnishes in part a solution to the question, which naturally arises, why the Court had not yet, after seven days, decided the plain question of law, which, as Judge Wright said, "was the only one before the Court, viz., whether the Board had the power to hear protests and contests," and why Democratic counsel did not dare to press for its decision. It is evident that a frightfully aggravating dilemma presented itself to the Democrats.

The face of the returns gave the control of the State Government to the Democrats, and, notwithstanding the frauds in Edgefield and Laurens, the Electoral ticket to Hayes. If, on motion of Democratic counsel, the Court denied to the Board the power to hear protests and contests, then, though they would have gained their great end, the possession of the State, they would at the same time have dealt an almost fatal blow to the important, but to them secondary, end—the success of Tilden.

If, on the other hand, the Court had decided that the Board had the power in question, they would have endangered the possession of the State, and could hardly then have hoped to make out a case for the rejection of the Hayes Electors, and the threats and intimidations of the rifle clubs, the massacres of Hamburg and Ellenton would have been in vain.

But, as we shall see, the effrontery of the counsel and their advisers was equal to the emergency, as it is an open secret that the proceedings in Court were daily transmitted by telegraph to New York, and the action of Democratic counsel inspired from thence.

On the statement of the Board of State Canvassers being received, the Democratic counsel requested time to examine the statement and consult. They then asked the Court to grant two orders (one for each horn of the dilemma). The first, "that the Board do certify to be correct the statement of the whole number of votes for members of General Assembly, . . . and determine and declare what persons have been by the greatest number of votes elected to such offices, . . . make certificate of their determination, and deliver it to the Secretary of State, who shall transmit a copy to each person declared to be elected, . . . and that they shall do the same in reference to members of Congress." . . .

This order, if granted, would give them a Democratic Legislature, and consequently the Governor and Lieutenant Governor and two members of Congress, which was all they needed, and more than their most sanguine hopes had expected.

The second order was the one of the previous day, now brought up again, "to compel the Board to surrender to the Court *all* official documents showing the nature and character of errors and irregularities." So that the Court, after by the former order giving them the State, might at last pass upon the original question, and so decide whether the Board had power to go behind the face of the returns as to the Republican Electors and Republican State officers. The plain meaning of these two orders is :

1. We have the State Legislature ; issue the certificates and don't go behind the returns.

2. We have lost the Presidential Electors and most of the State officers ; send us the papers, and then we will decide whether you shall go behind the returns or not.

When the Court entertained such motions it already indicated what answer it would give, but it at least preserved the faint show of dignity by not granting the orders at once, and adjourned after long arguments.

But delay was all in favor of the Democrats. It was well known to all concerned that the statute defining the powers and duties of the Board limited their sitting to ten days. This period expired about noon the next day. If the Board had not fulfilled its duties by that time, and certified its determination and made certificate of election according to the statute, it would no longer have had legal existence—would have been incompetent to perform a single function, could not have given validity to any certificate, and would not, as a Board, be longer amenable to judicial control.

What would have been the inevitable result? The Supreme Court, the only legally constituted body in possession of the records of the election, though illegally wrung from the Board, would have assumed, with alacrity, the responsibility of declaring the result of the election. Was not the accomplishment of this desirable end the object of the deliberate policy of the Democrats, and would not its success have been a source of the gravest peril to the Republicans ?

We now come to the 22d November—the last eventful day. The Board of State Canvassers, having obeyed the only mandate of the Supreme Court addressed to them, in full view of the plain requirements of the statute, with but a few hours left them of legal existence, and being without further express instructions or orders of the Court, met at 10 A.M. to complete their duties. Their minutes show :

That they corrected the errors referred to in their statement to the Court, namely, counting the votes cast for F. C. Dunn as Comptroller General and John B. Tolbert as Superintendent of Education, for T. C. Dunn and John R. Tolbert, respectively, for said offices.

The following certificates and determination of the Board were submitted and adopted : [Here follow the certificates as to Presidential Electors and State Congressional, Circuit, and County officers].

On the question as to whether the statement of the County Canvassers of Edgefield and Laurens counties should be included in the statement and determination of the Board, the majority voted in the negative. The Board then adjourned *sine die*—about 1 P.M.

In the meantime the Supreme Court, having dallied with the main question of law until within a few hours of the determination of the Board's legal existence, met at 11 A.M. and granted the principal part of the order asked on the previous day, viz.: That a writ of peremptory mandamus do issue, directed to the Board of State Canvassers and the Secretary of State, commanding them to forthwith declare duly elected, and to issue certificates to the persons who received the greatest number of votes for the offices of Senators and members of the House of Representatives (State).

There is so far no evidence that the members of the Board, individually or in their collective capacity, had any knowledge of this writ until after their adjournment *sine die*.

The Court, after a short recess to give Democratic counsel opportunity to amend or divide their second order of the previous day, met at 1 P.M., and then on very lengthy affidavits and motions (or suggestions) presented by counsel, reciting "the irregularities in certain counties as to Presidential Electors, and neglect or failure to act on the part of the Board, and asking that the Board shall proceed according to law and submit to the Court their report, and that the Board shall bring into Court all official papers and documents, etc.," the Court ordered that a rule do issue requiring the Board of State Canvassers to show cause on Friday, the 24th (two days after the time when the Board would cease to exist), why a writ of mandamus should not issue in accordance with the prayer of the said suggestion.

The Court then took up other business.

The wrath of the Court and the Democrats when they discovered that the Board of State Canvassers had performed its duty and terminated its legal existence while yet uninformed of the ultimate decision of the perplexed and procrastinating Court, is indescribable. The Court avenged itself for its mortification by consigning all the members of the Board to prison for contempt, the contempt consisting in having obeyed the Constitution and laws in the absence of any order communicated to them enjoining them from the performance of their duty in their own discretion. The anger of the Democrats was hardly restrained within bounds by the earnest efforts of leaders who realized the importance of keeping the peace. Their spirit and conduct plainly indicated that the action of the Board had defeated some cherished scheme, and it was quickly and probably accurately judged that the real motive of the long delays and peculiar orders of the Court was to secure that no determination could be reached by the Board within the period of ten days prescribed by law ; when the Court would have decided that its members were without power to act further, and would assume the duty of canvassing the returns itself, in which case, undoubtedly, they would have been revised in a manner to elect the entire Democratic State ticket, with a majority of the Legislature, and also the Democratic candidates for Presidential Electors. That plot, if it existed, was effectively foiled.

The declaration of the Board of Canvassers that the irregularities and frauds in Edgefield and Laurens counties had been such that they were unable to determine who had been chosen to the Legislature, was equivalent to a declaration that the election in those counties was void, and left them without representation. Certificates were issued by the Secretary of State to all others who appeared on the face of the returns made by the County Canvassers to be elected, although there were other counties from which protests had been received that were worthy of consideration, and, under other circumstances, would have been considered. Owing to the harassment to which the Board was subjected, and the excitement prevailing, no attempt was made to consider the large number of cases involving the legality of the voting at district polling places.

Two days before the date of the meeting of the Legislature the following instructions were sent to General Ruger, commanding the United States troops in South Carolina:

WASHINGTON, November 26, 1876.

Gen. Thomas H. Ruger, or Col. H. M. Black, Columbia, S. C.:

The following has been received from the President:

EXECUTIVE MANSION, November 26, 1876.

Hon. J. D. Cameron, Secretary of War:

SIR—D. H. Chamberlain is now Governor of the State of South Carolina beyond any controversy, and remains so until a new Governor shall be duly and legally inaugurated under the Constitution. The Government has been called upon to aid with the military and naval forces of the United States to maintain republican government in the State against resistance too formidable to be overcome by the State authorities. You are directed, therefore, to sustain Governor Chamberlain in his authority against domestic violence until otherwise directed.

U. S. GRANT.

In obeying these instructions you will advise with the Governor, and dispose your troops in such a manner as may be deemed best in order to carry out the spirit of the above order of the President. Acknowledge receipt.

J. D. CAMERON,
Secretary of War.

For some days before the meeting of the Legislature the Democrats in Columbia were expressing confidence that they would control the organization and obtain immediate possession of all departments of the State Government. They asserted that more than enough Republicans would be absent to give them a majority, and that the Democrats from Edgefield and Laurens would be admitted at once. If the Republicans were not all there, then the excluded members would demand to have their names called, and would enforce the demand. A Democratic Speaker would be elected, and the Legislature would declare the election of Hampton, who would be inaugurated forthwith, although it had been usual to inaugurate the Governor on the Thursday after the meeting of the Legislature.

Certificates of election to the House of Representatives had been issued by the Secretary of State to fifty-nine Republicans and fifty-seven Democrats, leaving eight vacancies,—the number of the members to which the counties of Edgefield and Laurens, whose elections had been declared null, were entitled. The Senate, with two vacancies, had a Republican majority of five.

The Legislature met on Tuesday, the 28th of November. The following special despatch to the New York *Times* gives an account of the proceedings, which were attended by much confusion, at times threatening to culminate in riot, especially in the House of Representatives:

COLUMBIA S. C., November 28th.

Last night a company of United States troops took charge of the Capitol. The streets had been full of rumors, and threats that the roughs in the city from almost every county in the State would take possession of the corridors, and prevent the Republican members of the House from entering the chamber until an organization was effected by the Democrats. The Republicans, and especially the colored men, were excited and alarmed, and had begun to gather in some places near the Statehouse. The inflammability of the community was apparent to every observer. White men in red shirts swaggered in the streets of the town, displaying their revolvers, while there were some colored men talking wildly. No local authority would have been of the least use in quelling the riot, if one had started. It was in the interests of peace and order, and as a purely preventive measure, that General Ruger, at the request of the Governor, sent a small force to the Statehouse. All well-disposed persons are glad to feel safer because of their presence.

Both houses of the Legislature met at 12 noon. The Democratic members marched down to the Statehouse by twos, with Gen. Wade Hampton and the Chairman of the Democratic Executive Committee bringing up the rear. The persons claiming to have been elected from Edgefield and Laurens counties were refused admission to the hall, whereupon one of the Edgefield members read the following protest :

COLUMBIA, November 28th.

We, a majority of the House of Representatives elect, protest against the refusal to admit us to the Hall of Representatives. We protest against the military power of the United States barring the passage into the Statehouse of members-elect of the

Legislature. We protest against the legality of the proceedings, and especially against the Army of the United States being placed for the purpose of this exclusion under the command of John B. Dennis, a partisan of Governor Chamberlain. We protest against the said Dennis' instructions to the guard to admit no one to the Statehouse except upon his own pass or a pass of A. O. Jones, the former Clerk of the House, who may thus exclude all except his own partisans, and who, by the Republican programme, is to organize the said House.

We have presented ourselves with the judgment of the highest Court of South Carolina, certified to by its Clerk, with the great seal of the Court attached. As to our right to participate in the organization of the said House, we are refused, by the orders of the said Dennis, admission to said hall except upon his pass, the pass of said Jones, or the certificate of H. E. Hayne, Secretary of State, who is now under condemnation of said Court for refusal to issue certificates in accordance with its judgment and mandate.

In protesting against this barefaced usurpation, this trampling on the laws and Constitution of the State, this defiance of the highest tribunal of the State, it is our purpose to offer no resistance to this armed intervention, but to make our solemn appeal to the American people, without distinction of party. Our veneration for law, our respect for the Supreme Court and the usages of all legislative assemblages, forbid our participation in such unprecedented and revolutionary proceedings.

[Signed by all the Democratic members, sixty-four in number.][1]

During the excitement an immense crowd had assembled in front of the Statehouse, when the Federal officer in charge approached General Hampton, who was in the Statehouse, with a request to prevent the crowd from pushing in. General Hampton immediately appeared upon the front steps of the Capitol, and addressed the crowd as follows :

My Friends :—I am truly doing what I have done earnestly during this whole exciting contest, pouring oil on the troubled waters. It is of the greatest importance to us all, as citizens of South Carolina, that peace should be preserved. I appeal to you all, white men and colored, as Carolinians, to use every effort to keep down violence or turbulence. One act of violence may precipitate bloodshed and desolation. I implore you, then, to preserve the peace. I beg all of my friends to disperse, to leave the grounds of the Capitol, and I advise all the colored men to do the same. Keep perfectly quiet, leave the streets, and do nothing to provoke a riot. We trust to the law and the Constitution, and we have perfect faith in the justness of our cause.

The Democratic members, with one exception, then withdrew to the rifle company's hall, and organized as a House of Representatives. The Republican members entered the hall in the Statehouse, and at the hour of 12 the Clerk called the roll, omitting Edgefield and Laurens counties. General Wallace, of Union, a Democrat, was present, but refused to vote. Hon. E. W. M. Mackey, of Charleston, was elected Speaker, and A. O. Jones, Clerk. The other officers were elected, and the Senate was informed that the House was duly organized. In reply to a question from a member, the Speaker informed the House that there were sixty members present, and that it was a constitutional majority of all the members elected, as the Board of Canvassers had declared that no valid election had occurred in Laurens and Edgefield counties ; consequently the full House now consisted of only 116 members, instead of 124.

The Senate organized at once, with Lieutenant Governor Gleaves in the chair, and every member present. The Democrats took no active part in the business. The Senators from Edgefield and Laurens were in their seats, but were not recognized and

[1] Including those claiming election from Edgefield and Laurens.

did not vote. The Senate elected S. A. Swails President *pro tem*. Protests were made against the members from Aiken and Barnwell, on the ground that they were elected by force and fraud. There was perfect order and apparent good-humor on all sides in the Senate. Both houses adjourned until 10 to-morrow.

The city is full of men but all is quiet so far. A company of troops remain in the Capitol to-night.

The returns of the Governor's election will be sent to the House promptly to-morrow. It is thought that the regular House will declare Chamberlain elected, and the Democratic House Hampton, while the Senate is expected to recognize Chamberlain.

To-night the Democrats held a mass-meeting in front of the Wheeler House, which was addressed by General Gary and Judge Mackey. The proceedings of the Republicans, and especially the use made of the United States troops, were bitterly denounced. There seems to be no danger of trouble to-night. The barrooms are closed, and the leading Democrats seem to be disposed to quiet the turbulent members of their party. A cold rain helps to keep the peace. The programme for to-morrow on the part of the Democrats is unknown, save by rumor. It is certainly their intention to keep up a House of their own, and to trust to accidents. They are using every art of threat and bribery to seduce some Republicans to their side.

The Democratic members fitted up Carolina Hall, and held a secret caucus to-night.

They fully organized by the election of General W. H. Wallace, of Union, as Speaker. Sixty-six members are said to have been present, including two Republicans, who joined in the organization of the Republican House this morning, and the eight members from the excluded counties. It is said that if they get a clear majority, without counting the Edgefield and Laurens men, they will go to the Statehouse in the morning, and join in the joint Assembly to count the vote for Governor.

The same despatch contained the following report of an interview with the Governor regarding the events of the day:

I saw Governor Chamberlain to-night, and said, "What do you think of the situation?"

"I think [said he] the result of the events here to-day is very favorable to the cause of Republicanism and public justice. In the first place, the United States troops have performed their proper functions in preserving the peace and maintaining an attitude of perfect neutrality between the two parties. The effect of their presence has, of course, been favorable to the Republicans, because the chief reliance of the Democrats has been, and is now, in overawing the Republicans, or by some violent means preventing them from securing their rights. I know of no act done by the military forces to-day which has abridged or denied any right of a Democrat."

"What is your opinion of the organization of the House?"

Governor Chamberlain—"I think the House, as at present organized, is as valid a legislative body as there is in America. Why is it not? Every man who held a credential entitling him to a seat would have been admitted without question, and out of the one hundred and sixteen members elected, sixty were present, answered to the call of the Clerk, and fifty-nine of these voted for Speaker. The language of the Constitution of South Carolina upon the subject of a legislative quorum is absolutely identical with that of the Constitution of the United States : ' A majority of each House shall constitute a quorum to do business.' The great congressional precedent of 1861, as stated in ' Barclay's Digest,' is to the effect that a quorum consists of a majority of all the members chosen. It is plain, therefore, that the House of Representatives has been organized in a perfectly lawful and constitutional manner. As to the Senate there is no question. The Democrats have remained and taken part in its organization, and that body has exchanged messages with the House of Representatives. Thus, you see, we have a House and Senate in working order. No arbitrary or unlawful step has been taken."

" Do you expect to be sustained at Washington ? "

Governor Chamberlain—" As to that, I can only say that I do expect to be sustained at Washington if I stand on the law and the facts of the case, and upon no other condition. If I am the lawful Governor of the State, President Grant will sustain me, and I shall never ask him to do more than that. I propose, from beginning to end, to put my case, and that of the Republican party, upon strict law and actual facts. I shall attempt no usurpation, and I want none attempted for me."

That evening the Governor sent the following despatch to the President :

COLUMBIA, S. C., November 28th.

His Excellency, U. S. Grant, President of the United States, Washington, D. C. :

The House and Senate organized to-day. The Democrats, on the refusal to admit the members from Edgefield and Laurens counties, withdrew, leaving sixty members in the House, a quorum of all the members chosen. The House then proceeded to business. The Senate organized without delay. General Ruger has preserved the peace, and acted with perfect impartiality and great good judgment.

D. H. CHAMBERLAIN,
Governor of South Carolina.

On the 30th of November the whole body of Democrats constituting the pretended House of Representatives marched in a body to the State Capitol, and effected an entrance to the hall of the legitimate House while the Legislature was in session, having previously ascertained from General Ruger that he would exercise no authority with reference to determining the rights of members, but only to preserve the peace in case of riot. How the entrance was effected was described in a special despatch to the New York *Herald :*

Upon reaching the door, it was found guarded by a United States Deputy Marshal and the colored Republican Sergeant-at-Arms of the House. The Democratic visitors in front asked for admission, and were refused on the ground that none but members could go in. The members who were in front drew their certificates from the Secretary of State and presented them. The doorkeeper not suspecting the crisis at hand, the doors were opened to pass the few with papers in their hands. As soon as some half dozen had crossed the threshold they turned, flung open the doors, placed their backs against them, and in walked the entire Democratic body and took their seats. The doorkeeper made a desperate struggle to keep them out.

The Speaker of the Democratic House, so called, attempted to take the chair. The result was a scene of noisy confusion, two bodies attempting to control the proceedings. Fear of interference by General Ruger prevented violence. The Associated Press despatch of the same evening contained the following account of proceedings subsequent to this action.

About three o'clock this afternoon General Ruger sent his staff officer to the Speaker's stand, and notified Democratic Speaker Wallace that at twelve o'clock to-morrow the Democratic members form Edgefield would not be permitted on the floor of the House. Upon the receipt of that order the following letter was sent to General Ruger :

General T. H. Ruger, Commanding United States Troops in South Carolina ·

DEAR SIR—We have just heard through Major McGinnis, of your staff, your order communicated to William Wallace, Speaker of the House of Representatives, that at twelve o'clock to-morrow the members elect from Edgefield would not be allowed upon the floor of the House.

To say that we are surprised at such an order, after the explanations and pledges made by you to each one of us, is to use very mild language. When the outrage of Tuesday last was committed by the placing of armed sentinels at the door of the House of Representatives, who decided upon the admission of members to their seats, and when the provisions of the Constitution and the decision of the Supreme Court were brought to your attention, you distinctly and warmly asserted, again and again, that your orders were misunderstood ; that you did not intend to have sentinels at the door of the hall ; and that you had not and did not intend to assume to decide upon the legality of any man's seat, or upon his right to enter the hall. You were then reminded by us that your guard received instructions from one Dennis, a citizen, and partisan of Governor Chamberlain, to admit parties upon his own pass or that of one Jones, and had, through armed forces, excluded all Democrats from the hall until the Republican organization was completed.

You assured us again that such were not your orders, and were told by us that, notwithstanding the perpetration of this inexpressible shame upon our free institutions and the rights of the people, the evils could still be remedied without violence or bloodshed by a simple withdrawal of your guard from the doors of the hall, and that a majority of votes decides all questions in accordance with law and the usage of legislative bodies. You stated that no troops should be at the door, and that under no circumstances would you interfere, except there should occur a serious disturbance of the peace. You affirmed your determination to exercise no supervisory control whatever over the body or bodies claiming to be the House of Representatives. All this occurred on yesterday. Last night, in a later interview with Senator Gordon, you made the same assurances, and this morning after both bodies were assembled in the hall, you assured General Hampton that under no circumstances would you interfere, except to keep the peace.

What now can justly measure our astonishment at the issuance of such an order as the one just sent by you ? There is no breach of the peace and no prospect of its disturbance. You had it officially brought to your notice that absolute good humor prevails in that hall. We cannot refrain from expressing the apprehension that the fact that a number of leading Republicans are taking issue with the legality of the proceedings of the Republican House has changed your views as to your line of duty. It is proper that we should say, in conclusion, that we relied upon your honor as a man and your character as a soldier to maintain your pledged position of non-intervention.

The Democratic members from Edgefield and Laurens are entitled to their seats by the judgment of the Supreme Court of this State, and we have advised them to remain in that hall until removed by your troops, that the issue may be made in this centennial year of American independence whether we have a Government of law as construed by Courts, or a centralized despotism whose only law is force. Let the American people behold the spectacle of a Brigadier General of the Army seated by the side of Governor Chamberlain in a room in the Statehouse, and issuing his orders to a legislative body peacefully assembled in one of the original thirteen commonwealths of this Union.

Respectfully yours,

J. B. GORDON,[1]
WADE HAMPTON,
A. C. HASKELL,

COLUMBIA, S. C., November 30, 1876.

General Ruger explained his action in the following despatch:

COLUMBIA, December 1, 1876.

Gen. W. T. Sherman, or the Secretary of War, Washington, D. C.:

I have carefully abstained from interference with the organization of the House from the first. On the application of the Governor, and my own belief for the necessity therefor for the preservation of the peace, I placed troops in the Statehouse (but not in the rooms of assembly of either of the Houses) on the day of meeting. It came about that for a time soldiers were placed on either side of the door of entrance to the Hall of Representatives under the following circumstances : A person at the door of the House, and who claimed authority to examine the certificates of those claiming to be members prior to their admission to the hall, but who, I think, had no legal authority for so doing, applied to the officer in command of the troops placed in the corridor for the preservation of the peace, for assistance, on the ground that he was being pressed upon and could not perform his duty. The soldiers were placed as stated. As soon as I was fully informed of the circumstances, I ordered the soldiers withdrawn. As I had previously informed Gov. Chamberlain that I should confine my action to the preservation of the peace, and should do nothing with reference to keeping the doors of the rooms of meeting of the Houses, or the rooms themselves, unless it became necessary because of a breach of the peace which the civil officers of the Houses should be unable to quell. No act was done by the soldiers except that of their presence, as stated, but while they were so present, persons claiming the right of entrance under certificate of the Clerk of the Supreme Court were refused admission.

THOMAS H. RUGER,

Commanding Department.

General J. B. Gordon, of Georgia, and other prominent Democrats from Southern States and Northern States, representing Mr.

[1] Of Georgia, United States Senator.

Tilden and the Democratic party, were in Columbia advising with
General Hampton and his supporters, and sending abroad daily
bulletins giving partial and perversive accounts of the situation,
shrewdly adapted to befog and perplex public sentiment regarding the course of events and current phases of the contest. To
some of these misleading representations Governor Chamberlain,
who, in the complications thickening about him, had need to be
"well-eyed as Argus was," replied in the following telegraphic
letter to the New York *Tribune*, published December 5th:

To the Editor of the Tribune:
    The zealous and heroic despatches with which Senator Gordon and
other persons, who have suddenly landed here with their carpet-bags to
take charge of South Carolina, are flooding the country, make it proper
that I should give an exact and faithful statement of the facts.
    First: It is not true, as charged, that the United States army officers
have assumed any duties here without being properly called upon to
do so. The orders of the President to the commanding officers here,
dated November 25th, are well known. Acting in view of those orders,
I called upon Col. Black on Monday, the 27th ult. for a force sufficient
to protect the Statehouse against the intrusion of armed and violent
men on Monday night and Tuesday morning prior to the hour for the
Legislature to assemble. This I did upon evidence that a plan was matured to take forcible possession of the halls of the Legislature and carry
out the "shotgun" policy in the organization of the two Houses. Col.
Black, as he was bound to do, responded by ordering a company of soldiers to guard the Statehouse. To say that I ought to have done this
myself is to speak without knowledge of the condition of affairs here.
There is no State force available for such a purpose—a fact perfectly
well known here.
    On the morning of Tuesday, the 27th ult., I detailed a State officer
to take charge of the admission of persons to the Statehouse, with instructions to admit only such persons as had official business in the
Statehouse, or who held the certificates of the Secretary of State as
members of the General Assembly. These orders were enforced, whenever necessary, by the military officers on duty in the Statehouse. Later
in the forenoon it seemed best to relax these orders and admit persons
generally into the Statehouse. This was done. Subsequently when the
Democratic members reached the door of the House of Representatives
the Sergeant-at-Arms and his assistants, who were in charge of the door
and acting under the orders of the Clerk of the former House, found
themselves pressed upon and about to be overpowered by a body of
Democrats demanding admission. The Clerk had properly given
orders to admit only those who held the certificates of the Secretary
of State. In this emergency the Sergeant-at-Arms called upon the military officers in charge of the United States troops to aid him in guard-

ing the doors against the intrusion of unauthorized persons, and such aid was granted. It is true that after conference with me upon the point, Gen. Ruger properly intended that this call for aid at the doors should be submitted to him before the aid was given ; and this is, so far as I know, the only act done by the military forces which was not previously sanctioned by Gen. Ruger. This act, however, was in no sense in excess or violation of his orders from the President. No person holding the certificate of the Secretary of State was at any time refused admission to the Statehouse or to the House of Representatives.

Second : It is not true, as charged, that the military commander here has assumed to decide upon the certificates of members of the General Assembly. The Clerk of the former House had decided that no persons except those holding certificates signed by the Secretary of State were entitled to enter the hall of the House or to participate in the organization. Whatever has been done by the military forces in this respect has been done to enforce this decision and order of the Clerk. To say that all this is not the business of the military forces is to say that the President's orders to enforce my authority and to protect the State against domestic violence are improper. It was certainly my duty to enforce the authority of the Clerk if I had the power ; and if, as was the fact, I had no adequate force to do this, then, if my authority was unquestioned, the action of the military force would seem to be warranted.

Third : It is not true, as stated, that any persons hold certificates of election from the Supreme Court. The Court on application refused to issue any certificates. What the persons from Edgefield and Laurens counties hold are mere evidences from the Clerk of that Court that the Court made an order requiring the Canvassers and the Secretary of State to do what they have never done. If such papers are said to be valid certificates of election, entitling the bearers to be recognized as members of the House, I take issue, and appeal to the judgment of courts and lawyers. The Democratic members holding valid certificates refused on Tuesday, doubtless under the advice of Senator Gordon and our other Democratic strangers, to go into the House, because their friends from Edgefield and Laurens counties, without certificates, were refused admittance. No impediment other than this was placed in their way by any civil or military officer.

Fourth : The House now presided over by Mr. Mackey was organized with 60 present holding the certificates of the Secretary of State based on the action of the Canvassers, 59 of whom voted in the election of Speaker. This is a majority of 116, the whole number holding the certificates of the Secretary of the State.

Fifth : The body presided over by Mr. Wallace has never had more than 57 persons holding the certificates of the Secretary of State—less than a majority of 116.

Sixth : The present position of affairs is caused by the attempt of the Democrats to escape from the effects of the blunder committed by them on Tuesday, in refusing to take part in the organization of the

House. They have forcibly injected themselves, including the persons (holding no certificates of election) from Edgefield and Laurens, into the House presided over by Mr. Mackey, and the Edgefield and Laurens men refuse to retire. That the whole force of the State, if any force was available, ought to be employed by me in enforcing the lawful orders of Mr. Mackey as Speaker, I entertain no doubt. As such force is not available, what alternative is left except a call upon the President for aid in suppressing domestic violence? To call this a "parliamentary struggle" is to do violence to language as well as to misstate facts. If a body of men can be permitted, without credentials and without right to take their places in a legislative body already duly organized, and call their refusal to retire on the order of the lawful officers of that legislative body and their usurpation of the Speaker's chair, a mere parliamentary struggle, the results are plain. This is, in fact, domestic violence now, and will soon be revolution. To yield to such violence is to abandon lawful government.

Seventh : The Republicans desire a speedy and peaceful settlement of the present difficulties, but they will never, with my consent, yield one hair's breadth of their legal rights to secure peace, especially under the present menaces of the South Carolina Democracy. I have fought corruption in my own party, and shall not blanch before violence in the Democratic party.　　　　　D. H. CHAMBERLAIN.

COLUMBIA, S. C., Dec. 4, 1876.

P. S.—Since preparing the above statement the Democrats have again withdrawn from the Statehouse. What further issues are to arise I cannot say.　　　　　D. H. C.

The vote for Governor and Lieutenant Governor was canvassed without disturbance by the two Houses sitting in joint convention on the 5th of December, 1876. The reported vote of Edgefield and Laurens counties was not counted; but no other counties were thrown out, although the Legislature had, upon evidence of gross frauds in two or three other counties, considered and reported upon by the proper committee, given seats to Republicans claiming to be chosen in place of Democrats, to whom certificates had been given on the report of the Board of State Canvassers. The result of the vote for Governor was declared as follows:

D. H. Chamberlain received 86,216
Wade Hampton received 83,071

And for Lieutenant Governor:

R. H. Gleaves received 86,620
W. D. Simpson received 82,521

Governor Chamberlain's reëlection was by a majority, ascertained and declared by the only body having authority to canvass the vote, of 3,145.

CHAPTER XXVI.

ON the 10th of December, 1876, Governor Chamberlain was inaugurated as Governor for a second term, and delivered the following Address:

Gentlemen of the Senate and House of Representatives:

I accept the office to which, by the voice of a majority of the people of this State, I have a second time been called, with a full knowledge of the grave responsibilities and difficulties by which it is now attended. No considerations, except the clearest convictions of duty, would be sufficient to induce me to accept this great trust under the circumstances which now surround us. I regard the present hour in South Carolina as a crisis at which no patriotic citizen should shrink from any post to which public duty may call him. In my sober judgment, our present struggle is in defence of the foundations of our Government and institutions. If we fail now, our Government—the Government of South Carolina—will no longer rest on the consent of the governed, expressed by a free vote of a majority of our people. If our opponents triumph—I care not under what guise of legal forms,—we shall witness the overthrow of free government in our State.

My chief personal anxiety is, that I may have the firmness and wisdom to act in a manner worthy of the great interests so largely committed to my keeping. My chief public care shall be to contribute my utmost efforts to defend the rights, to guard the peace, and to promote the welfare of the people of our State.

The constant occupation of my time with other duties, which I could not postpone, has prevented me from preparing the usual statements and recommendations respecting our public affairs. At the earliest practicable day I will discharge this duty. Our greatest interest, our most commanding duty now, is to stand firmly, each in his appointed place, against the aggressions and allurements of our political opponents. Our position up to the present time has been within the clear limits of our Constitution and laws. Nothing but the cowardice, or weakness, or treachery of our own friends, can rob us of the victory.

I state what facts show, what overwhelming evidence proves, when I say that, if we yield now, we shall witness the consummation of a deliberate and cruel conspiracy on the part of the Democratic party of this State to overcome by brute force the political will of a majority of thirty thousand of the lawful voters of this State. I have mourned over public abuses which have heretofore arisen here. I have, according to the measure of my ability, labored to make the conduct of our public affairs honest and honorable. But I stand appalled at the crimes against freedom, against public order, against good government, nay, against government itself, which our recent political experience here has presented. And I am the more appalled when I see the North, that portion of our country which is secure in its freedom and civil order, and the great political party which has controlled the Republic for sixteen years, divided in its sympathies and judgment upon such questions. It is written in blood on the pages of our recent national history, that no government can rest with safety upon the enforced slavery or degradation of a race. In the full blaze of that great example of retributive justice which swept away a half million of the best lives of our country, we see the American people divided by party lines upon the question of the disfranchisement and degradation of the same race whose physical freedom was purchased at such a cost. And what is more astonishing still, there are Republicans who permit the errors which have attended the first efforts of this race in self-government to chill their sympathies to such an extent that they stand coldly by, and practically say that the peace of political servitude is better than the abuses and disquiet which newly acquired freedom has brought.

I denounce the conduct of the recent election on the part of our political opponents in this State as a vast brutal outrage. Fraud, proscription, intimidation in all forms, violence—ranging through all its degrees up to wanton murder—were its effective methods. The circumstances under which we have assembled to-day show us how nearly successful has been this great conspiracy. It is for us, in the face of all dangers, in the face of false or timid friends, in the face of open enemies, to show that we understand the cause in which we are engaged, and that no earthly sacrifice is too great to secure its triumph.

The gentleman who was my opponent for this office in the late election has recently declared, as I am credibly informed, that he held not only the peace of this city and State, but my life, in his hand. I do not doubt the truth of his statement. Neither the public peace nor the life of any man who now opposes the consummation of this policy of fraud and violence is safe from the assaults of those who have enforced that policy.

My life can easily be taken. I have held it, in the judgment of all my friends here, by a frail tenure for the last three months. But there is one thing no man in South Carolina can do, however powerful or desperate he may be, and that is to cause me to abate my hatred or cease my most vigorous resistance to this attempted overthrow and enslavement of a majority of the people of South Carolina. "Here I stand ; I can do no otherwise : God be my helper." Wife and children, —dearer to me than "are the ruddy drops that visit my sad heart"—all other considerations must give way before the solemn duty to resist the final success of that monstrous outrage under whose black shadow we are assembled to-day.

The character and spirit of this brief address, which was published in almost every newspaper in the land, not less than the extraordinary circumstances under which it was delivered, made a profound impression on the public mind, and there were few journals which did not make it the theme of editorial comments. In the excited state of political and partisan feeling these comments were colored by prejudice, no doubt. The time was unpropitious for calm and just estimates of merit in act or speech. But those who have followed thus far this record will not fail to appreciate the high and cordial tribute to Governor Chamberlain expressed in the following editorial article from the Rochester (N. Y.) *Democrat* of December 16, 1876 :

It is impossible to read the Inaugural Address of Governor Chamberlain, the full text of which appears in another place, without being impressed with the utter sincerity and devotion of its author. For the moment, we may ignore the legal controversies, in which he is involved, to pay our tribute of respect to the courage with which he is inspired. That Governor Chamberlain is of the mould in which heroes are cast, both his words and his works show forth. That he believes he is right, is a moral demonstration to those who have watched his course and studied his purpose. That, believing he is right, he will fearlessly tread the path of duty, is certain. No sacrifices seem to him too great, no dangers too imminent, to deter him from the mission to which he thinks he is called. That mission, in his view, is to give good government to all the citizens of South Carolina, and to protect them in each and every right. Not more deeply conscious of the right they contended for, or the liberty they intended, was the grim Covenanter, or the soldier of Naseby, than is this gallant representative of constitutional freedom, battling for a despised race against the hosts of his oppressors.

We need not, in analyzing the quality of this man, maintain that all that he has done can be reconciled with the strict technicalities of the law. This is a separate issue, which, however, his friends need not fear to discuss. We are dealing with his animus, rather than with his acts—and this, we assert, challenges the admiration of all loyal and liberty-loving Americans. The speech before us, while informed with the noblest sentiments and the most inflexible determination, is free from undue self-exaltation. Governor Chamberlain states only the exact truth when he says that he has held his life by a frail tenure, for the last three months. The testimony of correspondents from South Carolina is uniform as to the deadly feeling with which desperate men regard him, and the country would not be surprised at any time to hear that a tragedy similar to that which ended the career of Henry IV., or terminated the usefulness of William the Silent, at the summit of his greatness, had occurred in the streets of Columbia, or in the Executive Chamber of the "Palmetto State." And yet, the testimony is as uniform concerning the bravery with which Governor Chamberlain has carried himself through the trying times in which he has been placed—the resolution which has nerved him to dare obloquy and reproach and to face peril and death in behalf of the principles he professes.

All this appears in the Address, in which he once more dedicates himself to the cause of good government in the State whose affairs he has wisely administered. He speaks deliberately; he addresses a nation, when he arraigns the party of opposition in South Carolina as seeking through fraud, proscription, and all forms of violence to compass the overthrow and practical enslavement of a majority of the people of South Carolina; and it is against this monstrous outrage that he protests and which he promises to resist even at the sacrifice of all that man holds dearest—his life. If it shall occur that out of the tumult and confusion that now obtains in South Carolina —the fierce war of words and the portents of the fiercer strife of arms—the State shall come with her Constitution intact, her laws supreme, and her peace assured, she will owe much to the firmness and the fearlessness of Daniel H. Chamberlain, once honored by all citizens with a valid title to respectability, as a discreet and honest ruler, now denounced by the whole body of electors opposed to him as an adventurer and a thief. . . . Governor Chamberlain is precisely the same man he was a year ago, impelled by the same motives and pledged to the same ends. His courage has indeed been strikingly exemplified by the ordeal through which he has passed, but his fealty to principle remains unchanged.

If it did not, he would shake the dust from his feet and leave the troubled State behind him. He would seek rest and safety among the people of the North. It cannot be an enviable lot to remain in a community where his name is traduced and his person endangered. He is a gentleman of refinement and culture. In one of the best of our Northern universities he was a scholar of high rank. As a writer and an orator he has few superiors in the nation. In his profession, at the North, he would easily win fame and fortune. Did he here seek political honors he could obtain them. With the reputation he has already acquired, his future would be guaranteed in any Northern State. He is not one of the ordinary "carpet-baggers," whom even we of the North have been taught to despise for their rapacity. No enemy claims that his gubernatorial record is blotted by corruption. Even the most violent of his foes has, at least until recently, freely admitted the honesty and the fidelity with which he has administered his office. He has been scrupulously correct in his official capacity.

What then has he personally to gain by continued consecration to the principles he has already so conspicuously vindicated? Nothing save the good of those whom he serves. This is for him sufficient stimulus. This equips him for the contest in which he is engaged ; and this will make him faithful to the end, whatever that end may be. This will enable him to bear up against vituperation. This will be the compensation for the abuse with which he is visited. This will encourage him to face all perils awaiting him. When impartial history writes the record of the Reconstruction of the Southern States, she will award to few a higher meed of praise than to Daniel H. Chamberlain, the bold and sagacious Governor of that Commonwealth which first essayed to disrupt the Union. This may seem to some extravagant eulogy, but it is uttered calmly and conscientiously, in view of the qualities he has displayed in the extraordinary circumstances that have confronted him.

One passage in Governor Chamberlain's address was the occasion of a public denial by General Wade Hampton. The whole matter is distinctly set forth in the following communication to the Columbia *Union-Herald.*

COLUMBIA, December 12, 1876.

To the Editor of the Union-Herald,

Sir : I have to request that you publish in the *Union-Herald* the enclosed papers.

The statements of General Elliott and Judge Settle are confirmed by the remarks of Senator Nash made yesterday in the Senate, as well as by the statements of Judge Denny made to me and to many other persons here.

Very respectfully,

D. H. CHAMBERLAIN.

To the Public :—The following paragraph appears in an address of D. H. Chamberlain, delivered in tne Capitol to-day :

The gentleman who was my opponent for this office in the late election declared, as I am credibly informed, that he holds not only the peace of this city and State but my life in his hands. I do not doubt the truth of his statement. Neither the public peace nor the life of any man who now opposes the consummation of this policy of fraud and violence is safe from the assaults of those who have opposed that policy.

I pronounce this statement infamously false. I, by my unwearied exertions, have endeavored to preserve the peace of this State, and I have thus contributed to shield from popular indignation one who has proved himself a disgrace to his rank and a traitor to his trust. His conscience may make him tremble, but neither I nor the men with whom I act countenance the hand of the assassin.

WADE HAMPTON.

COLUMBIA, S. C., December 9, 1876.

His Excellency D. H. Chamberlain, Governor of South Carolina,

Dear Sir :—In response to your request that I should state, as nearly as I can, my recollection of a conversation between General Wade Hampton and myself, I have the honor to say :

That on Thursday, 30th ult., while standing near the door of the House of Representatives, General Hampton approached me and enquired if I were Mr. Elliott. I replied in the affirmative ; whereupon he expressed a desire to confer with me for a moment. We then walked across the lobby to the glass door between the rooms of the President of the Senate and the Speaker of the House of Representatives. Speaking of the condition of affairs, General Hampton said that all his efforts, from the inception of the campaign up to that moment, had been employed in the interests of peace and order, and that he hoped for a peaceful solution of the difficulties surrounding us. I joined him in the expression of such hopes, and said that the efforts of the leading men on our side had been employed in like endeavors to maintain the peace, and assured him that they would always be so employed. I also said that I was pleased to be able to say that I fully believed that he had done much to preserve the public peace.

After defining his position more fully, he remarked that he regarded you as being largely responsible for the present situation of affairs, and that it was the duty, as well as the interest, of leading colored men like myself to refuse our support and countenance to you ; for, said he, " I can and will protect the people of this State, black and white alike, while Governor Chamberlain cannot protect either." Continuing, he said further : " *Governor Chamberlain cannot protect his own life. I have had to protect him from the just indignation of the people, and if I were now to take my hands off the brakes for an hour, his life would not be safe.*"

After a few more words between us, he then entered into conversation with Senator Nash, who was on his way towards the Senate Chamber, while I walked towards the House of Representatives, stopping awhile to converse with Mr. T. C. Dunn and Senator Cochran, of Anderson.

The above is the substance of the conversation to which you refer. In addition to the impressions made on my mind at the time, my recollection of it was strengthened, a day or two after, by the fact that Judge Settle, in my presence, detailed a conversation which took place between General Hampton and himself, in which the same words, which I have above italicized, were used almost *verbatim*. As soon as these words were uttered by Judge Settle, I immediately informed him of the conversation between General Hampton and myself, and remarked upon the similarity of the expressions used in each instance.

I have the honor to be, very respectfully, your Excellency's obedient servant,

ROBT. B. ELLIOTT.

GREENSBORO, N. C., December 9, 1876.

His Excellency D. H. Chamberlain,

Dear Sir :—In answer to your request of the 8th instant, to state a conversation I with others had with General Hampton, in which he referred to protecting your life, I have the honor to say : Judge Denny and myself called on General Hampton, accompanied by General Bradley T. Johnson. During the interview both Judge Denny and myself expressed the opinion that, in view of the threatening aspect of affairs in Columbia, the life of Governor Chamberlain was not safe in South Carolina.

General Hampton remarked that his efforts to preserve the peace had been incessant ; that he had constantly advised moderation, and that by doing so he had doubtless protected your life

I will not now say that what is given above is the exact language used by either side, but it is the substance of the conversation on that head.

During the conversation General Gordon came into the room, but I cannot state how much or what part of the conversation he heard.

I have the honor to be, your obedient servant,

THOMAS SETTLE.

———

General Gordon, of Georgia, persisted in his voluntary undertaking to enlighten the country regarding the situation in South Carolina, and provoked another communication from Governor Chamberlain to the New York *Tribune.*

To the Editor of the Tribune:

Sir—I should make an unworthy use of your permission to reply to Senator Gordon's last despatch if I did not confine myself to such matters as clearly affect the merits of the issues now presented to the country by recent events here. The temptation to retort is great, but I put it aside and say:

First: Senator Gordon now says that his complaint is not against the direct action of army officers here, but against the placing of the army under my control and that of Dennis. I trust this admission will be noted by the public and contrasted with the letter to General Ruger of December 1st, signed by J. B. Gordon, Wade Hampton, and A. C. Haskell, in which General Ruger is assailed in unmeasured terms, personally and officially, and his direct action denounced as personally dishonorable and officially tyrannical. The writers of that letter did not then relieve General Ruger of responsibility by putting it upon me and my confederate. But Senator Gordon's last refuge fails when the fact is stated—a fact which I here challenge Senator Gordon and his confederates to disprove in any particular—that no United States troops have at any time been placed under my control or that of any other persons than the proper officers of the army. General Ruger has acted wholly independently of me and upon his own judgment and responsibility as an officer; and it is certainly time that any pretence to the contrary be withdrawn or proved.

Second: My information as to the design of the Democrats to take forcible possession of the halls of the Legislature prior to the hour for assembling on November 27th was received from members of the rifle clubs here. Whether this information was correct or not, Senator Gordon doubtless knows better than I do. But I repeat that my information was direct, abundant, and worthy of belief. I will add that events which have since taken place confirm me in the opinion that such a design was formed and matured.

Third: Senator Gordon seeks to throw discredit on my statement that no effective State force was available for the protection of the State Government, by declaring that I have control of all the ordinary lawful agencies for enforcing the laws; and he considers my statement a suggestive acknowledgment. It is indeed suggestive. It is suggestive of the fact that there exist here agencies outside the law, organized and equipped, armed and officered, too powerful to be resisted by any lawful force at my command. The Republicans here rely upon the law. So completely have they relied upon the law that they are now without the means of resisting or overcoming the unlawful agencies which threaten them. Neither Senator Gordon nor any man acquainted with the facts doubts that the State Government is unable to protect itself against the force now acting in opposition to it here. What then? Does this impair the validity of the State Government or its right to be protected? When Senator Gordon asserts that General Hampton can keep the peace with no force except the civil tribunals and public opinion, he simply asserts that the Republicans here are law-abiding and peaceful; and when, on the other hand, he asserts that with all the lawful agencies on my side I cannot keep the peace, he asserts what is true—that the Democrats are not law-abiding, and, if left to their own will, would break the peace and overthrow the law. This is a correct picture of the relations of the two parties here.

Fourth : The statements which I desire to repeat under this head are these : First, that no person holding the certificate of the Secretary of State, or even the certified copy of an order of the Supreme Court, failed to obtain admittance to the Statehouse on the 28th of November; and, second, that no person holding the certificate of the Secretary of State was refused admittance to the hall of the House of Representatives. I repeat these statements in view of what Senator Gordon now asserts. There may have been delay in admitting persons who applied, until their right to enter was ascertained, but nothing more. It was a precaution necessary to the public peace and the peaceful organization of the Legislature, that persons not having official business in the Statehouse should be excluded on that day ; and it was a precaution necessary to the same end that only persons declared elected by the State Canvassers should be admitted to the hall of the House of Representatives. The former order was issued by me and enforced by General Dennis as my officer ; and the latter was issued by Mr. Jones, the Clerk of the former House, and enforced by the officers of the House under his control. The exclusion of Democratic members was self-imposed. They chose to retire because persons not entitled to admittance were not admitted with them. This is the exact statement of the whole case, and we stand upon it.

Fifth : Senator Gordon seeks to divert attention from the real issue and to represent the Republicans here as acting against the judgment of our State Supreme Court as well as the United States Supreme Court. He will not succeed. We say that the only power competent to declare the elections was the Board of State Canvassers, and no court has decided otherwise. Senator Gordon is a stranger here. He is not familiar with the decisions of our Supreme Court. This is not his fault, perhaps, but it is certainly his misfortune when he comes forward to argue this case before the country. He represents our Supreme

Court as declaring, nearly three years ago, that the County Canvassers' returns were sufficient. Sufficient for what purpose ? To entitle a person to take his seat in the General Assembly ? He means this, or his reference is pointless. But our Supreme Court has never decided that County Canvassers' returns are sufficient to entitle a person to a seat in the General Assembly ; nor have they made any decision equivalent to this. Senator Gordon incidentally betrays his want of familiarity with the decisions of our Supreme Court in expressing his belief that none of the decisions have ever been reversed on appeal to the Supreme Court of the United States. In this he is mistaken ; but it is a mistake of little importance compared with the error into which he falls when he undertakes to refer to the decision of our Supreme Court on the subject of a legislative quorum. He says that " this Court decided in a case not political, and when the Court and Governor Chamberlain were in accord, that a majority of 124 members constituted a quorum, and not a majority of 116, as decided by Governor Chamberlain." I am aware that this statement has been made by others who have less excuse than Senator Gordon for making erroneous statements ; but it is nevertheless a total error. In the case of Morton, Bliss, & Co. against Comptroller General (4 South Carolina Reports, 430) the Court had occasion to consider whether a constitutional provision requiring " a vote of two thirds of each branch of the General Assembly " meant two thirds of a quorum or two thirds of all the members. They decided that it meant two thirds of a quorum—that and nothing more. They did not decide that 63 were necessary to form a quorum. They did not decide that a majority of 124 members were necessary to form a quorum.

Senator Gordon regards my idea of a quorum of the House as " the essence of absurdity." I will present my idea and leave it for others to judge whether it is absurd or not. Our State Constitution says : " The House of Representatives shall consist of one hundred and twenty-four members." It also says : " A majority of each House shall constitute a quorum." The latter provision is identical with the provision of Section 5 of Article I. of the United States Constitution. Now it is admitted that the United States House of Representatives has decided that this provision of the Constitution means a majority, not of the whole number of Representatives who may be chosen, but a majority of all the members actually chosen. This is my idea of a quorum. In our present case the Board of State Canvassers, the only body competent to declare the election, have declared that only one hundred and sixteen members were chosen in the late election. My idea of a quorum therefore is a majority of one hundred and sixteen, and for this I have the most commanding precedents, while Senator Gordon has not a precedent whatever for his idea. When the objection is made to this view that the whole representation in our House is fixed, while by the United States Constitution the number is left to be fixed by Congress, the utter folly of the objection is apparent. The number of Representatives in Congress is always fixed at any given time as much as the number of our House. The same rule, therefore, which is applied to the National House of Representatives becomes a controlling authority over the question presented under our Constitution.

Lastly : I feel no necessity of replying to Senator Gordon's closing remarks. I trust, however, that I shall not be considered too unkind if I say that when he charges me with treason he is upon ground with which he should be familiar. My personal experience has not required me to study this subject deeply, and possibly I ought to feel alarmed at Senator Gordon's charge. Our modest claim, however, is that we are now, as on former occasions, resisting an effort to subvert our Government, destroy our institutions, and enslave a majority of our people, and that in this struggle Senator Gordon aspires to leadership, as before, on the wrong side.

D. H. CHAMBERLAIN.

COLUMBIA, S. C., December 14, 1876.

The group of Democrats who maintained a pretence of being a House of Representatives, with the Democratic Senators who sat, as occasion served, either with the Senate in session at the Statehouse or with the company of Democrats meeting in Armory Hall, went through a form of canvassing returns for Governor and Lieutenant Governor, and declared Wade Hampton and his associate candidate on the Democratic ticket duly chosen, whereupon General Hampton and his associate went through a ceremony of inauguration, General Hampton making a brief and unimportant address, while some of his adherents celebrated the occasion by vehement and incendiary speeches against Governor Chamberlain. One sequel of this performance was the following interesting correspondence :

STATE OF SOUTH CAROLINA,
EXECUTIVE CHAMBER,
COLUMBIA, December 18, 1876.

Sir :—As Governor of South Carolina, chosen by the people thereof, I have qualified in accordance with the Constitution, and I hereby call upon you, as my predecessor in the office, to deliver up to me the Great Seal of the State, together with the possession of the Statehouse, the public records, and all other matters and things appertaining to said office.

Respectfully, your obedient servant,

(Signed)   WADE HAMPTON,
Governor.

D. H. CHAMBERLAIN, Esq.

STATE OF SOUTH CAROLINA,
EXECUTIVE CHAMBER,
COLUMBIA, December 18, 1876.

Sir:—I have received the communication in which you call upon me to deliver up to you the Great Seal of the State, etc., etc.

I do not recognize in you any right to make the foregoing demand, and I hereby refuse compliance therewith.

I am, sir, your obedient servant,

(Signed)   D. H. CHAMBERLAIN,
                                  Governor of South Carolina.

WADE HAMPTON, Esq.

This Legislature had the duty of choosing a United States Senator in place of Hon. T. J. Robertson, whose term would expire on the 4th of March. Hon. David L. Corbin was chosen on the 12th of September. Other candidates voted for by Republicans were ex-Congressman Elliott, lately chosen Attorney General, C. C. Brown of Charleston, and F. A. Palmer, a member of the Legislature. No Democrats voted in the lower branch, but in the upper branch all the Senators of that party voted, complimenting by their suffrages General M. C. Butler of Edgefield County, and General Gary of the same county. On the same day the pretended Legislature took one ballot. On the 19th the Democratic Senators joined the pretended House of Representatives in a so-called joint ballot, and General M. C. Butler was chosen on the part of this body. His conspicuous services to the cause of the " Straight-outs, ' particularly his connection with the Hamburg crime, appear to have marked him for early honor and reward. Major Corbin, a native of Vermont, was graduated at Dartmouth College in 1853, served in the Union army throughout the war, except while a captive in Libby Prison, was severely wounded in battle, was detailed by General Sickles for duty in the Freedman's Bureau in South Carolina, and had remained in the State. He had served in the State Senate, and had been United States District Attorney for South Carolina for several years. He was an able lawyer, an outspoken supporter of the reform policy of Governor Chamberlain, and a gentleman whose high character and various accomplishments qualified him for an honorable career in the National Legislature.

Soon after the meeting of the Legislature, while the excitement caused by the existence of a pretended Legislature was at its height, some four or five Republicans were prevailed upon to join the Democratic body, but when they discovered that the real Legislature did not collapse they soon returned.

At this time Committees of both Houses of Congress were in South Carolina investigating the conditions and circumstances of the election. A majority of the committee of the House of Representatives were Democrats whose chief aim was to discover some pretext for counting the vote of the State for the Democratic candidate for President, but they were quite unsuccessful. They did a large business, however, in disseminating, by means of reported conversations, letters, and despatches, calumniating reports regarding the Governor and the Republican party, and contributed not a little to a confusion of public opinion throughout the country with regard both to the questions at issue and the circumstances of the case. Not the least preposterous and harmful of the reports which gained currency at that time were those diligently propagated to the effect that Governor Chamberlain was seeking a compromise and anxious to make terms with the usurping and insurrectionary forces. These reports finally took such a form as made it expedient to quash them once for all, which was effectually done by the following article in the Columbia *Union-Herald* of December 26th, entitled " The Governor on Compromise ":

Governor Chamberlain was interviewed yesterday respecting the recent reports of a compromise of the present difficulties here. Being asked if he was responsible for any offers of compromise he answered that he was not ; that he had never suggested or authorized the suggestion of compromise. Being asked to give his views of the question of a compromise he answered that he saw no room for any compromise. There might be surrender, but of compromise, meaning by the term a mutual yielding of advantage, there could be none. The Governorship was the strategic aim of each party. That office alone commanded the whole situation. The Governor continued :

" I have no purpose in holding my present position except to prevent the success of a great crime, namely, the success of the Democratic party here, conducted on the plan of brute force. I despise the man who would not fight for such a cause, and I have much more respect for Gary and Butler than I have for Republicans who want to purchase peace by consenting to recognize as valid the apparent results of the late campaign. It is precisely like the conduct of the " Union Savers " from 1850 to 1860. They were ready always to sacrifice for the Union the very things the Union was framed to secure, namely, liberty, justice, good government. Just so do we hear a great deal about the ' sacred forms of law,' but very little about the sacred substance of justice. I do not intend to break the law or to overstep the law, but I do intend to exhaust all lawful remedies and defences before I yield, and if I have to choose between the letter and the spirit of the law I shall choose the spirit."

The Governor was asked if he had seen the report that he would accept the United States Senatorship if a compromise could be effected. He answered that such a story was absurd. There were many reasons why such a report could not be true. In the first place, there was no such place to bargain away. Mr. Corbin was duly elected to that place, and no one else could be elected until a vacancy arose. In the second place, he (the Governor) would not be a candidate for the place under any circumstances.

"Finally," said the Governor, "I want it distinctly understood that I will accept no office or place, great or small, as the result of yielding my present position. I shall be Governor or nothing, and it is an insult to me to suggest that I should take any office as the price or reward or result of giving up this contest. I am not trading in my position, nor shall I allow others to trade for me."

There are several official Reports which set forth with more or less fulness the situation at this troublous period and the conditions precedent out of which it sprung, as well as the steps of its progress, among them the Report of the Special Committee of the House of Representatives of South Carolina relative to the organization of their body and the constitutional validity thereof, adopted December 21, 1876," the Reports of the Committees of Congress who visited the State, and the memorials to Congress of both parties. All these are of record and accessible to persons who may have occasion to examine them. None of them, however, presents a more graphic or trustworthy view of affairs at this stage than a report by Mr. James Redpath of a conversation with Governor Chamberlain, that was published in the Chicago *Tribune*, of December 26th and December 28th, in two communications dated Columbia, December 22d and December 23d, from which extracts are here given. Mr. Redpath stated at the end of the two letters that "the conversation was reported by a stenographer, word for word, as it occurred, and is now given without amendment or revision." What is here quoted is but a fragment of the whole which filled many columns of the *Tribune*. The above statement of Mr. Redpath affords a key to the method by which Governor Chamberlain was able to accomplish so much communication with the public while taxed with other labors.

The Legislature adjourned on the 22d, the day on which the first of these letters was written. "Every thing," says Mr. Red-

path, in the beginning of the letter, "is quiet—on the surface.
But if it were not for the presence of the national troops there
would be a revolution that would wet the soil of the State with
Republican blood before twenty-four hours were passed."

Although Governor Chamberlain in this talk speaks as a
Republican and an interested party, his statements of fact are
characterized by his habitual care and accuracy, and tally with
the official findings. His opinions and reasoning may be left to
make their own impression. What the Governor says regarding
the net results of Republican rule in South Carolina, is pertinent
and permanently valuable.

Q.—"Governor, will you give us a brief statement of the present
political complication, or, what they call in the North, the 'South Carolina Muddle'?"

Governor Chamberlain—"The actual facts of the present situation
are these: According to the Republican view, the last campaign resulted in the election of all the Republican State officers, as well as the
Republican Presidential Electors, and three out of the five Congress-
men. The Board of State Canvassers have declared this result, and
the Republicans have acted upon it, and have proceeded to inaugurate a
Governor and Lieutenant Governor, who are now in possession of these
offices. The other Republican State officers have qualified and are in
possession of their respective offices. And both branches of the Legislature are now in session in the Statehouse, engaged in the ordinary
work of legislation.

"On the other hand the Democrats have claimed that the result of
the election gave Hampton and Simpson, their candidates for Governor
and Lieutenant Governor, a small majority of about 1,000 over the
Republican candidates. They have disregarded the declaration of the
Board of Canvassers, and have proceeded, first, to organize a House
of Representatives, outside of the legal House, and finally, with long
delay and much hesitation, they advanced to the step of declaring the
election of Hampton and Simpson, as Governor and Lieutenant Governor, upon certified copies of the returns obtained from the Clerks of
the Courts in the various counties, and have inaugurated these two
officers. Their Government is at best fragmentary, and they are wholly
unable to discharge any of the functions of a State Government, except so far as they may do it through the Governor alone. They do not
claim to have the Legislature, nor to be able to do any acts of legislation.

"Of course there are the gravest questions of constitutional law
involved in the statement I have just made, about some of which there
is more or less controversy. The leading question concerns the validity of the organization of the legal House of Representatives. The

fact is that inasmuch as the Board of State Canvassers declared that only 116 members were elected to the House of Representatives, the Republicans regard that number as comprising *all* who had any proper claim to act in the organization of the House or to take any part in the action of that House at all, until whatever claim they might have should be passed upon by the House itself after its organization. The Constitution of the State declares that the House of Representatives shall consist of 124 members ; and if all the members had been elected a quorum would have consisted of a majority of 124, but as only 116 were actually chosen, the Republican view is, that a quorum, in this instance, consists in a majority of 116.

" On the 28th day of November, 1876, when the House of Representatives was organized, there were present sixty members declared elected by the Board of State Canvassers. Of these, fifty-nine, just a majority of 116, took part in the organization, and, according to the view just presented, had a right to do so, because they constituted a quorum.

" On the other hand, the Democrats have claimed, as I have before said, that a majority of 124, namely, sixty-three, was the lowest number that, under the Constitution, could form a quorum to do legislative business."

LEGISLATIVE PRECEDENTS REVIEWED.

" In considering this question, of a legislative quorum under the Constitution, it will be found that in all essential respects the case is precisely like a similar case which might arise, and in fact has arisen, under a corresponding provision of the United States Constitution, the only difference between the two being unimportant, so far as local practice and rule is concerned. For instance, the United States Constitution provides, simply, that the House of Representatives shall consist of a certain number of members, to be apportioned by Congress, based upon a certain basis of population. The basis of population varies with each decade, and the whole number of Representatives varies with each decade, but all the time the whole number of Representatives in the House of Representatives at Washington, is just as fixed and definite as if a specified number were named in the Constitution. The provisions respecting a quorum of the United States Constitution are identical with those of the State of South Carolina. Now, in 1861, owing to a failure to elect Representatives to Congress in the seceding States, it became necessary to determine whether, in order to transact legislative business, it was necessary that there should be present in the House of Representatives a quorum of the whole number provided for by the statutes passed in conformity with the Constitution, or whether some other rule was the true test of a legislative quorum. It was decided repeatedly (a conclusion acquiesced in fully by both parties) that a quorum consisted of a majority of the members actually chosen. Again, in the next Congress, in the session of 1862–63, the same question arose in the Senate, when it was elaborately argued and decided by a formal resolution that a quorum of the Senate consisted of a majority of the members actually chosen. This resolution was adopted by the vote of the ablest men of both parties, among them on the Republican side, Charles Sumner, Fessenden, Wilson, and Wade, and on the Democratic side, Reverdy Johnson and Lyman Trumbull (now a Democrat), and others. We here have regarded these precedents as controlling, and have acted upon them. We had a majority of all the members actually chosen when the House of Representatives was organized. After the organization, the House proceeded to decide contested seats in several of the counties, and seated the Republican claimants, so that the whole number of new members acting with the present House has been as high as seventy-three. At one time five of these men were induced to secede from the legal House and join temporarily the secession House ; two of them have since returned to their proper allegiance. The legal House now consists of seventy members, which, under any view of the question of a quorum, would be sufficient. The Senate is unquestionably Republican. One half of them are elected every two years, the present political division being eighteen Republicans to thirteen Democrats. The two vacancies were caused by the failure to elect in the counties of Edgefield and Laurens. The Senate has from the first recognized the legal House. The two bodies have coöperated in acts of legislation ; have recognized me as Governor, invariably ; have met in joint assembly, first, for the declaration of the vote for Governor and Lieutenant Governor ; and second, for the confirmation of the election of United States Senator—as well as to witness my inauguration as Governor. It will thus be seen that the only alleged defect in the Republican measures for the Government of the State grows out of a claim that no less than sixty-three members could constitute a quorum of the lower House.

" I have before stated substantially the defects in the Democratic situation. They claim to have had a valid House of Representatives from the first, but make no claim to the Senate, or to any State officers, except Governor and Lieutenant Governor. In the face of all this they have, notwithstanding, proceeded to inaugurate their Governor, but have been unable, of course, to accomplish any legislative work, and Hampton, so far as I know, has not yet assumed to perform any Executive functions.

" I regard the legal situation as entirely safe and satisfactory for the Republicans. There are grave practical difficulties that may be thrown in our way by the Democrats. And it is too early to predict how we shall find our way through all the difficulties before us. One thing is certain : the situation is much more satisfactory now than it has been at any time since the election."

THE TERROR AND THE FRAUD.

Q.—" Gen. Gordon, Senator from Georgia, stated in a telegram addressed *at* the President (and published by the Associated Press, I believe, before the President saw it) that ' during the late exciting canvass in this State no blood had been shed except by the partisans of

Chamberlain.' If my memory serves me rightly, Wade Hampton also signed the despatch. What is your answer to that statement?"

Gov. C.—"Such a statement is a monstrous falsehood, by whomsoever stated. When I say a falsehood, I mean untrue in fact, and I am unable to see how it is not an untruth in intent, by any person who has the slightest familiarity with the history of the last four months in South Carolina. My own belief is that over one hundred Republicans have lost their lives, purely on account of their political opinions, since the 1st of last July in this State, and I know that more than fifty well-authenticated cases of political murder have occurred in this State.

* * * * * * *

"On the day of election, however, the most effective means employed for overcoming the Republican majority was repeating. This was practised by bands of Georgians, who raided from poll to poll throughout the county [Edgefield], as well as by many of the white people residents of the county, who voted at different polls, and oftentimes repeated at the same poll. There was hardly a precinct in the county where the managers were not so much in fear of bodily injury or death as not to allow them to discharge the duties of their office properly. In some instances the ballot-boxes were taken possession of during the day, and carried away from the polls, probably for the purpose of stuffing them with Democratic votes, and in other instances they were taken possession of at the close of the polls, and no count as required by law was allowed until those who had them in charge were ready.

"The United States Supervisors and Deputy Marshals that were detailed for the various polls were in many instances prevented from being present or even in sight of the ballot-boxes, and they were so completely intimidated by the evidences of violence around, that they rarely dared to make any report of the violence and disorder they witnessed.

"What was not accomplished by actual repeating was accomplished in the making up of returns, and here again the officers of the election were threatened, and so much violence was threatened, that they were required in very many instances to sign returns which they knew to be false.

"And, finally, when the commissioners of election at the Courthouse aggregated the returns from the polls, two of this Board of Canvassers considered themselves in such danger of injury or death that they signed the returns, knowing them to be false, and did n't even dare to send up to Columbia any protest against the returns, or any evidence of the violence and disorder which attended the election.

"Unfortunately, on the day following the election, the United States troops were ordered away from Edgefield, and it was not until by special authority a company of United States troops were ordered back, that any progress was made toward obtaining any evidence of the violence and disorder in this county. I recollect well that the first messenger who brought us any evidence from Republican sources of the election was a colored woman who was sent over because no man dared to expose himself to the danger of travelling from Edgefield Courthouse to Columbia."

*   *   *   *   *   *   *

Q.—" How did the returns of the last election compare with the returns of previous elections at which there was no intimidation, or but little intimidation, and with the male white and male colored population of the county ?   I ask this question because General Gordon has described the throwing out of the ' heavy Democratic majorities ' of this county and Laurens as a ' great outrage ' on the part of your authorities."

Gov. C.—" The returns were in startling contrast to the returns of any previous election held in this county.   For instance, the entire vote of this county, Republican and Democratic, in 1874, was a little over 6,000, which was a decidedly full vote for that county ; and, in the present election, the aggregate reported vote is over 9,300.   In the election of 1874 the Republican majority was 1,200 ; and, in this election, the reported Democratic majority is over 3,200.   Besides this, the reported vote of the county is over twenty-six hundred in excess of all [male] persons, white and colored, over twenty-one years of age, in the county, according to the State census of 1875, which shows a large excess of population over the United States census of 1870.

" In view of these facts, the Board of State Canvassers decided as to the county of Edgefield that no legal and valid election had taken place on the 7th of November, and that they could not decide that any persons had been elected in that county at that election.

" The Board reached the same conclusion as to the county of Laurens, upon grounds generally the same as those in Edgefield, and with this notable addition : that the returns of the Board of County Canvassers in Laurens County were signed by only two of the three members of the Board, one of these two signing under written protest, and afterwards making his affidavit before the Board of State Canvassers that he signed simply to save his life until he could get to Columbia, or some other place of safety.   The election was, therefore, not only void in itself, but there were no returns of the election that could be taken notice of by the Board of State Canvassers.   In this way it came about that only 116 members of the House of Representatives received certificates of their election from the Board of Canvassers.   These two counties had eight representatives, five from Edgefield, and three from Laurens—with the one Senator from each."

THE LEGISLATURE.

Q.—" All were rejected ?"

Gov. C.—" Yes, all were rejected from both counties."

Q.—" How many Democrats were elected at the late election to the House, exclusive of these two counties ? "

Gov. C.—" Fifty-seven."

Q.—" A minority of the House ?"

Gov. C.—" Yes, a minority, under *any* view of the question of a quorum—I mean to say a minority of 116, and of course a minority of 124. The only pretext that the Democrats have that they had a quorum when they organized their House came from their including the claims of persons who appeared on the face of the returns to have been elected from Edgefield and Laurens."

Q.—" From whom do your members-elect to the House of Representatives receive their certificates?"

Gov. C.—" From the Secretary of State. He issues them upon the declaration of the election made by the Board of State Canvassers."

Q.—" To how many of these Democrats did he issue certificates?"

Gov. C.—" To only fifty-seven."

Q.—" Then how did these fifty-seven members, who do not constitute a quorum of the House, seat the eight members from these two counties? Is there any law of South Carolina that authorizes them to do so?"

Gov. C.—" No law whatever; they simply did it without law and without precedent, and in defiance of the law. In fact it was a sheer assumption that because the members from Edgefield and Laurens appeared by the returns, as *originally* sent in to the Board of State Canvassers, to have been elected, that they therefore *were* elected, notwithstanding the Board of State Canvassers had declared otherwise, and the Secretary of State had refused to give them certificates of election."

Q.—" I understand you to say that the seceding body claiming to be the Democratic House has no legal quorum under any interpretation of the law, and also that it has no Senate at all? How does it get along without a Senate? Do any of the Democrats in the legal Senate act with the secessionists' Senate, or have they seceded from the legal Legislature altogether?"

Gov. C.—" No, they have no Senate whatever, and no portion of the Senate which coöperates with the legal House of Representatives pretends in any way to coöperate with the secession House. They are simply holding daily sessions of their secession House without having any pretence to a Senate."

Q.—" Have the Democratic Senators who were elected at this last election taken seats in the legal Senate which recognized you as Governor, or do they hold a 'rump' Senate in the secession halls?"

Gov. C.—" All the Senators-elect have actually qualified, and taken their seats in the Senate which meets in the Statehouse, and which recognizes me as Governor, and the persons claiming to have been elected from the two counties of Edgefield and Laurens are also clamoring for seats in the same Senate."

* * * * * * *

Q.—" How does this legislative " Hampton Legion " pretend to be able to elect United States Senators with only one branch of their Legislature, even if it should be admitted that *it* had a legal quorum?"

Gov. C.—" That I may call an insoluble Democratic mystery. Plainly, they have no grounds on which to claim that they are competent to elect a United States Senator."

Q.—" Is it true that Democratic Senators sitting and voting daily in the Legislature that recognizes you as Governor, and addressing your Lieutenant Governor every time they rise as the President of the Senate, have gone over to the secession Legislature and voted for General Butler ? "

Gov. C.—" Yes, they have done precisely that. They actually voted on the day of the election of Mr. Corbin, they actually voted in the Senate in the Statehouse, and yet they have since, as you have reminded me, gone to the secession House and voted again for M. C. Butler."

*　　*　　*　　*　　*　　*　　*

THE " CARPET-BAG " GOVERNMENTS.

Q.—" The Democrats have made great complaints of what they call the misrule of the "carpet-bag" Government of South Carolina. They claim also that you have been the most vehement in denunciation of that negro misrule, although you are now its representative. Have you any objection to talking on that subject ? "

Gov. C.—" No ; I have no objection whatever to stating my own views, as well as my own course, upon any of these matters

" It is quite too much the custom in speaking of what are called the carpet-bag' Governments of the South to present only one side of the picture. I freely admit that there is one side which is to a large degree discreditable to the State Governments of South Carolina for some part of the time since 1867. And I have during my own Administration considered it my duty, for the best interests of the State, of the Republican party, and especially of both races of people living on this soil, without regard to party, to oppose and discountenance many of the practices that have grown up under our State Government since reconstruction. In consequence of being engaged somewhat conspicuously in this work of correcting Republican abuses, it has been very erroneously supposed that I was a wholesale denouncer of the Government which has existed here since reconstruction.

" The fact is that I have never lost sight of the benefits the new order of things has conferred upon this State. And I say now, very deliberately, that in my judgment the so-called ' carpet-bag' Governments of South Carolina have done more for the permanent prosperity and progress of South Carolina than any other agency which has ever existed in this State.

" Now, I am willing to catalogue all the abuses against good government which have existed here under Republican rule since the war. I admit that the State debt has been needlessly increased, and large sums of money raised by taxation have been expended in unnecessary amounts upon unnecessary objects, and that many ruthless, incompetent, and dishonest persons have crept into public office ; although, as a strict matter of justice, I think I ought to say here that quite as many of such persons have been natives as otherwise. Yet when this tale is all told, I still say there are certain indisputable facts which ought always to be stated as the other side of this picture and essential to a just and accurate judgment of what has taken place in this State since the war. I refer now to such remarkable facts as these—that under Republican influences that system of representation in South Carolina which threw the whole political power of the State into the hands of comparatively few persons, numerically speaking, which gave political power and influence to one class of citizens and placed the burden of supporting the Government almost exclusively upon another class, has been completely revolutionized. And we have now a just system of representation, giving just influence and power to every class of the community and to each individual, and laying the burdens of taxation and the support of the Government equally and justly upon all classes of the people and upon all descriptions of property.

*　　*　　*　　*　　*　　*　　*

"But still, over and above all these evils, we have this to show for Republican rule in South Carolina : A free and just Constitution under which, so far as the organic law can effect it, the rights of all the people of South Carolina are secured ; a just distribution of the political power of the State between both the races and among all the people ; a system of taxation which is, in my judgment, as correct as has been devised in any State in the Union ; a system of local affairs and local administration which is simple, convenient, and as unexceptionable as can be devised ; a system of public education which embraces and extends to all the people of the State alike ; and now, after the first eight years' experience under that Constitution, a habit of self-government, and to the exercise of political power on the part of all the people of the State, which would never have dawned upon the State except under Republican rule, and under what, as I have said, is so universally called the 'carpet-bag' Administrations.

"Now, put in one scale the virtual stagnation and practical oppressions of the old systems, and in the other scale the free and open prospect, and the actual progress in all the habits and methods of self-government, which we have seen since 1868, and along with it the great abuses of which I have spoken, and I submit that no man who values political freedom, or who is capable of striking a just balance between the two systems, will hesitate to say that at the end of eight years more of experience under the free government in South Carolina, but will confess, what a few of us are able to see to-day, namely, that Republicanism, with all its faults, has made South Carolina its debtor in a sum greater than that earned by any other political agency known to our history. And I am not saying this to-day for the first time, nor am I influenced by recent events in now saying it, but simply because, when the enemies of the Republican party flaunt in the face of the nation the sins of the former 'carpet-bag' Governments of South Carolina, it is proper that somebody should tell them that along with these abuses South Carolina has in fact been making the greatest progress that she has ever made in the same number of years. . . ."

Q.—"Was there any general system of free education in South Carolina before the war—either for whites or blacks ?"

Gov. C.—"No, sir ; there was *none at all.*"

The following extracts from newspaper correspondence sent from Columbia during this exciting period are of a nature rather private and personal than public and official, but they throw a strong light on some phases of the trial through which Governor Chamberlain was then passing:

[From a letter to the Cincinnati *Commercial* by Dr. H. V. Redfield.]

Chamberlain is conspicuously the one South Carolina Republican who has never used politics to make money. His Republicanism is from conviction, and he has done all that mortal man could do to make it respectable in that State. He has wasted his law practice, endangered his life, and fooled away all his money trying to be Governor, not because he wanted to be, or because the place was at all desirable, but he got into the harness, and from his view of things there was no way but to pull through. His instincts as a reformer are so earnest, and his desire to make the Republican name respectable in South Carolina so strong, that he went before the Legislature and urged them to reduce his own salary to $3,000, a beginning in the work of retrenchment. He pleaded for economy and reform with tears in his eyes, and for the selection of decent and competent men for judges. But talk of this sort to the South Carolina Legislature is about as effective as the reading of Watts' hymns to a drove of mules. He has been serving as Governor the past four months without pay and without prospect of pay. His treasury is empty. Tens of thousands of dollars have rolled into Hampton's coffers, because the tax-paying portion of the community recognize him, while Chamberlain's treasury has received but $900. He is a man of decided ability and culture—a graduate of Yale—and was pronounced by the late Reverdy Johnson to be one of the best lawyers in America. He has an interesting family, and the relief they will feel should his claims to the Governorship be decided adversely cannot be measured in words. For months his devoted wife has lived in daily and nightly dread that the hand of an assassin would take her husband. What satisfaction is such a life to a cultivated, quiet, domestic man, a natural scholar and student, having little in common with South Carolina politics and pistols? He has only sought to maintain his position through the most devoted loyalty to the principles of civil liberty to all men.

[From a letter to the New York *Times* by Mr. Howard Carroll.]

The beautiful and accomplished wife of Daniel H. Chamberlain had even a more terrible experience. Never, so long as I live, shall I forget a night after the election in Columbia, when the Democrats, believing they had elected their national ticket, went wildly through the streets, drunk with joy and mad with whisky. The Governor sat in the Executive Chamber of the desolate Statehouse, calm and collected as ever, but with a pale face and quivering lip, which were not usual to him. There was no one in the chamber but he and I, and as we sat waiting for good news of the election which did not come, a great crowd of yelling red-shirted rifle-club Democrats, drunk like the rest of those in the town, came about the building and under the Governor's windows cursing, shouting, discharging their guns and pistols, and with jeers and threats of violence, calling upon Chamberlain to show his Radical head that they might blow it off. Fearing for his life—and it was in continual danger—a number of friends came in and urged him to go home. " No, no," he said, " my duty is here, and I will stay." Then they went out, and he, turning to me, exclaimed, as if his brave, true heart would break : " Oh, my God, if I only could go ! My poor wife ! my poor wife ! " At that time I did not understand nor appreciate the full meaning of his words. I did both when, some days later, it was announced that Mrs. Chamberlain had given birth to a child. It was born amid the shouts and curses, the cheers and imprecations of lawless men who were at any moment ready to send its father into another world. Who can tell of the agony that was suffered by that father and mother? And after all, their suffering was as nothing compared to the trials which the black men and women of the South have been subjected to because of their fidelity to the Republican party.

CHAPTER XXVII.

The Trying Condition Prolonged for Two More Months—Governor Hayes Becomes President—Surprising Communication Despatched to Governor Chamberlain on the Day of the Inauguration—Governor Chamberlain's Reply—His Despatch to Hon. D. T. Corbin—Mr. Evarts Explains—Previous Action of Senator Matthews in the Character of Conciliator—Governor Chamberlain and General Hampton Invited to Washington by the President—Governor Chamberlain's Statement of the Case to the President—The Administration Determines to Withdraw the United States Troops from Columbia—Governor Chamberlain Declares It Useless to Make Further Contest—Governor Chamberlain's Address to South Carolina Republicans on Abdicating His Office—Accompanying Documents—Transfer of the Executive Office to General Hampton—Conclusion.

IN this strained and perilous condition the State of South Carolina continued through January and February while the whole nation awaited with painful anxiety and apprehension the issue of the proceedings in Washington to determine the disputed election of President. There was no doubt at any time that if Mr. Tilden became President he would recognize Hampton as Governor and promptly withdraw the United States troops, leaving the Republican majority at the mercy of the South Carolina rifle clubs. But there was no expectation that if Governor Hayes became President he would pursue a similar course. President Grant continued to recognize Governor Chamberlain as the Chief Magistrate, and the body that sat in the Statehouse as the legal Legislature. Upon Governor Chamberlain's call he had directed the United States troops, as has been seen, to prevent any outbreak of violent disorder, or insurrection. But for the hope entertained that Mr. Tilden would be inaugurated, the *simulacrum* of government maintained by General Wade Hampton and his supporters would have dissolved and vanished. While ,no pressure was needed to induce the Governor to maintain his rights, there was an abundance of approbation, counsel, and exhortation to stand firm, volunteered by leading Republicans, justly supposed to represent the wish and sentiment of the Republican candidate for President, throughout that difficult and perilous period up to the time of the ratification by Congress of the decision of the Electoral Commission, when the succession of General Hayes to President Grant was assured.

On the day of the inauguration of President Hayes, the following note, written by an attached personal friend of the new President, was despatched to Governor Chamberlain, by a special messenger, the person selected for this confidential service being Colonel A. C. Haskell, Chairman of the Democratic State Committee of South Carolina, the same gentleman whose misrepresentation of the situation in South Carolina before the election the Governor had convincingly exposed.

WASHINGTON CITY, March 4, 1877.

Hon. D. H. Chamberlain, Columbia, S. C. :

MY DEAR SIR—I have not the honor of a personal acquaintance with you, but have learned to respect you from my knowledge of your reputation. I take the liberty of addressing you now, with great distrust of the propriety of doing so, prefacing it by saying that I speak without authority from any one, and represent only my own views. The situation of public affairs in South Carolina is too complicated to be discussed at length in a note, and yet impresses me as one that ought to be changed by the policy of Republican statesmen in such a way as not only to remove all the controversies that disturb that State, but to remove the embarrassments arising from it to the party in other parts of the country. It has occurred to me to suggest, whether by your own concurrence and co-operation, an arrangement could not be arrived at which would obviate the necessity for the use of Federal arms to support either Government, and leave that to stand which is able to stand of itself. Such a course would relieve the Administration from the necessity, so far as Executive action is concerned, of making any decision between the conflicting Governments, and would place you in a position of making the sacrifice of what you deemed your abstract rights for the sake of the peace of the community, which would entitle you to the gratitude not only of your own party, but the respect and esteem of the entire country. I trust you will pardon the liberty I have taken, as my motive is to promote not only the public but your personal good. With great respect,

STANLEY MATTHEWS.

DEAR GOVERNOR :—I have read this letter, and conversed with Colonel Haskell and Senator Gordon on this subject, so interesting to us all. I should be very glad to aid in a solution of the difficulties of the situation, and especially to hear from you speedily. With my compliments to Mrs. Chamberlain, yours, very truly,

WM. M. EVARTS.

As Mr. Evarts was about to become Secretary of State, his postscript to Judge Matthews' letter gave it an Administration sanction.

To this communication of a surprising import, the Governor replied as follows:

COLUMBIA, S. C., March 7, 1877.

MY DEAR SIR:—Your note of the 4th instant was handed to me last evening by Colonel Haskell.

I feel grateful for the interest you manifest in the public welfare here, as well as in my personal good. To give you my views of the situation here, and my duty in connection therewith, with any thing approaching fulness would require a conversation. I can only say here, in substance, that I am wholly unable to see any line of conduct on my part, consistent with personal honor or public duty, which would permit me to yield my claims to the Governorship. I am equally unable to see any course which can be pursued by the National Administration toward the Government here which I represent, consistent with political or constitutional duty, which will not require it to support, against violence or overthrow, the lawful Republican Government.

I certainly wish most devoutly that I could relieve myself of this duty. I have been exposed to personal danger by day and night constantly for five full months, and I am wearied nearly to death ; but there are one or two things dearer to me than comfort or life—one is my honor as a public man, and another is my duty to the Republicans of this State. Neither of these, in my judgment, would permit me to accept any accommodation or compromise which was not forced upon me by a power which it would be idle to resist. I desire to aid and relieve President Hayes, but this is a life or death struggle, and I know that I should consign myself to infamy in the eyes of all Republicans here, who know the situation by fearful experience, if I were to accept any terms or do any act which could result in the success of the monstrous conspiracy against law and humanity which the Democracy of this State embody and represent.

There are better ways than this to conciliate and pacify the South. Let the present Administration, while firmly standing by the law and the right for Republicans, manifest a spirit of charity and sympathy for our opponents here, as countrymen and citizens, in the thousand ways open to an Administration, and peace will come and will abide— the peace of justice and law, the only peace worth fighting for. To permit Hampton to reap the fruits of a campaign of murder and fraud, so long as there remains power to prevent it, is to sanction such methods.

All this I say, my dear sir, with feelings of profound respect for you, but as in duty bound to declare the truth as I understand it. Of one thing I am sure, neither you nor any man moved by a sense of justice can understand the situation here and be willing, for any political advantage or freedom from embarrassment, to abandon the Republicans to the fate that awaits them whenever Hampton becomes the undisputed Governor of this State.

I despair of being able to set our case in its true light before those who have had no such experience, but I do feel that if I had the privilege of personal conversation I could do much more toward it.

I have written hurriedly, and beg that you will believe me to be,

Yours, very truly,

D. H. CHAMBERLAIN.

Hon. STANLEY MATTHEWS,
Washington.

Immediately upon receiving the letter of Judge Matthews, the Governor sent this despatch to Hon. D. T. Corbin, then in Washington:

COLUMBIA, S. C., March 6, 1877.

To Hon. D. T. Corbin :

I have just had a long interview with Haskell, who brings letters to me from Stanley Matthews and Mr. Evarts. The purport of Matthews' letter is that I ought to yield my rights for the good of the country. This is embarrassing beyond endurance. If such action is desired I want to know it authoritatively. I am not acting for myself, and I can not assume such responsibility. Please inquire and telegraph me to-night.

D. H. CHAMBERLAIN.

The following note, which was made public, indicates that Mr. Evarts had some compunctions regarding the part he was acting :

WASHINGTON, March 8th.

Hon. J. G. Blaine :

DEAR SIR—Hon. W. M. Evarts begged me to say to you that he did not endorse the letter of Stanley Matthews to Governor Chamberlain to the extent implied by the telegram of Governor Chamberlain to me ; that the letter was presented to him by Mr. Haskell, of South Carolina, and he wrote upon it substantially as follows : That he had read the foregoing letter ; that he desired to see the troubles in South Carolina composed, and he desired to hear from Governor Chamberlain upon the subject.

Very respectfully,

D. T. CORBIN.

It is pertinent to say in this place that this was not the first occasion when Senator Matthews had attempted to smooth the way before the steps of his friend. On the 27th of February, while the count of the electoral vote was in progress, he, conjointly with Hon. Charles Foster, Representative in Congress, and also an Ohio friend of the President-elect, addressed a written communication, in the terms following, to Senator Gordon, of Georgia, and Representative Brown, of Kentucky.

We can assure you in the strongest possible manner of our great desire to have him [Hayes] adopt such a policy as will give to the people of the States of South Carolina and Louisiana the right to control their own affairs in their own way, subject only to the Constitution of the United States and the laws made in pursuance thereof ; and, to say further that, from an acquaintance with, and knowledge of, Governor Hayes and his views, we have the most complete confidence that such will be the policy of his Administration.

The affairs of South Carolina, and of Louisiana as well, were promptly taken under advisement by the Administration. The papers of the day bear witness of the fact that the uppermost matter in all men's minds at Washington was their settlement. There were frequent conferences in which leading Southern Democrats were conspicuous; and at length it began to be charged by them that the " agreement " was not being kept. The President promptly disclaimed having in any way committed himself to any agreement, alleging that whatever might have been said by his friends had been said on their own responsibility. As the result of all this, so far as it concerned South Carolina, the following letter was sent to Governor Chamberlain :

> EXECUTIVE MANSION,
> WASHINGTON, March 23, 1877.

SIR:—I am instructed by the President to bring to your attention his purpose to take into immediate consideration the position of affairs in South Carolina, with a view of determining the course which, under the Constitution and laws of the United States, it may be his duty to take in reference to the situation in that State as he finds it upon succeeding to the Presidency. It would give the President great pleasure to confer with you in person, if you shall find it convenient to visit Washington and shall concur with him in thinking such a conference the readiest and best mode of placing your views as to the political situation in your State before him. He would greatly prefer this direct communication of opinion and information to any other method of ascertaining your views upon the present condition and immediate prospect of public interests in South Carolina. If reasons of weight with you should discourage this course, the President will be glad to receive any communication from you in writing, or through any delegate possessing your confidence, that will convey to him your views of the impediments to the peaceful and orderly organization of a single and undisputed State Government in South Carolina, and of the best methods of removing them. It is the earnest desire of the President to be able to put an end as speedily as possible to all appearance of intervention of the military authority of the United States in the political derangements which affect the Government and afflict the people of South Carolina. In this desire the President cannot doubt he truly represents the patriotic feeling of the great body of the people of the United States. It is impossible that the protracted disorder in the domestic Government of any State can or should ever fail to be a matter of lively interest and solicitude to the people of the whole country. In furtherance of the prompt and safe execution of this general purpose, he invites a full communication of your opinions on the whole subject in such one of the proposed forms as may seem to you most useful.

By direction of the President I have addressed to Hon. Wade Hampton a duplicate of this letter.

I am, very respectfully, your obedient servant,

W. K. ROGERS,
Private Secretary.

To Hon. DANIEL H. CHAMBERLAIN.

Upon receipt of this letter the Governor started for Washington, where he arrived on the 27th of March. General Hampton followed a day or two later. When he left South Carolina he made the following address to his supporters in Columbia :

> I go to Washington simply to state before the President the fact that the people of South Carolina have elected me Governor of that State. I go there to say to him that we ask no recognition from any President. We claim the recognition from the votes of the people of the State. I go there to assure him that we are not fighting for party, but that we are fighting for the good of the whole country. I am going there to demand our rights—nothing less—and, so help me God ! to take nothing less.

His journey was made the occasion of frequent demonstrations of partisan sympathy on the part of the communities through which he passed, and he repeated in various forms substantially the same sentiment in several addresses.

During the two or three days after Governor Chamberlain's arrival in Washington he had protracted interviews with the President, the members of the Cabinet, and prominent public men. The following letter to the President, embodying his view of the situation, was written in accordance with a request communicated to him.

WASHINGTON, March 31, 1877.

His Excellency, the President :

SIR—I have been invited by Mr. Evarts to lay before you my views of the results to be expected to follow the withdrawal of the United States forces now stationed in the Statehouse at Columbia, together with such statement of any reasons therefor as I may deem it proper to make. A brief preliminary statement of the circumstances under which these forces were stationed at the Statehouse will be of service in responding to this request.

In October, 1876, I made an official call upon the President for the aid of the United States in suppressing domestic violence and insurrection. In response the President ordered a considerable number of troops to various points within the State, distributing them in such manner as seemed likely not only to suppress the actual existing violence or insurrection, but to prevent similar outbreaks in other localities. The causes and objects of the violence now referred to were purely political. An effort had been made at that time by the Democratic party to secure political control of the State by the use of physical force and violence. A large number of armed military companies had been organized and made effective for this work in violation of the laws of the State. To overcome the actual open violation inaugurated by these organizations, and hold them in check pending the election, and thus to receive a fair expression of the will of the people at the election in November, was the sole object of my call upon the President and his action in response. Under these circumstances the election took place. Unfortunately the election did not close the political struggle, but rather intensified it.

About the 25th of November last, on the eve of the assembling of the State Legislature, I deemed it my duty to call upon the President to assist me in protecting the State Capitol against the violence of the organizations already referred to, in order to permit the Legislature to assemble and organize itself peacefully. In response to this call the President gave orders which resulted in stationing a small military force in the Statehouse. The force was shortly after reduced to one company, numbering from twelve to twenty men. The single object in placing this force in the Statehouse, as well as the sole use which it served, was to secure the State Government and Legislature against attack and overthrow by the unlawful organizations already described.

The effort to organize the House of Representatives resulted in the organization of two Houses, one of which remained in the Statehouse, and, in conjunction with the Senate, formed the Legislature, while the other occupied a hall at some distance from the Statehouse. The complete Legislature thus organized at the Statehouse in due course of procedure canvassed the votes for Governor and Lieutenant Governor, declaring me to have been elected agreeable to the provisions of the State Constitution. From that time until the present the presence of the United States troops at the Statehouse has resulted in protecting the Legislature, while it remained in session, and the various State officers associated with me, in the enjoyment of their official rights and the discharge of their official duties. In the meantime my present competitor for the office of Governor had proceeded, under a declaration of his election made by the House of Representatives in political affiliation with himself, to assume the office of Governor and to exercise its functions. Owing to causes not requiring present statement, no settlement of conflicting claims to the office of Governor was made during the term of your immediate predecessor, and thus, after your accession to the Presidency, the conflict remained unsettled, and the United States forces at the Statehouse were then, and are now, discharging the function or duty which I have already stated.

From what has now been stated, it follows that, in my judgment, the United States forces at the Statehouse are there in pursuance and execution of a constitutional duty or practice of the Government of the United States in its constitutional relations to the State of South Carolina. They are there for the protection of the State Government, of which I am the head, against domestic violence and insurrection, not now flagrant, but held in check only by the presence of the force referred to.

In the meantime the dispute respecting the office of Governor continues, and no available power or mode of settling it has been found. Under these circumstances my opponents desire and demand the withdrawal of the United States forces from the Statehouse, and I am invited to state my objection to such action on the part of your Excellency.

My first objection is that the withdrawal of these forces from the Statehouse would be a withdrawal of support and aid against domestic violence by the Government of the United States to which the State and State Government which I represent are entitled under the Constitution and laws of the United States. The claim here made does not, in my judgment, involve an assertion of a claim to the permanent presence and aid of the United States in upholding a State Government. The cause of the present condition of affairs is the disputed title to the office of Governor. Two rival Governments are contending for possession of the Executive office and its property, in order that they may possess the proper facilities for exercising the office. If the Government of the United States cannot properly, under the present circumstances, determine which of the two contending State Governments is the lawful one, the forces at the Statehouse are not, in any proper sense, acting to the disparagement of the rights of either of the contending claimants, but, on the contrary, they are holding the rival parties in an attitude in which each can pursue its proper remedies and seek a proper settlement of its claims. If, on the other hand, it is within the power and duty of the Government of the United States to determine, as a political fact and question, which of the two rival State Governments is the lawful one, and to confirm its political conduct to such a determination, then at whatever moment such a determination shall be reached and announced, all probable necessity for the actual presence of armed forces of the United States to further sustain the Government, thus decided to be the lawful Government of the State, will cease.   If further necessity for aid from the Government of the United States shall arise, such aid will be demanded, and extended or denied under the well known provisions of the Constitution of the United States.

My next objection to the withdrawal of the United States forces from the Statehouse is that such withdrawal at the present time, pending the decision of the question of validity of one or the other of the two Governments will be a practical decision in favor of my opponent. By this I mean that my opponent is at this moment fully prepared, in point of physical strength, to overthrow the Government which I represent.   Why is this ?   The cause is honorable to the political party which I represent.   They are law-abiding ; they are patient under the infliction of wrong ; they are slow to resort to violence, even in defence of their rights ; they have trusted that a decent regard for law, a decent respect for rights conferred by the Government of the United States, would restrain their opponents from the violence which has now overtaken them.   They know now that they can expect from their political enemies neither justice nor mercy.   They have relied with unshaken faith upon the protection of the United States.   If, therefore, the United States forces now stationed at the Statehouse shall be withdrawn, they will regard that act, under the circumstances now existing, as leaving them exposed to the power and vengeance of the armed, illegal, military organizations which cover the State and constitute the political machinery of the Democratic party.   They will regard that act—I speak now only of the fact—as a declaration by the United States that no further protection can be hoped for except such as they hold in their own hands.   They cannot alone maintain the unequal contest.   I certainly cannot advise further resistance.   That which would be an imperative duty under other circumstances would become madness now.

If it be said in reply that such use of the United States forces is merely giving a political advantage to one of the two contending parties in the assertion of its claims, I answer that, in my view, it is rather the preservation to each party of their right to a chance in the struggle if it must go on, or if the Government which I represent is the lawful Government it is the protection of the Government against domestic violence in accordance with the Constitution.

My opponent demands the withdrawal of the United States forces from the Statehouse.   It will be of service in judging what results will follow compliance with this demand to ask why the demand is made. I suppose neither courtesy nor charity will warrant the suggestion that it arises from a zealous regard for constitutional limitations on the part of my opponent.   On the other hand, the demand is plainly made for the purposes of political advantage in the present struggle.   What is this advantage ?   It has been suggested it is to enable my opponent to pursue his legal remedies in the premises.   It is a sufficient answer to this to say that no hindrance of any kind now exists to the peaceful and complete enforcement of all legal remedies whatever. Every legal right and remedy which belongs to my opponent under any circumstances is within his unobstructed reach to-day, and has been on all days. This fact points at once to the conclusion that in demanding the withdrawal of the troops from the Statehouse my opponent does not desire thereby to secure his own right by lawful means or peaceful agencies, but to rob me and my associates and constituents of our rights by unlawful means and violent agencies.

If reference be made to the profession of those who demand the withdrawal of the troops, that they seek only to secure their rights by lawful means, I respectfully answer that I am familiar with such professions. They have been made with endless iteration during a campaign of unprecedented length, marked from the opening to the close by every degree and form of physical violence. To one not familiar with the condition of South Carolina, the statements I have now made may seem extravagant. I refer for confirmation of all I have stated to the testimony taken by the Congressional committees during the past winter, and I affirm that my present acquaintance with the facts compels me to say that this testimony falls short of the truth. The Republicans of South Carolina have carried on a struggle up to the present time for the preservation of their rights; their hope has been that they might continue to live under a free Government. The withdrawal of the troops from the Statehouse will close the struggle,—will close it in defeat to a large majority of the people of the State, in the sacrifice of their rights, in the complete success of violence and fraud as agents in reaching political results.

To restate the results which will follow the withdrawal of the troops from the Statehouse I say :

First—It will remove the protection absolutely necessary to enable the Republicans to assert and enforce their claim to the Government of the State.

Second—It will enable the Democrats to remove all effective opposition to the illegal military forces under the control of my opponent.

Third—It will place all the agencies for maintaining the present lawful Government of the State in the practical possession of the Democrats, through the admission it will require.

Fourth—It will lead to the quick consummation of a political outrage against which I have felt and now feel it to be my solemn duty to struggle and protest so long as the faintest hope of success can be seen.

Very respectfully, your obedient servant,

D. H. CHAMBERLAIN.

The President and Cabinet had also before them for consideration the following propositions, previously submitted, looking to the ascertainment of the legal result of the disputed election in South Carolina by a method somewhat similar to that by which the disputed right of the President to his office had been determined :

To the President :

The Republicans of South Carolina are actuated now, as at all times heretofore, by an earnest desire to adjust all political differences as to lawful government in that State upon the basis of justice and right. To that end the undersigned now submit the following propositions, agreeing to abide by the results thus to be reached :

First, All the returns of election for Governor and Lieutenant Governor, together with all the papers connected therewith, shall be submitted to a Commission of five persons, who shall have power, upon said returns and papers, and upon such other evidence, if any, as said commission may obtain relating to said election, and to any allegations of fraud or irregularities which may be made, to find and declare the result of the election for Governor and Lieutenant Governor ; or—

Second, All the returns of the election of members of the House of Representatives, together with all the papers connected therewith, shall be submitted to a Commission of five persons, who shall have power upon said returns and papers, and upon such other evidence, if any, as said Commission may obtain relating to said election and to any allegations of fraud and irregularities which may be made, to find and declare what persons have been duly elected members of the House of Representatives, and such persons shall assemble and organize as a legislative body, and thereupon the returns for Governor and Lieutenant Governor shall be submitted to the Senate and House of Representatives so constituted, and the election of Governor and Lieutenant Governor shall thereupon be ascertained and declared in the manner provided for by the Constitution of the State.

Respecting the manner of appointing said Commission, the undersigned submit the following propositions : First, the Commission shall be appointed by the President of the United States in such manner as he shall deem best ; or, second, two persons shall be chosen by each party respectively, which persons, with the Chief Justice of the United States, shall constitute the Commission ; or, third, two persons shall be chosen by each party respectively, and the fifth person shall be drawn by the other four by lot or otherwise, as they may deem best.

The foregoing propositions are presented solely with a view to a practical adjustment of the present difficulties, and the undersigned, on behalf of the Republicans of South Carolina, while submitting them, affirm that their course heretofore in relation to the election of Governor and Lieutenant Governor, and the organization of the House of Representatives, has been strictly just and legal, and that the State Government which the undersigned represent is in all respects the lawful and only lawful Government of South Carolina.

JOHN J. PATTERSON.
DANIEL H. CHAMBERLAIN.
DAVID T. CORBIN.

Governor Chamberlain's letter was read in a meeting of the Cabinet held on the 2d of April. The correspondent of the New York *Times* sent the following account of subsequent proceedings to that paper :

After freely discussing the foregoing paper, it was unanimously decided that the Federal Government has no constitutional right to intrude the army into the official headquarters of a State Government, except to quell riot or suppress domestic disturbance when the Government of a State is powerless to protect itself. This exception, in the opinion of the Cabinet, does not now apply to South Carolina ; and the determination of the President, therefore, to withdraw the troops from the State-house, was unanimously approved, and Secretary McCrary was instructed to issue an order in accordance with this decision. The Secretary was engaged this afternoon in preparing the necessary order, which will probably be promulgated to-morrow, although the actual removal of troops will not take place until after the return of Hampton and Chamberlain to South Carolina.

The order will recite that there being no domestic violence, and no apprehension of any, the parties on both sides having given solemn pledges that none is intended, and having announced their intentions to amicably settle the dispute before the Courts, in accordance with the laws of the State, the President has no alternative but to abstain from interference. Hampton and Chamberlain were both notified of this decision of the Cabinet. Hampton had an interview to-day with Postmaster General Key and other members of the Cabinet, to whom he reported his assurances that he would not resort to violence, but would proceed against Chamberlain in the regular manner through the Courts ; and until the question can be judicially settled he will allow no interference with Chamberlain or his supporters in their occupation of the Statehouse. Hampton says that as soon as the troops are withdrawn from the State-house he will station his own officers about it, and permit no one to interfere in any way with Chamberlain until the controversy shall be regularly decided by due process of law.

On the next day it was determined in a Cabinet meeting that the troops should be withdrawn on the 10th instant. Governor Hampton had pledged himself in a communication to the President not only, as stated above, that no violence should be used to oust Governor Chamberlain and the other State officers, but that the constitutional rights of all classes of citizens should be respected, and no violence done to any.

The correspondent of the Boston *Daily Advertiser*, in his despatch of this date, said :

Nothing but praise is heard from members of the Cabinet of the manner in which Chamberlain has acted during the progress of this settlement. He has shown no bitterness, and while protesting against the policy laid down, has been on the very best of terms with the President and all the members of the Cabinet, and conceding to them the purest and most patriotic motives in their actions. Chamberlain has said to all who called on him to-day that it will be useless to make a further contest, and that he shall return home and advise his friends to succumb to the inevitable, and to do what they can to aid Hampton in trying to administer the duties of Governor in an honest manner. Chamberlain does not hesitate to say that he believes the Republicans of the State cannot recover from the defeat which they have just received, and that hereafter South Carolina will be a Democratic State.

The expected order for the withdrawal of the troops from the Statehouse at Columbia on the 10th of April was promulgated in due time. Governor Chamberlain thereupon published the following address, and withdrew from office.

To the Republicans of South Carolina :

By your choice I was made Governor of this State in 1874. At the election on the 7th of November last, I was again, by your votes, elected to the same office. My title to the office, upon every legal and moral ground, is to-day clear and perfect. By the recent decision and action of the President of the United States, I find myself unable longer to maintain my official rights, and I hereby announce to you that I am unwilling to prolong a struggle which can only bring further suffering upon those who engage in it.

In announcing this conclusion, it is my duty to say for you, that the Republicans of South Carolina entered upon their recent political struggle for the maintenance of their political and civil rights. Constituting, beyond question, a large majority of the lawful voters of the State, you allied yourselves with that political party whose central and inspiring principle has hitherto been the civil and political freedom of all men under the Constitution and laws of our country. By heroic efforts and sacrifices which the just verdict of history will rescue from the cowardly scorn now cast upon them by political placemen and traders, you secured the electoral vote of South Carolina for Hayes and Wheeler. In accomplishing this result, you became the victims of every form of persecution and injury. From authentic evidence it is shown that not less than one hundred of your number were murdered because they were faithful to their principles and exercised rights solemnly guaranteed to them by the nation. You were denied employment, driven from your homes, robbed of the earnings of years of honest industry, hunted for your lives like wild beasts, your families outraged and scattered, for no offence except your peaceful and firm determination to exercise your political rights. You trusted, as you had a right to trust, that if by such efforts you established the lawful supremacy of your political party in the nation, the Government of the United States, in the discharge of its constitutional duty, would protect the lawful Government of the State from overthrow at the hands of your political enemies. From causes patent to all men, and questioned by none who regard truth, you have been unable to overcome the unlawful combinations and obstacles which have opposed the practical supremacy of the

Government which your votes have established. For many weary months you have waited for your deliverance. While the long struggle for the Presidency was in progress, you were exhorted by every representative and organ of the National Republican Party, to keep your allegiance true to that party, in order that your deliverance might be certain and complete.

Not the faintest whisper of the possibility of disappointment in these hopes and promises ever reached you while the struggle was pending. To-day—April 10, 1877—by the order of the President whom your votes alone rescued from overwhelming defeat, the Government of the United States abandons you, deliberately withdraws from you its support, with the full knowledge that the lawful Government of the State will be speedily overthrown. By a new interpretation of the Constitution of the United States at variance alike with the previous practice of the Government and with the decisions of the Supreme Court, the Executive of the United States evades the duty of ascertaining which of two rival State Governments is the lawful one, and by the withdrawal of troops now protecting the State from domestic violence, abandons the lawful State Government to a struggle with insurrectionary forces too powerful to be resisted. The grounds of policy upon which such action is defended are startling.

It is said that the North is weary of the long Southern troubles. It was weary, too, of the long troubles which sprung from the stupendous crime of chattel slavery, and longed for repose. It sought to cover them from sight by wicked compromises with the wrong which disturbed its peace, but God held it to its duty until, through a conflict which rocked and agonized the nation, the great crime was put away and freedom was ordained for all.

It is said that if a majority of a State are unable by physical force to maintain their rights, they must be left to political servitude. Is this a doctrine ever before heard in our history? If it shall prevail, its consequences will not long be confined to South Carolina and Louisiana. It is said that a Democratic House of Representatives will refuse an appropriation for the army of the United States, if the lawful Government of South Carolina is maintained by the military forces. Submission to such coercion marks the degeneracy of the political party or people which endures it. A Government worthy the name, a political party fit to wield power, never before blanched at such a threat. But the edict has gone forth. No arguments or considerations which your friends could present have sufficed to avert the disaster.

No effective means of resistance to the consummation of the wrong are left. The struggle can be prolonged. My strict legal rights are, of course, wholly unaffected by the action of the President. No Court of the State has jurisdiction to pass upon the title of my office. No lawful Legislature can be convened except at my call. If the use of these powers promised ultimate success to our cause, I should not shrink from any sacrifices which might confront me. It is a cause in which by the light of reason and conscience a man might well lay down his life.

But, to my mind, my present responsibility involves the consideration of the effect of my action upon those whose representative I am.
I have hitherto been willing to ask you, Republicans, to risk all dangers
and endure all hardships until relief should come from the Government of the United States.   That relief will never come.   I cannot ask
you to follow me further.   In my best judgment I can no longer serve
you by further resistance to the impending calamity.

With gratitude to God for the measure of endurance with which He
has hitherto inspired me, with gratitude to you for your boundless confidence in me, with profound admiration for your matchless fidelity to
the cause in which we have struggled, I now announce to you and to
the people of the State that I shall no longer actively assert my right to
the office of Governor of South Carolina.

The motives and purposes of the President of the United States in
the policy which compels me to my present course are unquestionably
honorable and patriotic.   I devoutly pray that events may vindicate
the wisdom of his action, and that peace, justice, freedom, and prosperity may hereafter be the portion of every citizen of South Carolina.

D. H. CHAMBERLAIN,
Governor of South Carolina.

With the Governor's Address the following documents were
published:

EXECUTIVE DEPARTMENT,
OFFICE OF ATTORNEY GENERAL,
COLUMBIA, S. C., April 10, 1877.

*To His Excellency, D. H. Chamberlain, Governor of South Carolina,
Columbia, S. C. :*

DEAR SIR—Recurring to the views severally expressed by us during the personal conference which we had the honor to hold with you
yesterday in regard to the political complications which have grown
out of the late canvass in this State, we beg leave to apprise you
formally of the conclusions we have reached, after mature deliberation
and the gravest reflection which we have been able to bestow upon the
subject.

Whilst we are no less inspired with admiration for the dignified and
resolute manner in which you have consistently maintained your claims
to the gubernatorial chair, by virtue of the election held in November
last, than we are solemnly impressed with the validity of your title to
the office, we are unanimous in the belief that to prolong the contest,
in the absence of that moral aid to which we feel ourselves and
our party justly entitled at the hands of a National Administration installed, in large measure, through the same agencies which are now
held to be insufficient for our maintenance, will be to incur the responsibility of keeping alive partisan prejudices which are in the last degree
detrimental to the best interests of the people of the State, and perhaps
of precipitating a physical conflict that could have but one result to
our defenceless constituency.   We cannot afford to contribute, however

indirectly, to such a catastrophe, even in the advocacy of what we know to be our right.

We are agreed, therefore, in counselling you to discontine the struggle for the occupancy of the gubernatorial chair, convinced as we are that, in view of the disastrous odds to which its maintenance has been subjected by the action of the National Administration, your retirement will involve no surrender of principle, nor its motive be misapprehended by the great body of that political party to which, in common with ourselves, you are attached, and whose success in the past in this State has been ennobled by your intelligent and unselfish services.

We have the honor to be, very respectfully, yours,

> ROBERT B. ELLIOTT, Attorney General.
> JOHN R. TOLBERT, Superintendent of Education.
> JAMES KENNEDY, Adjutant and Inspector General.
> THOMAS C. DUNN, Comptroller General.
> F. L. CARDOZO, Treasurer.
> H. E. HAYNE, Secretary of State.

STATE OF SOUTH CAROLINA,
EXECUTIVE CHAMBER,
COLUMBIA, S. C., April 10, 1877.

SIR—Having learned that you now purpose to turn over to me the Executive Chamber, with the records and papers belonging to the Executive Office, now in your possession, I beg to inform you that I will send a proper officer to receive the same at any hour you may indicate as most convenient to yourself.

I am, very respectfully, your obedient servant,

(Signed)   WADE HAMPTON,
Governor

Hon. D. H. CHAMBERLAIN.

STATE OF SOUTH CAROLINA,
EXECUTIVE CHAMBER,
COLUMBIA, S. C., April 10, 1877.

SIR—Replying to your note of this date, I have to say that my Private Secretary will meet such officer as you may designate, at twelve meridian to-morrow, at the Executive Chamber, for the purpose indicated in your note.

Very respectfully,

(Signed)   D. H. CHAMBERLAIN,
Governor S. C.

Hon. WADE HAMPTON.

The following comment on the abdication is taken from the editorial columns of the Boston *Daily Advertiser :*

The reports current of Governor Chamberlain's intention to prolong a hopeless struggle for the benefit of those who desire that the Administration should be antagonized, and have not seen the wisdom of openly opposing it themselves, turn out, as we suspected they would, to be groundless.   Probably the mistake was made in supposing that Chamberlain purposed doing what the Hampton crowd feared he would do, and what weak malignants like Patterson assumed he would do.   His conduct has been exactly consistent with what he uniformly told the President and all others who consulted him in Washington concerning his intentions.   And there never was any good reason to believe it would be different.   From beginning to end he has acted the manly part.   His sincerity, courage, and wisdom are apparent to the country.

His letter announcing to those who elected him his retirement from the contest is characteristic of the man.   He asserts what he believes to be the right bravely and with a confidence which has its root in sincere conviction.   He arraigns what appears to him to be the mistake of those who have decided this matter for him sharply, as one who feels that he owes allegiance to truth rather than to party chiefs, however strongly sustained.   Speaking for himself, and for the people whom he thinks the Government has betrayed, he does much less than justice to its motives, and holds the President and his advisers responsible for results which, under the Constitution, they have neither the right nor the power to control.

But let it be remembered that he has stood for years in the thick of an unequal fight, contending with great courage against a powerful, well organized, and desperate opposition in front, and at the same time maintaining a not less watchful and vigorous conflict in the party of his supporters, to repress their ignorant and sometimes vicious excesses, and make them worthy of the cause in which they are enlisted.   He won the hard fight, and when all the resources of fraud and intrigue were employed to prevent the consummation of the victory, he baffled the conspirators.   It was natural that he should expect the support of the national authority against attempts to oust him.

But objects and principles of paramount importance have made it necessary to throw upon the people themselves the responsibility for their own government, and withdraw the military support on which he was obliged to rely.   That he should be bitterly disappointed is natural.   That he does not surrender his judgment at the same time he surrenders his office, proves his own confidence in its correctness. That, in spite of his sense of wrong, he still bears frank testimony to the honorable and patriotic purpose of the President, mistaken as he believes it to be, and prays that the results may vindicate its wisdom, shows that he is capable of a generous renunciation.

This protracted struggle was for a weak and ignorant race, whom he hoped to be instrumental in leading to a right appreciation of their duties and responsibilities as citizens vested with equal political rights.   He has not the opportunity to complete his work, but it does not follow that what he has done will be without large and permanent results, which may appear sooner than we think.   South Carolina has passed under the control of the men who, by leading the State into rebellion, brought upon her extreme humiliation.   For generations her politicians had been extreme and malignant in their antagonism to every maxim of freedom.   The men who now come into power are pledged as strongly as professions and promises can bind men to rule justly, and to defend and promote the equal rights of all,—white or black.   If they keep their plighted faith they will in time dissipate the fears of those who now regard the experiment with anxiety, not without reasonable cause. And we venture to say that there will be no man in the State or in the nation more rejoiced to see South Carolina wisely governed in the spirit of impartial liberty than Governor Chamberlain.

The following account of the last scene in a long and exciting drama is from the Charleston *News and Courier*, a despatch from its correspondent in Columbia :

COLUMBIA, April 11th.

The transfer of the Government of South Carolina, with all the momentous interests involved in that proceeding, was effected to-day with as little pomp and circumstances as though the two prominent characters, parties to the ceremony, were exchanging photographs or jack-knives. These two gentlemen were Messrs. Wade H. Manning and C. J. Babbitt, Governor Hampton's and Mr. Chamberlain's respective secretaries.

Mr. Chamberlain left his office a few minutes after 11 A.M., and after bidding farewell to his officers and clerks in the Capitol, entered his carriage, in company with Mr. J. G. Thompson, and was driven through Main Street to his residence. The streets were densely crowded at the time by thousands who had assembled to witness a circus pageant which was then passing, and the carriage picked its way slowly along almost unnoticed. The cold, handsome face of the ex-Governor might have been seen for a moment as he went by, but if he felt any natural emotion in view of his suddenly altered circumstances, no evidence of it could be detected in the expression of his pale, quiet features. The familiar portfolio, without which he has never, or seldom, been seen, in his daily journey to and from the Statehouse, was as usual under his arm, and even while you noted these slight details he was gone.

At five minutes to 12 M. Mr. Manning presented himself at the Executive office and was politely met by Mr. Babbitt, of whom he requested the surrender of the Governor's office in the name of Governor Hampton. Mr. Babbitt replied that he was directed by Governor Chamberlain to make the transfer at twelve precisely, and would do so when that hour had arrived. As the first stroke of noon was heard, Mr. Babbitt handed over the seal and keys of the office, accompanying the action with the usual verbal formula, and Governor Hampton was in possession of his office. A few minutes more were spent in explaining the details of books, papers, etc., and both gentlemen retired from the premises, leaving the office locked, as it will remain until the key is turned to admit Governor Hampton himself. He will probably take possession in person to-morrow. A few idlers were present about the building, but only one or two gentlemen were allowed to be present at the ceremony as witnesses.

The day has been strangely quiet, barring the circus, after the events of yesterday. There have been no flags displayed, no hurrahs heard, nothing beyond a quiet, satisfied acceptance of the new era so long expected, so often despaired of, but at last arrived.

I have been reliably informed that Mr. Chamberlain's sudden change of purpose was brought about by the earnest representations and advice of his chief executive officers, whose names appeared attached to the letter addressed to him and published in the *News and Courier* yesterday. The cogent arguments used are fully recounted in Mr. Chamberlain's own letter published at the same time. It is said his final determination was arrived at only after long deliberation,[1] and that he finally yielded directly in the teeth of most urgent advices from Washington to stick to his first resolution.

The other officers in the Statehouse consider it their duty to hold their ground, subject to the decision of the Supreme Court. I do not think they care or hope to remain very much longer. The Democratic contestants for the same offices will move into the Capitol at once, and occupy others of the numerous vacant rooms therein until duly recognized.

This story of a brave attempt, a good fight, and a .baffling, cruel defeat, is told. So ended Governor Chamberlain's Administration in South Carolina. From first to last it was a battle waged with dauntless energy and fortitude for two great causes which he represented with an ardor and fidelity equal towards each—the cause of EQUAL RIGHTS and the cause of HONEST GOVERNMENT. From beginning to end it illustrates the candor of his avowal of his ambition and hope which is placed on the title-page of this volume, and not less the sincerity of his declaration : " Public duty is my only master."

His misfortune was that so many of the party upon whose support he depended did not perceive that their misdoing would invite their destruction. If they had coöperated in advancing the reforms he toiled to achieve, the reorganization of the Democratic party for the purpose and on the basis proposed by the " Straight-out " leaders, would have been impossible. Their persistent, vicious folly afforded the occasion and the pretext wanted by their political opponents to gain party ascendancy. They made it impracticable for the wisest and most capable political leader the Republican party in the Southern States ever had, to save them from political overthrow. Their greedy abuse of power annulled the high and hopeful endeavor to establish their political freedom on a foundation both honorable and permanent. By the same acts they made it easy for their enemies at home to attack them, and hard for their allies in the North to defend

---

[1] There was no foundation, except in the imagination of fearful persons, for the assumption that Governor Chamberlain would attempt forcibly to prevent what had been decreed. He announced before leaving Washington that he should not longer resist the inevitable end. No one knew better than he that those who advised him to continue the fight were powerless to render effectual assistance under existing circumstances.

them. Thus they prepared the catastrophe which overwhelmed reformers and corruptionists in a common and indiscriminating disappointment.

The two and one third years of Governor Chamberlain's Administration, years burdened with responsibilities, perplexed with anxieties, harassed with care, vexation, and strife, and crowded with exacting duties, must have been for him wearisome years. How he endured all and how he acquitted himself will be judged finally by the full record, substantially included in this volume, as it shall interpret itself to the intelligence and the judgment of men capable of candid appreciation. It is now first presented in its entirety to the contemplation and scrutiny of his countrymen, not without a hope that when party prejudices, still violent, shall be as obsolete as is the factional bitterness of Washington's Administration, the truth-loving and philosophical historian of these troublous times may find in it (if perchance some library preserve a dusty copy) material of worth and usefulness in his labor of tracing the springs and impulses of the developed greatness of that New South which had its birth into freedom by painful throes of civil war and political reconstruction.

APPENDIX.

I.

THE CHARGES AFFECTING GOVERNOR CHAMBER-LAIN'S INTEGRITY AND HONOR, AND HIS ANSWER THERETO.

VARIOUS references appear in the preceding pages to charges affecting the personal and official integrity of Governor Chamberlain. They all relate to a period prior to his Administration as Governor, and form no proper part of the record of that Administration. But inasmuch as these charges have pursued him since his retirement from office, the following public statements embodying the charges, and his answers to them are here given.

The following letter was published in the Columbia *Union-Herald* in the summer of 1874:

TO THE PUBLIC :

It is now nearly two years since I ceased to be a State officer. During this interval I have closely followed my profession, taking no part whatever in public or political affairs, and seeking no return to official position. No man living has ever heard me, directly or indirectly, solicit office ; nor can a single act of mine during the last two years be pointed out which could reasonably indicate that I sought any office in this State. Notwithstanding my constant and studious avoidance of politics, many friends have, from time to time, expressed their desire that I should be a candidate for the office of Governor. Within the last few months a large number of prominent gentlemen of the Republican party have urged that candidacy upon me as a matter of grave and urgent duty which I owed to the State as well as to my political party. I have laid before them my reasons for not wishing to share in political affairs at the present time, and have earnestly endeavored to show them that others could serve the public better than I in the office of Governor.

Their judgment has apparently remained unchanged, and I have, up to the present time, simply maintained this position—that if the Republican party should, when duly assembled in State Convention, tender me its nomination for Governor, I should not decline it.

In that sense, and to that extent only, I am a candidate now. I have not sought or desired the office. It is a burden from which I shrink, and which I shall take up only at the unsolicited call of the best men of my party as expressed in the coming State Convention.

Such being my unvarying attitude toward this question, I have, as I think reasonably, felt no solicitude to repel adverse criticisms, or to deny or disprove charges made against me for the purpose of defeating my nomination. I have now lived in this State for nine years, and for the last six years this community [1] has had full opportunity to note my personal character and to estimate my worth as a man and a citizen. I am one of those who still believe, amidst the fiercest storms of detraction, that an honorable and correct personal life is the best answer to all such charges as are now hurled at me. Of this I have constant and touching evidence in the numberless assurances which come to me from those who are in strenuous political opposition to me, that the charges now made against me and the attempt to drag me down to the level of others whom I might name, are regarded by all who know me as a temporary expedient to accomplish a political end. Personally, I am wholly indifferent to the charges recently made against me. Those who care to examine them will find them to be baseless, and those who do not care to examine them are not objects of anxiety to me. I am sufficiently an egotist to firmly believe that no man who knows me believes that I am, in public or private affairs, a dishonest man.

I have yielded to the wishes of my friends in this case, however, to the extent of now setting forth, briefly and emphatically, my answer to the charges which have recently been put forth against me as a candidate.

The charges, so far as they have taken an answerable shape, concern my actions as a member of various public Boards or Commissions from 1868 to 1872. During that period I was, *ex officio*, a member of the Financial Board, of the Board known as the Commissioners of the Sinking Fund, of the Advisory Board of the Land Commission, and of the Board to take charge of the congressional land scrip for an agricultural college.

In connection with the first-named Board, one of the charges most constantly repeated is, that I was specially responsible for the appointment of Mr. Kimpton as the Financial Agent of the State in New York. Beyond the single fact that Mr. Kimpton was a college classmate of mine, there is not the slightest ground for such a statement. Mr. Kimpton came to this State without my knowledge, and without any reference to me or to any employment by the State. I had not seen him nor communicated with him since leaving college. He brought his own recommendations, made his own impressions, and was never urged by me upon the other members of the Board. Acting upon what I regarded as good evidence of his capacity and character, I voted for him, in common with the other members of the Board, and that is the full extent of my responsibility for his appointment. That the Financial Board acted reasonably in this matter can now be shown by

---

[1] Columbia, S. C.

numerous commendations of Mr. Kimpton's management during the first three years of his agency, by the highest financial authorities in New York, as well as by the very great success which he certainly achieved in many respects during those years. I am not called upon, in this connection, to defend the entire transactions of the Financial Agent, but I do affirm that the Financial Board were warranted, by good and sufficient evidence, in the appointment of Mr. Kimpton, and that I had no larger share of influence in his appointment than each of the other members of the Board.

Another charge made against me is, that as a member of the Financial Board, and as Attorney General, I am specially responsible for the issue of what are known as the "conversion" bonds. This charge seems to rest chiefly on the fact that I was a member of that Board, and it is, therefore, needful to refer to the constitution and powers of that Board.

The Financial Board were never charged with any duty in connection with the issue of bonds of any kind.

By the Act of the General Assembly to issue bonds to redeem the "bills receivable," the Governor was authorized to borrow a certain sum of money. The bonds were to be signed by the Governor and countersigned by the Treasurer, and sealed with the seal of the State. The only duty placed by this Act upon the Attorney General was to fix, together with the Governor and Treasurer, the price at which the bonds should be sold, and the time for the redemption of the "bills receivable." Every bond issued under this Act was signed by the Governor and Treasurer, and sealed by the Secretary of State, and the Attorney General had no part or duty in the issue or execution of a single bond.

The same is true of the bonds issued under the Act to authorize a loan to pay interest on the public debt. By this Act the sole duty of the Financial Board in connection with the bonds was to fix the price at which they should be sold.

The next Act which authorized the issue of bonds was the "Act for the relief of the Treasury." Under this Act the sole duty of the Attorney General was, in conjunction with the Governor, Comptroller General, and Treasurer, to give directions for the use of the bonds issued under this Act as collateral security, and to fix the price at which they should be sold.

The "Act for the conversion of State securities" imposed no duty and conferred no power on any officer except the Treasurer, who was charged with the work of conversion, and the Governor, who was to sign and the Treasurer to countersign the conversion bonds.

The four Acts now specified are all the Acts under which it is pretended that the Financial Board had any powers, or has exercised any functions.

The Attorney General had no duty or power in the issuing of bonds ; neither had the Financial Board.

But it has been said that I gave an opinion, as Attorney General, to Mr. Cardozo, then Secretary of State, in which I claimed authority for the Financial Board to issue bonds without limit. As this alleged opinion has recently been made the ground for fixing upon me the "sole responsibility for the issue" of the conversion bonds, it is necessary for me to state precisely what that opinion contained.

Mr. Cardozo applied to me to know whether his action in sealing bonds was merely ministerial or not, and whether by sealing bonds he incurred any legal responsibility for the use made of such bonds by the Treasurer or the Financial Agent. To those inquiries I replied that I thought his duty in the matter of sealing bonds was merely ministerial, and that he was not in any way responsible for the issue of bonds to the Financial Agent, or the use he might make of them. In that opinion I asserted no authority in the Financial Board to issue bonds at all, nor did I say a word which could be construed into a claim, as has been recently charged, that it was Mr. Cardozo's "duty to seal as many bonds as the Treasurer, instructed by the Financial Board, requested."

I can further say that I believe from all the knowledge which I possess, that the action of the other members of the Financial Board, both as members of that Board and as individual State officers, in connection with the bonds of the State, was dictated by honest motives, and was intended to avoid the very results which finally took place.

Another charge is that, as a member of the Financial Board, I joined in directing the Financial Agent to make fictitious entries in his books so as to disguise the affairs of the agency. I take it upon myself to say that the Financial Board never gave such instructions, nor any instructions which were intended to deceive or mislead the public in regard to the affairs of the agency. So far as I am aware, the books of the Financial Agent have at all times been truly and faithfully kept. If they were not it did not arise from any instructions to which I was a party, or of which I had any knowledge.

In connection with the Sinking Fund Board, it has been charged that I was a party to a fraudulent sale of the State stock in the Greenville and Columbia Railroad Company. This charge I deny in every particular. In the first place there was no fraudulent sale of that stock, so far as my knowledge or belief extends. The sale was made at a price fully equal to the value of the stock at that time, and was made to a party wholly without connection with me, or, so far as I know, with any member of the Sinking Fund Board. The statement, by whomsover made, that I joined in a sale of that stock to any person who acted for me, or under any arrangement or agreement with me, tacit or expressed, that I was to have any interest in the stock when purchased by him, is wholly false and utterly incapable of being sustained by any evidence.

Another charge is that I engaged in a disastrous sale of the State stock in the Blue Ridge Railroad Company. The truth is that I was not present when that sale was made, and never in any manner took part in it. My views as to the proper terms and conditions of a sale of that stock were laid before the Board in writing, but they were not adopted by the Board.

The purchases of bonds made by order of the Sinking Fund Board were made in good faith, and the funds in the hands of the Board were applied in payment of such purchases. It is true, I think that the second purchase of $100,000 of State bonds was ordered before the funds were in the hands of the Board; but this was done in the expectation, on the part of the Board, that sufficient funds would come into the hands of the Board to pay for the purchases as rapidly as payment should be necessary. This may have been an imprudent act, but it certainly has no element of dishonesty or fraud in it.

To all other statements which impute to me any improper action in connection with this Board, I give an unqualified denial. I was never a party to any note given for purchases made from this Board. I never received a fee for any service done in connection with this Board or as a member of it; and I have never been a party to any disposition of the proceeds of sales either in money or bonds, made by this Board, which was not strictly in accordance with law. If any illegal disposition has been made of any property in the hands of this Board, it was not done with my consent, as the present Attorney General, who was directed to institute legal proceedings to recover property illegally disposed of by the Sinking Fund Commissioners, can testify.

I am charged with responsibility for the losses arising to the State from the transactions of the Land Commission. Upon this point I frankly say that I have always regretted exceedingly the action which I was led to take in some instances as a member of the Advisory Board of that Commission, but I deny that in any instance I acted carelessly or dishonestly. I was, as a member of that Board, charged with the duty of consenting to the purchases of land recommended by the Land Commissioner. Of course I could have no personal knowledge of the lands. I never in a single instance had any personal knowledge of any tract of land purchased for the State. I acted, from the necessity of the case, solely upon the information and representations of others. Subsequently I learned that some of the lands purchased were not worth the price paid, but no member of that Board can be charged with dereliction of duty on that account, unless it can be shown that he had some knowledge, or had some reason to believe or suspect, that the information presented to him was incorrect, or that the purchases were improper or undesirable at the time they were made. In the case, for instance, of the Schley purchases, so called, the Board was informed by persons who were certainly competent to judge, and who were directed by the Board to make inquiries concerning those lands, that those lands were desirable. In that case I acted upon evidence which I was as well warranted in trusting as any evidence for any other purchase.

If there be a man anywhere who can say that I ever had any personal connection of any sort with any purchase made by this Board, or that I communicated or acted with any party to any sale, with a view to promote such sale, or that I was ever remotely interested in any sale

of land to this Board, let him be named.   Once for all I say there is no
shadow of foundation for such charges or insinuations.   No man can
prove them, and no man will undertake to prove them.

Of the charges made against me in connection with the Board appointed to take charge of the agricultural land scrip, little need be said.
Every act of that Board was in strict accordance with law.   The sale
of the scrip was made at a full and fair price, and after careful consideration and inquiry by the Board.   The proceeds were immediately
invested in State bonds as directed by law.   Subsequently those bonds,
while in the hands of the agent of the Board, were pledged for State
loans, and are still held in New York as collateral security for about
$57,000 lent to the State.   Of the legality of this use of these bonds it
is not now necessary to speak.   They were pledged by the Agent
under a claim of authority conferred by an Act of the General Assembly.   The Board were not consulted in this matter, and never in any
way consented to the pledging of these bonds.

The thousand other idle tales, born of the personal and political
malice and mendacity with which this community is so remarkably
afflicted—such as my reported partnership with Mr. Kimpton, my present or past pecuniary interest in various schemes which were intended
to draw money from the Treasury, and the pecuniary benefit derived
by me from my connection with the State Government—do not deserve
even a denial.   They are, each and all, false in every particular and
every sense.   Not only have I not received pecuniary profit from any
transactions in which I have had an official duty to perform, and not
only have I never been interested in any scheme which was hostile to
public interests, but I can say, with honest pride, that no man ever yet
in South Carolina approached me with a bribe in any form, or solicited
my official or personal consent or coöperation in any dishonest measure or action.   Such a degree of respect has at least been shown me.
While denouncing me in public as a corrupt official, my defamers have
never ventured to solicit the aid which they would now convince the
public I have been swift to extend to all corrupt and fraudulent measures.   The little property which I now possess I have acquired neither
by corruption nor speculation ; but I have earned it by honest and honorable labor, and I defy the world to produce evidence sufficient to
excite a shadow of a presumption to the contrary.   I acknowledge mistakes, and I regret the consequences of some acts in my official career.
I desire to see those consequences repaired, and I desire it all the
more because they have resulted in part from my acts, but to every
specific and every general charge involving moral delinquency or conscious wrong in my official action in this State, I give my absolute and
solemn denial.   D. H. CHAMBERLAIN.

Columbia, August 19, 1874.

The following letter was published in the New York *Tribune*.
Governor Chamberlain had been nominated by the Republicans
and was engaged in prosecuting his canvass, pledging himself in

public addresses throughout the State, as the platform of the party pledged all the candidates, to a policy of retrenchment and reform.[1] The writer of the letter to which this communication is a reply is understood to be Mr. E. V. Smalley:

To the Editor of the Tribune :

SIR—The present political campaign in South Carolina is attracting the attention of the country to a degree which I am sure will induce you to publish a brief statement from me in reply to the letter of your correspondent " S.," writing from Philadelphia in the *Tribune* of September 21st. Having been absent from home in the upper portions of this State for a fortnight past, I did not read the letter referred to until to-day. I find that it consists of a " conclusion " that I am not innocent of certain alleged frauds in connection with South Carolina bonds, based upon certain alleged " facts" which are " briefly outlined " by your correspondent. The " conclusion" of course rests upon the "facts." I shall give my attention entirely to the "facts" and let the " conclusion" take care of itself.

I pass by the numerous minor inaccuracies, to use the mildest term, into which your correspondent has fallen in his outline of "facts," and notice only those leading statements which are relied upon to connect me with the alleged frauds.

First—Your correspondent asserts as a matter of fact that :

All the Acts for the increase of the State debt were drawn by Chamberlain. They were very cunningly worded. Instead of authorizing the issue of bonds to a definite amount they authorized a sufficient amount to be issued to raise a given sum of money. A wide door was purposely left open for fraud here.

In reply to this statement, I say that I did not draw any of the Acts in question, and I make this offer to your correspondent—that if he will support the assertion that I drew all or any of the Acts referred to by any thing besides his own assertion, I will prove the fact which I now state by incontestable evidence. Truth permits me to go further, and to say that I not only did not draw those Acts, but that I was not consulted in regard to their form or phraseology, nor did I know their phraseology until I saw them when duly published as Acts of the Legislature.

But the remainder of your correspondent's statement, as above quoted, is not less unfounded and indicative of culpable haste or ignorance. He says the Acts in question were " very cunningly worded," and that "a wide door was purposely left open for fraud." Let us see how this is. The Acts are to be found on pages 17, 18, and 182 of the fourteenth volume of the Statutes At Large of this Sate. By the first section of each Act authority is given to a designated officer or officers " to borrow, on the credit of South Carolina, a sum not exceeding —— dollars." This is the exact language of each Act, the amount to be

[1] See Chapter I., page 8.

borrowed being precisely fixed in each Act. This is the alleged
" cunning " and " wide door for fraud " which is charged upon me Now,
if you or your correspondent will refer to page 259 of the Statutes At
Large of the United States of 1861, and to page 709 of the Statutes
At Large of the United States of 1862–63, it will be found that the
alleged " cunning " wording and " wide door to fraud " are simply *literal
copies from the Acts of Congress under which the present bonded debt
of the United States was authorized and contracted.* The late Chief-
Justice Chase, as you are aware, is the reputed author of each of those
Acts.

I leave this statement of your correspondent without further answer,
and I respectfully submit to a candid public whether such a statement
does not entitle me and all affected by it to the benefit of the maxim,
"Ab uno disce omnes." I think such reckless and injurious assertion
ought to recoil on its author with fatal effect.

Second—Your correspondent asserts as a matter of fact :

Finally, when the credit of the State was exhausted ; when the Railroad Ring,
under the lead of John Patterson, had stolen all the valuable interest of the State in
the Blue Ridge, Greenville, and Columbia, and Spartanburg and Union railroads ;
when the Real Estate Ring had made way with all the landed property of the State
which they could put their hands on ; when the Legislative Ring under Moses had
emptied the treasury and put out certificates of indebtedness by the ream ; when the
Land Commission Ring had sucked that orange dry, the Bond Ring, as the four
officials above named, their New York agent, and their Columbia bankers were popularly designated, hit upon a shrewd expedient to raise money. The bonded debt of
the State had been run up to about $9,000,000, and it was plain that Wall Street
would not touch a new issue adding to the total of the debt. A bill was prepared by
Chamberlain, and put through the Legislature in February, 1872, if I remember right,
known as the Conversion Bond Act.

Here are two principal substantive allegations : first, that the " Conversion Bond Act " was passed in 1872, or in other words, after the
events as described in the words above quoted took place. The alleged
design of the Act is an inference from the time of its passage. What,
then, shall be said of your correspondent's accuracy or truthfulness
when I inform you that the " Conversion Bond Act " referred to is to
be found on page 241 of the 14th volume of the General Statutes of
this State, and was passed March 23, 1869, instead of February, 1872—
within less than seven months after the passage of the first bond Act in
the fall of 1868, and three years before the date named by your correspondent as showing that this Act was a " shrewd expedient to raise
money " after every thing else had been stolen ?

The second principal allegation contained in this extract from your
correspondent's letter is, that the " Conversion Bond Act " was " prepared by Chamberlain." This is likewise a total error. The Conversion Bond Act is a just and necessary Act of legislation, and I might
have drawn it without a shadow of blame ; but as a matter of fact, the
statement which I have made respecting the drawing of the other bond

Acts is true of this Act. Absolute proof of this statement will be furnished, if it is denied.

Third—Your correspondent asserts as a matter of fact that "on Chamberlain's sole recommendation H. H. Kimpton, a college classmate of his, was appointed Financial Agent to negotiate State loans in New York." Your correspondent is fortunate here in being correct in saying that Mr. Kimpton was a college classmate of mine, but beyond that single fact he is wholly mistaken in his statement. I deny that Mr. Kimpton was appointed on my "sole recommendation," and all fair-minded men will agree that I am entitled to be believed until some evidence to the contrary is adduced. I say that I had no more to do with his appointment than each and every other member of the Board, either in power or influence. The appointment was made on the "sole recommendation" of financial authorities in New York, whose recommendations were furnished to the Board, and in proof of this I refer to Mr. Kimpton and the other members of the Board. They are competent witnesses familiar with the facts and not likely to assume responsibility which does not belong to them.

Your correspondent further asserts that Governor Scott stated to him that he accepted Mr. Kimpton's bond "because Chamberlain had told him it was all right." I know nothing of such a statement of Governor Scott, and it will be seen to have very little significance when other facts are properly stated. The Act authorizing the appointment of a Financial Agent is to be found on page 18 of the fourteenth volume of the General Statutes of this State. No bond of any kind is authorized or required to be taken of the Financial Agent. The Board did, however, of their own motion require of the Agent his own personal bond in the sum of $200,000 for the faithful performance of his duties. That bond was given, and if I stated to Governor Scott that the bond was all right, I stated the truth the whole truth, and nothing but the truth. That bond is now good and binding, and is an evidence that the Financial Board were at least more careful of the State's interests than the law required them to be. The statement that I misrepresented any matter connected with Mr. Kimpton's bond is destitute of truth, or any basis of probable truth.

I might go on to show other instances in your correspondent's letter of what I think should be considered unpardonable inaccuracy ; as, for instance, his statement that "the Legislature at its next session repudiated the entire issue of conversion bonds." Whereas the fact is that the Legislature at that session, instead of repudiating those bonds, formally "validated" them by an Act to be found at page 278 of the fifteenth volume of the General Statutes of this State.

It will be conceded, I think, that the foregoing are the principal "facts" upon which the "conclusion" of your correspondent respecting me rests. Of all or nearly all the rest it may be said that it is hearsay, repeated by your correspondent, and not evidence nor "facts" which demand more than a denial, and I forbear to claim further space for comment or argument. I quite agree with your correspondent when he says that "if he (I) had been a member of a band of assassins who had committed a murder, he (I) could not escape punishment on his (my) own statement that the others throttled the victim against his (my) protest"; but I hope your correspondent is sufficiently familiar with the principle of law to which he appeals to know that it is always necessary, first, to establish the "fact" of the conspiracy and who are its members, before each can be made responsible for the acts of the others.

I am happy to believe that you do not wish to do injustice to me or to any man, and if the ordinary avenues by which the facts on both sides of our present political controversy here might be presented to the country were not practically closed to the side on which I stand, I should not have felt called upon to offer you this statement.

D. H. CHAMBERLAIN.

COLUMBIA, S. C., October 12, 1874.

After Governor Chamberlain had left South Carolina and settled in New York, there appeared in one of the journals of that city a pretended "confession" by Niles G. Parker, who had held the office of State Treasurer of South Carolina in the term of Governor Scott. The only notice taken of it by the Governor appears in the following report of an interview, published in the New York *Tribune* :

Ex-Governor Chamberlain, of South Carolina, was visited at his office, No. 346 Broadway, yesterday afternoon, by a *Tribune* reporter, who asked him if he had any statement to make in reply to the charges made against him by Niles G. Parker, ex-Treasurer of the State of South Carolina, of complicity in a ring to rob the State. Mr. Chamberlain said that he had carefully read Parker's statement, or so-called "confession," and emphatically denied all the charges therein contained. He was ready and willing at all times to answer to the proper authorities for his acts while in South Carolina. He then made the following statement, which, he said, was all he was willing to say at present :

Niles G. Parker, during my term of office as Governor, was sued by the State of South Carolina to recover for a large amount of coupons which he was charged with stealing, and afterward converting into State bonds. In this suit he was arrested and held to bail, which he was unable to give. The case was tried in June, 1875, and a verdict rendered against Parker for $75,000. He was finally released from jail on *habeas corpus* and instantly fled from the State and has never returned. Since that time he has diligently sought to implicate me, in order to obtain money and immunity for himself. His agents and attorneys have visited Columbia repeatedly on this errand, and through one of them, Parker now actually confesses, he sold certain papers, to be used against me politically, for $4,000. I know, also, that his wares were offered to those Republicans who were hostile to me for my course as Governor. They were likewise offered to the Democratic committees last fall, and, I am glad to say, they found no market there. I have also the best reasons for stating that he has over and over offered his testimony against me to the officers of the present Administration in South Carolina, and I can only conclude that they found it as unworthy as did others.

Having failed to realize further upon his stock of scandal, and being himself now under new indictments at Columbia, he comes forward in a fresh effort to palm off his budget upon the general public. Now, I, for one, do not feel called upon to notice Parker or his statements, further than to give the foregoing facts, and to pronounce his charges against me, one and all, maliciously false. None of them are, in fact, new, except the charge that he bribed me with $2,000 to do something which was so base that even he could not name it. With this exception, they have all been repeatedly published in South Carolina for political effect in the last four years. If anybody demand of me that I should do more now than deny such charges, put forward by such a man as Parker confesses himself to be, he will not be gratified by me. I am amenable to the laws of South Carolina at all times for my acts, and whenever the officers of the law in that State wish to call me to account, I shall respond and meet my accusers. In the meantime, I shall trust to the evidence I have given to the country that I have been the friend of good government and the foe of dishonest men of all parties in South Carolina,—evidences which, less than one year ago, men of all classes and parties in that State accepted as conclusive,—to protect my character with those whose good opinion is valuable.

II.

INDICTMENT OF GOVERNOR CHAMBERLAIN.

ON November 6, 1878, eighteen months after Governor Chamberlain had left the State, the Grand Jury of Richland County, sitting at Columbia, returned an indictment of Governor Chamberlain with four others (the Land Commissioner, the other two members of the Advisory Board of the Land Commission, and the Financial Agent of the State in New York) for conspiracy to defraud the State. The transactions upon which the indictment appeared to be founded occurred in the year 1870, while the Governor was the Attorney General and *ex officio*, a member of the Advisory Board of the Land Commission. Immediately upon the announcement in the press despatches of the day, that an indictment against him had been returned, Governor Chamberlain telegraphed to the Attorney General of the State, asking what bail was desired, and announcing his readiness to meet the trial. Bail was fixed and given for $20,000. It was understood and believed by the public that all those indicted with Governor Chamberlain, with the exception perhaps of Kimpton, the Financial Agent, would have been offered and would have accepted immunity in consideration of giving testimony against the Governor.

The history of the proceedings upon this indictment is a short one and is given in the following transcript of the Court records at Columbia :

STATE OF SOUTH CAROLINA, }
    RICHLAND COUNTY. }

Wednesday, November 6th, 1878.

*   *   *   *   *   *   *

The Grand Jury returns Bills as follows :

The State, }
vs.   } Indictment for Conspiracy.
Charles P. Leslie ; John S. Neagle, Niles G. Parker, }
Daniel H. Chamberlain and Hiram H. Kimpton. }

True Bill,

J. G. GRAHAM, Foreman.

The Court adjourned until 10 o'clock A.M., to-morrow :

D. B. MILLER, C.C.C.P. & G.S.

THE STATE OF SOUTH CAROLINA :

At a Court of General Sessions for the County of Richland, begun to holden at Columbia on the fourth Monday in March (being the (24th) Twenty-fourth day of the month), Anno Domini eighteen hundred and seventy-nine.

Present His Honor Thomas Thomson, presiding.

*   *   *   *   *   *   *

No. 26.

The State. }
vs.   } Conspiracy Cont. by deft.
Charles P. Leslie, John L. Neagle, Niles G. Parker, } Chamberlain
Daniel H. Chamberlain, and Hiram H. Kimpton. } 24 March, 1879.

*   *   *   *   *   *   *

The Court adjourned until 10 o'clock A.M. to-morrow.

D. B. MILLER, C.C.C.P. & G.S.

THE STATE OF SOUTH CAROLINA :

At a Court of General Sessions, in and for the County of Richland, begun to be holden at Columbia, in the County and State aforesaid, on the fourth Monday in March (being the twenty-eight day of the month), in the year of our Lord one thousand eight hundred and eighty-one.

Present the Honorable A. P. Aldrich, Judge of the Fourth Judicial Circuit presiding.

*   *   *   *   *   *   *

Same. }
vs.   } Indictment Conspiracy Nol.
C. P. Leslie, D. H. Chamberlain, Niles G. Parker, } Pros.
and Hiram H. Kimpton. }

The Court adjourns until to-morrow at 10 o'clock A.M.

E. R. ARTHUR, C.C.G.S.

SOUTH CAROLINA }
RICHLAND COUNTY. }

I, E. R. Arthur, Clerk of the Circuit Courts, for the County and State aforesaid, do hereby certify that the foregoing are true extracts from the Sessions Journal for Richland County, and State aforesaid, as will more fully appear by a reference to said Journal at pages 259, 267 and 380.

In witness whereof, I have hereunto set my hand and affixed the seal of the said Courts at Columbia, S. C., this 18th day of April, A.D., 1887.

E. R. ARTHUR,

Clerk of Circuit Courts.

The indictment itself as it stands in the files of the Court at Columbia, bears this indorsement :

"*Nol : Pros :*—Bonham, Solicitor, 28 March, 1881."

III.

TWO LETTERS BY GOVERNOR CHAMBERLAIN REGARDING HIS ADMINISTRATION AND RETIREMENT.

THE two personal letters following are given a place here, because they seem to have a certain public interest in connection with the record contained in this volume.

GOVERNOR CHAMBERLAIN TO WILLIAM LLOYD GARRISON.

NEW YORK, June 11, 1877.

DEAR MR. GARRISON :—. . . Your prophecy is fulfilled ; and I am not only overthrown, but as a consequence I am now a citizen of New York. It seems to me a remarkable experience indeed, though I hope I do not egotistically exaggerate it, for I am sure it will soon be forgotten by most men in the press and hurry of new events. Why I write this line now and send it to Boston when I know you are in Europe, is because I feel like putting on record now my main reflections on my experiences of the last three years, and because I know, or think I know, that you will be interested in what I shall now write.

First, then, my defeat was inevitable under the circumstances of time and place which surrounded me. I mean here exactly that the uneducated negro was too weak, no matter what his numbers, to cope with the whites.

We had lost, too, the sympathy of the North, in some large measure, though we never deserved it so certainly as in 1876 in South Carolina.

The Presidential contest also endangered us and doubtless defeated us. The hope of electing Tilden incited our opponents, and the greed of office led the defeated Republicans under Hayes to sell us out. There was just as distinct a bargain to do this at Washington as ever existed which was not signed and sealed on paper. And the South is not to be blamed for it, if anybody is ; but rather those leaders, like Evarts, who could never see their Constitutional obligations towards the South till the offices were slipping away from their party.

So the end came ; but not as you expected. I find many sources of consolation. For my family I can only rejoice; and for myself, if I could at all separate my interests from theirs, I shall now lead a life better suited to my tastes and probably to my talents. . . .

One other word only: I need not say to you that I look back on my record as Governor, even to its last hour, with pride and satisfaction. There is not in it all one act or effort which, in its intention, I would now change. It will lie open to scrutiny whether I will or not, but I submit it confidently to the inspection of all men.

Yet I must close with a remark which may surprise you. It is this : I made a grave mistake in that I did not refuse to run on a ticket with R. B. Elliott. I saw it then, but not so clearly as now. I do not mean that this excuses, or tends to excuse, the conduct of those who have overthrown us. What I mean is that Elliott's bare presence on the ticket justly gave offence to some honest men of both races. He had opposed me brutally, especially in the nominating convention. Unable to defeat me, he determined to foist himself on the ticket with me to cover his defeat. I saw at once the bearing, in part, of this, and I took the resolution unknown to any friends, to walk into the Convention and throw up my nomination and avow that I did it because I would not run on a ticket with Elliott. I knew it would result in putting him off the ticket. I had actually risen in my office to go into the hall for this purpose when I was met at the door by a dozen or more of my most devoted colored supporters who came to congratulate me on *the surrender of Elliott in seeking to stand on a ticket with me !* I was disarmed of my purpose and relinquished it. It was a mistake. Whether it affected the result which has now come I do not know. But I ought to have made Elliott's withdrawal the condition of my acceptance. This incident is now known only to *you and me.* . . .

Yours faithfully,

D. H. CHAMBERLAIN.

GOVERNOR CHAMBERLAIN TO HON. B. O. DUNCAN.

MUNICH, August 25, 1882.

MY DEAR DUNCAN :—. . . It does seem a little strange, does it not ? that we should renew our acquaintance here in Europe ; but as I have just determined to stay over till spring, I shall see you in Naples (D. V.) about February on our " grand tour " of Italy. Your letter has brought back South Carolina to me in a most vivid way. I am now paying the long-deferred penalty of my life there. Malaria, overwork, nervous tension, and all that attends these, have invalided me for I know not how long, though lately I have good hope I am going to be fairly well again.

But, after all, whether I am or not, I cannot say I really regret my work in South Carolina. If I had sought it from ambitious or other causes, I should certainly have to regret it bitterly;—for failure, I suppose, is the verdict of the rest of the world upon it, so far as it notices it at all; but as it now looks to me, and as it did at the time, my career there was laid or forced upon me at every step. Others do not see this as clearly as I do. I remember that after the inauguration of Hampton, while I was still " holding the fort," Judge Magrath and Mr. Campbell of Charleston called on me at the Governor's room. In the course of conversation, they alluded to my throwing away so recklessly my political preferment at the hands of the white people, saying what was so often said to me, that I might have been Senator, and, as I remember it, might still be, if I would bow to events, or words to that effect. I knew they were sincere, and at heart friends of mine, and I took the occasion to tell them how I looked at things from a personal standpoint :—that I was, and had been, throughout, fighting no fight of my own or for myself, but for my party, which represented to me freedom, *with* good government, in South Carolina ;—that I had dreamed the dream of making the Republican party, even in South Carolina, and made up, as it was, mostly of negroes, the source and symbol of good government for *all* the people;—that I had not seen, and could not then see, how their party, by their plan of rifle clubs and suppression of a free ballot, could preserve freedom, even if in all other respects they secured good government;—that I did not yet see the end, but at any rate I saw no path of honor for me but the one I was pursuing ;—that neither the coming National Administration nor the Democratic party in South Carolina could tempt me to voluntarily swerve from it ;—that I could be, and probably was already, beaten in my public hopes and plans, but that, so much the more, was nothing left for me but to stand where I was till the end came. They were impressed, as I saw, by what I said, and one of them came back a half hour later to tell me, for both, how fully they respected my motives and position.

But one thing followed my defeat which I did not count upon. I did not think any Court would ever be found in South Carolina to indict me. I fancied that their victory would recall, rather than blot out, the recollection of two years of plaudits and praise and support of my Administration. Still I can see now that this result was to them almost a necessity of the situation, for, political necessity, real or imagined, like other kinds of necessity, *knows no law.* . .

Thank God, however, that is all past, and has left no bitterness in my heart ! I have just seen that Hugh Thompson has been nominated for Governor. It is the best nomination that could have been made. He is progressive, and especially concerned with education, and I am heartily glad he is to be Governor.

I believe now that with peace, even if it has been in some sense the peace of the sword at first, prosperity will come to the State. Time is the all-healer. The negro is remitted to work, and the white man to power. These, with honest administration and low taxes, will keep the peace, and time will heal the wounds and blot out even the scars of old strifes. The great resources of the State, her great permanent staples, the indomitable spirit of our people—which you even, native as you are, do not know so well as I do—will bring a noble future to South Carolina. That it may be so and that I may live to see it, is my earnest hope, and I am sure you will believe me when I say so. . . .

Yours faithfully,

D. H. CHAMBERLAIN.

IV.

A DISCUSSION OF PRESIDENT HAYES' SOUTHERN POLICY.

On the 4th of July, 1877, Governor Chamberlain delivered an address at Woodstock, Conn., on President Hayes' Southern Policy, the only occasion when he has given fully his views upon the constitutional, political, and personal questions involved in that policy. The following portions of this speech are given here as a discussion of questions which will always have interest in connection with the topics and events of which this volume contains the record :

. . . I have already sufficiently informed you that I must speak in condemnation of what is known as President Hayes' Southern Policy. The question will be asked : " Why attack that policy now ? It is irrevocable. Criticism cannot recall it. Denunciation cannot change it. Attacks upon it will distract the party and promote only the success of our political opponents." I answer, that if a political party is a contrivance for seizing and holding the government of the country, regardless of any broad or fixed political principles, I ought to hold my peace. But if, as I have believed, a political party is a means or agency for promoting the welfare of all the people by the enforcement, in the affairs of government, of certain political principles, then, whenever the citizen finds those principles abandoned by the party professing them, it is the simple dictate alike of duty and honor to oppose and attack those who are betraying the party which has trusted them. This duty I shall try to discharge. Party success is not always possible. Party honesty is. I know well that there are tides in the affairs of parties, great refluent waves of sentiment or opinion, which sometimes overpower the strongest political organizations. There is no permanent loss in such reverses. Principles remain and vitalize organizations into fresh life after every defeat ; but woe to that party which bends silently under the blow of treachery to its own principles !

I am to discuss a *Presidential* policy. It is one of the peculiarities, as well as misfortunes, of our political life that heretofore, as well as now, we have heard of Presidential policies. The expression discloses a dislocation of the proper relations between a President and the party which he represents. If you say the President should represent no party, but the whole people, the answer is, he must represent the whole people through fidelity to principles approved and accepted by him as the representative of his political party. Political parties, in the sense in which we use the term, are the outgrowth of freedom. The experience of free peoples has devised no other effective mode of steadily influencing and controlling public affairs. It is essential to the life of a party, to an honest or useful relation between a party and its leaders, that the latter should faithfully represent the principles of the former. No man is ever trusted as a party leader upon any other basis. A *Presidential* policy, if the term is descriptive, is an anomaly and offence. It savors of bad faith. It has a native and historical odor of treachery and intrigue.

But, fellow-citizens, what is the President's Southern policy?

In point of physical or external fact, it consists in withdrawing the military forces of the United States from the points in South Carolina and Louisiana where they had been previously stationed for the protection and support of the lawful Governments of those States.

In point of immediate, foreseen, and intended consequence, it consists in the overthrow and destruction of those State Governments, and the substitution in their stead of certain other organizations called State Governments.

In point of actual present results, it consists in the abandonment of Southern Republicans, and especially the colored race, to the control and rule not only of the Democratic party, but of that class at the South which regarded slavery as a Divine Institution, which waged four years of destructive war for its perpetuation, which steadily opposed citizenship and suffrage for the negro—in a word, a class whose traditions, principles, and history are opposed to every step and feature of what Republicans call our national progress since 1860.

In point of general political and moral significance, it consists in the proclamation to the country and the world that the will of the majority of the voters of a State, lawfully and regularly expressed, is no longer the ruling power in our States, and that the constitutional guaranty to every State in this Union of a republican form of government and of protection against domestic violence, is henceforth ineffectual and worthless.

Does not such a policy challenge attention? Does it not justify iree discussion? The statement which I have now made is drawn with a fair and judicial hand. It contains nothing but clear, visible, actual facts. And yet I ask you, fellow-citizens, does it not sound like an indictment?

In discussing such a policy it will not be necessary to do more than to recall well known and undisputed facts.

When President Hayes assumed his office, he found in Louisiana a State Government complete in all its departments, executive, legislative, and judicial, with Governor Packard as its Chief Executive. That government rested for its legal title upon an election held and conducted according to law, the results of which had been ascertained and declared in the manner provided by law. Those results and the mode of their legal ascertainment and declaration had been subjected to the examination and judgment of an august special tribunal. By the judgment of that tribunal, the agencies established by the laws of Louisiana for the conduct and declaration of that election had been declared legal and competent for those purposes. That judgment was an indispensable support to the President's title to his own office. Without it he was himself a usurper, without a shadow of legal right or semblance of lawful authority.

It is another unquestioned fact that by the same election and the same agencies which had thus resulted in securing the electoral vote of Louisiana for President Hayes, a Legislature had been chosen composed of a large majority, in both branches, of Republicans. This Legislature had assembled, and with an unquestioned quorum of lawfully elected members in both branches, had proceeded in exact and unquestioned conformity to the Constitution and laws of Louisiana, to declare Governor Packard the lawfully elected Governor. He had assumed the office, and was in its lawful exercise. Not an element of legal regularity or validity was wanting to his title. From the moment Governor Packard became clothed with that office under the Constitution and laws of Louisiana, no lawful authority existed in Louisiana or elsewhere to destroy or mar or impeach his title. It was irrevocable and unassailable by any lawful agency.

President Hayes found the State Government, as I have said, complete in its organization, unquestionable in its validity, except upon grounds which directly and equally impeached the validity of his own title. He found it, however, menaced and beleaguered by an armed, violent, and revolutionary organization, calling itself a State Government, which had already forcibly seized a considerable part of the public offices and property at the capital, and stood in avowed readiness to complete its usurpation, whenever this could be done without actual collision with the military forces of the United States. Not only was every feature of this situation known to President Hayes, but he was subsequently, in due constitutional form, informed of it by the Legislature of Louisiana, then in session, in its demand, under the fourth section of the fourth Article of the Constitution of the United States, for protection against domestic violence.

Now, I undertake to say that no public exigency ever arose in which the Constitutional and political duty of the President of the United States was clearer or more imperative than in Louisiana at the time to which I have referred. I leave out of view, for the moment, all consideration of that most peculiar, and to many most humiliating feature of this business, which consists in a willingness, on the part of the President, to accept for himself the fruits of the election of Louisiana, although it is an indisputable fact that the vote in that State for the Hayes electors fell short of that for Governor Packard by several hundreds, and yet, while clutching those fruits with a ready, if not eager hand, to plan and carry out the overthrow of Governor Packard. I leave out of view here also the general question of party fealty, of which I shall hereafter speak, as well as of the general consequences of the President's conduct. I do not stop now to inquire what manner of man Governor Packard was, or what party he represented. If Governor Packard had been a corrupt poltroon, instead of a man whose honor and courage matches that of any in the Union, the President's duty would have remained the same. I inquire only, at this point, what was the official duty of President Hayes towards the State of Louisiana? And I answer that it is beyond intelligent dispute or reasonable question that it was his duty to protect the lawful Government of that State from domestic violence by the military forces of the United States, and to make the measure of that protection, as well as its continuance, the extent necessary to render Governor Packard's authority effective throughout the State of Louisiana.

Our Government is a Union composed of separate States; in the impressive judicial phrase of Chief-Justice Chase, it is "an indestructible Union composed of indestructible States." The powers of the General Government are limited and special. Beyond these it cannot go. Its powers limit and measure its duties. The Constitution in its opening sentence declares the great purposes of its own creation, and among these we find "to insure domestic tranquillity." By the concurrence of all respectable authorities the true construction of the whole instrument and the true interpretation of its separate provisions or phrases is that which secures, on the one hand, the efficient exercise of all the powers of the General Government which are essential to the attainment of the purposes for which the Union was formed, and on the other hand, and at the same time, leaves to the people of each State the free exercise of all the powers not delegated by the Constitution to the General Government. The gravest constitutional discussions, both parliamentary and judicial, which have marked our history have had reference to the line which should separate State rights from national rights.

In defending the President's action towards Louisiana and South Carolina, great efforts have been made to cover his action with the mantle of State rights. The President himself has proclaimed his policy to be "local self-government," and we hear it described on all sides as "home-rule." It is in truth the exact opposite of this; but what I wish to remark now is, that the question involved in this discussion is not one, primarily, of State rights or national rights, but of national duty. The relations of the General Government and of the President as the Chief Executive to the present question, arise under the provisions of Section 4 of Article 4 of the Constitution, which declares that "The United States shall guarantee to every State in this Union a republican form of government, and shall protect each of them against invasion; and on application of the Legislature, or of the Executive (when the Legislature cannot be convened), against domestic violence."

Whoever reads the Constitution will observe that almost every other section is concerned with the granting, or defining, or regulation of the several powers designed to be conferred on the General Government, or the denial or restriction to the States of powers which might interfere with the great objects of the Union. In the present section we find a purpose, primarily, not to enlarge the powers of the General Government nor to deny powers to the States, but the solemn imposition of a great duty to be discharged by the United States towards each State. As to other sections the State and the nation are left to adjust their respective powers under the light of the language of the Constitution, and by the modes provided by that instrument. This section raises no such question. Its terms are clear, broad, unmistakable. " The United States *shall* . . . protect every State in this Union, on application, etc., against domestic violence." It does not say that the United States shall have power to protect each State. It does not say that each State shall have the right to demand protection. It is not a question of powers or rights. It is a plain command addressed by the Constitution to the Government which it created, requiring it to do a plainly specific duty.

In discharge of the duty imposed by this section Congress, by the Acts of 1795 and of 1807, authorized the President, whenever the exigency described in this section should arise, or, to use the exact language of the Acts,—" in case of an insurrection in any State against the Government thereof "—to call forth such number of the militia of any other State or States as he deems sufficient to suppress the insurrection, or to employ for the same purposes such part of the land or naval forces of the United States as he deems necessary.

This duty, therefore, originally imposed upon the United States, is now imposed on the President.

This section and the Act of 1795 have received judicial examination and application in the Supreme Court of the United States in the well-known case of *Luther v. Borden*, (7 Howard, 1). Referring to this section of the Constitution, Chief-Justice Taney, speaking for the Court, says : " It rested with Congress to determine upon the means proper to be adopted to fulfil this guaranty " ; and referring then to the Act of 1795, he says :

" By this Act, the power of deciding whether the exigency had arisen upon which the Government of the United States is bound to interfere, is given to the President. He is to act upon the application of the Legislature or of the Executive, and consequently he must determine what body of men constitute the Legislature, and who is the Governor, before he can act. The fact that both parties claim the right to the Government cannot alter the case, for both cannot be entitled to it. If there is an armed conflict, like the one of which we are speaking, it is a case of domestic violence, and one of the parties must be in insurrection against the lawful Government. And the President must, of necessity, decide which is the Government, and which party is unlawfully arrayed against it, before he can perform the duty imposed upon him by the Act of Congress."

Now I submit that before any intelligent audience or tribunal, no argument is needed to make plainer the President's duty towards Louisiana. Read the section of the Constitution, and the Act of 1795, with the opinion of Chief-Justice Taney, and I do not see how any man with an honest purpose to do his duty could miss his path. The simple inquiries to be made before acting were : Has application been made by the Legislature or the Executive according to the constitutional requirements? If yea, does domestic violence or insurrection exist? If yea again, then the President is false to his trust, derelict of his plain constitutional duty, if he fails to protect the State to whatever extent in degree of force or length of time may be requisite to subdue the insurrection or violence. Since no other provision of the Constitution, as we have seen, is so imperative in enjoining a duty, so the discharge of no other constitutional duty by the President is so essential to the preservation of our dual system of government. It is the bulwark not of State rights alone, but of State life.

And now, let me inquire what was the action of the President under the circumstances stated? Did he discharge his constitutional duty by protecting the State of Louisiana against domestic violence? He made no attempt to do it. Being called upon by the Legislature of Louisiana in strict conformity to the Constitution, did he inquire and "determine," to use the words of Chief-Justice Taney, "what body of men constitute the Legislature, and who is the Governor"? No, he did not. Assuming the right to preserve the peace in Louisiana by the military forces of the United States pending his negotiations, a right the exercise of which was a bold and flagrant usurpation unless derived from the duty which he was at the very moment refusing to perform, he enters upon negotiations with those who by armed violence and in military array are menacing the lawful Government of the State. Sir, I have seen the hot indignation of outraged patriotism poured upon the weak old man in whose feeble hands the great rebellion found the powers of this Government in 1860, because he treated with the leaders and agents of that rebellion and could find no warrant in the Constitution for "coercing a State." I could frame an excuse for James Buchanan. He was the decaying fruit of half a century of Northern subservience to Southern dictation, the poor dregs of a worn-out politician whose life had been spent in cowering submission to the will of those whom he was now called to confront. But what shall be said of this President, educated by the events of the last seventeen years— the long and perilous struggle to save the nation to freedom and justice,—the representative of a party whose life and inspiration in every hour of its existence has been political justice and freedom for all American citizens,—a President who had literally climbed to his high seat over the dead bodies of hundreds of loyal men in Louisiana, who had met death in forms far more terrible than any battle-field in order that the liberty of which they had tasted might be kept for their children? James Buchanan could say he negotiated with those who were in arms against the United States, in order that he might by peaceful agencies preserve the integrity of the Union and avoid a fratricidal war. The President enters upon his negotiations with those who are in arms against the lawful Government of Louisiana, in order that he might the more surely betray the friends who had trusted him and the cause he was sworn to uphold.

You are familiar with the story. President Hayes, instead of seeking to discharge his constitutional duty according to the plain letter of the Constitution and law; instead of inquiring, if he had doubts, "what body of men constitute the Legislature, and who is the Governor"; instead of recognizing the palpable fact that an armed insurrection against the lawful Government of Louisiana existed and had been arrested in mid career solely by the presence of the military forces of the United States, and was still literally resting on its arms, despatches to New Orleans a Commission of five—for what? Let the elaborate letter of instructions of his Secretary of State answer. Is it to inquire "what body of men constitute the Legislature and who is the Governor"? No, that inquiry was foreign to his purpose. Is it to inquire whether in point of fact an insurrection had arisen against the Government of which Packard was the head? No. That inquiry was already answered by the fact avowed on the one hand and admitted on the other, that Governor Packard held his place against the insurrectionary forces solely by the protection of the military forces of the United States. The President's Commission went to New Orleans under instructions which forbade their discharging the duties appropriate to such an occasion, and which directed them to enter upon work foreign to any just conception of the President's duties or powers. They were directed to make "no examination into or report upon the facts of the recent State election, or the canvass of the votes cast at that election." They were told that it was important to learn "the *real impediments* to regular legal and peaceful proceedings under the laws and Constitution of Louisiana." They were told that "the President desires that you should devote your first and principal attention to the removal of the obstacles to an acknowledgment of one Government." "If," says the Secretary, "those obstacles should prove insuperable, it should be your next endeavor to accomplish the recognition of a single Legislature as the depository of the representative will of the people of Louisiana. This great department rescued from dispute, the rest of the problem could be gradually worked out." The Commission is further informed of the "extreme solicitude" of the President to avoid using his authority in influencing or determining "contested elections" in a State, and to "put an end to even the appearance of military intervention in the domestic affairs of the State"; and they are again urged to secure a single Legislature, with the significant hint that the President will thus be relieved of his embarrassment, since the Legislature can alone call for his aid under the Constitution.

Now, fellow-citizens, we cannot do better than to pause here long enough to consider the most extraordinary nature of these instructions. We shall see, if we look with our eyes and not with our prejudices, a disregard not merely of the constitutional duty which then confronted the President, but a greater disregard of the proper line which limits the powers and functions of the General Government in its relations to the States. We shall see that as the final result of this business was a disastrous blow at State rights as well as human rights, so the methods employed to reach the end were conceived and executed in fitting disregard of constitutional powers and limitations.

Recall now, what has already been shown, that the only possible warrant which the President had for any action or policy towards Lousiana was the duty imposed by the 4th Section of Article 4 of the Constitution. Observe again that the only inquiries to be made by the President under the call of the Legislature of Louisiana were, Does domestic violence, in the sense intended by the Constitution, exist in Louisiana? or, Which of the two organizations claiming to be State Governments is the true and lawful one? When the President of the United States is thus summoned to this duty, what right, what warrant of Constitution or law, I ask, can he have or find, for pushing aside the proper inquiries, and inquiring, either by himself or by a Commission of five, how he may " remove the obstacles to the acknowledgment of one Government in Louisiana," or how he may " accomplish "—in the sounding phrase of the Secretary—" the recognition of a single Legislature as the depository of the representative will of the people of Louisiana " ? Of what concern was it to him—I speak in a constitutional sense—to know how two Governments could be reduced to one, or two Legislatures combined in one? We hear much from the President and his advisers and defenders, of a new-born zeal for constitutional limitations. The same lips which in recent years have been wont to come to the consideration of constitutional questions with no narrower rule of construction than " *salus populi suprema lex*," are now tremulous with assurances of their " extreme solicitude " lest they should give " even the appearance of military intervention." Sir, hold them to their new tests. Ask the President under what power, express or implied, he enters Louisiana to secure one Legislature or one Government? No man can answer you. It was bold, arrant usurpation, without even an excuse that it was undertaken in a good cause. He had been called upon by the Legislature which recognized Governor Packard, to protect this State against domestic violence. It was under this warrant alone that he could enter Louisiana except as a usurper. He could have refused aid to Governor Packard, as Tilden would have done, because he was not the lawful Governor. He could have withdrawn the troops from the vicinity of the Statehouse on the ground that no domestic violence existed, and left the controversy to settle itself. In either course his action would have had the merit of being an exercise of powers undoubtedly committed to him. It might also have been characterized as open and straightforward. But the course which he did pursue was, first by his Commission to undermine Governor Packard, and then to withdraw the support of the United States troops. He dared not question Governor Packard's title ; but he thought, in the face of an intelligent people, to accomplish by indirection the purpose to which he stood committed. When, by the direct influence of his Commission and the pre-announcement of his purpose to withdraw the United States troops, he had gained for the Nichols Legislature a Returning Board quorum, he proclaims his discovery that no case of domestic violence exists in Louisiana warranting his intervention, and withdraws the troops.

Now, fellow-citizens, I exercise the right of an American citizen,— no more,—when I say that a review of this chapter of our history leaves me in no doubt that the real purpose of the Louisiana Commission and of the whole conduct of the Louisiana case by the President, was to accomplish the overthrow of Governor Packard and his authority. Called upon under the Constitution and laws of the country, as its Chief Executive, to discharge a grave public duty, a duty essential to the maintenance of the life of a great State, a duty equally essential to the maintenance of human rights and the principles of the political party which had elected him, the President not only declines the duty, but he stabs the State that sought his aid, and betrays the principles and men whom he was bound to uphold and protect.

Mark, too, the confession involved in the very effort to secure for Nichols a Returning Board Legislature. It was a confession that the foundation of the title of Governor Packard was impregnable ; that, in order to gain any semblance of authority for Nichols, Governor Packard's legislative department must be broken up,—a piece of policy as shallow as it was disreputable. Does any man say or suggest in terms, that the State Government of which Governor Packard was the head, was any the less the lawful State Government when a majority of the members declared elected by the Returning Board had taken seats in the Nichols Legislature ? Whenever any member of the Packard Legislature deserted his post, he left a vacant seat behind him. He carried nothing with him. It was then the prerogative of those who remained to cause the vacant seat to be filled. Or, if by the number of desertions no quorum was present, the result was a temporary paralysis of the legislative arm. It remained for this obstacle to be removed by new elections, as provided by the laws of Louisiana as of all other States. It is an evidence of the confusion of ideas bred by such efforts to circumvent political justice, that the country has been deluded into a less degree of reprobation of the President's policy by the fact that under the influence of the President's Commission and his own pre-announced purpose, a majority of the members of the lawful Legislature vacated their seats and joined the unlawful and revolutionary body called together by Nichols. The legal and parliamentary fact is that the action of those members neither took away any lawful authority from the one body, nor added any lawful authority to the other. Still less did such action change in any respect the constitutional duty of the President towards the State of Louisiana.

Fellow-citizens, I do not intend to overlook any plausible or prominent argument by which the President's Southern policy is defended, and I therefore propose to consider the question of the actual existence of " domestic violence " in Louisiana. The President, in his order removing the troops on the 20th day of April last, after, as I have shown, a Returning Board quorum had been obtained for the Nichols Legislature, declared that he did not find in Louisiana a condition of "domestic violence " such as is contemplated by the Constitution. He had, of course, been familiar with every feature of the situation there during the whole period of his delay, and he had not waited till April 20th to satisfy himself whether domestic violence existed or not. But such is the ground on which he places his removal of the troops. Let us examine this ground. Let us ask what is " domestic violence," and did " domestic violence " exist, in the constitutional sense, in Louisiana when the President was called upon to determine his action ?

*　　*　　*　　*　　*　　*　　*

I shall not object to allowing the present question to rest upon the doctrines and principles laid down by Mr. Webster. I have an habitual reverence for that most commanding authority in all our constitutional history.

When Mr. Webster speaks of " merely threatened domestic violence," or of " anticipating insurrectionary movements," what does he mean ? His meaning cannot well be expressed in clearer terms, but it may be said that he has in mind the broad and obvious distinction between the avowal of a purpose to resort to violence or the belief that violence will be used, on the one hand, and the actual exhibition or use of violence on the other. If a purpose were formed by a large number of the citizens of this State to overthrow or resist your Government,—if organizations for that purpose existed, but their members had not yet appeared as actual organized bodies or openly moved to the accomplishment of their purposes,—Mr. Webster would not regard this as "domestic violence " within the meaning of the Constitution,—a proposition which no one will dispute. The purpose must appear in acts. Whenever this condition of affairs arises, it is insurrection, and the moment for interference is the moment when the insurrection shows by its acts the power and the will to carry out its purpose. If a column of men, armed or unarmed, are found marching upon your Courthouse or your Statehouse with the known purpose of expelling your officers and your Government from their places, and if they possess the power to execute their purpose, are we to be told that this is not domestic violence because the column has not yet captured your public buildings or dispossessed your lawful officers, or because it has not yet come into actual collision with the lawful authorities ? This is not reason nor law, and no respectable authority can be produced to support such a theory. The simple test is : Is there an actual exhibition of physical force sufficient and designed to assault the lawful Government, or oppose its authority with success ? If there is, domestic violence exists, insurrection exists—not latent, but patent—not constructive, but palpable ; and if at such a juncture the President is called upon by the lawful Government to intervene, he is bound to protect the State. Must a lawful State Government, conscious that the force arrayed against her is beyond her power to control or subdue, still be told to wait till the violence has struck her before she can demand protection? The first blow may overthrow her, render her helpless, inflict irreparable injury upon all the great interests she is bound to guard.

But, sir, the great authority of Mr. Webster must not be claimed for such doctrines. Let me vindicate his fame from this undeserved imputation. In 1848 Mr. Webster appeared in the Supreme Court of the United States, in the celebrated case of *Luther v. Borden*, involving a discussion of the controversy connected with the attempt in 1842 to displace the old Charter Government of Rhode Island. His argument has justly been regarded as one of the ablest efforts of his forensic life, and I ask you to listen to his views upon the identical question we are now discussing.

Speaking of the section of the Constitution which we are now considering, Mr. Webster says: "I cannot but think this a very stringent article, drawing after it the most important consequences *and all of them good consequences*. The Constitution, in this section, . . . speaks of cases in which violence is practised or *threatened* against a State—in other words, 'domestic violence,'—and it says *'the State shall be protected.'*"

Continuing his argument, Mr. Webster quotes the law of 1795, together with the section of the Constitution under discussion, and says: "These constitutional and legal provisions make it the indispensable duty of the President to decide, in cases of commotion, what is the rightful Government of the State. He cannot avoid the decision." Again, he says:

My learned adversary has shown a rightful Government. Suppose it to be rightful. Suppose three fourths of the people of Rhode Island to have been engaged in it, and ready to sustain it. What then? How is it to be done without the consent of the previous Government? How is the fact that three fourths of the people are in favor of the new Government to be legally ascertained? And if the existing Government deny that fact, and if that Government hold on and will not surrender till displaced by force, *and if it is threatened by force, then the case arises,* and the United States must aid the Government that is in, *because an attempt to displace a Government by force is "domestic violence."* It is the exigency provided for by the Constitution.

We see now that in Mr. Webster's opinion the Constitution and laws of the United States have reference in this matter to a case where violence is "practised or threatened"; to a case where "commotion" arises; to a case where a State Government is "threatened by force"; to a case where "an attempt is made to displace a State Government by force." In these cases he declares with just and honest emphasis that the Constitution commands that "*the State shall be protected.*" He declares, too, that in such cases "it is the indispensable duty of the President to decide what is the rightful Government of the State." He declares that the President "cannot avoid the decision."

Read these statements of constitutional principles and duty, fellow-citizens, and then read the letter of the Secretary of State to the Louisiana Commission, the Report of that Commission to the President, and the final action of the President, and you will see how far Mr. Webster's great name can be borrowed to cover the cowardice and treachery of President Hayes' Southern policy

It will be useful here to notice the action taken by the President of the United States, when called upon for aid by the Governor of Rhode Island in the case which Mr. Webster was discussing. President John Tyler replied that, in his opinion, the time had not arrived to apply force, but he directed his Secretary of War to confer with the Governor of Rhode Island, and when it appeared to them to be necessary, to call out from Massachusetts and Connecticut a sufficient force of the militia *to terminate at once this insurrection.* He decided that the Charter Government was the lawful Government, and, while awaiting further events, he proclaimed his purpose to uphold the lawful Government whenever the power of the United States should be necessary to that end. I invite you to contrast this course with that of President Hayes towards Louisiana.

But, fellow-citizens, what were the facts of the situation in Louisiana as respects this question of domestic violence ? Was there actual or only threatened violence ? I simply state facts known to every man when I say that actual violence, armed insurrection, military organizations under arms, moving and acting under orders of officers, had attacked the Government represented by Governor Packard, had wrested from it by actual overpowering force a large part of the public offices and buildings at New Orleans, and had paused only when they had shut him and all that remained of his Government within the walls of one building in that city. This armed force had been stayed from further progress only by the actual presence of the military forces of the United States acting under orders which required them to permit no further violence. Now, fellow-citizens, is it not mockery and insult to ask whether this is domestic violence ? But it is said the violence had ceased. How had it ceased ? Why had it ceased ? Had the insurgent forces been disbanded ? Had they relinquished their purpose to resist the authority of Governor Packard ? Had his rightful authority been restored in the places from which it had been expelled ? No ; the insurgent forces maintained their ground, maintained their organizations, maintained their purpose, held possession and use of all they had gained by force, and openly and at every hour, from the 4th of March to the 20th of April, defied the lawful Government of the State, resisting by actual force every effort of the lawful Government to subdue them, and actually seizing and imprisoning the State officers who attempted to exercise or assert the authority of the lawful Government. Will any man dispute this statement ? I challenge him to come forward. But we are told, we are especially assured by Col. Higginson, that there was peace at this time ; perhaps, he says, a "hollow peace," but still "peace." Now, I say that, as a matter of fact, or of reason, or of law, there was no more peace in Louisiana at this time than there was in Virginia in the winter of 1863 to '64, when the armies of General Meade and General Lee lay silently confronting each other on the banks of the Rapidan. I mean exactly what I say. The authority of the lawful Government of Louisiana was as much assailed, the peace of that State was as much disturbed, by armed resistance, from March 4th to April 20th, as was the government and peace of the United States when active military operations were suspended, for any cause, during the four years of the rebellion.

Fellow-citizens, much more might be said in support of views already presented, but enough has now been presented to warrant the conclusion that President Hayes' action towards the State of Louisiana, was a plain and palpable disregard of the rights of that State under the Constitution, and of the duty imposed by the Constitution upon the President of the United States.

You have already, no doubt, asked why I have tested the President's Southern policy solely by his conduct toward Louisiana. I will answer you. I have preferred to speak of a case in which I was not a party. In addition to this, I have presented the case of Louisiana instead of South Carolina, because the facts of the Louisiana case were in some respects clearer than those of the South Carolina case. Unfortunately for us in South Carolina, the *apparent* result of the election was the election of a part of the Democratic State officers, including the Governor. The legal safeguards for the protection of the election from the effects of fraud and violence were likewise less perfect than in Louisiana. The validity of one branch of the Legislature of South Carolina was in controversy. The question of the existence of domestic violence, in the constitutional sense, was less clear than in Louisiana ; and I frankly admit now, as I have always admitted, that the situation in South Carolina presented questions upon which there may have been occasion for difference of opinion. The President's duty, in this case, to have examined and decided, in the language of Chief-Justice Taney, "what body of men constituted the Legislature, and who was the Governor," a duty which Mr. Webster declared the President "could not avoid," was as clear and imperative as in the Louisiana case. If upon such examination he had decided that Governor Hampton represented the lawful Government of South Carolina, his conduct in removing the troops would have been justifiable or otherwise, according to the facts and evidence upon which his conclusion rested. This he did not do. I shall not now enter upon a discussion of this question. I have only to say that I regard the legality of the Government of South Carolina, which I represented, and my own title to the office of Governor of that State, as perfect. I therefore regard the action of the President towards South Carolina with the same disapproval as I regard his action toward Louisiana.

We have now seen what are the features of what is well called *President Hayes'* Southern policy. I ask no one to go with me further than arguments which I present shall fairly carry him. For myself, I take leave to denounce it, here and now, as unconstitutional and revolutionary, subversive of constitutional guaranties, and false to every dictate of political honor, public justice, and good morals. There is no point, feature, or form of this policy that has support in a fair construction of the Constitution, or an honest view of facts which are involved ; and I believe it requires only a careful examination, uninfluenced by mawkish sentiment or the cowardice which shrinks from attacking the conduct of one who was chosen by our own party, to convince all who have ever sympathized with the principles of the Republican party, that such a policy deserves, upon all legal and constitutional grounds, the condemnation which I have pronounced upon it.

But when we look further and inquire what other defences of this policy are offered, we are lost in a maze of subterfuges, contradictions, falsehoods, fallacies, and inanities. Conspicuous in this list is the claim made by the President himself and echoed by his defenders, that this Presidental policy is in accord with the platform of the Republican party, with the President's letter of acceptance, and with his known views at the time of his nomination and during the canvass. I call this the chief of subterfuges, if not of falsehoods. I confess I cannot understand or measure the audacity which prompts such a claim. When, where, by whom, before the nomination, or after it, during the canvass or during the long agony of suspense which succeeded the canvass, will you find from President Hayes or any representative of him or of the Republican party, high or low, a hint of such a policy ? It cannot be found. Never till the country heard with amazement the first whisperings of the machinations of Stanley Matthews and the Ohio clique who stood nearest the President,—the basest passage I have ever read in our political history,—did any portion of the public, or of the Republican party, imagine that the President would enter upon such a policy or course of action. It is impossible to overstate this general fact. Especially is it impossible to overstate the deliberate, long-continued, unremitted efforts, made at every stage of the struggle from November 7th to March 4th, to inspire the Southern Republicans with fidelity to the Republican cause. If doubts arose, with electric speed came new assurances that Hayes, if elected, would vindicate the rights of those who were fighting his battles at the South. Is the despicable suggestion here made that President Hayes knew nothing of all this ? Sir, it is incredible. He did know it ; and he stood by, willing to see men risking, by day and by night, for months which seemed longer than years, their lives ; aye, losing their lives by hundreds, to lift him, to the Presidency, upon the lying assurances, if what he now says be true, that he would protect and rescue them by the great powers of the office he should receive. Every man who stood near to the President, every man whom the public had a right to regard as his faithful representative, joined in these assurances,— assurances which carried no doubtful meaning,—assurances which meant to the beleaguered and fainting soldiers on those outposts of freedom, that succor and help would come if only they defended to the last the ground which they had won. Sir, when I think of these things, my heart grows hot with indignation, and a curse comes unbidden to my lips, for the men who thus played with the blood of brave men and women as the gambler plays with his dice. Such treachery passes my comprehension. . . .

V.

THE ADDRESS AT GREENVILLE, S. C.

THE following article is preserved here because it contains so distinct a recognition of what appeared probably to most of the white citizens of South Carolina, as well as to the writer of the article, the "hopeless incongruities" of Governor Chamberlain's position.

[Editorial article in the Charleston *News and Courier*, May 6, 1876.]

Governor Chamberlain's visit to Greenville in December last is memorable because his absence from Columbia was turned to such evil account by the bandit factions in the Legislature, who seized the occasion to elect Moses and Whipper to be judges in South Carolina. This catastrophe engrossed public attention for the time, and the Governor's speech in Greenville, together with the whole subject of the Whitsitt prizes, received but little notice, far less than was due.

Now, therefore, in the calm of politics, we welcome heartily the neat pamphlet, reprinted from the pages of the *New Englander*, which places us in possession of his beautiful "Address on the Value of Classical Studies." The style and substance of the address are in Governor Chamberlain's best vein ; and the occasion, the speaker, the theme, the scenes in the midst of which it was composed, and the audience to whom it was delivered, combined to render it one of the most remarkable of his efforts.

It would have been difficult to have brought together anywhere in the State an assemblage presenting so striking a view of the manner in which time and circumstances have harmonized what, some years ago, must have seemed hopeless incongruities, and even now are hardly removed from paradox. Had this assemblage occurred but a few months earlier, it could scarcely have failed to excite either passion or derision ; yet on the occasion of the award of the Whitsitt prizes for proficiency in Greek, neither propriety nor decorum seems to have ruffled a feather.

Greenville, the first town in the State and the metropolis of the white counties, has never been in vassalage to policy, nor has she been required to pay to political expediency the galling tribute of bated speech or ambiguous language ; hence from no other quarter could an invitation have come to Governor Chamberlain more free from the color of insincerity, and therefore more complimentary to his personal worth.

He came to Greenville as a scholar, not as a politician ; as a distinguished citizen, not as Chief Magistrate of the State ; and the tact which has always sat at the helm during his public career guided him safely amidst the intricacies of so anomalous a position.

When Daniel H. Chamberlain stood before a select audience of South Carolinians in the capital of the up-country as their chosen orator and the advocate of the humanities, he might well have felt proud of the intellect which had achieved such a success ; and he could with great appropriateness extol the course of study by which his mind had been instructed and its faculties trained and developed. He must have felt that all who now hailed him as the champion of culture, knew him also to be the chief exponent in South Carolina of the social and political forces which had overthrown the culture and the refinement of the State and had established igno- rance and vulgarity in supreme control. He must have been aware that within sound of his voice were many familiar with his ordinary surroundings in Columbia, and keenly sensible of the contrast they present to the features of society at the capital at a period when nearly all who served the State had been nurtured at her own college, and were accustomed to illustrate in personal demeanor and in official conduct how well their Alma Mater had fulfilled her modest profession, " *Emollit mores nec sinit esse feros.*"

The orator must have had these thoughts in his mind, but he was unmoved by them. There are two qualities which, when harmoniously blended and thoroughly incorporated in a man's character, establish his dignity and command deference in every company. These are courage and courtesy. These same qualities, even when found apart, have always been honored in South Carolina ; hence it is easy to under- stand how Governor Chamberlain captivated his audience, first by his courage in calmly stepping upon the pedestal which seemed to have so narrow a base in the fit- ness of things, and secondly by the graceful compliment he paid to the State in calling up from the cherished memories of her people the name of Hugh S. Legare to intro- duce and commend the subject and the speaker.

From this point one who reads the Address loses sight of orator and audience, place and time. The mind retires into its garden, which is the imagination, and there, reposing under the shade of college recollections, takes in argument and illus- tration, narrative and figure, mingled with breezy memories of delightful days, and flecked with, now and then, the shadow of a passing remembrance—a cloud now— once the light of a comrade's face.

It is well for South Carolina that somewhere in her borders a new spring of literary culture has made its way through the crust of material utility into which the surface of society has been trodden by the ceaseless feet of men toiling for their daily bread ; it is well that the precious fountain has been recognized and protected ; it is well that the Governor of the State has publicly honored it ; but better than all is it, that through the guidance of an over-ruling Providence this worn and wasted State should just at this juncture have received at the hands of such an organization as the Republican party of South Carolina a Chief Magistrate worthy to raise again an altar to the classical muses, and able to pour upon the fane so acceptable a libation.

There are still in South Carolina men who have not bent the knee to the Baal of expediency ; there are still children who have not passed through the fire of prema- ture " sharpening " ; and to these the demonstration at Greenville is like the little cloud that rose out of the sea foretelling redemption, when the broken altars shall be repaired and the neglected sacrifices resumed.

The Alumni of the South Carolina College will hear with especial satisfaction of the revival of classical studies in the State, and it may be that the time will soon be propitious for them to ask to be embodied under a State charter, and to have recommitted to their pious hands the future of their revered Alma Mater. This would, indeed, be the beginning of the end of the supremacy of ignorance and vulgarity.

VI.

BIOGRAPHICAL SKETCH.

DANIEL HENRY CHAMBERLAIN was born in the town of West Brookfield, Worcester County, Massachusetts, June 23, 1835. His father was a farmer, in moderate pecuniary circumstances, of great firmness and even sternness of character, and his mother a woman of unusual intellectual force and religious culture. He was the ninth of ten children, nine of whom—six sons and three daughters—are now living. All the children of the family achieved a good education, two of the brothers being Rev. J. M. Chamberlain, of Iowa College, and Rev. L. T. Chamberlain, D.D., of Brooklyn. Until he was fourteen years of age Governor Chamberlain's life was passed in work on his father's farm and in attendance on the common schools of his native town. In 1849 and 1850 he spent a few months at the academy in Amherst, Mass., beginning there his Latin and Greek, and in 1854 he passed part of a year at Phillips Academy, Andover, Mass., teaching school each winter from 1852. In 1856, at the age of twenty-one, he entered the High School in Worcester, Mass., then under the charge of Homer B. Sprague and Wolcott Calkins, where, in 1857, he completed his preparation for college; but being then without the money to go on, he remained a year as teacher in the same school, and in 1859 he entered Yale College. His college course was marked by great industry in all directions. In 1862 he was graduated with the highest honors in oratory and English composition, while in general scholarship he held the fourth place in his class, which at graduation numbered 110 members. Among his classmates who have since become known to the world were Franklin McVeagh, of Chicago; Rev. Dr. Edward B. Coe, of New York; W. H. H. ("Adirondack") Murray; Flavius Josephus

("Joseph") Cook; Dr. George M. Beard; Frederick Adams, of Newark, N. J.; Rev. H. H. Stebbins, of Oswego, N. Y.; Robert K. Weeks, S. B. Eaton, Henry Holt, Buchanan Winthrop, and Melville C. Day, of New York City; John W. Alling, of New Haven; George C. Ripley, of Minneapolis; Prof. John P. Taylor, of Andover Theological Seminary; and Prof. Henry P. Johnston, of the College of the City of New York.

From the age of fifteen he was, in sentiment and sympathy, an abolitionist of the Garrison-Phillips type, though believing in political action, and taking keen interest in the leaders and the triumphs of the political parties called Free Soil and Republican. At New Haven, in 1860, he cast his first vote for Abraham Lincoln. On the breaking out of the Rebellion, he was on the point of quitting college and entering the army, but was dissuaded by friends whose judgment he was bound to regard, who urged that he could not afford to sacrifice his collegiate course. Upon the completion of his college course he entered the Harvard Law School, where he remained but little more than a year, until the fall of 1863, when he could no longer resist the duty of entering the army. The following extract from a letter written by him to a college friend, in November of that year, shows his motive and feeling in thus abandoning his uncompleted professional studies:

I am going to the war within the next two months. January, 1864, shall see me "enlisted for the war." I have no plans beyond that; do not know how or where I shall go, but go I must. I ought to have gone in '61, but the real reason I did n't was, that I was then, as I am now, in debt for my college expenses to those who cannot possibly afford to lose what I have borrowed from them. I am told that it is foolish for me to go; that I can do no more in the army than the less educated. I know all that, but years hence I shall be ashamed to have it known that for *any* reason I did not bear a hand in this life-or-death struggle for the Union and for Freedom. I find I can insure my life for enough to cover the $2,000 I owe, and nothing shall hinder me longer than is necessary to get the money to do this.

Accordingly, obtaining the loan of $250 from his instructor and friend, the late Professor Emory Washburn, for that purpose, he insured his life, and by the interest of the same good friend he received a Lieutenant's commission in the 5th Massachusetts Cavalry, a regiment of colored volunteers, then forming under the command of Col. Henry S. Russell, of Boston, and under the special patronage of Governor John A. Andrew. He left for the seat of war in Virginia in the spring of 1864. His army life, until the end of hostilities, was spent at Point Lookout, Maryland, and in the Army of the James, at City Point, and before Petersburg. On the early morning of April 3, 1865, he entered Richmond with his regiment, then under the command of Col. Charles Francis Adams, Jr. He passed the remainder of the year on the Rio Grande, with Weitzel's corps, and in December, 1865, was mustered out of the service at Boston.

Early in January, 1866, he went to Charleston, S. C., to settle the affairs of a classmate, James Pierpont Blake, of New Haven, drowned at Edisto Island. While so engaged he visited the Sea Islands near Charleston, where he was led to engage in cotton planting, in the hope of being enabled in this way to pay his college debts; but the two years he spent in this occupation proved pecuniarily unsuccessful. In the Fall of 1867, he was chosen a member of the Constitutional Convention, called under the Reconstruction Acts, and took his seat in that body in January, 1868. He was a member of its Judiciary Committee, and an influential member in all its deliberations. He so acquitted himself in these duties that all the friends of the new Constitution desired him to be one of the State officers who were to establish in practical operation the new organization of government. The office of Attorney General, being in the line of his chosen profession, was the only one he would consent to take, and to this he was chosen, holding it for four years continuously. This Attorney General, whose law studies had been prematurely broken off, who had never had a day's practice in the courts, was almost immediately brought into conflict with some of the foremost lawyers of a community always distinguished for the learning and ability of its Bar, in the trial of causes of great moment, involving the highest constitutional and legal questions, a strenuous endeavor being made to secure fulfilment of the prediction that the new State could not live. It was soon discovered that their inexperienced opponent was a man of whom it was not wise to presume any weakness that could be overcome by tireless industry and sound thinking. The pages of this book bear ample testimony to the standing he achieved at the Bar of South Carolina.

At the close of his service as Governor, he removed to New York City, where he resumed and has continued the practice of his profession.

INDEX.